Elements of Computer Music

F. Richard Moore

University of California
San Diego

P T R Prentice Hall, Upper Saddle River, NJ 07458

Library of Congress Cataloging-in-Publication Data

Moore, F. Richard.
    Elements of computer music / F. Richard Moore.
       p.   cm.
    Bibliography: p.
    Includes indes.
    ISBN 0-13-252552-6
    1. Computer sound processing. 2. Computer music–Instruction and
study. I. Title.
MT723.M6 1990
786.7'6--dc20
                                    89-8679
                                    CIP
                                    MN

Editorial/production supervision: MARY P. ROTTINO
Cover design: BEN SANTORA
Manufacturing buyer: RAY SINTEL

© 1990 by P T R Prentice Hall
Prentice-Hall, Inc.
A Pearson Education Company
Upper Saddle River, NJ 07458

The publisher offers dicounts on this book when ordered
in bulk quantities. For more information, write:

    Special Sales/College Marketing
    College Technical and Reference Divsision
    Prentice-Hall
    Upper Saddle River, NJ 07458

Printed in the United States of America
10 9 8 7 6 5 4 3

ISBN 0-13-252552-6

Prentice-Hall International (UK) Limited, London
Prentice-Hall of Australia Pty. Limited, Sydney
Prentice-Hall Canada Inc., Toronto
Prentice-Hall Hispanoamericana, S.A., Mexico
Prentice-Hall of India Private Limited, New Delhi
Prentice-Hall of Japan, Inc., Tokyo
Pearson Education Asia Pte. Ltd., Singapore
Editoria Prentice-Hall do Brasil, Ltda., Rio De Janeiro

To Cynthia and Amanda.

Contents

Foreword

F. Richard Moore is one of the pioneers of computer music. He contributed to the Music V program, one of the early foundations of this field. He later collaborated in the writing and development of the Groove system, which first demonstrated the possibility of using a computer as a musical instrument for live performance in real time. Groove used an analog synthesizer because no digital machine at the time was powerful enough to calculate interesting music in real time. As part of his doctoral thesis at Stanford, Moore made one of the first all-digital music synthesizers. Since 1979 he has directed the computer music research at University of California at San Diego, one of the leading computer music institutions in the world. One of his first projects there was to write cmusic, the first computer music program to be written in the C language. cmusic is the first general music program to be written in powerful modern language that is almost universally available. As a result, cmusic can be run on almost any computer.

In addition to being one of the technical founders and an expert in all aspects of computer music, Moore is a superb teacher and an excellent writer. He has done a great service to this field by taking the time to write a book that covers the entire field lucidly and completely. The book will become a standard work both as a textbook and as a reference source. It is a much needed and very important addition to the discipline of computer music.

Max V. Mathews
Stanford University

Preface

This book is for anyone interested in learning how to use computers to extend the boundaries of music. It is necessary to assume that the reader is already familiar with the basics of computers and music—this book does not deal with these subjects separately. I have necessarily made several assumptions, some of which are designed to lighten the reader's load as much as possible.

First, this book concentrates on how computers can analyze, process, and synthesize musical sounds and structures. It is therefore necessary to assume that the reader is musically literate at the level of being able to read and write common practice music notation. The general issues pertaining to how to make good music are the subject of traditional music training, which is not covered in this book.

Second, many of the detailed explanations in this book are couched in terms of computer programming. I assume, therefore, that the reader is computer literate at the level of being able to read and write computer programs in some "high-level" computer language. The examples in this book are written in the C programming language, which should be understandable to anyone who is familiar with Pascal, Fortran, Algol, or any similar language. Readers with little or no programming experience may wish to consult any of the myriad books for beginning programmers (such as the author's *Programming in C with a Bit of UNIX*, Prentice Hall, 1985). Readers who already know how to program but are not familiar with C may wish to consult *The C Programming Language* by B. W. Kernighan and D. M. Ritchie (Prentice Hall, 1978, 1988), which is the defining document for the language.

Third, the mathematics in this book should be understandable—perhaps with some effort—to anyone who has taken high school courses in algebra and trigonometry. I assume, however, that the reader is not afraid of mathematics. Because computers can only add, subtract, multiply, divide, and make simple decisions, it is usually unnecessary to invoke higher forms of mathematics such as calculus, provided that the programming examples are understood. Extended mathematical concepts are explained in basic terms as they are needed, often with the support of programming examples. Readers whose mathematical skills are "rusty" may wish to consult any of a wide variety of excellent review books (such as *Integrated Algebra, Trigonometry, and Analytic Geometry* by R. C. Fisher and A. D. Zieber, Prentice-Hall, 1982).

Fourth, one of the great problems of writing about any subject that involves computers is the rapid rate of change of computer technology, which tends to make specific information obsolete very rapidly. This presentation therefore attempts to build the concepts of computer music from the first principles of music, acoustics and psychoacoustics. I have adopted this approach in an attempt to provide a firm theoretical basis for computer music concepts that transcends any particular computer language, system, synthesizer, or way of making music. An excellent introduction to the principles of musical acoustics and psychoacoustics written for the general reader is *The Science of Musical Sound* by J. R. Pierce (W. H. Freeman, 1983).

Fifth, many figures and diagrams are provided to aid in the visualization of abstract concepts. I have attempted to describe computer music concepts as concretely as possible—often in terms of complete computer programs. Someday, perhaps, a better form of book will allow figures and diagrams to be interactive, allowing readers to pose alternatives and to see and hear the results of their choices. In the meantime, readers must still work out such alternatives by hand, ideally while programming a computer according to the principles described in this book. I have not, however, included explicit exercises (though many are suggested implicitly). The typically divergent academic backgrounds of computer music students make it necessary for the task of designing appropriate exercises based on the text to be in the hands of an insightful instructor.

Finally, the book acts in many ways as an introduction to the literature of computer music and related topics. It is therefore incomplete because this literature is growing rapidly and often in surprising directions. Music is a sophisticated art and in many ways an ideal area of application for findings in other fields such as computer science, digital signal processing, psychological and physical acoustics, and mathematics. At the same time, the practice of computer music teaches us much about music and digital technology by giving us new perspectives on both. As in many other application fields, the computer acts as a mirror of our understanding. By explaining music, or attempting to explain music, to a computer we discover—sometimes with exasperating precision—where our understanding begins and ends. So far, the computer has provided more interesting questions about music than answers. But these questions often lie at the very heart of the art-making process, where the computer is simultaneously the ultimate tool for exploring the oceans of the mind and the ultimate challenge for the artist.

LEGAL MATTERS

The following statements regarding legal matters appear in slightly different form in the preface to *Numerical Recipes: The Art of Scientific Computing* by W. H. Press, S. A.

Teukolsky, B. P. Flannery, and W. T. Vetterling (Cambridge University Press, 1986). Because these statements apply equally well to the contents of this book, they have been adapted for presentation here (with permission, of course).

Some registered trademarks appear in the text of this book: VAX is a trademark of the Digital Equipment Corporation, and UNIX is a trademark of AT&T Bell Laboratories.

Like all artistic and literary compositions, computer programs can be protected by copyright. Generally it is an infringement for you to copy into your computer a program from a copyrighted source. It is also not a friendly thing to do, because it deprives the program's author of compensation for his or her creative effort. Although this book and its programs are copyrighted, the author and publisher specifically authorize you, a reader of this book, to make one machine-readable copy of each program for your own use. Distribution of the machine-readable programs to any other person is not authorized.

Copyright does not protect ideas, only the expression of those ideas in a particular form. In the case of a computer program, the ideas consist of the program's methodology and algorithm, including the sequence of processes adopted by the programmer. The expression of those ideas is the program source code and its derived object code.

If you analyze the ideas contained in a program and then express those ideas in your own distinct implementation, that new program implementation belongs to you. Some of the programs in this book are based on copyrighted sources, while others are entirely of the author's own devising. When programs in this book are said to be "based" on programs published in copyrighted sources, this means that the ideas are the same. The expression of these ideas as source code is the author's. The author believes that no material in this book infringes on an existing copyright.

The fact that ideas are legally "free as air" in no way supersedes the ethical requirement that ideas be credited to their known originators. When programs in this book are based on known sources, whether copyrighted or in the public domain, published or "handed down," I have attempted to give proper attribution in each case.

ACKNOWLEDGMENTS

Many people have had a direct or indirect impact on the material presented in this book. As a graduate music student at the University of Illinois, I had the good fortune to

know and become familiar with the pioneering work of Lejaren Hiller, James Beau-
champ, Salvatore Martirano, and Herbert Brün. At AT&T Bell Laboratories I had the
great luck to collaborate with Jean-Claude Risset, Pierre Ruiz, Joe Olive, Emmanual
Ghent, Vladimer Ussachevsky, and Lillian Schwartz. Without question, though, my
biggest debt of gratitude is to the two men who really gave the computer its infinitely
malleable musical voice, John Pierce and Max Mathews, both of whom are now on the
faculty of music at Stanford University.

At Stanford University I had the privilege of working closely with and learning
much from John Chowning, James Angell, James Moorer, Loren Rush, Leland Smith,
Julius Smith, John Snell, Michael McNabb, John Strawn, and Tovar.

At the University of California, San Diego, I have had the good fortune to have
worked closely with two people who deserve special acknowledgment. Without the
vision and savoir-faire of Roger Reynolds, the UCSD Center for Music Experiment,
which provides a nearly ideal home for the Computer Audio Research Laboratory,
would never have existed. Without the tireless dedication and reliable insight of Gareth
Loy, the Computer Audio Research Laboratory might never have worked.

For all these people and the many more with the courage to try to tame our most
powerful of technologies in the service of art, I am profoundly grateful.

I also wish to acknowledge the financial support that has been provided for the
work described in this book, and to the field of computer music in general, by the
Rockefeller Foundation; The University of California, San Diego; the National Endow-
ment for the Arts; the Ford Foundation; the California Arts Council; and, especially, the
System Development Foundation.

Finally, I thank David Wessel, Gareth Loy, Robert Willey, and Durand Begault
for their many useful comments on the manuscript of this book and Cynthia Moore for
her invaluable help with the mechanics of authoring.

F. Richard Moore
La Jolla, California

1

Introduction

> First and above all, an explanation must do justice to what is being explained, must not devaluate it, misinterpret it, belittle it, or distort it, in order to make it easier to understand. The question is not "What view of the phenomenon must be acquired so that it can be comfortably explained in accordance with one or another philosophy?" but precisely the reverse: "What philosophy will be required in order to live up to the subject, be on the same level with it?" The question is not how the phenomenon must be turned, twisted, narrowed, or crippled, so that it can be made explicable according to principles that we have in any case resolved not to go beyond, but: "To what point must our thought be enlarged in order to stand in proportion with the phenomenon?"
>
> —F. W. J. von Schelling, *Philosophie der Mythologie* (1857)

Every human culture has developed—along with language—at least some form of visual art and music. Little can be said of the true origins of music because its roots are shrouded in the remotest of human antiquities. Music is, perhaps, more a *defining* characteristic of human beings than a passing phase in the evolution of intelligence.

The significance of music has been debated with varying degrees of heat throughout recorded history. All such debates, however enlightened, have ultimately failed to capture the essence of music for the simple reason that music expresses properties and states of mind that cannot be expressed in words.

The inability to state its significance in words has earned music both respect and a certain amount of trepidation. Among the ancient Greeks, the great philosopher-poet Plato repeatedly revealed his disquiet regarding music.

Now we must not omit the full explanation of the difficulty with music. There is much more talk about musical imagery than about any other kind, and this is the very reason why such imagery demands more cautious scrutiny than any other. It is here that error is at once most dangerous, as it encourages morally bad dispositions, and most difficult to detect, because our poets are not altogether on the level of the Muses themselves. The Muses, we may be assured, would never commit the grave mistake of setting masculine language to an effeminate scale, or tune, or wedding melody, or postures worthy of free men with rhythms only fit for slaves and bondsmen, or taking the prose of a free man and combining it with an air or words of inappropriate rhythm. Not to say that they would never make a pretended presentation of a single theme out of a medley of human voices, animal cries, noises of machinery, and other things. Whereas our mere human poets tend to be only too fond of provoking the contempt of us who, in the phrase of Orpheus, are "ripe for delight," by this kind of senseless and complicated confusion. In fact, not only do we see confusion of this kind, but our poets go still further. They divorce rhythm and figure from melody, by giving metrical form to bare discourse, and melody and rhythm from words, by their employment of cithara and flute without vocal accompaniment, though *it is the hardest of tasks to discover what such wordless rhythm and tune signify, or what model worth considering they represent* [emphasis added]. Nay, we are driven to the conclusion that all this so popular employment of cithara or flute, not subordinated to the control of dance or song for the display of speed and virtuosity, and the reproduction of the cries of animals, is in the worst of bad taste; the use of either as an independent instrument is no better than unmusical legerdemain. So much for the theory of the thing.[1]

Plato, it would seem, was among the first and most significant to fall into the trap of confusing knowledge with language. For a musician "to discover what such wordless rhythm and tune signify" is among the easiest—not the hardest—of tasks, provided, of course, that the musician is not required to translate this significance into words. Words, no matter how skillfully employed, are impoverished when compared to the full range of human experience. To confound knowledge that can be stated in words with all knowledge is to confuse the map with the territory.

To be sure, knowledge is conveyed through its expression, but expression, like knowledge, has many forms. In modern science, for example, mathematics is often used both to investigate and to express fundamental concepts about nature. It is usually possible to recouch a mathematical statement in words without loss of any essential detail. But mathematics represents more than a precise and convenient shorthand. The power of mathematics is that it captures the essence of certain types of relationships in a way that reveals more than it conceals to anyone who is fluent in its principles. Yet it would be in most cases difficult, if not impossible, to attain mathematical insights through the use of words alone.

Without mathematics, for example, the study of the stars is called *astrology*, derived from the Greek roots *astro*, meaning "star", and *logos*, meaning "word or speech." *Astrology* therefore signifies "what can be said about stars." The scientific study of the stars, however, is called *astronomy*, from *astro* plus *nomy*, from the Greek

---

[1]Plato, *Laws*, as trans. by A. E. Taylor, in *The Collected Dialogues of Plato*, ed. E. Hamilton and H. Cairns, (Bollingen Foundation, 1966). Reprinted with the permission of the copyright owners, J. M. Dent and Sons, London.

némein, meaning "distribute." *Astronomy* therefore signifies the system of laws governing or sum total of knowledge regarding the stars. Even though they are not used consistently in this way today, the *-logy* and *-nomy* suffixes distinguish neatly between the part of knowledge that can be expressed in words and the sum total of knowledge about a field.

The establishment of astronomy came, however, not with the advance of mathematics but with the advance of the telescope. Despite the fact that he is often miscredited with its invention, the Italian scientist Galileo Galilei (1564–1642) *applied* the telescope to the study of the stars, discovering along the way the four "Galilean" moons of Jupiter and the rings of Saturn. Galileo's real contribution to astronomy, however, was not the establishment of a few new facts about our natural environment but the correct *interpretation* of these observations as confirmation of the revolutionary ideas of Polish scientist Nicolaus Copernicus (1473–1543). Copernicus believed and taught—contrary to popular and official opinion at the time—that the earth was *not* the center of the universe but instead revolved around the sun, thereby contributing both a fundamental scientific insight and a new word to the English language to describe such radical ideas, that word, of course, being *revolutionary*. The Copernican revolution—as it came to be called—rested on an untested theory until Galileo actually saw its confirmation through a telescope; today Copernicus is honored as the father of astronomy and Galileo as the founder of experimental physics and astronomy. Both were persecuted for the entirety of their lifetimes.[2]

It may seem strange to begin a discussion computer music with the distinction between astrology and astronomy, because music is a purely human activity, whereas the stars have existed since a few astronomical moments after the Big Bang. But the parallel is a strong one, for computers allow investigation of purely musical issues in a way that permits observations more precise than those available to the "naked ear" alone.

If I were to attempt the ostensibly impossible task of stating in words what music really is, I would suggest that music addresses a sense for which our minds are the primary (if not the only) organ: our sense of *time*. Music draws our attention to a detailed progression of moments, the significance of which is apprehended as an abstraction of the succession of momentary awarenesses that make up a human lifetime. Physiologically, our senses of hearing and touch are similar, because the basilar membrane in the ear is basically a highly enervated piece of skin with a correspondingly fine ability to discriminate vibrations at frequencies in a range that overlaps slightly with the sense of touch at our fingertips. We find music "touching" in the metaphorical sense partly because we perceive it through physical contact with mechanical vibrations of the atmosphere.

So much for the theory of the thing. The important parallel between astrology and astronomy on the one hand and music on the other is that the computer represents a technological advance that has clear application to the study of music in a way that has not been possible in the past. Because music is a temporal art, its proper study

---

[2]It is interesting to note that the works of Galileo were removed only recently from the Index (a list of forbidden works) of the Roman Catholic church, the teachings of which he contradicted.

necessarily includes a method for capturing, representing, and interpreting information about successive moments of time.

One such technological advance occurred about a century ago with the advent of means for recording sound. Not only has sound recording drastically transformed the study of music (it is now possible to study music from all over the world by listening to recordings, for example), but it has also transformed the methods by which music is made in fundamental ways. In a 1925 composition titled *The Pines of Rome*, Italian composer Ottorino Respighi (1879–1936) incorporated a part for a "gramophone" recording of the songs of nightingales during an orchestral evocation of a predawn moment. This use of recorded sound in music was a precursor to the development of *musique concrète* in France, which was based on the juxtaposition of recordings of the "concrete" sounds of nature (as opposed to the "abstract" sounds of traditional musical instruments). Describing their 1952 composition of *musique concrète* titled *Erotica (Symphonie pour un homme seul)*, French composers Pierre Schaeffer and Pierre Henry wrote: "To record a symphony of human sounds. The man by himself becomes his own instrument: his voice, his shout, his breathing, his laugh, the sound of his throat being cleared."

Electrical and electronic musical instruments have also graced the musical horizon practically since the turn of the twentieth century. At first rather impractical due to the relatively large size of electrical and electronic components,[3] improvements in electronics technology allowed serious composers of the 1950s to begin the exploration of new types of "synthetic" sound as material for music, such as the historically significant *Studien* created by German composer Karlheinz Stockhausen.

What, then, is significantly different about computer music? The full answer to that question is the topic of the rest of this book, but the essential quality is one of *temporal precision*. Computers allow precise, repeatable experimentation with sound. In effect, musicians can now design sounds according to the needs of their music rather than relying on a relatively small number of traditional instruments. Further, computers act as an instrument of the mind, extending the principles of musical composition to the simultaneous consideration of many more levels of organization than is practicable with the "naked mind" alone. Computers also extend the capabilities of musicians to control the production of sound during live performance.

With that said, it should be quickly noted that we are not used to dealing with music with such an enriched means to control its every aspect. We still live in an age where the primary theory of music comes under the heading of "musicology." With computers we are gradually entering the age of "musiconomy."

To complicate matters, computer music is one of the most strongly interdisciplinary fields in existence, because it includes significant aspects of art, science, and technology. Which of these is emphasized depends largely on the objectives of each practitioner, although some elements of art, science, and technology come constantly into play to some extent. Insofar as the objective is to produce music, computer music

[3]The Dynamophone, an inductance-based electrical musical instrument constructed in 1906 by Dr. Thaddeus Cahill, for example, apparently required several railroad cars for its transport.

is an art; if the objective is to understand music as a human activity, computer music is definitely more like a science. Finally, all computer music activity involves the use of the computer, with all of the associated technological implications.

In a famous lecture on the relationship between physics and mathematics, noted physicist Richard P. Feynman started with an apology to those in the audience who knew nothing about physics or nothing about mathematics because to discuss their relationship it is necessary to begin by assuming familiarity with what is being related.

We necessarily adopt the same approach here. It would be impractical to discuss the basics of music and the basics of computers while at the same time attempting to relate computers to music. It is therefore necessary to assume that the reader is both musically literate and "computer literate" from the outset in the sense of being able to read and write both music and computer programs. If you know music well but do not know how to program computers, do not despair, for computer programming is much easier to learn than music. If you know how to program computers but not how to read and write music, you might despair slightly, for acquiring musical fluency generally takes a long time. Fortunately, computers are ever more prepared to help in music instruction, but that is another topic.

From a musical point of view, computers turn abstractions into concrete perceptions. Computers are of interest to musicians, therefore, not in themselves but insofar as they provide a vital link between musical imagination and reality.

Simply stated, computer music is the art of making music with digital computers. Because computers have no fixed function, their role in music-making processes varies greatly. To develop a coherent view of how computers can be applied to music, we begin with a bird's-eye-level examination of the processes that constitute music. In this context it will be convenient to define a *process* as any agent or activity that transforms information from one form to another. This definition leaves open the possibility that the processor may alternatively be a machine, a human being, or some cooperative combination of both.

1.1 MUSICAL DATA AND PROCESSES

Figure 1-1 is a "word picture" that depicts primary relationships among various types of information (data) that exist in music, together with processes (defined here as transformations of information) that act on this information. The flow of information is characteristically clockwise around the circle shown, although interactions occur at every level. General information about music (called the "musical" knowledge base in Figure 1-1 is used as needed in the listening, composing, and performing processes, any of which may be interpreted here as actions of a human being, a machine, or a combination of both. General properties of sound and vibration (collectively referred to as the "physical" knowledge base in the figure) is relevant primarily to the operation of musical instruments and performance spaces. The instrument and room processes may rely on physical objects, or they may be abstractions of these objects embodied in computer programs.

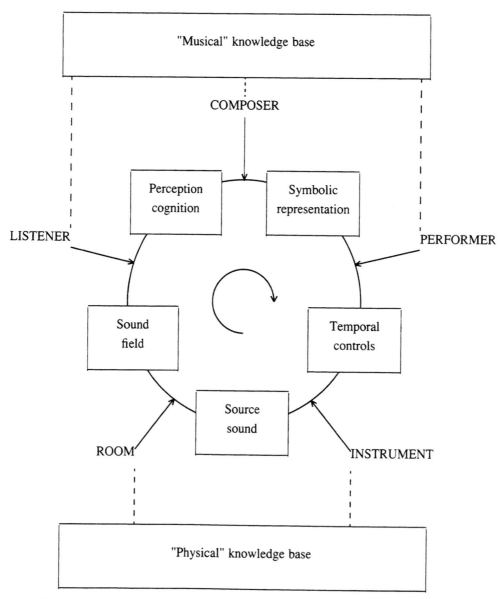

Figure 1-1 Musical data (in boxes) and processors (in capital letters). Data is information that may exist in many forms; processors may be human beings, machines, or a combination of both.

Stating that the process of musical composition may be undertaken by either a human being or a machine does not, of course, imply that people and computers are in any way equivalent. Rather, this definition is based on the premise that people and machines may at times carry out *equivalent tasks.* Although the distinction between what someone or something *is* versus what someone or something *does* would seem to be self-evident, it can sometimes be a source of confusion.[4]

1.2 MUSICAL THOUGHT

We start our exploration of computer music with consideration of the nature of musical thought. The box bearing the labels "perception" and "cognition" in Figure 1-1 does little to explain the profound nature of musical sensation and imagination.

On the most basic level, our senses gather information about our environment— this is the process of perception. Sensory information is used to aid in the various sub-tasks of survival. We must be able to detect dangerous situations in order to avoid falling off cliffs, being struck by moving objects, being attacked by dangerous beasts, and so on.

On a higher level, sensory information forms the basis for communication. While not all senses seem equally suited to communication, any available sense may be used, in principle, to pass messages. Spoken and written languages provide, among other things, the possibility of indirect knowledge about a great deal more than we could or would wish to experience directly.

On a yet higher level, sensory information forms the basis of the arts, with the most acute senses providing the most variegated forms of potential expression. The nature of artistic expression is a deep and multifaceted subject that goes well beyond the scope of this book. It is helpful to recall at this point, however, that virtually every human culture has developed—along with language—one or more forms of visual art and one or more forms of music.

Art is therefore a kind of commentary on human existence, one that extensively exercises the interpretive mechanisms (cognition) to which sensory information flows. Through art we gain not only indirect experience of actual existence but indirect experience of potential existence as well. In other words, art portrays imagination.

Acts of imaginative portrayal are limited in at least two important ways. The more fundamental of these limitations is human imagination itself. A simple example of such a limitation is to be found in the pervasive anthropocentrism that impedes our ability even to think about communication with intelligent nonhumans.

---

[4]An example of such confusion occurred to me when I read the following prose in the introductory section of the fourteenth edition of the famed *CRC Standard Mathematical Tables*: "**Four-Place Antilogarithms**—Some computers prefer to use separate tables for determining antilogarithms; the table being entered from the margins with the logarithm and the number being found in the body of the table." I found "Some computers prefer" to be curious indeed until I learned from the preface to the volume that the Chemical Rubber Company first published this collection of mathematical tables and formula in the year 1938—the "computers" referred to were people!

A less fundamental but no less important limitation on artistic portrayal involves the artist's quest to forge the means to express what has already been imagined. In short, we can easily conceive of things that we do not know how to realize. The annals of literary fiction—especially so-called science fiction—are filled with such imaginings. The importance of such expressed imaginings lies in the fact that they are necessary precursors to their eventual realization. In this sense, human imagination is the driving force behind human technology, not the other way around.

Computers are useful in the creation of music, therefore, because they allow the creation of music that cannot be realized in any other practical way. Consider, for example, the transformation of one sound into another.

The notion of a *Klangfarbenmelodie* ("tone-color melody") is not new in music, yet the manner of its realization has generally been limited to the orchestral technique of gradually fading in one instrument while another fades out—a kind of instrumental "crossfade" (see Figure 1-2). At each intermediate point in time during the crossfade, we hear a sound mixture whose characteristics are dependent on the capabilities of the performers and instruments involved.

Other types of transformations are easily imagined, however. Suppose we imagine a clarinetist who begins to play middle C, but shortly after the beginning of the note the instrument gradually begins to take on the physical form of an oboe playing the same note (we ignore the physical—not to mention cognitive—difficulties such a transformation, might provide for the player). During each intermediate temporal interval in the transformation, we would hear a sound that gradually changes from that of a clarinet to that of an oboe. Such a transition would sound quite different from a crossfade.

We can construct a visual analogy to these two types of timbral transitions in the following way. During a crossfade, we perceive either or both of two well-defined shapes, as in the following diagram, where the square might represent the sound of the clarinet and the circle the sound of the oboe.

The following diagram represents not a crossfade but a gradual transformation of one shape (the square) into the other (the circle).

We can imagine an infinite number of "paths" by which we might transit from one sound to another, some of which might visit familiar sounds along the way but all of which visit the vast, largely unexplored territory that exists between the familiar ones. This is but one example of how computers enlarge the realm of musical possibility by allowing the realization of what otherwise can only be imagined.

Figure 1-2 "Farben (Sommermorgen an einem See)" from *Fünf Orchesterstücke* by Arnold Schönberg (Opus 16, 1909). In this landmark composition of twentieth-century music, Schönberg produces a "melody" of tone colors by continual reorchestration of sustained pitches. Reprinted with the permission of the copyright owners, C.F. Peters Corporation, New York. (© C. F. Peters, Leipzig. All rights reserved.)

1.3 COMPOSING

Traditional music composition, as we have defined it, is the process of producing symbolic representations of musical thought. Musical thought appears to be based on subjective interpretation of the temporal relationships of audible events. These relationships are perceived in at least three ways according to associated human sensory modalities involving the sense of hearing and short- and long-term memory.

The most rapid temporal events in music are associated with the vibrations of sound itself. Audible sound usually consists of a periodic or semiperiodic mechanical disturbance of the planetary atmosphere at rates of about 20 to 20,000 vibrations per second. Vibrations that occur at rates faster than about 20,000 times per second are not perceived as sound, and atmospheric disturbances that occur less frequently than about 20 times per second are perceived individually, if at all. Atmospheric vibration patterns that repeat themselves in regular, periodic patterns in the sonic regime tend to give rise to the sensation of definite *pitch*, while irregular vibration patterns tend to give rise to indefinitely pitched sonic sensations, often described as various qualities of *noise*. The strength, or *amplitude,* of these vibration patterns is generally related to the subjective sensation of loudness, while the detailed *shape* of sonic vibration patterns is perceived as tone quality, or *timbre.* Sounds are also perceived differently according to *spatial relationships* between sound sources and listeners, allowing us to form subjective impressions of the directions and distances from which sounds emanate. These four physical characteristics of sound,

- Vibration pattern repetition rate
- Vibration pattern amplitude
- Vibration pattern shape and
- Sound source location relative to the listener

together with their subjective correlates,

- Pitch (definite or indefinite)
- Loudness
- Timbre
- Localization

form the psychophysical basis for musical sound.

On a broader temporal level, sounds begin and end in patterns that are perceived as musical events such as notes, rhythms, tempo, and meter. Music is often organized around a periodic event rate called a beat, or *pulse.* The range of acceptable pulse rates in music is related to characteristic periodicities of the human body, especially by comparison to the rate of the "natural" visceral human clock, that is, the rate at which the human heart pumps blood (about 72 beats per minute, or 1.2 beats per second). Pulse rates in music vary around this frequency over about the same range as the heart rate also varies, from about 30 beats per minute (0.5 Hz) during sleep or deep meditation to about 200 beats per minute (3.33 Hz) during vigorous exercise. The establishment of a pulse rate in music serves the important function of allowing performers to play together, because the regularity of the pulse can be used to anticipate sonic events in the immediate future as well as to suggest the organization of events in the immediate past. For these reasons, a musical pulse may go no faster than human performers can readily synchronize and may go no slower than human listeners can immediately remember.

Musical pulses are typically organized into further temporal groupings, or *meters*, thereby establishing a yet slower periodicity (or quasi-periodicity) in music. Pulses are also subdivided harmonically to provide the basis for *rhythm*. Harmonic subdivisions of the pulse may extend upward in frequency to about 10 to 15 events per second and are limited mainly by the physical characteristics of human performers and musical instruments. Temporal event patterns may synchronize well with expectations induced in the listener by an obvious pulse, or they may purposely thwart such expectations, giving rise to the "offbeat" musical concept called *syncopation*. Certain types of music, especially traditional dances, are based not only on particular meters but on particular rhythms as well. A musical meter may be regular, like the consistent triple-pulse grouping of a waltz or duple-pulse grouping of a march, or it may be consistently irregular, such as the constantly shifting meter of the great ballets of Igor Stravinsky.

Some composers have explored other types of temporal organizations for music in the five-octave range from 0.5 to 15 Hz. The pseudorhythms of human speech have often been employed in this context, as well as various other types of continuous (rather than harmonic or hierarchical) subdivisions of pulses. Such methods of temporal organization are often plagued with difficulties of synchronization among multiple performers but work well for solo performers or in cases where precise synchronization is irrelevant.

Longer-term temporal organizations occur in music at the level of the *phrase*, which is associated with the time between breathing during human speech (normally about 2 to 15 seconds). Musical phrases are continuous utterances, not in any strict sonic sense but in the sense of continuous availability of breath and hence connectivity. Of course, musical phrases for certain instruments are not necessarily limited to human lung capacity, but short-term human memory has about the same temporal proportions, making musical "phrases" a common constituent of much music. Other long-term musical effects include the gradual change of some overall musical characteristic such as loudness (*crescendo* and *diminuendo*), and tempo (*accelerando* and *rallentando*).

The longest-term level of musical organization is commonly called *form*. Forms include the "ABA" phrase structure of simple songs (such as "For He's a Jolly Good Fellow") to complex and involved "dramatic" forms such as sonatas (exposition-development-recapitulation-coda, typified in much keyboard music by Mozart) and "narrative" tone poems (such as Richard Strauss's *Till Eulenspiegel's Merry Pranks* and Modest Mussorgsky's *Pictures at an Exhibition*).

The following table summarizes the categories of temporal variation in music.

Approximate Levels of Temporal Variation in Music

Duration (Period)	Repetition Rate (Frequency)	Typical Examples
> 1 hour	(once per evening)	Grand opera
5 – 60 minutes	(a few per evening)	Symphonies, sonatas
0.5 – 20 minutes	(a few per composition)	Formal musical structures, movements
2 – 60 seconds	(many per composition)	Phrases
0.067 – 10 seconds	0.1 – 15 Hz	Events (notes, rhythms, pulses, meters)
50ms–50μs	20–20,000 Hz	Sound (pitch, loudness, timbre, localization)

This, then, is the temporal domain of the composer of music. The task of composing, as we have defined it, lies in finding symbolic representations for musical events on some or all of these temporal levels of variation.

Alternative notations for music may be characterized by the ways they encode musical thought. Some notations can represent specific qualities of perceived sound (such as pitch) in terms of what should be heard as a function of time. Other notations represent specific instructions to performers regarding actions they are to take with their instruments (such as fingerings, bowings, mutings, and articulatory instructions). Still other notations describe general and often abstract qualities of the music (such as tempo markings and intended emotional states to be induced).

By far the most common notation for musical thought is the traditional and well-entrenched system of staves, clefs, quarter notes, flats and sharps, and barlines. So-called common practice notation (CPN) for music has the built-in advantage of being well-understood by virtually everyone who has received formal training in Western music as well as countless others who have "picked up" music notation as one "picks up" a second or third written language. Another advantage of CPN is that the bulk of an extremely rich and varied musical literature ranging from about the sixteenth century to the present is expressed in it.

CPN is essentially a highly encoded abstract representation of music that lies somewhere between instructions for performance and representation of the sound. Before the advance of CPN, music was commonly notated with so-called *tablature* symbols that described more or less directly what a performer had to do to play it on a particular instrument.

Some forms of tablature notation survive today, most notably the symbols that show actual (if somewhat simplified) fingerings for guitar chords on popular sheet music. The disadvantage of tablature notation, then, is its limitation to specific instruments—the same composition would have to be notated differently for a guitar and a piano, for example.

Because it encodes just pitch, duration, and dynamics, a CPN score may be more easily carried from instrument to instrument as long as the instruments have similar capabilities: harpsichord music may be played on the piano, flute music may be played on the oboe, and so on. Instruments of dissimilar capabilities may all share a fairly compatible notation as well, making it relatively straightforward to arrange a piano score for orchestra and vice versa. Special extensions to CPN can be made for specific instruments as well, such as allowing two five-line staves for pianos and harps, three staves for the pipe organ, and a variety of convenient clefs (today only the treble, alto, tenor, and bass are in common use) according to the pitch range of the instrument.

CPN encodes music in much the same way as written language encodes spoken language. The proper correspondent of CPN in written language is not the text of a novel, however, but the script for a play. Music notation is not meant to be "read"; it is meant to be "read aloud." The CPN equivalents of stage directions are given, typically in quaint Italian terms such as *"presto con fuoco," "largo e mesto,"* and (one of my favorites) *"allegro giusto, nel modo russico; senza allegrezza, ma poco sostenuto."*

Despite its considerable advantages, CPN has disadvantages as well, especially as a notation for computer music. For one thing, CPN is built around the (historically reasonable) idea that instrumental timbres and other characteristics remain fixed in time. CPN therefore does little to represent tone quality, or timbre. It would be difficult to extend CPN to describe the transformation of timbre discussed earlier. A lengthy written description of the intended effect could be attached to a CPN score (such descriptions are often found in modern scores), but that is just the point: the basic notation no longer serves to describe the intentions of the composer very well.

Another disadvantage of CPN is that it describes pitches organized in two basic types of systems: *tonal* systems in which single pitches are primary, and *well-tempered* systems, which admit enharmonic equivalents. Pitch, however, is a *continuum*, while its representation in CPN is inherently *categorical*. Such restrictions on the notation of pitch are entirely appropriate to instruments whose pitch properties remain fixed in time (such as keyboard instruments), but they become increasingly intolerable as the pitches obtainable from instruments become more precisely controlled.

The reasons to retain CPN as a music representation break down altogether when a composer is notating music for machine realization. In the generalized context of computer music, CPN remains useful as a link to human performers (when they *are* human) and little else.

1.4 PERFORMING

Performing music, as we have defined it, is the task of transforming symbolic representations of musical thought into the physical actions necessary to operate a musical instrument so that the specified musical thoughts are realized in sound. While much is known about the symbolic representations (scores) themselves, and a great deal is known about the operating characteristics of musical instruments, very little is known about the nature of performance itself. Clearly, a performer may use a score as a guide to the performance of a particular composition of music. In addition, performers use a great deal of general knowledge about music to make decisions about the most effective manner in which to perform a particular composition. Performers also use acoustic feedback to adjust their actions to the circumstance of a performance.

Consider the notion of a *staccato* (literally, "detached" or "separate") note. In CPN, a composer specifies that a note is to be played staccato by placing a dot over or under it, indicating that it is to sound disconnected from notes that follow it. Such disconnection is typically achieved by operating a musical instrument so that the duration of the note is shortened relative to its "normal" duration, placing a tiny region of silence (or near-silence) between that note and the next. It is the performer's task to decide whether this shortened version of the note is to have 10, 50, or 90 percent of its nominal duration. How does a performer make such a choice?

Among the factors that will determine the "duty cycle" of the staccato note are the operating characteristics of the instrument. Some musical instruments such as the piccolo flute and violin "speak" relatively quickly, giving the performer a broad range of choice in determining note durations even at rapid tempi. Other instruments such as the tuba and contrabass speak relatively slowly, which places a lower bound on the range of available durations.

Even more important, though, is the reverberant quality of the listening room in which the music is played. In a room with a long reverberation time such as a cathedral, notes of even brief duration tend to "ring" for protracted periods of time. In a dry recording studio, notes die out almost immediately after the instrument stops vibrating. In the former environment, a performer is likely to play the same staccato note much shorter than in the latter, because the responses of the rooms will tend to make these two "interpretations" sound equivalent to a listener. Furthermore, the performer will be justified in doing so, because the different manners of performance will both produce precisely what is indicated in the score: a note detached from its successor by a little silence. At least in a certain sense, the room itself is part of the instrument that the performer has to play.

The details of performance have been little studied in any quantitative way because musical performance, unlike composition, occurs in real time. Until recently, therefore, it has been virtually impossible to unravel with any degree of precision what performers actually do . A basic part of musical training consists of learning to take musical dictation, which is the act of writing down CPN to describe a musical performance. Sufficient practice in dictation allows musicians to reconstruct the musical score from which players read by listening. But as in taking dictation of human speech, the notation reveals only the stimulus to which the performers are presumably reacting and not the nature of the reaction itself. In other words, CPN represents much less information than is contained in an actual performance.

Musicians use at least four basic types of information during standard performance:

- Information from the score prepared by a composer
- Information about the nature and response of musical instruments
- General knowledge about musical performance practice
- Acoustic feedback from the performance as it unfolds in a particular room

Performers may also monitor the sounds and actions of other musicians with whom they play in concert, including a conductor whose purpose is to resolve performance interpretation issues during rehearsals and to provide reminders (cues) and interpretive synchronization gestures during performance.

The result of all of these considerations is some type of *inflection* for virtually every note executed by a musician during performance, for example:

- Notes may be accented slightly with tonguing or bowing articulations.
- Rhythms may be distorted slightly (*rubato*) to provide agogic accentuation or de-accentuation of certain notes.
- Pitches may be inflected by a characteristic but variable trajectory.
- Vibrato or tremolo may be applied in a dynamically changing manner during note events.
- Dynamic levels may be adjusted to match those of other instruments or to enhance contrast.
- Specific but unindicated playing techniques may be invoked, consciously or unconsciously, (such as bowing or plucking near the fingerboard or bridge rather than the usual place), to enhance brightness, contrast, or manual feasibility.

This virtually endless list of techniques for expressive innuendo comprises the performer's art and task. Performers are at once beset by the composer's specifications, the historical weight of performance practice, the gestural indications from a conductor, the sounds and mechanical functions (and malfunctions) of an instrument, the vagaries of room acoustics, and the expressions on the faces of the audience.

Performers also are known at times to dispense with composers altogether and to undertake improvisatory control of the formal aspects of the music as well. This is necessary to make sure that they have enough to do during performance. More seriously, it is clear that musical performance is one of the most complex tasks of which human beings are capable, and a better understanding of it will undoubtedly require considerable further research.

1.5 INSTRUMENTS

Musical instruments transform the actions of one or more performers into sound. The characteristics of the sound generated depend on the structure of the instrument as well as the manner in which it is played.

According to the lore of musical acoustics, traditional musical instruments fall into one or more basic categories according to their construction:

- *String instruments*, in which one or more stretched strings are made to vibrate, typically by bowing, plucking, or striking, in conjunction with resonating boxes or sound boards (or both)
- *Wind instruments*, in which fipples, pressure-excited reeds, or buzzing lips are coupled with resonating air columns
- *Percussion instruments*, which include virtually any object that may be struck, typically consisting of bars, plates, or stretched membranes and associated resonators

- *Voices*, which consist of the vocalizing mechanisms of human beings and other animals

In each case, a typical traditional musical instrument consists of an *excitation source* that can be made to oscillate in controllable ways and a *resonating system* that acts to couple these vibrations to the surrounding atmosphere; in so doing, the resonating system also affects the precise patterns of vibration.

Traditional musical instruments are characterized by the range of available pitches under various types of playing conditions, the manners in which the instrument may be usefully played together with the types of sounds associated with these playing techniques, and "personality" characteristics related to musical traditions and idiosyncrasies associated with each instrument.

Computers have been used extensively both to study the operation of traditional musical instruments and to explore nontraditional ways to pattern sound vibrations in musically useful ways. Computer sound synthesis for music generally falls into one or more of four basic categories:

- *Additive synthesis models*, in which elemental sound components (such as sine waves) are added together in time-varying ways
- *subtractive synthesis models*, in which complex sound sources (such as harmonic-rich waveforms, white noise) are subjected to the "whittling away" effect of time-varying digital filters
- *Nonlinear synthesis models*, in which a nonlinear process (such as frequency modulation) is used to synthesize a complex waveform in ways controlled by time-varying parameters
- *Physical synthesis models*, in which the mechanical operation of a real or imaginary instrument is simulated via the (differential equation) techniques of mathematical physics

In addition to these four basic methods of synthesis, the techniques of *digital signal processing* may be applied to virtually any digitally recorded sound, creating the possibility of a kind of *computer musique concrète*. Any and all of these techniques may be—and often are—combined.

The use of the computer as a musical instrument, both in real time and in nonreal time—is one of the most extensively explored subtopics of computer music to date. Even so, the surface of the sonic possibilities of the computer as a source of musical sound has only been scratched.

1.6 ROOMS

No matter how sound is synthesized with a computer, we normally hear it over loudspeakers or headphones. The sound that comes from the loudspeakers can be conceived either as a source (the loudspeaker) in a room (the listening space) or as a reproduction of a sound source in a different (and possibly synthetic) sonic environment.

In the first case, the only room acoustics that come into play are those of the room in which we listen. This situation is analogous to listening to any electronic instrument (such as a Hammond organ) in a sonic environment (such as a concert hall) and is essentially similar to listening to any other instrument playing in that room.

In the second case, however, we can simulate the action of a sonic environment with properties different from those of the playback space. A simple example of this involves listening to almost any orchestral recording played back over loudspeakers in a living room. We hear not only the sounds produced directly by the instruments but the reverberant effects of the concert hall in which the recording was made as well. Without too much imagination (it sometimes helps if we close our eyes), it is possible to hear the orchestra as it sounded in, say, Carnegie Hall, as opposed to how it would sound in our living room (assuming it would fit). A good playback system and recording may even allow us to locate individual instruments in this unseen acoustic space in terms of the distance and direction from where we are listening to the sound source, or instrument.

Limited synthesis of illusory acoustic space can be achieved with echo and reverberation units such as those commonly used in conjunction with electric guitars. A by-now classic debate in sound recording technique deals with whether it is better to place a few (ideally two) microphones at propitious locations in a concert hall or whether the music is better served by "close-miking" every instrument so that the balance of the instrumental sounds is brought under control of the recording engineer as well as the performers. This debate could never have survived long enough to become "classic" unless both methods had true advantages as well as disadvantages, not to mention the fact that the ultimate evaluation of the results is highly subjective and therefore variable according to individual tastes.

The techniques of digital signal processing can be brought to bear on the simulation of the reverberant characteristics of unseen listening environments, giving rise to the notion of an illusory acoustic space into which sounds may be projected. Thus it is possible to compose computer music in terms of the auditory spatial relationships among sounds as well as their pitch, timbre, duration, and so on. Even more striking is the ability to synthesize spatial relationships in a dynamic manner, so that sounds may seem to "move around" in an illusory acoustic space whose properties may vary arbitrarily as time goes by.

1.7 LISTENING

Our ability to use computers to affect perceived properties of sound rests on our understanding not only of sound but on the way in which it is heard by listeners as well. The relationship between the physical properties of sound and the manner in which it is perceived and understood by human beings is a subtopic of the general interdisciplinary field of psychophysics known as *psychoacoustics*. Because the physical properties of sound and the perceptual mechanisms of human beings are complicated in themselves, their interrelationship can be quite complex. The three basic elements of hearing may be represented schematically as follows:

$$\text{Sound waves} \rightarrow \text{auditory perception} \rightarrow \text{cognition}$$

Sound waves normally travel in three dimensions, though we often simplify discussions of them by assuming that they travel only in one. Furthermore, a musical instrument such as a violin emits slightly different sounds simultaneously in all directions. The sound radiation pattern of a given instrument interacts with nearby objects to form a sound *field* in a given listening enclosure. Because music is normally played indoors, the properties of this sound field are quite complex, being affected by the temperature,[5a] humidity,[5b] composition,[5c] and density[5d] of the air; the size,[5e] shape, surface texture,[5f] and composition[5g] of walls, floors, and ceilings; and similar properties of any objects within the listening space. At every point in a listening space, the air pressure varies slightly above and below the atmospheric mean[6] in a slightly different way.

When we listen to a performance in a concert hall, we are literally "bathed" in a complex sound field. Our ears "sample" this sound field at two points separated by less

[5a]A useful formula showing the relation of sound propagation speed to temperature is

$$c \approx 331.7\sqrt{1 + T_C/273} \approx 331.7 + 0.61 T_C$$

where c is the speed of sound in meters per second and T_C is the air temperature in degrees Celsius (°C). This equation states that the speed of sound in a freezing room (0°C) is about 331.7 meters per second, while the speed of sound in a hot room (40°C) is $331.7 + 0.61 \times 40 = 356.1$ meters per second, a variation of just over 7.3 percent. At "normal" room temperatures of around 20°C, sound travels at about 344 meters per second.

[5b]Sound travels slightly faster in wet than in dry air, but the range of speed variation is only on the order of 1.5 percent from 0 to 100 percent relative humidity, so this effect can be ignored under most circumstances. Even this small effect, however, can affect the "spectrum balance" of the reverberant sound in a concert hall.

[5c]Normal dry air is approximately 78 percent nitrogen, 21 percent oxygen, and 1 percent argon by volume, except, perhaps, in Los Angeles.

[5d]It is interesting to note that variations in air pressure do not substantially affect the speed of sound and that all frequencies travel at essentially the same rate, though high frequencies are more readily absorbed and scattered by molecular processes than low frequencies.

[5e]Sound waves readily *diffuse* around objects that are small compared to the sound wavelength, making it possible, among other things, to hear around corners.

[5f]Rough surface textures tend to "trap" sound, especially at high frequencies, while smooth textures tend to reflect sound according to the basic physical law that the angle of reflectance is equal to the angle of incidence.

[5g]Diffraction effects cause more sound to be reflected from surfaces made of a material in which sound travels faster than from a material in which sound moves more slowly. Thus more sound is reflected from a smooth steel wall, than from a smooth wooden wall (sound travels at about 5250 meters per second in steel, about 4100 meters per second in maple wood).

[6]The smallest variation in air pressure that the ear can detect is on the order of 10^{-10} (one ten-billionth) of the mean atmospheric pressure, making it a very sensitive instrument indeed. Furthermore, the largest pressure variation that the ear can tolerate without pain is on the order of 10^{-4} of the mean atmospheric pressure, allowing the ear to operate over an amplitude range of 10^6 to 1. Because sound *intensity* is proportional to the square of the pressure variation, the numbers can seem even more impressive: the ear can detect certain sounds with an intensity of about 10^{-12} watts per square meter and withstand sounds at an intensity of about 1 watt per square meter, for an intensity range of 10^{12} to 1.

than 20 centimeters. The irregular shape of our *pinnae* (outer ears) allows us to distinguish slightly among sounds coming from different directions (front, above, and behind), and the two ears oriented in nearly opposite directions differentiate between sounds coming from the left and right.

Sound waves travel through the air, past the pinna, and into the outer ear canal (meatus), where they strike the timpanic membrane (eardrum), which vibrates sympathetically (see Figure 1-3). A chain of three small bones (middle ear) attached to the inner surface of the timpanic membrane transmits the vibrations to another membrane stretched across one of the openings of the inner ear, or cochlea (so called because it has a spiral shape similar to that of a snail). This membrane is called the oval window.

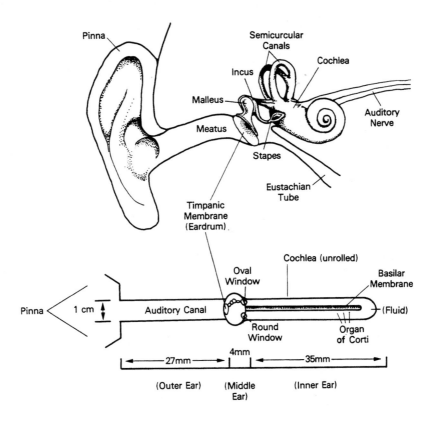

Figure 1-3   The ear.

The cochlea is hollow and filled with fluid. When the oval window vibrates, it produces compression waves in the cochlear fluid. Running through the center of the cochlea is the basilar membrane, which is lined on both sides with about 30,000 hair cells called the organ of Corti. These hair cells are actually frequency-specific nerve endings that are sensitive to forces produced by motion in the cochlear fluid. They generate electrical nerve impulses that exit the cochlea via the massive nerve bundle known as the auditory nerve. The auditory nerves from both ears run toward each other and into the auditory cortex where the signals are interpreted as speech, noise, music, and so on. There is increasing evidence that information from both ears is temporally correlated via "crossover" connections between the two auditory nerves before they enter the brain; this correlation information thereby enters the brain at practically the same time as the information from the ears themselves.

The eventual awareness of sound as music occurs on the highest level of nervous system processing—in the brain. It is essential to distinguish among the physical characteristics of the sound itself, the way in which the sound is perceived, and the eventual recognition and interpretation of the sound on a cognitive level (see Table 1-1).

Table 1-1 Physics→perception→cognition correlates of musical sound

Physics	Perception	Cognition
Air	Ear	Mind (knowledge + judgment)
Existence	Detection	Awareness
Sound	Sensation	Music
Intensity	Loudness	Musical dynamic
Frequency	Pitch	Pitch class
Spectrum	Timbre	Instrument recognition
Radiation	Localization	Subjective spatial map
Content	→	Form

As an example of the trichotomy among the physical, perceptual, and cognitive aspects of musical sound, consider the differences among sound intensity level, loudness, and musical dynamic.

Sound *intensity level* (IL) is measured in decibels above the threshold of hearing at 1000 Hz for acute listeners (10^{-12} watts per square meter) according to the formula

$$\text{IL (in dB)} = 10 \cdot \log_{10} \frac{I}{I_{\text{ref}}} \qquad (1\text{-}1)$$

where I is the intensity in watts per square meter and I_{ref} is 10^{-12} watts per square meter.[7] The well-known Fletcher-Munson curves shown in Figure 1-4 portray the variable sensitivity of human hearing at different frequencies, particularly at low intensity levels. Each Fletcher-Munson curve relates the physical intensity levels needed at various frequencies to produce a perceived sensation of equal loudness. By convention, the individual curves are labeled with their value at 1000 Hz—this value is called the *loudness level* (LL) expressed in *phons*. Thus a loudness level of 60 phons refers to all of the intensity levels along the 60 phon curve in Figure 1-4 (a sound with an intensity level of about 70 dB at 100 Hz is as loud as a sound with an intensity level of about 58 dB at 4000 Hz; both sounds have a loudness level of 60 phons).

[7]Intensity level is equivalent to decibels of sound pressure level (dB SPL) measured with respect to a pressure variation of 0.0002 dynes per square centimeter, or 2×10^{-5} newtons per square meter.

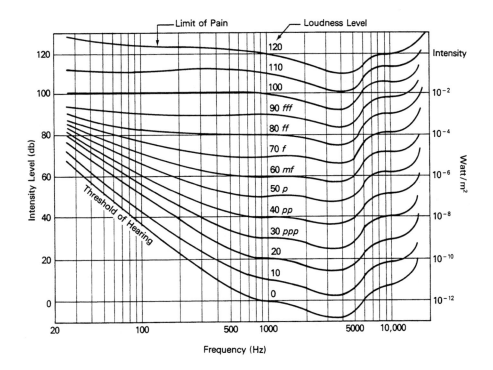

Figure 1-4   Fletcher-Munson curves of equal loudness level (isophons).

Both intensity level and loudness level refer only to the *physical* intensity of a sound. Knowing the intensity level of a sound is not sufficient to determine its perceived loudness, because that will depend on frequency. The loudness level of a sound tells us the intensity level of a 1000-Hz tone that will be equally loud. Does knowing the loudness level of two tones allow us to conclude anything about the relationship between their perceived loudnesses? In other words, because each 3 dB is an approximate doubling of intensity, can we conclude that a tone with a loudness level of 53 phons is twice as loud as a tone with a loudness level of 50 phons?

Unfortunately, the answer is no. The subjective scale of comparative loudness has nothing whatever to do with the so-called loudness level. To compare the loudnesses of two or more tones, we must use the measure of subjective *loudness* (L), which has units called *sones*. On this scale, a sound with a loudness of 2 sones is twice as loud as a sound with a loudness of 1 sone, a sound with a loudness of 100 sones is twice as loud as one with a loudness of 50 sones, and so on. Loudness has been shown to be approximately proportional to the cube root of intensity according to

$$L \approx C \times \sqrt[3]{I} \qquad (1\text{-}2)$$

where L is (subjective, perceived) loudness, I is intensity in watts per square meter, and C is a constant that depends on frequency. According to this relationship, a doubling of loudness requires an eightfold increase in intensity. Because

$$10 \log_{10} 8 = 9.03 \ \ldots$$

we see that a doubling of perceived loudness requires an intensity level (or loudness level) increase of about 9 dB.

In other terms, we might increase the sound intensity eightfold by enlisting eight identical instruments to play the same note. According to relationship (1-2), these eight instruments playing together will sound just twice as loud as a single instrument playing alone—a prediction that is in good accord with musical experience. If the instruments play different notes, however, the situation is more complicated.

The loudness of two or more frequency components is proportional to the cube root of their total intensity only when the frequency components fall within the same *critical band* according to the relationship

$$L \approx C \times \sqrt[3]{I_1 + I_2 + I_3 + \ \cdots} \tag{1-3}$$

where I_1, I_2, . . . , are the intensities of the individual components.[8] If the frequency differences among the components exceeds the critical band, a better prediction of the total subjective loudness is obtained by adding up the loudnesses of each individual component according to

$$L \approx C \times \sqrt[3]{I_1} + C \times \sqrt[3]{I_2} + C \times \sqrt[3]{I_3} + \ \cdots \tag{1-4}$$

Two frequency components of equal intensity will therefore sound louder if they are separated by a perfect fourth (more than a critical band) than if they are separated by a minor second (less than a critical band).[9] Finally, when the separation of the frequency components is very large, the loudness of multiple tones is approximated well simply by the loudness of the loudest among them.[10]

From this discussion we can see that the relationship between perceived loudness and physical intensity is fairly complicated. If we now forge ahead into how the mind attributes a musical dynamic level to the complex tone of a musical instrument, we find that the situation becomes still more complicated.

The tone quality, or *timbre*, of most traditional musical instruments changes with dynamic level. The tone of a trumpet, for example, is "brighter" when it is played *fortissimo* than when it is played *piano* because more high-frequency components are excited when the instrument is blown harder. Our listening experience with this property of a trumpet allows us to distinguish between, say, the sound of a trumpet played softly near the listener and that of a trumpet played loudly but farther away, even though the total intensity of the two sounds might be equal. In other words, we simply cannot turn the sound of a softly played trumpet into that of a loudly played one by turning up a volume control, that merely increases the intensity of the sound. Even assuming a

---

[8]Frequency components separated by less than a critical band interact to produce a "rough" or "beating" sound. At frequencies above about 500 Hz, the size of the critical band is between a major second and a minor third. Below 500 Hz, the critical band becomes progressively larger.

[9]It is important to keep in mind that a *frequency component* is essentially a sinusoidal vibration pattern. The loudness of complex tones such as those of musical instruments will be determined by the interactions of all of the frequency components in both tones.

[10]This effect is attributed primarily to masking of the softer components by louder ones.

constant distance between sound source and listener, we find that intensity is but one factor in determining the overall sense of musical dynamic level.

Musical imagination tends to work in terms of desired interpretations that a musician wishes to impart to the listener on a cognitive level. To produce a desired effect with a computer, we must be acutely aware that the end effect of a synthetic sound will be determined first by how it is perceived and that it will be perceived according to what is physically there. The computer allows us to manipulate the physical properties of the generated sound with great precision, but it is the responsibility of the musician to understand the mapping of these properties through the perceptual and cognitive processes of the listener.

1.8 THE DISCIPLINARY CONTEXT OF COMPUTER MUSIC

Most academic disciplines are disciplines of thought. They exist in order to define a "correct" (or at least useful) view of some subset of human knowledge. Computer music, however, is strongly interdisciplinary. In computer music, therefore, a "correct" view is one that does justice to several points of view simultaneously. An awareness of these points of view is important not so much because ignorance of any one of them makes it impossible to do anything but because what may be done will eventually be limited by that lack of awareness. A great deal has been discovered in different places, and in using the computer to make music, artists are obliged to master as much of this medium of expression as possible.

What are these "several" points of view? In computer music, they start with an awareness of the principles of music (see Figure 1-5). Music is a complicated and very technical subject, the study of which involves the acquisition of as much skill as knowledge. Development of skill generally requires much practice, making it take a long time to learn about music. Practically every facet of music comes into play in the act of its creation. A lack of knowledge of the history of music would give a serious composer certain distinct liabilities, for example. Similarly, a lack of knowledge of music theory, compositional principles, or performance practice would eventually place a limitation on the music produced by any individual.

In programming the computer to make music, we must deal with what philosophers would call objective knowledge about music. While the design of the musical result may include purely subjective components, the accurate reflection of these components in objective choices determines the quality of the resulting musical work. Some fluency in the realm of what is objectively known about music is therefore necessary.

Sound, for instance, is the objective manifestation of music. A great deal is known about sound in general, though perhaps not as much as musicians might like. The science of acoustics—a branch of physics—deals systematically with the objective properties of sound.

Because music is an art produced by humans for the appreciation of other humans, we must also deal with the perceptual qualities of sound, which are in the

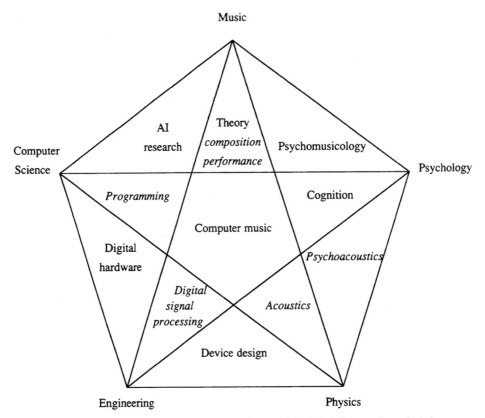

Figure 1-5 Disciplinary context of computer music (essential subdisciplines are shown in *italics*).

purview of psychoacoustics. Many of the most profound problems of computer music lie in the development of new understandings relating what we perceive to what is there. Quite often we are after a particular musical effect, but the properties of the sound are all we can manipulate. Understanding the relation between the objective and subjective properties of sound are at the heart of computer music.

In addition to recognizing the objective properties of sound, the computer requires instructions about how to manipulate it. This is in the realm of digital signal processing, a branch of electrical engineering. Without some knowledge of digital signal processing techniques, all the knowledge of acoustics in the world would not allow us to manipulate sounds with a computer.

Finally, all of the knowledge and skill brought to bear on the problems of computer music must eventually be realized in the form of one or more computer programs. Computer programming is a branch of the more general field of computer science, and it is becoming an increasingly sophisticated art in itself. If the programs required for music production were simple, a rudimentary knowledge of programming would probably suffice in most cases. But the problems of generating music often stretch the capabilities of computers to their limits, making programming skill a determining factor in the viability of many musical plans.

In this treatment of computer music, therefore, we will concentrate on elements that have proved to be useful in the analysis, modification, and synthesis of musical sounds and structures. While much less is known in these areas than we as musicians might like, a great deal is known, though much of it is couched in terms that are not traditionally musical. To be on the same level with the phenomenon of computer music, we shall need the resolve to go considerably beyond musical tradition, into the realms of digital signal processing, acoustics, psychoacoustics, and nontraditional musical structures, all of which is unified by the rich cross-fertilization of music and computers.

1.9 PREREQUISITES

As we have seen, computer music is so strongly interdisciplinary that it would be virtually impossible to describe it in any comprehensive way "from scratch" in a single volume. It is therefore important to make any assumptions about background explicit from the outset.

First and foremost, you must have at least a rudimentary knowledge of musical composition and performance. This includes a familiarity with music notation and the essentials of music theory, including harmony, counterpoint, and orchestration, possibly extending to contemporary serial, aleatoric, and notational techniques.

Second, you must have a rudimentary knowledge of musical acoustics and psychoacoustics. Fortunately, such basic information about sound and its perception is obtainable from a number of well-written and readily available textbooks. Unfortunately, most courses of music study do not include acoustics or psychoacoustics, even though it is hard to imagine anything more useful to a practicing musician than a basic understanding of sound and its perception.

Third, you must know at least the fundamentals of computer programming. All programming examples in this book will be written in the C language, which should be readily understandable if you have programming experience in any structured "algorithmic" language such as Pascal, PL/I, Ratfor (structured FORTRAN), or Algol.

Finally, a word about mathematics. To make the information in this book as widely accessible as possible, mathematical discussions will generally avoid calculus. Only standard high school–level algebra and trigonometry are needed to understand most of the mathematical techniques used in this book. It will sometimes be necessary, however, to define and use mathematical terminology and techniques that go beyond those normally encountered in high school math. Fortunately, there are many excellent review books written on the subject of mathematics that you may find useful from time to time.

With a basic knowledge of music, acoustics, programming, and elementary mathematics, you should find the concepts and techniques of computer music readily accessible. Even dubious preparation in any one of these areas should not hinder you from making good progress, provided you keep a good reference handy.

REFERENCES

1. J. H. Appleton and R. C. Perera, eds., *The Development and Practice of Electronic Music* (Prentice-Hall, Englewood Cliffs, N. J., 1975).

2. J. B. Davies, *The Psychology of Music* (Hutchinson & Co., London, 1978).

3. D. Deutsch, ed., *The Psychology of Music*, Academic Press, Orlando, Fla., (1982).

4. R. C. Fisher and A. D. Ziebur, *Integrated Algebra, Trigonometry, and Analytic Geometry*, (Prentice-Hall, Englewood Cliffs, N. J., 1982).

5. H. L. F. Helmholtz, *On the Sensations of Tone as a Physiological Basis for the Theory of Music* (Dover, New York, 1954).

6. B. W. Kernighan and D. M. Ritchie *The C Programming Language* (Prentice-Hall, Englewood Cliffs, N.J., 1978, 1988).

7. D. E. Knuth, *The Art of Computer Programming. Vol. 1: Fundamental Algorithms* (Addison-Wesley, Reading, Mass., 1968).

8. —*The Art of Computer Programming. Vol. 2: Seminumerical Algorithms* (Addison-Wesley, Reading, Mass., 1969).

9. —*The Art of Computer Programming. Vol. 3: Sorting and Searching*, (Addison-Wesley, Reading, Mass., 1973).

10. M. V. Mathews, F. R. Moore, and J.-C. Risset, "Computers and Future Music," *Science*, *183* (1974): 263–268.

11. H. McGilton and R. Morgan, *Introduction to the UNIX System* (McGraw-Hill, New York, 1983).

12. F. R. Moore, "The Futures of Music" *Perspectives of New Music*, *19* (Fall-Winter 1980, Spring-Summer 1981): 212–226.

13. — *Programming in C with a Bit of UNIX* (Prentice-Hall, Inc., Englewood Cliffs, N.J.,1985).

14. J. R. Pierce, *The Science of Musical Sound* (Freeman, New York, 1983).

15. J. G. Roederer, *Introduction to the Physics and Psychophysics of Music*, (Springer-Verlag, New York, 1975).

16. S. S. Stevens, "Measurement of Loudness," *J. Acoust. Soc. Amer. 27*, (1955): 815.

17. — "Neural Events and Psychophysical Law," *Science 170* (1970): 1043.

18. E. Zwicker, G. Flottorp, and S. S. Stevens, "Critical Bandwidth in Loudness Summation," *J. Acoust. Soc. Amer. 29*, (1957): 548.

2

Digital Audio

A familiarity with the basic ideas of music and computers is a good starting place for the study of their interrelationship. A few additional concepts are needed, however, before one can apply computers effectively to real musical problems. Some of these concepts deal with how computers can synthesize, analyze, and manipulate musical sounds. Because contemporary practice in music does not limit "musical" sound in any particular way, the study of computer applications to musical sound is essentially the study of digital audio.

2.1 SOUND REPRESENTATIONS

In order to manipulate sound directly with a computer, it must be represented in a manner suitable for computer processing. Because computers can manipulate information only in discrete packets of binary digits (*bits*) such as *bytes* or *words*, it is necessary to develop representations for sound that can be expressed in such forms. While considering methods for treating sound with computers, keep in mind that what computers manipulate is not sound itself but representations of sounds called *digital signals*. The first step in understanding digital audio is therefore understanding the correspondence between sound and its representation as a digital signal.

As usual, the same thing can be represented in a variety of ways. For example, to help a traveler to a particular destination, we might draw a map or give a set of directions, which are alternative representations of the information requested by the traveler. Though the map and the directions are not the same, they are equivalent in two ways:

- The result of applying the information, one hopes, will be the same in either case (that is, the traveler will find his destination).
- Either representation may be transformed into the other without information loss.

The information is more abstract than its representation, because the underlying route to the destination may be represented in more than one way.

In considering digital audio methods for computer music, we will encounter important examples of *transformation of representation*. Sound vibrations may be transformed into digital signals in more than one way, each of which will result in a different representation of the "same thing." While the alternative representations are equivalent, they may exhibit different detailed properties. Maps may or may not be drawn to scale, for instance, just as distances specified in a list of directions may be exact or not.

We can convert sounds into digital signals that can be manipulated with a computer. The digital signal, however, may be expressed either as a waveform or as a unique spectrum associated with that waveform. Using computers, we can work with sound in terms of either its waveform or its spectrum. We can convert from one representation to the other at will. The waveform and spectrum representations may correspond to sounds that we have recorded for the purposes of analysis or manipulation, or we can invent arbitrary representations that may or may not correspond to sounds that exist outside the computer.

There are two basic reasons for transforming one representation into another, one having to do with interpretation, the other with manipulation. Because alternative representations vary as to how they depict the same information, it is often true that alternative representations reveal different aspects of the same phenomenon. In effect, choosing a representation is like choosing a point of view (a person may be easier to recognize from the front than say, from behind). Similarly, it may be easier to manipulate the represented information in a particular way from one point of view than another (it is likely to be easier to shake a person's hand from the front as well).

Waveform representations are often convenient to use when temporal aspects are of interest, while spectrum representations are helpful in dealing with frequency aspects. A particular waveform may be transformed into a corresponding spectrum, and vice versa, in a way that causes no loss of information. In effect, the waveform and its associated spectrum are merely two alternative representations of the same phenomenon: the sound itself. This is not surprising if we consider that time and frequency are reciprocals.[1]

---

[1]We say the same thing, for example, when we describe a waveform as having a period of 1 second or a frequency of 1 hertz, because 1 second per cycle is equivalent to 1 cycle per second.

We can convert sound into a digital representation of its waveform by means of an analog-to-digital conversion (ADC) system. Conversely, we can convert a digital representation of a sound into a real sound with a digital-to-analog conversion (DAC) system. Thus we have a practical way to create *digital recordings* of sound because the digital representation of the waveform may be stored in memory that is relatively permanent and transportable. Digital waveform data may also be conveniently transmitted from one location to another, forming the basis for the *digital telecommunication* of sound. Some forms of digital memory may be optimized for compactness, permanence, and weight, such as the currently popular *compact disk*. Other forms of memory are designed to allow ready manipulation of the stored data, such as semiconductor, optical, and magnetic memories used with computers. The type of memory used to store a digital waveform will depend primarily on how we wish to use the data.

Fourier transformation can be used to associate a unique spectrum with any waveform. The spectrum shows, in effect, how to construct the analyzed waveform out of a set of sinusoidal harmonics, each with a particular amplitude and phase. Though it originated as an abstract mathematical technique, Fourier transformation can readily be accomplished by a computer program operating on stored waveform data. A particularly efficient way of calculating the Fourier transform, called the *fast Fourier transform* (FFT), is in common use today and is the mainstay of a subfield of electrical engineering called *digital signal processing*. Much of the theory of digital signal processing is applicable, directly or indirectly, to the manipulation of musical sounds with a computer.

For many musicians, as for many other people, reading that we are about to discuss a subfield of electrical engineering brings a certain tense trepidation. If engineers require intensive training in basic science and mathematics before even beginning to consider the seductive complexities of digital signal processing, how can someone without such training expect to comprehend such a discussion?

The answer to this question, and a host of others like it about music, computers, psychology, and acoustics, is an important issue in the field of computer music. It is, of course, neither possible nor necessary to learn everything about these fields in order to practice computer music effectively. But it is also neither possible nor necessary to practice computer music effectively by learning nothing of the fields that surround it.

To garner as much utility as possible from our consideration of digital audio, we will restrict ourselves to a minimum set of conceptual tools at first, building as much as possible on these. Any relevant mathematics beyond standard high school algebra and trigonometry will be explained before anything is based on it, and calculus will generally be avoided. Fortunately, a knowledge of computer programming is sufficient in itself to allow most digital audio concepts to be grasped from a practical standpoint. Some justifications will necessarily be omitted in order to preserve maximum accessibility. After all, if we had to rederive Euclid's division algorithm every time we wanted to divide one number by another, most people would be unable to settle a check in a restaurant. Mathematicians create mathematics, in part, so that the rest of us can simply use it. Using mathematics in this way hardly makes us mathematicians, to be sure, but it benefits us enormously.

We now proceed to survey digital audio by examining key concepts of sound, its representations in digital form, transformations among these representations, and their interpretation.

2.1.1 Transducers

A *transducer* converts energy or information from one form to another. The ear is a transducer because it converts the physical energy in a sound wave into encoded electrical nerve impulses. The apparent form of these nerve impulses bears little resemblance to the apparent form of the sound wave. The *information* contained in the nerve impulses, however, reflects certain properties of the sound wave with remarkable accuracy.

A microphone is also a transducer. Like the ear, a microphone "samples" a complex sound field at a particular position in space—ideally at a single point. A microphone may respond equally to sounds coming from all directions, or it may "prefer" some directions to others in various ways. We could even place a microphone in a "dummy head" replete with pinnae and ear canals. The diaphragm in a microphone corresponds conceptually to the timpanic membrane in an ear. Beyond the diaphragm, however, the structure and function of a microphone begins to diverge from that of the ear, which tends to become increasingly analytic from stage to stage. The microphone, by contrast, has but a single purpose: to convert air pressure variations into analogous variations in electrical current (or, equivalently, electrical voltage). The accuracy with which the microphone does its task strengthens the analogy between the air pressure and electrical signal variations. Thus the electrical signal produced by a microphone is called an *analog signal*.

Analog signals can be transmitted or transduced further. At audio frequencies, they travel well through wires. They can be amplified or attenuated in well-understood ways. An ideal amplifier multiplies the analog signal by a constant dimensionless value called the *gain* of the amplifier. Real amplifiers introduce small amounts of noise and distortion into the output signal as well. The art of amplifier design includes methods by which noise and distortion are held to perceptually acceptable levels.

The inverse transducer to the microphone is the loudspeaker, which converts electrical energy back into sound energy. To accomplish this transduction, a moving coil loudspeaker first converts the electrical energy of the analog signal to a time-varying magnetic field that causes an electrical inductor called a *voice coil* to move back and forth according to the electrical variations in the analog signal. The voice coil is attached to a diaphragm made of paper or polypropylene that disturbs the adjacent air. The sound energy produced by a loudspeaker thereby reproduces the original sound field at the point measured by the microphone.

An ideal loudspeaker is a point source of sound that matches precisely the one measured by the microphone. Real loudspeakers introduce far more distortion into the generated pressure wave than microphones or amplifiers. Real loudspeakers also cannot produce a very broad range of frequencies simultaneously, making it necessary to use a system of at least two or three of them to cover the range of human hearing adequately.

Electronic circuits called *crossover networks* are used to apportion energy at various frequencies in the analog signal to separate "drivers" that individually operate over limited frequency ranges.

2.1.2 Analog Signals

Suppose that the pressure variation at a single point in the sound field—the one measured by the microphone—is denoted $p(t)$ and that the output of the microphone is a time-varying voltage, $v(t)$. Ideally, we would like to have the relationship

$$v(t) \propto p(t) \tag{2-1}$$

where $\propto$ means "is proportional to". That is, when $p(t)$ changes, $v(t)$ also changes precisely by some corresponding amount. All real microphones, however, introduce a certain amount of distortion and noise into the analog signal. Mathematically, we can describe the effects of distortion and noise with the relationship

$$v(t) \propto D[p(t)] + n(t) \tag{2-2}$$

where $p(t)$ and $v(t)$ are defined as before, $n(t)$ is a function that describes the *noise* added to the signal by the system, and $D[\,\cdot\,]$ is a system function that characterizes *distortion*. Obviously, if

$$D[x] = x \tag{2-3}$$

then there will be no distortion, and the system is said to be *linear*. In fact, if the right side of equation 2-3 describes *any* straight line (that is, if it has the form $mx + b$, where m is the slope and b is the intersection of the line with the vertical axis), then the system will be linear and distortion-free (we will see plots of other possible system functions later).

The amount of noise added by the system effectively limits the useful dynamic range of a microphone, because the noise has an essentially constant average amplitude. Mechanical and electrical limitations effectively limit the frequency response of microphones and introduce small nonlinearities into the detailed shape of the analog waveform. We will return to these limitations later; for now, let us assume that relationship (2-3) holds precisely.

Because the electrical output of a microphone represents an air pressure variation at a single point in space, we can graph it conveniently in two dimensions. By convention, such a waveform plot consists of a horizontal axis that measures time in arbitrary units with an arbitrary ($t = 0$) starting point. The vertical axis measures amplitude in arbitrary units. The information about the sound in such a graph is contained in the detailed shape of the waveform.

Waveforms come in an infinite variety of shapes. Of special interest are waveforms that consist of repetitions of particular patterns—so-called *periodic* waveforms—because these give rise to the musical sensation of *definite pitch*. In mathematics, a periodic function is one that repeats the identical pattern over and over again for all time:

$$f(t + \tau) = f(t) \qquad\qquad (2\text{-}4)$$

The smallest nonzero value of τ for which equation (2-4) is true *for all values of t* is called the *period* of periodic function $f(t)$.

Musical sounds are never periodic in this mathematical sense, if only because they have beginnings and endings (that is, they do not exist in *all* time). Furthermore, sound waveforms change over time—the waveform in the middle of a note with a single musical pitch may vary considerably from the waveform near the beginning or end. Nevertheless the idealized periodic function described by equation (2-4) is a very useful tool for describing sounds because it is simple and understandable, and because it approximates the behavior of large portions of many musical waveforms.

To develop a more concrete example, let us assume that $p(t)$ is a sinusoidal sound pressure wave measured at a particular point in space with a frequency of 440 Hz and a peak amplitude of 2 pascals (Pa),[2] that is, the maximum deviation in pressure is 2 pascals above and below the mean atmospheric pressure level (this corresponds to a sound with an intensity level of about 100 dB SPL, which is just a bit louder than the loudest note a trombone can produce). We may describe this pressure wave by assuming that time is measured (arbitrarily) from a zero point corresponding to a moment when the pressure rises above the atmospheric mean with the formula

$$p(t) + a = 2 \cdot \sin(2\pi\, 440\, t) + a \qquad \text{Pa} \qquad (2\text{-}5)$$

where a is the mean atmospheric pressure in pascals.[3] For example, suppose that a particular electret microphone has a typical sensitivity rating described as −60 dB with respect to 1 volt per dyne per square centimeter, meaning that it will produce an electrical signal at its output with a peak of ±1 millivolt when measuring a sound pressure waveform with a pressure that varies ±1 dyne per square centimeter from the atmospheric mean.

The peak amplitude of the sound pressure wave described in equation (2-5) is 2 pascals, or 20 dynes per square centimeter. Our microphone will therefore produce an analog signal with a peak amplitude of 20 millivolts in response to the sound, which might be described with the formula

$$v(t) = 20 \cdot \sin(2\pi\, 440t) \qquad \text{mV} \qquad (2\text{-}6)$$

Again we have ignored the noise and distortion introduced into the analog signal by the operation of the microphone. We now turn to a characterization of these effects.

2.1.3 Noise

For our present purposes we may define *noise* as any unwanted signal added to the analog signal that bears the waveform information. *Broadband noise* consists of energy

---

[2]Metric units are defined in Appendix B.

[3]One standard atmosphere is a pressure equal to 101,325 pascals, or 1,013,250 dynes per square centimeter. Because 1 pascal is defined as 1 newton per square meter and 1 newton is equal to 10^5 dynes, we may convert from pascals to dynes per square centimeter by simply multiplying by 10.

at many frequencies—so-called *white noise*, for example, consists of all frequencies simultaneously in equal proportion.

A common figure of merit for analog systems is the so-called *signal-to-noise ratio* (SNR), which is usually defined as the ratio between the amplitudes of the largest useful signal and the amplitude of the inherent noise in a system. Because inherent noise tends to have a constant amplitude (that is, it does not depend on the strength of the signal), it tends to provide a lower limit to the range of useful signal amplitudes. Similarly, noise introduced by imperfect operation of an analog system (such as power supply hum) also provides a "floor" (minimum value) to the range of useful signal amplitudes.

Noise waveforms may be periodic or nearly so, as in the case of hum, or they may be aperiodic, as in the case of broadband noise introduced by the random heat dance of matter. Peak amplitude is not a useful measure of random waveforms precisely because they are random: a momentarily large peak noise amplitude is of less significance than the average noise amplitude. The term *average* has several interpretations, all of which get at different aspects of the subtle problem of replacing a set of numbers by a single number that is somehow "the same."

For example, what is the "average" value of the voltage described by equation (2-6)? Because $v(t)$ is a sine wave, half of its values are positive and the other half are negative. Due to the inherent symmetry of the sine wave, the negative-going half cycle has exactly the same shape as the positive-going half. If we were somehow to "add up all the amplitude values" in one period of a sinusoid in order to calculate its average value, we would perforce get zero. The procedure of calculating the arithmetic mean does not seem to distinguish the amplitude of one sinusoid from any other, regardless of their peak amplitudes.

What exactly does the phrase "add up the amplitude values" mean? A sinusoid is not a number or a collection of numbers; it is a smoothly, continuously varying waveform. To interpret the phrase "add up the amplitude values," we can substitute a list of numbers for the smoothly varying waveform. Consider one period of a pure sine waveform with amplitude equal to 1. If we take four equally spaced values of one period of a sine curve starting from the beginning, the resulting list of amplitude values will be 0, 1, 0, and –1. The arithmetic mean of these four values is just

$$\frac{0 + 1 + 0 + (-1)}{4} = 0$$

Taking eight equally spaced values results in the list 0, 0.707, 1, 0.707, 0, –0.707, –1, and –0.707, which also have an arithmetic mean of zero. As long as we choose to measure the period at equally spaced intervals that represent the positive and negative portions of the cycle equally well, we will clearly obtain the same result.[4]

---

[4]We would not obtain the same result if we were to choose three equally spaced measurements because the first two measurements (at 0/3 and 1/3 of the cycle) would occur in the positive half of the waveform while the last measurement (2/3 of the way through the cycle) would occur in the negative half-cycle. Note that this is a property of the sine waveform and not of the measurements.

We might obtain the average difference between the amplitude of a sinusoid and zero by adding up all the *absolute values* of amplitude and taking their arithmetic mean. Using this method for the case of four equally spaced measurements would yield an average difference of

$$\frac{|0| + |1| + |0| + |-1|}{4} = 0.5$$

If we apply the same method to the eight equally spaced measurements, though, the answer changes to

$$\frac{|0| + |0.707| + |1| + |0.707| + |0| + |-0.707| + |-1| + |-0.707|}{8} = 0.603 \ldots$$

A far more common approach to measuring the average value of a waveform is to use the so-called *root-mean-square* (rms) method. As implied by the name, we square each measurement value (this converts each measurement into a related positive value), find the arithmetic mean of the square values, and take the square root of the result. Applying the rms method to the four measurement values (recalling that the square root of a quantity x may be written either as $\sqrt{x}$ or $x^{1/2}$) results in a value of

$$\left[\frac{0^2 + 1^2 + 0^2 + -1^2}{4} \right]^{1/2} = 0.707 \ldots$$

Similarly, applying the rms method to the list of eight measurements given previously yields the same result:

$$\left[\frac{0^2 + 0.707^2 + 1^2 + 0.707^2 + 0^2 + -0.707^2 + -1^2 + -0.707^2}{8} \right]^{1/2} = 0.707 \ldots$$

We therefore say that the rms amplitude of a sinusoid with a peak amplitude of 1 is equal to 0.707 . . . The rms amplitude of the voltage waveform described by equation (2-6) is therefore[5]

$$20 \times 0.707 = 14.14 \text{ mV (rms)}$$

The 0.707 factor applied in general, but only for *sinusoidal* waveforms; a square waveform that alternates between steady values of ±10 volts, for example, has an rms amplitude of 10 volts.

To define the signal-to-noise ratio of an analog system (such as a microphone), then, we take the ratio of the rms amplitude of the maximum useful signal level and the rms amplitude of the noise rather than their peak amplitudes:

$$\text{SNR} = \frac{\text{maximum signal amplitude}}{\text{noise amplitude}} \qquad (2\text{-}7)$$

[5]One reason for the widespread use of the rms method of measuring the average signal amplitude is that the rms value expresses the precise level of a steady, nonvarying signal of *equivalent power*. Thus 120 V.A.C. household current can deliver the same amount of power as 120 V.D.C. because 120 is actually the *rms* value of the voltage in a wall socket: the peak value of household voltage is actually $120/0.707 \approx 170$ volts.

Rather than use the simple ratio as expressed in equation (2-7) it is common practice to express the signal-to-noise ratio in decibels (dB) thus:

$$\text{SNR (in dB)} = 20 \cdot \log \frac{\text{maximum signal amplitude}}{\text{noise amplitude}} \qquad (2\text{-}8)$$

What determines the "maximum useful" signal amplitude? Most electronic devices introduce *distortion* into the signal being processed, where distortion refers to some type of undesired change in the *shape* of the waveform. Distortion usually increases as the amplitude of the signal increases; the "maximum useful" signal amplitude is therefore usually one at which distortion effects are kept below some maximum tolerable level.

2.1.4 Distortion

Distortion may generally be divided into three types: frequency distortion, amplitude distortion, and phase distortion.

Frequency distortion is caused by the inability of an electronic device to perform equally well at all frequencies. For example, our microphone may be able to maintain a response of –60 dB with respect to 1 volt per dyne per square centimeter only over a range of frequencies from, say, 50 Hz to 13,000 Hz. Outside this range the output of the microphone will probably drop off gradually to no response at all. Even inside the operating range of 50–13,000 Hz, the microphone may not respond *exactly* the same way to all frequencies, causing its response not to be perfectly "flat." Electronic devices are typically characterized by a range of operating frequencies over which their response is relatively flat to within a tolerance of plus or minus a few decibels or less. Significant deviation from flat response results in "coloration" of the processed signal wherein some frequencies are emphasized and others attenuated.

Another example of frequency distortion is the inability of the ear to respond equally well to all frequencies within the range of human hearing. The Fletcher-Munson curves we saw in Chapter 1 show how the physical intensity of sounds must change at various frequencies in order to produce the same perceived loudness level.

Amplitude distortion is introduced by nonlinearities in the response (system function) of a device to various values of input signal amplitude. In a linear system, if an input amplitude of X produces an output response of Y, then an input of $2X$ should produce an output of $2Y$. In other words, a linear system maps its input to its output with a linear (straight-line) mapping function (see Figure 2-1). More generally, if input X_1 gives rise to output Y_1 and input X_2 gives rise to output Y_2, then any input consisting of a weighted combination of X_1 and X_2 should result in the same linear combination of outputs Y_1 and Y_2. Stated in mathematical terms, a system is linear if input $aX_1 + bX_2$ gives rise to output $aY_1 + bY_2$, where a and b are arbitrary constant values.

Nonlinear distortion occurs, for example, when an amplifier is pushed beyond its limits. Suppose that the voltage gain of the amplifier is 100 and that an input signal has a peak amplitude of 0.1 volt. The output signal should then have a peak amplitude of 10 volts. But as the peak amplitude of the input signal grows, the maximum output of the amplifier will eventually be exceeded (see Figure 2-2). Let us say that the

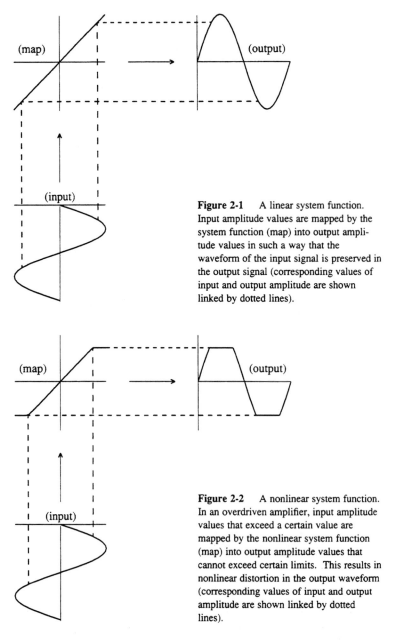

Figure 2-1   A linear system function. Input amplitude values are mapped by the system function (map) into output amplitude values in such a way that the waveform of the input signal is preserved in the output signal (corresponding values of input and output amplitude are shown linked by dotted lines).

Figure 2-2   A nonlinear system function. In an overdriven amplifier, input amplitude values that exceed a certain value are mapped by the nonlinear system function (map) into output amplitude values that cannot exceed certain limits. This results in nonlinear distortion in the output waveform (corresponding values of input and output amplitude are shown linked by dotted lines).

maximum voltage output of our particular amplifier is ±20 volts. An input signal with a peak amplitude of 0.2 volts would, given our supposed voltage gain of 100, push the amplifier to its maximum output limit. What happens if the input signal grows to have a peak amplitude of 0.3 volts? As the input signal goes from 0 to 0.2 volts, the output of the amplifier would grow from 0 to 20 volts, but as the input signal continues to grow, the output would simply remain *saturated* (effectively "stuck") at its maximum value. When the input signal recedes below 0.2 volts, the amplifier output would again be able to express its value proportionally.

Now let us compare the input and output waveforms of the overdriven amplifier. Suppose for simplicity that the input signal is sinusoidal. The output signal under the conditions we have described would look like a sinusoid with its extreme values "clipped" by the inability of the amplifier to produce them and would therefore look something like a square wave (albeit with slightly rounded transitions between the extreme values). Clearly, the shapes of the input and waveforms are not the same.

Nonlinearities in the system function can distort the shape of the waveform in a wide variety of ways. Figure 2-3 shows how a particular type of nonlinearity can transform a sinusoid—in this case a cosine waveform—into another waveform that consists of equal parts of the input fundamental and its second harmonic. We will study such transformations in detail when we take up the topic of computer sound synthesis.

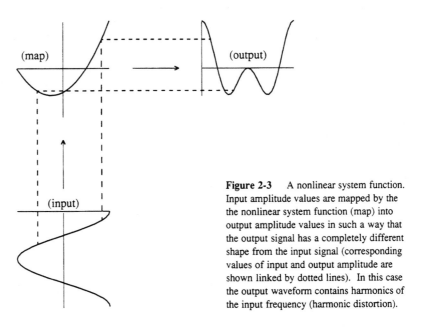

Figure 2-3 A nonlinear system function. Input amplitude values are mapped by the the nonlinear system function (map) into output amplitude values in such a way that the output signal has a completely different shape from the input signal (corresponding values of input and output amplitude are shown linked by dotted lines). In this case the output waveform contains harmonics of the input frequency (harmonic distortion).

Signal processing devices may operate quickly, but not instantaneously: a small but measurable time delay occurs between the input and the output. If several frequencies are present simultaneously in the input signal, an ideal device will maintain their time alignment in the output signal. *Phase distortion* occurs when this time delay is not the same for all frequencies (see Figure 2-4). A typical loudspeaker system, for example, might consist of three drivers for low, middle, and high frequencies (they would be called a *woofer*, a *squawker*, and a *tweeter* in hi-fi parlance). Suppose that the input signal to the loudspeaker system is a signal consisting of the sum of three sinusoids at

100, 1000, and 10,000 Hz and that they are all in sine phase (that is, their positive-going zero crossings all occur simultaneously at an arbitrary reference time $t = 0$). If the high-frequency driver is recessed into the loudspeaker cabinet, placing it slightly farther from a listener than the other two drivers, the signal coming directly from that driver will reach the listener slightly after the other two signals. This delay may be quite small, but the wavelength of the 10,000-Hz waveform is a mere 3.44 centimeters. Recessing the driver by one-fourth of this amount (less than 1 cm) would introduce a 90° phase shift at 10,000 Hz. The waveform at the listener's position would have a different time alignment than the input signal, resulting in a completely different waveform.

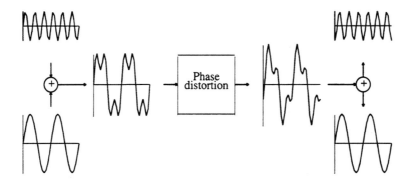

Figure 2-4   Phase distortion. The input signal consists of the sum of two frequency components at X Hz and $3X$ Hz, both in sine phase. The phase distortion stage introduces slightly more delay at $3X$ Hz than at X Hz, thereby changing the time alignment of the frequency components in the output signal, with a resulting distortion of the waveform. In this example, the $3X$ Hz component is delayed by a quarter cycle (90° at $3X$ Hz) more than the X Hz component.

The perceptual effects of various types of noise and distortion are subtle and complex. Each type of noise and distortion produces a different type of perceptual effect whose relevance depends on the type of sound used to test the effect. For steady, complex tones, the auditory system seems to be fairly insensitive to phase distortion, more sensitive to frequency distortion, and even more sensitive to amplitude distortion. The waveform of a sound therefore seems to be a poor predictor of its subjective effect because two waveforms that appear very similar but are amplitude-distorted with respect to each other can sound quite different. Conversely, two extremely different waveforms that are phase-distorted with respect to each other can sound quite similar. Tones with rapid transients, however, seem to be perceptually degraded by phase distortion under certain circumstances. Fairly large amounts of broadband noise will often be tolerated more readily than fairly small amounts of narrowband noise. In general, we may conclude only that the less noise and distortion a given system introduces, the better and that state-of-the art audio equipment is capable of keeping noise and distortion to a level that affords electronically processed sound a high degree of verisimilitude with respect to reality.

2.1.5 Recording

To transmit sounds through time as well as space, it is necessary to store the analog signal in some form of memory for later recall. By far the most commonly used medium of analog recording is magnetic tape. The analog signal generated by a microphone is converted into a time-varying magnetic field through the action of a magnetic recording head. A magnetically sensitive material such as iron oxide is passed at a uniform rate of speed through the time-varying magnetic field, resulting in a magnetic "impression" that remains after the magnetic force is removed. The process is also reversible: passing the magnetized recording past a magnetic playback head induces in it a time-varying electrical signal that is ideally identical to the analog signal that was recorded.

As before, noise and distortion are introduced when the original analog signal is transduced into magnetic form and once again when the magnetic impression on the tape recording is transformed back into electrical form. The most serious type of noise is a broadband noise that tends to sound like hiss because of the nonuniform frequency response of the ear. Nonuniform response of the magnetic tape introduces frequency distortion, and the recording process itself introduces unavoidable types of phase distortion, both of which require compensating circuitry. Furthermore, the magnetic impression degrades with time because of exposure to heat, light, stray magnetic fields, and other forms of radiation. Magnetic tape recordings even tend to affect themselves, the magnetic impression from one part of a recording tending to impress nearby parts of the same recording through the phenomenon known as *print-through*. Nonuniformities in the distribution of magnetically sensitive substances invariably lead to "dead spots" on the tape that cause *dropouts* in the recorded signal.

To combat the most insidious problem endemic to analog recording, noise reduction devices may be used. The Dolby system, for example, preemphasizes certain regions of frequency in the analog signal at which tape noise is most noticeable. On playback, precisely the same frequency regions are deemphasized by the same amount, thereby restoring the frequency balance of the original signal while simultaneously attenuating the tape noise.

Except for computer-aided composition for traditional instruments, the key to almost every application of computers to music lies in the ability to represent sound digitally, that is, with numbers that can be manipulated by a computer. The key elements relevant to audio signals are shown in Figure 2-5.

The upper part of the figure, labeled "Analog Transmission," depicts electronic means that allow sounds to be transmitted through space; the elements shown form the basis of a one-way telephone hookup, for example. The middle part of the figure shows a means whereby sounds may be transmitted through time, that is, stored (recorded) for later audition; the basic elements of a tape recorder are shown. The bottom part of the figure shows the basic elements needed for digital audio; the output of the ADC might be connected directly to the input of the DAC for spatial transmission, or a digital

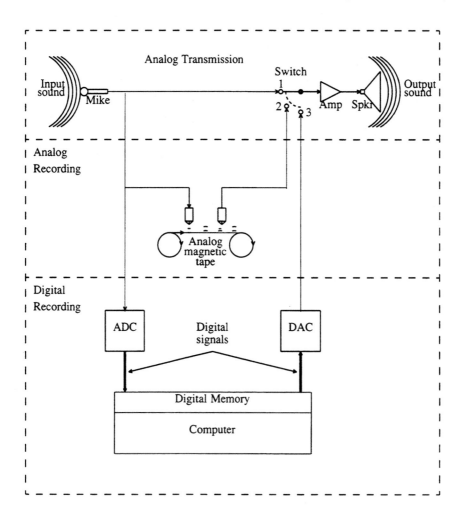

Figure 2-5   Audio signal relationships.

memory may be used to store the digital signal for later audition or manipulation via the computer. The three-position switch in the upper part of Figure 2-5 allows the output sound to be switched among the three basic possibilities shown: analog transmission, analog recording, and digital recording.

2.2 SOUND DIGITIZATION

The Dolby noise reduction system achieves its results by recording a signal derived from the analog signal. The derived signal is said to be *encoded*, because it is not the same as the original analog signal. Reconstruction of the analog signal from the Dolby-encoded one requires a *decoding* process. The encoding process is useful only insofar as it is possible to reconstruct the original analog signal from the encoded one as degraded by the magnetic recording process. The encoding and decoding processes must be precisely complementary; that is, the decoded signal must match the original analog signal to within tolerable limits of noise and distortion.

2.2.1 ADC and DAC Systems

A more extreme form of analog signal encoding is analog-to-digital conversion. In a particular form of analog-to-digital conversion called *pulse code modulation* (PCM), the original analog signal is replaced by a sequence of binary digits (*bits*) that represent precisely the waveform of the original signal. One of the fundamental advantages gained through the use of PCM is that the encoded (digital) signal has one of only two possible values at any given moment—one representing the value 0 and the other representing 1. To reconstruct the analog signal from the digital one, the decoder has only to be able to distinguish whether a 0 or a 1 was originally transmitted or recorded by the encoder. A PCM-encoded signal is therefore far more impervious to any noise that it might encounter in a transmission or recording medium.[6]

2.2.2 Sampling

Analog-to-digital conversion is conceptually a three-stage process (see Figure 2-6). The analog signal is first processed by a lowpass filter to remove any frequency components above $R/2$ Hz, where R is the sampling rate to be used in the next stage.[7] It is necessary to remove high-frequency components from the analog signal because of the basic rule of sampling, called the *sampling theorem* (or the *Nyquist theorem* after Harry Nyquist, its inventor):

SAMPLING THEOREM

To represent digitally a signal containing frequency components up to X Hz, it is necessary to use a sampling rate of at least $2X$ samples per second.

---

[6]Besides PCM, other encoding schemes occasionally employed for digitized signals include differential pulse code modulation (DPCM), pulse amplitude modulation (PAM), pulse width modulation (PWM), delta modulation (DM), and adaptive forms of most of these (such as ADPCM, adaptive differential pulse code modulation). PCM is by far the most commonly used scheme for digital audio, and all other schemes can be expressed in terms of an equivalent PCM signal. Furthermore, almost all processing methods for digital audio are more straightforward to implement with PCM-encoded signals than any other. We shall therefore restrict our consideration to PCM.

[7]A *lowpass* filter passes frequency components *below* some *cutoff frequency*. Similarly, a *highpass filter* passes frequency components *above* some cutoff frequency. A *bandpass filter* passes only frequency components lying within a certain range, while a *bandreject filter* rejects frequency components within a certain range.

Signal Representation

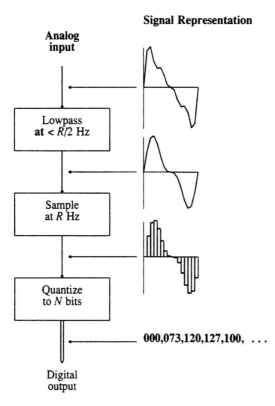

Analog
input

Lowpass
at $< R/2$ Hz

Sample
at R Hz

Quantize
to N bits

000,073,120,127,100, . . .

Digital
output

Figure 2-6   Analog-to-digital conversion system. The analog input signal is lowpass-filtered to remove any components above the Nyquist rate (one-half the sampling rate). The filtered signal is then sampled at R Hz; each sample is quantized to N bits of precision.

The sampling theorem states that if we wish to create a digital signal that contains all audible frequencies up to 20,000 Hz, we must use a sampling rate of *at least* 40,000 samples per second. Each sample consists ideally of an instantaneous measurement of the amplitude of a vibration pattern. Stated succinctly,

- The lowpass filter removes any frequency components in the analog signal that exceed one-half the sampling rate.

- The sampling process "measures" the instantaneous amplitude of the resulting vibration pattern at equally spaced intervals of time.

- The quantizer converts each measurement taken by the sampler into a corresponding numeric value.

The resulting sequence of numeric values is called a *digital signal*.

Possibly the easiest way to understand the sampling theorem is to consider that a vibration consists at the very least of some sort of back-and-forth, or to-and-fro pattern. In order for the digital signal to represent such a vibration pattern, it must contain at least one value for "back" and one value for "forth"; therefore, the digital signal must contain at least two numbers for each cycle of any input signal frequency component.

If the sampled signal contains any frequency components that exceed one-half the sampling rate (the *Nyquist rate*), the sampling process will essentially misrepresent the information in the sampled signal in a particular way, leading to a phenomenon known as *foldover* or *aliasing*. To understand the aliasing phenomenon, we must consider how the analog signal is reconstructed from the digital one.

Reconstruction of the analog signal from the digital signal is accomplished in the corresponding decoding process known as digital-to-analog conversion. The digital-to-analog conversion system shown in Figure 2-7 consists of essentially the same three types of operations involved in analog-to-digital conversion, applied in reverse order.

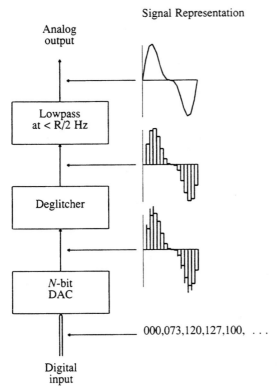

Figure 2-7   Digital-to-analog conversion system. The digital signal is converted to a time-varying voltage by the DAC module, whose output is a time-varying voltage proportional to the sequence of numbers at its input. Switching noise ("glitches") introduced by the DAC at transitions from one value to another are removed by the deglitcher (essentially a sample and hold circuit). The resulting staircase signal is smoothed by a lowpass filter whose cutoff frequency is at or below one-half the sampling rate.

The first stage is digital-to-analog conversion itself, which is accomplished by a digital-to-analog converter (DAC) stage. Conceptually, the DAC operation is very simple: the DAC emits a voltage proportional to the number at its input. New sample values are applied to the input of the DAC at the sampling rate.

We have assumed the sample values to be in binary form; that is, each numeric value consists of N bits, which we may designate as follows:

$$b_{N-1}\ b_{N-2}\ \cdots\ b_2\ b_1\ b_0$$

For example, if $N = 8$ bits, the binary representation for the value 1_{10} would be 0000 0001, 2_{10} would be 0000 0010, 24_{10} would be 0001 1000, and so on. Clearly, 8-

bit samples can take on any of $2 \times 2 \times 2 \times 2 \times 2 \times 2 \times 2 \times 2 = 2^8 = 256$ different values.

Because each binary digit can only be either 1 or 0, DAC construction is conceptually very simple. Each bit simply operates a binary switch that is either open or closed, depending on whether the corresponding bit is 1 or 0. The output of switch k is either a voltage proportional to 2^k volts (if the corresponding input bit b_k is a 1) or 0 volts (if the corresponding input bit is a 0). If we add up the voltages output by all switches in response to a binary input value, this voltage will be proportional to the numeric value of the input. This is essentially the way the DAC circuit operates—the switching is done by transistors that are turned on and off by the individual bits of the binary input value.

When a binary value is input to such a circuit, all the switches require a small amount of time (perhaps just a few microseconds or even nanoseconds) to operate. It is, however, nearly impossible for each switch to operate in exactly the same amount of time as all the other switches, because individual transistors are not identical, and each one in a DAC circuit has to switch a different amount of voltage on or off. Nonuniformities in the operation time of these switches cause the output voltage to vary wildly for a short time until all switches "settle down" to the correct output value. These short-lived and unpredictable variations that occur during transitions from one output value to another are called *glitches*.

The glitches must be removed from the output of the DAC because they have essentially nothing to do with the information in the digital signal. A sampling circuit is used to accomplish glitch removal—the samples are taken near the center of each sample period after the glitches have died out and before the value begins to change again. The resulting staircase waveform is essentially identical to the output of the sampling circuit during analog-to-digital conversion.[8]

The lowpass filter in the digital-to-analog conversion system serves the purpose of *smoothing* the abrupt transitions in the staircase waveform. The resulting analog signal is nearly identical to the one output by the lowpass filter during analog-to-digital conversion. Ideally, the only remaining difference is because of the operation of the quantizer.

2.2.3 Aliasing

We now return to the question of how aliasing works.[9] If we attempt to represent a frequency digitally with a magnitude greater than $R/2$ Hz, where R is the sampling rate, we find that the digital-to-analog reconstruction process misrepresents that frequency as some other frequency inside the range from $-R/2$ to $+R/2$ Hz. Figure 2-8 shows sinusoids at three different frequencies, one less than the Nyquist rate ($R/2$ Hz), one at the Nyquist rate, and one above the Nyquist rate. Frequency components sampled more than once per period are called *oversampled*, those sampled exactly twice per period are

---

[8]Sampling circuits for high-quality digital audio also smooth the transitions from one sample value to the next in an exponential way in order to maximize the linearity of the digital-to-analog conversion process.

[9]Additional details on aliasing can be found in Moore (1978b/1985b).

called *critically sampled*, and those above half the sampling rate are referred to as *undersampled*. The dotted waveform in Figure 2-8 represents how the undersampled sinusoid would be reconstructed during digital-to-analog conversion. We see that, as predicted, the reconstructed waveform in the undersampling case has a frequency *lower* than the one that was sampled. This aliasing effect occurs because the samples of the actual frequency component are *indistinguishable* from those that would be obtained from sampling the dotted waveform.

The frequency of the reconstructed waveform depends on the relation of the sampling rate to the original waveform frequency according to the formula

$$f_r = f + kR \qquad (2\text{-}9)$$

where f is the frequency of the component, f_r is the frequency of the component reconstructed during digital-to-analog conversion, and k is an integer that satisfies the relation

$$\frac{-R}{2} < f + kR < \frac{R}{2} \qquad (2\text{-}10)$$

If f lies inside the range $\pm R/2$ Hz, inequality (2-10) will be satisfied with k equal to 0. The reconstructed frequency is then equal to the *component* frequency (that is, no foldover occurs). If f is undersampled, then either $f > R/2$ or $f < -R/2$ Hz. For example, if R is set to 10,000 Hz and f to 6000 Hz, then k must be equal to -1 to satisfy the inequality and the reconstructed frequency will occur at -4000 Hz (do not let the idea of negative frequencies bother you—they sound just like positive ones except for a possible 180° phase shift).

We can solve inequality (2-10) generally by setting k as follows:

$$k = -\text{int}\left[\frac{2f}{R}\right] \qquad (2\text{-}11)$$

where int means "the integer part of." We can then restate inequality (2-10) as

$$f_r = f - \left[\text{int}\left[\frac{2f}{R}\right]\right]R \qquad (2\text{-}12)$$

Equation (2-12) states that in the absence of lowpass filtering, a reconstructed sinusoid of continuously increasing frequency would sound like an upward pitch glide until the Nyquist frequency is reached, after which it would sound like a downward pitch glide.[10]

2.2.4 Audible Effects of Aliasing

In terms of musical sounds, there are three basic cases in which the aural effects of aliasing may range from mild to devastating.

---

[10]Such effects are readily verified by making a plot of equation (2-12). Perform this as an exercise.

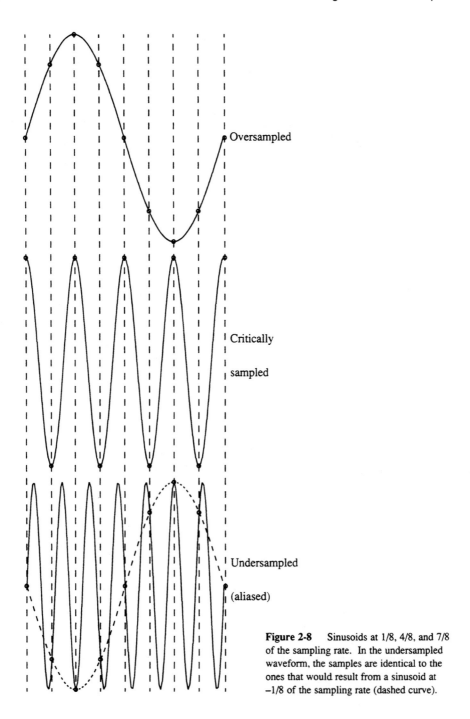

Figure 2-8   Sinusoids at 1/8, 4/8, and 7/8
of the sampling rate. In the undersampled
waveform, the samples are identical to the
ones that would result from a sinusoid at
−1/8 of the sampling rate (dashed curve).

Component Amplitude Distortion.   In the first case, aliased components might fall precisely on top on unaliased components in the sound. We might observe such an effect if we tried to synthesize a non-band-limited waveform with many strong harmonics and a fundamental frequency integrally related to the sampling rate. A non-band-limited square wave, for example, with a fundamental at one-fourth the sampling rate would generate aliased components for all its harmonics starting with the fifth. The fifth harmonic, according to our formula, would fall at minus the frequency of the third, the seventh would fall at minus the frequency of the fundamental, the ninth would fall at one-third the fundamental frequency, and so on. Not only would the interaction of the aliased and unaliased components distort the amplitude relationships of the square wave (that is, it would no longer *be* a square waveform), but new frequencies have been introduced as well. The audible effect of aliasing always depends on the relative strengths of the aliased components—if they are weak, they may be masked by other ones. Strong aliased components, however, are likely to be quite noticeable and objectionable, even in this relatively benign case.

Beating and Nonlinear Distortion.   Most of the time, signal component frequencies are unrelated to the sampling rate. Aliased components are therefore likely to fall at predictable but arbitrary frequencies in relation to fundamentals, some of which are likely to be close to those of unaliased components. If the fundamental of the non-band-limited square waveform in the last example happened to be 1 Hz greater than one-fourth the sampling rate, for instance, the fifth harmonic would fold over to a frequency just below that of the third harmonic, causing audible beating.[11] Other fundamental frequencies would cause aliased components to be removed sufficiently from that of unaliased components so that beating would not occur. In that case, however, the waveform would no longer consist of harmonically related frequencies. Such aliased, inharmonic waveforms would certainly have a timbre different from that of their unaliased counterparts and might not even have the same pitch characteristics. Again, the relative strengths of aliased and unaliased components would determine the extent to which such effects would be masked.

Heterodyning.   Most musical sounds are not constant in pitch because of vibrato, glides between pitches, or other performance inflections. As component frequencies increase, inspection of equation (2-12) reveals that the frequencies of some aliased components are likely to decrease. This can lead to a particularly noticeable effect called *heterodyning* in which an increasing pitch is accompanied by aliased components gliding downward simultaneously, and vice versa.

It should be obvious by now that because aliased components can fall among and even on top of unaliased components, they may not generally be removed from the digital signal (for example, by digital filtering) once they have been introduced. This underscores the importance of the antialiasing filter in the analog-to-digital conversion

---

[11]Acoustic beats are caused by alternating constructive and destructive interference of two components of nearly equal frequency. The rate of this beating is equal to the difference in frequency between the components.

process to remove frequencies above the Nyquist rate and the need for great care to avoid strongly aliased components in digital waveform synthesis.

It is also important to understand the difference between a band-limited and a non-band-limited waveform. A band-limited waveform will not be liable to aliasing provided that all of its frequency components lie within the range $\pm R/2$ Hz, where R is the sampling rate. Non-band-limited waveforms (such as impulsive, square, or triangular) or band-limited waveforms containing frequency components outside the permissible range will *always* cause aliasing. During the digital recording process, proper band limiting is usually assured by lowpass-filtering the analog signal before it is sampled. Aliasing can also be a problem, however, even during direct digital synthesis when the result is not band-limited, as when frequency modulation is used. Since aliased components cannot generally be removed from a digital signal (if only because they are mixed in among nonaliased components), care must be taken to minimize their effect when they are unavoidable.

2.2.5 Linear Quantization

The purpose of the quantizer is to determine which of several available amplitude ranges, or *regions*, the value of each sample falls within. For example, let us assume that the samples are voltage values that lie within an overall range of $\pm E$ volts, for a total range of $2E$ volts. To associate an N-bit value with any sampled voltage value v within this range, the quantizer must map the overall range into 2^N regions. A common mapping method is simply to divide the total amplitude range into 2^N regions, each of size $2E/2^N$ volts. Each region can then be associated with a precise minimum and maximum amplitude value and a unique N-bit code. The quantizer then maps any amplitude value that falls within one of these 2^N regions to the binary number associated with that region. For example, a ± 10-volt signal may be quantized into 4-bit values as shown in Table 2-1.

Some information is lost in the quantization process, because *any* voltage between some minimum and maximum value will be mapped into a single binary code. In effect, the quantizer substitutes an amplitude value that we might think of as equivalent to the midpoint amplitude of each region for any sample value that falls within that region.[12] If the DAC produces a voltage associated with the midpoint of each region used during analog-to-digital conversion, it is evident that a small error will occur during reconstruction of the analog signal. This type of error is called *quantization error*.

Under most circumstances, the nature of this quantization error is random, because the sampled voltages are as likely to be near the midpoint of any region as they are likely to be near either of its boundaries (this is true unless the quantization error is correlated with the sampling process in some way). The maximum possible size of this error is one-half the size of each region.

---

[12]We need not be overly concerned with what happens when an amplitude value sits precisely "on the fence" between two regions because the probability of this happening is extremely small and if it does happen, it usually does not matter which region the quantizer chooses.

TABLE 2-1   Linear quantization of a ±10-volt signal into 4 bits. If the voltage level of a sample falls within the minimum and maximum values of a particular region, the binary code associated with that region will be generated. In linear quantization, each region has the same size (1.25 volts in this example).

Quantization Region	Voltage Minimum	Voltage Maximum	Possible Binary Code
1	−10.00	−8.75	0000
2	−8.75	−7.50	0001
3	−7.50	−6.25	0010
4	−6.25	−5.00	0011
5	−5.00	−3.75	0100
6	−3.75	−2.50	0101
7	−2.50	−1.25	0110
8	−1.25	0.00	0111
9	0.00	1.25	1000
10	1.25	2.50	1001
11	2.50	3.75	1010
12	3.75	5.00	1011
13	5.00	6.25	1100
14	6.25	7.50	1101
15	7.50	8.75	1110
16	8.75	10.00	1111

Because quantization error is sometimes positive, sometimes negative, sometimes large (up to one-half the size of a quantization region), and sometimes small, we may think of it as equivalent to a small amount of uncorrelated (that is, "white") noise added to the signal by the digitization process. If we compare the amplitude of the signal to the amplitude of this quantization error noise, we can derive a *signal-to-quantization-error-noise ratio* (SQNR) for the digitizing process that is similar to the standard signal-to-noise ratio (SNR) measurement for an analog signal.

To do this, we start again with the assumption that the sampled voltage values lie within the range $\pm E$ volts. A full-amplitude sine wave, therefore, would have a peak positive amplitude of $+E$ volts and a peak negative amplitude of $-E$ volts. The maximum amplitude of the quantization error will be one-half the region size, or $2E/2^N$. The SQNR for a full-amplitude signal will therefore be the signal amplitude divided by the noise amplitude, or simply 2^N.

$$\text{SQNR} = \frac{\text{maximum signal amplitude}}{\text{quantization error noise amplitude}} = \frac{2E}{2E/2^N} = 2^N \qquad (2\text{-}13)$$

Stated in decibels, we have

$$\text{SQNR (in dB)} = 20 \log_{10} 2^N \approx 6N \qquad (2\text{-}14)$$

Equation (2-14) states that each bit of precision in the sampling process adds about 6 dB to the signal-to-quantization-error noise ratio for a full-amplitude signal—at least in the case of uniformly spaced amplitude regions (linear quantizing).

Quantization error is the major type of noise introduced into a signal by the process of digitization. For uniform quantizers, 12-bit samples result in an SQNR of about $6 \times 12 = 72$ dB. Standard digital audio practice (at the time of this writing) uses 16-bit samples, yielding a theoretical SQNR of 96 dB. Note, however, that these figures compare the amplitude of a *full-amplitude* signal with that of the "background" quantization noise; signals with smaller amplitude will have a correspondingly smaller SQNR because the amplitude of the noise is essentially constant and independent of the signal amplitude. The SQNR gets worse as the signal amplitude gets smaller because, in effect, the number of regions available for quantization of the signal samples also decreases. Eventually, the minimum-amplitude signal will "exercise" only two regions in the quantizer and will therefore always be reconstructed as if the input signal had a square waveform. We see that like analog recording, digital recording adds both noise and distortion to the recorded sound. Both may be controlled much more precisely, however, by choosing the number of bits for the samples so that these degradations are tolerably inaudible.

2.2.6 Encoding

The quantization process associates amplitude samples with one out of several available amplitude regions. The final step in digitization is to generate a code that identifies which region was selected by the quantizer. In most cases, binary codes for successive numeric values are associated with successive quantization regions. However, the codes may represent binary integers (as shown in Table 2-1), they may represent positive and negative values in two's complement or sign-magnitude form, they may represent binary fractions, or they may represent some form of floating-point number. These N-bit codes are the information that can be transmitted from one place to another and/or stored in a digital memory. If they are based on uniform amplitude divisions and if they are transmitted as a series of on-off "pulses" (representing ones and zeros), we call the digitization process *linear pulse code modulation,* or *linear PCM.*

In addition to the sample value itself, extra bits are sometimes added to sample values during the encoding process. So-called *error-correcting code* (ECC) bits allow bit errors to be detected—and in some cases even corrected—making digital audio more nearly impervious to imperfections in transmission and storage media. For example, by adding 5 properly chosen ECC bits to a 16-bit sample value, it becomes possible to detect when any one or two bits in the resulting code word have been contaminated (this is called *double error detection*). In addition, the same 5 ECC bits will allow the determination of exactly *which* bit is in error if only one is (this is called *single error correction*). Thus the sample values may be may completely impervious to accidental changes in any one bit in any or all samples, and the presence of more than one erroneous bit in any or all samples may be detected so that corrective action may be taken. Additional ECC bits allow even greater numbers of errors to be detected and corrected.

We have observed that the average amplitude of the quantization error for linear PCM is essentially constant and independent of the signal amplitude as long as the signal and the sampling and quantization process are not correlated with each other. When we then compared the largest possible signal amplitude to the largest possible quantization error ("noise" amplitude), we found their ratio to be about $6N$ dB, where N is the number of bits in one sample. More generally, the SQNR of a linear PCM signal is given by

$$\text{SQNR (in dB)} = 6N + S \qquad (2\text{-}15)$$

where N is the number of bits per sample and S is the signal level with reference to full scale (a full scale signal has a peak amplitude of 0 dB, a half-scale signal has a peak amplitude of –6 dB, and so on). Equation (2-15) makes explicit the fact that for linear PCM, the SQNR value gets smaller as the signal amplitude diminishes. Soft sounds are therefore more severely degraded by linear PCM than loud sounds.[13]

At very low amplitudes, quantization error in linear PCM acts more like waveform distortion than noise, because at the lowest possible input amplitude, every analog waveform is represented by a digital signal that oscillates between just two numeric values. Although this is rarely a problem in practice, it is sometimes audible at the tail end of reverberation or as a *pizzicato* note fades into silence.

2.2.7 Nonlinear Quantization

One solution to the problem of reducing quantization error at low signal amplitudes is simply to use enough bits in each sample so that this effect is not objectionable. A 16-bit DAC, for example, has a theoretical SQNR of approximately 96 dB. If the loudest amplitude level is adjusted for playback at, say, 100 dB SPL over a loudspeaker system (equivalent to the level of a full orchestra playing at its loudest as heard at the conductor's podium), the softest signal would appear at about 90 dB softer than this level, which is barely above the threshold of hearing. This is the approach taken in current commercial digital recording.

Another solution is to use quantization regions of nonuniform size. If the quantization regions are more closely spaced around zero, for example, quantization error for signals with small amplitude can be mitigated at the expense of slightly increased quantization error at higher signal amplitudes. Nonlinear quantization effectively allows the SQNR and the *dynamic range* of a digital signal to be separated.

The dynamic range of a signal processing system is just the ratio (usually expressed in dB) between the softest and loudest representable sounds. Using reasoning similar to that for deriving the SQNR, we find that the dynamic range for an N-bit digital audio system is approximately $6N$ dB. In the case of nonlinear quantization, however, the expression for the SQNR is more complicated, because it depends on how the spacing of the quantization regions is chosen.

---

[13]You may be tempted to conclude here that quantization error noise for linear PCM acts just like tape hiss, but remember that quantization error noise is present only when a signal is present, unlike tape hiss.

Of course, the total number of regions for an N-bit nonlinear quantizer is still 2^N, even though the regions into which the overall amplitude range is divided are of unequal size. To gain additional accuracy in the representation of small amplitude signals, nonlinear quantization uses smaller regions near zero amplitude and larger ones for greater amplitude values. The SQNR of a nonlinear quantizer therefore depends on the amplitude of the signal.

There are two basic types of nonlinear quantizers: floating point and logarithmic.

Floating-point quantization may be understood as a way to extend the dynamic range of a linear quantizer without affecting its SQNR. A 12-bit linear quantizer, as we have seen, will have an SQNR and a dynamic range of approximately 72 dB. Let us add to this quantizer an extra bit that operates in the following way: If the sampled signal has a magnitude of 5 volts or less, set the extra bit to 0 and quantize the ±5-volt range into 2^{12} equally spaced regions, as before. If the sampled signal has a magnitude between 5 and 10 volts, attenuate it by a factor of 2, set the extra bit to 1, and quantize the attenuated signal as before (because its magnitude will now be 5 volts or less as required by the quantizer).

By attenuating the signal amplitude by a factor of 2, we in effect double the relative size of the quantization error compared with the largest signal amplitude. Nevertheless, signals with magnitudes between 5 and 10 volts are quantized into 2^{12} uniformly spaced regions, so the SQNR is still approximately 72 dB. We have, however, doubled the range of allowable input amplitudes, so the dynamic range is now approximately $72 + 6 = 78$ dB. This is entirely equivalent to using a 13-bit linear quantizer in which the least significant bit is forced to 0 if the signal magnitude is between 5 and 10 volts.

We can think of the extra bit as a shift factor for converting the remaining 12 bits into a 13-bit linear quantized value. If the extra bit is off (0), we simply treat the remaining 12 bits as the least significant 12 bits of a 13-bit linearly quantized value. If the extra bit is on (1), we treat the remaining 12 bits as the most significant 12 bits of a 13-bit linearly quantized value. By using more than one extra bit, we may shift the remaining bits by more than one position: two extra bits would allow for four possible shifts, three extra bits would allow for eight possible shifts, and so on. Mathematically, we may think of the extra bits as an exponent, because shifting a binary value to the left by one digit is equivalent to multiplying it by 2.

A floating-point quantizer, then, consists of an N-bit linear quantizer combined with P extra or shift bits and is used to extend the dynamic range of the linear converter above its theoretical SQNR, which stays the same. The SQNR of such a converter is approximately $6N$ dB, as before, while its dynamic range is approximately $6N + 6P$ dB (for example, a 12-bit linear quantizer combined with 4 shift bits would have an SQNR of 72 dB and a dynamic range of 96 dB). Provision must be made to attenuate the input signal during analog-to-digital conversion by any of the factors $2^0(=1)$, 2^1, . . . , 2^P, depending on which of 2^P ranges the signal amplitude (magnitude) is in. To reconstruct the analog signal encoded by a floating-point ADC, we must use a corresponding floating-point DAC, which amplifies (rather than attenuates) each N-bit sample value by a factor corresponding to its attenuation during analog-to-digital conversion.

Another approach to nonlinear quantization involves a smooth variation in quantizer region size from small to large as the signal magnitude increases, typically according to a logarithmic curve. The total number of regions determines the number of bits needed for digital encoding, as with linear PCM, but signals with small amplitudes are more finely resolved than those with larger amplitudes.

Logarithmic quantization schemes basically assign bit codes to equally spaced regions along a log-amplitude scale in various ways. For comparison, a good 8-bit logarithmic quantizer may achieve the same dynamic range as a linear quantizer of between 13 and 14 bits. The SQNR of the 8-bit logarithmic converter at low signal levels can be made better than that of an 8-bit linear converter at the expense of making the SQNR quantizer worse at high signal levels (Nature always takes her due!).

Nonlinear quantization has the advantage of lessening quantization error noise at low signal levels. Its audible effect is essentially like *companding*, whereby signals are compressed (low levels are boosted and high levels are attenuated) before transmission or recording and inversely expanded on reception or playback: the audible noise is greater when the signal is loud and less when the signal is soft. This is often acceptable in practice because of the tendency of the loud signal to mask the increased noise. When this is tolerable, nonlinear quantization can provide a method for reducing the storage needed for digital signals.

Logarithmic quantization has an important disadvantage if the digital signals are to be processed. Logarithmically quantized sample values may not be added directly together, for example, because the resulting signal would represent the logarithm of the *product* of the two component signals according to the mathematical laws of exponents. It is generally possible (if somewhat time-consuming) to "decode" such a signal into an equivalent linear form if processing is to be done.[14]

It is common today for linear analog-to-digital conversion systems to generate 12 to 16-bit samples in two's complement binary fraction form. Two's complement binary fractions are usually considered to lie in the half-open interval $[-1, 1)$, which is close enough to ± 1 that such signals may be multiplied together with the assurance that the result also lies within the same numeric range. Some applications (such as inexpensive sampling synthesizers) use 8-bit logarithmic quantization to save storage space and when little processing of the digitally recorded signals is required.

2.2.8 Digital Signal Characteristics

The basic advantages for audio work of digital signals over analog ones are few but extremely important. Once a signal is in digital form, it can be transmitted or recorded as a series of ones and zeros, typically represented by two distinct voltage levels. For example, a binary one may be represented by a level of 5 volts and a zero by 0 volts. A receiver for such a signal needs to determine only if a one or, a zero was originally transmitted or recorded. Thus any added noise with an amplitude of less than about 2.5 volts will be easily ignored by the receiver, which simply calls any received voltage

---

[14]All sample values in this book are assumed to be linearly quantized.

over 2.5 volts a one and any received voltage less than the same threshold level a zero. Digital signals are therefore far more impervious to added noise than their analog counterparts. This means that in many cases even a severely degraded digital signal may be reconstructed perfectly. ECC techniques may be used to gain a certain tolerance for noise that exceeds the threshold value—digital signals may be reconstructed perfectly even when an occasional bit value is completely obliterated. Thus digital recordings may be duplicated indefinitely without degradation.

When (linearly quantized) digital signals are added together, the quantization noise of the result will in general be the sum of the noise of the component signals, giving digital signals no qualitative advantage over analog ones in this regard. Quantitatively, however, quantization error noise levels are quite small in comparison with, for example, tape hiss noise levels, allowing relatively many digital signals to be mixed together before the noise level is audibly increased.

The basic considerations of digital audio we have made so far have a number of implications for the practice of computer music. Foremost among them is the amount of data needed to represent high-quality digital audio signals. Practical antialiasing filters that can remove essentially all frequency components above the Nyquist rate must have a cutoff frequency of about 40 percent of the sampling rate rather than half of it. An audio passband of 20,000 Hz therefore requires a sampling rate on the order of 50,000 samples per second. If we assume that each sample consists of 16 bits of data, we see that 1 second of high-quality sound requires about 100 kilobytes of data. For stereophonic sound, because the signal in each channel is different, about 200 kilobytes per second is required. One megabyte of computer memory therefore represents sufficient space to store about 5 seconds of a first rate stereophonic digital recording. At this rate of 12 megabytes per minute, a digital recording of Wagner's *Ring* would occupy quite a few floppy disks!

Not only must all of this data be stored, but for most computer music applications it must also be processed. A superminicomputer such as a VAX-11/780 can execute just under 1 million floating-point operations per second (MFLOPS). In a high-quality stereo digital audio signal, sample values fly by at a rate of about 100,000 per second, leaving a scant 10 microseconds to process each one in real time. In 10 microseconds a VAX-11/780 can scarcely do 10 arithmetic operations; if more are required, real time operation will not be possible (typically it is not).[15] If each sample requires the equivalent of 1000 computer operations, then at these rates 1 second of music would require about 100 seconds of dedicated (that is, non-time-shared) work by a reasonably fast computer. Program efficiency is obviously relevant when so much data must be processed.

---

[15]The situation is gradually improving, however, as computers get faster as well as cheaper. At the time of this writing, a typical high-end single-user computer workstation can provide about 10 times the computational power of a VAX-11/780. Only two or so additional orders of magnitude improvement would allow much general-purpose computer music processing to be accomplished in real time. There is little reason to doubt that every process described in this book will eventually be possible in real time on an average general-purpose computer.

2.2.9 Digital Waveforms

Consider the numeric sequence 0, 1, 0, −1, 0, 1, 0, −1, 0, 1, . . . What can we conclude about the nature of the sound that corresponds to this digital signal?

For one thing, we see that the sequence is apparently periodic; that is, it repeats the basic pattern 0, 1, 0, −1 over and over again. Because the numeric sequence is periodic, it must therefore correspond to a periodic vibration pattern. Because period vibration patterns are known to give rise to the psychophysical phenomenon of pitch, it makes sense to try to determine that pitch.

The period of our periodic digital signal is four samples. To know how much time four samples represents, we must know the sampling rate R. Even without knowing the sampling rate, however, we can reason that because the pattern repeats itself every four samples, it must correspond to a frequency that is one-fourth the sampling rate. The pitch would then be whatever pitch corresponds to $R/4$ Hz.

But pitch is also weakly affected by amplitude and waveform. We usually write the numbers in a digital signal in the range ±1. Because the numbers in our sequence visit the extremes of this range, they probably correspond to a signal with the greatest possible amplitude.

So far we have determined that our sequence represents a loud signal at R/4 Hz. The waveform of the signal is perhaps a bit less obvious. Simple observation of the sequence might lead us to the erroneous conclusion that each period of the corresponding waveform changes abruptly from 0 to 1, then back to 0, then to −1, and so on, resulting in a "squarish" wave at $R/4$ Hz. We must recall, however, that a mathematically "perfect" square wave consists of a weighted sum of odd-numbered harmonics.[16] Frequency components of a square wave at $R/4$ Hz would therefore lie at $R/4$ Hz, $3R/4$ Hz, $5R/4$ Hz, and so on. Because a proper DAC system includes a lowpass filter to remove all frequency components above the Nyquist rate ($R/2$ Hz), *all* of the harmonics of our apparent square wave will be removed except for the first, resulting in a pure sinusoid at $R/4$ Hz.[17]

Suppose now that we are told that the sampling rate R is 1760 Hz. We can conclude that our sequence of numbers represents a loud sinusoid at 440 Hz. Whether the pitch we hear will correspond to the A above middle C on a piano depends on the volume setting of the playback amplifier, because loud sinusoids tend to have a lower pitch than soft ones of the same frequency in this range.

We rarely examine the numbers in a digital signal directly, if only because there tend to be so many of them. Even so, the last example demonstrates that such examination can sometimes lead to useful insights into the nature of the corresponding sound. It is more common, however, to describe a waveform either mathematically or graphically. For mathematical descriptions, the basic functions of trigonometry are essential. These functions are so important to the mathematical description of sound that we will now review them briefly.[18]

---

[16]Harmonics are numbered from 1 (the fundamental). The Nth harmonic therefore has a frequency equal to N times the fundamental frequency.

[17]Another way to understand that the sequence represents a pure sinusoidal waveform is to consider the list of samples that would result if a sine wave at $R/4$ Hz were sampled by an ADC system.

[18]See also Appendix A.

2.2.10 Trigonometric Functions

The sine of an angle is defined as the ratio of two sides of a right triangle containing that angle at one of its vertices. In Figure 2-9, θ is any angle. Angles are portions of circles; their size is measured typically in degrees or radians. An ancient estimate of the length of one year in days is responsible for the number 360 as the number of degrees in a circle (the Babylonians were close!); the number of divisions is, however, arbitrary. We could measure angles in percentage, for example, in which case "25 percent" would describe a right angle. A natural measure for angles commonly used in mathematics is the radian, which is based on $\pi = 3.14159265 \cdots$, the ratio of the lengths of the *diameter* and *circumference* of any plane circle. Because the *radius* of a circle is half its diameter, we say that there are 2π radians in a full circle. One-fourth of this measure, $\pi/2$ radians, represents a right angle.

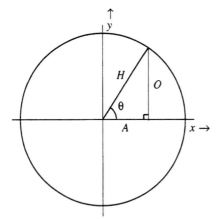

Figure 2-9   Defining trigonometric functions.

The *sine* of angle θ is defined as the ratio of the length of the side of the right triangle *opposite* angle θ to the length of its *hypotenuse*. In terms of Figure 2-9,

$$\sin\theta = \frac{O}{H} \tag{2-16}$$

The other basic trigonometric functions are similarly defined as

$$\cos\theta = \frac{A}{H} \tag{2-17}$$

$$\tan\theta = \frac{O}{A} \tag{2-18}$$

For convenience, we can choose to make measurements within a circle whose radius has a length of one (arbitrary) unit called the *unit circle*. The value of $\sin\theta$ is then just the length of side O in the same units for any angle θ.

Angles are by default measured as increasing counterclockwise from the positive horizontal axis. When the opposite side points upward from the horizontal axis, its length can be expressed as a positive number; when it points downward (for example, for angles greater than half a circle and less than a full circle), its length is expressed as negative. A graph of the sine of angle θ therefore traces one full cycle of the familiar sine curve as the angle increases from zero to one full circle (2π radians).

To connect the sine wave shape to the idea of time, we first multiply our notation for a full circle (2π) by t, which represents time in seconds. The quantity $2\pi t$ then goes once around the circle (that is, from zero to 2π) as t goes from zero to one. This corresponds to a frequency (or "oftenness") of one cycle per second, or 1 hertz. We represent an arbitrary frequency by multiplying this quantity by f, a frequency in hertz. The quantity $2\pi f t$ goes f times around the circle as t goes from zero to one, so a graph of sin $2\pi f t$ would go through exactly f cycles each time t increases by one unit.

The only additional features needed to represent arbitrary sinusoids are a starting point for the rotation when t is equal to zero, properly called the *phase offset*, and a quantity that scales the peak *amplitude* of the sinusoid to A (the normal sine curve, being defined on the unit circle, has a peak amplitude of ±1).

A one-dimensional sinusoidal pressure waveform with amplitude A, frequency f, and phase offset φ is typically described as a function of continuous time t according to

$$f(t) = A \sin(2\pi f t + \phi) \qquad (2\text{-}19)$$

or

$$f(t) = A \sin(\omega t + \phi) \qquad (2\text{-}20)$$

where $\omega = 2\pi f$ (because ω—the small Greek letter omega—is just the frequency multiplied by 2π, it is called the *radian frequency*). Because equations (2-19) and (2-20) are functions of the continuous independent variable t, they are appropriate mathematical descriptions of a sinusoidal analog waveform, at least for some range of values of t. The graphical equivalent of equations (2-19) and (2-20) is shown in Figure 2-10.

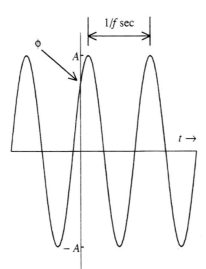

Figure 2-10   Graphical representation of the continuous function $f(t) = A \sin(2\pi f t + \phi)$. Continuous time t is plotted along the horizontal axis, increasing toward the right. At a frequency of f Hz, each period of the waveform lasts for $1/f$ seconds, as shown. Peak instantaneous amplitude values (± A) are marked on the vertical axis, along which amplitude is plotted. The phase offset value φ is arbitrarily chosen in this example to be π/4 radians, which causes the function to cross the $t = 0$ point one-eighth of the way through its cycle.

Notice that if the phase offset is one-fourth of a circle (that is, 90°, or π/2 radians), the sinusoid is a cosine wave, because

$$\sin{(\omega t + \frac{\pi}{2})} = \cos{\omega t} \qquad (2\text{-}21)$$

The sine and cosine waveforms are not very different from each other—they simply start in different places in the cycle. Nevertheless, it is useful to have two standard forms of the sinusoidal waveform for other reasons. For example, the sine and cosine functions exhibit the properties of oddness and evenness, respectively. A function is odd if it is inverted when reversed. In musical terms, oddness would correspond to a 12-tone row whose retrograde is also its inversion. Because $\sin{(-\theta)} = -\sin{\theta}$, sine is an odd function of θ. Similarly, the cosine function is even, because $\cos{(-\theta)} = \cos{\theta}$, corresponding to a tone row whose retrograde is identical to the original. We shall return to these even and odd properties later.

A related property of the sine and cosine is that they may be combined to represent amplitude and phase information such as that shown in equation (2-20). In general, combining any two sinusoids of the same frequency results in another sinusoid of the same frequency, but with a possibly changed amplitude and/or phase offset. Therefore, we may write

$$A \sin{(\omega t + \phi)} = a \cos{\omega t} + b \sin{\omega t} \qquad (2\text{-}22)$$

Clearly, if ϕ is equal to zero, then a is also zero and b is equal to A. If ϕ is equal to π/2 radians then b is zero and a is equal to A. In general we may find A and ϕ for any values of a and b and vice versa, with the following relations.

Given a and b,

$$A = \sqrt{a^2 + b^2} \quad \text{and} \quad \phi = \tan^{-1}\frac{b}{a}$$

Given A and ϕ,

$$a = A \cos{\phi} \quad \text{and} \quad b = A \sin{\phi}$$

The left and right sides of equation (2-22), as always, are just two ways to say the same thing.

The mathematical description of a digital signal is very similar, except that the independent variable t (continuous time) is replaced by a variable that takes on only discrete integer values. We may write

$$x(n) = A \sin{(2\pi f nT + \phi)} = A \sin{(\frac{2\pi f n}{R} + \phi)} \qquad n \in \mathbf{I} \qquad (2\text{-}23)$$

where $x(n)$ is a digital signal, T is the sample period (equal to $1/R$, where R is the sampling rate), and n takes on only *integer* (**I**) values, that is, $n = \ldots -2, -1, 0, 1, 2, 3, \ldots$ Here we have replaced the continuous time variable t with the discrete time quantity nT. It is common practice, however, to leave out any mention of the sampling rate or sampling period; thus

$$x(n) = A \sin{(2\pi f n + \phi)} \qquad n \in \mathbf{I} \qquad (2\text{-}24)$$

or

$$x(n) = A \sin(\omega n + \phi) \qquad n \in \mathbf{I} \qquad (2\text{-}25)$$

Because it is easy enough to remember that the relationship between the sample index n and time depends on the sampling rate chosen, we will usually use the latter form (shown in the last two equations) to describe digital signals. The graphical depiction of the corresponding digital signal appears in Figure 2-11. Because Figure 2-10 and Figure 2-11 are so similar, we rarely use the "dot and stick" symbols shown in Figure 2-11 except where we wish to make the digital nature of a signal explicit.

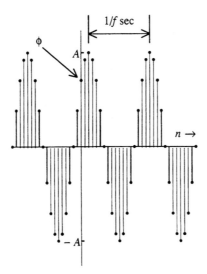

Figure 2-11   Graphical representation of the digital signal $x(n) = A \sin (2\pi f n + \phi)$. Peak amplitude ($A$), frequency ($f$), and phase ($\phi$) are shown as in Figure 2-10. Discrete time (n) is plotted along the horizontal axis, increasing toward the right. The relationship between sample index n and time depends on the sample rate (R) chosen—although in this example it is evident that $R = 16f$ because each period of $x(n)$ is sampled 16 times. Each increment in the value of n represents a time $T = 1/R$ seconds.

While we may be tempted to interpret such a plot by just connecting the dots to get a graph of the function it represents, such an interpretation would be incorrect if the connections were made with straight lines. The dot-and-stick plot represents samples of an underlying, smooth, continuous function. Rather than connecting the dots with straight lines, we must interpolate between the dots with a lowpass filter at half the sampling rate so that the transitions are properly "smoothed." While this may be somewhat difficult to do by eye, it is nevertheless essential to remember that this is the only way that the digital signal 1, −1, 1, −1, . . . can be interpreted as a *sinusoid* at half the sampling rate.

Waveforms may be added, subtracted, multiplied, and divided simply by combining corresponding points of two or more signals. As an example of waveform addition, consider the construction of a digital square wave.

The rule or "recipe" for the ideal (non-band-limited) analog square wave of frequency f is quite simple; it consists of an infinite number of odd harmonics, all in the same phase, with the amplitude of each present harmonic equal to the reciprocal of the harmonic number. Stated mathematically,

$$Sq(t) = \sum_{k=1}^{k=\infty} \frac{1}{k} \sin k \omega t \qquad k \quad \text{odd} \qquad (2\text{-}26)$$

where $\omega = 2\pi f$ as before. In other words, the sum notation of equation (2-26) states that we can obtain waveform $Sq(t)$ (a square wave) by adding together terms of the form shown on the right side of the equation for $k = 1, 3, 5, \ldots$ (k is the harmonic number). The sum notation is just a convenient shorthand for

$$Sq(t) = \sin \omega t + \frac{1}{3} \sin 3\omega t + \frac{1}{5} \sin 5\omega t + \ldots \qquad (2\text{-}27)$$

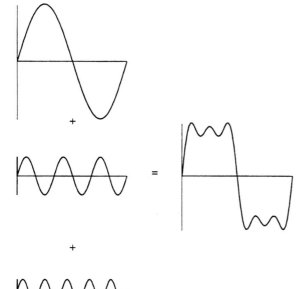

Figure 2-12   Graphical addition of the first three terms of a square wave. The frequencies of the three sine waves on the left are in the proportion 1 to 3 to 5 (from top to bottom), while their respective amplitudes are in the proportion 1 to 1/3 to 1/5. The waveform that results from adding together these three components is shown on the right.

Equation (2-27) tells us, in effect, how to construct a square wave by adding together sine wave components:

1. Start with a sine wave with amplitude 1.0 and radian frequency ω (ω refers to the fundamental frequency of the square wave times 2π).
2. Add to this another sine wave with three times frequency ω and one third the amplitude of the fundamental frequency component.
3. Add to this another sine wave with five times frequency ω and one fifth the amplitude of the fundamental frequency component.
4. Proceed in like manner for 7, 9, 11, and so on.

We can see in Figure 2-12 that this sequence converges rather rapidly to a more or less square waveform: the "sum" waveform on the right of the figure ripples above and below its maximum and minimum values by approximately $1/N$, where N is the highest-numbered harmonic included in the addition ($N = 5$ in Figure 2-12). We also know from the sampling theorem that we cannot represent a "true" square waveform in digital form (or in analog form, for that matter) because such a waveform would contain infinite frequencies. The frequencies of any of the components above half the sampling rate would cause aliasing. We must therefore replace the infinity symbol in equations such as (2-26) with a finite number N if we are using digital techniques. The maximum value for N that will avoid aliasing depends on the fundamental frequency f of the waveform and R, the sampling rate, according to

$$N \leq \frac{R}{2f} \tag{2-28}$$

2.3 SPECTRUM MEASUREMENTS

We have seen how complex waveforms can be built out of sinusoidal components. One of the most powerful and useful conceptual tools for understanding this process is the *Fourier transform*. The nineteenth-century mathematical physicist Jean-Baptiste Joseph Fourier made the remarkable discovery that *any* periodic waveform can be represented as a sum of harmonically related sinusoids, each with a particular amplitude and phase. In addition, Fourier derived a mathematical expression that transforms a waveform into its *spectrum*, showing explicitly the amplitudes and phases of the sinusoids that comprise it. No information is lost in this transformation—the spectrum may be transformed into the waveform just as well as the other way around.

That's just about all of the good news. The bad news about the Fourier transform is that, strictly speaking, it applies *only* to periodic waveforms. Though a musical sound may be roughly periodic, it is never truly periodic, if only because it has a beginning and an end. Periodicity, like circularity, is an abstract concept that is only approximated in the real world. To be truly periodic, a mathematical function must obey the relation

$$f(t) = f(t + \tau) \qquad -\infty < t < \infty \tag{2-29}$$

for some value of τ greater than zero. The smallest nonzero value of τ that satisfies Equation (2-29) is called the *period* of function f; if such a value exists, $f(t)$ is called a *periodic function of t*. If t represents time, we say that f is a periodic function of time.

The trigonometric functions sine, cosine, and tangent are all periodic in this mathematical sense—they are periodic functions of angle, with a full circle (360° or 2π radians) being the size of each period. If we let $f(t) = \sin t$, it is easy to see that equation (2-29) can be satisfied by setting τ to any integer times 2π, assuming that we measure our angles in radians; that is,

$$\sin t = \sin(t + k\,2\pi) \qquad k = \ldots -2, -1, 0, 1, 2, \ldots \tag{2-30}$$

Equation (2-30) holds for *any* value of t, all the way, from minus to plus infinity, and no person has ever played (or heard) a musical note for such a long time! In a way we might interpret this to mean that periodic functions do not exist in time at all—because they exist at all times, their only possible characteristics are frequency, amplitude, and phase relative at some arbitrary reference moment.

Once we introduce a beginning and ending time (call them t_1 and t_2), equation (2-30) no longer holds because our function is no longer truly periodic:

$$f(t) = \begin{cases} \sin t & \text{if } t_1 \leq t \leq t_2 \\ 0 & \text{otherwise} \end{cases} \qquad (2\text{-}31)$$

Strictly speaking, if $f(t)$ is not periodic, its Fourier transform does not exist, and without it, we cannot know the spectrum of the waveform described by equation (2-31).

Equation (2-31) can be viewed as the *product* of two even simpler functions, one of which is $\sin t$ and the other of which is called a *rectangular window function*, equal to 1 between t_1 and t_2 and zero elsewhere:

$$f(t) = w(t) \sin t \qquad (2\text{-}32)$$

where

$$w(t) = \begin{cases} 1 & \text{if } t_1 \leq t \leq t_2 \\ 0 & \text{otherwise} \end{cases} \qquad (2\text{-}33)$$

If we can compute the spectra of $\sin t$ and $w(t)$ separately, perhaps these two spectra can be combined in some way to yield the spectrum of $f(t)$ (we shall see later how to do this).

As simple as it is, $w(t)$ is not your run-of-the-mill function—it is what mathematicians call a *generalized function*, and special mathematical techniques are needed to find its spectrum. Because such window functions play an absolutely crucial role in the spectrum analysis of musical waveforms, we shall have to deal with them as well.

2.3.1 The Fourier Transform

We now begin our detailed examination of spectrum measurement as one of the key elements (with digital filtering) of digital signal processing. These are the power tools with which musical sound may be hewn, cajoled, coaxed, and caressed as never before by the power of computers to turn mathematical abstractions into audible results. We proceed by first examining the relevant mathematics, then turning this mathematics into computer programs, then using these programs to shape musical sounds. If you are unsure of your mathematical skills, you should probably pick up a pencil at this point—for this is the instrument of mathematics—and prepare to "play a few tunes" on paper.

Basic mathematical definitions for the Fourier transform are given by

$$X(f) = \int_{-\infty}^{\infty} x(t) e^{-2\pi i f t} \, dt \qquad (2\text{-}34)$$

and

$$x(t) = \int_{-\infty}^{\infty} X(f) e^{2\pi i f t} \, df \qquad (2\text{-}35)$$

where $x(t)$ is a (periodic) function of time t, $X(f)$—the *spectrum* of $x(t)$—is a function of frequency f, e is the "natural base of logarithms" (= 2.7182818 . . .), and i is the "imaginary unit," that is, by definition $i^2 = -1$ (do not worry if all the implications of these formulas are not immediately obvious to you—that is what this section is about!). If t is measured in seconds (the unit of time), then f will be in *cycles per second*, or Hertz (Hz, the unit of frequency). Equations (2-34) and (2-35) show the *reversibility* of the Fourier transform—we can compute the spectrum from the waveform, and vice versa. This means that the Fourier transform is really just a way to change the representation of the *same information*: we can see the information laid out in either the time or frequency domains.[19]

Equations (2-34) and (2-35) also show how similar the Fourier transform and the *inverse* Fourier transform are: they differ only by the sign of the exponent of e.

To understand equations (2-34) and (2-35) it is necessary to know another famous mathematical relation first worked out by the Swiss mathematician Leonard Euler called, aptly enough, *Euler's relation* (or *Euler's identity*):

$$e^{i\theta} = \cos\theta + i\sin\theta \qquad (2\text{-}36)$$

In words, Euler's relation says that the quantity e, when raised to an imaginary exponent is equal to a complex sum of cosine and sine functions (this relation is certainly no less remarkable than Fourier's transform). Setting θ to $2\pi ft$, as in the Fourier transform, yields

$$e^{i\,2\pi ft} = \cos 2\pi ft + i\,\sin 2\pi ft \qquad (2\text{-}37)$$

Similarly,

$$e^{-i\,2\pi ft} = \cos 2\pi ft - i\,\sin 2\pi ft \qquad (2\text{-}38)$$

because $\cos(-x) = \cos x$, whereas $\sin(-x) = -\sin x$.

2.3.2 Even and Odd Functions

Any function that has the property $f(-x) = f(x)$ (such as the cosine function) is called an *even function*—it is left-right *symmetrical* around the point $x = 0$. Any function that has the property $f(-x) = -f(x)$ (such as the sine function) is called an *odd function*—it is left-right *antisymmetrical* around the point $x = 0$. Functions may be even or odd or neither—only the "degenerate" function $f(x) = 0$ is, in a sense, both. Remarkably, however, *any* function may be broken down into the sum of two unique functions, one of which is purely even and the other purely odd:

$$f(x) = f_e(x) + f_o(x) \qquad (2\text{-}39)$$

where $f_e(-x) = f_e(x)$ and $f_o(-x) = -f_o(x)$, by definition of evenness and oddness, respectively. Of course, if $f(x)$ is purely even to begin with, its odd part will be zero, and vice versa.

To see that equation (2-39) does indeed hold true for all functions requires only a little simple algebra. Starting with equation (2-39) and the definitions of evenness and oddness just given, we may write

---

[19]As a simple analogy, we may likewise represent a positive numeric quantity in either the linear or logarithmic domain, using the formulas $X = \log_b x$ and $x = b^X$ to convert from one domain to the other. Knowing the logarithm of the number of chickens missing from a chicken coop is just as good as knowing how many chickens flew the coop—provided we understand the transform!

$$f(-x) = f_e(-x) + f_o(-x) = f_e(x) - f_o(x) \qquad (2\text{-}40)$$

If we now add equations (2-39) and (2-40), we obtain the formula for finding the even part of $f(x)$:

$$f(x) + f(-x) = f_e(x) + f_o(x) + f_e(x) - f_o(x) = 2f_e(x)$$

Therefore,

$$f_e(x) = \frac{1}{2}[f(x) + f(-x)] \qquad (2\text{-}41)$$

Subtracting yields the formula for finding the odd part of $f(x)$:

$$f(x) - f(-x) = f_e(x) + f_o(x) - f_e(x) + f_o(x) = 2f_o(x)$$

Therefore,

$$f_o(x) = \frac{1}{2}[f(x) - f(-x)] \qquad (2\text{-}42)$$

To show that equations (2-41) and (2-42) correctly add up to $f(x)$, we simply add them together:

$$f_e(x) + f_o(x) = \frac{1}{2}[f(x) + f(-x)] + \frac{1}{2}[f(x) - f(-x)] = f(x)$$

This demonstrates that equations (2-41) and (2-42) show us how to find the even and odd parts of $f(x)$. Furthermore, because we have placed no restrictions on the nature of $f(x)$ at all, these formulas apply to *all* functions. Isn't mathematics wonderful?

The reason that evenness and oddness are useful concepts for understanding the Fourier transform is that the complex exponential $e^{i2\pi ft}$ separates the waveform or spectrum by which it is multiplied into its even and odd parts with the real (cosine) part affecting only the even part of $x(t)$ or $X(f)$ and the imaginary (sine) part affecting only the odd part of $x(t)$ or $X(f)$. We shall see the details of this operation when we actually work out a Fourier transform in discrete form.

2.3.3 The Discrete Fourier Transform

Before proceeding with our investigation of the Fourier transform, we need to convert its representation into a form suitable for use with the digitized signals encountered in computer music. Instead of a continuous function of time $f(t)$, digital signals are represented as a list of discrete values indexed by sample index n. As usual, we will allow the sample period to remain implicit and refer to our sampled waveform simply as $x(n)$. In addition, time does not stretch from minus to plus infinity for a practical digital signal.

It is important to keep in mind that a digital signal is not identical to the underlying continuous waveform that it represents. The underlying waveform may be reconstructed precisely from the digital one to within the quantization error of the encoded samples and to the extent that aliasing has been avoided. Similarly, we can compute the *discrete Fourier transform* (DFT) of the digital waveform, which will represent samples of the underlying, continuous spectrum of the underlying, continuous waveform. The DFT is *sampled in frequency* in a manner precisely analogous to the way the digital waveform is *sampled in time*—neither representation says anything directly about what the underlying function does between the samples.

For example, the sampling theorem tells us precisely how to use the sampling process to avoid aliasing effects. The sampling process in the frequency domain is interpreted in an analogous manner: just as an increase in the number of samples per unit time leads to increased temporal resolution in the time domain, an increase in the number of samples per unit frequency leads to increased frequency resolution in the frequency domain. Because analog-to-digital conversion occurs in the time domain, an increase in temporal resolution is effectively just an increase in the sampling rate. The frequency domain, as we have seen, exists in all cases only over the fixed range $\pm R/2$ Hz. Increased resolution in the frequency domain generally requires an increase in the number of samples available. If the sampling rate remains fixed, therefore, we can increase the frequency resolution merely by analyzing a greater number of samples. We shall return to the ramifications of this issue later.

Suppose that we have N samples of a digital signal $x(n)$, $n = 0, 1, \ldots, N - 1$. Its DFT is defined by the formula

$$X(k) = \frac{1}{N} \sum_{n=0}^{N-1} x(n) e^{-2\pi ikn/N} \qquad k = 0, 1, \ldots, N-1 \qquad (2\text{-}43)$$

where k is a *frequency index* related to "true" frequency in a manner similar to the way in which the time index n is related to "true" time. The *inverse discrete Fourier transform* (IDFT) has a similar form:

$$x(n) = \sum_{k=0}^{N-1} X(k) e^{2\pi ikn/N} \qquad n = 0, 1, \ldots, N-1 \qquad (2\text{-}44)$$

As one might expect, $X(k)$ represents N samples of a continuous frequency spectrum, just as $x(n)$ represents N samples of a continuous time waveform (we couldn't get more information out of the transform than we put in, could we?). This implies that the discrete frequency spectrum obtained with the DFT often requires some care in its interpretation, just like digitized waveforms, even though the underlying continuous functions are "perfectly" represented in either case.

The DFT operates by constructing the analyzed waveform out of a unique set of harmonics. The actual calculation is done in terms of complex coefficients from which amplitudes and phases are readily extracted.

Which harmonics of what frequencies does the DFT use? The answer is both simple and subtle. If we take the DFT of N samples of a digital waveform, the fundamental frequency of the analysis will be the one associated with the duration of N samples. Thus if we analyze 1000 samples of a waveform sampled at 10,000 Hz, the DFT will show us how to construct that waveform out of the available harmonics of $10,000/1000 = 10$ Hz.

Which harmonics are "available"? The sampling theorem yields the answer: the available harmonics are those lying between minus and plus half the sampling rate, in this case −5000, −4990, . . . , −10, 0, 10, 20, . . . , 4990, 5000 Hz. This is consistent with the notion that the DFT treats the analyzed waveform as *one period* of an infinitely periodic waveform.

But, you may ask, what if the analyzed waveform really consists of a steady sinusoid at 333 Hz—how will it be represented in terms of the harmonics of 10 Hz? We shall return to this question later. For now, suffice it to say that in that case, the DFT would represent an *estimate* of the "true" spectrum of the waveform to within the available (10 Hz) frequency resolution.

2.3.4 Calculating the DFT

The DFT is usually calculated using a special technique called the *fast Fourier transform*, (FFT), which is an efficient method for evaluating equations (2-43) and (2-44) for certain restricted values of N. It is evident from looking at equations (2-43) and (2-44) that the DFT requires N complex multiplications for each value of k, and because there are N different values for k, the running time of the DFT is proportional to N^2. If N is only moderately large, say about 1000, then about a million complex multiply-adds would be required. By restricting N to highly composite numbers (usually powers of 2), the FFT is able to obtain the same result in a running time proportional to $N \log N$, which is much smaller than N^2 for moderate to large values of N.[20]

The following C programs show explicitly the steps in calculating the DFT and IDFT according to equations (2-43) and (2-44). Remember that these programs are given for purposes of understanding the DFT only—in almost every practical situation, the more efficient FFT algorithm would be used.

```
#include <stdio.h>
#include <math.h>
/*
 * define complex structure
 */
typedef struct {
    float re ;
    float im ;
} complex ;

#define LENGTH 16

main() {
 int N = LENGTH ;
 double pi2oN = 8.*atan( 1. )/N ; /* 2 pi / N */
 float x1[LENGTH], x2[LENGTH] ;
 complex X[LENGTH] ;
```

[20]A highly composite number is one that has many prime factors. Powers of 2 are the most highly composite numbers that exist.

```
 int n ;
/*
 * make up a test signal to analyze
 */
    for ( n = 0 ; n < N ; n++ )
        x1[n] = sin( pi2oN*1*n ) + .33*sin( pi2oN*3*n )
            + .2*sin( pi2oN*5*n ) ;
/*
 * take its discrete Fourier transform
 */
    dft( x1, N, X ) ;
/*
 * take inverse discrete Fourier transform of result
 */
    idft( x2, N, X ) ;
/*
 * print out the results
 */
    for ( n = 0 ; n < N ; n++ )
        printf(
          "[%2d] x1 = %6.3f, X = (%6.3f, %6.3f), x2 = %6.3f\n",
            n, x1[n], X[n].re, X[n].im, x2[n]) ;
}
/*
 * N (real) signal points reside in x[],
 * place their complex DFT in X[]
 */
dft( x, N, X ) float x[] ; int N ; complex X[] ; {
 double pi2oN = 8.*atan( 1. )/N ;
 int k, n ;
    for ( k = 0 ; k < N ; k++ ) {
        X[k].re = X[k].im = 0.0 ;
        for ( n = 0 ; n < N ; n++ ) {
            X[k].re += x[n]*cos( pi2oN*k*n ) ;
            X[k].im -= x[n]*sin( pi2oN*k*n ) ;
        }
        X[k].re /= N ;
        X[k].im /= N ;
    }
}
/*
 * N complex DFT values reside in X[],
 * place real signal in x[]
 */
idft( x, N, X ) float x[] ; int N ; complex X[] ; {
 double pi2oN = 8.*atan( 1. )/N ;
 double imag ;
 int k, n ;
```

```
    for ( n = 0 ; n < N ; n++ ) {
        imag = x[n] = 0.0 ;
        for ( k = 0 ; k < N ; k++ ) {
            x[n] += X[k].re*cos( pi2oN*k*n )
                    - X[k].im*sin( pi2oN*k*n ) ;
/*
 * check imaginary part of waveform
 * allow some tolerance for roundoff
 */
            imag += X[k].re*sin( pi2oN*k*n )
                    + X[k].im*cos( pi2oN*k*n ) ;
        }
        if ( fabs ( imag )  > 1.e-5 )
            fprintf( stderr,
                "warning: nonzero imaginary (%f) in waveform\n",
                    imag ) ;
    }
}
```

Compiling and executing this program produces the following output.

```
[ 0] x1 =   0.000, X = ( 0.000,   0.000), x2 =   0.000
[ 1] x1 =   0.872, X = ( 0.000,  -0.500), x2 =   0.872
[ 2] x1 =   0.799, X = ( 0.000,   0.000), x2 =   0.799
[ 3] x1 =   0.721, X = (-0.000,  -0.165), x2 =   0.721
[ 4] x1 =   0.870, X = ( 0.000,  -0.000), x2 =   0.870
[ 5] x1 =   0.721, X = (-0.000,  -0.100), x2 =   0.721
[ 6] x1 =   0.799, X = (-0.000,   0.000), x2 =   0.799
[ 7] x1 =   0.872, X = ( 0.000,   0.000), x2 =   0.872
[ 8] x1 =   0.000, X = ( 0.000,   0.000), x2 =   0.000
[ 9] x1 =  -0.872, X = ( 0.000,  -0.000), x2 =  -0.872
[10] x1 =  -0.799, X = (-0.000,  -0.000), x2 =  -0.799
[11] x1 =  -0.721, X = (-0.000,   0.100), x2 =  -0.721
[12] x1 =  -0.870, X = ( 0.000,   0.000), x2 =  -0.870
[13] x1 =  -0.721, X = (-0.000,   0.165), x2 =  -0.721
[14] x1 =  -0.799, X = ( 0.000,  -0.000), x2 =  -0.799
[15] x1 =  -0.872, X = ( 0.000,   0.500), x2 =  -0.872
```

Successive values in the x1 array represent the test input signal, defined here to be the sum of the first three components of a square waveform. The X array holds the complex-valued output of the DFT. The x2 array is computed from the X array with the IDFT as a check—it should match the x1 array to within the roundoff precision of the computations (it does!).

The results produced by our DFT program may be interpreted as follows. x1[n] is the *n*th sample of the digitized waveform expressed in the time domain.

Because the `LENGTH` macro in our C program is defined as 16, it is practical actually to print out the sample values themselves. For most practical audio applications, though, `N` would be much larger than 16, making it impractical or useless to print out the sample values in tabular form. We typically prefer to represent long lists of numbers in a more compact graphical form.

Just how should we represent waveform `x1`? One possibility would be simply to plot the numeric values, as shown in Figure 2-13. Although the figure looks somewhat like the first three nonzero components of our band-limited square wave, we should recall that it is more properly interpreted as 16 equally spaced samples of one period of that waveform. In other words, it would be inaccurate to interpret the waveform as equivalent to the waveform with the dots connected by straight lines, as shown in Figure 2-14. `x1` is correctly interpreted as 16 samples of the underlying waveform shown in Figure 2-15.

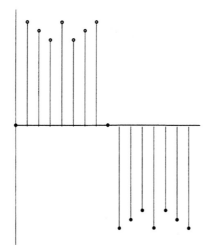

Figure 2-13   Graphical representation of waveform `x1`.

In other words, if the successive samples in array `x1` (or `x2`) were applied to the input of an ideal DAC, the action of the (ideal) lowpass filter (with a cutoff frequency equal to half the sampling rate) would result in the waveform shown in Figure 2-15 and not the linearly interpolated waveform shown in Figure 2-14.

2.3.5 Amplitude and Power Spectra

Given the improper and proper interpretations of Figure 2-13 as shown in Figures 2-14 and 2-15, respectively, how do we properly interpret the spectrum values in array X?

First, we see that each X value is complex; that is, each value consists of a real part and an imaginary part. Further, we also see that there are N such values,

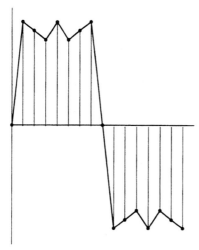

Figure 2-14   Incorrect interpretation of
graph of x1.

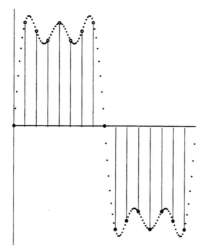

Figure 2-15   Correct interpretation of
graph of x1.

representing N samples of the spectrum of waveform x1. To interpret the X array, we
must understand

- How the real and imaginary parts of each value correspond to amplitude and
  phase values at particular frequencies
- The frequencies to which successive values of X correspond.

Fortunately, the rules for interpreting the output of the DFT are rather simple.
Each complex X value may be thought of as the rectangular coordinates of a point on
the two-dimensional *complex plane* in which the abscissa (horizontal axis) represents
the real part and the ordinate (vertical axis) represents the imaginary part of the value.

To convert from complex coordinate values to amplitudes and phases, we need only measure the length of a vector drawn from the origin of the complex plane to the described point to obtain the amplitude and measure the angle of that same vector to get the phase (angles are conventionally measured counterclockwise starting from the positive horizontal axis).

In Figure 2-16 we see a vector of length (amplitude) A and (phase) angle θ drawn from the origin to point (a, b) on the complex plane. a is the real part and b is the imaginary part of complex number (a, b). To find the length (amplitude) of the vector we need to use the well-known theorem of Pythagoras, namely, that the square of the length of the hypotenuse of any right triangle is equal to the sum of the squares of the lengths of the other sides; that is,

$$A = \sqrt{a^2 + b^2} \qquad (2\text{-}45)$$

From the basic definitions of trigonometry, the tangent of angle θ is equal to the ratio of the length of the opposite to the adjacent sides of a right triangle. Therefore,

$$\theta = \tan^{-1} \frac{b}{a} \qquad (2\text{-}46)$$

Equations (2-45) and (2-46), then, allow us to calculate the amplitude and phase values that correspond to complex numbers such as those produced by the DFT.

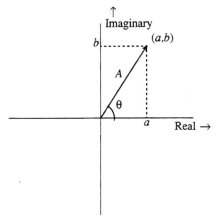

Figure 2-16   Interpreting the complex values of X.

In summary, we have this general rule:

> The complex spectrum $X(k)$ of a waveform $x(n)$ computed with the DFT (or FFT) may be equivalently expressed as a pair of real-valued functions of frequency called the *amplitude* (or *magnitude*) spectrum and the *phase* spectrum.

Because power is proportional to the square of amplitude, it is common to omit the square root operation in the calculation of the DFT. We then obtain the *power* spectrum instead of the amplitude spectrum.

It is also common practice to express power and amplitude values on a decibel scale because these quantities have such a wide range of variation.[21] Be careful to use the proper conversions into decibels. If a sound has certain intensity I, it also has a certain (root-mean-square) amplitude A, which are related according to

$$I = CA^2 \qquad (2\text{-}47)$$

where C is a constant of proportionality that depends on the units of measurement we prefer. Because intensity and power are both proportional to the square of amplitude we may choose an arbitrary reference value (for 0 dB) that we will call I_0. Decibel measurements are then defined as

$$\text{dB} = 10\log\frac{I}{I_0} = 10\log\frac{CA^2}{CA_0^2} = 10\log\left[\frac{A}{A_0}\right]^2 = 20\log\frac{A}{A_0} \qquad (2\text{-}48)$$

where $A_0 = \sqrt{I_0/C}$ (the corresponding amplitude reference). On a logarithmic (decibel) scale, then, the amplitude and power spectrum of a given function would look exactly the same, provided the proper form of the decibel conversion formula is used in both cases.

How do the complex values produced by the DFT correspond to frequency? For convenience, let us repeat our definition of the DFT:

$$X(k) = \frac{1}{N}\sum_{n=0}^{N-1} x(n)e^{-2\pi ikn/N} \qquad k = 0, 1, \ldots, N-1 \qquad (2\text{-}49)$$

$x(n)$ consists of N samples of an underlying continuous waveform, which is a function of time. At a sampling rate R, these N samples occur over a total duration of N/R seconds. $X(k)$ consists of N samples of the underlying continuous spectrum of the (underlying, continuous) waveform represented by $x(n)$. In other words, $X(k)$ is a *sampled spectrum* in the same sense that $x(n)$ is a *sampled waveform*. Just as the N samples in $x(n)$ represent evenly spaced amplitude measurements of the waveform taken over a duration of N/R seconds, the N samples in $X(k)$ represent evenly spaced amplitude and phase measurements of the spectrum taken over the entire range of frequencies that any digital signal can represent (from minus to plus one-half the sampling rate).

In other words, the DFT treats the N samples of the waveform as *one period* of an infinitely periodic waveform with period N/R seconds. The DFT will show us how to construct the waveform out of harmonics of the frequency with this period, that is, harmonics of R/N Hz. We call R/N Hz the *fundamental frequency of analysis* or, more simply, the *analysis frequency*. For example, if N is equal to R (that is, if we analyze one second's worth of the digital waveform), the DFT will show us how to construct the analyzed waveform out of the available harmonics of 1 Hz; if N is one-half of R

---

[21]Recall that the ear can detect sounds with intensities on the order of 10^{-12} W/m^2 and can withstand intensities as high as 1 W/m^2, giving it a dynamic range extending over 12 orders of magnitude in power, which is more usefully expressed as a range of 120 dB.

(that is, a half-second's worth), the DFT will show us how to construct the analyzed waveform out of the available harmonics of 2 Hz, and so on.[22]

The frequency represented by frequency index k is therefore given by the formula

$$F = \frac{kR}{N} \qquad k = 0, 1, \ldots + N - 1 \qquad \text{(2-50)}$$

According to equation (2-50) setting $k = 0$ corresponds to 0 Hz ("DC"), $k = 1$ corresponds to R/N Hz, $k = 2$ corresponds to $2R/N$ Hz, and so on. The only subtlety arises from the fact that for values of k greater than $N/2$, equation (2-50) refers to frequencies greater than half the sampling rate.

To interpret these frequencies, we have only to recall that the spectrum of a sampled waveform is *periodic in frequency* (just as the analyzed waveform is periodic in time), with the frequencies $(N/2 + 1)R/N$ Hz, $(N/2 + 2)R/N$ Hz, and so on, equivalent, respectively, to frequencies $(-N/2+1)R/N$ Hz, $(-N/2+2)R/N$ Hz, and so on. Furthermore, the frequency $(N/2)R/N$ Hz itself corresponds to *both* minus and plus half the sampling rate.[23]

Table 2-2 illustrates the correspondence between frequency index k and frequency in hertz for the case $N = 16$. It is evident from the table that the 16-point DFT is expressed in terms of (positive and negative) harmonics of the frequency $R/16$ Hz. In other words, if R (the sampling rate) is equal to 16,000 Hz, then the DFT of waveform $x(n)$, $n = 0, 1, \ldots 15$ will find the amplitudes and phases of 16 sinusoids harmonically related to 1000 Hz that will add up to the given waveform. The harmonic frequencies examined by the DFT in this case will be presented in the order 0, 1000, 2000, 3000, 4000, 5000, 6000, 7000, ±8000, −7000, −6000, −5000, −4000, −3000, −2000, and −1000 Hz.

In summary, the discrete Fourier transform $X(k)$ of an N-point waveform $x(n)$ computes spectrum values for N frequencies, kR/N Hz, for $k = 0, 1, 2, \ldots, N-1$; due to the periodicity (in frequency) of sampled waveform spectra, frequencies between the Nyquist rate and the sampling rate (R) are equivalent to those lying between minus the Nyquist rate and 0 Hz.

Armed with these insights, we can now interpret the output of the DFT as computed by our C program. X[0] is printed as (0, 0), indicating no component at 0 Hz. X[1] is given as (0, −0.5). The amplitude of this component is $(0^2 + 0.5^2)^{1/2} = 0.5$, and its phase is $\tan^{-1} -0.5/0 = \tan^{-1} -\infty = 90°$ (phase angles are measured here with respect to the cosine function; a phase of 90° therefore represents an inverted sine wave). This corresponds to a sinusoid in inverted sine phase with a period of 16 samples and an amplitude of 0.5. Referring to our C program, we see a component in the test waveform in sine phase at this frequency but with an amplitude of 1.0. Apparently the DFT amplitude is half the "true" amplitude of the component at this frequency. As a check on this

---

[22]The analysis frequency may also be thought as as the *frequency resolution* of the DFT, because its harmonics are all equally spaced along the frequency axis. Clearly, the frequency resolution is increased (made finer) by increasing N, and vice versa.

[23]There is no distinction between signal components at minus and plus half the sampling rate in a digital signal.

TABLE 2-2 Correspondence between
frequency index k and frequency for $N = 16$.

k	f (Hz)	=	$kR/16$		
0	0				
1	$R/16$				
2	$2R/16$	=	$R/8$		
3	$3R/16$				
4	$4R/16$	=	$R/4$		
5	$5R/16$				
6	$6R/16$	=	$3R/8$		
7	$7R/16$				
8	$8R/16$	=	$R/2$	$\equiv$	$-R/2$
9	$9R/16$	$\equiv$	$-7R/16$		
10	$10R/16$	$\equiv$	$-6R/16$	=	$-3R/8$
11	$11R/16$	$\equiv$	$-5R/16$		
12	$12R/16$	$\equiv$	$-4R/16$	=	$-R/4$
13	$13R/16$	$\equiv$	$-3R/16$		
14	$14R/16$	$\equiv$	$-2R/16$	=	$-R/8$
15	$15R/16$	$\equiv$	$-1R/16$	=	$-R/16$

hypothesis, let us see if there is a similar component at three times this frequency with 0.33 its amplitude. X[3] is shown as (0, –0.165), which corresponds to an amplitude of $0.33 \times 0.5 = 0.165$.

From this we might be tempted to conclude that the DFT expresses "half-amplitudes" rather than full amplitudes, and we would be almost right. The DFT component amplitudes are *half* their "true" values *except* at 0 Hz (D.C.) and half the sampling rate, where they are numerically "correct."

The reason for this "halving of amplitude" by the DFT is found in the way it distinguishes positive and negative frequencies. We see that X[15] is given as (0, 0.5), indicating a component at $-R/16$ Hz in addition to the one we have already noted at the corresponding positive frequency. The $-R/16$ Hz component is equal in amplitude to the positive frequency component (0.5) but has the opposite phase (–90°); that is, the amplitude of the negative frequency component is the same but is reversed in phase. This is due to the fact that the Fourier transform does not distinguish positive from negative frequency components except for the phase of *sine* components, because sine is an odd function—that is, $\sin(-x) = -\sin x$. The DFT, in effect, attributes half the amplitude to the negative frequency component and half to the positive frequency component.

This brings us to some extremely important conclusions regarding the interpretation of spectra obtained with the Fourier transform. As long as the waveform consists only of real values (true for all digital audio signals),

- The negative frequency amplitude spectrum is just the (left-right) mirror image of the positive frequency amplitude spectrum.
- Except at 0 Hz (D.C.) and the Nyquist rate, the amplitudes of all components are half of their "true" values (the Fourier transform in effect divides the amplitude equally between the positive and negative frequency components).

We have seen that the phase of sine (odd) components is reversed on the positive and negative frequency sides of the spectrum because $\sin(-x) = -\sin x$.

Table 2-3 shows the complete frequency, amplitude, and phase interpretation of the output of our DFT program.

TABLE 2-3   Frequency, amplitude, and phase output of the DFT program.

k	$X(k)$	Freqrency	Amplitude	Phase	
0	(0.000, 0.000)	0	0.00	—	
1	(0.000, –0.500)	R/16	0.50	90°	(–sine)
2	(0.000, 0.000)	2R/16	0.00	—	
3	(0.000, –0.165)	3R/16	0.1650	90°	(–sine)
4	(0.000, 0.000)	4R/16	0.00	—	
5	(0.000, –0.100)	5R/16	0.10	90°	(–sine)
6	(0.000, 0.000)	6R/16	0.00	—	
7	(0.000, 0.000)	7R/16	0.00	—	
8	(0.000, 0.000)	–8R/16	0.00	—	
9	(0.000, 0.000)	–7R/16	0.00	—	
10	(0.000, 0.000)	–6R/16	0.00	—	
11	(0.000, 0.100)	–5R/16	0.10	–90°	(sine)
12	(0.000, 0.000)	–4R/16	0.00	—	
13	(0.000, 0.165)	–3R/16	0.1650	–90°	(sine)
14	(0.000, 0.000)	–2R/16	0.00	—	
15	(0.000, 0.500)	–R/16	0.50	–90°	(sine)

Of course we could arrange for our C program to print such information directly. Again, however, this would be a practical solution only if the number of points in the sampled spectrum is small (such as 16). A far more common approach to spectrum display is to plot the amplitude or phase spectrum graphically (see Figure 2-17). Because the spectrum of digitized real-valued waveforms is *always* symmetrical around 0 Hz, it is also common practice to plot only the *positive frequency half* of the spectrum (see Figure 2-18).

As mentioned previously, we must be careful to interpret spectrum plots produced by the DFT as *N-point samples of an underlying continuous function*. This consideration is largely irrelevant when the waveform being transformed consists of harmonic components, an integral number of which "fit" in the number of samples being analyzed, as has been the case so far. In the previous program, for example, exactly one period of the sine wave at 1/16 the sampling rate "fits" into 16 samples; similarly, exactly three periods of three times this frequency also fit, and so on.

Now we can return to the question of analyzing waveforms that contain a nonintegral number of periods of a periodic waveform. As a first step, we can analyze such a waveform and observe the results of transforming it with the DFT program. Let us replace the C statement

```
for ( n = 0 ; n < N ; n++ )
    x1[n] = sin( pi2oN*1*n ) + .33*sin( pi2oN*3*n )
            + .2*sin( pi2oN*5*n ) ;
```

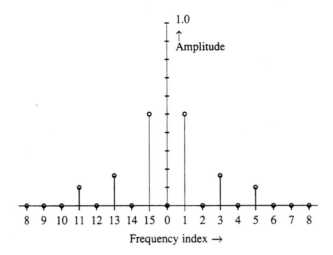

Figure 2-17   Plot of the amplitude spectrum represented by the X array. The plot extends from minus half the sampling rate on the left to plus half the sampling rate on the right. Values for the frequency index (k) are shown at their corresponding frequencies.

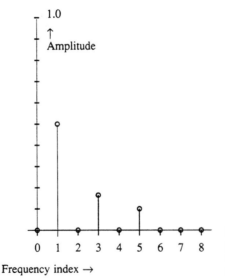

Figure 2-18   Plot of the positive-frequency amplitude spectrum represented by the X array.

with the statement

```
for ( n = 0 ; n < N ; n++ )
    x1[n] = sin( pi2oN*1.7*n ) ;
```

and rerun the program. The output now reads as follows:

```
[ 0]  x1 =   0.000,  X = ( 0.148,   0.000),  x2 =   0.000
[ 1]  x1 =   0.619,  X = ( 0.212,   0.082),  x2 =   0.619
[ 2]  x1 =   0.972,  X = (-0.294,  -0.269),  x2 =   0.972
[ 3]  x1 =   0.908,  X = (-0.033,  -0.068),  x2 =   0.908
[ 4]  x1 =   0.454,  X = (-0.003,  -0.038),  x2 =   0.454
[ 5]  x1 =  -0.195,  X = ( 0.008,  -0.024),  x2 =  -0.195
[ 6]  x1 =  -0.760,  X = ( 0.013,  -0.014),  x2 =  -0.760
[ 7]  x1 =  -0.999,  X = ( 0.015,  -0.007),  x2 =  -0.999
[ 8]  x1 =  -0.809,  X = ( 0.016,  -0.000),  x2 =  -0.809
[ 9]  x1 =  -0.271,  X = ( 0.015,   0.007),  x2 =  -0.271
[10]  x1 =   0.383,  X = ( 0.013,   0.014),  x2 =   0.383
[11]  x1 =   0.872,  X = ( 0.008,   0.024),  x2 =   0.872
[12]  x1 =   0.988,  X = (-0.003,   0.038),  x2 =   0.988
[13]  x1 =   0.679,  X = (-0.033,   0.068),  x2 =   0.679
[14]  x1 =   0.078,  X = (-0.294,   0.269),  x2 =   0.078
[15]  x1 =  -0.556,  X = ( 0.212,  -0.082),  x2 =  -0.556
```

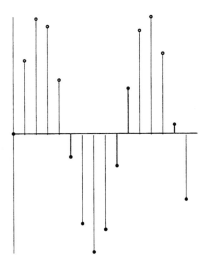

Figure 2-19   Waveform consisting of 1.7 periods of a sine wave.

Clearly, the program has worked in the sense that x2 (the IDFT of X) still matches x1 exactly—no information has been lost.   x1, however, now represents 1.7 periods of a sine wave, as we verify by examining its plot (see Figure 2-19).

X, the complex spectrum of this waveform, indicates nonzero values for every value of frequency index k, implying that several components must be added together to obtain this waveform. While it may seem surprising at first, the spectrum obtained is perfectly accurate *because we are no longer analyzing a sine wave!* This example underscores the point that the waveform being analyzed consists of 16 samples containing exactly 1.7 periods of a sine wave. If we treat these 16 samples as a *single period* of an infinitely periodic waveform (as the DFT does), it becomes clear that the waveform being analyzed is not a sine wave at all—it is, in fact, not even sinusoidal in shape. In other words, the waveform we are analyzing consists of the 16 samples shown in Figure 2-19 repeated infinitely many times. The DFT then proceeds to answer the question, how can we manufacture the infinitely periodic waveform with one period given in x1 by adding together harmonics of $R/16$ Hz? The X array (the complex spectrum) shows us the answer.

We now make another modification in our program so that it prints out amplitude and phase information directly by replacing the statement

```
for ( n = 0 ; n < N ; n++ )
    printf(
    "[%2d] x1 = %6.3f, X = (%6.3f, %6.3f), x2 = %6.3f\n",
        n, x1[n], X[n].re, X[n].im, x2[n] ) ;
```

with

```
for ( n = 0 ; n < N ; n++ )
    printf(
    "[%2d] x1 = %6.3f, X = (%6.3f, %6.3f), A = %6.3f, P = %6.3f\n",
    n, x1[n], X[n].re, X[n].im,
        sqrt( (double) X[n].re*X[n].re + X[n].im*X[n].im),
        360.*atan2( (double) X[n].im, (double) X[n].re )/pi2 ) ;
```

Rerunning our program now generates the following output.

```
[ 0] x1 = 0.000, X = ( 0.148, 0.000), A = 0.148, P =    0.000
[ 1] x1 = 0.619, X = ( 0.212, 0.082), A = 0.228, P =   21.121
[ 2] x1 = 0.972, X = (-0.294,-0.269), A = 0.398, P =-137.582
[ 3] x1 = 0.908, X = (-0.033,-0.068), A = 0.076, P =-115.943
[ 4] x1 = 0.454, X = (-0.003,-0.038), A = 0.038, P = -93.821
[ 5] x1 =-0.195, X = ( 0.008,-0.024), A = 0.025, P = -71.124
[ 6] x1 =-0.760, X = ( 0.013,-0.014), A = 0.019, P = -47.838
[ 7] x1 =-0.999, X = ( 0.015,-0.007), A = 0.016, P = -24.060
[ 8] x1 =-0.809, X = ( 0.016,-0.000), A = 0.016, P =  -0.000
[ 9] x1 =-0.271, X = ( 0.015, 0.007), A = 0.016, P =   24.060
[10] x1 = 0.383, X = ( 0.013, 0.014), A = 0.019, P =   47.838
[11] x1 = 0.872, X = ( 0.008, 0.024), A = 0.025, P =   71.124
[12] x1 = 0.988, X = (-0.003, 0.038), A = 0.038, P =   93.821
[13] x1 = 0.679, X = (-0.033, 0.068), A = 0.076, P =  115.943
[14] x1 = 0.078, X = (-0.294, 0.269), A = 0.398, P =  137.582
[15] x1 =-0.556, X = ( 0.212,-0.082), A = 0.228, P =  -21.121
```

We can now read the spectrum amplitude and phase values (in degrees) directly from the output of the program. Note that the amplitude values are still symmetrically arranged around 0 Hz because our input waveform consists only of real values. The phase values in this case appear to be *antisymmetrical* around 0 Hz as well. These values tell us directly how to construct waveform x1 out of sinusoids at frequencies that are all harmonics of $R/16$ Hz. In other words, the DFT of x1 tells us that it may be formed by adding together the following sinusoidal components:

$$x1(n) = 0.148 \cos 0 + 0.228 \cos (\frac{2\pi n}{N} + 21.121°) +$$

$$0.398 \cos (\frac{2\pi 2n}{N} - 137.582°) + 0.076 \cos (\frac{2\pi 3n}{N} - 115.943°) + \cdots$$

$$= \sum_{k=0}^{N-1} A_k \cos (\frac{2\pi kn}{N} + \phi_k)$$

where the A_k (amplitude) and ϕ_k (phase) values are taken directly from the program output shown previously.

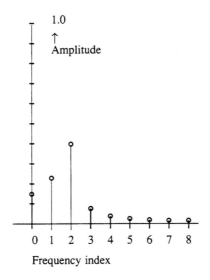

0 1 2 3 4 5 6 7 8

Frequency index

Figure 2-20   Positive frequency amplitude spectrum of waveform plot in Figure 2-19.

    A plot of the positive frequency side of this amplitude spectrum is shown in Figure 2-20. It may seem a little surprising that 1.7 cycles of a single sine wave could give rise to a spectrum with components at all available positive and negative frequencies until we reemphasize that the N-point DFT answers the question; What amplitudes and phases of all possible harmonics of R/N Hz will add up to the given waveform?

    Finally, a plot of this spectrum superimposed on a finer representation of the underlying spectrum is shown in Figure 2-21. We can observe from this plot that the eight positive frequency points of the $N = 16$ spectrum are samples of the underlying spectrum at equally spaced intervals of frequency and that in the underlying spectrum, an amplitude peak does occur at about $k = 1.7$. Nevertheless, the underlying spectrum is also filled with components at many frequencies because the transformed waveform still does not contain an integral number of cycles; therefore, the transformed waveform is still not sinusoidal.

    The foregoing discussion leads to the conclusion that if f_0 is not a subharmonic of the sampling rate R, the DFT spectrum of waveform $x(n)$ will invariably indicate

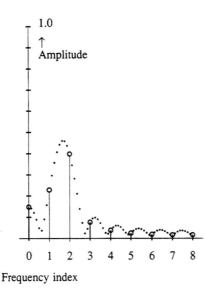

Frequency index

Figure 2-21 $N = 16$ Positive frequency spectrum superimposed on underlying spectrum (note the peak at approximately 1.7).

energy at frequencies other than the harmonics of f_0. Such discrepancies are often called *artifacts of analysis* because they arise from interactions among choices for sampling rates and analysis durations with the frequency content of a sound waveform rather than from the frequency content alone. The effects of such artifacts can be minimized through the use of windowing techniques, which we will discuss later. In all cases, it is correct to conclude that the DFT "treats" N samples of the waveform being analyzed as *one period* of a periodic waveform with period N/R seconds and computes the spectrum of this putative waveform in terms of necessary amplitudes and phases of the harmonics of R/N Hz.

To increase the frequency resolution (lower the analysis frequency) of a DFT spectrum, either R (the sampling rate) must be decreased or N (the length of the analysis window) must be increased (or both). Because we usually do not have a choice in setting R (the waveform may have already been sampled, for example), the frequency resolution is usually adjusted by varying the choice for N. There are two difficulties inherent in varying the value of N to achieve greater frequency resolution.

The first difficulty is that the spectrum amplitudes and phases reported by the DFT represent the *average* of these values over the duration of the waveform being analyzed. As long as the analyzed waveform remains absolutely steady over the period being analyzed, this presents no problem. But—as is often the case with musical waveforms and other sounds from the real world—it is most unlikely that such properties would remain constant for significant periods of time. All real sounds (as opposed to mathematical functions) have a beginning and an end that prevent them from being truly periodic in any absolute sense. At the beginning and end of real sounds, such waveforms exhibit *transient behavior* during which their properties vary according to rapidly changing mechanical states. Even during the middle section of most musical sounds, their spectrum properties may be changing due to vibrato, tremolo, and intended or unconscious variations in intensity.

Except for sounds resulting from electronic sources, then, there is virtually no such thing as a "steady state." If you desire information about how the spectrum of a sound *changes* as time goes by, there will be a constant trade-off between the available *frequency resolution* (which can be increased by increasing N) and *temporal resolution* (which can be increased only by decreasing N).

A second difficulty encountered in setting N according to the desired frequency resolution is more practical. From the definition of the DFT, it is evident that for each of N samples we must compute N frequency values. The amount of computation needed is therefore proportional to $N \times N = N^2$. Doubling the amount of data therefore *quadruples* the computation time, trebling the amount data increases the computation time by a factor of 9, and so on. If a certain DFT computation takes 10 seconds and results in a frequency resolution of 100 Hz, for example, then a 50 Hz resolution could be achieved with a DFT only with a computation that would take about 40 seconds. Eventually the practical limits of computing (and patience!) will be reached, often before the desired frequency resolution can be obtained.

2.3.6 The FFT Algorithm

A partial solution to the computation time problem is to use the so-called fast Fourier Transform algorithm (FFT), in place of the DFT. The FFT is simply another way to compute the DFT in less time, *provided* the value of N is a highly composite number—typically, it must be a power of 2.

The amount of computation required to compute the FFT grows as $N \log N$ instead of N^2 (the logarithmic base will be 2 if N is restricted to powers of 2). For small values of N, the FFT has only a small advantage (if any) over the DFT. For large values of N, however, the quantity $N \log N$ grows much more slowly than the quantity N^2, giving the FFT an enormous advantage over the DFT if high-frequency resolution (relatively large N) is desired. As we can see from Table 2-4, if the FFT algorithm takes 30 seconds to compute a 8192-point transform on a given computer, the DFT algorithm on that same computer would take over five hours to compute the same result! With the FFT, however, we are not free to chose just any value of N and thus may not set the analysis frequency (frequency resolution) arbitrarily. The usual technique for using the FFT with data sets of arbitrary length is to "pad" the data with zero-valued samples at the beginning and/or end until the next power of 2 is reached.

In general, we need not be concerned with the detailed operation of the FFT algorithm because the results it computes are precisely the same as those of the DFT. The basic idea of the FFT algorithm, however, is that it is possible to recouch the problem of transforming N samples as two subproblems, each of which involves transforming N/2 samples, one set consisting of all the even-numbered samples from the original, the other consisting of all the odd-numbered samples. Obviously, if this is possible, each of the subproblems can be similarly divided into subsubproblems, and so on, until the final subproblems involve transforming only single points! It is also obvious that for this recursive procedure to work, we must start with N samples where N is some power of 2. There will then be $\log_2 N$ "sets" of subproblems of lengths $N/2$, $N/4$, $N/8$, and so on.

TABLE 2-4 Comparison of $N \log_2 N$ (proportional to the amount of time the FFT requires) with N^2 (the amount of time needed by the DFT) for selected values of N. The last column shows how many times faster the FFT is than the DFT.

N	$N \log_2 N$	N^2	$\dfrac{N^2}{N \log_2 N}$
2	2	4	2.00
4	8	16	2.00
8	24	64	2.67
16	64	256	4.00
32	160	1,024	6.4
64	384	4,096	10.67
128	896	16,384	18.29
256	2,048	65,536	32.00
512	4,608	262,144	56.89
1,024	10,240	1,048,576	102.40
2,048	22,528	4,194,304	186.18
4,096	49,152	16,777,216	341.33
8,192	106,496	67,108,864	630.15
16,384	229,376	268,435,456	1,170.29
32,768	491,520	1,073,741,824	2,184.53
65,536	1,048,576	4,294,967,296	4,096.00

TABLE 2-5 Bit-reversed reordering for the case $N = 8$. The FFT "scrambles" its output into the order shown in the last two columns. The proper order can be recovered either by unscrambling the output or by bit-reverse-ordering the input before applying the FFT algorithm.

n_{10}	n_2	Bit-reversed n_2	Bit-reversed n_{10}
0	000	000	0
1	001	100	4
2	010	010	2
3	011	110	6
4	100	001	1
5	101	101	5
6	110	011	3
7	111	111	7

It happens that the FFT algorithm produces its results in an order that is scrambled in a certain way (see Table 2-5). The spectrum (or waveform, if we are doing an inverse transform) may be unscrambled by numbering the transformed samples from 0 to $N-1$ in binary and then *reversing the bits* in the binary index to get their proper position in the transformed data. Some FFT programs (using the so-called decimation-in-time algorithm) first scramble the original data into bit-reversed order to make the transformed data come out right; others (using the so-called decimation-in-frequency algorithm) compute the transform first and then rearrange the results into bit-reversed order.

A good general FFT program for complex input data is shown in the next example.[24] It is based on the technique of successively dividing the problem into two parts discussed previously, a procedure first described by Danielson and Lanczos in 1942. The program is quite general, because it always expects a complex input and provides a complex (transformed) output. For reasons of simplicity, the complex input values are represented in a **float** array x, of length 2 NC. x[0] contains the real part of the first complex value, x[1] contains the imaginary part of the first complex value, x[2] contains the real part of the second complex value, and so on.

The program transforms these values *in place*, meaning that the complex values are *replaced* by their Fourier transform, thus conserving storage. Furthermore, a Boolean argument to the program (forward) determines whether the forward Fourier transform or the *inverse* Fourier transform is performed. As before, the forward transform values are scaled by 1/*N*, where *N* is the number of *complex* input values. Note that the number of input complex values NC *must* be a power of 2. Note also that the program expects the value of variable TWOPI to be defined externally. This is done to prevent the program from having to compute it each time it is called.

```
#include <math.h>

extern float TWOPI ;
/*
 * cfft replaces float array x containing NC complex values
 * (2*NC float values alternating real, imaginary, and so on)
 * by its Fourier transform if forward is true, or by its
 * inverse Fourier transform if forward is false.  NC MUST be
 * a power of 2.  Based on program FOUR1 in Numerical Recipes:
 * The Art of Scientific Computing (Cambridge University Press,
 * 1986), copyright 1986 by Numerical Recipes Software.  Used
 * by permission.
 */
cfft( x, NC, forward ) float x[] ; int NC, forward ; {
  float wr, wi, wpr, wpi, theta, scale ;
  int mmax, ND, m, i, j, delta ;
     ND = NC<<1 ;
     bitreverse( x, ND ) ;
     for ( mmax = 2 ; mmax < ND ; mmax = delta ) {
         delta = mmax<<1 ;
         theta = TWOPI/( forward? mmax : -mmax ) ;
         wpr = -2.*pow( sin( 0.5*theta ), 2. ) ;
         wpi = sin( theta ) ;
         wr = 1. ;
         wi = 0. ;
         for ( m = 0 ; m < mmax ; m += 2 ) {
           register float rtemp, itemp ;
```

---

[24]The cfft and rfft programs given here are adapted from the FORTRAN programs FOUR1 and REALFT in Press et al. (1986).

```
    for ( i = m ; i < ND ; i += delta ) {
        j = i + mmax ;
        rtemp = wr*x[j] - wi*x[j+1] ;
        itemp = wr*x[j+1] + wi*x[j] ;
        x[j] = x[i] - rtemp ;
        x[j+1] = x[i+1] - itemp ;
        x[i] += rtemp ;
        x[i+1] += itemp ;
    }
    wr = (rtemp = wr)*wpr - wi*wpi + wr ;
    wi = wi*wpr + rtemp*wpi + wi ;
}
    }
/*
 * scale output
 */
    scale = forward ? 1./ND : 2. ;
    for ( i = 0 ; i < ND ; i++ )
        x[i] *= scale ;
}
/*
 * bitreverse places float array x containing N/2 complex values
 * into bit-reversed order
 */
bitreverse( x, N ) float x[] ; int N ; {
 float rtemp, itemp ;
 int i, j, m ;
    for ( i = j = 0 ; i < N ; i += 2, j += m ) {
        if ( j > i ) {
            rtemp = x[j] ; itemp = x[j+1] ; /* complex exchange */
            x[j] = x[i] ; x[j+1] = x[i+1] ;
            x[i] = rtemp ; x[i+1] = itemp ;
        }
        for ( m = N>>1 ; m >= 2 && j >= m ; m >>= 1 )
            j -= m ;
    }
}
```

In digital audio applications, it is most often the case that we wish to find the spectrum of a waveform that contains only real values. We could use the cfft program directly for such a waveform by using the real part of the input array to hold the waveform samples and setting the imaginary part of the input array to zero. We have seen, though, that the spectrum of a purely real waveform is always symmetrical around 0 Hz, with spectrum values for the negative frequencies the complex conjugates of the corresponding positive frequency values.[25] This fact suggests that it would be possible

[25]If $a + jb$ is a complex number, its complex conjugate is simply $a - jb$.

to fashion an FFT program that would replace $2N$ real waveform values with N complex values representing, say, only the positive frequency half of the waveform's spectrum. The negative frequency values could easily be inferred from the output of such a program if they are needed, and only half the storage would be required.

The following program example uses just such a method. It accepts $2N$ waveform values and replaces them with N complex values representing the positive frequency half of the Fourier transform of that waveform. However, a trick is necessary to squeeze the entire positive frequency spectrum into the N number pairs in the output of the forward transform. In the earlier examples of discrete Fourier transformation, we saw that there would actually be $N+1$ complex values that refer to positive frequencies, because the half sampling rate, or Nyquist, value ambiguously refers both to a positive and a negative frequency (it is simply not possible to distinguish a sampled cosine waveform at $+1/2$ the sampling rate from one at $-1/2$ the sampling rate). Furthermore, the spectrum value at half the sampling rate *must always be purely real* because a pure sine wave at that frequency would be sampled only at its zero crossings. Similarly, the spectrum value at zero frequency is also always purely real, because $\sin 0 = 0$. We can therefore use the imaginary part of the zero frequency value to hold the real part of the Nyquist value, thereby squeezing *all* the information about positive frequencies into exactly N number pairs. It is important to remember, though, that using this procedure means that the first number pair will represent two *real* values, the first being the amplitude of the zero frequency component, the second being the amplitude of the Nyquist frequency component. The second pair of the N number pairs represents the real and imaginary parts of the spectrum component at frequency $R/2N$, where R is the sampling rate and $2N$ is the number of *real* waveform samples being transformed.

Because the `rfft` program uses this trick to squeeze the entire positive frequency spectrum into N number pairs when doing the forward transform, it expects the input spectrum to be in this format when the inverse transform is specified. Note that `rfft` makes use of the `cfft` program given earlier. Also note that it expects the value of variable `PI` to be defined externally.

```
#include <math.h>



extern float PI ;
/*
 * If forward is true, rfft replaces 2*N real data points in x
 * with N complex values representing the positive frequency half
 * of their Fourier spectrum, with x[1] replaced with the real
 * part of the Nyquist frequency value.  If forward is false, rfft
 * expects x to contain a * positive frequency spectrum arranged
 * as before, and replaces it with 2*N real values.  N MUST be a
 * power of 2.  Based on program REALFT in Numerical Recipes: The
 * Art of Scientific Computing (Cambridge University Press, 1986),
 * copyright 1986 by Numerical Recipes Software.  Used by
```

```
 * permission.
 */
rfft( x, N, forward ) float x[] ; int N, forward ; {
 float c1, c2, h1r, h1i, h2r, h2i, wr, wi, wpr, wpi, temp, theta ;
 float xr, xi ;
 int i, i1, i2, i3, i4, N2p1 ;
     theta = PI/N ;
     wr = 1. ;
     wi = 0. ;
     c1 = 0.5 ;
     if ( forward ) {
         c2 = -0.5 ;
         cfft( x, N, forward ) ;
         xr = x[0] ;
         xi = x[1] ;
     } else {
         c2 = 0.5 ;
         theta = -theta ;
         xr = x[1] ;
         xi = 0. ;
         x[1] = 0. ;
     }
     wpr = -2.*pow( sin( 0.5*theta ), 2. ) ;
     wpi = sin( theta ) ;
     N2p1 = (N<<1) + 1 ;
     for ( i = 0 ; i <= N>>1 ; i++ ) {
         i1 = i<<1 ;
         i2 = i1 + 1 ;
         i3 = N2p1 - i2 ;
         i4 = i3 + 1 ;
         if ( i == 0 ) {
             h1r =   c1*(x[i1] + xr ) ;
             h1i =   c1*(x[i2] - xi ) ;
             h2r =  -c2*(x[i2] + xi ) ;
             h2i =   c2*(x[i1] - xr ) ;
             x[i1] =  h1r + wr*h2r - wi*h2i ;
             x[i2] =  h1i + wr*h2i + wi*h2r ;
             xr =  h1r - wr*h2r + wi*h2i ;
             xi = -h1i + wr*h2i + wi*h2r ;
         } else {
             h1r =   c1*(x[i1] + x[i3] ) ;
             h1i =   c1*(x[i2] - x[i4] ) ;
             h2r =  -c2*(x[i2] + x[i4] ) ;
             h2i =   c2*(x[i1] - x[i3] ) ;
             x[i1] =  h1r + wr*h2r - wi*h2i ;
             x[i2] =  h1i + wr*h2i + wi*h2r ;
             x[i3] =  h1r - wr*h2r + wi*h2i ;
             x[i4] = -h1i + wr*h2i + wi*h2r ;
```

```
            }
        wr = (temp = wr)*wpr - wi*wpi + wr ;
        wi = wi*wpr + temp*wpi + wi ;
    }
    if ( forward )
        x[1] = xr ;
    else
        cfft( x, N, forward ) ;
}
```

The `cfft` and `rfft` programs together form a general and useful set of tools for practical evaluation of the discrete Fourier transform using the FFT algorithm. As an example of their use, the following program exercises them to find the spectrum of a simple waveform and calculates the inverse transform as a check. Note the use of left and right shifts to avoid multiplications and divisions of integer values.

```
#include <stdio.h>
#include <math.h>

#define L 16

float TWOPI ;   /* needed for rfft and cfft */
float PI ;      /* needed for rfft and cfft */

main() {
 float x[L], y[L], z[L] ;
 int n ;
    PI = 4.*atan(1.) ;
    TWOPI = 8.*atan(1.) ;
    for ( n = 0 ; n < L ; n++ )
        x[n] = y[n] = 1. + cos( 8*n*TWOPI/L ) + cos( 3*n*TWOPI/L ) ;
    rfft( y, L/2, 1 ) ;
    for ( n = 0 ; n < L ; n++ )
        z[n] = y[n] ;
    rfft( z, L/2, 0 ) ;
    printf( "%4s%9s%10s%10s%10s\n",
        "n ", "x(n)", "y(2n)", "y(2n+1)", "z(n)" ) ;
    for ( n = 0 ; n < L ; n++ ) {
        if ( n < L/2 )
            printf( "[%2d] %9f %9f %9f %9f\n",
                n, x[n], y[n<<1], y[(n<<1)+1], z[n] ) ;
        else
            printf( "[%2d] %9f                        %9f\n",
                n, x[n], z[n] ) ;
    }
}
```

The preceding program produces the following output when run.

```
  n        x(n)      y(2n)     y(2n+1)       z(n)
[ 0]    3.000000   1.000000   1.000000    3.000000
[ 1]    0.382683  -0.000000   0.000000    0.382683
[ 2]    1.292893   0.000000   0.000000    1.292893
[ 3]   -0.923880   0.500000   0.000000   -0.923880
[ 4]    2.000000   0.000000   0.000000    2.000000
[ 5]    0.923880   0.000000   0.000000    0.923880
[ 6]    2.707107   0.000000   0.000000    2.707107
[ 7]   -0.382683  -0.000000  -0.000000   -0.382683
[ 8]    1.000000                           1.000000
[ 9]   -0.382683                          -0.382683
[10]    2.707107                           2.707107
[11]    0.923880                           0.923880
[12]    2.000000                           2.000000
[13]   -0.923880                          -0.923880
[14]    1.292893                           1.292893
[15]    0.382683                           0.382683
```

2.3.7 Convolution

One of the most important properties of spectra computed with the DFT (or FFT) is their behavior when two or more waveforms are combined. When two waveforms are added together, their spectra add as well. That is, if N samples of waveform $f(n)$ have the DFT spectrum $F(k)$ and N samples of waveform $g(n)$ have the spectrum $G(k)$, then

$$\text{DFT}(f(n) + g(n)) = F(k) + G(k) \qquad (2\text{-}51)$$

Furthermore, if we multiply a waveform by a constant, the spectrum of the waveform is scaled by the same constant, that is,

$$\text{DFT}(af(n)) = aF(k) \qquad (2\text{-}52)$$

where a is a constant.

Combining these properties, we may also describe the DFT as *linear*, because it obeys the necessary requirement

$$\text{DFT}(af(n) + bg(n)) = aF(k) + bG(k) \qquad (2\text{-}53)$$

where both a and b are constants.

When two waveforms are *multiplied*, however, the spectrum of the resulting waveform is *not* the product of the two spectra of the waveforms taken individually. The spectrum of the product of two waveforms is the *convolution* of the spectra of the individual waveforms:

$$\text{DFT}(f(n)g(n)) = F(k) \, * \, G(k) \qquad (2\text{-}54)$$

where $*$ indicates convolution.

The linear, or *aperiodic*, convolution of two finite-length sequences $f(n)$ and $g(n)$ of length N_f and N_g, respectively, is defined as

$$h(n) = f(n) * g(n) = \sum_{m=0}^{n} f(m)g(n-m)$$

(2-55)

where both f and g are considered to have zero values outside the range 0 to $N_f - 1$ and 0 to $N_g - 1$, respectively.

If the two sequences being convolved are considered to be *periodic* with periods N_f and N_g, respectively (and therefore *not* zero outside the intervals 0 to $N_f - 1$ and 0 to $N_g - 1$), the resulting convolution is said to be *circular*, or *periodic*. In the first (aperiodic) case, the resulting sequence h has a *length* of precisely $N_f + N_g - 1$ samples, while in the second (periodic) case, the resulting sequence has a *period* of precisely $N_f + N_g - 1$ samples.

So much for the theory of the thing. Equation (2-55) is readily understood by extending slightly our view of a sequence. We start with the fact that the linear convolution of any finite-duration sequence $f(n)$ with the unit sample function $u(n)$ results in a sequence identical to $f(n)$, that is,

$$f(n) * u(n) = f(n)$$

(2-56)

where $u(n) = 1$ for $n = 0$ and $u(n) = 0$ for all other values of n. In other words, convolving any sequence with the unit sample function leaves that sequence unchanged, much as multiplying it by 1 (or adding 0 to it) leaves it unchanged. If we delay the unit sample function by d samples, which we may notate by $u(n-d)$, and convolve it with sequence $f(n)$, the result is simply $f(n)$ delayed by the same number of samples:

$$f(n) * u(n-d) = f(n-d)$$

(2-57)

If we scale the unit sample function by a constant a, the convolution with sequence $f(n)$ similarly scales the sequence:

$$f(n) * au(n) = af(n)$$

(2-58)

As we might expect, these operations may be combined, as in

$$f(n) * au(n-d) = af(n-d)$$

(2-59)

These relations lead to a very simple and useful interpretation of the convolution operation. If we now consider an N-sample sequence to be a sum of N delayed, scaled unit sample functions, we see that the convolution of this sequence with any other can be thought of as the sum of the convolutions of that sequence with each of the delayed, scaled unit sample functions. We simply slide a copy of the other sequence to the position of each sample of the first (the $n = 0$ sample provides the reference point), scale it by that sample's value, and add it into the resulting sequence.

To provide a concrete example, let's say that $f(n)$ is the five-sample sequence $\{2, 2, 3, 3, 4\}$ and that $g(n)$ is the three-sample sequence $\{1, 1, 2\}$. From our earlier discussion, we expect the convolution of these two sequences to result in a sequence of length $5 + 3 - 1 = 7$. To compute the values in the convolved sequence, we simply write down, the $g(n)$ sequence five times, once for each value in $f(n)$; each time we write it down, we multiply the entire $g(n)$ sequence by the corresponding member of $f(n)$. These shifted, scaled versions of $g(n)$ are then simply added together.

$$f(n) * g(n) =$$

{	2	2	3	3	4	}	*	{	1	1	2	}

	2	2	4				
		2	2	4			
			3	3	6		
				3	3	6	
					4	4	8
	2	4	9	10	13	10	8

Convolution is *commutative*; that is, $f(n) * g(n) = g(n) * f(n)$, so we might just as well have computed the result as follows:

$$g(n) * f(n) =$$

{	1	1	2	}	*	{	2	2	3	3	4	}

	2	2	3	3	4		
		2	2	3	3	4	
			4	4	6	6	8
	2	4	9	10	13	10	8

Convolution is just another way to combine functions, like addition and multiplication. If the functions are sampled and real-valued (corresponding to digital audio waveforms), the simple procedure just described may be used to compute their convolution.[26] If the sampled functions are complex (such as spectra computed with the DFT), the procedure is exactly the same, but the rules for adding and multiplying complex numbers must be used.

We may also interpret convolution graphically. Suppose that we wish to find the spectrum of a waveform consisting of the product of two sinusoidal functions sampled at R Hz, x_1 and x_2, where

---

[26]The method shown is not the fastest way to compute the result for real waveforms, however.

$$x_1(n) = A_1 \cos\frac{2\pi f_1 n}{R} \qquad (2\text{-}60)$$

and

$$x_2(n) = A_2 \cos\frac{2\pi f_2 n}{R} \qquad (2\text{-}61)$$

Here, f_1 and f_2 represent the frequencies of the sinusoids (they are both in cosine phase), and A_1 and A_2 represent their respective amplitudes. We know from our previous considerations that the underlying spectrum $X_1(k)$ of $x_1(n)$ consists of a two spikes at plus and minus f_1 Hz with amplitude $A_1/2$ (if f_1 is a subharmonic of R, the DFT will show us the underlying spectrum precisely; if f_1 is not a subharmonic of the sampling rate, analysis artifacts will also be present). The spectrum of $x_2(n)$ is similar, with different values for the frequency and amplitude of the sinusoid. We wish to compute the spectrum of

$$x_3(n) = x_1(n)x_2(n) = A_1 \cos\frac{2\pi f_1 n}{R}\, A_2 \cos\frac{2\pi f_2 n}{R} \qquad (2\text{-}62)$$

For concreteness, let's suppose that the frequencies of our two sinusoids are 10 Hz and 100 Hz, respectively, and that both amplitudes are equal to unity. Plotted on a linear scale, the amplitude spectrum of x_1 then looks something like

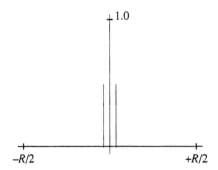

while the amplitude spectrum of x_2 looks like

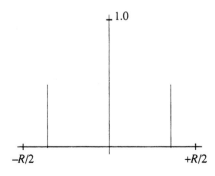

Given these two plots, we may construct a plot of the amplitude spectrum of x_3 as follows. We center a copy of X_1 (the first plot) around each component in X_2. We then scale the components of X_1 by the amplitude of the component around which it is centered. The resulting shifted, scaled components depict the result, which looks like this:

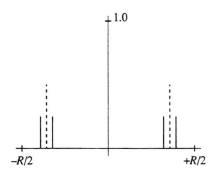

Notice that the dotted lines in the last plot are not part of the resulting spectrum—they simply mark the locations of the components of X_2 around which we centered the others. Also notice that the resulting components each have an amplitude of 0.25, because the components of X_1 and X_2 were all of height 0.5.

The resulting plot (X_3), obtained by graphical convolution, shows us that the spectrum of the product of two sinusoids consists of the sum and difference frequencies of the two original sinusoids. A well-known trigonometric identity (see Appendix A) states that

$$\cos A \, \cos B = \frac{1}{2}[\cos(A+B) + \cos(A-B)]$$

where A and B are arbitrary angles, which agrees well with our result. In terms of sound, if we multiply a 100-Hz sinusoid by a 10-Hz one of equal strength, we would expect to hear 90 and 110 Hz, each at half the original amplitude. Such multiplication is often accomplished in the realm of analog electronic music through the use of a device called a *ring modulator*.

With graphical convolution, some care must be taken with the phases of components that happen to land on top of each other. Referring to the amplitude spectra just presented, we may easily compute the amplitude of the sum of two sinusoids with identical frequencies but different phases by converting amplitudes and phases to rectangular (complex) coordinates before summing using the relations

$$a = A\cos\theta \tag{2-63}$$

and

$$b = A\sin\theta \tag{2-64}$$

Given two sets of amplitude and phase values for the same frequency, we simply convert them both to complex (real and imaginary) form, add the real and imaginary parts separately, and find the amplitude and phase of the result. Even with this proviso, graphical convolution can provide a quick and useful way to evaluate frequencies and amplitudes of product waveform spectra.

2.3.8 Working with Spectra

Combining knowledge of convolution—especially graphical convolution—with knowledge of the spectra of a few simple functions allows considerable insight into spectrum behavior.

Figure 2-22 shows several Fourier "transform pairs" about which we can make several useful observations.

Time and Frequency Domain Symmetry.   The Fourier transform associates a spectrum with a waveform and vice versa: we may consider the left column of Figure 2-22 to be waveforms; if so, the right column shows spectra. We could just as easily treat the right column as waveforms, in which case the left column shows associated spectra. Thus we can see that a waveform consisting of a single pulse (a unit-sample function) has a spectrum consisting of all frequencies in equal proportion. Conversely, we see that a constant-valued waveform (steady "DC") has a spectrum consisting only of energy at 0 Hz.

Spectrum Spacing versus Waveform Spacing.   The relationship between time and frequency is inverse; that is, time has units of seconds (sec), so frequency has units of per second (sec^{-1}). Similarly, the period of a periodic waveform has units of seconds per cycle while the frequency of the same waveform is measured in units of cycles per second (hertz). It is evident, therefore, that squeezing features more closely together in one domain has the effect of spacing the corresponding features farther apart in the other domain by a proportionate amount. In the case of the pulse train, for example, if we halve the spacing between pulses on one side of the picture, we would double it on the other.

Spectrum Shape versus Waveform Shape.   It is evident from inspection of Figure 2-22 that smooth, gradual behavior in one domain corresponds to sharp, confined behavior in the other. Smoothly varying sinusoids, for example, have sharp lines for correspondence in the other domain (recall that this means that the spectrum of a waveform consisting of two symmetrically spaced impulses has a sinusoidal shape as well as vice versa). The most "unsmooth" impulse and random functions, taken as waveforms, are associated with absolutely uniform (constant!) spectra.

In addition, the high-frequency (long-term) behavior of spectra (waveforms) is intimately connected with their shape in the other domain. For example, periodic waveforms exhibiting impulsive behavior (such as the pulse train) have spectra that do not decrease in energy with increasing frequency. If we smooth the impulse function by a mathematical process known as integration, it becomes a step function (that is, it is zero on one side and a nonzero constant on the other side of an arbitrary time or

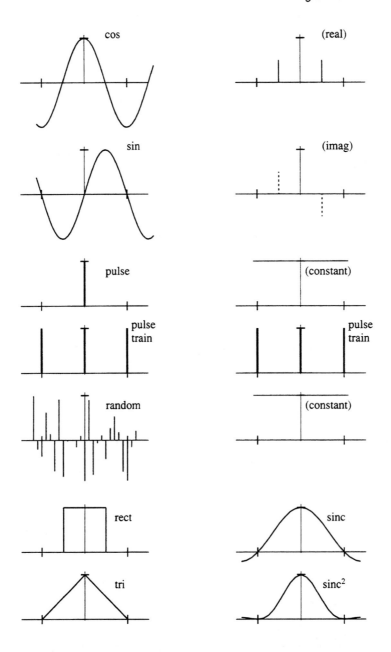

Figure 2-22   Fourier transform pairs. Functions on the left and right transform into each other, making it possible to think of either column as waveforms and the other as spectra. Unit values of time (or frequency) and amplitude are marked on the axes to show the relationships among these values.

frequency value). Periodic waveforms that exhibit step behavior (such as square waves) have spectra that contain components that gradually decrease in energy as the frequency goes up. In fact, the strength of harmonics decreases as the reciprocal of the harmonic number (that is, the N-th harmonic is $1/N$ as strong as the fundamental), which means that the spectrum gradually "rolls off" at the rate of 6 dB per octave. Integrating the square wave again leads to a triangular wave, whose harmonics decrease in amplitude as the reciprocal of the square of the harmonic number (that is, the third harmonic is one ninth the strength of the fundamental), indicating that the spectrum rolls off at a rate of 12 dB per octave.

We can summarize these observations as follows:

- Waveforms exhibiting *impulsive behavior* tend to have spectra that *do not decrease* with increasing frequency.
- Waveforms that tend to have *sharp steps* tend to have spectra that roll off at the rate of *6 dB per octave*.
- Waveforms that tend to have *sharp corners* tend to have spectra that roll off at the rate of *12 dB per octave*.

Examples of similar behavior can be seen in Figure 2-22 by comparing the spectra of the rect waveform and the tri waveform. Note that these are *not* periodic functions because they consist of only a single "box" or "triangle" rather than a periodic succession of such features. The transforms of the rectangular and triangular functions will be discussed in section 2.3.9.

Another useful observation we can make at this point is the potential of using spectrum transformation techniques for both analysis and synthesis. As we have seen already, the waveform may be transformed into its corresponding spectrum, and this spectrum may similarly be transformed into its corresponding waveform. From the standpoint of digital waveforms, we may interpret the first of these two steps as an analysis procedure and the second as a synthesis procedure. In our first programming example, we verified that the output of the synthesis step can be identical to the input supplied to the analysis step; that is, the inverse transform essentially undoes what the transform does.

There is nothing to prevent us from modifying the spectrum in some useful way before resynthesizing the waveform. For example, we could filter the waveform by multiplying its spectrum by some desired frequency response, or we could modify the phases of the spectrum components in some desired way. In Figure 2-23, we see this modification procedure represented as multiplication of the spectrum of the input with a spectrum-modifying function $H(k)$. The resynthesized waveform will be the convolution of the input waveform $x(n)$ with the inverse transform of $H(k)$; that is,

$$y(n) = x(n) * h(n) \qquad (2\text{-}65)$$

where $h(n)$ is the inverse transform of $H(k)$ and $*$ represents convolution.

Care must be taken in specifying the type of spectrum modification to be introduced in that we must be aware of what $h(n)$ is. It might be tempting to try to produce

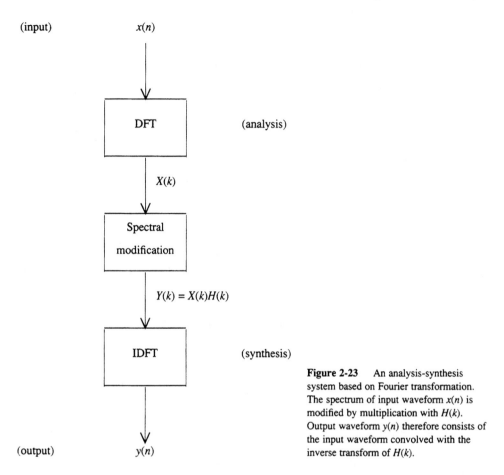

(input) $x(n)$

DFT   (analysis)

$X(k)$

Spectral
modification

$Y(k) = X(k)H(k)$

IDFT   (synthesis)

(output) $y(n)$

Figure 2-23   An analysis-synthesis
system based on Fourier transformation.
The spectrum of input waveform $x(n)$ is
modified by multiplication with $H(k)$.
Output waveform $y(n)$ therefore consists of
the input waveform convolved with the
inverse transform of $H(k)$.

a "perfect" notch filter, for example, by simply setting $X(k)$ to zero for a particular frequency. Unfortunately, the inverse spectrum of a function that is equal to one
everywhere except for a single point where it is equal to zero is in many ways very
similar to that of a pulse function. Because the pulse function is very narrow, its
transform is very wide. If we convolve a waveform with a wide function, we learn the
reason why the convolution operation is often referred to as the "smearing" operation.[27]
Because each sample of the input waveform would be "smeared" over all samples of the
output, we see that the result is *aliasing in time*, which is in every way equivalent to
aliasing in frequency. We shall return to this question later when we discuss time-
varying spectrum measurements.

---

[27]Recall that convolving a function with a single pulse leaves that function unchanged. By the same
token, convolving a function with a string of pulses effectively copies the entire original function to each pulse
position. If the pulse string is essentially a sequence of identical values, these copies could easily overlap;
their sum would form the result.

2.3.9 Convolution and the Sampling Theorem

The Fourier transform and convolution concepts may be combined to gain new insight into the sampling theorem. If the pulses shown in the pulse train function in Figure 2-22 are extremely narrow and of unit height, its continuous form is sometimes called the *sampling function*.[28] The frequency at which pulses occur is the sampling rate. Clearly, if we multiply an arbitrary (continuous) waveform by this sampling function, the result will be a string of pulses. The height of each of the resulting pulses will be equal to the instantaneous amplitude of the original waveform at the time each sampling pulse occurs.

What is the spectrum of the sampled waveform? We can now state with confidence that it will be the convolution of the spectrum of the original waveform with the spectrum of the sampling function. But the spectrum of the sampling function is simply an infinite progression of components at all integer harmonics of the sampling rate. The convolution process associated with sampling effectively centers a copy of the spectrum of the original waveform around all multiples of the sampling frequency. The spectrum of the sampled waveform is therefore just an infinite progression of copies of the spectrum of the original (continuous) waveform. For these copies not to overlap, they must extend no farther than half the distance to the center of the next copy, or half the sampling rate. But that is just another way of saying that the sampling rate must exceed twice the highest-frequency component in the sampled waveform.

The antialiasing lowpass filter in the analog-to-digital conversion process ensures that the infinite progression of copies of the spectrum of the original waveform created by the sampling process is nonoverlapping. The smoothing lowpass filter in the digital-to-analog conversion process removes all copies of the sampled waveform spectrum except for the one centered around 0 Hz.

2.3.10 Windowing

We have seen the so-called artifacts that arise when we use the DFT to analyze N samples of a waveform containing frequency components that are not integrally related to the sampling rate R and/or the analysis frequency R/N. We have also seen that such artifacts are due to the fact that the samples being analyzed do not contain an integral number of periods of the frequencies they "really" contain. While such artifacts cannot be eliminated entirely (making it important to understand them), their effect can be minimized through the use of *window functions*.

Recall that simply choosing N samples from a digital waveform is equivalent to specifying an infinite-time DFT on the waveform multiplied by $w(n)$, where $w(n) = 1$ for $n = 0, 1, \ldots, N - 1$ and 0 elsewhere. This multiplication effectively convolves the spectrum of the waveform with the spectrum of the rectangular window function before the transformation is accomplished.

---

[28]The sampling function is the "idealized" train of impulses, each with unit area and infinitesimal duration.

The spectrum of the rectangular window function has the form of a well-known function called

$$\text{sinc } x = \frac{\sin x}{x} \qquad (2\text{-}66)$$

We can observe from the definition of sinc x that it consists of a cosine-like waveform that decreases in amplitude as x moves away from zero in either direction (see Figure 2-24).

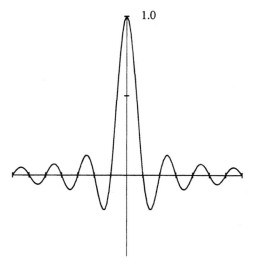

Figure 2-24   Graph of sinc x. The zero crossings of this function occur at intervals of π along the horizontal axis.

Recalling that convolution replaces each component in one spectrum with a scaled copy of the other spectrum centered at the same frequency does much to explain how an implicit multiplication by a rectangular window function can yield the type of artifact we have so far. When an integral number of periods are present, the harmonics of the analysis frequency line up with the zero crossings of the sinc function spectrum of the rectangular window, yielding a single spectrum line at the center only. If a nonintegral number of periods are present, the sinc function is centered about each component in the underlying spectrum. Because these components lie generally in between the harmonics of the analysis frequency, the zero crossings of the sinc function are not aligned on analysis frequency harmonics, resulting in spurious components (artifacts) in the resulting spectrum.

Alternatively, we may view the sinc function as the response of each harmonic measurement of the DFT to all frequencies. When the DFT makes its measurement for the amplitude of the kth harmonic, this measurement is affected by components of the signal as described by the sinc function. A component precisely at the frequency of the kth harmonic would have its amplitude scaled by 1. If all other frequency components fall on zero crossings of the sinc function response curve, they will not affect the measurement. But any component in the underlying spectrum that does not fall on a zero crossing will contaminate the measurement to a degree expressed by the sinc curve.

Thus it is possible to interpret the DFT as the output of a *bank of filters*, each of which responds to frequencies in a manner shown by the sinc function curve. The central lobe of each filter's response is centered around the harmonics of the analysis frequency, and the zero crossings are spaced at intervals of the analysis frequency.

The first zero crossing occurs, in terms of the sinc function as defined here, when x has traversed half a circle. Therefore, the first side lobe has a peak where $x = 3\pi/2$, implying that on a dB scale it has an amplitude response of

$$20 \log_{10} | \operatorname{sinc} \frac{3\pi}{2} | \approx -13.5 \text{ dB}$$

compared with that of the central (0-dB) lobe. In other words, the putative filter centered around each harmonic of the analysis frequency would also "hear" a frequency component located 1 1/2 harmonics away at an amplitude attenuated by less than 14 dB. In these terms we may also observe that the amplitudes of the side lobe peaks fall off rather slowly with frequency on either side, indicating that the rectangular window is particularly prone to artifacts, because each DFT measurement is responding to many frequencies besides the one at its center.

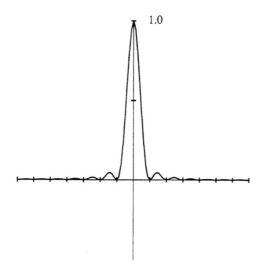

Figure 2-25   Graph of sinc^2 x. The peak amplitudes of the side lobes of this function are significantly smaller than those of sinc x.

Many other window functions may be used instead of the rectangular one. For example we may double (in dB) the rejection at the side lobe peaks by simply squaring the sinc function. The sinc^2 function (see Figure 2-25), of course, is the spectrum corresponding to the rectangular window function convolved with itself. The waveform corresponding to a sinc^2 spectrum therefore has a triangular shape and *double the time width* of the corresponding rectangular window.

The effect of window functions is achieved by their characteristic shape, which almost always starts from zero, reaches a maximum, and symmetrically falls back to zero at the end. A moment's thought will reveal that this minimizes the effect of any discontinuities at the endpoints of the analyzed waveform due to a nonintegral number of periods. Window functions effectively "link up" the beginning and ending of the analyzed segment of the waveform, helping them to behave like single periods of a periodic function even if they are not. By contrast, a rectangular window function turns on and off so rapidly at the beginning and end that it actually provokes high frequencies in the spectrum estimate obtained with the DFT.

Many window functions have names. Each is distinguished by some charming property such as a narrow central lobe, fast rolloff of side lobe peaks, or advantageous worst-case side lobes. The choice of a window function is usually not critical and is often simply a matter of taste, familiarity, or convenience. For most spectrum estimation tasks, though, the use of almost any window function other than rectangular is highly recommended.

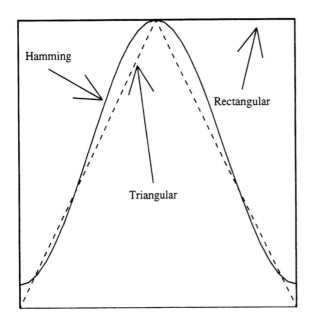

Figure 2-26 The rectangular (heavy line), triangular (broken line) and Hamming windows. Note that the Hamming window does not go to zero on both sides; the others do.

A commonly used window for audio applications is the *generalized Hamming window*, which is defined by the equation

$$w_H(n) = \alpha + (1 - \alpha)\cos\frac{2\pi n}{N}, \qquad -\frac{N-1}{2} \le n \le \frac{N-1}{2} \qquad (2\text{-}67)$$

If α in equation 2-67 is set to 0.54, the resulting window is called a *Hamming* window—if α is set to 0.5, it is called a *hanning* window.[29] Another commonly used window is the triangular, or *Parzen*, window. Figure 2-26 shows the relationships

---

[29]If you find these terms confusing, you are in good company—they are often confused in the literature as well.

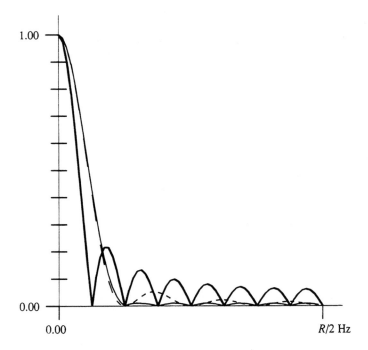

Figure 2-27   Positive frequency amplitude spectra (linear scale) of the rectangular (heavy line), triangular (broken line), and Hamming windows. Note that the rectangular window has more zeros than the others but much greater side lobe amplitude. When used with the DFT, the Hamming and triangular windows allow comparatively less contamination by energy from distant frequencies than the rectangular window.

between the shapes of the Hamming, triangular, and rectangular windows. Note that the Hamming window does not go to zero on both ends, whereas the others do. Figure 2-27 compares the spectra of these three windows. It is apparent from this figure that the "leakage" from other frequencies is most pronounced for the rectangular window.

To demonstrate the effect of windowing in a concrete way, we can observe the effect of using a Hamming window on our example waveform consisting of 1.7 periods of a sine wave. Immediately after the waveform is computed with the statement

```
for ( n = 0 ; n < N ; n++ )
    x1[n] = sin( pi2oN*1.7*n ) ;
```

we add the following statement to multiply it by a Hamming window:

```
for ( n = 0 ; n < N ; n++ )
    x1[n] *= ( 0.54 - 0.46*cos( n*pi2oNm1 ) ) ;
```

where variable `pi2oNm1` has the value 2π divided by $N - 1$ (the length of our transform minus 1) to assure that the window is symmetrical.

When we transform the windowed waveform using either the DFT or FFT program, we get new results. Table 2-6 shows a comparison between the unwindowed amplitude and phase values and the windowed ones.

TABLE 2-6 Comparison between DFT results using rectangular and Hamming windows.

	Amplitude		Phase	
k	Rectangular Window	Hamming Window	Rectangular Window	Hamming Window
0	0.148	0.039	0.000	180.000
1	0.228	0.176	21.121	28.300
2	0.398	0.238	−137.582	−140.452
3	0.076	0.067	−115.943	49.782
4	0.038	0.001	−93.821	16.657
5	0.025	0.001	−71.124	−59.227
6	0.019	0.001	−47.838	−45.724
7	0.016	0.001	−24.060	−24.110
8	0.016	0.001	0.000	0.000
9	0.016	0.001	24.060	24.110
10	0.019	0.001	47.838	45.724
11	0.025	0.001	71.124	59.227
12	0.038	0.001	93.821	−16.657
13	0.076	0.067	115.943	−49.782
14	0.398	0.238	137.582	140.452
15	0.228	0.176	−21.121	−28.300

We see from Table 2-6 that the relative amplitudes of most of the "spurious" components in the amplitude spectrum have been attenuated by the Hamming window. However, all of the component amplitudes have been made smaller. The largest value at $k = 2$, for instance, has 59 percent of its previous value. Note that even though most of the other components have a much smaller percentage of their rectangularly windowed values, the ones immediately adjacent to the largest one are actually relatively larger than before (at $k = 1$, the Hamming window amplitude is 77 percent of the rectangular window value, and at $k = 3$, the similar value is 88 percent). This is the effect of the relatively wider central lobe of the spectrum of the Hamming window. The amplitudes at the remaining frequencies are very small, however. Thus we see that the "concentrating" effect of the Hamming window comes at the price of broadening the response of the analysis filter to nearby frequencies while making it less sensitive to frequencies further removed from its central lobe.

We also note that the phases are not the same. The DFT is reporting the amplitudes and phases of the sinusoids needed to construct the *windowed* waveform. An inverse transform of the windowed spectrum would result, of course, in the windowed version of the original waveform. To recover the original waveform from its windowed version, we could divide the windowed version by the window, provided that the window itself is nowhere exactly equal to zero. This is one advantage of the Hamming window over many other window functions described in the literature (such as the triangular window): it nowhere has a zero value.

The concepts discussed so far are sufficient for making many useful spectrum measurements. We can combine the idea of windowing with the FFT programs presented earlier. First, we choose a window length equal to a power of 2. If the number of waveform samples to be transformed is not a power of 2, we simply pad the data up to the next power of 2 with zero-valued samples. We then apply the window function to the data. The data then can be transformed in place with the `rfft` program, resulting in a representation of the positive frequency side of the complex spectrum. If array x contains N waveform samples, the C statement

```
rfft( x, N/2, 1 ) ;
```

will effect this transformation. To print out the result or to place it in a form suitable for plotting, we probably want to transform the data further from rectangular form to either amplitude on a linear or decibel scale or to a phase representation. The C statement

```
/*
 * Compute amplitude spectrum from complex values
 */
for ( i = 1 ; i < N/2 ; i++ )
 x[i] =
  sqrt( (double) x[2*i]*x[2*i] + x[2*i+1]*x[2*i+1] ) ;
```

will convert the N real and imaginary values into $N/2$ real amplitude values (note that the amplitude of the Nyquist frequency component would be omitted by this conversion according to the conventions of the `rfft` program).

To observe amplitude on a decibel scale, we must first choose a reference value for 0 dB. Common choices are arbitrarily to set 0 dB to correspond to a linear amplitude of 1.0 or to find the maximum amplitude present in the spectrum and use this as the 0 dB reference value, as in

```
/*
 * Find largest amplitude value for ref (dB reference)
 */
for ( ref = x[0], i = 1 ; i < N/2 ; i++ )
    if ( x[i] > ref )
        ref = x[i] ;
```

The amplitude measurements could then be converted to dB by the statement

```
/*
 * Convert amplitude scale from linear to dB
 */
for ( i = 0 ; i < N/2 ; i++ )
 x[i] =
  x[i] > 0. ? 20.*log10( (double) x[i]/ref ) : -HUGE ;
```

Recall that care is needed when taking the logarithms of nonpositive numbers.

A simpler conversion to dB is possible, however, because the square root operation is not needed. Given the x array as returned by rfft, the following C code would express the amplitude (power) spectrum in dB using the maximum value as the 0 dB reference. This code uses shifting and temporary register variables for efficiency.

```
N2 = N>>1 ;
/*
 * Compute power spectrum from complex values
 */
for ( i = 1 ; i < N2 ; i++ ) { register float a, b ;
    a = x[i<<1] ;
    b = x[(i<<1)+1] ;
    x[i] = a*a + b*b ;
}
/*
 * Use largest power value for dB reference
 */
for ( ref = x[0], i = 1 ; i < N2 ; i++ )
    if ( x[i] > ref )
        ref = x[i] ;
/*
 * Convert from linear to dB scale
 */
for ( i = 0 ; i < N2 ; i++ )
 x[i] =
  x[i] > 0. ? 10.*log10( (double) x[i]/ref ) : -HUGE ;
```

Similarly, the C statements

```
/*
 * Compute phase spectrum from complex values
 */
N2 = N>>1 ;
x[0] = 0. ;
for ( i = 1 ; i < N2 ; i++ )
    x[i] = atan2( (double) x[(i<<1)+1], (double) x[i<<1] ) ;
```

would convert the complex values returned by the rfft program into $N/2$ real phase values in the range $-\pi$ to $+\pi$ for printing or plotting.

2.3.11 Time-varying Spectrum Measurements

The spectrum of a musical sound is not constant over time. In other words, the waveform of a musical sound is not strictly periodic. A single note played on a typical musical instrument usually consists of an initial *attack*, a roughly periodic sustained portion often miscalled a *steady state*, and a release or *decay* portion. During the attack and decay portions of the note, the waveform and its associated spectrum change rapidly as time goes by. Even during the so-called steady state, most musical tones vary over a considerable range of amplitude due to intended variations such as *tremolo* or unintended but nonetheless natural variations in the strength of the excitation. The pitch may also vary due to intended (*vibrato* or pitch inflection) or unintended effects. Minor variations in *timbre* also occur, as when a violin vibrato causes spectrum components to move independently into and out of regions of resonance associated with the violin body. Such variations over time are largely responsible for the auditory richness of musical sounds. They also support our perceptual ability to recognize subtle differences between individual musical instruments of the same kind as well as our acute ability to distinguish natural from synthetic musical tones.

A considerable amount of computer music research has concentrated on the time-varying properties of musical sounds, both from the standpoint of understanding what makes traditional musical instruments sound "musical" and on how to use this understanding to create new synthetic sounds that are as musically satisfying to the refined ear as traditional instruments.

To study the time-varying properties of musical sounds, it is useful to have a way to make the Fourier transform of a waveform time-dependent. This is usually done in computer music applications by combining the ideas of the discrete Fourier transform with that of a time-dependent window function.

If $x(n)$ represents a digital audio waveform of arbitrary duration and $w(n)$ is a window function such as those described earlier, the product of the window positioned at time n along the waveform can be defined as

$$w_n(m) = w(n-m)x(m) \qquad (2\text{-}68)$$

Notice that this definition has the effect of reversing the window in time (which does not matter if the window is left-right symmetrical in shape) and that the value of n determines which sample of $x(n)$ is aligned with $w(0)$ (see Table 2-7).

TABLE 2-7   Alignment of window w with waveform x according to equation (2-68).

		$m \rightarrow$					
	$\cdots$	-2	-1	0	1	2	$\cdots$
n 0	$\cdots$	$w(2)x(-2)$	$w(1)x(-1)$	$w(0)x(0)$	$w(-1)x(1)$	$w(-2)x(2)$	$\cdots$
↓ 1	$\cdots$	$w(3)x(-2)$	$w(2)x(-1)$	$w(1)x(0)$	$w(0)x(1)$	$w(-1)x(2)$	$\cdots$
2	$\cdots$	$w(4)x(-2)$	$w(3)x(-1)$	$w(2)x(0)$	$w(1)x(1)$	$w(0)x(2)$	$\cdots$

If both the waveform and the window have finite duration (as in all practical applications), we simply consider out-of-range indices to refer to zero-valued sampled or window values. If we define N_w to be the length of the window function, Table 2-8 shows the windowed waveform w_n for $N_w = 3$. This example makes it clear that for a window function of length N_w, $w_n(m)$ "picks out" N_w samples of the waveform *ending* at time n, which are weighted by window function w. If w is rectangular, w_n is simply a certain portion of waveform x.

TABLE 2-8　ω_n According to equation (2-68) for $N_\omega = 3$ and $n = 0, 1, 2, 3, 4$.

		$m \rightarrow$			
$w_0(m) =$	$w(0)x(0)$	0	0	0	0
$w_1(m) =$	$w(1)x(0)$	$w(0)x(1)$	0	0	0
$w_2(m) =$	$w(2)x(0)$	$w(1)x(1)$	$w(0)x(2)$	0	0
$w_3(m) =$	0	$w(2)x(1)$	$w(1)x(2)$	$w(0)x(3)$	0
$w_4(m) =$	0	0	$w(2)x(2)$	$w(1)x(3)$	$w(0)x(4)$

We can use the selecting property of windows to define a time-dependent discrete Fourier transform in the following way:

$$X_n(e^{j\omega}) = \frac{1}{N_w} \sum_{m=-\infty}^{\infty} w(n-m)x(m)e^{-j\omega m} \qquad (2\text{-}69)$$

Note the difference between this definition and the ones given previously. The imaginary unit is here written as j, which is common practice in much literature dealing with this subject. Radian frequency ω is defined as $2\pi f T$, where T is the sampling period and f is frequency in hertz. Because window function w is assumed to be zero everywhere except over the interval 0 to $N_w - 1$, the scale factor is now set to $1/N_w$. Even though the summation takes place over all values of m, the finite duration of the window assures that in fact only N_w values of the summand are possibly nonzero.

The time-dependent DFT is clearly a function of three variables instead of two. For a fixed value of time n, however, it is still just the familiar spectrum of a (windowed) waveform. It is interesting to note that for a fixed value of frequency, equation (2-69) also describes a filter tuned to that frequency, with the filter having a response described by the spectrum of the window function and an input equal to the waveform (we shall return to this idea later).

For now, we consider the time-dependent DFT to be the spectrum at time n of windowed waveform x. Clearly, this spectrum depends on the properties of the waveform over a period of N_w samples ending at time n. A possible way to use the time-dependent DFT would be to let n vary sample by sample, resulting in a spectrum to be associated with each sample of the waveform. This interpretation truly motivates the term *data explosion* to describe the relationship between the amount of data in such a time-varying spectrum compared with that in the associated waveform: Each sample of the waveform would be associated with N_w complex values in the spectrum domain (or $N_w/2$ complex values if we take advantage of the symmetry of the positive and negative frequencies in the spectrum of a purely real waveform).

In many cases, it is possible to reduce the amount of spectrum data (and the time needed to compute it) by hopping the window along the waveform instead of sliding it sample by sample. In the most extreme case, we can compute the spectrum of the first N_w samples, then advance the window to the next block of N_w samples for the next spectrum measurement, and so on. Each measurement would then describe the spectrum content of successive blocks of N_w samples. If N_w is fairly small, short-term temporal variations in the spectrum of the waveform would be readily discernible by observing the sequence of spectrum plots. However, because N_w also determines the frequency resolution of each measurement, each spectrum measurement in this case may not be adequately resolved. The major advantage of this method is that the amount of spectrum data can be made the same as the amount of waveform data (thus avoiding the data explosion), because the minimum $M_w/2$ complex spectrum values can be stored in the same amount of space (even the *same* space) required for the N_w waveform samples. The disadvantage of inadequate frequency resolution might not be readily overcome, however.

We could increase the spectrum resolution at each measurement by increasing the length of the window while still hopping the window along the waveform by the same amount. For example, if we set N_w to four times its previous value while still hopping by the same amount (now $N_w/4$ samples), we could obtain four times the frequency resolution, but would we actually retain the same temporal resolution?

The answer is, unfortunately, both yes and no. The Fourier spectrum computed over N_w samples shows the *average spectrum content* over that many samples of the waveform, so while we would encounter new spectrum features at a rate of every $N_w/4$ samples, these features would probably be one fourth as prominent as before. We see that there is a useful trade-off between the size of the window N_w and the size of skip factor S, which we can usefully express as a factor to be multiplied by N_w. If S is 1 (the maximum), we will have the minimum amount of spectrum data to deal with and the worst temporal resolution. If S is $1/4$ as discussed previously, we will have $1/S = 4$ times as much spectrum data to deal with, and 4 times the temporal resolution, albeit with features $1/4$ as prominent as before.

To make such trade-offs visible, let us examine some spectrum plots of a time-varying signal. To keep matters simple, let us compute a sinusoidal signal that lasts one second at a sampling rate of 8192 samples per second. Over this duration, the frequency changes linearly from 1000 to 3000 Hz, and the amplitude drops linearly from 1 to 0. A C program to generate such a signal follows.

```
#include <stdio.h>
#include <math.h>

#define R 8192

main() {
```

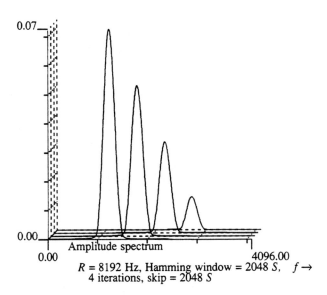

0.07

0.00

Amplitude spectrum

0.00   4096.00

R = 8192 Hz, Hamming window = 2048 S, $f \rightarrow$
4 iterations, skip = 2048 S

Figure 2-28   Time-dependent amplitude spectra of sinusoidal waveform going from 1000 to
3000 Hz in frequency and 1 to 0 in amplitude over 1 Second (R = 8192 samples per second).
Four nonoverlapping blocks of 2048 samples each were selected with a Hamming window.

```
int n ;
double PI2T, theta ;
float dur, factor, amp ;
/*
 * calculate duration in samples
 */
    dur = R ;
/*
 * PI2T is 2 pi times sample period
 */
    PI2T = 8.*atan(1.)/R ;
/*
 * frequency goes from 1000 to 3000 over dur
 */
    for (
        theta = n = 0 ;
        n < dur ;
        n++, theta += PI2T*(1000.+2000.*factor)
    ) {
/*
 * factor goes from 0 to 1 over dur
 */
        factor = n/(dur - 1.) ;
```

```
/*

 * amp goes from 1 to 0 over dur
 */
        amp = 1. - factor ;
        printf( "%f\n", amp*sin( theta ) ) ;
    }

}
```

TABLE 2-9 Two ways of calculating $\theta(n)$, the argument to the sine function during signal generation. Note that as long as $f(n)$ is constant, both methods agree in the amount by which $\theta(n)$ changes at each step (defined as the *instantaneous frequency*), but that the first method gives incorrect results when $f(n)$ is changing.

n	$f(n)$	$\theta(n) = n2\pi f(n)/R$	$\theta(n+1) = \theta(n) + f(n)2\pi/R$
0	1	0	0
1	1	$2\pi/R$	$2\pi/R$
2	1	$4\pi/R$	$4\pi/R$
3	1	$6\pi/R$	$6\pi/R$
4	2	$16\pi/R$	$8\pi/R$
5	3	$30\pi/R$	$12\pi/R$
6	4	$48\pi/R$	$18\pi/R$
7	4	$56\pi/R$	$26\pi/R$
8	4	$64\pi/R$	$34\pi/R$

Notice that this program does not implement the signal generator as

$$x(n) = A(n)\sin\frac{n\,2\pi f}{R} \qquad (2\text{-}70)$$

which can be used only when frequency f is constant. Because f is changing, the proper implementation is based on

$$x(n) = A(n)\sin\theta(n) \qquad (2\text{-}71)$$

where

$$\theta(n+1) = \theta(n) + \Delta\theta(n) \qquad (2\text{-}72)$$

and

$$\Delta\theta(n) = \frac{2\pi}{R}f(n) \qquad (2\text{-}73)$$

This takes into account the fact that each time n increases by 1, $\theta(n)$ should increase by an amount $2\pi f(n)/R$. If f is a constant, there is no difference between the two procedures. When $f(n)$ is not a constant, however, the second procedure leaves $\theta(n)$ set to the correct values at each step, while the first does not. This can be understood by noting that for frequency to be a quantity that can change over time, it must have a well-defined *instantaneous value*. In discrete terms, *instantaneous frequency* is proportional to the amount by which $\theta(n)$ changes each time n increases by 1. The constant of proportionality is of course $2\pi/R$, because this is the amount by which $\theta(n)$ would change if $f(n) = 1$. A comparison of the values calculated by the two methods is shown in Table 2-9. We shall find this concept of instantaneous frequency useful later on.

We now analyze the output of the waveform produced by this *portamento* program in three ways for comparison. Figure 2-28 shows four nonoverlapping measurements, each of length 2048 ($= 2^{11}$) samples. Each measurement is therefore taken over a duration of 0.25 second. Each plot shows the amplitude of the discrete Fourier spectrum calculated with the FFT algorithm. A Hamming window was applied to each block of waveform samples before they were transformed. The plots are shown superimposed, with the origin moved up and to the right a little bit for each iteration—giving the visual impression that time recedes away (into the page) from the viewer. The averaging effect of the Fourier transform is evident in the broadness of the peaks due to the changing frequency and amplitude of the sinusoid during each measurement.

Figure 2-29 shows eight nonoverlapping measurements, each of length 1024 ($= 2^{10}$) samples, of the same waveform. The peaks are narrower in this picture because each measurement now represents a duration of 0.125 second, over which the time-varying sinusoid has less opportunity to vary. Each measurement in this case has half the frequency resolution of the previous plot, because the transform is taken over half as many samples.

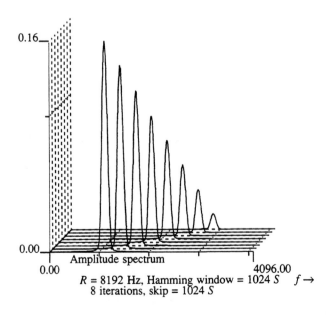

Figure 2-29 Time-dependent amplitude spectra of sinusoidal waveform going from 1000 to 3000 Hz in frequency and 1 to 0 in amplitude over 1 Second ($R = 8192$ samples per second). Eight nonoverlapping blocks of 1024 samples each were selected with a Hamming window.

Figure 2-30 shows eight *overlapping* measurements. In this case, each measurement was 2048 samples long, but the Hamming window was advanced by only 1024 samples for each new measurement. The peaks are broader in this picture because each measurement represents a duration of 0.25 second, and each measurement has a frequency resolution equal to that of the first plot (in fact, the first, third, fifth and seventh measurements are the same as the ones in the first time-varying plot).

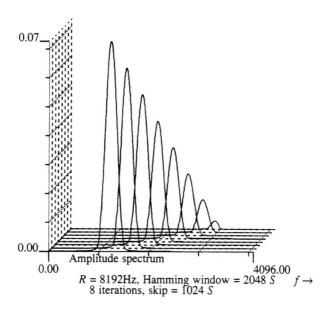

Figure 2-30   Time-dependent amplitude spectra of sinusoidal waveform going from 1000 to 3000 Hz in frequency and 1 to 0 in amplitude over 1 Second (R = 8192 samples per second). Eight blocks of 2048 samples overlapped by 1024 samples were selected with a Hamming window.

2.4 DIGITAL FILTERS

Digital signal processing may be roughly divided into two broad areas, one pertaining to spectral measurements, the other to digital filtering. The ideas of the Fourier transform and convolution presented so far provide a useful starting point for a discussion of digital filtering.

In the broadest terms, a *digital filter* can be almost any computational algorithm for processing a digital signal. The purpose of most digital filters, however, is to modify the spectrum of a digital signal in some useful way. Digital filters are often used as frequency-dependent gain elements to emphasize some frequencies and attenuate others. They may also be used to introduce frequency-dependent phase changes in a signal.

Because filters operate in frequency-dependent ways, their action is usually described in terms of frequency-dependent amplitude or phase functions—precisely the same kinds of functions used to describe waveform spectra computed with the Fourier transform.

2.4.1 The z Transform

The response of any digital filter can be characterized by its complex *transfer function*, usually denoted $H(z)$. z is the *complex frequency* variable and represents a slightly more general concept of frequency than we have encountered so far. However, we calculate the frequency and phase responses of a digital filter by setting z to the familiar $e^{j\omega}$, where ω varies between values representing minus to plus half the sampling rate. $H(e^{j\omega})$ is therefore very similar to a spectrum in that its *magnitude* (or *amplitude*), $|H(e^{j\omega})|$, describes the frequency response of the filter, while its *phase*, pha$[H(e^{j\omega})]$, describes the filter's phase response.

As we have said, the complex frequency domain, or z *domain*, is similar to the frequency domain accessible through the Fourier transform. To express a waveform in the z domain, however, we use the z *transform* rather than the Fourier transform. Given a discrete waveform $x(n)$ defined for all values of n, its z transform is defined as

$$X(z) = \sum_{n=-\infty}^{\infty} x(n)z^{-n} \qquad (2\text{-}74)$$

where z is a complex variable. The quantity z^{-1} is interpretable as the *unit sample delay operator* in the sense that $x(n)z^{-1} = x(n-1)$. Alternatively, we may note that the definition of the z transform suggests that if $X(z)$ is the z transform of $x(n)$, then the z transform of $x(n-k)$ is $z^{-k}X(z)$.

Also, if we set $z = e^{j\omega}$, we see that by definition,

$$X(e^{j\omega}) = \sum_{n=-\infty}^{\infty} x(n)e^{-j\omega n} \qquad (2\text{-}75)$$

which is the Fourier transform of $x(n)$, demonstrating that the Fourier transform is just a special case of the more general z transform (later we shall see that it is useful to consider other values and interpretations of z as well).

The utility of $H(z)$ is that it can be used to describe the action of any filter in a very simple way. If we know the transfer function $H(z)$ of a filter, we can calculate the z transform of its response to any signal by multiplying $H(z)$ by the z transform of the signal input to the filter (see Figure 2-31). $H(z)$ describes the exact relationship between the input and output of the filter. From Figure 2-31, it is evident that

$$H(z) = \frac{Y(z)}{X(z)} \qquad (2\text{-}76)$$

where $X(z)$ is the z transform of the input to the filter and $Y(z)$ is the z transform of its output.

We may also observe that $H(z)$ is the z transform of some waveform, $h(n)$. Because multiplication in the frequency domain (even the *complex* frequency domain)

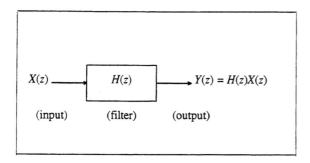

Figure 2-31   Operation of a digital filter in the z (complex frequency) domain.

corresponds to convolution in the time domain, we can calculate the output of any digital filter by convolving the input signal $x(n)$ with $h(n)$ (see Figure 2-32).

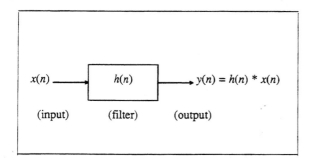

Figure 2-32   Operation of a digital filter in the time domain. The * operation in the diagram indicates convolution.

The signal $h(n)$ is called the *impulse response* (or more properly, the *unit sample function response*) of the filter, because it is the signal emitted by the filter in response to an impulse (or unit sample) input. Thus given a digital filter that we wish to analyze, we can do so in the following steps.

1. Feed the filter an impulse signal (the digital version of this signal is just 1, 0, 0, . . .).
2. Observe the response of the filter to the impulse function; call this response $h(n)$.
3. Either find the z transform of $h(n)$ with equation (2-74) and call this function $H(z)$ (the *transfer function* of the filter), or take the Fourier transform of $h(n)$.
4. If $H(z)$ was calculated in step 3, set $z = e^{j\omega}$, making the transfer function equivalent to the Fourier transform as in equation (2-75); if the Fourier transform was taken in step 3, call the result $H(e^{j\omega})$.
5. The magnitude of the transfer function $|H(e^{j\omega})|$ is the *frequency response* of the filter.[30]
6. The phase of the transfer function, pha[$H(e^{j\omega})$] is the *phase response* of the filter.

[30]What we call the frequency response is also sometimes called the *amplitude response, magnitude response,* or *modulus* of a filter. All of these refer to the *gain* of the filter as a function of frequency.

It is apparent from the list that if we wish to determine only the frequency and phase responses of a filter (which is often the case), we can avoid taking the z transform altogether. Obviously, there must be other characteristics of a filter that can be determined with the z transform. These other characteristics are essentially the locations of the filter's *resonances*, or *poles*, and its *antiresonances*, or *zeros*, in the complex frequency domain. Poles are located at frequencies the filter tends to emphasize, zeros at frequencies the filter tends to deemphasize.

It might seem that knowledge of the frequency response of a filter would tell us the same thing as knowledge of the locations of its poles and zeros, but strictly speaking, this is not the case. The locations of the poles and zeros *determine* the frequency response, to be sure, but they can also interact in ways that are not evident in the frequency response of a filter. For example, poles and zeros can be located so as to cancel each other exactly. Such an arrangement would result in a so-called *allpass filter* because it would have a "flat" (constant) frequency response while possibly exhibiting a complicated phase response.

2.4.2 The Digital Filter Equation

An important subclass of digital filters has the remarkable property of being defined by a single mathematical relationship. A digital filter is said to be *linear* if it obeys the so-called *principle of superposition*. If $y_1(n)$ is the output produced by a filter in response to input signal $x_1(n)$ and $y_2(n)$ is the filter's response to input $x_2(n)$, then the filter is said to be *linear* if its response to input $ax_1(n) + bx_2(n)$ is $ay_1(n) + by_2(n)$, where a and b are arbitrary constants. Basically, linearity assures us that if we add two (scaled) inputs to a filter, the response of the filter to that signal will be just the sum of the (scaled) outputs due to the inputs taken separately.

If the output of the filter depends only on its present and past inputs as well as its past outputs, the filter is said to be *causal*. The output of a *noncausal* filter, by implication, might depend on future inputs as well. Digital filters need not be causal if they are processing a sequence of waveform samples stored in a computer memory, because this would allow the filter to "look ahead" in time to see its future inputs—it could, in effect, begin to respond to something before it happens! Noncausal filters obviously could not be made to work in real time without introducing a delay in the output equal to the time needed for such look-ahead.

If the response of a filter does not change as time goes by, it is said to be *time-invariant*. A filter may be either time-variant or time-invariant.

If a digital filter is linear, causal, and time-invariant, it may be described with the equation

$$y(n) = \sum_{i=0}^{M} a_i x(n-i) - \sum_{i=1}^{N} b_i y(n-i) \tag{2-77}$$

where a_i and b_i are *constant coefficients* that determine the characteristics of the filter. We will refer to equation (2-77) as the *digital filter equation* because it describes *all* filters that we will have any occasion to deal with in this book. The first part of equation (2-77) specifies how the output of the filter depends on its present and past inputs; the second part specifies how the output depends on past outputs.

A *stable* filter is one whose output dies away, however gradually, once the input becomes all zero. If some part of the output is fed back into the filter's input, the filter is said to be *recursive*. Such feedback may cause the filter's output to grow without bound, in which case the filter is said to be *unstable*. In any case, a filter that uses feedback always has an impulse response that lasts (at least in theory) forever. Such *infinite impulse response* (IIR) filters are ones in which one or more of the b_i coefficients in equation (2-77) is nonzero.

If all of the b_i coefficients in equation (2-77) are zero, the filter's output will depend only on its present and past inputs. It is then guaranteed to be stable, because setting the input to zero would eventually cause the output to go to zero. Because the output is guaranteed to become zero in a finite amount of time after the input goes to zero, such filters are called *finite impulse response* (FIR) filters.

The $M+1$ a_i coefficients in equation (2-77) determine the positions of M zeros in the complex frequency domain; the N b_i coefficients determine the positions of N poles. An FIR filter therefore has only zeros (antiresonances), while an IIR filter contains one or more poles (resonances).

FIR filters have the special property that under certain circumstances, they can exhibit an exactly *linear phase* response, meaning that they introduce no phase distortion into the filtered signal, thus preserving the time alignment of all frequency components exactly. *All* IIR filters exhibit nonlinear phase response, meaning that they introduce some phase distortion into the signals they process. Whether this phase distortion is objectionable depends greatly on the application.

2.4.3 Digital Filter Analysis

The basic ideas discussed so far allow us to analyze many digital filters. One of the simplest cases is the IIR filter described by the equation

$$y(n) = x(n) + Ky(n-1) \qquad (2\text{-}78)$$

Equation (2-78) is just a special case of equation (2-77) with $M = 0$, $a_0 = 1$, $N = 1$, and $-b_1 = K$. We readily construct the impulse response of the filter described by equation (2-78) as

n	$x(n)$	$y(n) = h(n)$
0	1	1
1	0	K
2	0	K^2
3	0	K^3
4	0	K^4
.	.	
.	.	
.	.	

In general, we see that for $n \geq 0$, the impulse response is $h(n) = K^n$.

The z transform of the impulse response is therefore

$$H(z) = \sum_{n=0}^{\infty} h(n)z^{-n} = 1 + Kz^{-1} + K^2 z^{-2} + \cdots = \frac{1}{1 - Kz^{-1}} \qquad (2\text{-}79)$$

The last step in equation (2-79) is possible due to the general relation (see Appendix A)

$$\sum_{k=0}^{\infty} ar^k = a + ar + ar^2 + \cdots = \frac{a}{1 - r} \qquad (2\text{-}80)$$

Setting z to $e^{j\omega}$ yields

$$H(e^{j\omega}) = \frac{1}{1 - Ke^{-j\omega}} \qquad (2\text{-}81)$$

The right side of this equation is complex, which is to say that it has both real and imaginary parts. To compute the frequency response, we need to find the magnitude of this expression. A useful device in calculating the magnitude is to note that the square of the magnitude of any complex quantity is equal to that quantity multiplied by its complex conjugate, as in

$$(\alpha + j\beta)(\alpha - j\beta) = \alpha^2 + \beta^2 \qquad (2\text{-}82)$$

The magnitude is just the square root of this quantity. We therefore proceed as follows:

$$|H(e^{j\omega})| = [H(e^{j\omega})H(e^{-j\omega})]^{1/2} = \left(\frac{1}{1 - Ke^{-j\omega}} \frac{1}{1 - Ke^{+j\omega}} \right)^{1/2} \qquad (2\text{-}83)$$

$$= \frac{1}{(1 - Ke^{j\omega} - Ke^{-j\omega} + K^2)^{1/2}} \qquad (2\text{-}84)$$

$$= \frac{1}{[1 + K^2 - K(e^{j\omega} + e^{-j\omega})]^{1/2}} \qquad (2\text{-}85)$$

We now make use of Euler's relation $(e^{j\omega} = \cos\omega + j\sin\omega)$ to conclude that $e^{j\omega} + e^{-j\omega} = 2\cos\omega$. Substituting this into our equation yields the final result

$$|H(e^{j\omega})| = \frac{1}{(1 + K^2 - 2K\cos\omega)^{1/2}} \qquad (2\text{-}86)$$

To find the phase response, we need to separate the real and imaginary parts of $H(e^{j\omega})$ so that we can divide one by the other. Another useful mathematical device in this context is to note that because

$$\text{pha}(\alpha + j\beta) = \tan^{-1}\frac{\beta}{\alpha} \qquad (2\text{-}87)$$

we also can easily show that

$$\text{pha}\left(\frac{1}{\alpha + j\beta} \right) = \text{pha}\left(\frac{\alpha - j\beta}{\alpha^2 + \beta^2} \right) = \tan^{-1}\frac{-\beta}{\alpha} \qquad (2\text{-}88)$$

We therefore proceed by expanding $H(e^{j\omega})$ according to Euler's relation in order to separate its real and imaginary parts.

$$H(e^{j\omega}) = \frac{1}{1 - Ke^{-j\omega}} = \frac{1}{1 - K(\cos\omega - j\sin\omega)} \qquad (2\text{-}89)$$

$$= \frac{1}{1 - K\cos\omega + jK\sin\omega} \qquad (2\text{-}90)$$

Applying equation (2-88) yields

$$\text{pha}(H(e^{j\omega})) = \tan^{-1}\frac{-K\sin\omega}{1 - K\cos\omega} \qquad (2\text{-}91)$$

We can make plots of these results for various values of K in order to observe frequency and phase responses of our filter. To do this, we note that the frequency range from minus to plus half the sampling rate corresponds to running ω from $-\pi$ to $+\pi$.

Another approach would be to write a C program that implements this filter. We could then use this program to calculate the impulse response and observe the amplitude and phase of its Fourier transform to discover the frequency and phase responses of our filter. A very simple C program for computing the first 128 points of the impulse response of this filter for $K = 0.8$ follows.

```
#include <stdio.h>

main() {
 float input, output, K ;
 int i ;
/*
 * Set initial value of output and set K
 */
    output = 0. ;
    K = 0.8 ;
/*
 * Compute 128 points of the impulse response
 */
    for ( i = 0 ; i < 128 ; i++ ) {
/*
 * Use impulse (unit sample) function for input
 */
        input = ( i==0 ? 1. : 0. ) ;
        output = input + K*output ;
        printf( "%f\n", output ) ;
    }
}
```

The frequency and phase responses of our filter are shown in Figure 2-33. They were obtained by using the FFT algorithm to compute the discrete Fourier transform of the filter's impulse response (note that a rectangular window was used) and plotting the amplitude and phase spectra of the result. It is evident from the figure that this filter exhibits a lowpass characteristic.

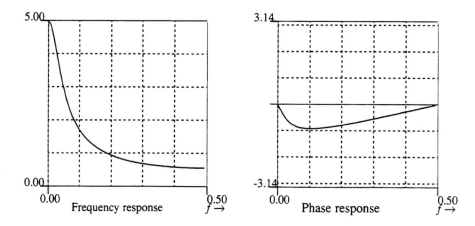

Figure 2-33   Frequency and phase response (in radians) of $y(n) = x(n) + K y(n-1)$ for $K = 0.8$. Note the lowpass characteristic. 128 points of the impulse response of this filter (generated with the program given in the text) were transformed with an FFT algorithm (rectangular window). The magnitude and phase of the resulting spectrum were used to obtain these plots.

If, however, we use a different value for K, the response of the filter will be different. Figure 2-34 shows the frequency and phase responses for $K = -0.9$, which is evidently a highpass characteristic.

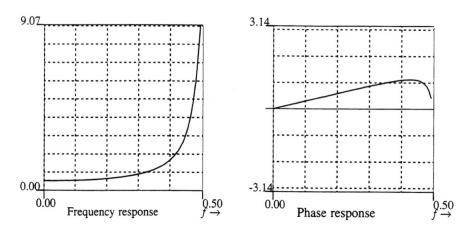

Figure 2-34   Frequency and phase response (in radians) of $y(n) = x(n) + K y(n-1)$ for $K = -0.9$. Note the highpass characteristic.

It should be evident from inspecting the impulse response of this filter that the magnitude of K must be less than one for the filter to be stable, because its output would otherwise grow without bound, even after the input signal has become zero. It may be evident that setting K to zero will make the output equal to the input, but the fact that setting K to positive values gives it a lowpass characteristic while setting it to negative values gives it a highpass characteristic may be less than obvious.

We have the conceptual tools necessary (basically, windows, the FFT, and amplitude and phase spectra) to continue to experiment with our filter. To develop a firmer basis for understanding this and all other digital filters, however, we need to explore further the concept of poles and zeros.

2.4.4 Poles and Zeros

Using the general property that the z transform of

$$x(n - k) = z^{-k}X(z) \tag{2-92}$$

we can take the z transform of equation (2-77), which yields

$$Y(z) = \sum_{i=0}^{M} a_i z^{-i} X(z) - \sum_{i=1}^{N} b_i z^{-i} Y(z) \tag{2-93}$$

Collecting all the $Y(z)$ terms on the left side and factoring out the common $Y(z)$ and $X(z)$ terms yields

$$Y(z)(1 + b_1 z^{-1} + \cdots + b_N z^{-N}) = X(z)(a_0 + a_1 z^{-1} + \cdots + a_M z^{-M}) \tag{2-94}$$

Recalling equation (2-76), we may now write the transfer function of any filter described by equation (2-77) in the general form

$$H(z) = \frac{Y(z)}{X(z)} = \frac{a_0 + a_1 z^{-1} + \cdots + a_M z^{-M}}{1 + b_1 z^{-1} + \cdots + b_N z^{-N}} = \frac{N(z)}{D(z)} \tag{2-95}$$

where the a_i and b_i coefficients and M and N values are the same as in equation (2-67), $N(z)$ is the numerator polynomial, and $D(z)$ is the denominator polynomial. Any value of z that makes $N(z)$ zero will cause $H(z)$ to be zero (a zero of the transfer function), while any value of z that causes $D(z)$ to become zero will cause $H(z)$ to become infinite (a pole of the transfer function).

The values of the independent variable that make a polynomial zero are called the *roots* of that polynomial. The *fundamental theorem of algebra* states that any Nth degree polynomial has exactly N roots, which may or may not be distinct (that is, different from each other); they may also be complex. To find the locations of the poles and zeros of a filter with transfer function $H(z) = N(z)/D(z)$, then, we have only to find the roots of the polynomials $D(z)$ and $N(z)$, respectively.

There are several ways to find the roots of a polynomial—much of the subject of algebra is about just that problem! One of the most useful ways when it is possible is to *factor* the polynomial into a product of terms; if any of these terms is zero, the polynomial is also zero. The filter gain is scaled by the a_0 coefficient; we can see if we factor out a_0 from the numerator of the transfer function thus:

$$H(z) = \frac{a_0 + a_1 z^{-1} + \cdots + a_M z^{-M}}{1 + b_1 z^{-1} + \cdots + b_N z^{-N}} = a_0 \frac{1 + \alpha_1 z^{-1} + \cdots + \alpha_M z^{-M}}{1 + b_1 z^{-1} + \cdots + b_N z^{-N}} = \qquad (2\text{-}96)$$

where $\alpha_i = a_i / a_0$. The factored polynomials can then be expressed in the following form:

$$H(z) = a_0 \frac{N(z)}{D(z)} = a_0 \frac{\displaystyle\prod_{i=1}^{M} (1 - Z_i z^{-1})}{\displaystyle\prod_{i=1}^{N} (1 - P_i z^{-1})} \qquad (2\text{-}97)$$

where Z_i are M zeros of $H(z)$ and P_i are N poles of $H(z)$ ($\prod$ is the product operator, indicating that all the specified factors are to be multiplied together). When M (the number of zeros) and N (the number of poles) is small, factoring can often be accomplished directly.

Equation (2-97) implicitly shows the relationships of the transfer function, the locations of the poles and zeros, and the frequency and phase response of a filter. The roots of the numerator are the zeros of the filter. The roots of the denominator are the poles. Furthermore, equation (2-97) can be interpreted graphically when we evaluate the frequency or phase response for some frequency ω by setting z to $e^{j\omega}$.

For example, consider the general two-pole filter

$$y(n) = a_0 x(n) - b_1 y(n-1) - b_2 y(n-2) \qquad (2\text{-}98)$$

We may now write the transfer function directly according to equation (2-85) as

$$H(z) = \frac{a_0}{1 + b_1 z^{-1} + b_2 z^{-2}} \qquad (2\text{-}99)$$

Because the order of the denominator polynomial is 2, we call this a *second-order* filter. It will have two poles, because the fundamental theorem of algebra guarantees us that the denominator polynomial has two roots. The *quadratic formula* of algebra may be used to solve for these roots.[31] As long as b_1 and b_2 are real numbers, the rules of algebra also assure us that if the two roots of the denominator polynomial are complex, they are complex conjugates of each other. We could solve the transfer function for the frequency and phase response as before, but first let us consider the roots of the denominator polynomial. The denominator may be written in factored form, according to equation (2-97), as

$$D(z) = 1 + b_1 z^{-1} + b_2 z^{-2} = (1 - P_1 z^{-1})(1 - P_2 z^{-1}) \qquad (2\text{-}100)$$

where the two roots, P_1 and P_2 are in general complex. Because they will have to be complex conjugates of each other (because b_1 and b_2 are real), we can write them in

---

[31]The general solution to the quadratic equation $ax^2 + bx + c = 0$ is $x = (-b \pm \sqrt{b^2 - 4ac})/2a$. If $4ac$ is not greater than b^2 the roots are real, otherwise they are complex.

polar form as $P_1 = Re^{j\theta}$ and $P_2 = Re^{-j\theta}$. We can locate these two points on the complex plane by moving outward from the origin by a distance R at the angles θ and $-\theta$. These are the *locations of the poles in the complex frequency domain*. Using the results we have obtained so far, we can substitute these roots back into the transfer function to yield

$$H(z) = \frac{a_0}{(1 - P_1 z^{-1})(1 - P_2 z^{-1})} = \frac{a_0}{1 - 2R\cos\theta z^{-1} + R^2 z^{-2}} \qquad (2\text{-}101)$$

where it is evident that $b_1 = -2R\cos\theta$ and $b_2 = R^2$.

The usefulness of knowing where the poles and zeros are comes when they are plotted on the complex z plane. It is customary to show the position of a *unit circle* (a circle with radius 1) on the z plane because the unit circle is a graph of the solution to the equation $z = e^{j\omega}$ (see Figure 2-35). The z transform maps frequencies in the range $(-R/2, +R/2)$ Hz into angles in the range $(-\pi, +\pi)$ radians on the complex plane. Locations along the perimeter of the unit circle represent possible frequencies in a digital signal. As we traverse the upper half of the unit circle from right to left, we traverse the frequencies from zero to half the sampling rate. If we traverse the lower half of the circle from right to left, we traverse the frequencies from zero to minus half the sampling rate. Notice that aliasing is represented accurately by the unit circle concept, because moving more than 180° from the right-hand axis lands us precisely on the correct (aliased) frequency value. The unit circle thus represents the periodicity of frequency in the digital domain—it is impossible to have a frequency in a digital signal that is not between minus and plus half the sampling rate.

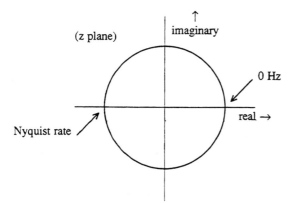

Figure 2-35   The unit circle on the complex z plane. 0 Hz is represented at the point $z = 1$; the Nyquist rate is located at $z = -1$. Traversing the unit circle along the top traverses positive frequencies; traversing along the bottom half of the circle traverses negative frequencies.

Poles and zeros are points anywhere on the z plane. They may lie inside, on, or outside the unit circle. If any pole of a filter lies *outside* the unit circle, however, the filter will be unstable. We can use the unit circle on the complex z plane to understand filter behavior in various other ways. Equation (2-82) informs us that the distance of a pole from any point on the unit circle is the *reciprocal* of that pole's contribution to the gain of the filter at that frequency. This is the graphical equivalent of evaluating the denominator of equation (2-97) at $z = e^{j\omega}$. For example, we have already found that

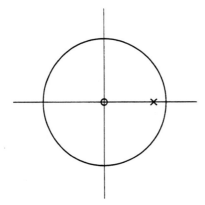

Figure 2-36   Pole-zero diagram for the
filter $y(n) = x(n) + Ky(n - 1)$ for $K = 0.8$.
The position of the pole is marked X. The
position of a "theoretical" zero is marked O.

the gain of the filter $y(n) = x(n) + 0.8y(n - 1)$ at zero frequency is 5 (see Figure 2-34).
The transfer function of this filter exhibits a pole at $z = 0.8$ as well (see Figure 2-37).
The filter also has a theoretical zero at $z = 0.$[32]

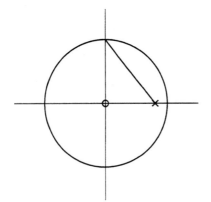

Figure 2-37   Calculating the gain of a
one-pole filter at one-fourth the sampling
rate. The length of the line from the pole to
the point on the unit circle representing this
frequency is the *reciprocal* of the gain.

The gain of the filter at zero frequency, we have said, is the reciprocal of the
length of the line from the pole to the point on the unit circle representing zero frequency ($z = 1$), or $1/0.2 = 5$, just as we saw in Figure 2-34. Furthermore, the gain of
the filter at *any* allowable frequency may be found by drawing a line from the pole to
the point on the unit circle representing that frequency. For example, the gain at one-
fourth the sampling rate would be the reciprocal of the length of the line shown in Figure 2-37. The reciprocal of the length of this line is easily calculated (by solving the

[32]Such theoretical poles and zeros arise when M and N are unequal in equation (2-67). All digital filters
theoretically have the same number of poles and zeros. If $M > N$ (more zeros than poles), we simply add $M
- N$ extra poles at $z = 0$. If $N > M$ (more poles than zeros), we simply add $N - M$ extra zeros at $z = 0$. This
accounts for the zero at $z = 0$ in the pole-zero diagram of the one-pole filter (see Figure 2-36). Such theoretical poles and zeros do not contribute materially to the frequency response of the filter, although they may introduce a pure delay in the phase response.

triangle with the Pythagorean formula) to be $1/(1 + 0.8^2)^{1/2} \approx 0.78$, which also agrees well with Figure 2-34.

For more complicated cases in which several poles and zeros are present, equation (2-97) tells us that to find the magnitude of $H(z)$, we must take the distances of all zeros from the desired frequency point on the unit circle, multiply them together, and divide that number by the product of the distances of all poles from that point. For example, in the case of the two-pole filter we derived, we first plot the pole locations on the z plane, then find the distance from each pole to any frequency on the unit circle. The reciprocal of the product of these distances yields a number proportional to the gain of the filter at that frequency (see Figure 2-38). The filter gain is scaled by the a_0 coefficient.

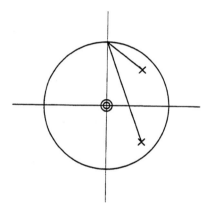

Figure 2-38   Calculating the gain of a two-pole filter at one-fourth the sampling rate. The product of the lengths of the lines from the poles to the point on the unit circle representing this frequency is the *reciprocal* of the gain (notice the theoretical zero pair at $z = 0$).

In more precise terms, if L_{Z_i} is the length of the line from the ith zero to a point $e^{j\omega}$ on the unit circle, and L_{P_i} is the length of the line from the ith pole, then

$$|H(e^{j\omega})| = a_0 \frac{\displaystyle\prod_{i=1}^{M} L_{Z_i}}{\displaystyle\prod_{i=1}^{N} L_{P_i}} \qquad (2\text{-}102)$$

From this relation, it is easy to see that the closer a pole is to the unit circle, the greater will be the gain of the filter near that pole's frequency. The closer a zero is to the unit circle, the smaller will be the gain of the filter near that zero's frequency.

Similarly, if θ_{Z_i} is the angle of the line from the ith zero to a point $e^{j\omega}$ on the unit circle, and θ_{P_i} is the angle of the line from the ith pole, then

$$\text{pha}[H(e^{j\omega})] = \sum_{i=1}^{M} \theta_{Z_i} - \sum_{i=1}^{N} \theta_{P_i} \qquad (2\text{-}103)$$

From this relation, we see that because poles are constrained to lie inside the unit circle (if the filter is to be stable), only certain types of phase responses are possible if a filter contains poles. Furthermore, poles lying near the unit circle will affect the phase response more radically than poles lying farther from the unit circle.[33] An all-zero filter may have an arbitrary phase response because zeros may lie *anywhere* on the z plane. We shall return to this point later on.

Poles and zeros can interact in a variety of interesting ways. Consider what would happen if a pair of poles were located very near but inside the unit circle while a pair of zeros at the same frequency were located just outside the unit circle (see Figure 2-39). If the distances of the poles from the origin were just the *reciprocals* of the distances of the zeros from the origin—in other words, if the zeros were located at $Re^{\pm j\theta}$ and the poles were located at $(1/R)e^{\pm j\theta}$— their mutual effects on the gain of the filter would exactly balance. The filter would therefore exhibit a constant gain at all frequencies, making it a so-called *allpass filter*.

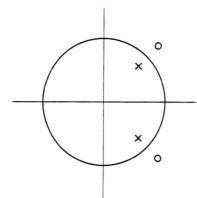

Figure 2-39 Pole-zero diagram for an allpass filter. Such filters have a constant frequency response while exhibiting nonuniform phase behavior.

A second-order allpass filter therefore has a transfer function of the form

$$H(z) = a_0 \frac{(1 - Re^{j\theta}z^{-1})(1 - Re^{-j\theta}z^{-1})}{[1 - (1/R)e^{j\theta}z^{-1}][1 - (1/R)e^{-j\theta}z^{-1}]} \qquad (2\text{-}104)$$

As we have seen, this indicates that the filter coefficients are as follows:

$$a_1 = -2R\cos\theta$$

$$a_2 = R^2$$

$$b_1 = -2/R\cos\theta$$

$$b_2 = 1/R^2$$

To see the allpass effect mathematically, we need to show that the frequency response does not depend on frequency; that is, we need to establish the relationship

---

[33]A pole "maximally distant" from the unit circle in a stable filter would be located at the theoretical point $z = 0$. The contribution of such a pole to the phase response of the filter at frequency ω would simply be $-\omega$, corresponding to a pure delay in the filter's response.

$$|H(e^{j\omega})| = \text{constant} \tag{2-105}$$

To see that this is so, we calculate the frequency response in the usual way. We start by choosing $a_0 = 1$ for convenience and then set z to $e^{j\omega}$.

$$H(e^{j\omega}) = \frac{(1 - Re^{j\theta}e^{-j\omega})(1 - Re^{-j\theta}e^{-j\omega})}{[1 - (1/R)e^{j\theta}e^{-j\omega}][1 - (1/R)e^{-j\theta}e^{-j\omega}]} \tag{2-106}$$

$$= \frac{(1 - Re^{j(\theta-\omega)})(1 - Re^{j(\theta+\omega)})}{[1 - (1/R)e^{j(\theta-\omega)}][1 - (1/R)e^{j(\theta+\omega)}]}$$

We may view the last form of $H(e^{j\omega})$ as a product of two factors:

$$H(e^{j\omega}) = H_1(e^{j\omega})H_2(e^{j\omega}) \tag{2-107}$$

We can calculate the magnitudes of these two factors separately—the product of the separate magnitudes will then be the magnitude for the entire transfer function:

$$|H(e^{j\omega})| = |H_1(e^{j\omega})| \; |H_2(e^{j\omega})| \tag{2-108}$$

We find the square of the magnitude of the first factor by multiplying it by its complex conjugate:

$$|H_1(e^{j\omega})|^2 = \frac{1 - Re^{j(\theta-\omega)}}{1 - (1/R)e^{j(\theta-\omega)}} \; \frac{1 - Re^{-j(\theta-\omega)}}{1 - (1/R)e^{-j(\theta-\omega)}} \tag{2-109}$$

$$= \frac{1 + R^2 - 2R\cos(\theta - \omega)}{1 + 1/R^2 - (2/R)\cos(\theta - \omega)}$$

The last expression may be rewritten as

$$|H_1(e^{j\omega})|^2 = \frac{R^2[(1/R^2 + 1 - (2/R)\cos(\theta - \omega)]}{1 + 1/R^2 - (2/R)\cos(\theta - \omega)} = R^2 \tag{2-110}$$

Similarly, we can show that

$$|H_2(e^{j\omega})|^2 = R^2 \tag{2-111}$$

Therefore,

$$|H(e^{j\omega})|^2 = R^4 \tag{2-112}$$

and

$$|H(e^{j\omega})| = R^2 = \text{constant} \tag{2-113}$$

We see that the frequency response of our allpass filter is indeed a constant that is independent of frequency, which is what we wanted to verify. We could, if we wished, force this constant gain to unity by setting a_0 to $1/R^2$.

To demonstrate the operation of this filter, we can set $1/R$ to 0.9 (the poles, as usual, must remain inside the unit circle for the filter to be stable) and θ to 45°. This yields the second-order allpass filter

$$y(n) = x(n) - 1.571348x(n-1) + 1.234568x(n-2) \qquad (2\text{-}114)$$

$$+ 1.27279y(n-1) - 0.81y(n-2)$$

The frequency and phase responses of this filter—obtained by taking the DFT of its impulse response—are shown in Figure 2-40. Note that the frequency response is constant at 1.23 ($= R^2$, as predicted) and that the phase response "wraps around" at about one eighth the sampling rate (corresponding to placing the poles and zeros at 45°, as specified). This is due to the way in which the inverse tangent function is evaluated in terms of principal values that lie, in this case, between $-\pi$ and $+\pi$.

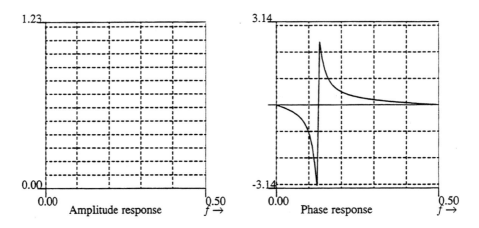

Figure 2-40   Frequency and phase response (in radians) of an allpass filter. Note the wraparound in the phase characteristic.

The phase response of this allpass filter can be calculated graphically according to equation (2-103). If θ_1 and θ_2 are the angles of the lines running from the zeros to a frequency ω on the unit circle and θ_3 and θ_4 are the angles of the lines running from the poles to the same frequency, then in accordance with equation (2-103), the phase response of the filter at that frequency would be $\theta_1 + \theta_2 - \theta_3 - \theta_4$ (see Figure 2-41).

We can easily construct C programs for general pole-zero filter analysis based on the principles developed in this section. The following program, for example, accepts an arbitrary number of pole-zero locations as input and prints the associated filter amplitude response at a list of frequencies that are evenly spaced around some portion of the unit circle. We can use this program to design arbitrary digital filters in terms of their pole-zero locations.

```
#include <stdio.h>
#include <math.h>
/*
 * Polar coordinates for pole and zero locations
 */
struct polar {
```

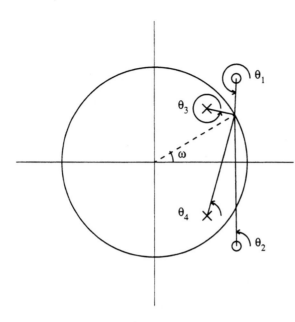

Figure 2-41   Measuring the phase response of an allpass filter at frequency ω. The zero angles are added and the pole angles are subtracted. In this case, ω is 30° ($\pi/6$), corresponding to one-sixth of the sampling rate, indicating that the phase response is $\theta_1 + \theta_2 - \theta_3 - \theta_4 \approx 267.3 + 90.7 - 347.7 - 74.3 \approx -64°$ ($\approx -0.36\ \pi$).

```
    double mag ;
    double ang ;
} ;
/*
 * M is number of zeros, N is number of poles;
 * K is number of equally spaced frequency points
 * to evaluate between omin and omax (in radians)
 */
#define M 2
#define N 2
#define K 32

struct polar zero[M+1] ;
struct polar pole[N+1] ;

main()
{
  double PI = 4.*atan(1.) ;
  double omin = 0. ;
  double omax = PI ;
  double ostep = (omax - omin)/K ;
  double omega, length() ;
  double gain, amp, num, den ;
  int i ;
/*
 * Set gain (a0) term ;
 */
```

```
    gain = 1. ;
/*
 * Set pole-zero locations
 *
 * Complex conjugate pole-pair at one fourth the Nyquist rate;
 * pole magnitude is 0.8.  Note that pole[0] is not used.
 */
    pole[1].mag = 0.8 ;          pole[1].ang = 0.25*PI ;
    pole[2].mag = pole[1].mag ; pole[2].ang = -pole[1].ang ;
/*
 * Zeros at 0 hertz and at the Nyquist rate.
 * Note that zero[0] is at z = 0.
 */
    zero[1].mag = 1. ;           zero[1].ang = 0. ;
    zero[2].mag = -1. ;          zero[2].ang = 0. ;
/*
 * Evaluate pole-zero diagram at K equally spaced points
 * from omin to omax
 */
    for ( omega = omin ; omega <= omax ; omega += ostep) {
        for ( num = 1., i = 0 ; i <= M ; i++ )
            num *= length( omega, zero[i] ) ;
        for ( den = 1., i = 1 ; i <= N ; i++ )
            den *= length( omega, pole[i] ) ;
        num *= gain ;
/*
 * Take care with possibly zero denominator value
 */
        if ( den != 0. )
            amp = num/den ;
        else if ( num >= 0. )
            amp = HUGE ;
        else
            amp = -HUGE ;
/*
 * Print result as function of frequency
 */
        printf( "%f %f\n", omega, amp ) ;
    }
}
/*
 * Returns length of line from pole or zero location (given by
 * point) to frequency omega (on unit circle)
 */
double length( omega, point )
 double omega; struct polar point ;
{
 double a, b ;
```

```
    a = point.mag*cos( point.ang ) - cos( omega ) ;
    b = point.mag*sin( point.ang ) - sin( omega ) ;
        return( sqrt( a*a + b*b ) ) ;
}
```

Note that the method used in the program just given is entirely analogous to the graphical method described earlier for finding the amplitude response of a filter given its pole locations. The following program similarly uses the method developed in this section to evaluate the phase response of the identical filter (redundant comments are omitted).

```
#include <stdio.h>
#include <math.h>

struct polar {
    double mag ;
    double ang ;
} ;

#define M 2
#define N 2
#define K 32

struct polar zero[M+1] ;
struct polar pole[N+1] ;

main()
{
 double PI = 4.*atan(1.) ;
 double omin = 0. ;
 double omax = PI ;
 double ostep = (omax - omin)/K ;
 double omega, angle() ;
 double gain, pha ;
 int i ;
    gain = 1. ;
    pole[1].mag = 0.8 ;          pole[1].ang = 0.25*PI ;
    pole[2].mag = pole[1].mag ; pole[2].ang = -pole[1].ang ;
    zero[1].mag = 1. ;           zero[1].ang = 0. ;
    zero[2].mag = -1. ;          zero[2].ang = 0. ;

    for ( omega = omin ; omega <= omax ; omega += ostep) {
        for ( pha = 0., i = 0 ; i <= M ; i++ )
            pha += angle( omega, zero[i] ) ;
        for ( i = 1 ; i <= N ; i++ )
            pha -= angle( omega, pole[i] ) ;
        printf( "%f %f\n", omega, pha ) ;
    }
```

```
}
/*
 * Returns angle (in radians) of line from pole or zero location
 * (given by point) to frequency omega (on unit circle)
 */
double angle( omega, point )
 double omega ; struct polar point ;
{
    return(
        atan2(
            sin(omega) - point.mag*sin(point.ang),
            cos(omega) - point.mag*cos(point.ang)
        )
    ) ;
}
```

Knowledge of the locations of the poles and zeros of a filter is tantamount to knowledge of the transfer function. However, the transfer function must be computed from the pole-zero locations according to equation (2-97). The following program evaluates equation (2-97) by direct multiplication of the numerator and denominator factors.

```
#include <stdio.h>
#include <math.h>

struct polar {
    double mag ;
    double ang ;
} ;

#define M 2
#define N 2

struct polar zero[M+1] ;
struct polar pole[N+1] ;
struct polar acoef[M+1] ;
struct polar bcoef[N+1] ;
double PI ;

main()
{
 int i ;
 PI = 4.*atan(1.) ;

    pole[1].mag = 0.9 ;         pole[1].ang = 0.25*PI ;
    pole[2].mag = pole[1].mag ; pole[2].ang = -pole[1].ang ;
    zero[1] = pole[1] ;         zero[1].mag = 1./zero[1].mag ;
    zero[2] = pole[2] ;         zero[2].mag = 1./zero[2].mag ;
```

```
/*
 * Find and print coefficients of numerator and denominator
 * of transfer function.
 */
    getcoef( acoef, zero, M ) ;
    getcoef( bcoef, pole, N ) ;
    printf( "              1. " ) ;
    for ( i = 1 ; i <= M ; i++ )
        if ( acoef[i].mag != 0. )
            printf( " %+fz[-%d] ", acoef[i].mag, i ) ;
    printf( "\nH(z) = a[0] -----------------------------\n" ) ;
    printf( "              1. " ) ;
    for ( i = 1 ; i <= N ; i++ )
        if ( bcoef[i].mag != 0. )
            printf( " %+fz[-%d] ", bcoef[i].mag, i ) ;
    printf( "\n" ) ;
}
/*
 * Multiply polynomial factors of form (1 - root[i]*x)
 * to find coefficients.  Note that these coefficients
 * may not be real if complex poles or zeros do not
 * always occur in conjugate pairs.
 */
getcoef( coef, root, Nroots )
 struct polar coef[], root[] ; int Nroots ;
{
 struct polar cadd(), cnegmult() ;
 int i, j ;
/*
 * Initialize coefficient vector
 */
    for ( i = 0 ; i <= N ; i++ )
        coef[i].mag = coef[i].ang = 0. ;
    coef[0].mag = 1. ;
/*
 * Recursive multiplication to find polynomial coefficients
 */
    for ( i = 1 ; i <= Nroots ; i++ ) {
        coef[i] = cnegmult( root[i], coef[i - 1] ) ;
        for ( j = i - 1 ; j >= 1 ; j-- )
            coef[j] =
                cadd( coef[j], cnegmult( root[i], coef[j - 1] ) ) ;
    }
}
/*
 * Return complex product of -a and b
 */
struct polar cnegmult( a, b )
```

```
 struct polar a, b ;
{
 static struct polar v ;
    v.mag = -a.mag*b.mag ;
    v.ang =  a.ang + b.ang ;
/*
 * Negate magnitude when phase of result is 180 degrees
 */
    if ( fabs( fabs( v.ang ) - PI ) < 1.e-6 ) {
        v.mag = -v.mag ;
        v.ang = 0. ;
    }
    return( v ) ;
}
/*
 * Return complex sum of a and b
 */
struct polar cadd( a, b )
 struct polar a, b ;
{
 static struct polar v ;
 double x, y ;
/*
 * Convert to rectangular form for complex addition
 */
    x  = a.mag*cos( a.ang ) ;
    y  = a.mag*sin( a.ang ) ;
    x += b.mag*cos( b.ang ) ;
    y += b.mag*sin( b.ang ) ;
    v.mag = sqrt( x*x + y*y ) ;
    v.ang = atan2( y, x ) ;
    if ( fabs( fabs( v.ang ) - PI ) < 1.e-6 ) {
        v.mag = -v.mag ;
        v.ang = 0. ;
    }
    return( v ) ;
}
```

We recognize in the last example the poles and zeros for the allpass filter described earlier in this section. Running this program results in the following output:

```
              1.  -1.571348z[-1]  +1.234568z[-2]
H(z) = a[0] ---------------------------------------
              1.  -1.272792z[-1]  +0.810000z[-2]
```

which verifies equation (2-114).

All these examples could be combined into a single program that obtains pole-zero locations from a variety of sources (possibly through interaction with the user) and produces a variety of useful results. The output of the amplitude or phase response programs might be piped to a graphics program to obtain a frequency response plot. For example, the UNIX command

```
a.out | graph | plot -Tcrt
```

where a.out is the compiled and loaded version of the frequency or phase response program given previously, will produce a crude plot of its output on almost any interactive terminal.

2.4.5 IIR Filters

Poles are associated with feedback terms in the digital filter equation, making the filter output dependent on one or more of its previous outputs. This feedback causes the impulse response of the filter to have an infinite duration; such filters are therefore called infinite impulse response (IIR) filters.[34] An IIR filter may also contain one or more zeros in its transfer function.

An IIR filter will be *stable* if all of its poles lie strictly *inside* the unit circle when their locations are plotted on the complex plane. IIR filters can also be *unstable* if one or more of their poles lies *outside* the unit circle. An IIR filter can also be *conditionally stable* if one or more of its poles lies exactly *on* the unit circle, meaning that its impulse response neither dies away nor grows as time goes by. Most of the time we are interested in using only stable filters.

The frequency response of an IIR filter typically contains peaks, or *resonances*, associated with frequencies that the filter tends to emphasize. The frequencies of such resonances are associated with the locations of the poles. For the coefficient of a digital filter to be real numbers, poles must either be purely real (that is, they must lie on the real axis), or they must occur in complex conjugate pole pairs of the form $Re^{\pm j\omega}$. A single pole lying inside the unit circle on the real axis can therefore give rise to a resonance only at 0 Hz or at the Nyquist frequency, indicating that a one-pole filter can have either a lowpass or highpass characteristic. A pole pair at $z = Re^{\pm j\theta}$ can place a resonance at any frequency between these two values. The center frequency of this resonance will be determined by θ, and the height of the peak, or *gain*, associated with the resonance will be determined by the distance of the poles from the perimeter of the unit circle. We can determine the gain of the filter at the resonance point by referring to equation (2-101). The poles are located at $z = Re^{\pm j\theta}$. Evaluating $H(z)$ at $z = e^{j\omega}$ and setting ω to θ (the resonance frequency) yields the following expression for the peak gain:

$$|H(e^{j\theta})| = \frac{a_0}{[(1-R)^2(1-2R\cos 2\theta + R^2)]^{1/2}} \tag{2-115}$$

We see from this relationship that the peak gain depends on the value of θ, achieving a maximum possible value when both poles lie on top of each other at $z = 1$ or $z = -1$ in

[34]Such filters are also sometimes referred to as *recursive* or *autoregressive* filters.

which case it is equal to $a_0/(1 - R)^2$. For example, when $R = 0.9$ and $\theta = 0$, equation (2-105) yields a value of $1/(1 - 0.9)^2 = 100$, while for the same value of R and $\theta = \pi/2$ (half the Nyquist rate), the peak gain is equal to about 5.26. As R approaches unity (that is, as the poles approach the perimeter of the unit circle), the peak gain in all cases becomes progressively larger (see Figure 2-42).

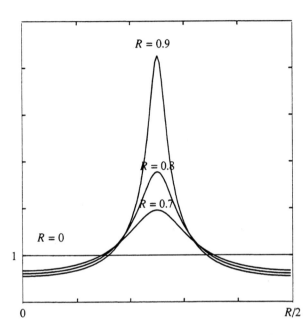

Figure 2-42   Frequency response of a two-pole filter for various values of R. The center frequency is set to one half the Nyquist rate in all cases. Note how the bandwidth of the resonance decreases as the peak gain increases.

Another useful concept associated with resonance is that of *bandwidth*, usually defined as the difference between the frequencies where the filter gain has fallen by 3 dB from its peak value at the center frequency. In other words, if a filter has two poles at $z = Re^{\pm j\theta}$, its peak gain G will occur at center frequency $\omega_c = \theta$. There usually will be some frequency $\omega_+ > \omega_c$ where the gain of the filter is 3 dB less than the peak gain, that is, $G/\sqrt{2}$. Similarly, there will usually be some frequency $\omega_- < \omega_c$ where the filter also has gain $G/\sqrt{2}$. The bandwidth B of the filter is then given by $B = \omega_+ - \omega_-$. The exact mathematical relationship between R and the bandwidth is quite complicated. However, when R is close to 1, the bandwidth B is approximately $-2\ln R$ radians.

Because its poles must lie within the unit circle for stability, the phase response of an IIR filter is always nonlinear, meaning that it will tend to distort the phase of any processed signal. This implies in turn that the time alignment of the frequency components in the input signal will differ from the time alignment of those same components in the output signal. The amount of phase distortion in a two-pole filter generally increases as the peak gain of the resonance increases (that is, as the bandwidth decreases). An IIR filter can be used to change both the relative amplitudes and the relative phases of signal components simultaneously. Conversely, no IIR filter can alter the frequency content of a signal while simultaneously preserving the time alignment of its frequency components exactly.

It is interesting to note at this point that any analog filter can be implemented as an IIR digital filter. One upshot of this fact is that many decades of theoretical work on the design of analog filters may be applied directly to the design of IIR digital filters; one simply works out the required filter design in the analog domain and then applies one of several standard mathematical transformations to obtain the equivalent digital filter.[35] Analog filter design techniques exist for

- *Butterworth filters*, which have maximally flat frequency response at low frequencies
- *Bessel filters*, which have maximally linear phase response at low frequencies
- *Chebyshev filters*, which have equal-sized errors above and below some desired passband *or* some desired stopband specification (the so-called *equiripple* criterion)
- *Elliptic filters*, which have equal-sized errors above and below both the desired passband *and* stopband specifications

Design techniques for all these filter types can be found in specialized books.

The techniques developed in section 2.4.4 form a simplified but practical basis for the design of IIR digital filters. Using these techniques, we can specify the locations of poles and zeros directly and compute the associated filter response curves. It is surprising how even a little experience at pole-zero specification can lead to effective filters, especially for musical applications in which maximally flat or optimally equiripple performance in a passband or stopband is of little relevance.

We can further simplify the filter design problem by noting that it is possible to *decompose* higher-order filters into simpler forms. There are two basic methods for decomposing digital filters. The *cascade* method involves connecting the output of one filter to the input of another. In this case, the output of the first filter will become the input for the second, and we would hear the result of the second filter's response to the output of the first. If the first filter has a transfer function $H_1(z)$ and the transfer function of the second filter is $H_2(z)$, then their cascade interconnection forms another filter whose transfer function is

$$H(z) = H_1(z)H_2(z) \qquad (2\text{-}116)$$

Thus if both the component filters are of second order, the composite filter will be of fourth order, offering the possibility of two resonant regions in its frequency response. This approach may be carried on for any number of constituent filters. In general, we find that only first- and second-order filters are necessary as basic building blocks for filters of arbitrarily high order.

Another basic approach to filter decomposition is the *parallel* interconnection of multiple filters in which the outputs of two or more filters, each receiving the same

---

[35]These transformations include differential mapping, impulse-invariant transformation, bilinear transformation, and matched z transform techniques.

input signal, are added together. In this case, we would hear the outputs of the consti-tuent filters simultaneously. Again, we find that only first- and second-order filter sec-tions are necessary to implement arbitrarily complex filters.

2.4.6 FIR Filters

If a digital filter contains only zeros, it will depend only on its past inputs. An *M*th order all-zero filter can therefore have an impulse response of *M* samples. Because *M* is a finite number we refer to such filters as finite impulse response (FIR) filters.[36]

An FIR filter is always stable because its impulse response is guaranteed to become zero after at most a finite number of samples. This has the important implica-tion that the zeros of the transfer function of an FIR filter may lie anywhere on the *z* plane; that is, unlike the case with the poles, zeros are *not* constrained to lie inside the unit circle.

The frequency response of an FIR filter is composed of one or more dips, *antiresonances*, which are associated with frequencies the filter tends to deemphasize. The frequencies of the anitresonances are associated with the locations of the zeros of the filter's transfer function on the complex plane. As in the case of poles, these zeros must occur either on the real axis of the complex plane, or they must appear in complex conjugate pairs if the coefficients of the filter are to be real. A single zero can therefore deemphasize either 0 Hz or the Nyquist frequency, depending on whether it lies closer to $z = 1$ or $z = -1$ on the real axis. A single complex conjugate zero pair at $Re^{\pm j\omega}$ can deemphasize any frequency ω in between, with the gain, or depth of the antiresonance, associated with the zero being given by its distance from the unit circle, $1 - R$. Notice that because R can have any value, this gain can be either negative or positive.

FIR filters have the important property that they can achieve an exactly *linear phase* response characteristic. This means that they can alter the amplitude of fre-quency components in signals that they process while preserving exactly the time align-ment of these components (there may be an overall delay of all components, however). Generally speaking, practical analog filters cannot be designed to have a finite duration impulse response because such filters would have to contain time delay elements that do not exist in analog form. Therefore, analog filters cannot in general exhibit linear phase responses, although they may in fact exhibit *nearly* linear phase responses over a partic-ular frequency band of interest.

The impulse response of an *M*th order FIR filter

$$y(n) = a_0 x(n) + a_1 x(n-1) + \cdots + a_M x(n-M) \qquad (2\text{-}117)$$

is seen to be a simple listing of its coefficients; that is, the impulse response is a_0, a_1, For an FIR filter to have a linear phase response, it can be shown that it is sufficient for its impulse response to be *left-right symmetrical;* that is, $a_0 = a_M$, $a_1 = a_{M-1}$, and so on. The *center of symmetry* will lie either on the middle sample if *M* is an odd number or between two samples if *M* is even. The overall *phase delay* or *group delay*, which expresses the overall delay between the input and output of the filter, will therefore be

---

[36]Such filters are also sometimes called *nonrecursive*, *transversal*, or *moving average* filters.

$(N - 1)/2$ samples, where N is the length of the impulse response of the filter. This delay will not be an integer if N is even. For this reason, FIR filters are often designed with an odd number of coefficients.

In terms of the locations of the zeros on the complex frequency (z) plane, it can be shown that linear phase FIR filters obey certain simple rules. For each zero located at $Re^{j\omega}$, a corresponding zero must be present at $1/Re^{j\omega}$ for the filter to have linear phase. Zeros lying on the unit circle ($R = 1$) are the only exception, because $1/1 = 1$. Thus each real zero of the form $z = \alpha$ must be accompanied by another real zero at $z = 1/\alpha$, and each complex conjugate zero pair of the form $z = Re^{\pm j\omega}$ must be accompanied by another zero pair at $1/Re^{\pm j\omega}$.

There are several methods for designing linear phase FIR filters. One of the simplest methods is based on the equivalence between the discrete Fourier transform and the evaluation of the z transform at equally spaced points around the unit circle. In effect, we can design a linear phase FIR filter by specifying its frequency response directly in terms of the DFT of its impulse response. We then take the inverse DFT of this frequency response to obtain the impulse response, which, as we have seen, is the same as the coefficients of the desired FIR filter. For example, if we wish to design a linear phase FIR filter of length N, we divide N into two halves representing the positive and negative frequencies. For the coefficients to be real, the frequency response must be left-right symmetrical and the phase must be antisymmetrical around zero frequency. The linear phase characteristic is satisfied by choosing a particular value of slope for the phase:

$$\theta(\omega) = -\alpha\omega \qquad -\pi \leq \omega \leq \pi \qquad (2\text{-}118)$$

The frequency response may then be set arbitrarily within these constraints and the inverse DFT will provide the filter coefficients. The resulting filter will have a finite impulse response and a linear phase characteristic. It will not be optimal in any sense, because the frequency response between the specified values may vary above and below the straight line connecting adjacent amplitude specifications. Relatively smooth frequency response curves will be matched fairly well, but abruptly changing response curves (as in an "ideal" lowpass filter with a passband response of 1 and a stopband response of 0) will exhibit considerable "ripple" in both their passbands and stopbands. The optimal apportionment of this ripple is one of the profound problems of FIR filter design. However, for arbitrary linear phase filter responses that are not too abrupt, the following C program works quite well. The `idft` program is the same as the one given previously.

```
#include <stdio.h>
#include <math.h>
typedef struct { float re ; float im ; } complex ;

#define NMAX 1025

main() {
 int N, n ;
 double PI2 = 8.*atan( 1. ) ;
```

```
float h[NMAX], alpha ;
complex X[NMAX] ;
/*
 * make up a frequency response (symmetrical around zero)
 * use X[].re to hold magnitude
 */
    N = 65 ;
    for ( n = 0 ; n < (N + 1)/2 ; n++ ) {
        X[n].re = sin( PI2*n/N ) + 0.333* sin( 3.*PI2*n/N ) ;
        X[N - n].re = X[n].re ;
    }
/*
 * set phase for linearity
 * use X[].im to hold phase angle
 */
    alpha = -(N - 1.)/2. ;
    for ( n = 0 ; n < (N + 1)/2 ; n++ ) {
        X[n].im = alpha*n*PI2/N ;
        X[N - n].im = -X[n].im ;
    }
/*
 * convert from polar to rectangular values
 * divide by N to normalize filter gain
 */
    for ( n = 0 ; n < N ; n++ ) { float a, b ;
        a = X[n].re*cos( (double) X[n].im )/N ;
        b = X[n].re*sin( (double) X[n].im )/N ;
        X[n].re = a ;
        X[n].im = b ;
    }
/*
 * take inverse DFT
 */
    idft( h, N, X ) ;
/*
 * h now contains filter coefficients
 * print symmetrically to avoid roundoff errors
 */
    for ( n = 0 ; n < N ; n++ )
        if ( n < (N + 1)/2 )
            printf( "%f\n", h[n] ) ;
        else
            printf( "%f\n", h[N - 1 - n] ) ;
}
```

The filter designed by this program will always have a linear phase delay of $(N - 1)/2$ samples. Note that if N is even, the phase delay of the filter will not be an integral number of samples. As in all cases, it is best to check the impulse, frequency, and phase responses of the designed filter before using it.

The impulse and frequency responses of the filter designed by the program just given are shown in Figure 2-43. Note the rather novel frequency response curve purposely chosen to have the shape of the first two components of a square wave to demonstrate the arbitrariness of the filter specification. This specification works well using this design technique because it is relatively smooth; that is, there are no abrupt jumps in the frequency response.

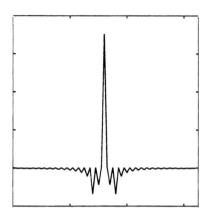
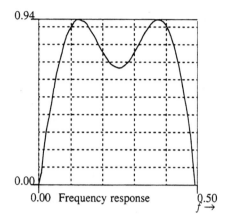

Figure 2-43 · Impulse and frequency response of a length 65 linear phase FIR filter. This filter was designed by the program given in the text. Note the left-right symmetry of the impulse response. The phase (or group) delay of this filter is a constant 33 samples.

We can demonstrate the difficulty with abrupt jumps in the following manner. Let us create an arbitrary lowpass filter by substituting the following filter specification into the program.

```
N = 33 ;
for ( n = 0 ; n < (N + 1)/2 ; n++ ) {
    X[n].re = n < 8 ? 1. : 0. ;
    X[N - n].re = X[n].re ;
}
```

The impulse and frequency responses for the resulting filter are shown in Figure 2-44. The abrupt transition between the passband and stopband cause considerable ringing to occur, and the filter exhibits considerable ripple in both bands, making it a rather poor choice for straightforward lowpass filtering applications (it may be useful for some novel musical effect, however).

As always, it is possible to combat such ringing behavior with windowing techniques. In other words, we can improve the performance of the filter whose response is shown in Figure 2-44 by multiplying its impulse response with a length 33 window function. Such windowing will have the effect of broadening the transition between the passband and stopband, but the rippling in both bands will be considerably suppressed.

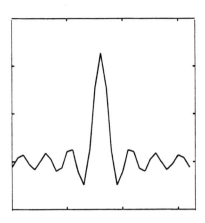
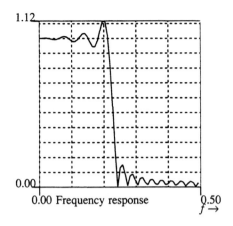

0.00 Frequency response   0.50
                                          $f \rightarrow$

Figure 2-44   Impulse and frequency response of a length 33 linear phase FIR filter. The abrupt transition between the passband and stopband of this lowpass filter causes considerable ringing to occur in the frequency response, making this a rather poor filter. Notice also that its odd length does not allow an antiresonance to be placed at exactly the Nyquist rate.

Any of the window functions we have discussed so far (triangular, Hamming, hanning) may be used. Figure 2-45 shows the effect of multiplying the impulse response of our lowpass filter by a Hamming window, together with its improved frequency response. The Hamming window was applied merely by changing the printout statement in the program to read as follows:

```
for ( n = 0 ; n < N ; n++ )
    printf( "%f\n", (0.54 - 0.46*cos(n*PI2/(N-1)))*h[n] ) ;
```

Whenever a filter response appears nearly flat in any of its bands, it is usually a good idea to check that response on a dB scale in order to observe small details more readily. Figure 2-46 shows the same frequency response plotted on a dB scale, in which it is evident that the passband is flat to within a fraction of a dB, and the stopband rejection is everywhere at least on the order of –50 dB or more, indicating that the windowing operation really has done considerable good.

2.4.7 Nonlinear Phase Cancellation

As we have seen, all the poles of an IIR filter must lie inside the unit circle if the filter is to be stable. Zeros need not lie inside the unit circle to maintain stability, however, and by balancing each zero inside the unit circle with one outside the unit circle, FIR filters can attain an exactly linear phase characteristic for any specifiable frequency response. It is interesting to observe in this context that a nonlinear phase characteristic of any filter can be exactly canceled, allowing exact phase alignment to be maintained, by a very simple technique. Phase nonlinearities simply cause some frequencies to come out either ahead of or behind the time that other frequencies arrive at the output.

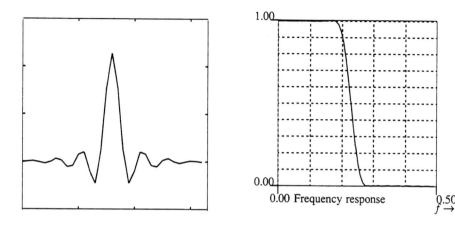

Figure 2-45   Improved frequency response obtained by applying a Hamming window to the impulse response of the filter. The transition between the passband the stopband of this lowpass filter is broadened by the window, but the ringing in the passband and stopband is considerably reduced.

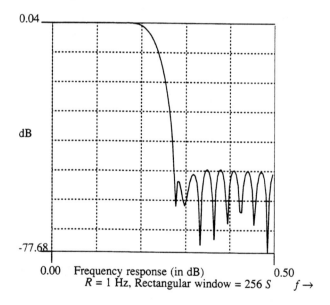

0.04

dB

-77.68

0.00   Frequency response (in dB)   0.50
$R = 1$ Hz, Rectangular window $= 256\ S$ $f \rightarrow$

Figure 2-46   The frequency response of Figure 2-45 plotted on a dB scale. The dB scale allows detailed behavior in the passband and stopband to be observed more readily. In this case, we see that the passband is quite flat and that all frequencies in the stopband are attenuated by about 50 dB.

If we simply process the signal twice—once *forward* in time and once *backward* in time—through any filter, any phase nonlinearities in the response of the filter will be exactly canceled. The effective frequency response will simply be the square of the one obtained by passing the signal through the filter once. Any frequencies advanced in time by the first operation will be retarded in time by the same amount in the second pass through the data, and vice-versa.

Obviously, this technique cannot work in real time. If, however, we are processing a digitally recorded signal (as is often the case), the nonlinear phase characteristics of *any* filter may be easily removed in this manner, provided that we can benefit from the square of its frequency response.

2.4.8 Fast Convolution

We generally think of filters as spectrum modifiers in the sense that they emphasize or deemphasize certain frequencies in their input signals, modify their phase characteristics, and so on. In the frequency domain, we have seen that the operation of any filter can be described by the relationship

$$Y(z) = H(z)X(z) \tag{2-119}$$

where $X(z)$ is the z transform of input signal $x(n)$, $Y(z)$ is the z transform of output signal $y(n)$, and $H(z)$ is the z transform of impulse response $h(n)$ of the filter.

We have also seen that multiplication in the frequency domain corresponds to convolution in the time domain, implying that equation (2-119) is entirely equivalent to the relationship

$$y(n) = h(n) \ ^{*} \ x(n) \tag{2-120}$$

where * denotes convolution.

General convolution is defined by the relationship

$$y(n) = \sum_{m=-\infty}^{\infty} h(m)x(n-m) \tag{2-121}$$

This relationship applies only to the case where all the functions involved have infinite duration. As we have seen, however, if $h(n)$ is a sequence of N_h samples and $x(n)$ is a sequence of N_x samples, then we may rewrite equation (2-121) as

$$y(n) = \sum_{m=0}^{N_h-1} h(m)x(n-m) \tag{2-122}$$

This linear, or aperiodic, convolution results in a sequence $y(n)$ of length $N_h + N_x - 1$.

What if, as in the case of an FIR digital filter, only $h(n)$ is of finite duration while $x(n)$ is of arbitrary—but typically large—duration? In other words, how can we implement an FIR filter? There basically are two ways: by direct convolution, as implied in the digital filter equation, or by *fast* convolution using the FFT.

Using direct convolution, an FIR filter requires N_h multiplies and adds to compute each sample of its output. Thus to apply an FIR filter to N_x samples of input, the direct convolution method would require about $N_h(N_h + N_x - 1) = N_h^2 + N_h N_x + N_h$ multiply-adds. If N_h is small, direct convolution is reasonably efficient. The following subprogram shows how such a process could be implemented using a *circular buffer* technique to keep track of the past N_h inputs. Each time the subprogram is executed it receives a single sample of input, an array containing M filter coefficients, and an array of length M to hold the necessary history of previous inputs (this array and the `now` variable are assumed to contain zeros the first time the subprogram is called). Note that the filter order is $M - 1$.

```
float convolve( x0, h, xn, M, now )
 float x0, h[], xn[] ; int M, *now ;
{
 register int i, j ;
 float y ;
    xn[*now] = x0 ;
    y = 0. ;
    j = *now ;
    for ( i = 0 ; i < M ; i++ ) {
        y += h[i]*xn[j++] ;
        if ( j >= M )
            j = 0 ;
    }
    (*now)-- ;
    if ( *now < 0 )
        *now = M - 1 ;
    return( y ) ;
}
```

This subprogram uses a pointer-to-integer `now` to keep track of where current input value `x0` will be stored in the `xn` array. To avoid moving M pieces of data by one location in the `xn` array on each call, the subprogram simply decrements `now` at the end of each call, wrapping around to the end of the `xn` array as needed. At the beginning of each call, therefore, `xn[now]` is set to the current input, `xn[(now + 1)%M]` will contain the previous input, and so on. Simple comparison operations are employed to avoid using the modulus (%) operator, which can be quite slow because it generally requires an integer division operation to compute the remainder.

The subprogram could be made more efficient by recognizing that the comparison operation need not be done each time the main loop is executed, because the value of `j` is reset only once during each call. The following version of the same program is more optimized, efficient, and (as usual in such cases) obtuse. It behaves exactly the same way from the calling program's perspective, however.

```
float convolve( x0, h, xn, M, now )
 float x0, *h, *xn ; int M, *now ;
{
 register float y, *endh, *endx ;
    endh = h + M ;
    endx = xn + M ;
    *( xn += *now ) = x0 ;
    y = *h++ * *xn++ ;
    while ( xn < endx )
        y += *h++ * *xn++ ;
    xn -= M ;
```

```
    while ( h < endh )
        y += *h++ * *xn++ ;
    if ( (*now -= 1) < 0 )
        *now = M - 1 ;
    return( y ) ;
}
```

Regardless of their optimization and simplicity, our programming examples have implemented direct—or slow—convolution. A much more efficient method—known as *fast* convolution—is available when N_h is fairly large (more than 30 or so). Fast convolution is based on the FFT, which, as we have seen, operates on N data points in a computation time proportional to $N \log_2 N$ rather than N^2.

To implement an FIR filter, for example, we wish to convolve the impulse response $h(n)$ of the filter with a digital waveform $x(n)$ of arbitrary length. A useful technique—called the *overlap-add method*—for doing this consists of sectioning $x(n)$ into equal-length blocks of samples, each with a length L_x, which is on the same order as L_h.

We know that the length of the linear (aperiodic) convolution of two sequences of length L_h, and L_x respectively, is $L_h + L_x - 1$. To use the DFT to effect such a linear convolution, it is necessary that both $h(n)$ and the selected block of $x(n)$ be at least $L_h + L_x - 1$ samples long. To ensure this, we can simply append $L_x - 1$ samples to $h(n)$ and $L_h - 1$ samples to the block taken from $x(n)$. We now can compute the convolution by taking the inverse DFT of the product of the DFTs of the two sequences. The first $L_h + L_x - 1$ samples of the result will contain the result. Furthermore, if we choose the first power of 2 not less than $L_h + L_x - 1$, we can use the FFT algorithm to compute the DFTs. The first L_x samples of the result will overlap with the previous $L_h - 1$ samples from the previous computation. Thus we need to overlap the final $L_h - 1$ samples of the first $L_x + L_h - 1$ samples produced by each inverse FFT with the following computation. The FFT of the (possibly zero-padded) $h(n)$ sequence need be computed only once.

The following C program example implements fast convolution by reading in an impulse response $h(n)$ and determining its length (called Lh in the program). Lh is then used for the size of the input signal block as well. The FFT length N is chosen to be the smallest power of 2 not less than Lh + Lh - 1. The transform of the impulse response H is computed from $h(n)$ padded to length N with zeros. The input signal is then read in blocks of length Lh. Each block is zero-padded to length N and transformed with the FFT. A complex multiplication is then done in the frequency domain, and the result is transformed back into the time domain. Only the first Lh + Lh - 1 samples of this signal are nonzero, as required by the convolution operation. Call the first Lh samples block A and the remaining Lh - 1 samples block B. Block A overlaps block B from the previous inverse transformation—these two blocks are added and output. The current block B is then saved for addition to the beginning of the next inverse transformation.

```
#include <stdio.h>
#include <math.h>
```

```
float PI ;              /* needed for rfft and cfft */
float TWOPI ;           /* needed for rfft and cfft */

main() {
 int Lh, Lhm1, L, N, N2, n, Nread ;
 float *H, *X, *Y, *B ;
 char *malloc(), *calloc(), *realloc() ;
 FILE *impulse, *input, *output, *openfile() ;
    PI = 4.*atan(1.) ;
    TWOPI = 8.*atan(1.) ;
/*
 * open files containing h and x
 * output goes to file y
 */
    impulse = openfile( "h", "r" ) ;
    input   = openfile( "x", "r" ) ;
    output  = openfile( "y", "w" ) ;
/*
 * read impulse response of length Lh
 */
    Lh = readin( impulse, &H ) ;
    Lhm1 = Lh - 1 ;
/*
 * L is length of linear convolution
 * N (FFT length) is first power of 2 >= L
 */
    L  = 2*Lh - 1 ;
    for ( N = 1 ; N < L ; N <<= 1 ) ;
    N2 = N>>1 ;
/*
 * input and output share memory to conserve space
 */
    X = Y = (float *) malloc( N*sizeof( float ) ) ;
/*
 * zero pad impulse response to length N
 */
    H = (float *) realloc( H, N*sizeof( float ) ) ;
    for ( n = Lh ; n < N ; n++ )
        H[n] = 0. ;
/*
 * transform and scale for unity gain
 */
    rfft( H, N2, 1 ) ;
    for ( n = 0 ; n < N ; n++ )
        H[n] *= N ;
/*
 * B holds overlapped segments--initially zero
 */
    B = (float *) calloc( Lhm1, sizeof( float ) ) ;
    do {
```

```
/*
 * read up to Lh samples of input waveform--pad to length N
 */
        Nread = readblock( input, X, Lh ) ;
        for ( n = Nread ; n < N ; n++ )
            X[n] = 0.0 ;
/*
 * perform convolution in frequency domain
 */
        rfft( X, N2, 1 ) ;
        cmult( Y, H, X, N ) ;
        rfft( Y, N2, 0 ) ;
/*
 * overlap-add the results
 */
        for ( n = 0 ; n < Lhm1 ; n++ ) {
            Y[n] += B[n] ;
            B[n]  = Y[Lh + n] ;
        }
/*
 * write out accumulated output
 */
        writeblock( output, Y, Nread ) ;
    } while ( Nread == Lh ) ;
/*
 * flush last segment when done
 */
    writeblock( output, &Y[Nread], Lhm1 ) ;
}
/*
 * open file name in requested mode--abort if error
 */
FILE * openfile( name, mode ) char *name, *mode ; {
 FILE * fp ;
    if ( ( fp = fopen( name, mode ) ) != NULL )
        return ( fp ) ;
    else {
        fprintf( stderr, "Error opening file %s\n", name ) ;
        exit ( -1 ) ;
    }
}
/*
 * read file into stretched array--return array size
 */
readin( file, array ) FILE * file ; float **array ; {
 float value ;
 char *malloc(), *realloc() ;
 int count ;
    for( count = 0 ;
      fscanf( file, "%f", &value ) != EOF ;
```

```
        count++ ) {
        if ( count == 0 ) {
            *array = (float *)
                malloc( sizeof( float ) ) ;
            **array = value ;
        } else {
            *array = (float *)
                realloc( *array, (count + 1)*sizeof( float ) ) ;
            *(*array+count) = value ;
        }
    }
    return ( count ) ;
}
/*
 * read up to size samples into array from file if possible--
 * return number of samples actually read
 */
readblock( file, array, size )
 FILE * file ; float array[] ; int size ;
{
 float value ;
 int count ;
    for ( count = 0 ; count < size ; count++ ) {
        if ( fscanf( file, "%f", &value ) == EOF )
            break ;
        array[count] = value ;
    }
    return ( count ) ;
}
/*
 * write out size samples from array to file
 */
writeblock( file, array, size )
 FILE * file ; float array[] ; int size ;
{
 int i ;
    for ( i = 0 ; i < size ; i++ )
        fprintf( file, "%f\n", array[i] ) ;
}
/*
 * c, a, and b are rfft-format spectra each containing n floats--
 * place complex product of a and b into c
 */
cmult( c, a, b, n ) float c[], a[], b[] ; int n ; {
 int i, j ;
 float re, im ;
    c[0] = a[0]*b[0] ;
    c[1] = a[1]*b[1] ;
    for ( i = 2, j = 3 ; i < n ; i += 2, j += 2 ) {
        re = a[i]*b[i] - a[j]*b[j] ;
```

```
        im = a[i]*b[j] + a[j]*b[i] ;
        c[i] = re ;
        c[j] = im ;
    }
}
```

2.5 DIGITAL AUDIO: SUMMARY

Musical sound propagates as a pressure disturbance in the atmosphere at frequencies between about 20 and 20,000 hertz. Microphones may be used to measure sound waves at fixed points in space by transducing the mechanical disturbance of the air into analogous variations in electric current. Loudspeakers transduce these analog signals, after suitable amplification, back into atmospheric pressure waves. All transducers, amplifiers, and transmission lines introduce small amounts of noise and linear and nonlinear distortions into the information that passes through them.

An analog signal may be converted into digital form with an analog-to-digital conversion system, which samples and quantizes according to various encoding schemes such as linear pulse code modulation. The sampling rate R of the digital signal must be at least twice the highest frequency in the analog signal (an analog antialiasing filter is used to ensure this), or foldover will result. Foldover causes frequencies outside the range $\pm R/2$ Hz to appear erroneously inside that range when the analog signal is reconstructed during digital-to-analog conversion. The amplitude of each sample is encoded as a binary number by the quantizer, which introduces small errors into the digital signal generally heard as noise when the analog signal is reconstructed. Neither foldover nor quantization error noise may usually be removed from the digital signal once it is there.

Spectral properties of a digital waveform may be observed with the discrete Fourier transform, which shows how to construct the waveform as a sum of harmonics of the analysis frequency, each with a particular amplitude and phase. Because the waveform and spectrum may be obtained equally well from each other (to within the numeric precision of the computer), no information loss is associated with the transformation in either direction. The amplitude (or, equivalently, the power) portion of the spectrum is most often displayed on a linear or logarithmic (decibel) scale. Phase spectrum plots are sometimes usefully viewed as phase delay or group delay.

Fourier transformation, convolution, and windowing form the basis of many of the digital signal processing techniques used in computer music. Multiplication in the time domain corresponds to convolution in the frequency domain, and vice versa. Waveform multiplication (modulation) leads to convolution of the spectra associated with the individual waveforms. Similarly, spectral multiplication (filtering) leads to convolution of a waveform with the unit sample (impulse) response of a filter. Digital filters may have either infinite (IIR case) or finite (FIR case) duration impulse responses, and FIR filters can exhibit the important property of linear phase response.

Waveforms are often multiplied by time domain window functions to minimize analysis artifacts caused by the sampled nature of digital spectral measurements. By sliding or hopping windows in time along a waveform, time-varying spectral measurements can be made. Given such time-varying measurements of the phase, instantaneous frequencies can be measured, leading to interesting and useful musical tools such as the phase vocoder. Other methods of time-varying spectral estimation include linear prediction, which has been especially useful for the analysis and synthesis of the human voice.

REFERENCES

1. R. N. Bracewell, *The Fourier Transform and Its Applications* (McGraw-Hill, New York, 1986).

2. F. R. Moore, "An Introduction to the Mathematics of Digital Signal Processing, Part I: Algebra, Trigonometry, and the Most Beautiful Formula in Mathematics," *Computer Music Journal*, 2(July 1978): 38–47. Reprinted in *Digital Audio Signal Processing: An Anthology*, ed. J. Strawn (W. Kaufmann, Los Altos, Calif., 1985).

3. ———"An Introduction to the Mathematics of Digital Signal Processing, Part II: Sampling, Transforms, and Digital Filtering," *Computer Music J.* 2 (September 1978b): 38–60. (Reprinted in *Digital Audio Signal Processing: An Anthology*, ed. J. Strawn (W. Kaufmann, Los Altos, Calif., 1985b).

4. A. V. Oppenheim and R. W. Schafer, *Digital Signal Processing*, (Prentice-Hall, Englewood Cliffs, N. J., 1975).

5. W. H. Press, B. P. Flannery, S. A. Teukolsky, and W. T. Vetterling, *Numerical Recipes: The Art of Scientific Computing* (Cambridge University Press, Cambridge, 1986).

6. L. R. Rabiner and B. Gold, *Theory and Application of Digital Signal Processing* (Prentice-Hall, Englewood Cliffs, N. J., 1975).

7. L. R. Rabiner and R. W. Schafer, *Digital Processing of Speech Signals* (Prentice-Hall, Englewood Cliffs, N. J., 1978).

8. J. O. Smith, "An Introduction to Digital Filter Theory," in *Digital Audio Signal Processing: An Anthology*, ed. J. Strawn (W. Kaufmann, Los Altos, Calif., 1985).

9. M. R. Spiegel, *Mathematical Handbook* (McGraw-Hill, New York, 1968).

3

Instruments

We have also our sound-houses, where we practice and demonstrate all sounds, and their generation. We have harmonies which you do not, of quarter-sounds, and lesser slides of sounds. Divers instruments of music likewise to you unknown, some sweeter than any you have; together with bells and rings that are dainty and sweet. We represent small sounds as great and deep; likewise great sounds extenuate and sharp; we make divers tremblings and warblings of sounds, which in their original are entire. We represent and imitate all articulate sounds and letters, and the voices and notes of beasts and birds. We have certain helps which set to the ear do further the hearing greatly. We have also divers strange and artificial echoes, reflecting the voice many times, and as it were tossing it: and some that give back the voice louder than it came; some shriller, and some deeper; yea, some rendering the voice differing in the letters or articulate sound from that they receive. We have also means to convey sounds in trunks and pipes, in strange lines and distances.

—Francis Bacon, *The New Atlantis* (1624)

Computers allow us to turn ideas into actions. By connecting a computer to a loudspeaker through a digital-to-analog converter, for example, not only can we think about mathematical relationships such as those presented in Chapter 2, but we can perceive them directly through our sense of hearing as well. Mathematical relationships can become, in effect, musical instruments.

There are usually many ways to represent the same relationship. Each representation brings out some aspect of the relationship while perhaps making other aspects less apparent. Much of the subject of mathematics is about expressing relationships in various alternative forms, some of which are very revealing, others less so. For example, the mathematical statement

$$x^2 = 1 \qquad\qquad (3\text{-}1)$$

describes the square of one quantity, x, as equal to another quantity, 1. The identical relationship is also expressed by the statements

$$x = \sqrt{1} \qquad\qquad (3\text{-}2)$$

and

$$x^2 - 1 = 0 \qquad\qquad (3\text{-}3)$$

and

$$(x + 1)(x - 1) = 0 \qquad\qquad (3\text{-}4)$$

and

$$x = \pm 1 \qquad\qquad (3\text{-}5)$$

and so on, ad infinitum. We have often been told that the last form is called the *answer*, in the sense that it expresses a value of the quantity x directly. But we might equally well regard equation (3-5) as a *question*, one that might be answered equally well by all the other statements and many more besides. Each of the statements is a different representation of the same relationship. More important, each of the other statements also reveals a unique aspect of the relationship that they all embody. In mathematics, not only can we say the same thing infinitely many ways, but we can prove it.

The ancient Greeks regarded music as a kind of audible mathematics. The laws that govern the vibrations of stretched strings, for example, are related in many ways to the properties of numbers. We might adopt the view that pure and simple numeric relationships capture only a small part of what exists in real music, or we might decide that real music is only a very loose approximation of mathematical ideals. The prevailing contemporary view leans toward the former, while the ancient Greeks apparently preferred the latter. Unlike mathematics, very little has been proved about the essential nature of music.

Computers provide unprecedented opportunities to create music according to either of these complementary viewpoints and many others as well. We may synthesize sounds from purely mathematical relationships, or we may use "real" sounds that have been digitized as basic materials. This dual approach is reminiscent of the origins of electronic music in the mid-twentieth century, when the French school of *musique concrète*—based on manipulation of the "concrete" sounds of nature as opposed to the "abstract" sounds of traditional musical instruments—was for a time distinguishable from the German school of "pure" electronic music, which championed electronic devices such as oscillators as sound sources. Not only are both procedures possible using computers, but they are possible with an audio fidelity and a degree of precise control that far exceeds any earlier methods for manipulating sound.

Just as questions and answers are not always readily distinguishable from each other, we are only at the beginning of understanding the full implications of the musical precision offered by computers. To learn to use this great ship to explore musical realms, we must understand how it can be used as a musical instrument. In this chapter, we examine the relationships among mathematical concepts, their many revelations through alternative representations, and musical sound materials.

3.1 REPRESENTING INSTRUMENTS

To turn concepts into musical instruments, it will be useful to define some notation. We start with the simplest possible notation for describing the kinds of operations developed in Chapter 2.

Let us repeat the digital filter equation here for convenience.

$$y(n) = \sum_{i=0}^{M} a_i x(n-i) - \sum_{i=1}^{N} b_i y(n-i) \tag{3-6}$$

Viewing this equation as a prescription for computation rather than as a mathematical relationship, we see that we may compute the current output $y(n)$ of any digital filter if we know precisely four things:

- The $M+1$ values of the a_i coefficients
- The N values of the b_i coefficients
- The values of the present and past M filter inputs $x(n-i)$, $i = 0, 1, \ldots, M$
- The values of the past N filter outputs $y(n-i)$, $i = 1, 2, \ldots, N$.

3.1.1 Flow Diagrams

In Chapter 2, we saw how to relate the filter coefficients to the actions of the filter in the frequency domain. To perform the computation itself, however, we need only to be able to add and multiply and keep track of previous things. To construct putative "instruments" using these concepts, we need to be able to describe such operations in a simple, manipulable way. We start by describing the addition operation with the graphic symbol

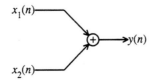

The output of the add operation is the sum of its inputs, that is, $y(n) = x_1(n) + x_2(n)$. For example, if $x_1(n)$ is equal to the sequence 1, 2, 3, 4, . . . , and $x_2(n)$ is equal to the sequence 2, 4, 6, 8, . . . , then $y(n)$ as output by the addition element would be 3, 6, 9, 12, and so on.

Similarly, we can describe multiplication of a signal by a constant, similar to passing a signal through a constant gain element, with the symbol

The output of the gain operation is the input times the gain factor, that is, $y(n) = gx(n)$. For example, if $x(n)$ is equal to 1, 2, 3, 4, . . . , and g is equal to 2, then $y(n)$, the output of the gain element, would be equal to 2, 4, 6, 8, and so on.

Finally, we can describe a one-sample delay of a signal with the symbol

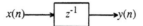

The output of the unit sample delay operation is simply the input delayed by one sample, that is, $y(n) = x(n - 1)$. For example, if $x(n)$ is equal to 1, 0, 0, 0, . . . , then $y(n)$, the output of the unit sample delay element, would be equal to 0, 1, 0, 0, and so on.

Using these three simple symbols, we can build up symbolic representations for virtually any digital filter. For example, we see that the following interconnection of these elements describes a one-zero filter.

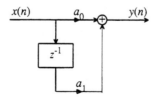

We interpret this diagram by observing that it defines the output $y(n)$ as the sum of two quantities: the first is the input $x(n)$ scaled by a_0; the second is the input $x(n)$ delayed by one sample and scaled by a_1. In other words, $y(n) = a_0x(n) + a_1x(n - 1)$.

Such figures are often used in digital signal processing discussions because they describe a complicated process (such as a digital filter) in terms of an interrelationship of simpler subprocesses, (for example, addition, scaling, and delay). Because they show explicitly and precisely how information moves among these subprocesses, they are referred to as *flow diagrams*.

Flow diagrams do not represent how a process is implemented. Instead, they represent *what happens* when a process is carried out. They can also be rearranged in alternative ways that suggest various forms of implementation. For example, the general two-zero filter might be represented with the following diagram.

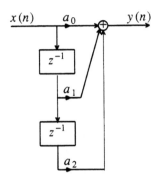

A few moments' observation of this diagram allows us to conclude that it does indeed correspond to a two-zero filter because $y(n) = a_0 x(n) + a_1 x(n-1) + a_2 x(n-2)$, as required. A simple rearrangement of the same diagram yields a quite different view of the same process.

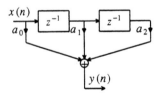

The definition of the output is still the same, but the different visual representation makes clear that an FIR filter consists of a delay line through which the input signal is passed (even though the delay line is short in this case, it is obvious that it could in principle be of any length). After each stage of delay, the signal may be "tapped off" through a gain element—the sum of these "taps" constitutes the output of the filter. This representation of the filter makes it fairly easy to see why an FIR filter is sometimes called a *tapped delay line filter*. It also shows how the impulse response of any such filter will be a simple listing of its coefficients, a_0, a_1, a_2, and so on.

A two-pole filter has the following flow diagram:

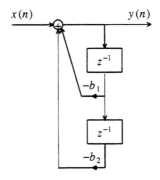

This diagram is very similar to the one for the two-zero filter. However, the taps on the delay line now flow back toward the input, because they are *feedback* taps (as opposed to the *feedforward* taps used in an FIR filter). The gains for these feedback taps are appropriately labeled $-b_1$ and $-b_2$, resulting in a representation of the filter $y(n) = x(n) - b_1 y(n-1) - b_2 y(n-2)$ as required (notice that there is an *implicit* a_0 coefficient here with a value of 1).

If we feed the output of the two-pole filter into the input of the two-zero filter, we obtain a filter whose z transform is the product of the two filters taken individually.

$$H(z) = \left[\frac{1}{1 + b_1 z^{-1} + b_2 z^{-2}}\right](a_0 + a_1 z^{-1} + a_2 z^{-2}) = \frac{a_0 + a_1 z^{-1} + a_2 z^{-2}}{1 + b_1 z^{-1} + b_2 z^{-2}} \quad (3\text{-}7)$$

The rightmost expression in this equation assures us that the resulting filter is indeed a second-order filter with two poles and two zeros. However, when we connect the filters as shown here:

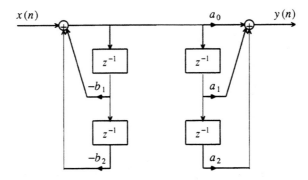

it becomes immediately apparent that the contents of the two delay lines would be identical in this configuration. The flow diagrams show us that the required process may just as well be accomplished in the following manner.

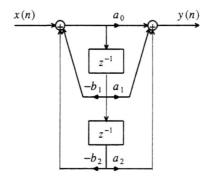

This diagram shows what is sometimes called the *canonical form* of the second-order filter because it contains the minimum number of delay, add, and gain elements. This diagram also represents a *direct form* for implementing the filter equation because it is obvious that it may be extended to any number of poles and zeros, always with the minimum number of delays.

Flow diagram notation is well suited to hierarchical definitions. For example, we can simply draw a box around the flow diagram for a one-zero filter and define it as such ("OZF"), with input $x(n)$, output $y(n)$, and parameters a_0 and a_1, as follows:

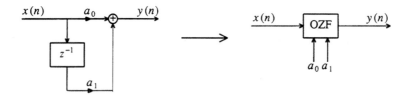

The only difficulty with the OZF box is that it tells nothing about what it does or how it works. Once defined, however, the OZF symbol may be used to replace the diagram on the left in all cases. The OZF diagram retains only the characteristics of the one-zero filter pertaining to signal flow and settable parameters. Once we understand the OZF function, such signal and parameter information is all we need to specify fully its operation in any practical context. The diagram on the left defines the operation of a one-zero filter in terms of basic operations; the diagram on the right symbolizes the one-zero filter as an abstract *instrument* that can be used as part of more complex instruments.

How can we "play" such an abstract instrument in the musical sense? Because the OZF box accepts a signal input and two parameter inputs, we can essentially play it by choosing values for all of its inputs—the output signal would then be the result. We may set the parameters to fixed values, or we may decide to vary them as time goes by.

3.1.2 The Click Problem

One of the most pervasive problems in digital sound synthesis and processing is the intrusion of unwanted discontinuities, or clicks, into the audible signal. Such clicks almost always introduce an unexpected diversion in a sound design procedure. We begin our discussion of this niggling problem with this diversion on the subject, which will reappear from time to time throughout the rest of this book.

If we choose an input signal $x(n)$ containing N samples, we may decide that for samples 0 through $N/2 - 1$, the a_0 and a_1 coefficients of our OZF instrument should be set to 0.5 and 0.5, respectively, and for input samples $N/2$ though $N - 1$, the coefficients should be 0.5 and –0.5, respectively. Thus the first half of $y(n)$ would be a lowpass-filtered version of $x(n)$, while the second half would be a highpass-filtered version of $x(n)$.

Even in this extremely simple example of playing an abstract instrument, however, there is a problem associated with the moment when the a_1 coefficient is switched from 0.5 to –0.5: by instantaneously introducing a change in the filter coefficient, we are also likely to introduce a discontinuity in the output signal $y(n)$ that was not present in the input signal $x(n)$. The following table illustrates the occurrence of such an output discontinuity for $N = 8$ and a gradually increasing input signal.

n	$x(n)$	$a_0(n)$	$a_1(n)$	$y(n) = a_0 x(n) + a_1 x(n-1)$	
0	1	0.5	0.5	0.5	
1	2	0.5	0.5	1.5	
2	3	0.5	0.5	2.5	
3	4	0.5	0.5	3.5	
4	5	0.5	–0.5	0.5	← Occurrence of discontinuity
5	6	0.5	–0.5	0.5	
6	7	0.5	–0.5	0.5	
7	8	0.5	–0.5	0.5	

Such discontinuities are generally heard as clicks in the output signal and present a fundamental problem in digital sound synthesis. We find that while such clicks are often signal-dependent in the sense that they may or may not occur depending on the specific waveform of the input signal, if clicks *can* occur, they generally *will* occur.

How do we know when a given waveform discontinuity will be perceived as an audible click? It is often very difficult to know, because the same discontinuity may produce a click in one waveform and not in another. In general, very smooth, continuous waveforms are the most susceptible to click contamination, while very complex or jagged waveforms are less susceptible. However, a potential click may occur when a waveform happens to be crossing zero or at some other propitious point that tends to mitigate (or even obliterate) the effect of the discontinuity.

The general solution to the click problem is not based on predicting when discontinuities will occur but on varying parameters in such a way that they simply cannot occur. The discontinuity in the output of the OZF box shown earlier was possible only because one of its inputs (the a_1 parameter) changed abruptly. If we change the value of this parameter gradually instead of abruptly, the size of any discontinuity in the output waveform due to this change can be controlled. The output signal may still have clicks in it if the input signal itself contains discontinuities, but that would no longer be the fault of the OZF box.

How gradual is gradual enough to avoid an audible click? The answer is unfortunately circular: the change is gradual enough when no objectionable click is audible in the output. Some musical waveforms contain clicks that are properly part of the sound (consider the onset of a xylophone note, for example). The definition of a click is therefore entirely context-dependent. The extent to which waveform discontinuities will be audible as clicks is related to the phenomenon of masking. A pure sinusoidal waveform would have a very weak ability to mask even a small discontinuity, while a complex waveform might tolerate superimposed discontinuities of considerable amplitude without noticeable degradation.

Another problem associated with click fighting is the nature of the gradual change. In our filtering example, for example, we wish to change from a setting of $(0.5, 0.5)$ to $(0.5, -0.5)$ for (a_0, a_1). If we gradually change a_1 from 0.5 to -0.5 by a process of linear interpolation over a duration of K samples, halfway through the change a_1 will likely have the value 0 if K is odd or very nearly 0 if K is even. When a_1 is 0 (or nearly so), the filter will have a transfer function $H(z) = 0.5$. Obviously, the gain of the filter at this point will be one-half at all frequencies. For a value of a_1 besides 0, however, the gain of the filter will depend on frequency. For low frequencies, the gain will decrease during the transition, while for high frequencies, the gain will increase. If there is a maximum allowable gain (the output signal may become distorted if it exceeds a certain amplitude, for example), we must be careful to take this into account during the transition. Also, the gain at half the Nyquist frequency for both the filters $y(n) = [x(n) + x(n-1)]/2$ and $y(n) = [x(n) - x(n-1)]/2$ is equal to unity. By just changing a_1 from 0.5 to -0.5, a steady sinusoid at one-half the Nyquist frequency would undergo a corresponding amplitude change from 1 to 0.5 and back to 1 again. We may wish to compensate for this effect by changing a_0 as well so that the gain at this frequency remains a constant 1 during the transition.

More serious problems occur if the filter contains poles as well as zeros. In an FIR filter, we are assured that no matter what the values of the coefficients, the filter will always be stable, even if the gain changes at particular frequencies. With an IIR filter, however, we have to consider the additional issue of whether the filter is stable for all combinations of coefficient values during the transition. If one or more of the poles of the filter should wander outside the unit circle during the transition, the filter output could grow (without bound) for as long as this condition persists. For this reason, we must exercise extra caution when using time-varying IIR filters. We will return to this problem later.

Given an appropriate set of definitions, then, we may begin to treat graphical representations such as our OZF box as abstract instruments that can be played in musical ways. Before we can construct instruments of useful complexity for building musical sounds, however, we need to define a few more symbols. In the case of the OZF box, we simply prestidigitated an input signal. To synthesize musical sounds, we will also need controllable signal *sources*. The most basic—and certainly one of the most important—among such sources is the *oscillator*, to which we now turn our attention.

3.1.3 Table Lookup Oscillators

The workhorse of digital music synthesis is the *table lookup oscillator*. Ideally, we would like to have a single, completely general version of the oscillator that does everything. In practice, however, we find that only certain features of the oscillator are needed for certain applications. In nonrealtime synthesis, unnecessary computation is translated into unnecessary waiting time to hear the result. For example, if a digital oscillator running in software takes 50 microseconds to compute a sample of output on a general-purpose computer and 1000 oscillators are needed to implement some kind of synthesis, then to a first approximation 20 samples of output can be produced in a second of computation. If 20,000 samples are needed per second of sound (a modest sampling rate by today's standards), the software will be running 1000 times slower than real time. If we are doing realtime synthesis, unnecessary computation is translated into fewer available functions.

Oscillators exist in many forms, each having some combination of features and associated computational costs. The basis for the table lookup oscillator is the table lookup procedure for evaluating an arbitrary mathematical function. Basically, there are two ways to specify a mathematical function. The first method is to specify a rule by which a given value of one or more independent variables is to be mapped into a value for the function. For example, the rule

$$f(x) = 3x + 2 \tag{3-8}$$

specifies that to find the value of $f(x)$, we multiply x by 3 and add 2 to the result. Similarly,

$$f(t) = \cos(2\pi f t + \phi) \tag{3-9}$$

specifies that for an arbitrary value of t, we find the value of $f(t)$ by multiplying t by $2\pi f$, adding ϕ to the result, and taking the cosine of that result. To compute the cosine, either we look up the required value in a table published in a book, or we use a mathematical expansion of the cosine function, such as

$$\cos x = 1 - \frac{x^2}{2!} + \frac{x^4}{4!} - \frac{x^6}{6!} + \cdots \tag{3-10}$$

to compute the value to the required precision.[1]

---

[1]The option of using a calculator is not available because we are in fact considering the problem of how to program the calculator!

The second basic method for specifying a mathematical function is the table lookup procedure, in which a table is set up to display corresponding values of all independent variables and the function. For example, we might specify the function sign x as follows:

$$\text{sign} \, x = \begin{cases} 1 & \text{if } x > 0 \\ 0 & \text{if } x = 0 \\ -1 & \text{if } x < 0 \end{cases} \qquad (3\text{-}11)$$

The specification is really just a list of all the possible values that sign x can have together with the (mutually exclusive) conditions needed to qualify for each condition.

3.1.4 Wave Tables

An even more explicit table might relate the values of independent variable x with function $f(x)$ as follows:

x	$f(x)$
0	0
1	1
2	0
3	-1

Here it is quite clear that when x is 0, $f(x)$ has the value 0, and so on. Two basic questions are inevitably raised by this type of specification:

- What about the value of $f(x)$ for values of x less than 0 and greater than 3?
- What about the value of $f(x)$ for values of x *between* 0 and 1, 1 and 2, and so on?

The table remains silent on these matters, so without further information, we would be forced to conclude that $f(x)$ is *undefined* unless x has the value 0 or 1 or 2 or 3.

We might *define* the value of the function $f(x)$ to be 0 everywhere except for the range $0 \le x \le 3$, or we might define $f(x)$ to be a periodic function of x with a period of 4—the table would then contain exactly *one period* of the function. We might similarly declare that $f(x)$ is undefined for noninteger values of x, or we might decide that $f(x)$ is a continuous function of x, with noninteger values of x corresponding to values of $f(x)$ determined by *linear interpolation* between the values given in the table. This would effectively specify that $f(2.5) = -0.5$, because 2.5 lies halfway between 2 and 3 and -0.5 lies halfway between $f(2)$ and $f(3)$.

There are other possible interpolation rules as well. We may specify, for example, that the values in the table correspond to the values of a digitized sine wave at one-fourth the sampling rate, in which case linear interpolation would clearly give incorrect results for noninteger values of x.

If we need to generate just a few values of a function such as $\sin x$ or $\cos x$ with a computer, we can usually find subprograms in the system library that can compute these functions in a fairly efficient way, based on some variation of trigonometric expansions such as equation (3-10). If, however, we need to calculate such values millions or billions of times, even efficient subprograms begin to use a significant amount of computation time. In this case, we can speed up the computations considerably by computing a table for the function in the form of an array. The index for the array then corresponds to the value of the independent variable, and the data stored in the array gives the corresponding function value.

For example, we can make a table of length L consisting of one period of a sine waveform with the following C program fragment:

```
float table[L] ;
double TWOPI = 8.*atan( 1. ) ;
    .

    .

    .
for ( i = 0 ; i < L ; i++ )
    table[i] = sin( TWOPI*i/L ) ;
```

Clearly, as `i` goes from 0, 1, ..., $L-1$, the quantity `i/L` goes linearly from 0 to almost 1, causing the argument to the `sin` function to go from 0 to almost 2π. Why "almost" 1 and "almost" 2π instead of these values exactly? Because we wish to make a table consisting of only *one period* of the sine waveform and because $\sin x$ has a period of 2π, the value $\sin 2\pi$ corresponds exactly to $\sin 0$, meaning that $\sin 2\pi$ is really the beginning of the next period and *not* the end of the first.

`L`, the lookup table length, must be large enough for the table lookup procedure to give accurate results. For instance, if we set `L` to 4, the table array will contain the following values:

i	table[i]
0	0
1	1
2	0
3	−1

Clearly, such a small value of `L` would make the table much too inaccurate to use as a substitute for the sine function except, perhaps, at frequencies above half the Nyquist rate. As `L` is made larger, however, the accuracy of the table grows accordingly. Doubling the length of the table effectively doubles the accuracy of the representation of the function. In terms of the information in the table, each doubling of the table length adds one bit of precision to the representation of the function.

Viewed another way, consider what would happen if we were to output the information stored in the table to a digital-to-analog converter. With $L = 4$ as before, the converter would need to have only 2 bits to represent fully the information stored in the table, no matter which value we decide to output, because 2 bits can select from among any four prespecified possibilities.

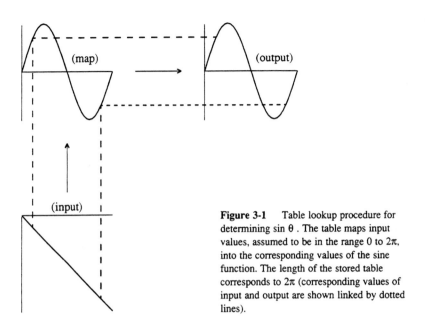

Figure 3-1   Table lookup procedure for determining sin θ . The table maps input values, assumed to be in the range 0 to 2π, into the corresponding values of the sine function. The length of the stored table corresponds to 2π (corresponding values of input and output are shown linked by dotted lines).

3.1.5 Table Lookup Procedure

Now let us consider the determination of $\sin \theta$ using a table of length L that contains one period of the sine waveform. The basic process is shown in Figure 3-1. If θ (the phase input) is measured in radians, we need to consider three issues in accessing the table:

- We must check whether θ is in the range $0 \le \theta < 2\pi$. If it is not, we need to adjust θ so that it does lie within this range.
- We must convert from radians in the range $0 \le \theta < 2\pi$ to a table index value i in the range $0 \le i < L$.
- We must decide how to access the table in case the index is not an integer.

The first step can be implemented by dividing θ by 2π and testing whether the integer part of the result is zero. If it is, θ is in the range $0 \le \theta < 2\pi$. If it is not, the integer part of the result tells us how many factors of 2π to subtract from θ to place it in this range. For example, the following C program fragment could be used to implement this step.

```
int k ;
double INVERSETWOPI = 1./(8.*atan( 1. )) ;
 .
 .
 .
k = theta*INVERSETWOPI ;
if ( k != 0 )
    theta -= k*TWOPI ;
```

This procedure is quite general and efficient if θ is likely to have any value. If, however, we know that θ will usually be inside the required range or that it is not likely to lie far outside this range, the following C statements may be more efficient because they avoid the multiplication by $1/(2\pi)$.

```
while ( theta < 0 )
    theta += TWOPI ;
while ( theta >= TWOPI )
    theta -= TWOPI ;
```

To map linearly a value in the range 0 to 2π into the range 0 to L is straight-forward. If θ lies p percent of the way from 0 to 2π, we want the table index to lie P percent of the way from 0 to L. That is, we want to preserve the relationship

$$\frac{\theta}{2\pi} = \frac{index}{L} \tag{3-12}$$

where *index* is a real value. Solving this relationship for the table index yields the following C statement:

```
index = theta*L*INVERSETWOPI ;
```

If we are concerned about computational efficiency (and we usually are), we could precompute the value `L*INVERSETWOPI` to avoid an unnecessary multiplication. The value of variable `index` is now greater than or equal to 0 and less than `L`, as required.

In the unlikely event that the table index computed by the last C statement is an integer, we can obtain the value of sin θ simply by accessing `table[index]`. If the index value is not an integer, we have three basic choices about how to access the table to obtain an approximate value for sin θ:

- *Truncation.* We can simply truncate the index (ignore its fractional part) and treat `table[ (int) index ]` as our approximation of sin θ.
- *Rounding.* We can round the index value to the nearest integer and treat `table[ (int) (index + 0.5) ]` as our approximation of sin θ.
- *Linear Interpolation.* We can use various methods of interpolation, most conveniently linear interpolation, to calculate a better approximation of sin θ than either of the other two methods.

The nature of the approximation error is different using each of these three methods. For a given table length, the error is largest with the truncation method (because the index can be off by almost 1), slightly smaller with rounding (because the index can be off by ±0.5), and smallest with interpolation.

However, we should also note that the truncation method is the fastest method, rounding is slightly slower, and interpolation requires considerably more computation than the other two methods. Because we can reduce the size of the approximation error by increasing the length of the table (no matter which lookup method is used), the issue usually becomes one of determining whether we can make the table long enough so that the errors introduced by the truncation lookup method are acceptably small. If so, the truncation method will allow for the fastest evaluation of the function. If the error cannot be made sufficiently small by increasing the table length, the interpolation method must be considered despite its greater computational complexity.

3.1.6 Approximation Errors

We can gain insight into the nature of the approximation errors for these table lookup methods by considering the values given in Table 3-1.

As the table shows, the errors introduced by the three methods are quite different. A useful way to characterize such errors is to regard them as a kind of noise added to the correct signal. We can then compute a signal-to-error noise ratio according to

$$SN_eR = 20 \log_{10} \frac{S}{N_e} \quad \text{dB} \tag{3-13}$$

where S is the signal amplitude and N_e is the amplitude of the error noise.

TABLE 3-1 Comparison of values and error produced by truncation, rounding, and linear interpolation methods of table lookup for evaluating sin θ. Phase angle θ is given in degrees, and the table length is assumed to be 360. θ is incremented by 0.75˚ for each sample. The truncation method produces sin ⌊θ⌋, the rounding method produces sin ⌊θ + 0.5⌋, and the linear interpolation method produces sin ⌊θ⌋ + (θ - ⌊θ⌋)[sin(⌊θ⌋ + 1) - sin⌊θ⌋], where ⌊x⌋ stands for "floor" of x (the largest integer not larger than x). All values shown are rounded to four decimal places. * indicates an extremely small nonzero value.

			Table Lookup Method Error Comparison					
Sample	Phase Angle	Correct Value	Method			Error		
			Truncation	Rounding	Interpolation	Truncation	Rounding	Interpolation
0	0.00	0.0000	0.0000	0.0000	0.0000	0.0000	0.0000	0.0000
1	0.75	0.0131	0.0000	0.0175	0.0131	–0.0131	0.0044	*
2	1.50	0.0262	0.0175	0.0349	0.0262	–0.0087	0.0087	*
3	2.25	0.0393	0.0349	0.0349	0.0393	–0.0044	–0.0044	*
4	3.00	0.0523	0.0523	0.0523	0.0523	0.0000	0.0000	0.0000

If we notate the wave table index as I.F, where I is its integer part and F is its fractional part, we see that for the truncation method, the maximum error that can occur will occur when F is equal to .999 . . . , because I.999 . . . would be treated the same as

I.0. The instantaneous truncation method error is therefore potentially as large as the greatest difference between any two adjacent wave table entries. For rounding, the maximum error that can occur will occur when F is equal to .5, because I.5 is treated the same as $(I + 1).0$. For the rounding method, then, the instantaneous error is potentially as large as *half* the greatest difference between any two adjacent table entries. The linear interpolation method is considerably more accurate than either rounding or truncation.

Because the rounding method introduces errors into the generated waveform that are potentially half as large as those introduced by truncation, we might be tempted to conclude that the rounding method should be used whenever possible. It is important to note, however, that for purposes of sound synthesis, the difference between the results yielded by the rounding and truncation table lookup methods affects only the phase of the resulting waveform. If we ignore this phase difference (as our ears are likely to), the truncation and rounding methods produce waveforms with equivalent purity of shape—the *audible* error will be the same for both.

Recent theoretical investigations (Hartmann, 1987) have shown that to a good approximation, the signal-to-error noise ratio for the rounding method may be written as

$$SN_e R_{rnd} \approx 20 \log L - 5 \quad \text{dB} \tag{3-14}$$

For example, if a sine wave table length L is 360 (as in Table 3-1), both the truncation and rounding methods will generate a waveform in which the error noise *sounds* about 46 dB below the signal level. If the table length is equal to 2^B (that is, if L is a power of 2), we may restate this relationship as

$$SN_e R_{rnd} \approx 6B - 5 \quad \text{dB} \tag{3-15}$$

In cases where phase errors cannot be ignored (for example, when the table lookup method is used for the mathematical evaluation of a sine function), the truncation method must be considered to have a performance about 6 dB worse than this:

$$SN_e R_{trunc} \approx 6B - 11 \quad \text{dB} \tag{3-16}$$

The corresponding figure for the linear interpolation (Moore, 1977/1985) is approximately

$$SN_e R_{interp} \approx 12(B - 1) \quad \text{dB} \tag{3-17}$$

We can conclude that for sound synthesis, we need only consider the truncation and interpolation methods. Table 3-2 shows several achievable signal-to-error noise ratios for all three methods.

3.1.7 The Table Lookup Oscillator Algorithm

Given these table lookup procedures for the efficient evaluation of sin θ, we can complete our oscillator by finding the relationship between θ and the frequency of the generated signal. Equation (3-12) makes it clear that the fundamental correspondence is between θ and *index*, in that having θ go from 0 to 2π corresponds to having *index* go

TABLE 3-2 Approximate signal-to-error noise ratios for truncation, rounding and interpolation table lookup methods as a function of wavetable length. For sound synthesis work, the figures for the rounding method ($SN_e R_{rnd}$) generally apply to both the rounding and truncation methods. All of these figures assume that wave table entries are specified to a precision sufficient to avoid quantization errors.

Wave Table Length	$SN_e R_{trunc}$ (dB)	$SN_e R_{rnd}$ (dB)	$SN_e R_{interp}$ (dB)
32	19	25	48
64	25	31	60
128	31	37	72
256	37	43	84
512	43	49	96
1,024	49	55	108
2,048	55	61	120
4,096	61	67	132
8,192	67	73	144
16,384	73	79	156
32,768	79	85	168
65,536	85	91	180

from 0 to L. We learned in Chapter 2 that to control the frequency of an oscillator in a time-varying manner, we need to control its *instantaneous frequency*. This allows the phase angle θ to be calculated as the sum of all instantaneous frequency values up to time n according to the recursive relation

$$\theta(n+1) = \theta(n) + \Delta\theta(n) \tag{3-18}$$

where $\Delta\theta(n)$ is the instantaneous radian frequency. $\theta(n)$ is the time-varying phase angle for a sinusoid

$$\theta(n) = \frac{2\pi f n}{R} + \phi \tag{3-19}$$

where f is the frequency, R is the sampling rate, and ϕ is the phase offset. For a given frequency, $\theta(n)$ will increase by $2\pi f/R$ each time n increases by 1. $2\pi f/R$ therefore *is* the instantaneous frequency. Using this information, it is possible to make an oscillator out of the recursive relation

$$y(n) = A(n) \sin[\theta(n)] \tag{3-20}$$

$$\theta(n+1) = \theta(n) + \Delta\theta(n)$$

where $y(n)$ is the output, $A(n)$ is a (possibly time-varying) amplitude value, $\sin[\theta(n)]$ is evaluated by the table lookup method described previously, and

$$\Delta\theta(n) = \frac{2\pi[\Delta f(n)]}{R} \tag{3-21}$$

where $\Delta f(n)$ is the instantaneous frequency at time n. To scale the instantaneous frequency value properly for the table lookup procedure, we must recast equation (3-12) in terms of instantaneous values, as follows:

$$\frac{\Delta\theta(n)}{2\pi} = \frac{\Delta index(n)}{L} \qquad (3\text{-}22)$$

Combining this result with equation (3-21) yields

$$\frac{\Delta\theta(n)}{2\pi} = \frac{2\pi[\Delta f(n)]/R}{2\pi} = \frac{\Delta f(n)}{R} = \frac{\Delta index(n)}{L} \qquad (3\text{-}23)$$

The appropriate increment to the index for the table lookup procedure is therefore L/R times the desired instantaneous frequency. That is,

$$y(n) = A(n)\text{table}[index(n)] \qquad (3\text{-}24)$$

$$index(n+1) = index(n) + \Delta index(n)$$

where

$$\Delta index(n) = [\Delta f(n)]\frac{L}{R} \qquad (3\text{-}25)$$

We must take appropriate care to limit $index(n)$ to the range $0 \le index(n) < L$ via modulus arithmetic and access the table according to the truncation, rounding, or interpolation method.

An alternative method of understanding the operation of the table lookup oscillator is to consider what happens when $\Delta index(n)$ is equal to 1. In this case, the modulus arithmetic simply causes the contents of the table values (scaled by the amplitude factor) to be output in sequence over and over again. Because the period of a waveform generated in this manner will be L samples, it is easily seen that the corresponding frequency will be R/L Hz; that is, we have the relationship

$$\Delta f(n) = \Delta index(n)\frac{R}{L} \qquad (3\text{-}26)$$

Solving this equation for $\Delta index(n)$ then yields equation (3-25).

The complete algorithm for the truncating table lookup oscillator may now be stated as follows:

$$y(n) = A(n)\,\text{table}[\lfloor S(n)\rfloor] \qquad (3\text{-}27)$$

$$S(n+1) = [S(n) + I(n)] \bmod L$$

where

$y(n)$	is the oscillator output signal
$A(n)$	is a time-varying peak amplitude value
table[ ]	is a waveform table of length L containing samples of exactly one period of any periodic waveform $f(\theta)$ with period 2π sampled at $\theta = 0, 2\pi/L, 4\pi/L, \ldots, (L-1)2\pi/L$

$S(n)$ is the table index value at time n (often called the oscillator sum location)

$\lfloor x \rfloor$ is the floor function, equal to the largest integer not larger than x

$I(n)$ is the increment to the table index value at time n, which controls the oscillator's (possibly time-varying) instantaneous frequency according to $I(n) = f(n)L/R$, where $f(n)$ is the frequency to be generated at time n, L is the table length, and R is the sampling rate

$a \bmod b$ is the generalized modulus operation, equal to $a - \left\lfloor \dfrac{a}{b} \right\rfloor b$.

It is necessary to use the generalized modulus operation rather than the standard modulus (wherein $a \bmod b$ is defined simply as the remainder of a divided by b) because the general procedure is well defined for both positive and negative values of a and b, whereas the standard procedure is not. This allows the oscillator to generate both positive and negative frequencies, the need for which will become evident when we examine sound synthesis techniques later on.

Figure 3-2 shows the flow diagram for the truncating table lookup oscillator. Such oscillators may be implemented quite efficiently in software and hardware to provide the basic waveform synthesis element for computer music synthesis. For example, the following C subprogram example, given current values for amplitude (amp), increment (incr), and a table index (index), along with an arbitrary waveform table (table) of length L, returns a single sample of oscillator output.

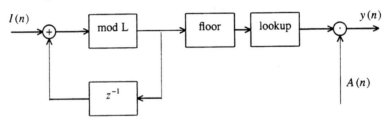

Figure 3-2 Flow diagram for a truncating table lookup oscillator. The lookup table contains L samples of one period of a periodic waveform. $A(n)$ is an arbitrary (time-varying) peak amplitude scale factor. $I(n)$ controls the frequency of output signal $y(n)$ according to $I(n) = f(n) L/R$, where $f(n)$ is the frequency to be generated at time n and R is the sampling rate.

```
float
osc( amp, incr, table, index, L )
 float amp, incr, table[], *index ;
 int L ;
{
    float output ;
    output = amp*table[ (int) *index ] ;
    *index += incr ;
    while ( *index >= L )
        *index -= L ;
```

```
   while ( *index < 0 )
       *index += L ;
   return( output ) ;
}
```

We could use this `osc` subprogram to generate a digital signal representing a steady sine wave at 440 Hz with a peak amplitude of 1 and a duration of 5.5 seconds at a sampling rate of 32,768 Hz by exercising it as shown in the following programming example.

```
#define L 4096
#define R 32768.0

main() {
 float index, table[L], osc() ;
 int i, duration ;
 double TWOPI = 8.*atan(1.) ;
/*
 * initialize table and signal duration
 */
    for ( i = 0 ; i < L ; i++ )
        table[i] = sin( TWOPI*i/L ) ;
    duration = R*5.5 ;
/*
 * generate signal
 */
    for ( index = i = 0 ; i < duration ; i++ )
        printf( "%f\n", osc( 1.0, 440.0*L/R, table, &index, L ) ) ;
}
```

3.1.8 Table Lookup Oscillator Applications

As before, it is convenient to define a single symbol for the oscillator that retains only essential information about its inputs and outputs. The most commonly used symbol for such oscillators in the computer music literature is the elongated half-circle, showing the amplitude and table index increment inputs at the top, and the signal output at the bottom.

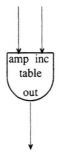

The interior of the oscillator symbol may contain either a notation defining its table contents or a simple graph of the waveform stored in the table:

Of course, there is nothing to restrict such an oscillator to the generation of sinusoidal waveforms. The only restriction on the waveform table is that it contain a single *period* of an arbitrary periodic waveform. It is also convenient to restrict the values in the wave table to lie within the range ±1 so that after multiplication by the amplitude input, the output is guaranteed to lie within the range ± amp.

If the waveform stored in the oscillator wave table contains multiple harmonics, we must of course use caution to make sure that none of these harmonics occur at frequencies that will cause foldover or aliasing. If the wave table contains a waveform consisting of just a fundamental plus a second harmonic, for example, the maximum fundamental frequency that we can specify without causing foldover will be one-fourth the sampling rate.

If we wish to produce the digital equivalent of a square waveform, for example, we must take into account the highest-frequency component in relation to the Nyquist rate in order to avoid aliasing. The following C code initializes the table for our oscillator to contain a waveform consisting of the first nine harmonics of a square waveform. Such a waveform is called a *band-limited* square waveform because the ideal square waveform contains an infinite number of frequency components. After the waveform components are summed into the table, the values in the table are divided by the maximum table entry in order to scale all table entries so that they lie within the range ±1.

```
/*
 * clear table
 */
for ( i = 0 ; i < L ; i++ )
    table[i] = 0. ;
```

```
/*
 * form bandlimited squarewave in table
 */
max = 0. ;
for ( h = 1 ; h <= 9 ; h += 2 )
    for ( i = 0 ; i < L ; i++ ) {
        table[i] += (1./h)*sin( TWOPI*h*i/L ) ;
        if ( fabs( (double) table[i] ) > max )
            max = table[i] ;
    }
/*
 * normalize table to +-1 range
 */
for ( i = 0 ; i < L ; i++ )
    table[i] /= max ;
```

After these statements are executed, the `table` array contains one period of a band-limited square wave containing harmonic energy at 1, 3, 5, 7 and 9 times the fundamental frequency (the square waveform contains only odd harmonics in sine phase). Even though it is evident from the C statements that the ninth harmonic has only 1/9 the amplitude of the fundamental, it is still quite strong relative to the fundamental frequency component (a factor of 9 in amplitude is roughly a factor of 19 dB). Thus, if this waveform is used in a table lookup oscillator with a fundamental frequency greater than $R/18$ Hz, audible foldover is likely to occur. Of course, this is much better performance than the case where the table contains a *non-band-limited* waveform, such as the one defined in the following C statement:

```
for ( i = 0 ; i < L ; i++ ) {
    table[i] = i < L/2 ? 1. : -1. ;
```

Because the waveform in the earlier programming example jumps abruptly from +1 to −1 in midcycle (and back again at the end of each cycle), it is easily seen to have a spectrum that does not stop at the Nyquist rate. Such a waveform would produce foldover at *any* fundamental frequency, although the amplitude of the aliased components may be small if the fundamental frequency is very low and the Nyquist rate is sufficiently high.

The output of the truncating table lookup oscillator may be used to generate control signals for other oscillators as well as basic waveforms. For example, we may use a table lookup oscillator to generate an amplitude envelope signal by defining an appropriate envelope shape and feeding the output of one oscillator into the amplitude input of another. Such an interconnection may be represented using the oscillator symbols as follows:

The output of one oscillator is used to supply the amplitude input of another. The graph in the upper oscillator is shown as a waveform that gradually rises from 0 to 1, then gradually falls from 1 to 0 at the end of the cycle. If we set the increment of the envelope oscillator to a value corresponding to a frequency $1/D$ Hz, where D is the desired duration of the digital signal in seconds, it will generate exactly one period of its waveform over a period of D seconds.

The following C program uses the `osc` subprogram defined earlier both to generate an amplitude envelope control function and to use this function to control the amplitude of a second oscillator producing a sinusoid at 220 Hz. The note duration is set to 1.5 seconds.

```
#define L 4096
#define R 32768.0

main() {
  float D, index1, index2, envtable[L], sintable[L], osc() ;
  int i ;
  double TWOPI = 8.*atan(1.) ;
/*
 * initialize tables
 * envtable contains trapezoidal envelope function
 * sintable contains sinewave
 */
    for ( i = 0 ; i < L ; i++ ) {
        if ( i < L/4 )
            envtable[i] = 4.*i/L ;
        else if ( i >= 3*L/4 )
```

```
            envtable[i] = 4.*(L - i)/L ;
        else envtable[i] = 1. ;
        sintable[i] = sin( TWOPI*i/L ) ;
    }
    D = 1.5 ;
/*
 * generate signal with envelope control
 */
    for ( index1 = index2 = i = 0 ; i < D*R ; i++ )
        printf( "%f\n",
            osc(
                osc( 1., (1./D)*L/R, envtable, &index1, L ),
                220.0*L/R,
                sintable,
                &index2,
                L
            )
        ) ;
}
```

In this programming example, we see that there are two wave tables, one to hold the amplitude envelope and one to hold the sine wave. The output of the oscillator producing the envelope control function is fed into the amplitude input of the oscillator producing the sine wave. The frequency of the envelope control oscillator is set to $1/D$, as explained. Each oscillator has its own wave table and index variable for keeping track of where it is in its own table from sample to sample. The separate variables for the sample index values allow the oscillator routine to be reentrant, that is, to execute multiple copies of itself "simultaneously."

The example demonstrates that the truncating table lookup oscillator can be a powerful tool for music synthesis. First, the basic oscillator algorithm itself is capable of generating an arbitrary periodic waveform at an arbitrary frequency (within the constraints of a digital signal) and an arbitrary amplitude. It would be a simple matter to introduce a phase offset by giving the index variable a nonzero initial value. Furthermore, the signals of such oscillators may be precisely controlled and combined in arbitrary ways. Oscillator outputs may be summed together, multiplied by each other to produce modulation effects, and used as control signals at arbitrarily low frequencies.

It would clearly be useful to have a means for manipulating signal generating and modifying subprograms such as truncating table lookup oscillators, adders, multipliers, delays, filters, and so on, in the form of conveniently interconnectable units. Such a system should also include some means for conveniently specifying the contents of wavetables in various ways and for specifying parameters to the subprograms each time they are needed to produce a waveform.

Such programs exist in many forms. The first such program to be generally distributed was called MUSIC V, written by Max V. Mathews and others (including myself) at AT&T Bell Laboratories in the late 1960s. MUSIC V was of course a descendant of MUSIC IV and was the progenitor many of its own descendants, including cmusic.

3.2 cmusic

I wrote the cmusic program in 1980 as part of the basic computer music software developed at the Computer Audio Research Laboratory (CARL), a computer music research project located at the University of California, San Diego, Center for Music Experiment and Related Research (CME). cmusic (it is always spelled with a small letter) is loosely based on the earlier MUSIC V program and is in many ways similar to other software music synthesis programs. cmusic is written in the C programming language and runs under Berkeley UNIX.[2]

The basic signal generating and processing elements in cmusic, such as truncating table lookup oscillators, adders, multipliers, and filters, are for historical reasons, called *unit generators*. Many cmusic unit generator subprograms have been written over the years, and the list is still growing.

The cmusic user specifies one or more computer instruments, each of which is composed of arbitrarily interconnected unit generators taken from the cmusic unit generator library. In addition to specifying putative instruments in this way, the cmusic user also specifies the contents of one or more tables containing waveforms, control functions, and so on. Once the "orchestra" (the collection of instruments to be used) and the associated wave tables are defined, the cmusic user then "plays notes" on these instruments, each of which consists of an arbitrary starting time and duration specification as well as a list of parameter values required by the instrument being played. Of course, the word *note* need not have the same meaning as it does in common practice music, because cmusic notes are generalized sonic events of arbitrary complexity. For example, one kind of cmusic note might synthesize a brasslike tone on middle C for 2.1 seconds, another may consist of a brief noise burst that simulates a consonant in some synthetic speech, a third may synthesize an entire phrase with variegated pitch and amplitude transitions between adjacent melodic elements, while a fourth may provide information for all sounding instruments on the auditory shape of a gradual increase in loudness (a *crescendo*). A note in cmusic is really just an arbitrary signal event that has a beginning and a duration.

Programs like cmusic are sometimes referred to as *acoustic compilers* because they essentially translate the acoustic specifications for a given set of sounds into a digital signal—possibly with multiple channels for stereophonic or quadraphonic effects—representing the waveform of the specified sounds. Because the computations involved are arbitrarily complicated and therefore arbitrarily time-consuming, programs such as cmusic do not run in real time, which would allow them to be played by live performers like traditional musical instruments. Once the input specification—called the user's *score*—is complete, cmusic simply computes the corresponding digital signal as quickly as possible, storing the waveform sample values in the bulk memory of the computer such as a disk or tape file. When the waveform output is complete, it may be

---

[2]cmusic is available as part of the CARL Software Distribution, which can be obtained for a nominal distribution fee from the Center for Music Experiment, University of California, San Diego, La Jolla, CA 92093.

transformed into sound by feeding it into a digital-to-analog conversion (DAC) system at the appropriate sampling rate. The resulting sound may then be audited directly over loudspeakers or headphones and/or recorded by analog or digital means for convenient transportation through space and time.

In addition to being able to generate sounds using artificial sources such as oscillators and critically stable filters, cmusic and similar programs can also process digital waveforms obtained from arbitrary sources. A digital waveform processed by cmusic may be the result of a previous cmusic computation, or it may be a digital recording of an arbitrary sound source at which a microphone has been pointed. Virtually any type of digital signal processing is possible with a program like cmusic because the unit generator library may be extended by the user. cmusic therefore represents a completely general musical instrument, one that can execute any known digital audio process on any type of sound. cmusic can be used to mix, edit, and rearrange digitized waveforms in arbitrarily complicated (or simple) ways. Its only real drawback is that it does not run in real time, which implies that all of its actions must be prespecified by the user, the results of which become audible only after the computations are complete.

The complete cmusic program is quite extensive and involved. A complete treatment of it, therefore, would go considerably beyond the scope of this book. Because you may have access to a similar but nonidentical acoustic compiler program, we will discuss cmusic only in general terms (see also Appendix D).

One of the principal values of acoustic compilers is that they provide a convenient framework for the discussion of computer music synthesis techniques. We will therefore develop this framework from the standpoint of using it as a descriptive language for musical sound synthesis and processing, leaving a comprehensive treatment of the specific details of cmusic to more specialized books.

3.2.1 cmusic Scores

To use cmusic, one prepares a file containing specifications of the sound to be produced. This input file—called the *score* in cmusic parlance—typically contains four major sections:

- An *initialization* section in which values for global parameters such as the sampling rate, and the number of channels, are specified
- An *instrument definition* section in which one or more instruments are defined in terms of interconnections of unit generators available from the unit generator library
- A *wave table definition* section in which one or more wave tables are defined for use as basic waveforms, control functions, and so on
- A *note list* section in which the defined instruments are played at certain times for certain durations throughout the synthesized composition, each note statement containing parameters according to the needs of the (user-defined) instrument that plays it

The cmusic program accepts the name of the score file as a UNIX command line argument (cmusic reads its standard input if no file is named) and produces the resulting digital signal on its standard output. This signal is usually piped to another program that stores the samples for later replay through a digital-to-analog conversion system in realtime. If its standard output is not piped to another program, cmusic simply lists the sample values of its output signal on the user's terminal.

3.2.2 Statements

cmusic scores contain a list of *statements*, each of which begins with a *command* and ends with a *semicolon* (;). Between the initial command and the final semicolon of each statement are a number of *fields*, each containing alphabetic and/or numeric expressions. Fields are separated from each other by *blanks* and/or *commas*; fields themselves, therefore, may not contain blank spaces.

3.2.3 Expressions

Whenever numeric information may be typed, cmusic accepts *expressions* containing numbers (with or without decimal points—all internal calculations are performed in floating point), and the usual assortment of + (plus), – (minus), * (times), and / (divide) operators. The caret symbol (^) is used for exponentiation. Exponentiation is normally done before multiplication and division, which are normally done before addition and subtraction. The order in which the operations is done may be altered with parentheses. For example, the expression

    2^(1/2)+1

stands for 1 plus the square root of 2.

In addition, cmusic recognizes a special set of *postoperators,* which are normally executed after all other operators. The Hz postoperator, for example, multiplies the expression of which it is a part by the current sampling rate divided by the current default wave table length. Thus the expression

    2+438Hz

stands for 440 Hz because the addition operation is done first (this action could be overridden with parentheses), and the result is converted into an increment value suitable for setting the frequency of a table lookup oscillator unit generator according to the prevailing default values for wave table length and sampling rate. Here are some other cmusic postoperators:

sec is exactly like Hz except that the value is treated as a duration in seconds instead of a frequency in hertz (3sec is equivalent to 1/3Hz);

K multiplies the expression by 1024

dB converts from a decibel scale referenced to 1 (the maximum cmusic amplitude)

Postoperators may be combined, allowing

```
1KHz
```

to stand for the oscillator increment corresponding to 1024 Hz.

3.2.4 Note Lists

cmusic note statements have the form

```
note <time> <instrument> <duration> <parameter_list> ;
```

where `<time>` stands for a numeric expression that specifies when the note is to begin
(in seconds), `<instrument>` is the (alphabetic) *name* of the instrument (previously
defined in the score) to be played, `<duration>` is the duration of the note event (in
seconds), and `<parameter_list>` is a list of numeric fields that specify parameter
values required by the selected instrument. The fields of this statement are numbered
p1 (the note command itself), p2 (the starting time), p3 (the instrument name), p4 (the
duration), p5 (the first parameter value on the `<parameter_list>`, and so on.
Numeric expressions in note statement fields may refer to the values of previously-
defined fields by using these names (for example, p10 may be set to p8/p9).[3]

The entire score is automatically passed through the C language preprocessor
before cmusic interprets it, allowing the user to use **#define** and **#include** statements exactly as in the C programming language. Score comments are enclosed
between braces ({ }) and may be nested.[4]

3.2.5 Instrument Definitions

cmusic instruments are defined in terms of unit generators, each of which represents a
digital signal processing or generating subprogram. The general form of a cmusic instrument definition is as follows:

```
instrument <time> <name> ;
    <unit_generator_statements>
end ;
```

where `<name>` is an arbitrary name supplied by the user for this instrument. Each unit
generator statement has a predefined name and parameter list that specifies how its inputs and outputs are to be interconnected with those of other unit generators, wave

---

[3]Forward references to note parameter values are allowed in cmusic but should be used with caution.
For example, if p10 is set to p11/p9, the resulting value will be computed from the most recent value to which
p11 was set (probably in the previous note statement) and the most recent value to which p9 was set (probably
in the current note statement).

[4]The C preprocessor also processes standard C comments, which are enclosed between /* and */ delim-
iters. C-style comments, however, may unfortunately *not* be nested. One must therefore exercise care when
using defined macro names inside cmusic comments because these are checked (by the C preprocessor) for the
proper number of arguments and so on.

tables, note statement parameters, and so on. The cmusic `osc` unit generator is a truncating table lookup oscillator. The general form of the `osc` unit generator statement is as follows:

```
osc output[b] amplitude[bvpn] increment[bvpn] table[fvpn] sum[dpv] ;
```

The meaning of the fields following the `osc` token is determined by their ordinal position. That is, the first field following the `osc` token determines how the oscillator's output is connected, the second field determines how the amplitude control input is connected, and so on (the sum location is the same as the table index described earlier). Enclosed in brackets ([ ]) after each field descriptor is a list of allowable field types. These field types have the following interpretations.

b An input-output *block* of the form *bN*, where *N* is an identifying integer (input-output blocks act like "patch cord" labels for tying outputs of one unit generator to inputs of others).

d A *dynamic variable* of the form *d* (or *dN*), which stands for a dynamically allocated memory location created by cmusic at the beginning of a note and initialized to 0. Such dynamic variables are useful for allocating space to hold intermediate computations that are needed by the unit generator but about which the user typically has no particular concern.

f A *function name* of the form *fN*, where *N* is an identifying integer, referring to wave table *N*.

n Any *numerical expression* that evaluates to a constant (in an instrument definition, the values of subsequent note statement parameters is not yet known, constant expressions may therefore not contain references to note parameters).

p A note *parameter* of the form *pN*, where *N* is an identifying integer (note parameters, as mentioned previously, refer to fields in a note statement that plays a cmusic instrument).

v A global *variable* of the form *vN*, where *N* is an identifying integer (global variables may be set to numeric values that can be referenced in various types of numeric expressions).

To attach a unit generator output to cmusic's output signal, a special unit generator called `out` is used. Its parameters are all inputs.

```
out input[bvpnd]*
```

The asterisk (*) indicates that a variable number of inputs may be supplied. In the case of the `out` unit generator, the number of inputs must be precisely equal to the number of output channels—in monophonic mode, only one input is used; in stereo, two inputs are used; and so on (the number of channels is set at the beginning of the score and is by default assumed to be 1). If two or more instruments play simultaneously into `out` unit generators, their signals will be added automatically to form the cmusic output signal.

p5   p6

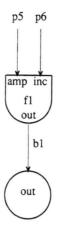

Figure 3-3   The instrument `toot`. `toot` consists of a single truncating table lookup oscillator unit generator (osc) feeding the cmusic output signal via the out unit generator. The output of the osc unit generator is connected to the input of the out unit generator via input-output block b1. The amplitude input to the oscillator is a number given by the fifth note parameter (p5) in a note statement that plays this instrument, and the increment input is given by p6. The wave table to which the oscillator refers is f1, which is defined elsewhere in the score (with a generate statement) typically to contain one cycle of a periodic waveform.

3.2.6 A Simple cmusic Score Example

We have now covered enough cmusic syntax to define and use a simple instrument. The following cmusic score defines and uses an instrument called `toot` consisting of a lone oscillator feeding the output signal. The `toot` instrument is described graphically in Figure 3-3. This instrument has only basic amplitude and increment controls. The amplitude values are given by note parameter p5, the increment values by note parameter p6. Wave table f1 is set to hold one period of a sine wave and is referenced by the `osc` unit generator in `toot`. After the instrument is defined and the wave table filled, the score specifies that exactly one note should be played for 1 second at an amplitude of one-half full scale and a frequency of A440.

```
instrument 0 toot ;              {begin definition at time 0 of toot}
    osc  b1 p5 p6 f1 d ;  {osc out=b1 amp=p5 inc=p6 table=f1 sum=d}
    out  b1 ;                             {out input=b1}
end ;                                     {end of toot}

generate 0 gen5 f1 1 1 0 ;       {fill wavetable f1 with sinewave}

note 0 toot 1 -6dB 440Hz ;             {p1=note p2=start at time 0
                                         p3=use toot p4=duration 1
                                      p5=amp is .5 p6 freq is 440 Hz}

terminate ;                              {end of score}
```

Because we have not specified any sampling rate, cmusic will use its default value of 16,384 (16K) samples per second. Monophonic output is also assumed. Note that the amplitude is specified in dB with respect to a reference value of 1.0, which represents the *largest* possible instantaneous amplitude value (just as 0 dB represents full scale on a recording level meter). The sixth field in the note statement (p6) is specified as 440Hz (recall that there may be no blank space within the field). The `Hz` postoperator multiplies the value 440 by the quantity 1024/16384, corresponding to the default wave table length divided by the default sampling rate. The resulting number is fed into the `osc` unit generator when the note is played as the table index increment.

3.2.7 Wave Table Generation

The general form of a wave table generation statement in cmusic is

```
generate <time> <gen_name> <table> <parameter_list> ;
```

This statement directs cmusic to execute a free-standing program named `<gen_name>` with a list of command line arguments given in the `<parameter_list>`, preceded by the argument $-LN$, where N is the wave table length. The referenced program may be a standard wave table generation program supplied with cmusic (such as `gen5`), or it may be supplied by the user. For example, the `generate` statement in the score example causes cmusic to execute the UNIX command

```
gen5 -L1024 1 1 0
```

because 1024 is the default wave table length. The `gen5` program must then return 1024 binary floating-point values via its standard output, which will be stored internally by cmusic under the wave table name `f1`.

     `gen5` is a wave table generating program that expects triplets of arguments, each of which refers to a harmonic number, an amplitude, and a phase offset (in radians) relative to sine phase. If more than one triplet is given in the `parameter_list`, the specified components are added together by `gen5`. Thus the command `gen5` `-L1024 1 1 0` specifies that the associated wave table is to contain 1024 samples of one period of a sine wave with unity amplitude. We could specify that wave table f1 is to contain a cosine waveform with the cmusic statement

```
generate 0 gen5 f1 1 1 90Deg ;
```

where the `Deg` postoperator translates a value in degrees into radians. We could also specify that f1 is to contain the first three components of a band-limited square waveform with the cmusic statement

```
generate 0 gen5 f1 1 1 0 3 1/3 0 5 1/5 0 ;
```

which cmusic translates into the UNIX command

```
gen5 -L1024 1 1 0 3 0.33333333 0 5 0.2 0
```

Notice that cmusic evaluates the expressions on behalf of the specified wave table generation program so that its arguments are purely numeric instead of expressions. `gen5` then returns precisely the wave table values specified by

$$y(n) = \sin\frac{2\pi n}{L} + \frac{1}{3}\sin\frac{2\pi 3n}{L} + \frac{1}{5}\sin\frac{2\pi 5n}{L} \qquad n = 0, 1, \ldots, 1023 \qquad (3\text{-}28)$$

Because this wave table would contain values that go outside of the range ± 1 (the normal maximum amplitude range for cmusic signals), the wave table would generally have to be normalized to lie within this range. A special cmusic wave table service routine called `gen0` may be used to normalize that maximum magnitude of any previously defined wave table to ±N with the cmusic statement

```
generate 0 gen0 f1 <N> ;
```

where `<N>` is usually set to 1.   `gen0` looks through the a predefined wave table, finds the largest entry, then divides every wave table entry by this value, which results in the largest possible entry of ±1. The entire wave table is then scaled by `<N>`.

As the name implies, `gen5` is but one of several wave table generators available in cmusic.   `gen5` generates sums of harmonically related sinusoids with arbitrary amplitudes and phase offsets. As we have seen, `gen0` normalizes any previously generated wave table to lie within a range ±N. We will have occasion to use these and other cmusic wave table generators in various ways as we go along. Keep in mind, however, that wave table generators are free-standing programs that can also be supplied by the user. Thus a programmer may specify wave tables for use by cmusic in completely arbitrary ways.

Suppose that you wish to specify only the harmonics of a waveform that are to be present and that they all are to have equal strength.[5] Suppose further that the you have written a program called `mygen` to generate such wave tables. The user's program can be invoked to fill wave table f1 with a statement such as

```
generate 0 mygen f1 1 2 3 5 7 ;
```

Assuming the default wave table length, this causes cmusic to execute the UNIX command

```
mygen -L1024 1 2 3 5 7 ;
```

A simple C program may be written to implement this wave table generator as follows:

```
#include <stdio.h>
#include <math.h>

main( argc, argv ) int argc ; char *argv[] ; {
 int L, n, k ;
 float y ;
 double TWOPI = 8.*atan(1.) ;
 /*
  * pick up wavetable length from first argument
  */
    L = atoi( argv[1]+2 ) ;
 /*
  * generate L values as binary floats to stdout
  */
    for ( n = 0 ; n < L ; n++ ) {
 /*
```

[5]The same task could be accomplished using the `gen5` program. This example is included only to show how such a program could be implemented.

```
  * each value is sum of specified equal strength harmonics
  */
        for ( y = 0, k = 2 ; k < argc ; k++ )
            y += sin ( TWOPI*atoi( argv[k] )*n/L ) ;
        fwrite( &y, sizeof( float ), 1, stdout ) ;
    }
 /*
  * normal termination
  */
    exit( 0 ) ;
}
```

Note the final call to exit(0), indicating normal program termination. Because the
wave table values generated by this program will not always lie within the range ±1, a
call to gen0 would usually follow the score statement invoking this particular wave
table generation program.

3.2.8 Amplitude Control

The basic cmusic truncating table lookup oscillator unit generator has two primary control inputs—one for control of the amplitude of the output waveform and one for control of its frequency. As discussed earlier, a general and useful way to control the amplitude of a waveform is simply to connect the output of one oscillator to the amplitude
input of another. The wave table referenced by the control oscillator may then be set to
any desired amplitude envelope shape.

The following example shows an instrument (called env) that implements this
type of amplitude envelope control. A graphical description of the env instrument is
shown in Figure 3-4.

```
set functionlength = 8K ;

instrument 0 env ;
    osc  b2 p6 p5 f2 d ;    {osc out=b2 amp=p6 inc=p5 table=f2 sum=d}
    osc  b1 b2 p7 f1 d ;    {osc out=b1 amp=b2 inc=p7 table=f1 sum=d}
    out  b1 ;                                    {out input=b1}
end ;

generate 0 gen5 f1 1 1 0 ;          {fill wavetable f1 with sinewave}
generate 0 gen4 f2 0,0 -1 .1,1 0 .8,.5 -1 1,0 ;   {fill wavetable f2
                                        with amplitude envelope}

note 0 toot 1 p4sec -6dB 440Hz ;          {p1=note p2=start at time 0
        p3=use env p4=duration 1 p5=p4sec=(1/p4)Hz p6=peak amplitude
                                                    p7=frequency}

terminate ;                                        {end of score}
```

The first statement of this example sets the wave table function length to 8192.
This value becomes the default length of all wave tables used in this score.

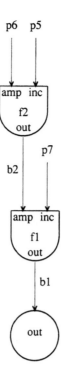

Figure 3-4   The instrument env. The output of one oscillator is used to control the amplitude of another via input-block b2. The peak amplitude of the note will be set by p6; the note frequency will be determined by p7. p5 is used to control the frequency of the oscillator generating the amplitude control function—it will normally be set to p4sec, equivalent to (1/p4) Hz. Because in a note statement p4 always specifies the note duration in seconds, this value will cause the control oscillator to generate exactly one period of its waveform over a duration of p4 seconds.

The only thing really new about this example is the type of specification used for wave table f2. A new wave table generation program named gen4 is invoked to fill f2 with an appropriate amplitude envelope control function. gen4 is a standard cmusic wave table generation program that accepts an arbitrary number of point specifications, each of which specifies a single point along the control function. The specified points are connected according to *transition parameters* specified between each point. In our score example, the user has specified that the four points (0, 0), (0.1, 1), (0.8, 0.5), and (1, 0) are to be used for the basic shape of the amplitude envelope control function. Each number pair consists of a relative horizontal position (starting from 0 and running to an arbitrary maximum value—in this case 1) and a vertical value. The transition parameter used between the first and last two points is –1; between the middle two points the transition parameter is given as –4. Thus the entire parameter list for the gen4 example in the cmusic score is interpreted as follows:

$\dfrac{0}{0}$	First point is (0, 0).
–1	Transition parameter
$\dfrac{0.1}{1}$	Second point is (0.1, 1).
–4	Transition parameter
$\dfrac{0.8}{0.5}$	Third point is (0.8, 0.5)
–1	Transition parameter
$\dfrac{1}{0}$	Last point is (1, 0).

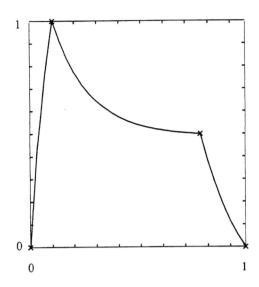

Figure 3-5   Graph of a cmusic gen4 wave table function. Four breakpoints were used to specify this function (each marked x's): (0,0), (0.1,1), (0.8, 0.5) and (1,0). Transition parameters specify the types of curves used to connect these points.

A graph of the wave table specified by this parameter list is shown in Figure 3-5.

gen4 allows an arbitrary number of points with intervening transition parameters to be specified. The exact interpolation used by gen4 between points $P_1 = (x_1, y_1)$ and $P_2 = (x_2, y_2)$ is

$$f(x) = y1 + (y2 - y1)\frac{1 - e^{I(x)\alpha}}{1 - e^{\alpha}} \qquad x_1 \leq x \leq x_2 \qquad (3\text{-}29)$$

where α is the transition parameter between P_1 and P_2 and $I(x)$ is a value that goes from 0 to 1 as x goes from x_1 to x_2 according to

$$I(x) = \frac{x - x_1}{x_2 - x_1} \qquad (3\text{-}30)$$

The value of transition parameter α determines the kind of curve used to connect the successive points (see Figures 3-6 and 3-7).

- If $\alpha = 0$, a *straight line* is used.
- If $\alpha < 0$, an *exponential curve* is used, where the magnitude of the transition parameter ($|\alpha|$) determines how many exponential time constants occur between the two endpoints of the curve.
- If $\alpha > 0$, an *inverse exponential curve* is used, where $|\alpha|$ determines how many exponential time constants occur between the endpoints of the curve.

All these curves transit from precise starting to ending values. An exponential curve approaches its ending value more rapidly than a straight line would, while an inverse exponential curve stays near its starting value longer than a straight line would. Such transitions between successive pairs of points are often useful for the specification

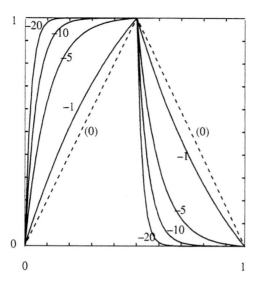

Figure 3-6   Exponential gen4 curves resulting from negative transition parameter values. This graph compares both positive-going [from (0, 0) to (0.5, 1)] and negative-going [from (0.5, 1) to (1, 0)] curves generated by setting α (the gen4 transition parameter) to 0 (dashed lines), –1, –5, –10, and –20. Note that as the magnitude of α is increased, such exponential curves approach their final values more rapidly.

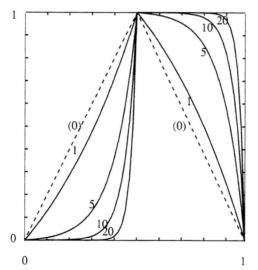

Figure 3-7   Inverse exponential gen4 curves resulting from positive transition parameter values. This graph compares both positive-going [from (0, 0) to (0.5, 1)] and negative-going [from (0.5, 1) to (1, 0)] curves generated by setting α (the gen4 transition parameter) to 0 (dashed lines), +1, +5, +10, and +20. Note that as the magnitude of α is increased, such inverse exponential curves remain near their initial values for more of the transition intervals.

of amplitude envelope curves, because many transitions occurring in nature are exponential or close to it.

3.2.9 Amplitude Modulation

As discussed in Chapter 2, whenever two waveforms are multiplied, the result has a spectrum equal to the convolution of the spectra of the two waveforms taken separately. The effect of multiplying a waveform by an amplitude envelope is therefore identical in all respects to the process of windowing, which results in a waveform whose spectrum is the convolution of the spectrum of the window (the amplitude envelope) with the spectrum of the windowed waveform.

The output signal of the `env` instrument defined in the previous cmusic score example may therefore be written as

$$y(n) = w(n)x(n) \qquad (3\text{-}31)$$

where $w(n)$ is the output of the control oscillator and $x(n)$ is the output of the controlled oscillator. $w(n)$ is a waveform with an arbitrary shape determined by f2, a peak amplitude determined by p6, and a frequency (duration) determined by p5. $x(n)$ is also a waveform with an arbitrary shape determined by f1, a (time varying) peak amplitude determined by $w(n)$, and a frequency determined by p7. If the amplitude control waveform $w(n)$ varies very slowly compared with the carrier waveform $x(n)$, then all of the frequency components in the spectrum of $w(n)$ will be at relatively low frequencies compared with those in the spectrum of $x(n)$. The convolution of the two spectra will therefore be very similar to the spectrum of $x(n)$ itself, because each component of the latter spectrum would be replaced by a shifted, scaled copy of the spectrum of $w(n)$.

We may interpret this waveform multiplication process in a slightly different way if the components of the spectrum of $w(n)$ are on the same order of magnitude as those in the spectrum of $x(n)$. For example, there is nothing to prevent us from setting wave table f2 to a sinusoid and setting p5 to a frequency in the audible range. In this case, it is clear that the result is simply the product of two sinusoids. If we shift and scale a copy of either spectrum around the components of the other, we find that the result of multiplying one sinusoid by another is a signal that contains frequency components at their sum and difference frequencies. The waveform multiplication process is clearly nonlinear, because frequencies are "coming out" that are not "going in," and is generally referred to as *amplitude modulation*, or simply *AM*.

In the analog signal realm, a simple gain element such as a voltage-controlled amplifier effectively multiplies a signal by a value G. A simple attenuator such as a volume control typically restricts the value of G to the range $0 \leq G \leq 1$. In the case of an analog amplifier, G may be either positive or negative and may also be greater than 1. If we wish to form the product of two analog waveforms, however, it is necessary to take into account the fact that either signal may be either positive or negative at any given instant in time, and the multiplication circuit must follow the usual rules of algebra wherein the result of multiplying two values of like sign (either both positive or both negative) is positive while the result must be negative if the multiplied values have unlike signs. An analog circuit that accomplishes such so-called *four-quadrant multiplication* (after the four possible sign combinations of two input signals) is called a *ring modulator*.

In the digital realm, almost every multiplication circuit is built in such a way that four-quadrant multiplication is automatic.[6] A typical digital multiplier is therefore

---

[6] It is possible to build digital multipliers in which either or both of the input values are restricted to positive numbers. Unlike the analog case, however, such digital multipliers are nearly as complicated as four-quadrant multipliers and are used only in very special circumstances.

entirely equivalent to an analog ring modulator because it can perform amplitude modulation just as easily as enveloping.

The processes of amplitude enveloping and amplitude modulation may be combined. Thus if $x_1(n)$ is a signal waveform that we wish to modulate with another signal waveform $x_2(n)$, with the result controlled by the amplitude envelope function $w(n)$, we have only to form the product

$$y(n) = w(n)x_1(n)x_2(n) \qquad (3\text{-}32)$$

A cmusic instrument suitable for implementing such a process is shown in Figure 3-8. Notice that it makes no difference which oscillator is used for envelope control or for either signal waveform because the terms in equation (3-32) may be multiplied in any order.

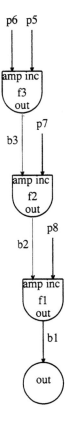

Figure 3-8   A cmusic instrument capable of combining amplitude envelope control with amplitude modulation.

3.2.10 Tremolo

The basic instrument shown in Figure 3-8 may also be used to implement a musical *tremolo*, defined to mean a periodic or nearly periodic variation in the loudness of a musical sound. A vibraphone, for example, consists of metal bars suspended over tuned resonating tubes inside of which are rotating disks that alternately close off and open the tubes at a rate controlled by a variable-speed electric motor. The loudness of the vibraphone therefore waxes and wanes according to how fast the disks are turning. The amount of loudness variation is fixed in the case of the vibraphone; only its rate (frequency) may be altered by the vibraphonist (who may, of course, turn the motor off altogether).

One way to synthesize such a *tremolo* effect would be to set f1 in the instrument shown in Figure 3-8 to a sinusoidal waveform for use as a carrier (a main, audible waveform), f2 to a tremolo control waveform, and f3 to an overall amplitude envelope for the note. We have seen that the cmusic score statement

```
generate 0 gen5 f1 1 1 0 ;
```

will store a sine wave in wave table f1. For synthesizing a vibraphonelike tone, we can specify an amplitude control envelope in wave table f3 consisting of a sharp attack followed immediately by an exponential decay with the statement

```
generate 0 gen4 f3 0,0 -10 .01,1 -2 1,0 ;
```

To provide the tremolo, we can use a waveform consisting of a sinusoidal variation above and below the midpoint value 1. If the waveform consists of values in the range 1±0.1, multiplying it by the other amplitude control functions will result in an amplitude variation of ±10 percent above and below the mean amplitude. But this amount of amplitude variation would result in a loudness level fluctuation of only $20 \log (1.1/0.9) \approx 1.74$ dB, which would be barely audible.

cmusic allows us to specify anything we like in terms of decibels with respect to the reference value 1. Therefore, we could approximate the amplitude of the sinusoidal variation above and below 1 directly in decibels by using the cmusic dB postoperator, as follows:

```
generate 0 gen5 f2    0 1 90Deg    1 (3dB)-1 0 ;
```

The first triplet in the parameter list specifies a harmonic number of 0, an amplitude of 1, and a phase offset of 90°—equivalent to $1 \cos 0$, or a constant 1. The second triplet specifies a harmonic number of 1, an amplitude of 3 dB–1, and a phase offset of 0—equivalent to one period of a sine wave with a peak amplitude of about 0.414. The waveform in f2 will therefore vary between about 1.414 and $1 - 0.414 = 0.586$ for a total amplitude variation of about $20 \log (1.414/0.586) \approx 7.7$ dB, which would be quite audible. If we wish to specify the exact total variation V directly in decibels, we have only to solve the relationship

$$V = 20 \log \frac{1+a}{1-a} \quad \text{dB} \tag{3-33}$$

for a, yielding

$$a = \frac{10^{V/20} - 1}{10^{V/20} + 1} \tag{3-34}$$

A total amplitude variation of 4 dB may then be specified directly by making use of the cmusic macro preprocessor, as follows:

```
#define VdB(V) (10^(V/20)-1)/(10^(V/20)+1)
generate 0 gen5 f2    0 1 90Deg    1 VdB(4) 0 ;
```

For a total amplitude variation of 4 dB, equation (3-34) (or the VdB macro) shows that a *tremolo* control in the approximate range 1 ± 0.226 is required.

Having now defined f1, f2, and f3, we have only to set note parameters p5 through p8 in order to play notes on our tremolo instrument. p8 will determine the main frequency of the note because it controls the increment for the oscillator referencing f1 (the sine wave). p7 will determine the tremolo rate because it controls the increment input to the oscillator referencing f2 (the tremolo control function). p5 will normally be set to p4sec or (1/p4)Hz because it controls the increment to the oscillator referencing f3 (the amplitude envelope control function). Note, however, that while p6 controls the peak value of the amplitude envelope control function, the maximum possible amplitude will be the product of this value and the maximum value generated by the tremolo control function. If, as in cmusic, we must take care not to generate an overall output amplitude greater in magnitude than 1, we can prevent possible overflows by dividing the p6 value by $1 + a$, which is easily accomplished by using our VdB macro.

The following is a complete cmusic score that defines the instrument described graphically in Figure 3-8, generates the wave tables described, and plays a brief musical phrase.

```
#include <carl/cmusic.h>

ins 0 vibes ;
    osc b3 p6 p5 f3 d ;
    osc b2 b3 p7 f2 d ;
    osc b1 b2 p8 f1 d ;
    out b1 ;
end ;

#define VdB(V) (10^(V/20)-1)/(10^(V/20)+1)

SINE(f1) ;
GEN5(f2)    0 1 90Deg    1 VdB(4) 0 ;
GEN4(f3) 0,0 -10 .01,1 -2 1,0 ;

{ p1  p2     p3    p4  p5           p6                     p7  p8 }
note  0    vibes  1  p4sec (-18dB)/(1+VdB(4))  4Hz A(0)   ;
note  0    vibes  1  p4sec (-18dB)/(1+VdB(4))  4Hz C(0)   ;
note  .75  vibes  1  p4sec (-18dB)/(1+VdB(4))  4Hz Bf(0)  ;
note  1    vibes  2  p4sec (-18dB)/(1+VdB(4))  4Hz B(0)   ;
note  1    vibes  2  p4sec (-18dB)/(1+VdB(4))  4Hz Ds(0)  ;

ter ;
```

This example introduces a few new features of the cmusic score language. The first line of the score incorporates a standard set of macro definitions available to all cmusic users (the precise name of this file may vary from installation to installation). The `cmusic.h` file contains macro definitions for many commonly useful cmusic score idioms. `SINE(x)` is defined, for example, so that it will set wave table `x` to a standard, normalized sine waveform. Similarly, `GEN5(x)` is defined so that wave table `x` will be set up by cmusic function generator `gen5`—only the definition need be stated, which in this case consists of a constant 1 (that is, a cosine waveform with amplitude 1 at 0 Hz) plus one period of a waveform in sine phase with an amplitude given by `VdB(4)`. The `GEN4` statement similarly sets up an amplitude envelope with a very rapid exponential attack (less than 1 percent of the note duration) and an immediate gradual exponential decay to zero.

In the note list, starting times are given by the second note parameter (p2), and note durations are given by the fourth note parameter (p4), as before. p5 is uniformly set to `p4sec`, causing one period of the amplitude envelope to be generated over the duration of each note. p6, the main note amplitude, is set as explained before, and the tremolo rate (frequency) is set to `4 Hz` in p7.

The pitches of the notes are given in note parameter p8 in terms of macros defined on file `cmusic.h` that allow convenient standard 12-tone pitch class name notation. In cmusic notation, `C(0)` stands for the frequency associated with middle C on the piano tuned with reference to A440, `Cs(0)` stands for C-sharp one half step above middle C, `Df(0)` stands for D-flat one half step above middle C, and so on. The number in parentheses gives the octave, with 0 referring to the octave from middle C up to B-natural, –1 referring to one octave lower, 1 one octave higher, and so on.[7] Straightforward modifications of these macro definitions allow an entire cmusic score to be transposed up or down in pitch by changing the reference pitch from 440 Hz to an arbitrary value. We might also easily specify a pitch one quarter tone above middle C with the notation `C(0)*2^(1/24)`, for example.

We could make the note list notation more compact by defining an appropriate macro. For example, the definition

```
#define VIBES(t,d,p)note t vibes d p4sec (-18dB)/(1+VdB(4)) 4Hz p
```

would allow the identical note list to be written in the form

```
VIBES(0,1,A(0)) ;
VIBES(0,1,C(0)) ;
VIBES(.75,1,Bf(0)) ;
VIBES(1,2,B(0)) ;
VIBES(1,2,Ds(0)) ;
```

The equivalent common-practice musical notation for this phrase might be written as follows:

---

[7]Note that cmusic pitch class notation differs from that used in the standard acoustics literature, which usually defines middle C as `c4`. This is done because pitch classes in cmusic are not limited to the range of the piano keyboard.

(vibes)   ♩ = 60 M.M.

mf (motor on)

3.2.11 Frequency Control

Just as the amplitude of the table lookup oscillator unit generator may be controlled with the output of another unit generator, its frequency may be similarly controlled. Time-varying frequency control is useful in the production of pitch glides such as *portamenti*, pitch inflections such as starting note with a slightly flat pitch, converging to and perhaps overshooting the main pitch, and pitch drop-offs at the end of the note. Pitch trajectories are often needed to connect one note to another smoothly within a musical phrase or to produce pitch ornamentations such as trills, mordents, and grace notes. Finally, time-varying pitch control is needed to produce *vibrato* and other frequency modulation effects.

Despite its extreme importance, time-varying frequency control of a cmusic oscillator unit generator is quite straightforward. The two basic cases are direct frequency control and basic frequency modulation.

In direct frequency control, the frequency input of the oscillator is connected to another unit generator that provides the time-varying frequency control signal. Figure 3-9 shows a simple example of one oscillator controlling the frequency of another. In this case, wave table f2 is scanned at a rate determined by p5, which is typically set to p4sec so that the duration of f2 matches the note duration. f2 is also scaled (multiplied) by p6. Because the p6 value is multiplied by f2 by the oscillator, we may think of p6 as a transposition factor to be applied to frequency control wave table f2—setting p6 to $\sqrt{2}$ would transpose the frequencies specified by f2 up a tritone, for example.

f2 must be specified in terms of the appropriate oscillator increment values to produce the desired frequencies. For example, if f2 is defined as

```
GEN4(f2) 0,440Hz 0 1,880Hz ;
```

the resulting waveform will have a frequency that moves up one octave in a straight line. The note statement

```
note 0 ins 3.5 p4sec 0.5 -20dB ;
```

would cause this transition to occur over a duration of 3.5 seconds at an amplitude of −20 dB with respect to 1, corresponding to a peak linear amplitude value of 0.1; the value given for p6 would cause the portamento to occur between A220 and A440.

Be aware that such a linear change in note frequency over the duration of a note will not be heard as linear in pitch because perceived pitch is related to the logarithm of frequency. Table 3-3 shows the approximate times at which chromatic pitches in the

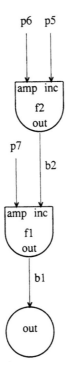

Figure 3-9   Direct time-varying frequency control. In this instrument, the output of one oscillator is used to control the frequency of another via input-output block b2. p5 determines the rate at which frequency control function f2 is scanned and is typically set to `p4sec`. p6 is multiplied by the frequency control function— setting it to 1 will render the control function without change, setting it to 2 will transpose the control function up one octave, and so on. The amplitude of the output signal is set by p7.

tempered scale would occur for a linear frequency change of one octave upward over a duration of 1 second. The table is couched in terms of a change from A440 to A880, but the time values shown apply equally well to any one-octave change. Note that only 59 milliseconds is required to traverse the first semitone (from A to A#), whereas about 112 milliseconds is required to traverse the final semitone (from G# to A). Exactly halfway through the portamento, the frequency would correspond to a pitch that is a *just perfect fifth* above the starting pitch—the tempered perfect fifth, being slightly flatter than a just perfect fifth, occurs slightly before the halfway point in time. Observing the times given in Table 3-3 lends insight into how the portamento will sound: it will rise more rapidly in pitch at the beginning than at the end.

We can use the `gen4` transition parameter value to specify frequency transitions different from straight lines. For example, if we wish to create a portamento that is linear in pitch rather than frequency, we need a transition curve that will require an equal amount of time to traverse each semitone. Equivalently, we could think of a linear-pitch portamento as one that requires a set amount of time to traverse any pitch interval. If we can find a `gen4` transition parameter value that requires 0.5 second to traverse the first tritone of the octave, it will also require 0.5 second to traverse the second tritone as well, yielding a linear-pitch portamento over its entire duration.

To find the required transition parameter, we have only to set the `gen4` transition curve equation to a required value and solve it for α. In other words, to obtain the transition parameter value that will cause the frequency to be a tritone above A440 half the way through the transition from A440 to A880, we must solve

TABLE 3-3 Time at which tempered pitches occur
during a linear frequency change of one octave over
a duration of 1 second.

Approximate Time of Occurrence	Frequency	Tempered Pitch Class Name
0.000	440.00	A
0.059	466.16	A#
0.122	493.88	B
0.189	523.25	C
0.260	554.37	C#
0.335	587.33	D
0.414	622.25	D#
0.498	659.26	E
(0.500)	(660.00)	(just perfect fifth)
0.587	698.46	F
0.682	739.99	F#
0.782	783.99	G
0.888	830.61	G#
1.000	880.00	A

$$f(x) = y1 + (y2 - y1)\frac{1 - e^{I(x)\alpha}}{1 - e^{\alpha}} \tag{3-35}$$

for α with $f(x)$ set to $440\sqrt{2}$ (the exact frequency of the pitch a tempered tritone above A440), $y1$ set to 440, $y2$ set to 880, and $I(x)$ set to 0.5. Unfortunately, equation (3-35) is a transcendental equation that cannot be solved by ordinary algebra! Without resorting to higher mathematics, however, we can guess various values for α and check the result either mathematically or with a computer program. With some luck, we can guess that the proper value of α is $\ln(y2/y1)$, where ln is the logarithm to the base e, which can be verified as follows. We first rearrange equation (3-35) like this:

$$\frac{f(x) - y1}{y2 - y1} = \frac{1 - e^{I(x)\alpha}}{1 - e^{\alpha}} \tag{3-36}$$

Substituting the required values into this relationship yields

$$\frac{440\sqrt{2} - 440}{880 - 440} = \frac{1 - e^{0.5 \ln\frac{880}{440}}}{1 - e^{\ln\frac{880}{440}}} \tag{3-37}$$

Factoring out 440 from the left side and dividing 880 by 440 on the right yields

$$\frac{440(\sqrt{2} - 1)}{440(2 - 1)} = \frac{1 - e^{\ln\sqrt{2}}}{1 - e^{\ln 2}} \tag{3-38}$$

Canceling the 440 factor and using the identity $e^{\ln q} = q$, we obtain

$$\frac{\sqrt{2} - 1}{1} = \frac{1 - \sqrt{2}}{-1} \tag{3-39}$$

$$\sqrt{2} - 1 = \sqrt{2} - 1 \tag{3-40}$$

which verifies that halfway through an octave transition, the frequency will be a tempered tritone above the beginning pitch if α is set to ln2.

TABLE 3-4 Time at which tempered pitches occur during a logarithmic frequency change of one octave over a duration of 1 second. These values were obtained by setting α to ln (880/440) in the `gen4` interpolation formula.

Exact Time of Occurrence	Frequency	Tempered Pitch Class Name
0	440.00	A
1/12	466.16	A#
2/12	493.88	B
3/12	523.25	C
4/12	554.37	C#
5/12	587.33	D
6/12	622.25	D#
7/12	659.26	E
8/12	698.46	F
9/12	739.99	F#
10/12	783.99	G
11/12	830.61	G#
1	880.00	A

If we change the definition of f2 to read as

```
GEN4(f2) 0,440Hz ln(880/440) 1,880Hz ;
```

and synthesize our portamento with the note statement

```
note 0 ins 1 p4sec 1 -20dB ;
```

the times at which the chromatic tempered scale pitches will be reached are given in Table 3-4. If we changed the duration of our note to 12 seconds, we would obtain a linear-pitch portamento that increases in frequency at the precise rate of one semitone per second. Cogitation over the mathematical verification allows us to conclude that the `gen4` transition parameter value $ln(end/start)$, where *end* is the final frequency and *start* is the starting frequency, will *always* yield a linear-pitch transition from frequency *start* to *end* that may be scaled to any duration. `gen4` transition parameters allow us to create pitch glides in terms of pitch intervals per unit time. For example, the definition and note statement

```
GEN4(f2) 0,G(-1) ln((C(-1))/(G(-1))) 1,C(-1) ;
```

```
note 0 ins 3.5 p4sec 1 -20dB ;
```

will create a linear-pitch transition from the G below middle C to the C below middle C at a rate of one semitone per half second, and the statements

```
GEN4(f2) 0,F(0) ln((G(0))/(F(0))) 1,G(0) ;

note 0 ins 6 p4sec 1 -20dB ;
```

would create a linear-pitch transition from F to G above middle C at the rate of one-third tone per second.

A pitch or frequency transition need not move at a uniform rate. A typical musical portamento from F to G would typically consist of a steady F pitch for a while, followed by the transition, followed by a steady pitch on G—otherwise, the beginning and ending pitches would not have time to become established in the ear of the listener. We could use direct frequency control to create such a transition with the following definitions:

```
GEN4(f2) 0,F(0) 0 .8,F(0) ln((G(0))/(F(0))) 1.1,G(0) 0 2,G(0) ;

note 0 ins 2 p4sec 1 -20dB ;
```

The result would be a sound that lasts for a total of 2 seconds. For the first 0.8 seconds, the pitch would be steady on F above middle C; for the next 0.3 seconds, the pitch would move linearly up a whole tone, then remain on G. This example exploits the arbitrary abscissa scale in the function definition to make the abscissa values in the function definition match the actual time values.

Pitch contours of arbitrary complexity can be built up merely by specifying more detail in the definition of wave table f2. In a practical instrument, however, pitch or frequency control would very likely be combined with amplitude envelope control in order to avoid clicks at the beginnings and ends of notes and to impart a musical dynamic contour as well as a pitch contour to the synthesized sound.

Some subtle issues are involved in such control, however. One is that in many musical contexts, no two pitch contours are likely to be the same. Furthermore, a long musical phrase might consist of dozens or even hundreds of transitions. We could define many wave tables with the requisite contours, but two extensions to the technique of direct frequency control are so often useful that they must be considered essential tools. One is waveform linking. The other is the direct generation of control functions that are not stored in wave tables. We shall discuss each in turn.

3.2.12 Waveform Linking

The dynamic (d) variable used to store the sum-of-increments value in the table lookup oscillator unit generator is automatically allocated and initialized to a zero value at the beginning of each note (this is how cmusic allows many notes to be played simultaneously on a single instrument). This is generally necessary to ensure that the waveform produced by the oscillator starts from the beginning of the wave table at the beginning of the note. It also implies that two notes may not be spliced "seamlessly"

without regard to the sum value, because resetting the sum to zero at the beginning of
each note is likely to produce a click in the resulting waveform. Instruments using oscillators with dynamic sum variables must therefore use amplitude envelopes that start
and end at zero in order to avoid such clicks. Such dynamic variables are allocated
(dynamically) by cmusic at the beginning of each note and are discarded (forgotten) at
the end of each note.

By using a static (v) variable for an oscillator sum location, however, we can
cause cmusic effectively to remember where it was scanning the wave table at the end
of one note. This position can then be saved for the next note played on the same instrument, allowing the waveform of the second note to start where the previous one left
off, thus avoiding a click. The disadvantage of this technique is that only one note may
be played at a time on such an instrument, because two sum values cannot be stored
simultaneously in the same static variable.

Using linked waveforms, we can, for example, separate the pitch transitions
between notes from the steady pitch portion of a melodic line. For example, in our example, the pitch of a single note started on F and remained there for 0.8 second, moved
from F to G over a duration of 0.3 second, then remained on G for 0.9 second. The
same result performed with linked waveforms is demonstrated in the following cmusic
score.

```
#include <carl/cmusic.h>

ins 0 port ;
    osc b3 p7 p5 p9 d ;   {amp control osc uses dynamic sum variable}
    osc b2 p6 p5 p8 d ;   {freq control osc uses dynamic sum variable}
    osc b1 b3 b2 f1 v1 ;          {main osc uses static sum variable}
    out b1 ;
end ;

SINE(f1) ;                                {main output waveform}
GEN4(f2) 0,1 0 1,1 ;       {wavetable containing constant unit value}
GEN4(f3) 0,1 ln(2^(2/12)) 1,2^(2/12) ;       {wholetone up portamento}
GEN4(f4) 0,0 -1 .1,1 0 1,1 ;                        {attack segment}
GEN4(f7) 0,1 0 .9,1 -1 1,0 ;                         {decay segment}

{
    in the following three notes the waveform at the end of each
    note is linked to the beginning of the following note through
    the use of static variable v1 for the sum location in the main
    output oscillator of instrument port
}
{p1   p2    p3    p4     p5     p6     p7    p8 p9}
note 0.0 port 0.8 p4sec F(0) -10dB 2 4 ;               {steady pitch}
note 0.8 port 0.3 p4sec F(0) -10dB 3 2 ;                {portamento}
note 1.1 port 0.9 p4sec G(0) -10dB 2 5 ;               {steady pitch}

ter ;
```

The instrument `port` is defined to include both amplitude and frequency control. The first note selects wave table f2 for frequency control and f4 for amplitude control (via note parameters p8 and p9, respectively). f2 is defined as a steady unit value—this value is scaled by p6, which is set to `F(0)`, resulting in a steady pitch. f4 is defined as an exponential amplitude rise from 0 to 1 over the first 10 percent of the note duration (0.8 second) and is scaled by p7 so that the maximum amplitude value is −10 dB.

The second note begins immediately when the first note stops. The instantaneous waveform value at the end of the first note depends on where wave table f1 (a sine wave) was being scanned at that moment—this value is stored in static variable v1. The value of v1 is retained (that is, it is not discarded) when the first note stops, allowing the second note to continue scanning wave table f1 at the place where the first note left off. The second note statement specifies f3 for frequency control and f2 (!) for amplitude control. f3 is defined as a normalized linear pitch transition up one whole tone; that is, it starts at a value of 1 (which will be scaled by the desired frequency) and ends with a value two semitones higher, or $2^{2/12} \approx 1.122$. The pitch control function is again scaled by p6, which is set to `F(0)`, so the portamento will start at F and proceed up to G over a duration of 0.3 second. The amplitude control function is again scaled by p7, which causes it to maintain a steady value of −10 dB over the duration of the note.

The third note starts when the second note is finished, again linking the output waveform via the sum value stored in static variable v1. Wave table f2 is specified to provide a steady pitch, because it is scaled by p6, this pitch will be `G(0)`. Wave table f5 is specified to provide an exponential drop in amplitude from its maximum value; this drop begins 90 percent of the way through the duration of the note (0.9 second). The values in this wave table are again scaled by p7, so the drop actually occurs from −10 dB to zero.

Note that f2 is used to provide both a steady frequency value and a steady amplitude value. It is scaled by the appropriate factor in each case.

3.2.13 Direct Control Function Generation

Wave tables are used in cmusic for efficiency. Computing one period of a periodic waveform and outputing it repetitively at varying rates is much more efficient than calculating the waveform point by point for the entire duration of the output signal. Control functions, by contrast, are often used only once or at most a few times in the synthesis of a musical composition or segment. A pitch inflection may be unique to a particular note or moment in a composition, for example, or an amplitude fluctuation may occur only a few times rather than for every note played by a particular cmusic instrument.

It is unnecessary and wasteful to store control functions in wave tables if they are to be used only once. cmusic therefore includes a unit generator version of the `gen4` program called `trans` that allows control function breakpoints and transition parameters to be specified within an instrument definition either as constants peculiar to that instrument or as note parameters that may be set for each individual note. Only the number of breakpoints must be fixed in the instrument definition.

The general form of the `trans` unit generator statement is as follows:

```
trans output[b] t1[dvp] t2[dpv] t3[dpv]
    [t[vpn] v[vpn] a[vpn]]* t[vpn] v[vpn] ;
```

The three temporary variables t1, t2, and t3 are normally dynamic variables (d). The rest of the statement gives a description of a transition path exactly as in a `gen4` definition—the generated control function always occurs over the duration of a note. Any number of time-value (t-v) breakpoint pairs may be specified, and the transition parameters (a) work as they do in `gen4`: 0 yields a straight line transition, negative numbers yield exponential transitions, and positive numbers yield inverse exponential transitions. The power of this unit generator lies in the fact that the breakpoints and transition parameters may be connected to note parameters, allowing such things as easy portamento specification, and loudness contouring on a note-by-note basis. For example, the following cmusic score plays a 1-second portamento from 440Hz to 880Hz, followed by a 2-second portamento to 100Hz.

```
#include<carl/cmusic.h>

ins 0 tport
    trans b2 d d d 0,p6 0 1/3,p7 0 1,p8;
    osc  b1 p5 b2 f1 d ;
    out  b1 ;
end;

SINE(f1) ;

note 0 tport 3 -6dB 440Hz 880Hz 100Hz ;

ter ;
```

A diagram of the instrument `tport` is shown in Figure 3-10. Note that only the *values* of the three breakpoints are connected to note parameters—the `tport` instrument is defined such that all transitions will occur in straight lines and the middle breakpoint always occurs one-third of the way through the note. It is possible to connect these specifications to note parameters as well, with the proviso that the time of the first breakpoint must always be zero (just as with `gen4`), and the total duration of the control function is always scaled to match the note duration. Also note that the `trans` unit generator should be used only in cases where each note is likely to require a different control function, because the `trans` computation is equivalent to running `gen4` for each note that the instrument plays.

3.2.14 Frequency Modulation

We have already seen how the frequency of a table lookup oscillator may be controlled in either a fixed or dynamic way over the duration of a note event. An important

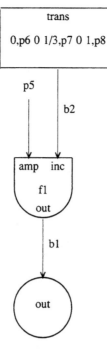

Figure 3-10   Direct frequency control with the `trans` unit generator. In this instrument, the output of the `trans` unit generator is used to control the frequency of an oscillator via input-output block b2. The control function generated by the `trans` unit generator will span the duration of any note played on this instrument. This function will start at a value given in note parameter p6, move in a straight line to a value given in p7 one-third of the way through the note, and then move to the value given by p8 at the end of the note.

extension of dynamic frequency control is the technique of *frequency modulation*, in which the frequency is made to vary about its main value in periodic or aperiodic ways.

The usual technique of frequency modulation involves adding a time-varying quantity to the main, or *carrier*, frequency. For example, if the frequency of an oscillator is controlled by a quantity

$$f(t) = f_c + \Delta f \sin 2\pi f_m t \qquad (3\text{-}41)$$

we see that the size of the frequency variation about carrier frequency f_c will be determined by Δf, while the rate of this variation will occur at the modulation frequency f_m (see Figure 3-11).

3.2.15 Periodic Vibrato

It is a simple matter to use the technique of frequency modulation to create the effect of a musical *vibrato*. In the simplest case the *frequency deviation* Δf can be used to control the *depth* of the vibrato, while the modulation frequency f_m controls the vibrato *rate*. Figure 3-12 shows a cmusic instrument in which note parameters are used to set values for the desired carrier frequency (p7), vibrato depth (p9), and rate (p8).

The instrument in Figure 3-12 uses a unit generator whose output is the sum of its inputs in order to form the frequency control signal (b3) used to control the carrier oscillator. In cmusic, this unit generator has the following general statement.

```
adn output[b] input[bvpn]* ;
```

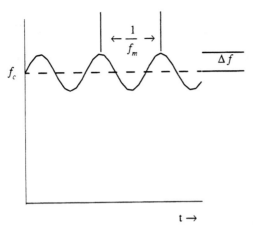

Figure 3-11   Graph of a time-varying frequency control function $f_c + \Delta f \sin 2 \pi f_m t$.

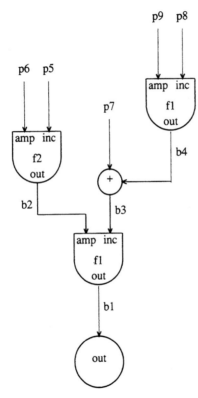

Figure 3-12   Basic frequency modulation instrument with amplitude envelope control. f1 is defined to be a sine waveform, and f2 is an appropriate amplitude envelope. The frequency produced by this instrument is then given by $f_c + \Delta f \sin 2 f_m t$, where p9 controls Δf, p8 controls f_m, and p7 controls f_c. p5 and p6 control the scanning rate and peak value of the amplitude envelope, respectively. As usual, all frequency values must be scaled by L/R (the wave table length divided by the sampling rate) in order to convert them into increments appropriate for the table lookup oscillators.

adn places the sum of all of its inputs (there may be any number of them) into its output. The complete cmusic definition for the instrument shown in Figure 3-12—together with appropriate wave table definitions—is therefore as follows:

```
#include <carl/cmusic.h>

ins 0 vibrato ;
    osc b4 p9 p8 f1 d ;   {frequency modulation control oscillator}
    adn b3 b4 p7 ;        {add modulation signal to carrier frequency}
    osc b2 p6 p5 f2 d ;   {amplitude envelope control oscillator}
    osc b1 b2 b3 f1 d ;                      {carrier oscillator}
    out b1 ;                                 {output signal}
end ;

SINE(f1) ;                                   {carrier waveform}
GEN4(f2) 0,0 -1 .1,1 0 .8,1 -1 1,0 ;         {envelope waveform}
```

For example, the note statement

```
{p1   p2    p3      p4   p5     p6   p7  p8     p9}
note  0 vibrato    2 p4sec -10dB A(0) 6Hz p7*.03 ;
```

if applied to the instrument shown in Figure 3-12, would produce a 2-second note with a peak amplitude of –10 dB (the overall amplitude envelope shape is determined by the definition of wave table f2). The carrier frequency (p7) will be A440, the vibrato rate (p8) will be 6 Hz, and the vibrato depth (p9) will be 3 percent of the carrier frequency, corresponding to a positive and negative excursion around the main frequency of about a quarter tone.[8]

An interesting and useful variation of this technique is to make the vibrato depth proportional to the amplitude of the note. That is, as the amplitude envelope builds up from zero to its maximum value, the vibrato depth will also build up from zero to its maximum value. Conversely, as the amplitude falls to zero at the end of the note, the vibrato depth will also go from its maximum value to zero. Such vibrato behavior more closely mimics that of a bel canto singer.

To create such vibrato behavior, we can simply multiply the amplitude envelope control signal by the vibrato depth—the result is fed into the amplitude input of the modulation control oscillator. An instrument that implements this procedure is shown in Figure 3-13. Note that this instrument can be played with exactly the same note statements as the last instrument presented.

We could similarly cause the vibrato rate to follow the shape of the amplitude envelope by applying the same treatment to the increment input of the modulation control oscillator. Rather than adding yet another oscillator to produce a third copy of the amplitude envelope scaled by the desired peak vibrato rate, we can alternatively use an oscillator to produce a single copy of the amplitude envelope control signal with a unity peak value. This signal can be scaled by using a unit generator that multiplies its inputs together to form its output. The general form of the multiplier unit generator statement in cmusic is similar to that for the adn unit generator.

```
mult output[b] input[bvpn]* ;
```

[8]The *total vibrato* width is therefore around 6 percent, or around a semitone.

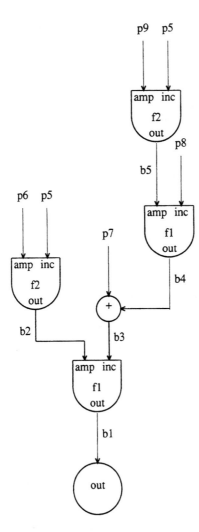

Figure 3-13   Frequency modulation instrument in which the amplitude envelope also controls vibrato depth. A separate oscillator is used to produce a copy of the amplitude envelope scaled by the desired peak vibrato depth given in p9.

mult simply forms the product of as many inputs as are stated and places the resulting value in its output.

Figure 3-14 shows such an instrument. Its cmusic definition is as follows:

```
ins 0 vibrato2 ;
    osc  b7  1 p5 f2 d ;     {produce normalized amplitude envelope}
    mult b5 b7 p9 ;                 {scale envelope for vibrato depth}
    mult b6 b7 p8 ;                  {scale envelope for vibrato rate}
    mult b2 b7 p6 ;                    {scale envelope for amplitude}
    osc  b4 b5 b6 f1 d ; {frequency modulation control oscillator}
    adn  b3 b4 p7 ;    {add modulation signal to carrier frequency}
    osc  b1 b2 b3 f1 d ;                        {carrier oscillator}
    out  b1 ;                                        {output signal}
end ;
```

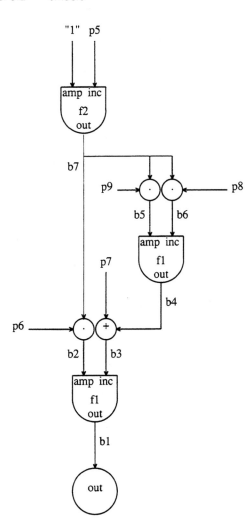

Figure 3-14 Frequency modulation instrument in which the amplitude envelope also controls vibrato depth and rate. A single oscillator produces a "normalized" version of the amplitude envelope with a unity peak value. This signal is scaled by the peak amplitude (p6), peak vibrato depth (p9), and peak vibrato rate (p8) note parameters.

Note the use of the constant value 1 in this instrument definition to control the amplitude of the oscillator that produces the "normalized" amplitude envelope curve (that is, the peak value of the signal generated by this oscillator will be a constant 1). As before, the same note statements may be used to play this instrument. However, note parameters p8 and p9 now specify *peak* values for vibrato rate and depth, respectively—the precise manner in which these parameters vary will be determined by these quantities together with the shape of the amplitude envelope curve (f2).

3.2.16 Random Vibrato

The vibrato imparted to the synthesized tone in the example sounds considerably more like that of a singer or a traditional musical instrument than one in which the vibrato rate and depth are held constant over the entire duration of the note. However, when the amplitude envelope is unchanging (as it is for 70 percent of the note duration, according to the envelope definition for f2 given earlier), the vibrato still sounds mechanically regular, lending a synthetic quality to the resulting tone. Vibrato produced by live performers is not so irregular that it sounds musically uneven, yet it is not so regular that it sounds artificial.

It is therefore useful to consider ways of making the vibrato pattern less regular while still retaining its basic sinusoidal shape. One way to impart irregularity to a process is to introduce a controlled amount of random behavior. For example, instead of setting the vibrato rate to exactly 6 Hz during the maximum amplitude part of the tone, we could specify that the vibrato rate is to be $6 + r(t)$ Hz, where $r(t)$ is a random quantity that changes over time within a specified range of values. For example, if $r(t)$ is a random quantity that changes over the range ± 2, we could set the vibrato rate to 6 ± 2 Hz.

In terms of waveform spectra, a random signal may be thought of as one in which discrete spectrum lines are replaced by regions centered about some frequency. The shape of the region determines the manner in which the spectrum is "spread" among the frequencies it covers. A random signal with a rectangular spectrum centered about 0 Hz, for example, would be equally likely to contain frequencies up to a given value, that value being analogous to the cutoff frequency of a lowpass filter. If the spectrum is centered around 0 Hz but falls off gradually to some cutoff frequency, the random waveform associated with that spectrum would be more likely to contain low frequencies (that is, frequencies close to 0 Hz) than frequencies close to the cutoff frequency.

A simple and very efficient way to generate a random signal with such properties is to create a signal consisting of random values chosen every τ samples (where τ need not be an integer) and to interpolate linearly sample values between adjacent random samples. Such a signal is similar to a non-band-limited triangular waveform at $1/\tau$ Hz in which the sample values at each "sharp corner" of the triangular waveform are replaced by random values. A plot of such a waveform and its associated power spectrum is shown in Figure 3-15. The pictured waveform consists of random values in the range ± 1 chosen every 100 samples at a sampling rate of 20,000 samples per second, corresponding to a new random value every 0.5 milliseconds, or at a frequency of 2000 Hz. Linear interpolation is used to fill in the sample values between the random choices. Because the waveform contains "sharp corners," its power spectrum falls off with increasing frequency at an asymptotic rate of about 12 dB per octave. The periodicity of the random waveform also shows up in the power spectrum as spectrum "dips" every 2000 Hz.

The waveform shown in Figure 3-15 was produced with the cmusic `ran` unit generator, which has the general statement

```
ran output[b] amplitude[bvpn] increment[bvpn] pos[dpv] from[dpv] to[dpv] ;
```

The output signal of `ran` consists of straight line segments that travel from one random value to another. The frequency with which new random values are chosen is determined by `increment`. A new random value is chosen every $L/\texttt{increment}$ samples, where L is the default wave table length, or at a rate of `increment`

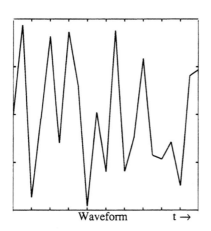
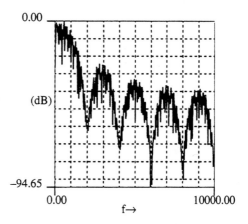

Figure 3-15   A random waveform and its associated spectrum. The plot on the left shows the first 10 milliseconds of a waveform consisting of random values in the range ±1 chosen every 0.5 milliseconds (that is, at a rate of 2000 Hz). Intermediate sample values are linearly interpolated between adjacent random values. The associated power spectrum—obtained by taking the FFT of 1024 samples of the waveform using a Hamming window—is shown on the right. Note that the spectrum dips every 2000 Hz and that the first side lobe amplitude is about 24 dB below the amplitude of the main lobe at 0 Hz.

$\times R / L$ Hz, where R is the sampling rate. The random values lie in the range ±1, and the output signal is scaled by amplitude. The last three arguments are typically dynamic variables and are used for temporary storage.

The waveform in Figure 3-15 was obtained by defining a cmusic instrument as follows:

```
ins 0 ranwave ;
    ran b1 p5 p6 d d d ;
    out b1 ;
end ;
```

and setting p5 and p6 with the note statement.

```
note 0 ranwave 1 1 2000Hz ;
```

The sampling rate was set to 20,000 Hz by running cmusic with the UNIX command

```
cmusic -R20000 score.sc | . . .
```

which overrides the default cmusic sampling rate of 16,384 Hz (as well as any statements that affect the sampling rate in the score file).

Although the waveform produced by the ran unit generator is not perfect lowpass-filtered noise, it can act as such in many cases. The strongest side lobe amplitude (which occurs in the example at about 3000 Hz) is about 24 dB lower than the peak amplitude of the main lobe (centered at 0 Hz). The remaining side lobes are lower still in amplitude than the first. The real utility of the ran unit generator is that the spacing of the side lobes is easily changed via the `increment` argument of `ran`, which mimics an oscillator frequency specification in order to set the bandwidth of the main lobe. In addition, it is a simple matter to shift the frequency of the main lobe to an arbitrary value by convolving the `ran` output spectrum with a line spectrum. In other words, if we simply multiply the `ran` output signal by a sine wave at f_c Hz, the main lobe will be centered around that frequency instead of 0 Hz.

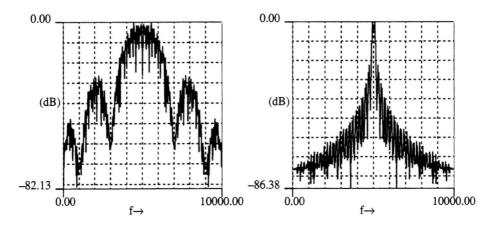

Figure 3-16   Power spectra of two random waveforms. Each plot shows the spectrum of a waveform consisting of `ran` output multiplied by a sinusoid at 5000 Hz. In the first spectrum, the increment input of `ran` was set to 2000 Hz; in the second plot, a `ran` increment value of 200 Hz was used. Each plot was obtained by taking an FFT of 1024 samples of the waveform under a Hamming window.

Figure 3-16 shows the spectra of two such signals. The corresponding waveforms were produced by defining a cmusic instrument and wave table as follows:

```
#include <carl/cmusic.h>

ins 0 noisy ;
    ran b2 p5 p6 d d d ;
    osc b1 b2 p7 f1 d ;
    out b1 ;
end ;

SINE(f1) ;
```

Note that the waveform multiplication (spectrum convolution) is achieved merely by feeding the `ran` unit generator output signal into the oscillator amplitude input via input-output block b2. This instrument was then played with the note statements

```
note 0 noisy 1 1 2000Hz 5000Hz ;
```

and

```
note 0 noisy 1 1 200Hz 5000Hz ;
```

The spectra in Figure 3-16 are the result of taking an FFT of 1024 samples of the waveforms resulting from these two note statements under a Hamming window. In each case, we see that the output spectrum is centered around the frequency of the sinusoid: 5000 Hz. In the first spectrum, however, the "bandwidth" of the noise signal produced by `ran` has a 2000-Hz spacing between spectrum nulls. In the second case, the spacing is 200 Hz, allowing many more side lobes to "fit" between 0 Hz and the Nyquist frequency.

The relevance of the `ran` unit generator to random vibrato is now clear. If we replace the modulation oscillator in the vibrato instrument with a `ran/osc` unit generator combination, we can set the oscillator frequency to the desired *average* vibrato rate and set the `ran` increment to the desired deviation from this rate. Because the spectrum of the `ran` output waveform drops off fairly rapidly on either side of the center frequency, we can think of its increment value as being approximately equal to the *bandwidth* over which the vibrato rate will range (the frequency could deviate further than this value, but such deviations are much less likely than one within the range $f_m \pm I/2$, where I is the `ran` increment input).

For example, the following vibrato instrument

```
ins 0 vibrato3 ;
    osc  b8  1 p5 f2 d ;    {produce normalized amplitude envelope}
    mult b6 b8 p9 ;         {scale envelope for vibrato depth}
    mult b7 b8 p8 ;         {scale envelope for vibrato rate}
    mult b2 b8 p6 ;         {scale envelope for amplitude}
    osc  b5 b6 b7 f1 d ;    {frequency modulation control oscillator}
    ran  b4 b5 p10 d d d ;{randomize fm control signal}
    adn  b3 b4 p7 ;         {add modulation signal to carrier frequency}
    osc  b1 b2 b3 f1 d ;    {carrier oscillator}
    out  b1 ;               {output signal}
end ;
```

when played with the note statement

```
{p1    p2    p3      p4   p5     p6   p7  p8    p9   p10}
note   0 vibrato3    2 p4sec -10dB A(0) 6Hz p7*.03 2Hz ;
```

will produce a tone with a vibrato rate and depth that follow the amplitude envelope. Furthermore, the vibrato rate will not be steady at 6 Hz during the steady state of the tone but will "wobble" around this value, mostly staying within the range from 5 Hz to 7 Hz. A diagram of instrument `vibrato3` is shown in Figure 3-17.

3.3 ADDITIVE SYNTHESIS

The basic notion of additive sound synthesis is that complex musical sounds can be created by adding together multiple sound components, each of which is relatively simple (see Figure 3-18). Such components are typically not perceived individually, but each component contributes materially to the overall quality of the resulting sound.

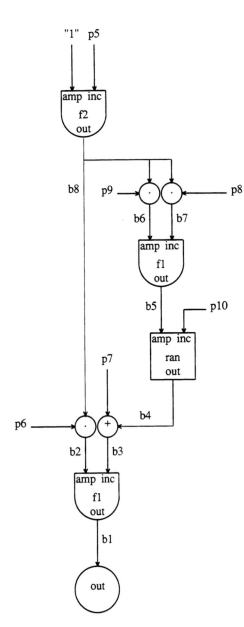

Figure 3-17   Frequency modulation instrument with amplitude envelope control of random vibrato width and depth. The range of variation of the vibrato rate is controlled by note parameter p10.

The greatest advantage of the additive method of synthesis is that it rests on the very well developed theoretical framework of Fourier analysis. For this reason, additive synthesis is sometimes called *Fourier synthesis*, though that description is more restrictive than the more general notion of additive synthesis.

Time Varying Component Parameters

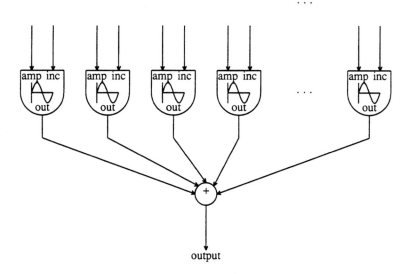

Figure 3-18   Processing model for additive synthesis. The complex sound is built up by adding together a number (possibly a large number) of sinusoidal components, each with independently varying amplitude, frequency, and phase, though in many cases the relative phase of the individual components is unspecified.

As we have seen, Fourier's theorem states that any periodic waveform that meets certain mathematical conditions[9] can be expressed as the sum of a number—possibly an infinite number—of harmonically related sinusoids, each with a particular amplitude and phase. Because we may find the amplitudes and phases of these sinusoidal components by using the Fourier transform, it is possible to think of such components as building blocks out of which any periodic waveform can be constructed. Therefore, all that is needed to construct any periodic acoustic waveform is an inexhaustible supply of sinusoidal waveforms, each with adjustable frequency, amplitude, and phase.

When two or more notes are played simultaneously on cmusic instruments, their waveforms are simply added together (provided they are connected to the same output channel). A simple cmusic instrument consisting of a table lookup oscillator referring to a sinusoidal wave table and connected to an `out` unit generator is thus a virtually inexhaustible supply of sinusoids, because the frequency, amplitude, and phase offsets of such an oscillator are all readily adjustable and because a single cmusic instrument can "play" an arbitrarily large number of "notes" simultaneously.

---

[9]These are known as the Dirichlet conditions. Because all acoustic waveforms automatically meet these conditions, they will not be discussed here.

Stated mathematically, Fourier's theorem assures us that if $f(t)$ is a waveform with a period of T seconds—that is, if $f(t) = f(t+T)$ for all values of t—then $f(t)$ may be expressed in the following form:

$$f(t) = \sum_{k=0}^{\infty} A_k \sin(k\omega t + \phi_k) \qquad (3\text{-}42)$$

where

A_k is the amplitude of the kth sinusoidal component of $f(t)$

ω is the fundamental frequency of the waveform ($= 2\pi/T$)

ϕ_k is the phase offset of the kth sinusoidal component of $f(t)$ (relative to sine phase)

Equation (3-42) may be rewritten in the equivalent form

$$f(t) = \sum_{k=0}^{\infty} (a_k \cos k\omega t + b_k \sin k\omega t) \qquad (3\text{-}43)$$

where $a_k = A_k \sin\phi_k$ and $b_k = A_k \cos\phi_k$,   or,   equivalently, $A_k = \sqrt{a_k^2 + b_k^2}$ and $\phi_k = \tan^{-1}(a_k/b_k)$. Equation (3-42) is more often used because the *Fourier coefficients* a_k and b_k can be found directly by applying the Fourier transform to $f(t)$ according to

$$\begin{cases} a_k = \dfrac{2}{T}\displaystyle\int_0^T f(t)\cos\dfrac{2\pi nt}{T}\,dt \\[2em] b_k = \dfrac{2}{T}\displaystyle\int_0^T f(t)\sin\dfrac{2\pi nt}{T}\,dt \end{cases} \qquad (3\text{-}44)$$

In Chapter 2, we saw how these Fourier coefficients may be found by using the discrete Fourier transform (DFT) or its especially efficient implementation known as the fast Fourier transform (FFT). Also in Chapter 2, we saw that the primary difficulty associated with Fourier methods arises in conjunction with the necessity for the waveform to be periodic. Most acoustic waveforms are not truly periodic even if they are nearly so, causing the spectrum of most musical waveforms to vary considerably over their durations. We must therefore resort in many cases to short-time Fourier analysis methods in order to capture the time-varying qualities of musical sounds. The main practical difference between classical and short-time Fourier methods is that the relevant frequencies, amplitudes, and phases of the sinusoidal components are fixed constants in the former and time-varying in the latter.

3.3.1 Periodic Waveform Synthesis

Truly periodic waveforms are quite simple to synthesize using additive synthesis. A single period of such a waveform may be specified with a wave table generating function such as cmusic's `gen5`. This waveform may then be produced at any frequency, amplitude, and phase offset using the table lookup oscillator algorithm embodied in the cmusic `osc` unit generator. We must take care to ensure that none of the harmonic components of such a waveform fall at a frequency that exceeds the Nyquist rate in order to avoid foldover. The amplitude, frequency and phase offset of the waveform may then be set via fixed constants—typically as cmusic note parameters—or they may be controlled in a time-varying manner using the outputs of other unit generators.

As mentioned, we may also synthesize a complex periodic waveform by playing several notes simultaneously on a cmusic instrument that emits a sinusoidal waveform.

The following cmusic score plays two notes in sequence. Each note consists of the first five components of a sawtooth waveform based on a fundamental frequency of 440 Hz. The first note is synthesized by creating a wave table consisting of one period of the required waveform and using a single oscillator to generate the sound for a duration of 2 seconds. The second note is synthesized by playing five simultaneous sinusoids with the proper frequencies and amplitudes (all in sine phase) to produce a waveform with a spectrum identical to that of the first.

```
#include <carl/cmusic.h>
{
    define instrument comp--a simple oscillator with amplitude
    envelope control.  p5 controls envelope duration, p6 is peak
    envelope amplitude, p7 is main note frequency, p8 selects main
    oscillator wavetable by number.
}
ins 0 comp ;
    osc b2 p6 p5 f1 d ;
    osc b1 b2 p7 p8 d ;
    out b1 ;
end ;
{
    generate wavetables--f1 is a simple amplitude envelope with
    exponential attack and decay and a 6dB sag during steady state,
    f2 is first 5 components of sawtooth waveform normalized to a
    peak amplitude of 1.0, f3 is a simple sine waveform.
}
GEN4(f1) 0,0 -1 .1,1 0 .8,.5 -1 1,0 ;
GEN5(f2) 1,1,0 2,1/2,0 3,1/3,0 4,1/4,0 5,1/5,0 ;
NORM(f2) ;
SINE(f3) ;
{
    FIRST MUSICAL NOTE: play instrument comp for 2 seconds with
    peak amplitude 1.0, fundamental frequency 440 Hertz, using
    wavetable f2.
}
note 0 comp 2 p4sec 1 440Hz 2 ;
{
    terminate this section of the score when note is finished and
    reset action time (p2) to 0.
}
sec ;
```

```
{
    generate a second of silence and reset action time (p2) to 0.
}
sec 1 ;
{
    define amplitude normalization constant equal to inverse of
    maximum possible amplitude
}
#define S (1/(1+1/2+1/3+1/4+1/5))
{
    SECOND MUSICAL NOTE: play instrument comp 5 times
    simultaneously for 2 seconds using wavetable f3.
    set relative amplitudes and frequencies of individual
    note components in same relation as the previous sound.
}
note 0 comp 2 p4sec   1*S 1*440Hz 3 ;
note 0 comp 2 p4sec 1/2*S 2*440Hz 3 ;
note 0 comp 2 p4sec 1/3*S 3*440Hz 3 ;
note 0 comp 2 p4sec 1/4*S 4*440Hz 3 ;
note 0 comp 2 p4sec 1/5*S 5*440Hz 3 ;
{
    terminate score when previous complex note is finished.
}
ter ;
```

While the timbres of the two musical notes produced by this cmusic score will be identical, their amplitudes will not be identical. The second note event has an amplitude about 3 dB lower than that of the first. While the amplitude scale factor S is set to the inverse of the sum of the peak amplitudes of each of the individual sinusoidal components, the peaks of the sine waves do not line up at the same moment during each of the resultant waveform periods.

Another important difference between these two additive synthesis procedures is that the first musical note event is computed roughly five times faster than the second because the first uses a single instrument while the second uses the same instrument five times (simultaneously).

If the second method is computationally so much less efficient, the question arises; Would anyone ever use it? In the example, computing a single period of the waveform to be used over and over again by a single oscillator clearly has a computation speed advantage. However, the relationships among the frequencies, amplitudes, and phases of the components are strictly fixed using the first method, whereas it is completely arbitrary (and possibly dynamically changing) using the second. If we wish to have the higher-frequency components die away more rapidly over the duration of the note than the low-frequency components (such effects are needed to simulate the behavior of plucked strings, for example), the first method would be inappropriate unless, of course, it were extended to include a lowpass filter with a time-varying response.

Even more important is the fact that the frequency components in the first method are constrained to be true and exact harmonics of a common fundamental frequency. That fundamental frequency need not be present, of course—we might, for example, create a complex tone consisting of only the third, seventh, and eleventh harmonics.

If we wish to simulate the "partials" of a piano string, however, which do not lie at exact integer multiples of a fundamental frequency but are slightly "stretched" because of stiffness in the vibrating string, we could not use the first method at all. Although the cmusic statement

```
GEN5(f2) 1,1,0 2.007,1/2,0 3.009,1/3,0 4.015,1/4,0 5.014,1/5,0 ;
```

is syntactically correct and matches published acoustical data regarding a proper amount of stretch to impart to each of the first five harmonics of a piano tone,[10] these numbers specify a nonintegral number of periods to be included in the wave table. When such a wave table is output repeatedly (as it must be when used as a waveform), such nonintegral periods give rise to discontinuities in the resulting sound, heard as clicks if they occur at a slow rate or as noisy distortion if they occur at rapid audio rates.

Using the second method of additive synthesis, however, each sinusoidal component is independent of all others. This allows frequencies to be set arbitrarily without concern about clicks or noise. We could easily modify the second note list from our example to read as follows to obtain the proper "stretched partials":

```
note 0 comp 2 p4sec   1*S      1*440Hz 3 ;
note 0 comp 2 p4sec 1/2*S 2.007*440Hz 3 ;
note 0 comp 2 p4sec 1/3*S 3.009*440Hz 3 ;
note 0 comp 2 p4sec 1/4*S 4.015*440Hz 3 ;
note 0 comp 2 p4sec 1/5*S 5.014*440Hz 3 ;
```

3.3.2 Data Reduction Techniques

Difficulties with additive synthesis are often not conceptual but practical. Because each component generally requires specification of an independent frequency, amplitude, and phase offset trajectory over the duration of each musical note event, the amount of control data soon becomes quite large. At a high-fidelity sampling rate of 48 kHz, for example, the Nyquist rate falls above the upper limit of human hearing. The number of components associated with a 1000-Hz complex tone, for example, is potentially 20 or more during the relatively periodic portion of the sound (transient, or aperiodic, portions of the sound may have spectrum energy distributed evenly at many more than 20 frequencies). A 100-Hz complex tone potentially carries 200 or more components below the Nyquist frequency. Viewed in this way, a single musical note event might require 200 or more control functions to specify the proper frequency, amplitude, and phase offset trajectories for a total of over 600 control functions in all. Furthermore, a subsequent nonidentical note event would typically require 600 *different* control functions.

[10]See, for example, Benade (1976).

For this reason, a good deal of attention has been paid to ways in which the amount of control data for additive synthesis may reasonably be reduced.

If such data reduction techniques are to succeed, they must have no objectionable effect on the resulting sound. Practically the entire subject of sound synthesis techniques turns on how *objectionable effect* is defined. One possible definition would be to require that the effect of the application of a data reduction technique must be completely inaudible. Such a criterion may be ideal in many ways, but it is often impractical and unnecessary.

A more relaxed criterion would be to require that the effect of a data reduction technique be unobjectionable musically rather than perceptually. For example, if two musical sound events are as alike as two such events performed on a traditional musical instrument by a musician who is trying to make them sound as much alike as possible, we may designate the events as *musically indistinguishable* (Moore, 1977/1985). It is self-evident that musically indistinguishable sound events may be substituted for one another in any practical musical context; otherwise, the traditional literature of music would be meaningless.

An even more relaxed criterion might be one of *musical acceptability*, in which the effect of a data reduction technique could be clearly audible but no more objectionable than, say, the substitution of one performer-instrument combination for another. Musical tradition admits to a great number of styles and performance techniques— traditional French and German playing techniques for wind instruments such as horns and oboes differ considerably, for example, with the French style tending toward timbral brilliance and virtuosic agility, while the German style tends toward timbral fullness and virtuosic smoothness. Clearly, such differences are musically acceptable, even when mixed together (as they often are in a live performance).

Relaxing the comparison criteria even more results in musically unacceptable results when the purpose of the data reduction is to preserve substitutability. In such cases, however, we often find that the "degraded" sound—while perhaps no longer acceptable in place of the original—takes on an identity independent of the original sound. In other words, such sounds are no longer substitutes because they are new. They may preserve one or more audible properties of the original sound, such as pitch contour or loudness contour, but they are no longer equivalent to the original sound in any musical way. Traditional instruments are themselves distinguished in this way, each having its own musical identity that makes confusion with another instrument unlikely (if not impossible).

Combining these criteria for comparison of musical sounds provides a useful vocabulary for discussing sound synthesis methods in general. To the four categories of distinguishability mentioned we must add two more: one for the case of true identity between musical sounds and the other for the case in which two sounds are unrelated in any evident way. These categories are listed in order of increasing differentiability in Table 3-5.

Applying such notions of differentiability to musical sounds is a subjective process in which the conscious judgment of a listener comes into play. Undoubtedly, many a golden-eared audiophile has argued with many a golden-eared musician about

TABLE 3-5   Categories of increasing subjective musical sound differentiability.

Category Number	Difference Criterion	Example
0	Physically indistinguishable	Identical waveforms
1	Perceptually indistinguishable	Identical percepts
2	Musically indistinguishable	Musically interchangeable sounds
3	Musically acceptable	Musically substitutable sounds
4	Musically different	Musically distinct identities (different instruments)
5	Musically independent	Completely unrelated sounds

the subjective qualities of one loudspeaker or amplifier or musical instrument or recording as compared with another, often to the bemused puzzlement of a bystander who fails to hear even the point of the argument. It is therefore generally necessary to verify subjective evaluations. What is surprising about subjective evaluations is not that they sometimes differ from individual to individual but that they are often surprisingly consistent from individual to individual.[11]

To reduce the amount of data needed for additive synthesis, one technique is to omit the synthesis of any component with an amplitude that is small compared with that of other components. This technique leads immediately to the question; How small is small enough? This question is unanswerable at this time, but several psychophysical findings shed light on parts of the answer.

About the least useful thing to consider in this context is the amplitude associated with the threshold of hearing, because our hearing mechanism is so sensitive that we are nearly able to hear the Brownian (heat) motion of air molecules under ideal conditions.[12] Even if energy were present in a sound at such levels, our ears are so much more sensitive than microphones and loudspeakers that we would be hard put even to detect it with electronic instrumentation, let alone remove it.

More important are the ways that the hearing mechanism determines the overall loudness of a sound and the auditory phenomenon known as masking. An important theoretical underpinning of such phenomena is the *critical band*, which corresponds roughly to the width of the region along the basilar membrane (about 1.2 mm except at low frequencies) that is excited by a tone consisting of a single frequency (a sinusoid). This critical bandwidth is about 15 percent in frequency, except at low frequencies in the audible range, where it is larger. In musical terms, this critical bandwidth is slightly

---

[11]The *sone* scale of subjective loudness, for example, is based on a surprising consistency among completely subjective judgments regarding when one sound may be regarded as "twice as loud" or "twice as soft" as another.

[12]The range of sensitivity of the human ear to pressure changes is quite impressive, with the smallest pressure changes being approximately a million times smaller than the largest ones that the ear can tolerate without immediate damage. The smallest audible pressure change causes the eardrum to move only about one-tenth the diameter of a hydrogen atom, which corresponds to an atmospheric pressure difference between that at sea level and that at about 1/3 inch above or below it!

less than a minor third over most of the frequency range but increases to almost an octave at frequencies below about 200 Hz.

Two frequency components will interact differently depending on whether they lie within a critical bandwidth of each other or not. In terms of pitch interactions, two frequency components falling within the same critical band will give rise to a sensation of roughness or beats, whereas two single frequency components falling in different critical bands will sound relatively smooth and independent.

In terms of loudness interactions, two single-frequency tones of identical intensity falling within the same critical band give rise to a subjective impression of loudness that is much less than when the tones are separated by more than a critical band. In other words, frequency components within a single critical band are once again seen to be *not independent* of each other.[13]

Masking effects also occur when two or more tones are heard simultaneously. In general, lower frequencies tend to mask higher frequencies (make them more difficult to hear) more effectively than vice versa. The masking effect diminishes as the tones become more widely separated in frequency. Two single-frequency tones with overlapping critical bands mask each other quite effectively because they cannot be perceived individually in any case. In the perception of a complex tone, the lower frequencies tend to mask the higher frequencies, and the higher harmonics that fall closer together than a critical band are not heard independently.

For the purposes of additive synthesis, then, it would seem that ideally, no more than one frequency component would be needed per critical band. Basing the properties of the synthesized sound around the properties of the listener is still a largely unexplored area, however, requiring a sophisticated translation of properties of the source sound into those of the received sound stimulus. Ultimately, such *receiver coding* of synthetic sound may reduce the amount of data needed for additive synthesis considerably. Until this process is better understood, however, it can be applied to additive synthesis only in limited ways.

A more tractable approach to additive synthesis is based on the idea of *source coding*, in which the acoustic properties of the signal are reproduced to a degree of approximation that preserves objective properties of the source sound such as its time-varying power spectrum. In his doctoral research on timbre perception, John Grey originated one such technique. Grey reasoned that the detailed behaviors of the frequency, and amplitude trajectories of each component of a musical sound were of less subjective importance than their overall, or average, behavior. Carried to an extreme, this method is equivalent to replacing the time-varying amplitude or frequency of a single component with a single number equal to the average value for that component over the entire duration of the musical note event. Rather than using a single number—equivalent

---

[13]This is the reason that two violins playing in unison do not sound twice as loud as a single violin. As long as they play in unison, about nine violins are needed to provide a sound judged subjectively to be twice as loud as that of a single violin. It is also the reason that an independent solo violin part can be heard easily against a background played by the rest of the violins in an orchestral string section.

to the setting for a drawbar on a Hammond organ—Grey replaced the variation for a single component by a small number of values representing breakpoints in a piecewise linear approximation to their "true" values determined via the techniques of short time spectrum measurement.

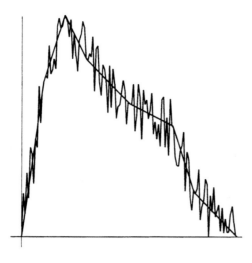

Figure 3-19   A time-varying amplitude trajectory and its piecewise linear approximation. The highly variable amplitude curve is typical of a component amplitude as reported by short time spectrum measurement techniques during a single musical note. It requires several hundred values to represent it precisely. The piecewise linear approximation to it requires only eight number pairs to represent it.

As an example of this technique, Figure 3-19 shows an amplitude trajectory for the fundamental frequency component of a single note played on a musical instrument. Exact resynthesis of an analyzed note would require that all the highly variable data in the amplitude, frequency, and phase offset curves be retained. Approximate resynthesis can be achieved by replacing the "noisy" curve with a piecewise linear approximation of it. Even though notes resynthesized in this way are not physically identical to the originals, the two are often musically indistinguishable.

A neat advantage of this data reduction technique is that it makes the additive synthesis parameters for a specific musical tone publishable as a list of numbers. Figure 3-20 shows a piecewise linear approximation to amplitude curves obtained from the analysis of a trumpet tone (Grey, 1975), together with numeric breakpoint information for the amplitude and frequency curves needed for synthesis. Resynthesis of this tone with cmusic is straightforward. A component-synthesizing instrument may be defined, for example, as a sinusoidal oscillator with `trans` unit generators controlling both its amplitude and its frequency. All transition parameters may be zero because the required functions are always piecewise linear. A few slightly different versions of this instrument may be used to accommodate the fact that not all of the control functions contain the same number of breakpoints. Alternatively, a single instrument that can accommodate the maximum number of breakpoints might be adapted to all cases.

The first (fundamental) component of the trumpet tone described in Figure 3-20 could be synthesized with cmusic as follows:

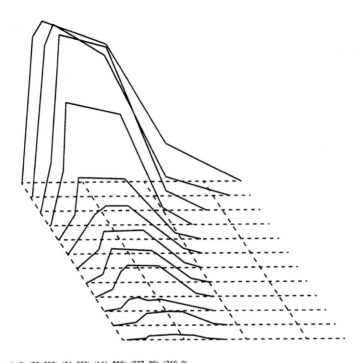

AMP 1 = (1, 0), (20, 305), (36, 338), (141, 288), (237, 80), (360, 0)
FREQ 1 = (1, 321), (16, 324), (32, 312), (109, 310), (317, 314), (360, 310)
AMP 2 = (3, 0), (25, 317), (39, 361), (123, 295), (222, 40), (326, 0)
FREQ 2 = (2, 0), (3, 607), (16, 657), (24, 621), (133, 621), (275, 628), (326, 628), (327, 0)
AMP 3 = (2, 0), (19, 100), (34, 369), (111, 342), (207, 41), (273, 0)
FREQ 3 = (2, 977), (5, 782), (15, 987), (24, 932), (128, 932), (217, 936), (273, 945), (275, 0)
AMP 4 = (1, 0), (3, 0), (24, 113), (29, 257), (118, 231), (187, 35), (235, 0)
FREQ 4 = (1, 0), (2, 0), (3, 718), (16, 1335), (24, 1243), (108, 1240), (199, 1248), (235, 1248), (236, 0)
AMP 5 = (1, 0), (27, 52), (34, 130), (110, 126), (191, 13), (234, 0)
FREQ 5 = (1, 1225), (9, 1569), (12, 1269), (21, 1573), (37, 1553), (97, 1552), (181, 1556), (234, 1566), (235, 0)
AMP 6 = (1, 0), (46, 83), (64, 100), (100, 100), (189, 11), (221, 0)
FREQ 6 = (1, 1483), (12, 1572), (23, 1988), (33, 1864), (114, 1864), (177, 1868), (221, 1879), (222, 0)
AMP 7 = (1, 0), (37, 39), (45, 77), (110, 79), (176, 11), (205, 0), (207, 0)
FREQ 7 = (1, 1792), (9, 1612), (29, 2242), (36, 2174), (93, 2176), (126, 2170), (205, 2188), (207, 0)
AMP 8 = (2, 0), (28, 17), (43, 71), (109, 66), (172, 8), (201, 0)
FREQ 8 = (2, 1590), (29, 2539), (36, 2491), (114, 2481), (153, 2489), (201, 2491), (203, 0)
AMP 9 = (2, 0), (29, 16), (43, 53), (54, 66), (105, 64), (165, 7), (191, 0)
FREQ 9 = (2, 1993), (25, 2121), (32, 2821), (37, 2796), (84, 2798), (105, 2792), (191, 2797), (192, 0)
AMP 10 = (1, 0), (27, 6), (41, 25), (56, 29), (72, 22), (95, 24), (180, 0)
FREQ 10 = (1, 1742), (12, 1849), (32, 3131), (37, 3111), (114, 3103), (164, 3116), (180, 3116), (181, 0)
AMP 11 = (2, 0), (37, 6), (55, 25), (88, 29), (114, 28), (164, 3), (186, 0)
FREQ 11 = (2, 1398), (41, 3419), (42, 3419), (91, 3419), (106, 3406), (150, 3421), (186, 3421), (187, 0)
AMP 12 = (7, 0), (39, 3), (43, 8), (88, 11), (118, 9), (138, 3), (165, 0)
FREQ 12 = (6, 0), (7, 1806), (23, 2942), (36, 2759), (37, 3746), (50, 3723), (84, 3731), (110, 3721), (156, 3741), (165, 3620), (167, 0)

Figure 3-20 Perspective plot and numeric breakpoint information for the piecewise linear approximation to a trumpet tone. Data for each of 12 amplitude and frequency curves is shown (the plot shows only the amplitude curves). The first number of each number pair is time in milliseconds. For the frequency curves, the second number is in hertz; for the amplitude curves, the second number is in arbitrary (linear) units.

```
#include <carl/cmusic.h>

ins 0 comp ;
    trans b2 d d d 0,0 0
        p5,p6 0 p7,p8 0 p9,p10 0 p11,p12 0 p13,p14 0 p15,p16 ;
    trans b3 d d d 0,0 0
        p17,p18 0 p19,p20 0 p21,p22 0 p23,p24 0 p25,p26 0 p27,p28 ;
    osc b1 b2 b3 f1 d ;
    out b1 ;
end ;


SINE(f1) ;

#define a(t,v)t/1000 v/4096
#define f(t,f)t/1000 (f)Hz

note 0 comp 0.360
    a(1,0) a(20,305) a(36,338) a(141,288) a(237,80) a(360,0)
    f(1,321) f(16,324) f(32,312) f(109,310) f(317,314) f(360,310) ;

ter ;
```

A comparison of the resynthesis of the tone based on the complete analysis data versus piecewise approximations to this data lead to two significant conclusions:

- The subjective quality of the approximation, though not always perceptually indistinguishable from the original tone, can be satisfactory at the level of musical indistinguishability.

- The amount of data needed to represent the approximation is on the order of a few number pairs (typically about eight) versus hundreds (typically 512 or more) numbers needed to represent the original data. This leads to a significant data reduction.

Synthesis based on piecewise linear approximation was sufficient to allow Grey to create a version of Robert Erickson's composition *Loops*. *Loops* is constructed as a musical "experiment" intended to investigate whether our sense of musical pitch is stronger in determining subjective organizations of musical patterns than timbre, or vice versa. The piece, originally composed for traditional instruments, consists of a single melodic line in which each successive note is played by a different instrument. The "instrumentation pattern" is organized into various repetitive groups, each group consisting of a sequence of I instruments, such as

1	saxophone
2	clarinet
3	trumpet
4	cello

for $I = 4$. The "pitch pattern" is similarly organized into various repetitive groups, each group consisting of a sequence of P pitches, such as

$$
\begin{array}{ll}
1 & G \\
2 & E\flat \\
3 & F \\
4 & D\flat \\
5 & B\flat
\end{array}
$$

for $P = 5$. When played in rapid succession, the sequence of I instrumental timbres is superimposed on the sequence of P pitches without rhythmic or dynamic accentuation (that is, all notes are of equal duration), producing a pattern such as this:

Note	Instrument	Pitch
1	1: saxophone	1: G
2	2: clarinet	2: E♭
3	3: trumpet	3: F
4	4: cello	4: D♭
5	1: saxophone	5: B♭
6	2: clarinet	1: G
7	3: trumpet	2: E♭
8	4: cello	3: F
9	1: saxophone	4: D♭
10	2: clarinet	5: B♭
11	3: trumpet	1: G
12	4: cello	2: E♭
13	1: saxophone	3: F
.	.	.
.	.	.
.	.	.

The key question posed by the piece is whether the melody is heard in temporal "groups" or patterns of I notes or P notes. If I-note groupings are reported by listeners, then tone quality is predominating over pitch; P-note groupings would tend to indicate that pitch predominates over timbre.

In one of its versions, the notes are played as even eighth notes at a tempo of about 120 quarter notes per minute. Both the instrumentation pattern and the pitch pattern are changed several times throughout the duration of the piece, making it a test of concentration for a group of human instrumentalists. Mistakes include not only playing wrong pitches or playing at the wrong time but also playing with any degree of dynamic emphasis that does not match that of the other players exactly. Live performance of Erickson's *Loops* is therefore quite challenging.

Computer synthesis of such a piece, by contrast, is straightforward—so much so that it is surprising that Erickson didn't synthesize this composition in the first place. Grey did this by choosing a single note that could be played by each of the several instruments at his disposal: the E above middle C. He then recorded and analyzed each instrument playing this note using short time spectrum measurement techniques. Each component of each note was then characterized by frequency and amplitude trajectories (Grey reasonably chose to ignore any phase contributions), which were replaced by piecewise linear approximations. The notes could then be resynthesized at different pitches by simple multiplication of the frequency values (such frequency modifications were generally small—on the order of a few semitones up or down). The loudness of each note was also matched to that of the others.

The results of the *Loops* experiment—though not in itself definitive—indicates that most listeners group the melody according to its pitch sequence rather than its timbre pattern. In other words, most listeners tend to hear the *Loops* melody in P-note rather than I-note groups.

3.3.3 Acoustical Illusions

Most synthetic sounds that do not resemble familiar sounds are easily identified as synthetic. This has prompted more than one observer of twentieth-century music to conclude that efforts to synthesize musical sounds have so far resulted in only one new timbre: electronic. Although such a conclusion is clearly false in the case of digital synthesis (if only in the case of the reconstruction of an analog signal from a sequence of digital samples), it is indeed remarkably difficult to synthesize a musical sound whose synthetic quality does not predominate over all others.

Sometimes, however, these synthetic qualities themselves become the foundation for surprising results. Such is the case with an interesting subclass of synthetic sounds called acoustical illusions. Like so-called optical illusions, acoustical illusions fool our perceptual mechanisms in some unexpected way.

One interesting and well-known acoustical illusion was discovered in the 1960s by Roger Shepard, a research psychologist who worked at AT&T Bell Laboratories while much of the early work on computer music was taking place. Shepard tones, as they are called, can be created using additive synthesis, though they are not based on sounds that occur in nature, nor are they based on tones produced by artificial musical instruments.

Shepard tones exhibit the peculiar property of *circular pitch* in the sense that if one constructs a musical scale out of them, the pitches eventually repeat themselves when the notes of the scale are played consecutively upward or downward. The illusion is that the notes have either continually increasing or decreasing pitch while simultaneously staying at or near the same place, similar to the optical barber pole illusion in which helical stripes painted on a rotating cylinder appear to move up or down as the cylinder rotates without ever moving off the ends of the pole.

Shepard created this effect by synthesizing a complex tone consisting only of components that are equally spaced on a log frequency scale. For instance, if all components are spaced an octave apart, their frequencies are constrained to lie at f, $2f$, $4f$, $8f$, $16f$, and so on, where f is the frequency of the lowest component.

The amplitude of each component is determined by a spectrum amplitude envelope curve such as the one shown in Figure 3-21. The shape of the amplitude

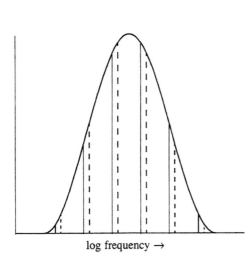

log frequency →

Figure 3-21   Spectrum amplitude envelope curve for Shepard tones. The amplitude of each sinusoidal component (whose frequencies are constrained to lie at equally spaced points along the log frequency axis—that is, they are separated by equal musical intervals) is given by the height of the spectrum amplitude envelope curve at that component's frequency. As many components are used as will fit under the amplitude envelope curve. The component frequencies and amplitudes for one tone are shown with solid vertical lines. The components for a second such tone are shown with dotted lines. As component amplitudes fall to zero (moving either upward or downward) at one end of the spectrum, they are replaced by new ones entering at the other end.

envelope curve in this case is a raised inverted cosine, equivalent to the hanning window function. Shepard demonstrated that by keeping the shape and position of the amplitude envelope curve fixed and by using octave-related components, one could play a chromatic 12-tone scale either upward or downward yet end up precisely where one began. Another researcher, Jean-Claude Risset, extended Shepard tones to the case where the frequency components glide continuously in an upward or downward direction while maintaining their frequency relationships precisely. In both cases, new components enter from one end and drop off at the other end, continuously maintaining the condition that as many components as will fit under the spectrum envelope curve are present at all times.

Shepard-Risset tone illusions can be extended in several ways. For example, if the component frequencies are held constant while the entire amplitude envelope curve is moved up or down along the log frequency axis, the tone will appear to become higher or lower in pitch while simultaneously remaining at the same pitch. If the components are moved in one direction, while the amplitude envelope is moved in the other direction, the result is a tone that seems to go up and down in pitch at the same time, and so on.

To synthesize Shepard-Risset tones, it is necessary to have a way to associate a given frequency with a corresponding amplitude. cmusic contains a unit generator called `lookup` that can associate input values with output values in an arbitrary way. The `lookup` unit generator simply uses a lookup table to associate input values with output values according to the general cmusic statement

```
lookup output[b] table[fvpn] input[bvpn] min[vpn] max[vpn] ;
```

The input value is clipped, meaning that if its value is less than `min`, it is set to `min`. Similarly, if the input value is greater than `max`, it is set to `max`. Input values between `min` and `max` are used to address wave table `table` by linearly mapping the input value into the index range 0 to $L - 1$, where L is the length of the wave table. Noninteger table addresses are resolved by linear interpolation between adjacent table entries. Thus we may think of the operation of the `lookup` unit generator as

```
if ( input < min ) input = min ;
if ( input > max ) input = max ;
integer_part = (int) (L - 1)*(input - min)/(max - min) ;
fractional_part = (L - 1)*(input - min)/(max - min) - integer_part ;
if ( integer_part < L - 1 )
   output = table[ (int) integer_part ] +
       ( table [ integer_part + 1 ] - table[ integer_part ] )
           * fractional_part ;
else
   output = table[ (int) integer_part ] ;
```

If the table is filled with a function $f(x)$, then the input value corresponds to x and the output value corresponds to $f(x)$.

A special function generator called `shepenv` is provided in cmusic to generate a spectrum amplitude envelope wave table that maps component frequencies into amplitudes. The general statement for this function generator is as follows:

```
gen <time> shepenv <wavetable> <cycles> <base> ;
```

This statement generates a wave table function suitable for the generation of Shepard-Risset illusions. The function produced by `shepenv` consists of a raised inverted cosine waveform that begins and ends with the value 0 and attains a single peak of 1 in between (that is, on a linear scale, $f(x) = 0.5 - 0.5 \cos x$, for $0 \le x \le 2\pi$). `shepenv` scales this function along a logarithmic abscissa, so that equal pitch intervals occupy equal intervals along the horizontal axis.

`shepenv` accepts two arguments: the number of logarithmic cycles and the logarithm base. For example, if the spectrum envelope is to be scaled over six octaves, `<cycles>` would be set to 6, and `<base>` would be set to 2; if the envelope is to span seven perfect fifths, `<cycles>` would be set to 7 and `<base>` to 3/2; and so on. cmusic.h contains a macro definition `SHEPENV(f)` that sets `<wavetable>` according to the `<cycles>` and `<base>` arguments that follow.

We can generate a single component for an upward-gliding Risset tone as follows. The pitch glide must start at the lowest frequency under the spectrum amplitude envelope. To be specific, let's suppose that we wish to construct a Risset tone glide over the four-octave range from A110 to A1760 [in cmusic notation, from A(-2) to A(2)]. Further, let's assume that only octave components are to be included, which implies that at any instant during the glide, at most four frequency components will be audible. Because we wish to create a spectrum amplitude envelope over four octaves, the statement

```
SHEPENV(f2) 4 2 ;
```

will create the appropriate lookup table for use in with the lookup unit generator (see Figure 3-22).

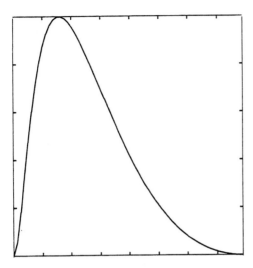

Figure 3-22 Output of the shepenv function generator for cycles = 4 and base = 2. The horizontal axis of this curve is linear frequency; the vertical axis is amplitude in arbitrary (linear) units. If plotted on a logarithmic frequency axis, this curve would exhibit the raised inverted cosine shape needed for the amplitude control of the components of a Shepard-Risset tone. The frequency (horizontal) axis of this curve is to be mapped with the lookup unit generator from min to max, where max lies four octaves above min.

We then use the trans unit generator to produce a frequency control function that will traverse one semitone per unit time for four octaves. If we choose a duration of 48 seconds, the glide will proceed at the rate of one semitone per second. So far we have determined the need for a trans unit generator to produce the (linear-pitch) frequency glide that feeds the frequency (increment) input of an oscillator to produce the output waveform (a sine wave). The same frequency control function can be fed simultaneously into a lookup unit generator to convert it into an associated amplitude according to the raised inverted cosine function produced by the shepenv wave table generator. The min and max values of the lookup unit generator may appropriately be set to A(-2) and A(2)—the range that the input signal will traverse. Thus a single component of the desired Risset tone could be produced with the cmusic score

```
#include <carl/cmusic.h>

ins 0 incomplete ;
    trans  b3 d d d 0,A(-2) ln((A(2))/(A(-2)) 1,A(2) ;
    lookup b2 f2 b3 A(-2) A(2) ;
    osc    b1 b2 b3 f1 d ;
    out    b1 ;
end ;


SINE(f1) ;
SHEPENV(f2) 4 2 ;


note 0 incomplete 48 ;


ter ;
```

As its name implies, however, this instrument is not yet complete. To create a Risset glide, more sinusoidal components must be added at different pitches. Also, an overall amplitude envelope is needed to avoid clicks at the beginning and end of the sound and also possibly to provide for inflection in the loudness of the tone over its total duration of 48 seconds.

In cmusic, we can provide overall (global) amplitude and frequency control for all sound components with a single instrument. Such a global control instrument provides control via input-output blocks that contain valid values for reference by other instruments over a duration specified in a cmusic score. For example, the instrument

```
ins 0 control ;    {amplitude (b5) and frequency (b6) control}
    osc   b5 p6 p5 f3 d ;
    trans b6 d d d 0,p7 p9 1,p8 ;
end ;
```

```
GEN4(f3) 0,0 -1 .01,1 0 .99,1 -1 1,0 ;    {amplitude envelope}
```

when played with the note statement

```
note 0 control 48 p4sec 1/4 A(-2) A(2) ln(p8/p7) ;
```

provides amplitude and frequency control via input-output blocks b5 and b6 that may be referenced by other instruments playing simultaneously in a cmusic score. To create a Risset glide, a second component an octave higher than the basic control frequency component must be added. This component will traverse the pitches from A(−1) to A(2) in the first three-fourths of the total note duration. After that it can reenter from A(−2) and ascend one octave. This component can be synthesized by multiplying the control frequency by 2 (one octave up) for the first three-fourths of the note duration and by one-eighth (three octaves down) for the final quarter of the note duration. Each of the two segments of this component can be synthesized with separate note statements—waveform linkage is not necessary because the abrupt change in the transposition factor (from an octave up to three octaves down) occurs when the amplitude of the component is zero.

To create such a component, we can define an instrument that receives its frequency control input from input-output block b6. Values in b6 will be set over a 48-second duration by the control instrument defined previously. To effect the transposition up or down, a `mult` unit generator may be used—the multiplication factor may then be set with a note parameter.

To use the overall amplitude envelope control information placed in b5 by the control instrument, we also add a multiplier unit generator between the lookup unit generator and the amplitude input of the main oscillator. The resulting component-synthesis instrument is shown in Figure 3-23.

A third component, two octaves higher than the basic component, will ascend from A(0) to A(2) over the first half of the total 48-second tone duration, after which it can be reset to A(−2) (two octaves lower than the control frequency) and ascend two octaves from there. A fourth component will start at a pitch three octaves higher than

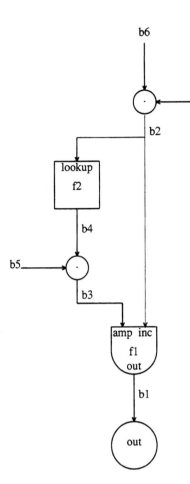

Figure 3-23   cmusic instrument to synthesize a Shepard-Risset tone component. Global amplitude and frequency control information is taken from input-output blocks b5 and b6 (this information must be provided by another instrument that plays simultaneously with this one). Note parameter p5 is used to scale the frequency control information, allowing the output waveform to be transposed up or down by an arbitrary musical interval.

A(–2) and after one-fourth of the note duration descend to the lowest frequency (one octave lower than the control frequency) and continue upward from there.

A complete cmusic score for the synthesis of a four-component Risset glide that ascends four octaves over a duration of 48 seconds follows. Note that the starting times for all notes are given in nondecreasing order (as required by cmusic).

```
#include <carl/cmusic.h>

ins 0 control ;    {amplitude (b5) and frequency (b6) control}
    osc   b5 p6 p5 f3 d ;
    trans b6 d d d 0,p7 p9 1,p8 ;
end ;

ins 0 component ;                          {component synthesis}
    mult   b2 b6 p5 ;        {scale frequency to proper value}
    lookup b4 f2 b2 A(-2) A(2) ;   {lookup amp for this freq}
    mult   b3 b5 b4 ;        {scale amp by global amp envelope}
```

```
    osc     b1 b3 b2 f1 d ;                    {waveform synthesis}
    out     b1 ;
end ;

SINE(f1) ;                                     {main waveform}
SHEPENV(f2) 4 2 ;                  {spectrum amplitude envelope}
GEN4(f3) 0,0 -1 .01,1 0 .99,1 -1 1,0 ;    {amplitude envelope}

{generate amp and freq control}
note 0 control 48 p4sec 1/4 A(-2) A(2) ln(p8/p7) ;

note  0 component 48 1    ;{component 1 (reference): glide up}
note  0 component 36 2    ;       {component 2A: 1 octave up}
note  0 component 24 4    ;       {component 3A: 2 octaves up}
note  0 component 12 8    ;       {component 4A: 3 octaves up}
note 12 component 36 1/2 ;        {component 4B: 1 octave down}
note 24 component 24 1/4 ;        {component 3B: 2 octaves down}
note 36 component 12 1/8 ;        {component 2B: 3 octaves down}

ter ;
```

3.3.4 The Phase Vocoder

Additive synthesis is clearly a powerful and general technique, but the quality of the result is determined (as usual) by the quality of the control data. In some cases—such as acoustical illusions—such control data is fairly easy to describe in a concise way. In most cases, however, the time-varying amplitude and frequency information required for additive synthesis must be based on the analysis of real tones through short time spectrum measurement techniques, as we have seen in the example of the data-reduced trumpet tone.

It is useful to have a practical means to analyze digital signals representing musical sounds. It is also highly desirable that the analysis data be in a form that is readily understood and manipulated. One such technique is the *phase vocoder*, which was originated and developed by James L. Flanagan and R. M. Golden at AT&T Bell Laboratories in the mid-1960s (Flanagan and Golden, 1966). As its name implies, the phase vocoder is a form of *vocoder*, a contraction of *voice encoder*. The original form of the device was the *channel vocoder* invented by Homer Dudley in the 1930s, also at AT&T Bell Laboratories (Dudley, 1939). All vocoders basically attempt to model their input signals—typically speech—in terms of multiple parallel channels, each of which describes activity in a particular region of the spectrum of the input signal. Because the activity in each spectrum region is usually much less complicated than the entire input spectrum, each channel may be transmitted or recorded using much less information than is required for the original signal; in many cases, a particular channel may even be omitted. Thus the original idea of the vocoder arose from the desire to find efficient ways to transmit as many simultaneous conversations as possible over individual telephone wires.

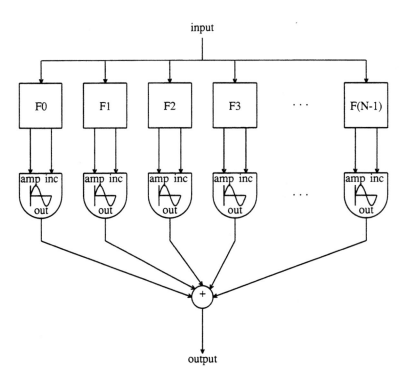

Figure 3-24　Block diagram of the phase vocoder. Each of N filters analyzes a small portion of the frequency spectrum of the input signal and produces time-varying amplitude and frequency signals that may be used to control a bank of table lookup oscillators. If the intermediate data is not modified, the sum of the signals produced by these oscillators (the output) will be identical to the input signal.

The musical utility of vocoders comes from the fact that vocoder channels contain information in a form that allows the input sound to be understood and manipulated in various useful ways. John Grey and James Moorer's pioneering work in use of the phase vocoder for musical purposes in the mid-1970s resulted in such analyses as the trumpet tone seen earlier (Grey and Moorer, 1977; Moorer, 1978). Around the same time, M. R. Portnoff clarified the use of the FFT for highly efficient time-varying spectrum measurements (Portnoff, 1980), speech analysis (Portnoff, 1981a), and time scale modifications using such techniques (Portnoff, 1981b). More recently, Mark Dolson, working at the University of California, San Diego, Computer Audio Research Laboratory, has implemented an advanced version of the phase vocoder that has been used in the creation of musical works by several composers (Dolson, 1986).

For our purposes, the phase vocoder may be viewed as an analysis-synthesis technique in which the intermediate data is couched in terms of time-varying amplitude and frequency signals suitable for the control of table lookup oscillators such as the cmusic `osc` unit generator. Phase vocoder operation can be generally described in terms of a filter bank connected to an oscillator bank (see Figure 3-24). Each of the putative filters analyzes a portion of the frequency range of an arbitrary input signal. Taken together, the bank of filters normally covers all possible frequencies in the input signal. Phase vocoder filters each produce dual signals that may be fed directly to the amplitude and frequency control inputs of a table lookup oscillator. Under certain circumstances, which we shall presently discuss, the sum of the signals produced by the oscillator bank may be used to reconstruct the input signal precisely. The phase vocoder analysis procedure is therefore a very useful source of additive synthesis parameters.

As an added benefit, the amplitude and frequency control signals may be manipulated in various ways to construct usefully modified versions of the input signal. For example, the phase vocoder allows the pitch of the input signal to be modified without changing its duration, or, equivalently, the duration of the input signal can be modified without changing its pitch. In addition, the spectrum of the signal may be modified in various useful ways. The intermediate data may also be so encoded as to reduce the storage needed for a parameterized representation of a musical sound (for example, by replacing it with piecewise linear approximations). Before delving into the detailed operation of the phase vocoder, it will be useful to elaborate on the notion of short time spectrum analysis.[14]

3.3.5 Fourier Transforms and Filterbanks

In Chapter 2, we defined the short time spectrum of an input signal $x(n)$ with the relation

$$X_n(e^{j\omega}) = \sum_{m=-\infty}^{\infty} w(n-m)x(m)e^{-j\omega m} \qquad (3\text{-}45)$$

(the scale factor before the summation is omitted here for convenience) where $w(n)$ is a window function of length N_w samples that selects a portion of $x(n)$, weighting the samples of that portion according to the shape of the window.

Equation (3-45) is clearly a function of both discrete time (n) and continuous frequency (ω). To interpret such a dual relationship, we either can hold time n fixed at a particular value and let frequency ω vary over its range of possible values, or we may choose a particular value for frequency variable ω and let time n vary. Both of these choices lead to alternative interpretations of equation (3-45). More important, however, the equation shows how these alternative interpretations lead to a *unification* of two seemingly independent concepts:

- *Fourier transform interpretation.* If we hold time n fixed, equation (3-45) describes the Fourier transform of a windowed portion of waveform $x(n)$:

$$w(n-m)x(m) \quad -\infty < m < \infty \qquad (3\text{-}46)$$

- *Filterbank interpretation.* If we choose a particular value for frequency ω that we

---

[14]The following technical discussion of the phase vocoder is partly based on Flanagan and Golden (1966) and Rabiner and Schafer (1978), to which you may refer for further details.

will denote as ω_k, equation (3-45) describes the time varying response of a band-pass filter whose properties (amplitude and phase response) are determined by its impulse response:

$$w(n)e^{j\omega_k n} \tag{3-47}$$

Taking the Fourier view, we have already seen in Chapter 2 how multiple spectrum measurements of $x(n)$ can be made by making various choices for n and using the discrete Fourier transform (DFT) to evaluate the Fourier transform at N equally spaced frequencies around the unit circle. By sliding or hopping the position of the window along $x(n)$ (with or without overlap), this procedure can reveal how the spectrum of $x(n)$ evolves over time—an important consideration if we are to capture whatever musical qualities it may possess.

By a change of summation index, equation (3-45) may be rewritten in the following mathematically equivalent form:

$$X_n(e^{j\omega}) = \sum_{m=-\infty}^{\infty} w(m)x(n-m)e^{-j\omega(n-m)}$$
$$= e^{-j\omega n}\sum_{m=-\infty}^{\infty} w(m)x(n-m)e^{j\omega m} \tag{3-48}$$

For a particular choice of ω (which we call ω_k), we can define

$$h_k(n) = w(n)e^{j\omega_k n} \tag{3-49}$$

For a fixed frequency, then, the summation in equation (3-48) expresses the *convolution* of $x(n)$ with $h_k(n)$, scaled by the time-varying quantity $e^{-j\omega_k n}$; that is,

$$X_n(e^{j\omega_k}) = e^{-j\omega_k n}\sum_{m=-\infty}^{\infty} x(n-m)h_k(m) \tag{3-50}$$

Equation (3-50) therefore describes a filtering operation on $x(n)$ in which the impulse response of the filter is given by $h_k(n)$ and the output of the filter is modulated by $e^{-j\omega_k n}$. In Chapter 2, we saw that the spectra of typical window functions (such as rectangular or Hamming windows) generally have the properties of lowpass filters. If we multiply such a window function by the complex sinusoid $e^{j\omega_k n} = \cos\omega_k n + j\sin\omega_k n$, the result will describe the impulse response of a bandpass filter with a frequency response centered around radian frequency $\omega_k = 2\pi f_k$ and a passband width and shape determined by the spectrum of $w(n)$.

We can implement equation (3-50) as a *bank* of filters by simultaneously choosing several center frequencies ω_k, $k = 0, 1, \ldots, N-1$ along with an appropriate window function w. Nothing in particular restricts us to using the same window function for all filter channels, but we will consider only the case where N equally-spaced frequencies are chosen around the unit circle and the window function for each filter channel is identical. Generally, we wish to choose the filter spacing and bandwidths in such a way that the entire spectrum of the input signal is covered uniformly; that is, we do not want our filter bank either to ignore or to overemphasize any particular region of frequency.

Figure 3-25 depicts the composite response of a filter bank for the case $N = 8$ and two idealized types of filter passbands. The upper part of the figure shows a "perfect" filter bank response in the sense that it is made up of "ideal" lowpass (or bandpass) filters spaced in such a way that all frequencies are covered and the filter passbands do not overlap. The lower part of the figure idealizes the cases where the overlapping passbands of the filter channels still allow the composite frequency response of the filter bank to be precisely flat at all frequencies.

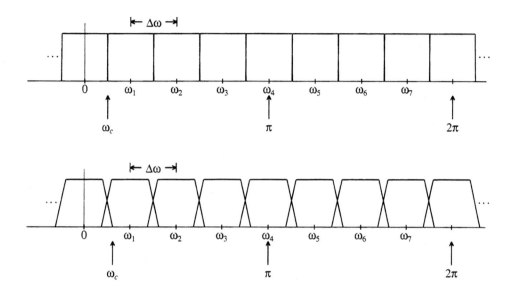

Figure 3-25 Idealized composite frequency responses for an $N = 8$ channel filter bank. All frequencies are shown in normalized radian units, with 2π corresponding to the sampling frequency. The center frequencies of the filter passbands (which are shown as having idealized trapezoidal shapes) are ω_i, $i = 0, 1, \ldots, 7$. The spacing between center frequencies is denoted as $\Delta\omega$ ($= \omega_1 = 2\pi/8$). The cutoff frequency of the lowpass filter function associated with the analysis window, denoted ω_c, is seen to be the half bandwidth of the bandpass regions. The upper part of the figure depicts nonoverlapping bands; the lower part shows overlapping between adjacent bands.

If we define the output of the kth channel of our filter bank as

$$y_k(n) = X_n(e^{j\omega_k})e^{j\omega_k n} \tag{3-51}$$

then we see from equation (3-50) that

$$y_k(n) = \sum_{m=-\infty}^{\infty} x(n-m)h_k(m) \tag{3-52}$$

Because $X_n(e^{j\omega_k})$ can be represented in alternative ways, so can the computation of $y_k(n)$. According to equation (3-50), $y_k(n)$ could be computed in the following way (the filter bank method):

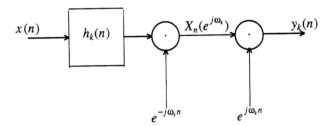

But, equation (3-45) implies that $y_k(n)$ could be computed according to the following diagram (the Fourier method).

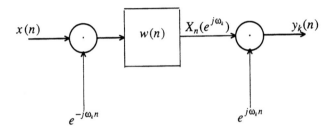

Equation (3-52) is satisfied using either method, because the exponential terms cancel, making the computation of $y_k(n)$ equivalent to the following flow diagram:

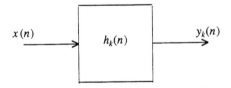

An important feature of short time spectrum analysis is that it can be shown that under certain conditions, the sum of all of the filter channel outputs (in the filter bank view) can be made precisely equal to the input signal. In other words, under these conditions, we can "break up" the frequency content of an input signal into N bands without worrying about losing any important information because we can reconstruct the input signal precisely by adding together the information in all the separate bands (see Figure 3-26). This result is so important that we must consider briefly the conditions under which it is true.

(Analysis)   (Synthesis)

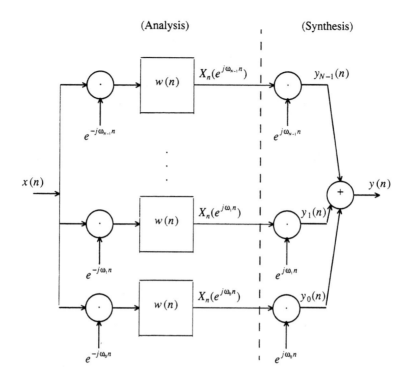

Figure 3-26 *N*-channel analysis-synthesis filter bank for short time spectrum analysis. The analysis for each channel consists of a complex modulator that shifts frequencies in the input signal *x*(*n*) to a region near 0 Hz, followed by a lowpass filter whose properties are determined by window function *w*(*n*). Synthesis consists of shifting the frequencies in the analysis channels back to their original position so that they can be added together to form the output signal *y*(*n*). Under certain conditions, the output signal can be identical to the input.

3.3.6 Sampling Rates in Time and Frequency

In Chapter 2, we saw from consideration of the highest frequency component in a signal that the sampling rate needed to avoid aliasing resulted in the *sampling theorem*, that is, $R \geq 2f_{max}$, where R is the necessary sampling rate and f_{max} is the highest frequency in an analog signal to be sampled. Because $X_n(e^{j\omega})$ is to be sampled both in time and in frequency (if we are to use digital signal processing techniques), we must consider the sampling rates along both the time and the frequency dimensions if we are to avoid aliasing in both domains.[15] If the *effective bandwidth* of the analysis window $w(n)$ is

---

[15]*Time aliasing* is entirely analogous to frequency aliasing as discussed in Chapter 2. The interchangeability of the time and frequency domains under the Fourier transform allows us to see that undersampling in frequency can result in time aliasing just as undersampling in time can result in frequency aliasing. Just as undersampling in time can cause spectrum features to appear at the wrong frequency, undersampling in frequency can cause temporal features to appear at the wrong time.

B Hz, then according to the sampling theorem, $X_n(e^{j\omega})$ must be sampled at a rate of at least $2B$ samples per second in order to avoid aliasing.

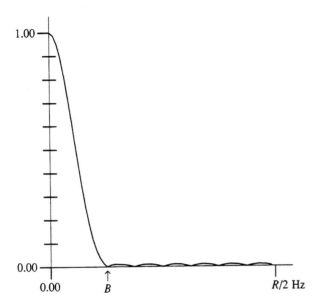

Figure 3-27   Positive frequency half of the amplitude spectrum of a Hamming window. The effective bandwidth of the window is marked at B Hz.

For example, if $w(n)$ is a Hamming window, then the effective bandwidth of $W(e^{j\omega})$ is given by

$$B = \frac{2R}{N_w} \quad \text{Hz} \tag{3-53}$$

where R is the sampling rate in hertz and N_w is the length of the Hamming window (see Figure 3-27).[16] Then, if N_w is 1024 samples and R is 16,384 samples per second, the effective bandwidth of the Hamming window is 32 Hz. According to the sampling theorem, to compute the short time Fourier transform $X_n(e^{j\omega})$ without aliasing, the input signal $x(n)$ must be sampled at a rate of at least $2B$ samples (windows) per second, or at a rate of 64 Hz. Therefore, $X_n(e^{j\omega})$ must be computed at a "window rate" of at least 64 Hz—at least once every 256 samples—using a Hamming window if we wish to be able to reconstruct the input signal from the short time spectrum measurements of it.

In the frequency domain, if window $w(n)$ is time-limited, then $X_n(e^{j\omega})$ can be viewed as a normal Fourier transform with an inverse transform that is similarly time-limited. The sampling theorem then requires that $X_n(e^{j\omega})$ be sampled in the frequency

---

[16]The effective bandwidth is taken to be the frequency of the first zero of the spectrum of the window function. Obviously, side lobes with significant peak amplitudes will exist at higher frequencies.

domain at a frequency "rate" of at least twice the "time width" of the window.[17] For a given value of n, $X_n(e^{j\omega})$ is just the Fourier transform of the windowed input signal $x(m)w(n - m)$, which has a duration of N_w samples—the length of the window function. Therefore, $X_n(e^{j\omega})$ must be sampled in frequency at a "rate" of at least $2\pi R/N_w$ Hz, that is, at the set of radian frequencies

$$\omega_k = \frac{2\pi k}{N_w} \qquad k = 0, 1, \ldots, N_w - 1 \qquad (3\text{-}54)$$

In other words, the sampling theorem requires that if $N_w = 1024$, $X_n(e^{j\omega})$ must in general be sampled at at least 1024 uniformly spaced frequencies around the unit circle to avoid time aliasing.

In practice, it is possible to use filters with bandwidths either greater or smaller than the ideal value, provided that we are able to tolerate some degree of nonuniformity in the composite response of the filter bank. We will discuss the special windowing techniques for doing this later.

From equations (3-53) and (3-54), we can see that the total number of samples that must be computed per second of $X_n(e^{j\omega})$ in order to avoid both time and frequency aliasing is given by

$$R_X \geq 2BN_w \qquad \text{samples per second} \qquad (3\text{-}55)$$

The ratio R_X/R is then a measure of the minimum extent of the data explosion encountered when a sampled signal $x(n)$ is replaced by its short time Fourier analysis $X_n(e^{j\omega})$. Using the frequency of the first zero of the window spectrum $W(e^{j\omega})$ to define B (the effective bandwidth of a window viewed as a lowpass filter), we see that $R_X/R = 4$ in the case of a Hamming window. The short time spectrum representation of $x(n)$ is therefore seen to require *at least* four times as much data as $x(n)$ itself.[18] However, the short time spectrum may be manipulated in both the frequency and time domain in ways that are not easy to accomplish directly on $x(n)$ itself.

3.3.7 Window Functions for Short Time Spectrum Analysis

We have seen that $X_n(e^{j\omega})$ must be properly sampled in both time and frequency if the output of the analysis-synthesis procedure is to be identical to the input. In addition to these constraints, there are some additional constraints on the window function $w(n)$ if the input signal is to be recoverable from the output of the analysis procedure.

---

[17]The longer the window, the narrower the bandwidth of the filters—the narrower the bandwidths, the more closely spaced the channel center frequencies must be to avoid gaps between adjacent bands; the more closely spaced the channel center frequencies, the more channels are needed to cover all available frequencies.

[18]The fact that the spectrum values are complex would seem to double this data requirement. However, we should recall that the spectrum of N real values is *symmetrical* around 0 Hz. The rfft program given in Chapter 2 provides a method by which all the complex spectrum information associated with N real-valued samples can be "shoehorned" into an array of length N.

In terms of the filter bank method, Figure 3-26 shows how the output signal is formed by adding together the outputs of the individual channels according to

$$y(n) = \sum_{k=0}^{N-1} y_k(n) = \sum_{k=0}^{N-1} X_n(e^{j\omega_k})e^{j\omega_k n} \qquad (3\text{-}56)$$

Assuming that window $w(n)$ is the same for all channels, it can be shown that if $X_n(e^{j\omega})$, is properly sampled in frequency (that is, when $N \geq N_w$),

$$y(n) = Nw(c)x(n) \qquad (3\text{-}57)$$

where $w(c)$ refers to the "midpoint value" of the window. This result holds regardless of the detailed shape of the window function chosen. Therefore, one constraint on the window function is that $w(c)$ be nonzero.

If $X_n(e^{j\omega})$ is undersampled in frequency, that is, if $N_w > N$, it can be shown that $x(n)$ is still perfectly recoverable (at least in theory) from $X_n(e^{j\omega})$ provided that $w(n)$ is equal to zero at intervals of N samples away from $w(c)$; that is,

$$w(c \pm rN) = 0 \qquad r = 1, 2, 3, \ldots \qquad (3\text{-}58)$$

In this case, we generally choose $w(n)$ so that its spectrum $W(e^{j\omega})$ approximates an ideal lowpass filter response as closely as possible. Recalling that the ideal lowpass filter has an impulse response of the form sinc $x = (\sin \pi x)/\pi x$ which is infinitely long (that is the problem with "ideal" lowpass filters!), we see that this response must be shortened to a manageable (finite) length for practical applications. As we saw in Chapter 2, one of the best ways to accomplish this is to multiply the sinc x function by a window function such as a Hamming window centered about $x = 0$. The resulting sequence ·can have any desired length. By multiplying the central N_w samples of the function

$$\text{sinc}\frac{x}{N} = N\frac{\sin(\pi x/N)}{\pi x} \qquad (3\text{-}59)$$

(which crosses through 0 every N samples from its midpoint at $x = 0$) by a Hamming window, we obtain an analysis window that has a unity midpoint value and has zero values as required. When N_w is an even number, care must be taken to assure that the resulting window is symmetrical, because in this case the midpoint of the sinc (x/N) function falls between two samples. Window functions with even and odd lengths are plotted in Figure 3-28 and spectra of typical window functions are shown in Figure 3-29.

Observation of Figure 3-29 makes it clear how increasing the window length N_w relative to the number of analysis channels N increases the sharpness of the cutoff of the filters, thus reducing the amount of overlap between adjacent bands. Reducing interband overlap has the generally desirable effect of decreasing the likelihood that a single sinusoidal component of the input signal could fall within the passbands of more than one filter bank channel. However, increasing the time width of the analysis window also has the effect of "smearing" temporal information regarding changes in the amplitudes and frequencies of the component sinusoids. In effect, filters with sharp sharp cutoff transitions take longer to respond to changes in the input signal than filters

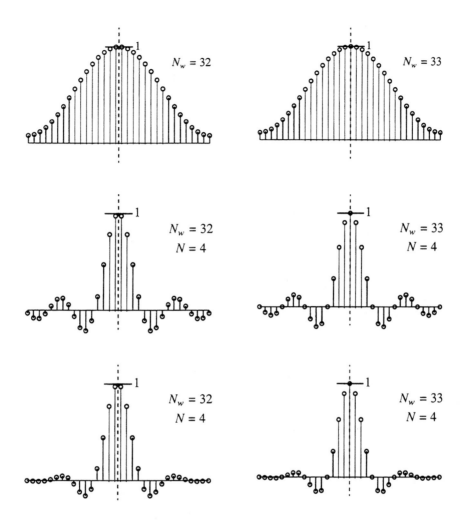

Figure 3-28 Window functions for short time spectrum analysis. Even and odd window lengths (time widths) are shown on the left and right, respectively. Midpoints are marked with dotted vertical lines. The uppermost plots show Hamming window functions. The middle plots show sinc (x/N) for $N = 4$ (N corresponds to the number of analysis channels). The bottom plots show the products of the two functions above them. Spectra of the three plots on the left are shown in Figure 3-29.

with more gradual cutoff transitions. In practical terms, this means that some experimentation with the N_w/N ratio may be necessary to find the best compromise between tracking rapid changes in the input signal versus minimizing interband overlap. Typical ratios generally lie in the range from 1 (for rapidly varying signals) to 4 (for more slowly varying signals).

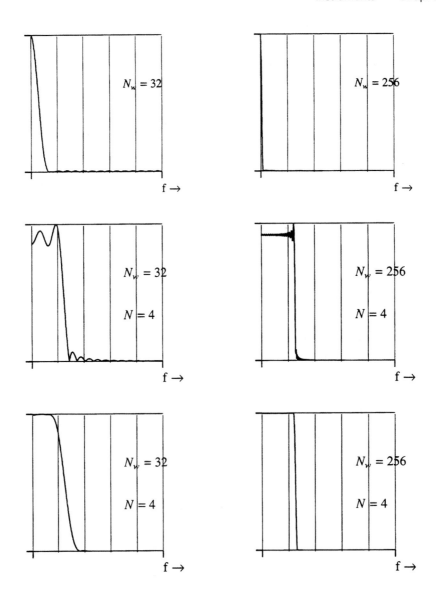

Figure 3-29 Analysis window spectra. The uppermost plots show positive frequency amplitude spectra of two time widths ($N_w = 32$ and $N_w = 256$) for a Hamming window. The middle
plots show sinc (x/N) for $N = 4$ and the same two time widths. The bottom plots show the convolutions of the two functions above them. Note the similarity of the bottom plots to the idealized filters shown in Figure 3-25.

3.3.8 Filterbank Analysis-Synthesis

We now can see that the definition given earlier for $y_k(n)$ represents a synthesis equation for a single channel of $X_n(e^{j\omega})$ when it is viewed as describing a filterbank. Analysis and synthesis operations for such a filterbank are shown in Figure 3-26.

Several observations are in order regarding the filter bank interpretation of short time spectrum measurements. First, the analysis consists of two basic steps: modulation by a complex sinusoid and lowpass filtering. To understand the modulation process, we have only to recall that multiplication of the input signal by a sinusoid at f Hz results in a signal that has a spectrum equal to the convolution of the spectrum of the input signal with the spectrum of the sinusoid. Viewed in terms of amplitude modulation, the resulting signal will contain components at all possible sum and difference frequencies among the components of the input signal and the sinusoid. For example, if the input signal is itself a sinusoid at f_1 Hz and the modulator for a particular filter bank channel is running at f_2 Hz, then the modulated signal will contain components at $f_1 + f_2$ Hz and $f_1 - f_2$ Hz according to the trigonometric identity

$$\cos A \cos B = \frac{1}{2}[\cos(A+B) + \cos(A-B)] \qquad (3\text{-}60)$$

If f_1 and f_2 are equal or nearly equal, the quantity $f_1 - f_2$ will be zero or nearly zero. In other words, the modulation process shifts the frequency components in the input signal that lie in the vicinity of the modulation frequency down to a very low (possibly zero) frequency. The lowpass filtering action of the window then attenuates any components above its cutoff frequency, leaving only information about signal components in the vicinity of the modulation frequency. Thus the identical lowpass filter (window function) can be used for all channels in the filter bank, because the modulation process essentially "shifts the attention" of the lowpass filter to a region of the spectrum centered around the modulation frequency.

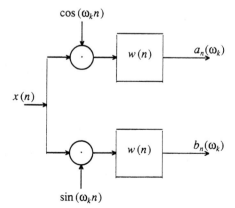

Figure 3-30   Implementation of a single channel of filter bank analysis.

Furthermore, the complex modulation process produces dual outputs corresponding to the real and imaginary parts of the complex sinusoid according to Euler's relation $e^{-j\omega_k n} = \cos(\omega_k n) - j\sin(\omega_k n)$. Viewed in terms of purely real operations, a single analysis channel of the filterbank has the form shown in Figure 3-30. This type of process is often called *quadrature modulation*, and the entire analysis procedure consisting of quadrature modulation at a selected frequency followed by fixed lowpass filtering is often called *heterodyning*.[19]

Another property of the filter bank analysis procedure worth noting is that because the filtered output signals ideally contain frequencies only up to the cutoff frequency of the lowpass filter, they need not be sampled at the same rate as the input signal. If the cutoff frequency of the filter were, say, 50 Hz, then according to the sampling theorem as few as 100 samples per second could be used to represent it.

If the sampling rate of $x(n)$ were, say, 50,000 Hz, then for a Hamming analysis window of length $N_w = 500$, we could lower the channel sampling rates either by running the modulators and filters at the input sampling rate and simply discarding 124 out of every 125 samples[20] or, by computing the analysis data only once for every 125 samples of input. This adds a minor complication to the synthesis procedure because in general we need $y_k(n)$ at the original sampling rate. This can be accomplished by inserting 124 zeros between the channel samples and using a suitable lowpass filter for interpolation.[21] These sample rate decimation and interpolation processes are depicted in Figure 3-31.

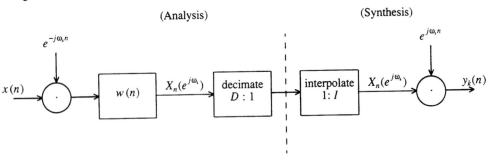

Figure 3-31 Complete implementation of a single channel of filter bank analysis-synthesis. In principle, the decimation ratio D can be set to $R/2f_c$ where R is the input (output) sampling rate and f_c is the cutoff frequency of the lowpass filter. If the interpolation factor I is the same as D, then $y_k(n)$ will be restored to the original sampling rate. Other choices for I allow shrinking and expanding the time scale during resynthesis.

[19]Because it is generally easier to construct variable-frequency oscillators than variable-frequency filters, and because heterodyning always produces output in the same (low) frequency range, it is a common technique for the detection of signals at selectable frequencies. Radio sets, for example, are often tuned in this way.

[20]Recall that for this case, the effective bandwidth of the Hamming window would be 200 Hz, implying that it should be applied at least 400 times a second, or at least once every 125 samples at a 50,000-Hz sampling rate.

[21]Due to its simplicity, linear interpolation, though far from ideal, can often be used for this process. The "ideal" interpolation filter for a 1:I interpolation has a sinc (n/I) response, as we shall see later.

3.3.9 FFT Implementation of Short Time Spectrum Analysis

Because, for fixed n, $X_n(e^{j\omega})$ can be viewed as the normal Fourier transform of the sequence

$$w(n-m)x(m) \qquad -\infty < m < \infty \tag{3-61}$$

it would be highly desirable to recouch its formulation so that the highly efficient FFT algorithm can be used to compute it. To accomplish this, we must substitute N equally spaced analysis frequencies of the form $\omega_k = 2\pi k/N$, $k = 0, 1, \ldots, N-1$ for the continuous frequency variable ω. This leads to the following form of the short time spectrum of $x(n)$:

$$X_n(e^{j(2\pi/N)k}) = \sum_{m=-\infty}^{\infty} w(n-m)x(m)e^{-j(2\pi/N)km} \tag{3-62}$$

If the limits of the summation in equation (3-62) were 0 to $N-1$, it could be evaluated with the DFT. To accomplish this transformation mathematically, we may rewrite equation (3-62) in the following form:

$$X_n(e^{j(2\pi/N)k}) = e^{-j(2\pi/N)kn} \sum_{m=-\infty}^{\infty} x_n(m)e^{-j(2\pi/N)km} \tag{3-63}$$

where the sequence $x_n(m)$ is defined as

$$x_n(m) = x(n+m)w(-m) \qquad -\infty < m < \infty \tag{3-64}$$

In other words, $x_n(m)$ represents the sequence $x(m)w(n-m)$ redefined to have an origin at sample n. For example, $x_0(m)$ is simply the sequence $x(m)w(-m)$ for all values of m, $x_1(m)$ is the sequence $x(m+1)w(-m)$ for all m, and so on. Notice that each of these sequences is only N_w samples long and that the negative index for $w(-m)$ specifies that the window is to be reversed in time, though the symmetry of most practical windows makes this reversal conceptually moot.

By substituting $m = Nr + q$, $-\infty < r < \infty$ and $q = 0, 1, \ldots, N-1$, equation (3-63) can be rewritten in the form

$$X_n\left[e^{j(2\pi/N)k}\right] = e^{-j(2\pi/N)kn} \sum_{r=-\infty}^{\infty} \left[\sum_{q=0}^{N-1} x_n(Nr+q)\right] e^{-j(2\pi/N)k(Nr+q)} \tag{3-65}$$

Interchanging the order of summation is permissible because $e^{-j2\pi kr}$ for integer values of k and r is equal to unity, yielding

$$X_n\left[e^{j(2\pi/N)k}\right] = e^{-j(2\pi/N)kn} \sum_{q=0}^{N-1} \left[\sum_{r=-\infty}^{\infty} x_n(Nr+q)\right] e^{-j(2\pi/N)kq} \tag{3-66}$$

Because $w(-m)$ is a finite-length sequence of length N_w, we can see that

$$u_n(q) = \sum_{r=-\infty}^{\infty} x_n(Nr+q) \qquad q = 0, 1, \ldots, N-1 \tag{3-67}$$

is also a finite-length sequence of length N. Therefore, we have

$$X_n \left[e^{j(2\pi/N)k} \right] = e^{-j(2\pi/N)kn} \sum_{q=0}^{N-1} u_n(q) e^{-j(2\pi/N)kq} \qquad k = 0, 1, \ldots, N-1 \quad (3\text{-}68)$$

which is just the DFT of $u_n(q)$ times $e^{-j2\pi kn/N}$.

Recalling that the DFT treats the N samples that are transformed as *one period* of an infinitely periodic waveform, we can apply the *shift theorem* for the DFT, which states that multiplication of the spectrum by a complex exponential is equivalent to taking the DFT of a *rotated* sequence of N samples according to

$$\text{DFT}[x((n-d) \bmod N)] = e^{-j(2\pi/N)kd} X(k) \qquad (3\text{-}69)$$

where d is a delay (shift factor) in samples. We can therefore write our expression for $X_n(e^{j2\pi k/N})$ as

$$X_n \left[e^{j(2\pi/N)k} \right] = \sum_{m=0}^{N-1} u_n((m-n) \bmod N) e^{-j(2\pi/N)km} \qquad (3\text{-}70)$$

which is the N-point DFT of a sequence easily derived from the windowed input sequence.

Although the foregoing mathematical steps may appear somewhat complicated, their implementation in terms of programming is quite straightforward. We start by forming the sequence $x_n(m)$ as defined in equation (3-64). A simple way to do this involves setting up an array `window[]` to hold the N_w values of window function $w(-m)$, recalling that the time reversal requirement is trivially satisfied for symmetrical window functions.

We have a choice regarding how to define $w(0)$. It can reasonably be placed at the beginning, end, or midpoint of the window. In terms of linear filtering theory, defining $w(n)$ over the interval 0 through $N_w - 1$ makes the window *noncausal* in the sense that aligning $w(0)$ with $x(n)$ makes the windowed sequence rely on knowledge of $x(n+0), x(n+1), \ldots, x(n+N_w-1)$: all but the first of these values of the input signal lies in the future with respect to time n. Defining $w(n)$ over the interval $-(N_w - 1)$ to 0 makes the window strictly *causal* by a similar argument. Finally, defining $w(n)$ over the interval $-M$ to $+M$, where $M = (N_w - 1)/2$, has the advantage of aligning the midpoint of the window with $x(n)$. Such a definition is sometimes called *symmetric*, though strictly speaking, it is just a special case of a noncausal window. In all cases, the window is N_w samples long, however.

We can also set up an input buffer `input[]`—also of length N_w—to hold the input samples. If we regard `window[0]` as holding $w(0)$, `window[1]` as holding $w(-1)$ (that is, the window is causal), and so on, we may form the sequence $x_n(m)$ by shifting samples into the `input[]` array from right to left (the value in `input[i]` is shifted into position `input[i-1]` throughout the array) and taking the product of the two arrays. When $x(0)$ has been shifted all the way to `input[0]`, the product of the two arrays will correspond to $x_0(m)$. Therefore, just before the first input sample is shifted into the right-hand end of `input[]`, the (all-zero) product of the two arrays would correspond to $x_{-N_w}(m)$ (we consider the input signal $x(n)$ to be all zero for negative values of n).

The product of the two arrays can then be formed with the C statement

```
for ( i = 0 ; i < Nw ; i++ )   /* all arrays of length Nw */
    product[i] = input[i]*window[i]
```

Equation (3-67) specifies that the `product[]` array is to be broken up into segments of length N, where N is the desired DFT length. These segments are simply added together to form a "folded" version of length N of the `product[]` array according to the C statements

```
for ( i = 0 ; i < N ; i++ )   /* folded array of length N */
    folded[i] = 0.0 ;
for ( m = i = 0 ; i < Nw ; i++ ) {
    folded[m] += product[i] ;
    if ( ++m >= N )
        m = 0 ;
}
```

Finally, the `folded[]` array is to be rotated circularly according to the value of time n (here we assume that variable `n` is a temporary copy of the time variable that may be modified as needed).

```
while ( n < 0 )
    n += N ;
n %= N ;
for ( i = 0 ; i < N ; i++ ) {
    rotated[i] = folded[n] ;
    if ( ++n >= N )
        n = 0 ;
}
```

An astute programmer reading this description will sooner or later notice that the three operations of windowing, folding, and rotating may easily be combined as follows:

```
for ( i = 0 ; i < N ; i++ )
    analysis[i] = 0.0 ;
while ( n < 0 )
    n += N ;
n %= N ;
for ( i = 0 ; i < Nw ; i++ ) {
    analysis[n] += input[i]*window[i] ;
    if ( ++n >= N )
        n = 0 ;
}
```

Here we name the result `analysis[]` to reflect the fact that it will next be submitted to a DFT routine. If N is chosen to be a power of 2, then the `rfft` program given in Chapter 2 can be used efficiently to compute the DFT of the `analysis[]` array with the FFT algorithm.

We have seen how $X_n(e^{j 2\pi k/N})$ can be computed for any value of n, any valid FFT length N, and any window length N_w. One of the important features of this process is that it can be reversed; that is, we can recover $x(n)$ exactly from successive computations of $X_n(e^{j 2\pi k/N})$ for increasing values of n. An especially important feature of this process is that $x(n)$ is precisely recoverable even when the value of n is incremented by more than one sample each time the analysis is done. In fact, we can recover $x(n)$ precisely—at least in theory—as long as the value of n is incremented for each analysis by an amount D that is less than or equal to N (the DFT length).

Assuming that $X_n(e^{j 2\pi k/N})$ is available for every D samples of $x(n)$, the computation of $y(n)$—the output of the analysis-synthesis procedure—would involve taking the inverse DFT of these spectrum measurements and summing the result in some way according to

$$y(n) = \sum_{k=0}^{N-1} Y_n(k) e^{j(2\pi/N)kn} \qquad n = 0, 1, \ldots, N-1 \tag{3-71}$$

$Y_n(k)$ is a (possibly modified) version of $X_n(e^{j 2\pi k/N})$ according to

$$Y_n(k) = P_k X_n\left[e^{j(2\pi/N)k} \right] \qquad k = 0, 1, \ldots, N-1 \tag{3-72}$$

where P_k is a complex weighting coefficient for modifying channel k (P_k may, for example, be set to zero in order to exclude the kth channel from the resynthesis). Because $X_n(e^{j 2\pi k/N})$ is available only for values of n that are integer multiples of D samples, we can think of each of its channels as a sequence pertaining to a particular frequency k that has an available value at multiples of D samples and is zero in between. The intermediate values for each channel must be interpolated from the data available for each channel. If we properly interpolate at the rate of once every D samples, $x(n)$ will be reconstructed precisely. If, however, we interpolate the samples for each channel at a rate of once every I samples, where $I \neq D$, modifications in the time scale are possibie. For example, if $I = 2D$, the output sequence $y(n)$ will contain twice as many samples as the input sequence $x(n)$. Even though the spectrum of $y(n)$ will evolve over time in exactly the same way as $x(n)$, it would take twice the amount of time to do it. Before we consider such time scale modifications, however, let us see how to reconstruct $y(n)$ in such a way that it is equal to $x(n)$.

We begin by defining the sequence

$$V_n(k) = P_k X_n\left[e^{j(2\pi/N)k} \right] \qquad n = 0, \pm D, \pm 2D, \ldots \tag{3-73}$$

For each value of k, $V_n(k)$ is a sequence that has values every D samples and is zero in between. To "fill in" these "missing" values, we have only to apply an interpolating lowpass filter to each channel of $V_n(k)$ that has a cutoff frequency of π/I radians, where I is the interpolation rate, taken for the moment to be equal to D. An ideal lowpass filter with this cutoff frequency has a now familiar impulse response of the form

$$h(n) = \text{sinc}\left[\frac{n}{I} \right] = I\frac{\sin(\pi n/I)}{\pi n} \qquad -\infty < n < \infty \tag{3-74}$$

This function again has the niggling disadvantage of having an infinite duration, so, as before, we multiply it by a finite-length window function. Because a Hamming window function has already been used in the analysis procedure, it may not be surprising to learn that we can create an appropriate synthesis window function by multiplying equation (3-74) by a Hamming window centered around $n = 0$. $h(n)$ will therefore have a total length of N_w samples. $Y_n(k)$ can then be reconstituted by convolving $h(n)$ with the zero-interpolated $V_n(k)$ sequences.

An overlap-add procedure can be used to synthesize the output signal very efficiently. Though it may have been modified somewhat, $Y_n(k)$ corresponds to $X_n(e^{j2\pi k/N})$. If no modifications have been applied and we are synthesizing at the analysis rate (that is, for the case $P_k = 1$ for $k = 0, 1, \ldots, N-1$ and $I = D$), the inverse DFT of $Y_n(k)$ will result in an N-point sequence precisely equal to the contents of the `analysis[]` array described in the last programming example. Let us call this N-point array `synthesis[]`, because it results from the inverse DFT operation.

To reconstruct the input sequence from this array, we can apply the windowing, folding, and rotating process more or less in reverse. The rotating process is simply a matter of starting at an array index determined by the output sample time value `nout`, which for $I = D$ is equal to the input sample time value `n`. The starting index in the `synthesis[]` array is simply the value of `nout` taken modulo N. Starting from this position, samples are read circularly out of the `synthesis[]` array N_w times, each time incrementing the array index and resetting it to zero whenever the end of the array is reached.

To these N_w values, the synthesis window $h(n)$ is applied, and the resulting partial product terms are *summed* into an output array `output[]`, which also has a length of N_w samples. After each such summation process, I samples are shifted out from the left of the `output[]` array while zeros are shifted in from the right (the samples shifted out constitute the output signal). We see that this process results in an output that consists of a sequence formed by successively summing sequences of length N_w that overlap by I samples.

This overlap-add process differs from the one used in Chapter 2 for fast convolution because I is likely to be considerably smaller than N_w, so each output sample (except for the first few) will be the sum of N_w/I samples. The multiplication by the synthesis window function combined with this overlap-add procedure essentially implements a convolution operation that applies the interpolation filter to each channel, as well as automatically summing the results of all channels to form the output signal. Given the N-point `synthesis[]` array resulting from the inverse DFT, the N_w-point synthesis window in an array called `synwindow[]`, and an initially all-zero output array of length N_w called `output[]`, the overlap-add process can be accomplished with the following C statements:

```
while ( nout < 0 )
    nout += N ;
nout %= N ;
for ( i = 0 ; i < Nw ; i++ ) {
    output[i] += synthesis[nout]*synwindow[i] ;
```

```
    if ( ++nout >= N )
        nout = 0 ;
}
```

After each such overlap-add step, *I* samples are shifted out of the left of the `output`
`[]` array, with a like number of zero-valued samples entering from the right.

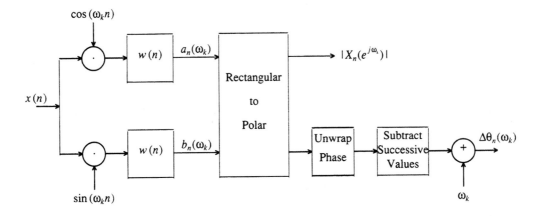

Figure 3-32   Analysis procedure for a single channel of the phase vocoder.

3.3.10 Calculating the Phase Vocoder Parameters

So far, the techniques of short time spectrum analysis-synthesis we have discussed have
been quite general. The phase vocoder, however, involves the rather specialized step of
converting the lowpassed quadrature output of each analysis channel into time-varying
amplitude and frequency parameters. The basic techniques for computing these parameters from the short time spectrum are shown in Figure 3-32. These parameters make
duration and pitch modifications of the analyzed signal especially convenient.

The operations needed to transform the output of the short time Fourier transform
into amplitude and frequency parameters are conceptually straightforward. The $a_n(\omega_k)$
and $b_n(\omega_k)$ parameters as defined in Figure 3-30 are first converted from rectangular to
polar coordinates, yielding a corresponding magnitude and phase. The magnitude value

$$|X_n(e^{j\omega_k})| = \sqrt{a_n^2(\omega_k) + b_n^2(\omega_k)} \qquad (3\text{-}75)$$

then represents the time-varying amplitude parameter needed to drive an oscillator for
resynthesis.

To calculate the frequency parameters, we must first obtain the phase angles associated with the rectangular coordinate values according to

$$\theta_n(\omega_k) = -\tan^{-1}\frac{b_n(\omega_k)}{a_n(\omega_k)} \qquad (3\text{-}76)$$

Ideally, we would like to compute the frequency parameter as the time derivative of the phase angle. As a first approximation, this time derivative is proportional to the first-order difference between successive values of $\theta_n(\omega_k)$ according to

$$\Delta\theta_n(\omega_k) = \theta_n(\omega_k) - \theta_{n-D}(\omega_k) \qquad (3\text{-}77)$$

$\Delta\theta_n(\omega_k)$ represents the phase difference in radians per D samples at the input sampling rate. Recalling that the quadrature modulation used in the analysis shifts all frequencies down to the vicinity of 0 Hz, the center frequency of each channel, ω_k $(= 2\pi k/N)$, scaled by a factor of $1/D$, must be added to the phase difference values for each channel in order to obtain the actual frequency value in radians per D samples. Multiplying the result by the sampling rate and dividing by 2π times D then renders the frequency values directly in hertz. These values can then be scaled appropriately (converted to increment values) to control the frequencies of table lookup oscillators.

A minor complication with this procedure is that the inverse tangent function must generally be computed in terms of its *principal values*, which typically lie between $-\pi$ and π. As time goes by, the "true" value of $\theta_n(\omega_k)$ increases without bound (for positive frequencies), causing the inverse tangent procedure to "wrap" around the extremes of its principal value range. Before the phase derivative can be calculated, therefore, it is necessary to "unwrap" the phase values returned by the inverse tangent procedure. This can generally be accomplished by adding and subtracting factors of 2π to and from $\Delta\theta_n(\omega_k)$ appropriately as it overflows the range of principal values.

3.3.11 A Practical Phase Vocoder Program

A practical phase vocoder program may be constructed using the `rfft` program given in Chapter 2 to do the required forward and inverse Fourier transforms. In addition to performing the basic analysis-synthesis operation, it allows the decimation and interpolation rates to be specified separately so that time scaling of the input signal may be accomplished. For example, if I is set to $2D$, the spectrum of the output signal will evolve over twice as many samples as in the input signal, thus effecting a temporal stretching of the input sound without otherwise modifying its pitch. Specifying an interpolation rate less than the decimation rate would shrink the time scale of the output signal relative to the input. The FFT length N, which also determines the number of channels, must be set to a power of 2. The window size N_w may be set to N, and it may be shorter or longer, corresponding to broadening or sharpening the frequency response of the bandpass filters used during the analysis-synthesis operations. In the case where N_w is chosen to be larger than N, windowed sinc-type filters are used for the analysis and synthesis windows. A Hamming window is used for both analysis or synthesis, although many other window functions are available (the so-called *Kaiser window* is often used for phase vocoder applications).

To demonstrate how the phase vocoder analysis data can be used to drive additive synthesis, the program includes both an overlap-add synthesis procedure and a table lookup oscillator bank for synthesizing the output signal. Because modification of the pitch of the input signal is often a simple matter of multiplying the channel frequencies by a transposition factor (we must, of course, observe the sampling theorem) before feeding them to an oscillator bank, the user of the program selects the synthesis method by setting a pitch transposition value P to a nonzero value in order to select oscillator bank resynthesis. If P is zero, the program will use the overlap-add method. If P is nonzero, the frequency values will all be multiplied by P, and oscillator bank resynthesis will be used.

Of course, many other types of modifications of the channel data are possible. We will discuss a few of them after examining the text of the phase vocoder program. Some observations on this text are relevant. First of all, the oscillator bank resynthesis method is considerably less efficient than the overlap-add method, because the latter exploits the efficiency of the FFT. The oscillator bank resynthesis method has some advantages, however. For one thing, the oscillators need not be the ones in this program but might just as well be unit generators in cmusic, for example. This allows the complete power of analysis-based additive synthesis, possibly with time, pitch, or spectrum modifications, to be combined with the completely general signal processing flexibility of an acoustic compiler program. The method by which phase vocoder analysis data may be made available to unit generators in an acoustic compiler program is an installation-dependent—typically, it is implemented by writing the analysis data on a temporary disk file for reading by cmusic or its equivalent, or, under UNIX, the data may be piped directly from the output of one program into the input of another. In either case, a special unit generator is needed that can read such data and present it in terms of time-varying input-output block signals, such as the bN variables in cmusic. It is then a simple matter to process the signal further, for example, by amplitude modulation or reverberation. By coupling it with an acoustic compiler, the phase vocoder creates a quite powerful analysis–modification–synthesis–further modification processing chain, especially because the further modification may include the addition of an arbitrary number of other signals, representing other sounds, that may arise from entirely synthetic or analysis-based sources.

In addition, pitch modifications are superior using oscillator bank resynthesis. To effect pitch changes using the overlap-add method, the lengths of the input and output DFT transforms must be different, which is tedious to implement and results in the availability only of pitch changes by factors of N_i/N_o, where N_i is the length of the input transform and N_o is the length of the output transform. Unless these numbers are quite large, pitch changes may not be made by perceptually arbitrary amounts. Furthermore, a dynamically varying pitch change is both difficult to accomplish and likely to sound "grainy" if the pitch changes at certain rates (of course, the overlap-add method works quite well and efficiently for time scaling, though the time scale factors are similarly restricted to ratios of I to D, which are usually small integers). An interesting possibility is to effect pitch modification and then to convert the sampling rate of the output signal until the original pitch is restored. If the pitch is modified by a factor P, this process would effect a similar modification on the duration without pitch change.

Some of the extra computation inherent in the oscillator bank resynthesis method can be avoided by omitting channels with small amplitudes. The following program uses a threshold value specifying the minimum amplitude a channel must have to be included in the resynthesis. Setting this threshold to zero forces all channels to be included. Setting it to a suitable small value (such as 10^{-6}) can save a considerable amount of computation without audible degradation of the result when the oscillator bank resynthesis method is used.[22]

Finally, note that the program is written for clarity rather than speed. In many cases, more abstruse code could be found that would run measurably faster. Because this program, like all programs in this book, is stated only to provide a starting point for musical additions and modifications, especially at the point marked "SPECTRUM MODIFICATIONS GO HERE," these efficiencies are left as an exercise.

```c
#include <stdio.h>
#include <math.h>

#define FORWARD 1
#define INVERSE 0

extern char *malloc(), *calloc() ;
float PI ;
float TWOPI ;
/*
 * memory allocation macro
 */
#define fvec( name, size )\
if ( ( name = (float *) calloc( size, sizeof(float) ) ) == NULL) {\
    fprintf( stderr, "Insufficient memory\n" ) ;\
    exit( -1 ) ;\
}

main( argc, argv )
    int argc ; char *argv[ ] ;
{
 int R, N, N2, Nw, Nw2, D, I, in, on, eof = 0, obank = 0 ;
 float P, synt, *Wanal, *Wsyn, *input, *buffer, *channel, *output ;
/*
 * pick up arguments from command line
 */
    R    = atoi( argv[1] ) ;   /* sampling rate */
    N    = atoi( argv[2] ) ;   /* FFT length */
    Nw   = atoi( argv[3] ) ;   /* window size */
    D    = atoi( argv[4] ) ;   /* decimation factor */
    I    = atoi( argv[5] ) ;   /* interpolation factor */
    P    = atof( argv[6] ) ;   /* oscillator bank pitch factor */
    synt = atof( argv[7] ) ;   /* synthesis threshold */
```

---

[22]The best value for this threshold is unfortunately data-dependent and time-varying in the general case. Heuristics, such as setting the threshold dynamically to a value, say, 60 dB below the amplitude of the strongest current amplitude component, are easily implemented.

```
    PI = 4.*atan( 1. ) ;
    TWOPI = 8.*atan( 1. ) ;
    obank = P != 0. ;
    N2 = N>>1 ;
    Nw2 = Nw>>1 ;
/*
 * allocate memory
 */
    fvec( Wanal, Nw ) ;         /* analysis window */
    fvec( Wsyn, Nw ) ;          /* synthesis window */
    fvec( input, Nw ) ;         /* input buffer */
    fvec( buffer, N ) ;         /* FFT buffer */
    fvec( channel, N+2 ) ;      /* analysis channels */
    fvec( output, Nw ) ;        /* output buffer */
/*
 * create windows
 */
    makewindows( Wanal, Wsyn, Nw, N, I ) ;
/*
 * initialize input and output time values (in samples)
 */
    in = -Nw ;
    on = (in*I)/D ;
/*
 * main loop--perform phase vocoder analysis-resynthesis
 */
    while ( !eof ) {
/*
 * increment times
 */
        in += D ;
        on += I ;
/*
 * analysis: input D samples; window, fold and rotate input
 * samples into FFT buffer; take FFT; and convert to
 * amplitude-frequency (phase vocoder) form
 */
        eof = shiftin( input, Nw, D ) ;
        fold( input, Wanal, Nw, buffer, N, in ) ;
        rfft( buffer, N2, FORWARD ) ;
        convert( buffer, channel, N2, D, R ) ;
/*
 *          SPECTRUM MODIFICATIONS GO HERE
 * at this point channel[2*i] contains amplitude data and
 * channel[2*i+1] contains frequency data (in Hz) for phase
 * vocoder channels i = 0, 1, ... N/2; the center frequency
 * associated with each channel is i*f, where f is the
 * fundamental frequency of analysis R/N; any desired spectral
```

```
 * modifications can be made at this point: pitch modifications
 * are generally well suited to oscillator bank resynthesis,
 * while time modifications are generally well (and more
 * efficiently) suited to overlap-add resynthesis
 */
        if ( obank ) {
/*
 * oscillator bank resynthesis
 */
                oscbank( channel, N2, R, I, output, P, synt ) ;
                shiftout( output, Nw, I, in+Nw2+D ) ;
        } else {
/*
 * overlap-add resynthesis
 */
                unconvert( channel, buffer, N2, I, R ) ;
                rfft( buffer, N2, INVERSE ) ;
                overlapadd( buffer, N, Wsyn, output, Nw, on ) ;
                shiftout( output, Nw, I, on ) ;
        }
    }
}
/*
 * make balanced pair of analysis (A) and synthesis (S) windows;
 * window lengths are Nw, FFT length is N, synthesis interpolation
 * factor is I
 */
makewindows( A, S, Nw, N, I )
    float A[], S[] ; int Nw, N, I ;
{
 int i ;
 float sum ;
 double TWOPI = 8.*atan(1.) ;
/*
 * basic Hamming windows
 */
    for ( i = 0 ; i < Nw ; i++ )
        A[i] = S[i] = 0.54 - 0.46*cos( TWOPI*i/(Nw - 1) ) ;
/*
 * when Nw > N, also apply interpolating (sinc) windows to
 * ensure that window are 0 at increments of N (the FFT length)
 * away from the center of the analysis window and of I away
 * from the center of the synthesis window
 */
    if ( Nw > N ) {
      float x ;
      double PI = 4.*atan(1.) ;
/*
```

```
 * take care to create symmetrical windows
 */
        x = -(Nw - 1)/2. ;
        for ( i = 0 ; i < Nw ; i++, x += 1. )
            if ( x != 0. ) {
                A[i] *= N*sin( PI*x/N )/(PI*x) ;
                S[i] *= I*sin( PI*x/I )/(PI*x) ;
            }
    }
/*
 * normalize windows for unity gain across unmodified
 * analysis-synthesis procedure
 */
    for ( sum = i = 0 ; i < Nw ; i++ )
        sum += A[i] ;
    for ( i = 0 ; i < Nw ; i++ ) {
     float afac = 2./sum ;
     float sfac = Nw > N ? 1./afac : afac ;
        A[i] *= afac ;
        S[i] *= sfac ;
    }
    if ( Nw <= N ) {
        for ( sum = i = 0 ; i < Nw ; i += I )
            sum += S[i]*S[i] ;
        for ( sum = 1./sum, i = 0 ; i < Nw ; i++ )
            S[i] *= sum ;
    }
}
/*
 * shift next D samples into right-hand end of array A of
 * length N, padding with zeros after last sample (A is
 * assumed to be initially 0); return 0 when more input
 * remains; otherwise, return 1 after N-2*D zeros have been
 * padded onto end of input
 */
shiftin( A, N, D )
    float A[] ; int N, D ;
{
 int i ;
 static int valid = -1 ;
    if ( valid < 0 )                /* first time only */
        valid = N ;
    for ( i = 0 ; i < N - D ; i++ )
        A[i] = A[i+D] ;
    if ( valid == N )
        for ( i = N - D ; i < N ; i++ )
/*
 * scanf is used to read one ASCII sample value from stdin;
```

```
 * a more efficient implementation would read binary values
 */
            if ( scanf( "%f", &A[i] ) == EOF ) {
                valid = i ;
                break ;
            }
    if ( valid < N ) {          /* pad with zeros after EOF */
        for ( i = valid ; i < N ; i++ )
            A[i] = 0. ;
        valid -= D ;
    }
    return( valid <= 0 ) ;
}
/*
 * multiply current input I by window W (both of length Nw);
 * using modulus arithmetic; fold and rotate windowed input
 * into output array O of (FFT) length N according to current
 * input time n
 */
fold( I, W, Nw, O, N, n )
    float I[], W[], O[] ; int Nw, N, n ;
{
 int i ;
    for ( i = 0 ; i < N ; i++ )
        O[i] = 0. ;
    while ( n < 0 )
        n += N ;
    n %= N ;
    for ( i = 0 ; i < Nw ; i++ ) {
        O[n] += I[i]*W[i] ;
        if ( ++n == N )
            n = 0 ;
    }
}
/*
 * S is a spectrum in rfft format, i.e., it contains N real values
 * arranged as real followed by imaginary values, except for first
 * two values, which are real parts of 0 and Nyquist frequencies;
 * convert first changes these into N/2+1 Pairs of magnitude and
 * phase values to be stored in output array C; the phases are then
 * unwrapped and successive phase differences are used to compute
 * estimates of the instantaneous frequencies for each phase vocoder
 * analysis channel; decimation rate D and sampling rate R are used
 * to render these frequency values directly in Hz.
 */
convert( S, C, N2, D, R )
    float S[], C[] ; int N2, D, R ;
{
```

```
static int first = 1 ;
static float *lastphase, fundamental, factor ;
float phase, phasediff ;
float TWOPI = 8.*atan(1.) ;
float PI = 4.*atan(1.) ;
int real, imag, amp, freq ;
double a, b ;
int i ;
/*
 * FIRST TIME ONLY: allocate zeroed space for previous phase
 * values for each channel and compute constants
 */
    if ( first ) {
        first = 0 ;
        fvec( lastphase, N2+1 ) ;
        fundamental = (float) R/(N2<<1) ;
        factor = R/(D*TWOPI) ;
    }
/*
 * unravel rfft-format spectrum: note that N2+1 pairs of
 * values are produced
 */
    for ( i = 0 ; i <= N2 ; i++ ) {
        imag = freq = ( real = amp = i<<1 ) + 1 ;
        a = ( i == N2 ? S[1] : S[real] ) ;
        b = ( i == 0 || i == N2 ? 0. : S[imag] ) ;
/*
 * compute magnitude value from real and imaginary parts
 */
        C[amp] = hypot( a, b ) ;
/*
 * compute phase value from real and imaginary parts and take
 * difference between this and previous value for each channel
 */
        if ( C[amp] == 0. )
            phasediff = 0. ;
        else {
            phasediff = ( phase = -atan2( b, a ) ) - lastphase[i] ;
            lastphase[i] = phase ;
/*
 * unwrap phase differences
 */
            while ( phasediff > PI )
                phasediff -= TWOPI ;
            while ( phasediff < -PI )
                phasediff += TWOPI ;
        }
/*
```

```
 * convert each phase difference to Hz
 */
        C[freq] = phasediff*factor + i*fundamental ;
    }
}
/*
 * oscillator bank resynthesizer for phase vocoder analyzer
 * uses sum of N+1 cosinusoidal table lookup oscillators to
 * compute I (interpolation factor) samples of output O
 * from N+1 amplitude and frequency value pairs in C;
 * frequencies are scaled by P
 */
oscbank( C, N, R, I, O, P, synt )
    float C[], O[], P, synt ;
    int N, R, I ;
{
 static int NP, L = 8192, first = 1 ;
 static float Iinv, *lastamp, *lastfreq, *index, *table, Pinc ;
 int amp, freq, n, chan ;
/*
 * FIRST TIME ONLY: allocate memory to hold previous values
 * of amplitude and frequency for each channel, the table
 * index for each oscillator, and the table itself (note
 * amplitude scaling); also compute constants
 */
    if ( first ) {
        first = 0 ;
        fvec( lastamp, N+1 ) ;
        fvec( lastfreq, N+1 ) ;
        fvec( index, N+1 ) ;
        fvec( table, L ) ;
        for ( n = 0 ; n < L ; n++ )
            table[n] = N*cos( TWOPI*n/L ) ;
        if ( P > 1. )
            NP = N/P ;
        else
            NP = N ;
        Iinv = 1./I ;
        Pinc = P*L/R ;
    }
/*
 * for each channel, compute I samples using linear
 * interpolation on the amplitude and frequency
 * control values
 */
    for ( chan = 0 ; chan < NP ; chan++ ) {
      register float a, ainc, f, finc, address ;
        freq = ( amp = chan<<1 ) + 1 ;
```

```
        C[freq] *= Pinc ;
        finc = ( C[freq] - ( f = lastfreq[chan] ) )*Iinv ;
/*
 * if channel amplitude under synthesis threshold, set it to 0
 */
        if ( C[amp] < synt )
            C[amp] = 0. ;
        ainc = ( C[amp] - ( a = lastamp[chan] ) )*Iinv ;
        address = index[chan] ;
/*
 * avoid extra computing
 */
        if ( ainc != 0. || a != 0. )
/*
 * accumulate the I samples from each oscillator into
 * output array O (initially assumed to be zero)
 */
            for ( n = 0 ; n < I ; n++ ) {
                O[n] += a*table[ (int) address ] ;
                address += f ;
                while ( address >= L )
                    address -= L ;
                while ( address < 0 )
                    address += L ;
                a += ainc ;
                f += finc ;
            }
/*
 * save current values for next iteration
 */
        lastamp[chan] = C[amp] ;
        lastfreq[chan] = C[freq] ;
        index[chan] = address ;
    }
}
/*
 * unconvert essentially undoes what convert does, i.e., it
 * turns N2+1 Pairs of amplitude and frequency values in
 * C into N2 Pair of complex spectrum data (in rfft format)
 * in output array S; sampling rate R and interpolation factor
 * I are used to recompute phase values from frequencies
 */
unconvert( C, S, N2, I, R )
    float C[], S[] ; int N2, I, R ;
{
 static int first = 1 ;
 static float *lastphase, fundamental, factor ;
 double TWOPI = 8.*atan(1.) ;
```

```
int i, real, imag, amp, freq ;
double mag, phase ;
/*
 * FIRST TIME ONLY: allocate memory and compute constants
 */
    if ( first ) {
        first = 0 ;
        fvec( lastphase, N2+1 ) ;
        fundamental = (float) R/(N2<<1) ;
        factor = TWOPI*I/R ;
    }
/*
 * subtract out frequencies associated with each channel,
 * compute phases in terms of radians per I samples, and
 * convert to complex form
 */
    for ( i = 0 ; i <= N2 ; i++ ) {
        imag = freq = ( real = amp = i<<1 ) + 1 ;
        if ( i == N2 )
            real = 1 ;
        mag = C[amp} ;
        lastphase[i] += C[freq] - i*fundamental ;
        phase = lastphase[i]*factor ;
        S[real] = mag*cos( phase ) ;
        if ( i != N2 )
            S[imag] = -mag*sin( phase ) ;
    }
}
/*
 * input I is a folded spectrum of length N; output O and
 * synthesis window W are of length Nw--overlap-add windowed,
 * unrotated, unfolded input data into output O
 */
overlapadd( I, N, W, O, Nw, n )
    float I[], W[], O[] ; int N, Nw, n ;
{
 int i ;
    while ( n < 0 )
        n += N ;
    n %= N ;
    for ( i = 0 ; i < Nw ; i++ ) {
        O[i] += I[n]*W[i] ;
        if ( ++n == N )
            n = 0 ;
    }
}
/*
 * if output time n >= 0, output first I samples in
```

```
 * array A of length N, then shift A left by I samples,
 * padding with zeros after last sample
 */
shiftout( A, N, I, n )
    float A[] ; int N, I, n ;
{
 int i ;
    if ( n >= 0 )
        for ( i = 0 ; i < I ; i++ )
            printf( "%f\n", A[i] ) ;
    for ( i = 0 ; i < N - I ; i++ )
        A[i] = A[i+I] ;
    for ( i = N - I ; i < N ; i++ )
        A[i] = 0. ;
}
```

If this program is compiled under the name pv, the following UNIX command will cause it to process the sample values (listed one per line) in file input, writing the result on file output.

```
pv  R N Nw D I P T < input  > output
```

where

R   is the sampling rate of the input and output signals (in hertz)

N   is the number of analysis channels (must be a power of 2)

Nw   is the desired window length

D   is the desired decimation factor (in samples)

I   is the desired interpolation factor (in samples)

P   is interpreted by the program to be a pitch transposition factor for
      oscillator bank resynthesis if it is nonzero (overlap-add resynthesis
      is used if P is set to zero)

T   is the minimum amplitude a channel must have to be included in the
      resynthesis (oscillator bank only)

Generally, we would specify N to be the first power of 2 large enough so that R/N is less than or equal to the lowest frequency component (the lowest fundamental) in the input signal. Nw is usefully set either to the same value as N or some integer multiple of it. D is conservatively set at one eighth the window size rather than the theoretical minimum of one fourth of it (for a Hamming window). If I is set to a value different from D, the duration of the output signal will differ from that of the input signal by a factor I/D. If P is set to zero, overlap-add resynthesis will be used, which is considerably faster than oscillator bank resynthesis. If P is set to a nonzero value, oscillator bank resynthesis will be used with all frequencies multiplied by P. Setting T to zero causes all channels to be included in oscillator bank resynthesis, even if they have zero amplitude. Setting T to a small nonzero value specifies the minimum amplitude an individual channel must have to be included in the resynthesis. Many types of spectrum modification are possible—these can be implemented by including C code at the point marked "SPECTRUM MODIFICATIONS GO HERE."

3.3.12 Using the Phase Vocoder

The phase vocoder models the input signal as a sum of sinusoids, each with a time-varying amplitude and frequency. To obtain satisfactory results, this model must apply at least reasonably well to the actual sound being processed. For example, a pitched musical sound such as a violin, flute, trumpet, or voice is more likely to be well modeled as a sum of sinusoids than a nonpitched percussion sound.

For the phase vocoder analysis procedure to work well, therefore, the filter center frequencies and bandwidths are ideally set in such a way that no more than one frequency component of the analyzed sound falls within any particular filter passband. Normally we want to minimize the number of filter bank channels so as to minimize the amount of necessary computation, and to minimize the time that the filters take to respond. Because a monophonic pitched sound source contains frequency components at (approximately) integer multiples of the fundamental frequency, the spacing of the filter passband center frequencies can usually be set according to the lowest fundamental frequency in the input signal.

If more than one frequency component falls within the response range of any individual filter, the sinusoidal oscillator driven by the filter's output can still reconstruct the input signal in the case where no modifications are made to the spectrum. This is so because the sum of two sinusoids can be represented as the product of two sinusoids—(see, for example, equation 3-60)—allowing a single oscillator to model the beating effect of two closely spaced components as a slowly amplitude modulated sinusoid. When spectrum modifications are performed before resynthesis, however, the fact that two or more components cannot be manipulated independently of each other when they fall within the passband of a single filter channel may keep the resynthesis from being acceptable.

Treating polyphonic sounds with a phase vocoder is problematic because the filter channels must be sufficiently numerous and selective as to separate out all components from each sound as much as possible. Two complex tones widely spaced in fundamental frequency may contain components at frequencies that are equal or very nearly so. For example, if two simultaneous complex tones lie a just perfect fifth apart at 200 Hz and 300 Hz, the third harmonic of the first tone lies at exactly the same frequency as the second harmonic of the second tone (600 Hz) and the phase vocoder cannot determine what portion of the 600 Hz component in the composite sound can be attributed to each tone separately. If the upper tone is a tempered fifth above 200 Hz, the situation is both better and worse: the upper frequency is now approximately 299.661 Hz. To separate the third harmonic of the first tone from the second harmonic of the second tone, the channel separation would have to be smaller than about 0.338 Hz, leading to an enormous number of required filter channels.

As we have seen, the bandwidth of each filter is determined by the length of the window function used—the longer the time width of the window function, the narrower its frequency bandwidth, and vice versa. Another way to put this is that the narrower the bandwidth of a filter, the longer it takes to respond to the input signal, and vice versa. Therefore if we wish the phase vocoder to track the behavior of components that are changing rapidly in time (as they would during an attack transient, for example), considerable overlap in the filter passbands would be necessary, thus increasing the possibility that an individual filter could respond to more than one component of the input signal.

To perform time scaling using the phase vocoder resynthesis, we can adjust the interpolation factor I to a value different from that of the decimation factor D. If I is set to twice D, for example, the amplitude and frequency information describing the input signal would be spread over a duration twice as long as the input signal. If the amplitude and frequency information is not otherwise modified, the output signal would then consist of the same spectrum information spread over twice the duration of the input signal. In other words, we would "stretch" the sound in time without changing its pitch. Similarly, by setting I to a value less than D, the original sound could be shortened in total duration without pitch change.

The subjective effect of large time stretch factors can be thought of as listening to the sound through a "temporal microscope" in the sense that we hear the temporal evolution of the sound over a greater duration without altering its pitch. This process is similar in subjective effect to that of a slow-motion movie. The phase vocoder has been used successfully to stretch musical sounds such as those of the violin and flute by factors of more than 200. The effect of hearing the temporal evolution of a 200-millisecond staccato note stretched over a duration of almost a minute can be quite striking.

Small time-scaling factors can also be useful for adjusting the effective tempo of a musical passage consisting of sounds amenable to phase vocoder analysis-resynthesis. Such temporal adjustments might be used to alter the total duration of a musical passage to fit a scene in a movie or play, for example, or to speed up the pace at which a passage is read by a speaker while maintaining excellent intelligibility.

The other side of the same coin is that the phase vocoder allows the pitch of a musical tone or passage to be changed without affecting its overall duration. We must of course take the usual precautions to avoid foldover in the resulting output signal.

It is interesting to observe that pitch transformation can lead to some surprising results when the amplitude information associated with each sinusoidal component "follows" that component to a new frequency location in the output spectrum. In the case of speech, for example, intelligibility can be lost with extreme pitch scaling (on the order of an octave or more) due to the fact that the formant regions in the output signal are altered by the same factor as the pitch transposition. Because the locations of these formant regions are responsible for our recognition of vowels, the shift in tone color can make the speech impossible to understand.

The subjective effect of such pitch scaling is one of shrinking or enlarging the physical dimensions of the person or instrument that is making the sound. Thus not only does a violin note transposed up an octave in pitch with this frequency-scaling procedure sound twice as high, but the instrument sounds twice as small. Speech transposed up in this manner sounds similar to "helium speech" in which the formant regions are similarly shifted. Downward pitch transpositions give impressions of giant instruments and speakers or singers.

One way to avoid the enlargement or shrinking effect is to retain the amplitude information associated with the original frequencies. For example, if we use oscillator bank resynthesis, we could shift the pitch of a speaker up an octave by multiplying all frequency control values by a factor of 2, then adjusting the corresponding amplitudes according to

$$A_k(n) = A_{Pk}(n) \qquad\qquad (3\text{-}78)$$

and

$$F_k(n) = PF_k(n) \qquad\qquad (3\text{-}79)$$

where $A_k(n)$ is the time-varying amplitude control data for the kth oscillator channel, $F_k(n)$ is the time-varying frequency control data for the kth oscillator channel, and P is the transposition factor. Note that in the case where P is not an integer the subscript on the amplitude channel may be truncated or rounded for constant pitch shifts with very little error in the resulting spectrum, although interpolation may be necessary for time varying pitch shifts. Such procedures can sometimes successfully preserve the overall shape of the spectrum, avoiding the vowel shifts while producing the speech at twice the original frequency. However, for noninteger values of P, this method has a severe problem: the phase vocoder analysis is very fine grained, and energy in one band does not necessarily mean that energy will be present in any other. Therefore, to retain the overall spectrum envelope while shifting the positions of the frequency components underneath it, a less highly resolved description of the spectrum would be useful. One such method is linear prediction, which will be discussed shortly.

Other spectrum modifications may be accomplished by altering the amplitudes or phases of the various channels to emphasize or attenuate some portion of the reconstructed signal. Such spectrum modifications may be either constant or time-varying. If they are constant, the effect is one of feeding the signal through a fixed filter with a response defined by the spectrum modifications. In this case it is necessary to consider the time width of the spectrum modification during the analysis-synthesis procedure—extremely sharp filtering (such as the notch-filtering effect of setting a single channel to zero) may result in a time width greater than N_w, in which case either time or frequency aliasing may result.

Remember that each channel responds to a wider portion of the frequency spectrum than the nominal width of a single channel due to the nonideal response of the channel filters—some "leakage" among channels is inevitable due to the nonzero response of the Hamming and sinc windows to frequencies greater than their effective bandwidths. Channels may often be entirely omitted from resynthesis without distorting the result unacceptably, especially if the amplitudes of the signals within these channels are small to begin with. A particularly useful type of spectrum modification is therefore

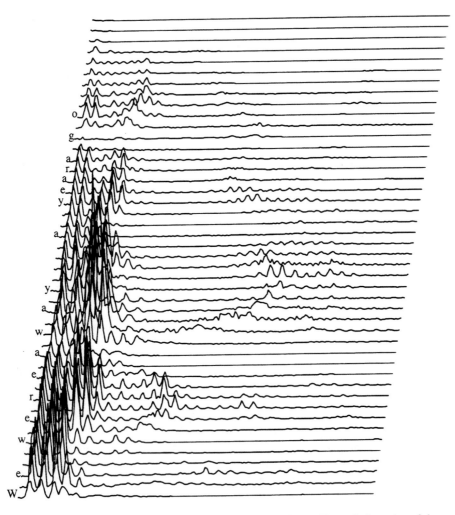

Figure 3-33 Graphical sound analysis with the phase vocoder. The analysis portion of the phase vocoder program given in the text was run with $R = 16384$, $N = N_w = 1024$, and $D = 512$. The plot was made by feeding the first 192 amplitude channels to standard UNIX plotting software, moving up and to the right for each new measurement. The plot therefore represents frequencies up to 3072 Hz, with the "slices" of the spectrum occurring at intervals of 1/32 second. The input signal was a digital recording of a male speaker saying "We were away a year ago" (the approximate timing of the speech is indicated in the figure). Individual spectrum components are clearly visible. The formant sweep between the words *away* and *a* is particularly evident near the center of the picture, as is the glottal stop (brief silence) associated with the *g* in *ago* near the top.

to remove channels from the resynthesis that have small amplitudes compared with that of the channels containing signal components. This can have the effect of attenuating unwanted broadband noise in the input signal, allowing the phase vocoder to act as a very effective noise reduction system. If the spectrum is modified in a time-varying manner, it is generally necessary to change the modifications to individual channels gradually to avoid clicks in the output signal.

Finally, note that even though the phase vocoder output signal will contain sinusoidal components with appropriate amplitudes and frequencies, the phases of these components will not often match those of the input signal. The process of transforming phase information into phase difference per unit time information (frequency) allows us to conclude that despite its name, the phase vocoder transmits everything *but* phase information from the analysis to the synthesis procedures. This amounts to introducing an arbitrary phase offset in each component of the output signal, which in many cases has little audible effect. When it is audible, however, this effect has been likened to that of making the signal sound relatively more reverberant than the original.

The phase vocoder is a powerful tool for the additive synthesis and manipulation of musical sounds. The analysis half of the phase vocoder may be used separately to produce a wide variety of types of plots of the temporal evolution of sound spectra (see Figure 3-33). Time, frequency, and spectrum features of many sounds may be treated in more or less independent ways during their resynthesis. Finally, the phase vocoder may be linked with an acoustic compiler such as cmusic to produce a very general sound analysis-synthesis-processing environment for musical applications.

3.4 SUBTRACTIVE SYNTHESIS AND PHYSICAL MODELS

Additive synthesis works by adding together time-varying sinusoidal components to produce the desired waveform. *Subtractive synthesis* is based on the complementary idea of passing a broadband signal through a time-varying filter to produce the desired waveform. Additive synthesis builds up complex sounds from elementary sound building blocks, while subtractive synthesis starts with a complex sound block and removes parts of it that are not in the desired sound—something like taking a sculptor's chisel to a block of marble. The characteristics of the filtered signal and those of the filter itself may again be specified directly or in a way that is based on the analysis of sounds that we wish to match in some way.

The basic processing model of subtractive synthesis consists of an excitation sound source feeding a resonating system (see Figure 3-34). Such a description fits many traditional musical sound sources rather well, as in the cases of a violin string (an excitation sound source) coupled through a bridge to a sound box (a fixed resonating system) or a trumpet mouthpiece feeding a pulse waveform (generated by the buzzing lips of the trumpeter) into a variable length of brass tubing (a variable resonating system). Even the sound of human speech can be fairly well modeled by an excitation source (either the buzzing of the larynx or hissing due to air from the lungs being forced through a constriction in the vocal tract) feeding a variable resonating system (the vocal tract itself, consisting of the throat, tongue, cheeks, teeth, tongue, lips, and nasal passages). To the extent that it models the operation of the physical mechanism by which a sound is produced, we see that subtractive synthesis can be viewed as a

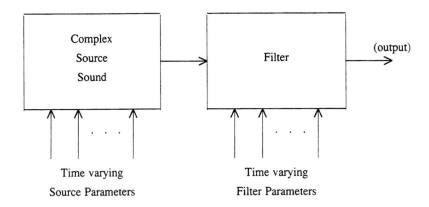

Figure 3-34   Processing model for subtractive synthesis of musical sounds. The complex source sound is typically a harmonic-rich waveform or some type of broadband noise—its parameters may include amplitude, frequency, bandwidth, and other factors. The filter is fed a set of time-varying parameters that determine the spectrum of the output signal.

special case of the more general sound synthesis technique known as *physical modeling*. We can therefore discuss subtractive synthesis and physical modeling together as restricted and general forms of the same basic idea.

3.4.1 Time-varying Digital Filters

One of the most important issues associated with subtractive synthesis is time-varying control of digital filters. For simple applications, it is useful to be able to vary the cutoff frequency of lowpass, highpass, bandpass, and bandreject filters, as well as the center frequency in the last two cases.

We usually think of the desired action of a filter in terms of its time-varying frequency response—for example, we may wish to sweep the cutoff frequency of a lowpass filter from 1000 to 3000 Hz over a duration of 1 second. We saw in Chapter 2 how to design a few kinds of filters: FIR filters can exhibit linear phase response, and IIR filters can be implemented quite efficiently. The problem of how to make a filter time-varying goes beyond the problem of how to design fixed filters, however. If we have, say, two lowpass FIR filters with cutoff frequencies at 1000 and 3000 Hz, we have specified the desired filters only at the two endpoints of the transition we wish to achieve. We cannot simply crossfade between the outputs of the two filters to achieve the effect of a time-varying filter—a time-varying filter would traverse intermediate values of cutoff frequency on its way from 1000 to 3000 Hz (if the change in cutoff frequency is linear with time, then halfway through the transition the filter would presumably have a cutoff frequency of 2000 Hz).

Therefore, the question naturally arises, How can digital filters be interpolated? A problem usually derives from the fact that we are trying to achieve a desired behavior in the frequency response of the filter, but what we usually have to work with is the time domain response of the filter (the filter coefficients). As an experiment, let us design two lowpass FIR filters using the techniques developed in Chapter 2—with cutoff frequencies of 1000 Hz and 3000 Hz—and observe the behavior of the frequency response as the filter coefficients are interpolated from one set of values to the other.

For this experiment, we can use the windowing technique in which we choose the FIR filter length N, a sampling rate R, and a cutoff frequency C. We then specify a frequency response that is unity up to the desired cutoff frequency and zero above that frequency by symmetrically filling the real part of a complex array of length N according to the C statement

```
for ( n = 0 ; n < ( N + 1 )/2 ; n++ ) {
    X[n].re = n < N*C/R ? 1. : 0. ;
    if ( n > 0 )
        X[N - n].re = X[n].re ;
}
```

Recall that the real part of array X[] is treated as a magnitude value during the specification process and the imaginary part holds the phase angle. The phase angles are specified in the following way to assure that the resulting filter will have a linear phase characteristic.

```
alpha = -(N - 1.)/2. ;
for ( n = 0 ; n < N/2 ; n++ ) {
    X[n].im = alpha*n*PI2/N ;
    if ( n > 0 )
        X[N - n].im = -X[n].im ;
}
```

Next, the magnitude and phase values are translated into rectangular complex coordinates with the statements

```
for ( n = 0 ; n < N ; n++ ) { double a, b ;
    a = X[n].re*cos( (double) X[n].im ) ;
    b = X[n].re*sin( (double) X[n].im ) ;
    X[n].re = a ;
    X[n].im = b ;
}
```

The X[] array now contains the complex Fourier transform of the impulse response of the desired filter, which is converted into an impulse response with the inverse DFT procedure given in Chapter 2.

```
idft( h, N, X ) ;
```

The h[] array now contains the unwindowed impulse response of the desired linear-phase filter. The Hamming-windowed impulse response can then be printed out with the statement

```
for ( n = 0 ; n < N ; n++ )
    printf( "%f\n", ( 0.54 - 0.46*cos( n*PI2/(N-1) ) )*h[n] ) ;
```

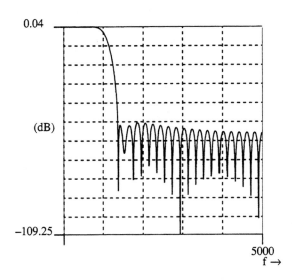

Figure 3-35 A length 51 lowpass linear-phase FIR filter with a cutoff frequency of 1000 Hz. A Hamming-windowed design procedure was used with a sampling rate specification of 10,000 Hz.

We design a lowpass linear phase FIR filter with a 1000–Hz cutoff frequency by setting N and R (arbitrarily) to 51 and 10,000, respectively, and C to 1000. The procedure then produces the required list of 51 filter coefficients. To verify our design, we implement the resulting filter (either in direct form or with the fast convolution technique described in Chapter 2), pass a digital impulse (unit sample function) through it, and observe the Fourier transform of the resulting signal. Figure 3-35 shows that the cutoff frequency may be regarded as the approximate 3-dB point and that the filter response falls off rapidly to a value of about –50 dB.

Figure 3-36 shows the frequency response of a second filter with identical design parameters except that the cutoff frequency is specified as 3000 Hz.

Suppose now that we have the 51 coefficients for the first filter (with a cutoff frequency of 1000 Hz) in an array called f1[] and the set of coefficients for the second filter in another array called f2[]. If we form a third array, f[] by linearly interpolating the values in the f1[] and f2[] arrays, will the frequency response of the filter corresponding to the f[] array fall between the responses associated with the f1[] and f2[] arrays? For example, if p is a value between zero and one, then the C statement

```
for ( i = 0 ; i < N ; i++ )
    f[i] = p*( f2[i] - f1[i] ) + f1[i] ;
```

would clearly set the f[] array according to the value of p: if p is 0, then f[] would be equal to f1[]; if p is 1, then f[] would be equal to f2[]; and if p is somewhere in between, then the values in f[] would be linearly interpolated between f1[] and f2[].

Figure 3-37 shows the frequency response of the filter that results from setting p to 0.5. If this procedure worked, we would expect to see a lowpass characteristic, ideally with a cutoff frequency of 2000 Hz. A glance at Figure 3-37 confirms that this

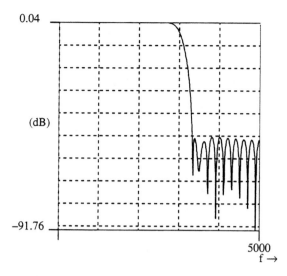

Figure 3-36 A length 51 lowpass linear-phase FIR filter with a cutoff frequency of 3000 Hz.

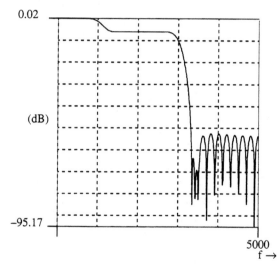

Figure 3-37 Frequency response of the length 51 FIR filter with an impulse response obtained by linearly interpolating the impulse responses of the previous two FIR filters.

is not the case. The interpolated impulse response results in a filter that does not exhibit a lowpass characteristic at all, let alone one between the two lowpass characteristics from which it was derived. However, because the symmetry of its impulse response is maintained, the interpolated filter still has a linear phase characteristic. Furthermore, like all FIR filters, the interpolated filter is stable.

This result is not too surprising if we recall that we are really trying to interpolate between two frequency responses rather than two impulse responses. In fact, the moral to the last example is that any intermediate filter settings in a time-varying filter must generally be obtained by interpolating its parameters in the frequency domain rather than its coefficients in the time domain. This could have been accomplished in the example by gradually changing the cutoff frequency in the design procedure and using the resulting impulse responses for the intermediate filtering operations.

This implies that for time-varying digital filters, it is useful to think in terms of successive *blocks* of samples during which the filter coefficients remain fixed. The duration of such blocks may be variable according to the rapidity with which the filter response is changing. In many circumstances, it makes little sense to change the filter coefficients at intervals shorter than the length of the impulse response of the filter, because the transient associated with changes in the coefficients is usually on the order of this length.[23]

Because the linear-phase FIR filter design procedure requires an inverse DFT operation, implementation of time-varying FIR filters can be computationally expensive. For this reason, IIR filters are usually chosen for time-varying filter operations, because the number of filter coefficients is typically much smaller than for FIR filters.

One of the simplest possible IIR filters is the two-pole resonator described by the filter equation

$$y(n) = a_0 x(n) - b_1 y(n-1) - b_2 y(n-2) \tag{3-80}$$

which has the transfer function

$$H(z) = \frac{a_0}{1 - 2R\cos\theta z^{-1} + R^2 z^{-2}} \tag{3-81}$$

where the center frequency of the filter is determined by pole angle θ and the bandwidth by pole radius R. For a sampling rate of S Hz, the center frequency in hertz, f_c, may be set with $\theta = 2\pi f_c / S$, and a useful approximation for a bandwidth of B Hz is given by $R \approx e^{-\pi B/S}$. As we saw in Chapter 2, however, one of the difficulties with this filter is that its gain at the center frequency varies inversely with its bandwidth (that is, small bandwidths result in large gains). A useful trick for "normalizing" the gain of this filter to unity over a broad range of center frequency and bandwidth specifications is to add two zeros to its transfer function (Smith and Angell, 1982) according to

$$H(z) = (1-R)\frac{1 - Rz^{-2}}{1 - 2R\cos\theta z^{-1} + R^2 z^{-2}} \tag{3-82}$$

The numerator shows that the two antiresonances (zeros) have been added at $z = -1$ and $z = 1$, corresponding to 0 Hz and the Nyquist frequency, respectively. The factor $1 - R$ is used to scale the entire transfer function because it can be shown that its magnitude at the resonance frequency ($|H(e^{j\theta})|$) is $1/(1 - R)$. This gives the entire filter a gain of unity at the resonance frequency, as long as the resonance frequency is neither at 0 Hz nor at the Nyquist rate. This filter may then be implemented directly with the equation

$$y(n) = (1-R)[x(n) - Rx(n-2)] + (2R\cos\theta)y(n-1) - R^2 y(n-2) \tag{3-83}$$

Equation (3-83), then, represents an IIR digital filter with unity gain at the resonance frequency $f_c = S\theta/(2\pi)$ Hz and a bandwidth of $B \approx -S\ln R/\pi$ Hz. We can

---

[23]For an IIR filter, the impulse can be considered to have an "effective length" determined by how long it takes to die away to a relatively small value, say by 20, 40, or 60 dB.

rewrite equation (3-83) as

$$y(n) = G[x(n) - Rx(n-2)] + b_1 y(n-1) + b_2 y(n-2) \qquad (3\text{-}84)$$

to make explicit that fact that the entire frequency domain behavior of the filter may be controlled by calculating only four numbers:

$$R \approx e^{-\pi B/S}$$

$$G = 1 - R$$

$$b_1 = 2R\cos(2\pi f_c/S)$$

$$b_2 = -R^2$$

Therefore, we can make a time-varying version of this filter by recalculating only these four filter parameters each time the values of B and θ change.

As before, we generally cannot interpolate between two settings for the time-domain filter coefficients and expect that the frequency response to follow suit. In addition, with IIR filters it is generally necessary to ensure that none of the poles of the filter wander outside of the unit circle as the filter parameters vary over time. If one or more poles do wander outside the unit circle, the filter will become unstable, which is to say that its output signal will begin to grow without bound. Fleeting filter instabilities are sometimes harmless, provided that the unstable condition does not last too long. This is true because the unbounded growth of the output of an unstable filter does not occur immediately but takes a while to build up. Whether the maximum allowable bounds on the output signal will be exceeded is usually difficult to predict, however, so purposely allowing an IIR filter to become unstable must be regarded as tantamount to playing with fire.

The filter described in equation (3-84) is implemented as a unit generator in cmusic under the name `nres`, which has the general statement

```
nres output[b] input[bvpn] gain[bvpn] cf[bvpn] bw[bvpn]
    t1[dpv] t2[dpv] t3[dpv] t4[dpv] t5[dpv]
    t6[dpv] t7[dpv] t8[dpv] t9[dpv] t10[dpv] ;
```

where `cf` and `bw` refer to center frequency and bandwidth values, respectively. Because the filter requires so many internal state variables (`t1` through `t10`), which are normally set to `d` variables, a macro is defined in the `<carl/cmusic.h>` file for use with this filter:

```
#define NRES(out,in,gain,cf,bw) nres out in gain cf bw\
                    d d d d d d d d d d
```

This macro allows the `nres` unit generator to be used as in the following example:

```
#include <carl/cmusic.h>

ins 0 test;
    osc  b2 1 p7 f2 d;
    osc  b1 p5 p6 f1 d;
```

```
    NRES(b1,b1,1.,b2,15Hz);
    out b1;
end;

SAWTOOTH(f1);
GEN4(f2) 0,400Hz 4 .5,1600Hz -4 1,400Hz; {define freq sweep}

note 0 test 4 0dB 200Hz p4sec; {sweep center freq over 4 seconds}

ter;
```

In this example, the `SAWTOOTH` macro defines wave table `f1` to contain the first eight harmonics of a normalized, band-limited sawtooth waveform while `f2` controls a sweep of the center frequency of the `nres` filter from 400 Hz up to 1600 Hz and back again, producing the kind of "harmonic arpeggio" commonly heard in analog synthesizer music. Note that the center frequency and bandwidth values are specified using the `Hz` postoperator exactly as if they were oscillator increment values.

3.4.2 Bandlimited Excitation Sources

Now that we have established the general necessity of specifying the behavior of a time-varying filter in the frequency domain rather than in the time domain, we turn to the issue of excitation signals for digital filtering. In our last cmusic score example, we noted that the filtered waveform consists of the first eight harmonics only of a sawtooth waveform. A "true" non-band-limited sawtooth waveform with a peak amplitude of π, a positive-going zero crossing at $x = 0$, and a period of 2π has the general formula

$$f(x) = 2(\sin x - \frac{1}{2}\sin 2x + \frac{1}{3}\sin 3x - \cdots) \qquad (3\text{-}85)$$

(The alternating signs are necessary to place the positive-going zero crossing at the origin; without them, the negative-going discontinuity is at the origin). We see from this formula that an infinite number of both even- and odd-numbered harmonics are present in a sawtooth waveform and that each harmonic has a peak amplitude that is inversely proportional to the harmonic number. Such harmonics might result in significant foldover if a non-band-limited sawtooth waveform were used as a digital signal. Therefore, we usually band-limit such waveforms as in the last example by omitting harmonics beyond some specific point.

The correct specific point depends on how the waveform will be used. If the highest fundamental frequency at which a given complex periodic waveform will be used is f_{max} Hz, we must take care that the highest included harmonic does not exceed the Nyquist frequency $R/2$ Hz, where R is the sampling rate; that is, we require

$$Nf_{max} \le \frac{R}{2} \qquad (3\text{-}86)$$

where N is the number of the highest included harmonic. Solving this inequality for N gives us an expression for the highest harmonic that *may* be included without fear of foldover.

$$N \leq \frac{R}{2f_{max}} \tag{3-87}$$

The number of included harmonics must generally be smaller for high-frequency tones than for low-frequency tones. However, if N is set according to the highest fundamental frequency that occurs over a considerable duration, such as an entire piece of music, low-frequency tones may be "harmonic-poor" in the sense that their spectra will be unnecessarily limited to low frequencies, making them sound dull or muted.

A possible solution to this problem is to use additive synthesis to add each sinusoidal component that is both desired and will "fit" underneath the Nyquist "ceiling." This solution is, however, computationally expensive (it would have replaced one of the oscillators in the previous example by eight oscillators, for example). Another solution is to define a few different versions of the required complex waveform, each containing a different number of included harmonics. This solution requires considerable memory space rather than computation time. We must take some care to normalize the amplitudes of the components in such a way that tones with more or fewer harmonics seem to have the same loudness (if all tones are normalized to the same peak value, for example, the relative loudness of the fundamental to the total sound of the waveform would be different).

A third alternative exists—one that is neither computationally expensive nor memory-intensive. To understand this alternative, we must take a brief detour into the realm of nonlinear synthesis techniques.

3.4.3 Closed-Form Summation Formulas

Closed-form summation formulas exist for many trigonometric functions (Jolley, 1961; Moorer, 1977; Stirling, 1749). Some of these mathematical relationships have a form that is useful for the efficient synthesis of band-limited complex waveforms. One of the simplest of these trigonometric relationships is given by the formula

$$\sum_{k=1}^{n} \sin k\theta = \sin \left[\frac{(n+1)\theta}{2} \right] \frac{\sin (n\theta/2)}{\sin (\theta/2)} \tag{3-88}$$

With θ set to $2\pi f t$ or $2\pi f n/R$, it is easy to see that equation (3-88) describes a waveform consisting of the sum of n equal-strength harmonics of frequency f. The left-hand side of the equation describes the additive synthesis approaches discussed previously—these may be implemented directly. The right-hand side describes a new way of computing this waveform, however, which involves two multiplications and one division of the sine functions of three quantities easily computed from θ and n. The major attraction of the right-hand side of equation (3-88) as a synthesis technique is its efficiency, because the amount of computation involved is independent of the values for θ and n. In other words, the "closed form" of the summation given on the right-hand side of equation (3-88) may be used to compute a waveform consisting of the sum of 100 harmonics with no more work than a waveform consisting of the sum of only two harmonics.

As might be expected, the implementation of such formulas is not without its subtleties, because the division of sin $(n\,\theta/2)$ by sin $(\theta/2)$ can be somewhat tricky when θ is equal to zero or, in fact, any integer multiple of π. One way of defining

$$B(n,\theta) = \frac{\sin(n\,\theta/2)}{\sin(\theta/2)} \tag{3-89}$$

to resolve this difficulty (Moore, 1977) is to note that

$$\lim_{\theta \to m\pi} B(n,\theta) = \begin{cases} +n & n \text{ odd} \\ +n & n \text{ even and } m \text{ even} \\ -n & n \text{ even and } m \text{ odd} \end{cases} \tag{3-90}$$

where m and n are any integers. Whenever θ approaches an integer multiple of π, we may simply replace the value of $B(n,\theta)$ by $+n$ or $-n$, depending on the circumstances.

$B(n,\theta)$ is such an interesting and useful function that it deserves further comment. For $\theta = 2\pi f_1 t$, it has a spectrum consisting of exactly n sinusoidal components—spaced at intervals of f_1 Hz—symmetrically arranged around 0 Hz. It also has a peak amplitude of precisely $\pm n$. Multiplying $B(n,\theta)$ by a sinusoidal waveform sin ϕ, where $\phi = 2\pi f_2 t$, has the effect of shifting the spectrum of $B(n,\theta)$ (by convolution in the frequency domain) so that it is centered around f_2 Hz. We are therefore not restricted to using the sinusoidal multiplier of $B(n,\theta)$ specified in equation (3-88), which sets f_2 to $f_1(n+1)/2$, thereby placing the lowest of the n frequency components at f_2 Hz, but may choose any appropriate frequency for f_2. For example, equation (3-88) may be rewritten in the following form:

$$\sum_{k=0}^{n-1} \sin(\theta + k\beta) = \sin\left[\theta + \frac{(n-1)\beta}{2}\right] \frac{\sin(n\beta/2)}{\sin(\beta/2)} \tag{3-91}$$

This equation describes a waveform with exactly n components that start at a frequency determined by θ and are spaced upward from that frequency at intervals determined by β. If θ is set equal to β, equation (3-91) is the same as equation (3-88).

A version of equation (3-91) is implemented in cmusic as the `blp` (for *band-limited pulse*) unit generator, which has the general statement

```
blp output[b] amp[bvpn] incr1[bvpn] incr2[bvpn] n[bvpn]
     sum1[dpv] sum2[dpv] ;
```

`blp` generates a band-limited pulse wave that contains n equal-amplitude sinusoidal components starting at frequency f1 (specified by `inc1`) and spaced upward by frequency f2 (specified by `inc2`). The only difference between the cmusic implementation of `blp` and equation (3-91) is that `blp` also automatically divides the output waveform by n so that the basic waveform is normalized to have a peak amplitude of unity (this peak amplitude is then further modified by multiplication by the `amp` input to `blp`).

Many other closed-form summation formulas exist, some of which are useful in the creation of band-limited waveforms such as those needed for excitation functions in the subtractive synthesis of musical tones. A few of the more useful ones are listed in Table 3-6.

TABLE 3-6 Useful summation formulas for computer music. The closed-form expressions on the right may be used for efficient computation of waveforms with a specifiable number of frequency components, such as band-limited pulse waveforms. Note that by definition, the cosecant function is the inverse of the sine function (that is, $\csc \theta = 1 / \sin \theta$).

Summation	Closed Form
$\displaystyle\sum_{k=1}^{n}\sin k\theta$	$\sin\left[\dfrac{1}{2}(n+1)\theta\right]\sin\left(\dfrac{n\theta}{2}\right)\csc\left(\dfrac{\theta}{2}\right)$
$\displaystyle\sum_{k=1}^{n}\cos k\theta$	$\cos\left[\dfrac{1}{2}(n+1)\theta\right]\sin\left(\dfrac{n\theta}{2}\right)\csc\left(\dfrac{\theta}{2}\right)$
$\displaystyle\sum_{k=0}^{n-1}\sin(\theta+k\beta)$	$\sin\left[\theta+\dfrac{1}{2}(n-1)\beta\right]\sin\left(\dfrac{n\beta}{2}\right)\csc\left(\dfrac{\beta}{2}\right)$
$\displaystyle\sum_{k=0}^{n-1}\cos(\theta+k\beta)$	$\cos\left[\theta+\dfrac{1}{2}(n-1)\beta\right]\sin\left(\dfrac{n\beta}{2}\right)\csc\left(\dfrac{\beta}{2}\right)$
$\displaystyle\sum_{k=0}^{n-1}a^{k}\cos k\theta$	$\dfrac{(1-a\cos\theta)(1-a^{n}\cos n\theta)+a^{n+1}\sin\theta\sin n\theta}{1-2a\cos\theta+a^{2}}$
$\displaystyle\sum_{k=0}^{n-1}a^{k}\sin(\theta+k\beta)$	$\dfrac{\sin\theta-a\sin(\theta-\beta)-a^{n}\sin(\theta+n\beta)+a^{n+1}\sin[\theta+(n-1)\beta]}{1-2a\cos\beta+a^{2}}$

3.4.4 Hornlike Tones

We can combine band-limited excitation sources with time-varying filters to create many musically interesting and useful effects. For example, in his pioneering work on the timbral qualities of brass tones done at AT&T Bell Laboratories in the late 1960s, Jean-Claude Risset determined that a subjectively important characteristic of brass tones is that their spectrum bandwidth varies proportionally to their amplitude (Risset and Mathews, 1969). That is, as the amplitude of a brass instrument builds up from zero at the beginning of a note, the number and strength of the higher harmonics builds up also, perceived as an increase in the "brightness" of the tone during the attack. Similarly, as the tone dies away at the end of a note, the number and strength of the upper harmonics decreases also, making the tail end of the note nearly a sinusoid.

We can simulate this behavior with the `blp` and `nres` unit generators in cmusic by placing the center frequency of the filter on the fundamental frequency of a band-limited pulse waveform and causing the filter bandwidth to track the amplitude envelope of the note (this general type of brasslike tone synthesis has been used extensively in the analog synthesis domain). By appropriate choice of amplitude envelopes and scale factors that determine the bandwidths associated with minimum and maximum amplitude values, we can create a simple instrument capable of a wide variety of brasslike tone effects.

The basic instrument consists of three elements: an envelope generator, a band-limited pulse-wave source, and a bandpass filter. We can use the `blp` and `nres` unit generators for the latter two functions, and though it would be possible to use an `osc` unit generator once again as an amplitude envelope controller, there is good reason not to do so in this case. Most musical instruments—especially those in the brass family—have a characteristic attack and decay time that is independent of the duration of the note being played. When an oscillator is used as an amplitude envelope controller, it is usually used in such a way that the entire envelope function is stretched over the duration of the note. If the attack portion of the envelope comprises the first 10 percent of the envelope function and the note lasts for 1 second, the attack *time* will be 100-milliseconds. However, using the same envelope function with an oscillator to play a 2-second note will result in an attack time of 200 milliseconds, which in many cases is undesirable. Either a great many envelope control wave tables must be available, or we must use a more sophisticated technique for controlling the amplitude envelope.

One general technique has already been discussed: the `trans` unit generator. Using the `trans` unit generator allows us to generate a unique amplitude control function for each and every note with all of the flexibility inherent in the `gen4` exponential wave table generator. However, this approach is more computationally expensive than necessary when we only wish to make the duration of the attack or decay transient portions of the amplitude envelope independent of the note duration. A more computationally efficient approach is to use a special version of the table lookup oscillator unit generator that can scan various portions of the wave table at different rates during a single note.

In cmusic, this unit generator is called `seg`, because it allows a single wave table to be broken up into an arbitrary number of segments, each of which can be scanned at different rates during a single note. For example, we can define a three-segment wave table in which each segment consists of one-third of the wave table. By scanning each of these segments at different rates, we can cause the attack portion of the envelope to last for a duration of, say, 50 milliseconds and the decay portion to last for 100 milliseconds, with the middle segment scanning rate adjusted to "fill" the remainder of the duration of the note. In this case, the total note duration would have to be greater than 150 milliseconds in order to leave time for the attack and decay portions of the amplitude envelope to occur.

The general cmusic unit generator statement for the `seg` unit generator is as follows.

```
seg output[b] amplitude[bvpn] table[fvpn] sum[dpv] increment[vpn]* ;
```

`seg` outputs a multisegment envelope based on the shape stored in `table`, which may be either a wave table function (such as `f3`), or a wave table function index (such as `3`). The wavetable is divided into N segments, where N is the number of increments given in the `seg` statement (typically `3`, corresponding to attack, steady state, and decay times). For use with `seg`, each of these N segments occupies 1/N th of the length of the wave table. Increments with zero values are used to signify that the corresponding segment duration is to be computed automatically from the duration that remains after all nonzero increments have been subtracted from the total note duration.

For example, the following instrument plays all notes with 100-millisecond attack and decay times, with the steady state adjusted to fill up the note duration.

```
#include <carl/cmusic.h>

ins 0 env ;
    seg b2 p5 f2 d .1sec 0 .1sec ;
    osc b1 b2 p6 f1 d ;
    out b1 ;
end ;


SINE(f1) ;
GEN4(f2) 0,0 -1 1/3,1 0 2/3,1 -1 1,0 ; {3 segment envelope}
```

The following instrument allows attack and decay to be varied for each note according to values specified in note parameters p7 and p8, with the steady-state duration computed automatically.

```
#include <carl/cmusic.h>

ins 0 env ;
    seg b2 p5 f2 d p7 0 p8 ;
    osc b1 b2 p6 f1 d ;
    out b1 ;
end ;


SINE(f1) ;
GEN4(f2) 0,0 -1 1/3,1 0 2/3,1 -1 1,0 ; {3 segment envelope}
```

In both of these examples, wave table f2 specifies that the attack and decay segments consist of simple exponential transitions and the steady state is a constant.

More than one segment may be computed automatically. In the next example, a four-segment envelope would be adjusted over a 1-second note duration thus: segment 1 = 0.1 second, segment 2 = 0.4 second, segment 3 = 0.4 second, segment 4 = 0.1 second. Once again, p7 and p8 control attack and decay times.

```
#include <carl/cmusic.h>

ins 0 env ;
    seg b2 p5 f2 d p7 0 0 p8 ;
    osc b1 b2 p6 f1 d ;
    out b1 ;
end ;


GEN4(f2) 0,0 -2 1/4,1 0 2/4,1 -1 3/4,.5 -1 1,0 ; {4 segment envelope}
SINE(f1) ;

note 0 env 1 -10dB 440Hz .1sec .1sec ;

ter ;
```

The total note duration given in note parameter p4 should be strictly greater than the sum of all specified segment durations.

Once again, we have a choice about whether to generate a "normalized" version of the envelope function that can be scaled separately for amplitude and filter bandwidth control, or we can allow the peak bandwidth to be scaled by the peak note amplitude. For simplicity, we can try the latter approach, which has the advantage of causing softer notes to have smaller peak bandwidths as well. This would cause softer notes to sound less bright as well as less loud—a behavior not unlike that of a real brass instrument. However, we must keep in mind that a rather large change in amplitude is necessary for a noticeable change in loudness, and a doubling or halving of amplitude may or may not correspond to a desired doubling or halving of filter bandwidth. Therefore, we must provide a means by which the bandwidth values can be scaled independently of the peak amplitude, which results in the following cmusic instrument. The following instrument is capable of producing somewhat hornlike or trumpetlike tones in the middle register, although the lack of pitch inflection, vibrato, or tremolo controls will cause it to sound more like a brass tone stop on an electronic organ than a real brass instrument.

```
#include <carl/cmusic.h>
{
    f1  = three segment amplitude envelope
    p5  = peak amplitude
    p6  = fundamental frequency
    p7  = number of harmonics
    p8  = attack time
    p9  = decay time
    p10 = minimum filter bandwidth
    p11 = peak - minimum filter bandwidth
}
ins 0 horn ;
    seg  b5 p5 f1 d p8 0 p9 ;
    mult b4 b5 p11 ;
    adn  b3 b4 p10 ;
    blp  b2 b5 p6 p6 p7 d d ;
    NRES(b1,b2,1,p6,b3) ;
    out  b1 ;
end ;
```

The operation of this instrument can be made clearer by considering its block diagram, shown in Figure 3-38. A great deal of experimentation is typically necessary with such an instrument to find reasonably useful settings for the note parameters, making it highly desirable to "tune" the instrument in a realtime interactive mode, if possible. In effect, given an instrument such as the one shown in Figure 3-38, we must discover how to "play" it. The problem is that even with a small number of parameters to adjust, the number of possible ways to play this instrument is enormous!

If the instrument can be implemented in real time (for example, with a programmable digital synthesizer), finding useful parameter settings is largely a matter of proceeding to twist knobs and listen, just as a string player tunes a violin or a guitar. If

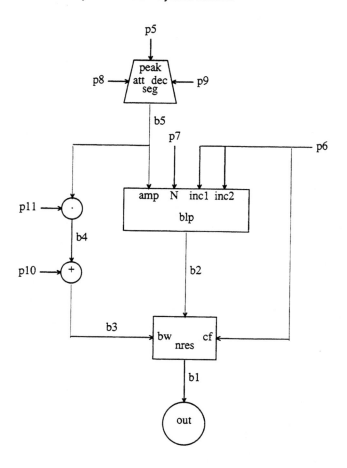

Figure 3-38   Instrument for producing brasslike tones. Note parameter p5 controls the peak amplitude, p6 controls the fundamental frequency, p7 controls the number of harmonics present in the band-limited pulse waveform, p8 controls the attack time (independent of the note duration), p9 controls the decay time, p10 controls the minimum filter bandwidth, and p11 controls the peak filter bandwidth in relation to the peak amplitude and p10.

realtime interactive operation is not available, however, it becomes necessary to organize a more methodical search of the parameter settings, eventually converging on useful ones. For the instrument in Figure 3-38, the following simple envelope and parameter definitions produce reasonably good results.

```
GEN4(f1) 0,0 -2 1/3,1 0 2/3,1 -2 3/3,0 ;

#define T (240MM)
#define HORN(dur,amp,pitch)\
 note p2+p4 horn (dur)*T amp pitch (1500Hz)/p6 .1sec .1sec 1Hz .5*p6
```

```
HORN(1,.7,C(0)); HORN(1,.7,F(0)); HORN(1,.7,G(0));
   HORN(2,1,Gs(0)); HORN(1,.7,A(0));

HORN(1,.7,C(0)); HORN(1,.7,F(0)); HORN(1,.7,G(0));
   HORN(2,1,Gs(0)); HORN(1,.7,A(0));
```

The envelope used in this score example is an extremely simple three-segment envelope with an exponential rise from zero to one, a steady state of one, and an exponential decay to zero. Score parameter T is defined as having the musical tempo value 240 MM—the MM postoperator translates the expression to seconds per beat at the indicated tempo. A note-playing macro called HORN is defined that allows the note list to be written succinctly in terms of note duration, amplitude, and pitch. In this macro definition, note parameter p2 is set to the sum of the most recent values assigned to p2 and p4, causing the note to begin immediately following the previous note. The duration is scaled by score parameter T, so that "beats" occur at the rate of 240 per minute, or 4 per second. As required by instrument horn, p5 is set to the required amplitude and p6 to the fundamental frequency. p7 is set so that blp will supply harmonics up to about 1500 Hz (the blp unit generator ignores any fractional part in the specification for the number of harmonics to generate). p8 and p9 are set so that a 100-millisecond attack and decay time is used with every note. p10 selects a minimum bandwidth value of 1 Hz—small enough to ensure that the waveform is sinusoidal at the beginning and end of any note.[24] Finally, p11 is chosen so that the peak bandwidth is equal to one-half the fundamental frequency of the note. Because the bandwidth of a resonating filter is defined as the width of the region around the center frequency over which the response is within 3 dB of the response at the center frequency, this implies that the harmonics will fall off at a rate of approximately 9 dB per octave.[25]

3.4.5 Plucked String Tones

Virtually any musical sound synthesis method may be characterized in terms of sound characteristics that it models and its computational complexity. The more insight we have into the fundamental properties of sound that are accessible through the model, the more easily we are able to control it in useful ways. Similarly, the more efficient the computational model, the more readily we can experiment with its sonic properties.

[24]Note that a zero bandwidth is not specified. A true zero bandwidth would require the filter to have an impulse response consisting of a sine wave that neither increases nor decreases in amplitude forever. Such requests are therefore usually deemed unreasonable.

[25] A simple way to figure the per-octave attenuation rate is as follows: Because the total bandwidth B is $f_c/2$, where f_c is the center frequency, the region where the filter attenuation is less than 3 dB must extend from approximately $f_c - f_c/4$ to $f_c + f_c/4$. The ratio $(f_c + f_c/4)/f_c$ is equal to 5/4, corresponding to the musical interval of a just major third. Because there are three major thirds in an octave, the filter attenuation on a per-octave basis is 3 dB per major third times three major thirds per octave, or about 9 dB per octave. Recalling that the bandwidth calculation is only an approximation of the width of the 3-dB region to begin with, it is easily shown that if p11 is set to $\alpha p6$, the overall spectrum will fall off as $Q = 3\log_{1+\alpha/2}2$ dB per octave. Solving this relation for α allows us to set p11 to achieve a roll-off rate of Q dB per octave: $\alpha = 2e^{3(\ln 2)/Q} - 2$.

Often, though, a synthesis method will doggedly resist improvement in the perceptual acceptability of its results. Most of the time this is due to one or both of two effects: I call them the "dumb machine" effect and the "dumb person" effect.

The dumb machine effect occurs with many types of machines, but it is particularly insidious in the case of the computer. People, places, and things can be influenced—perhaps even strongly—but basically most people, places, and things have a "mind of their own." A composer may write an E-flat to be sung by a professional vocalist who is quite skilled at producing accurate pitches (for a human), but any live performance of a piece of music is a kind of approximation that is based on a great many factors that merely include the composer's specifications. Written music is a kind of code that contains far less information than a typical performance of it. A fundamental problem in most types of electronic music—especially computer music—is that the machine producing the sound actually does what it is told to do, no less and *no more*. Because our sensory mechanisms are so acutely sensitive to changes in sensation, they are also acutely sensitive to lacks of change. One of the most striking characteristics of any unwavering sound is therefore its synthetic quality. A fundamental challenge of computer music is to impart a perceptible infrastructure to each and every sound by some means that will prevent it from sounding like distilled water tastes.

The dumb person effect results primarily from self-imposed limitations on what constitutes a musical sound. We may be so intent on creating a particular kind of sound that we fail to notice the portent of the sounds actually being produced. The well-developed tendency to "categorize and relegate" new sounds has undoubtedly rejected many a useful tone before its time. Labeling is bad enough (consider the names of the stops on most pipe organs), but mislabeling is more dangerous still. A mislabeled sound has been effectively mislaid and may never be found again.

It is therefore a happy conjunction indeed when both the dumb machine and dumb person effects are canceled entirely by a sound that is immediately striking and yet continues to provoke sustained interest after repeated hearings. Such accidents are made happier still when both people and machines express pleasure at a synthetic sound, the former with piqued musical interest, the latter with noticeably superior computational efficiency.

One such happy conjunction is the plucked string synthesis algorithm described by Kevin Karplus and Alex Strong (Karplus and Strong, 1983; Jaffe and Smith, 1983). This algorithm avoids the dumb machine effect by producing sounds with spectra that vary in constant, rapid, and varied ways. It avoids the dumb people effect by sounding alternatively very much like a struck or plucked string or drum and like a wide variety of other unnamable things. Finally, it is computationally efficient in the extreme, at least in its simpler forms. What more could a synthesis technique hope to offer?

The basic synthesis instrument consists of a recirculating delay line with a filter in the feedback loop. In qualitative terms, this instrument is played by filling the delay line with random values in the range $\pm A$, either by direct initialization or by feeding in p random values through the path marked "input" in Figure 3-39.[26] Once the delay line

---

[26]Methods for generating random numbers are described in Chapter 5.

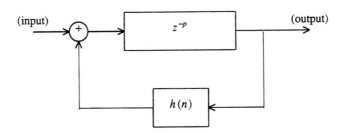

Figure 3-39 Basic flow diagram for the Karplus-Strong plucked string algorithm. The box labeled z^{-p} is a delay whose output is identical to its input delayed by p samples. The box labeled $h(n)$ is a digital filter with impulse response $h(n)$.

is filled with random values, the input may be disconnected (or, equivalently, set to zero).

What happens next is quite remarkable, both to the mind and to the ear. The random samples in the delay line circulate repeatedly through the feedback loop. If we temporarily ignore the action of the filter in the feedback loop, it is clear that these p samples would form a *periodic sample pattern* with a period of p samples. In this case, even though the pattern consists of random values, we would hear a steady, complex sound having a pitch associated with the period of this pattern, or R/p Hz, where R is the sampling rate.[27]

The filter in the feedback loop has two basic effects on the perceived sound. If the filter is a weak lowpass filter (one with a very gradual roll-off at high frequencies), then each time the p samples make a complete transit around the loop, they will be "robbed" of some of their high-frequency content according to the frequency response of the filter (see Figure 3-40). Because it is essentially random, the first period would contain all frequencies in more or less equal proportion, the second would contain a slightly greater preponderance of low frequencies, the third an even greater preponderance of low frequencies, and so on. Assuming that the gain of the filter is less than unity at the fundamental frequency, the sound is eventually robbed of almost all of its high-frequency content, leaving a nearly pure sinusoid at the fundamental frequency just before the sound decays to zero amplitude. This behavior—starting with a complex, harmonic-rich sound that gradually decays to a near-sinusoid—is precisely what happens in the sound of a typical plucked or struck string instrument such as a guitar, piano, or harpsichord. It also resembles the sonic behavior of many kinds of percussion instruments, notably drums. Figure 3-40 shows that the overall behavior of the spectrum of different notes—even those with identical specifications—will be the same, though the details differ, corresponding to different notes played on the same instrument. In other words, the two notes shown in Figure 3-40 would be *musically*

[27]This subjective effect is known as *periodicity pitch* and has been well studied in the field of psychoacoustics (see, for example, Roederer, 1975). Even pure, continuously varying white noise can exhibit periodicity pitch if it is presented to a listener along with a delayed copy of itself. This effect works even when the undelayed and delayed white noise is presented dichotically—that is, separately to each ear.

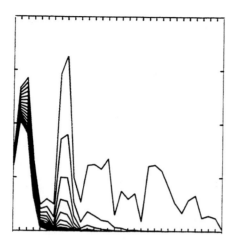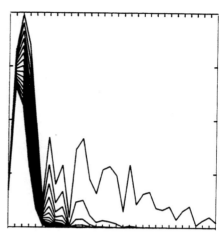

Figure 3-40   Time-varying amplitude spectra of two notes with identical specifications synthesized with the Karplus-Strong plucked string algorithm. The only difference between the two notes is the set of random numbers used to initialize the delay unit. Both notes have a frequency of 256 Hz, which, at a sampling rate of 16,384 Hz, corresponds to a period (total feedback delay) of 64 samples (the ticks along the horizontal axes mark the harmonics of 256 Hz). These plots were made by superimposing graphs of 16 successive 64-sample FFTs, skipping seven blocks between measurements. While the details of the two notes are quite different, their gross spectrum evolution characteristics are the same—high frequencies are attenuated according to the amplitude and phase response of the feedback loop.

indistinguishable, though they differ both physically and perceptually—a highly desirable feature of this algorithm.

The second effect of the filter is to alter slightly the delay associated with the feedback loop, thereby affecting the perceived pitch. If the filter has an impulse response described by

$$y(n) = \frac{x(n) + x(n-1)}{2} \tag{3-92}$$

the loop transit time will be increased by an amount that depends on the phase delay of the filter for each frequency.

Several questions must be answered before the behavior of this synthesis algorithm can be understood well enough to make it useful. One such question is, How long does it take the sound to die away? If the gain of the filter at frequency f is denoted $G(f)$, then for each loop period, a sound component at frequency f will suffer an attenuation of $G(f)$. Clearly, $G(f)$ had better be less than unity at all frequencies if the sound is to die away at all.

The transfer function associated with this filter is easily written directly from equation (3-92):

$$H(z) = \frac{1 + z^{-1}}{2} \tag{3-93}$$

$G(f)$ is simply the magnitude of this transfer function evaluated at frequency $\omega = 2\pi f / R$.

$$G(f) = |H(z)|_{z=e^{j\omega}} = |H(e^{j 2\pi f / R})| = \left| \frac{1 + e^{-j 2\pi f / R}}{2} \right| \qquad (3\text{-}94)$$

As shown in Chapter 2, we evaluate this expression by multiplying it by its complex conjugate and taking the square root, using various trigonometric identities (see Appendix A) to simplify the result.

$$G(f) = \left[\left[\frac{1}{2} + \frac{1}{2} e^{-j 2\pi f / R} \right] \left[\frac{1}{2} + \frac{1}{2} e^{j 2\pi f / R} \right] \right]^{1/2}$$

$$= \left[\frac{1}{2} + \frac{1}{4} (e^{j 2\pi f / R} + e^{-j 2\pi f / R}) \right]^{1/2}$$

$$= \left[\frac{1}{2} + \frac{1}{2} \cos(2\pi f / R) \right]^{1/2} \qquad (3\text{-}95)$$

$$= [\cos^2(\pi f / R)]^{1/2}$$

$$= \cos(\pi f / R)$$

The foregoing calculation shows that the simple averaging filter has a frequency response shaped like the first quadrant of a cosine wave; that is, it drops off from unity at 0 Hz to zero at the Nyquist rate.

The phase delay of a filter is defined as the phase of $H(e^{j\omega})$ divided by ω, as follows:

$$\frac{\text{pha } [H(e^{j\omega})]}{\omega} = \frac{\tan^{-1} \dfrac{\text{Im } [H(e^{j\omega})]}{\text{Re } [H(e^{j\omega})]}}{\omega}$$

$$= \frac{\tan^{-1} \dfrac{-\sin\omega}{1 + \cos\omega}}{\omega} \qquad (3\text{-}96)$$

$$= -\frac{\omega/2}{\omega} = -\frac{1}{2}$$

The delay through this filter is therefore 1/2 sample at all frequencies; that is, it exhibits *linear phase*, which is obvious if we note that its impulse response is finite and symmetrical around $n = 1/2$.

The total loop delay is the sum of the delays associated with the delay line and the filter, or $p + 1/2$ samples. If we think in terms of the harmonics of the fundamental frequency associated with the delay loop, $f_1 = R / (p + 1/2)$ Hz, then we can define f_k as $k f_1$; that is, f_k refers to the frequency of the kth harmonic of f_1. A component at frequency f_k is attenuated by a factor $G(f_k)$ in one transit around the loop; after two transits, it will have $1/[G(f_k)]^2$ of its initial amplitude, and so on. Clearly, it will have

$1/N$ of its initial amplitude after M transits, where $[G(f_k)]^M = N$. Following this line of reasoning, it can be shown that the time it takes for the component at the kth harmonic to die away by a factor of Q dB is given by

$$\tau_Q(f_k) = -\frac{\ln 10^{Q/20}}{f_1 \ln |G(f_k)|} \quad \text{seconds} \tag{3-97}$$

Equation (3-97) makes it clear that the decay time depends on both the fundamental frequency associated with the total loop delay and on which harmonic we are considering. Representative values of equation (3-97) are shown in Table 3-7. From this table, we can see that the upper harmonics decay more rapidly than the fundamental and that high pitches decay much more rapidly than low ones. It is also evident that the range of decay times varies greatly from low to high pitches—too greatly, in fact (such a simple algorithm has to have *some* disadvantages!).

TABLE 3-7   Representative values of $\tau_Q(f_k) = -(\ln 10^{Q/20})/[f_1 \ln |G(f_k)|]$ for $Q = 40$, $G(f) = \cos(\pi f/R)$, $R = 16{,}384$, $k = 1$ through 4, and $f_1 = 100$ through 1000 Hz in steps of 100 Hz. The first column shows the total loop delay required at fundamental frequency f_1.

Delay (samples)	f_1 (Hz)	$\tau_{40}(f_1)$ (sec)	f_2 (Hz)	$\tau_{40}(f_2)$ (sec)	f_3 (Hz)	$\tau_{40}(f_3)$ (sec)	f_4 (Hz)	$\tau_{40}(f_4)$ (sec)
163.840	100	250.489	200	62.611	300	27.818	400	15.641
81.920	200	31.305	400	7.821	600	3.472	800	1.949
54.613	300	9.273	600	2.314	900	1.026	1200	0.575
40.960	400	3.910	800	0.975	1200	0.431	1600	0.241
32.768	500	2.001	1000	0.498	1500	0.220	2000	0.122
27.307	600	1.157	1200	0.287	1800	0.126	2400	0.070
23.406	700	0.728	1400	0.180	2100	0.079	2800	0.043
20.480	800	0.487	1600	0.120	2400	0.052	3200	0.029
18.204	900	0.342	1800	0.084	2700	0.036	3600	0.020
16.384	1000	0.249	2000	0.061	3000	0.026	4000	0.014

To control note duration, we need ways both to shorten and to lengthen the decay times relative to those shown in Table 3-7. A simple way to obtain a shorter decay time (Jaffe and Smith, 1983) is to introduce a loss factor ρ into the filter, as follows:

$$y(n) = \rho \frac{x(n) + x(n-1)}{2} \tag{3-98}$$

Note that ρ must be less than 1 because otherwise the 0 Hz gain of the feedback loop will be greater than 1, causing the entire instrument to be unstable. This technique not only shortens the overall decay time for all frequencies but also has the advantage of decreasing the *range* over which the decay times vary from low to high pitches (see Table 3-8).

In many instances, especially at higher frequencies, we wish to lengthen the decay time rather than shorten it. This can be accomplished by modifying the filter in the feedback loop so that high frequencies are less severely attenuated during each loop

TABLE 3-8 Representative values of $\tau_Q(f_k) = -(\ln 10^{Q/20})/[f_1 \ln |G(f_k)|]$ for $Q = 40$, $G(f) = \rho \cos(\pi f /R)$, $\rho = 0.98$, $R = 16{,}384$, $k = 1$ through 4, and $f_1 = 100$ through 1000 Hz in steps of 100 Hz. The first column shows the total loop delay required at fundamental frequency f_1.

Delay	f_1	$\tau_{40}(f_1)$	f_2	$\tau_{40}(f_2)$	f_3	$\tau_{40}(f_3)$	f_4	$\tau_{40}(f_4)$
(samples)	(Hz)	(sec)	(Hz)	(sec)	(Hz)	(sec)	(Hz)	(sec)
163.840	100	2.259	200	2.199	300	2.107	400	1.990
81.920	200	1.100	400	0.995	600	0.858	800	0.719
54.613	300	0.702	600	0.572	900	0.436	1200	0.327
40.960	400	0.497	800	0.360	1200	0.245	1600	0.169
32.768	500	0.371	1000	0.238	1500	0.148	2000	0.096
27.307	600	0.286	1200	0.164	1800	0.095	2400	0.059
23.406	700	0.225	1400	0.116	2100	0.064	2800	0.038
20.480	800	0.180	1600	0.085	2400	0.044	3200	0.026
18.204	900	0.145	1800	0.063	2700	0.032	3600	0.018
16.384	1000	0.119	2000	0.048	3000	0.024	4000	0.013

transit, thus increasing the overall decay time. A filter that combines both decay-shortening and -lengthening capabilities is given by

$$y(n) = \rho[(1 - S)x(n) + Sx(n - 1)] \tag{3-99}$$

where S is a decay stretch factor and ρ is the decay-shortening factor. If $\rho = 1$ and $S = 1/2$, this filter is exactly the same as the one described in equation (3-92). For any other value of S between 0 and 1, $G(f)$ can be written as

$$G(f) = \rho\sqrt{(1 - S)^2 + S^2 + 2S(1 - S)\cos(2\pi f /R)} \tag{3-100}$$

Any value of S not equal to 1/2 results in a decay time *longer* than that for $S = 1/2$ (if S is set to either 0 or 1, the harmonics do not decay at all). We must also take account of the fact that for $S \neq 1/2$, the phase delay of the filter is no longer 1/2 sample but is given by

$$\frac{\text{pha}[H(e^{j\omega})]}{\omega} = \frac{\tan^{-1}\dfrac{-S\sin\omega}{(1 - S) + S\cos\omega}}{\omega} \tag{3-101}$$

Therefore, the pitch of the output signal is affected by our choice of S. Furthermore, for $S \neq 1/2$, the filter also no longer exhibits linear phase (every frequency is not delayed by the same amount), resulting in a slight sharpening (for $S < 1/2$) or flattening (for $S > 1/2$) of the upper harmonics relative to the fundamental.[28] At low frequencies, equation (3-101) is approximately equal to S. Representative values of $\tau_{40}(f)$ using the decay-stretching filter are shown in Table 3-9 (note the relatively longer decay times for the upper partials).

---

[28]This effect is not necessarily undesirable or unrealistic because the stiffness in real strings—especially metal strings such as those used in the piano—causes their upper partials to be stretched (sharp) with respect to the fundamental.

TABLE 3-9   Representative values of $\tau_Q(f_k) = -(\ln 10^{Q/20})/[f_1 \ln |G(f_k)|]$ for $Q = 40$, $G(f) = \rho\sqrt{(1-S)^2 + S^2 + 2S(1-S)\cos(2\pi f/R)}$, $\rho = 1$, $S = 0.1$, $R = 16{,}384$, $k = 1$ through 4, and $f_1 = 100$ through 1000 Hz in steps of 100 Hz. The first column shows the total loop delay required at fundamental frequency f_1. Note the stretching of the upper partials due to the nonlinear phase of the filter when $S < 1/2$ (this effect is more pronounced at high frequencies).

Delay (samples)	f_1 (Hz)	$\tau_{40}(f_1)$ (sec)	f_2 (Hz)	$\tau_{40}(f_2)$ (sec)	f_3 (Hz)	$\tau_{40}(f_3)$ (sec)	f_4 (Hz)	$\tau_{40}(f_4)$ (sec)
163.840	100	695.886	200	174.001	300	77.356	401	43.530
81.920	200	87.000	401	21.765	603	9.684	809	5.456
54.613	300	25.785	603	6.456	912	2.877	1229	1.624
40.960	400	10.882	807	2.728	1228	1.218	1671	0.690
32.768	500	5.575	1013	1.400	1555	0.627	2143	0.356
27.307	600	3.228	1223	0.812	1897	0.365	2655	0.208
23.406	700	2.034	1438	0.513	2258	0.231	3223	0.133
20.480	800	1.364	1657	0.345	2642	0.156	3863	0.091
18.204	900	0.959	1882	0.243	3055	0.111	4602	0.065
16.384	1000	0.700	2114	0.178	3505	0.082	5473	0.048

Tables 3-7, 3-8, and 3-9 indicate the total delay loop lengths required for various fundamental frequencies at a particular sampling rate. If we are to be able to tune the algorithm to arbitrary frequencies at arbitrary sampling rates, a means for achieving an arbitrary loop delay is needed, especially at high fundamental frequencies where adjusting the delay line length up or down by one sample can result in a relatively large pitch change. To tune the total loop delay, we may introduce an allpass filter into the feedback loop that has unity gain at all frequencies and a relatively flat phase delay, at least at low frequencies. By using both the decay-shrinking and -stretching filter given in Equation (3-99) and an allpass filter for delay loop length tuning, we can have complete control over the fundamental frequency and the decay length. A simple allpass filter with unity gain is given by

$$y(n) = Cx(n) + x(n-1) - Cy(n-1) \qquad (3\text{-}102)$$

which has the transfer function

$$H(z) = \frac{C + z^{-1}}{1 + Cz^{-1}} \qquad (3\text{-}103)$$

For stability, $|C|$ must always be less than 1.

The exact phase delay of this filter is given by

$$\frac{\text{pha}\,[H(e^{j\omega})]}{\omega} = -\frac{1}{\omega}\tan^{-1}\frac{-\sin\omega}{C + \cos\omega} \qquad (3\text{-}104)$$

which is approximately equal to $(1 - C)/(1 + C)$ at low frequencies. As before, the phase delay is not the same at all frequencies, which can lead to slight displacements in the frequencies of the upper partials relative to the fundamental (the upper partials are flattened slightly for values of C between 1 and 0 and sharpened somewhat more severely for values of C between 0 and -1). As long as $|C|$ remains less than 1, we

are free to move it about continuously, thereby providing a means for continuous fundamental frequency control that may be used for portamento and vibrato effects.

The loudness of the note produced by the algorithm may be controlled simply by
multiplying the output signal by a desired amplitude value. However, this provides
only a kind of "volume knob" control of loudness that affects all frequencies uniformly.
To simulate the difference between a string that is struck or plucked with much force
and one struck or plucked with little force, we can use the fact that softly plucked string
notes generally contain less high-frequency energy than loud notes. The overall amount
of high-frequency energy in the sound can be modified by applying a lowpass filter
directly to the random values used to initialize the delay line. Another approach would
be to let the samples circulate several times around the loop before starting to output
them, thus allowing some of the high-frequency energy to die away before the note "begins."

As the sound of a note dies away, the signal values approach the average value of
the random samples used to initialize the delay line. In addition, round-off errors in the
filter calculations can build up in various ways. Both of these effects contribute to the
possibility that the note will not die away to zero but to a nonzero constant. If the end
of the note is simply "shut off," a click may result. One way to avoid this possibility is
to superimpose a linear or exponential envelope on the entire note to assure that clicks
are avoided at both ends. Another possible technique would be to decrease the value of
p gradually as the end of the note draws near, thus causing the signal to decrease in
overall magnitude.

We may now combine this information to create a practical and efficient synthesis
technique. For orientation, we start with the simplest possible implementation of the
most basic form of the algorithm. If $d[]$ is an array containing p random floating
point values in the range ±1, the following C statement will output one cycle's worth of
samples (variable `lastsample` is assumed to be initially either zero or a random
value in the range ±1).

```
for ( i = 0 ; i < p ; i++ ) {
    sample = d[i] ;
    printf( "%f\n", sample ) ;
    d[i] = 0.5*( sample + lastsample ) ;
    lastsample = sample ;
}
```

(If we were to use integer sample values, the multiplication by 0.5 could be replaced
with a right shift of one bit position, making the algorithm very efficient indeed.) By
repeating this process, we can output as many cycles as desired.

```
for ( cycle = 0 ; cycle < Ncycle ; cycle++ )
    for ( i = 0 ; i < p ; i++ ) {
    sample = d[i] ;
    printf( "%f\n", sample ) ;
    d[i] = 0.5*( sample + lastsample ) ; /* filter */
    lastsample = sample ;
}
```

The pitch of the resulting waveform will be the one associated with the frequency $R/(p + 1/2)$ Hz, the duration will be $Ncycle \times p/R$ seconds, and the rms amplitude will probably be a little greater than 0.5 if a good uniform random number generator is used to compute the initial values for the delay buffer.

Whether the note will have died away to a small amplitude by the time the previous loop terminates depends on the length of the delay line (p) and to some extent on luck, which is to say, the particular random values initially chosen.

To control the decay time, we have to add the decay-shrinking and -stretching factors discussed earlier. To control the pitch, we must also add the allpass tuning filter. For clarity, we can apply the two filters separately in the programming statements.

```
for ( count = 0 ; count < duration ; )
    for ( i = 0 ; i < p ; i++ ) {
    sample = d[i] ;
    printf( "%f\n", sample ) ;
    if ( ++count >= duration )                      /* done? */
        break ;
    f1 = rho*( (1.-S)*sample + S*lastsample ) ; /* first filter */
    lastsample = sample ;
    f2 = C*f1 + lastf1 - C*lastf2 ;                 /* second filter */
    d[i] = f2 ;
    lastf1 = f1 ;
    lastf2 = f2 ;
}
```

The first filter implements the decay-shrinking and -stretching lowpass filter with parameters rho (shrink factor) and S (stretch factor), and the second filter is an all-pass fine tuning filter with phase delay parameter C. To operate this program, we have only to choose appropriate values for these variables according to our earlier discussion and decide on an appropriate value for variable duration. Care must be taken to ensure that all parameters lie within legal bounds, or an unstable loop may result.

One of the problems we have already mentioned with this algorithm is that the output waveform tends to shrink to a nonzero constant value. A practical way to ameliorate this effect is to use random values with a zero mean to initialize the delay line. This can be accomplished by computing the random values, calculating their mean (average) value, and subtracting this value from the list. Because we are often concerned with the peak amplitude values as well, we can scale the zero mean random values to have any desired peak amplitude, thus avoiding output samples that exceed a given range.

We can determine the need for decay length alteration by specifying a desired duration and decay factor (for example, we may specify that the sound should decay by a factor of 40 dB over a 2-second duration). We can then solve equation (3-97) for the required value of $G(f)$ to achieve this decay as follows:

$$G(f) = 10^{-Q/(20f\tau)} \tag{3-105}$$

where Q is the desired decay factor in decibels and τ is the desired duration over which this decay occurs at frequency f (we may use the fundamental frequency for f or that of any other harmonic). We then compare $G(f)$ as computed with equation (3-105) with the value $G_{norm} = \cos(\pi f/R)$, which is the gain of the lowpass filter at frequency f assuming that $\rho = 1$ and $S = 1/2$. If G_{norm} is greater than $G(f)$, decay shortening is indicated, in which case ρ can be set to $G(f)/G_{norm}$ to achieve the desired decay length. If G_{norm} is less than the desired gain $G(f)$, decay lengthening is indicated, which requires solving equation (3-100) for an appropriate value of S. This can be done by rearranging the equation into the form

$$(2 - 2\cos\omega)S^2 + (2\cos\omega - 2)S + 1 - [G(f)]^2 = 0 \qquad (3\text{-}106)$$

where $\omega = 2\pi f/R$ as before. Because equation (3-106) has the form $ax^2 + bx + c = 0$, the quadratic formula may be used to solve it. Generally, both solutions will lie between 0 and 1, on either side of 1/2. If we choose the solution that is less than 1/2, the resulting filter will tend to stretch the partials of the string tone, while the other solution will tend to flatten them. Because most real strings exhibit stiffness, which tends to stretch rather than flatten upper partials, we may prefer the lesser solution for S, though of course either may be used as long as $0 < S < 1$.

The approximate delay introduced by the lowpass filter, as we have noted, is S samples. To tune the delay loop to the proper period, we must calculate the difference between $p + S$ (where p is the length of the delay line) and R/f_1, which is the desired total loop delay in samples for fundamental frequency f_1. We can set p to the integer part of R/f_1 and then check to see if $p + S$ is less than the desired total length. If not, we simply reduce p by 1. Whether this reduction is needed or not, we then make up the difference in total loop length by choosing a value for C, the allpass filter parameter. In most cases, it is sufficient to use the fact that the delay D through the allpass filter is approximated by $(1 - C)/(1 + C)$, which is readily solved for C:

$$C = \frac{1 - D}{1 + D} \qquad (3\text{-}107)$$

where D is the desired delay in samples.

The following C program efficiently implements this procedure for playing single notes with arbitrary fundamental frequency, duration, amplitude, and decay factor at duration's end. The main loop for computing the output signal is also optimized to include fewer multiplies.

```
#include <stdio.h>
#include <math.h>

main( argc, argv ) int argc ; char *argv[] ; {
 int R, i, p, count ;
 float dur, amp, f1, s, rho, S, C, ls, f2, lf1, lf2 ;
 float delay, Q, Gf, G, m, loop, *d, *sp ;
 double a, a2, b, c, D, S1, S2, cosf1, PI = 4.*atan(1.) ;
 /*
  * seed random number generator with time of day so that
  * different random values will be used each time
  */
```

```
    srandom( time( 0 ) ) ;

    R = 16384 ;
    dur = atof( argv[1] ) ; /* desired duration in seconds */
    amp = atof( argv[2] ) ; /* desired peak amplitude */
    f1 = atof( argv[3] ) ;  /* desired fundamental frequency */
    Q = atof( argv[4] ) ;   /* desired decay in dB */
    loop = R/f1 ;
    p = (int) loop ;
    rho = 1. ;                    /* initial value */
    S = .5 ;                      /* initial value */
    C = .9999 ;                   /* initial value */
/*
 * Gf is the loop gain required at any frequency for a
 * Q dB loss over dur seconds
 */
    Gf = pow( 10., -Q/(20.*f1*dur) ) ;
/*
 * G is the loop gain without adjustments to rho and S
 */
    G = cos( PI*f1/R ) ;
/*
 * If smaller gain needed, reduce with rho, otherwise
 * stretch with S
 */
    if ( Gf <= G )
        rho = Gf/G ;
    else {
        cosf1 = cos( 2.*PI*f1/R ) ;
        a = 2. - 2.*cosf1 ;
        b = 2.*cosf1 - 2. ;
        c = 1. - Gf*Gf ;
        D = sqrt( b*b - 4.*a*c ) ;
        a2 = 2.*a ;
        S1 = (-b + D)/a2 ;     /* quadratic formula */
        S2 = (-b - D)/a2 ;     /* quadratic formula */
/*
 * use value of S that stretches rather than flattens partials
 */
        if ( S1 > 0. && S1 <= .5 )
            S = S1 ;
        else
            S = S2 ;
    }
/*
 * delay is approximate loop delay--adjust to equal loop with C
 */
    delay = p + S ;
```

```
   if ( delay > loop )
       delay = --p + S ;
   D = loop - delay ;
   C = `(1. - D)/(1. + D) ;
/*
 * check values for validity
 */
   if ( S <= 0. || S > .5 || rho < 0. || rho > 1. || fabs( C ) >= 1. ) {
       fprintf( stderr, "woops! S = %f, rho = %f, C = %f\n", S, rho, C ) ;
       exit( -1 ) ;
   }
/*
 * allocate delay line of length p samples
 */
   d = (float *) malloc( p*sizeof( float ) ) ;
/*
 * initialize delay line with random values uniformly
 * distributed between -1 and +1
 */
   for ( i = 0 ; i < p ; i++ )
       d[i] = 2.*( (float) random()/(0x7fffffff) ) - 1. ;
/*
 * compute average of random values
 */
   for ( m = i = 0 ; i < p ; i++ )
       m += d[i] ;
   m /= p ;
/*
 * subtract average so random values will have zero mean
 */
   for ( i = 0 ; i < p ; i++ )
       d[i] -= m ;
/*
 * scale random values to have maximum magnitude of amp
 */
   for ( m = i = 0 ; i < p ; i++ )
       if ( m < fabs( (double) d[i] ) )
           m = d[i] ;
   m = amp/m ;
   for ( i = 0 ; i < p ; i++ )
       d[i] *= m ;
/*
 * main loop--convert dur to samples
 */
   dur *= R ;
   S1 = 1. - S ;
   for ( count = ls = lf1 = lf2 = 0 ; count < dur ; )
       for ( sp = d ; sp < d + p && count < dur ; count++, sp++ ) {
```

```
        printf( "%f\n", *sp ) ;              /* output */
        f1 = rho*( S1**sp + S*ls ) ;         /* filter 1 */
        ls = *sp ;
        *sp = lf2 = C*(f1 - lf2) + lf1 ;     /* filter 2 */
        lf1 = f1 ;
    }

}
```

There are a great many variations on this technique. For example, sounds containing only even harmonics may be created by initializing the delay line in such a way that it contains two identical periods of random numbers. This doubles both the fundamental frequency and decay time, because each period of the sound now passes through the feedback loop at half the rate it would otherwise. Karplus and Strong (1983) suggest that by using a feedback filter with an equation

$$
y(n) = \begin{cases} +\dfrac{1}{2}[x(n) + x(n-1)] & \text{with probability } b \\[2mm] -\dfrac{1}{2}[x(n) + x(n-1)] & \text{with probability } 1-b \end{cases}
\tag{3-108}
$$

drumlike tones can be produced for values of b close to 1/2.

A final extension that has been explored is feeding an arbitrary sound into the input rather than using it solely for initializing the algorithm with random values. This creates a kind of "string resonator" that behaves somewhat like piano strings do when the damper pedal is held down and instruments are played nearby.

Many of these variations (and quite a few more) can be heard in David Jaffe's computer compositions *Silicon Valley Breakdown* and *May All Your Children Be Acrobats*, which have been commercially recorded, as well as Charles Wuorinen's *Bamboola Squared* for chamber orchestra and computer-generated sounds, which has not been commercially recorded to date. For such a simple synthesis technique, the Karplus-Strong plucked string algorithm represents a virtual cornucopia of musical sounds.

3.4.6 Formant (Vowel) Synthesis

Although a comprehensive treatment of the acoustic properties of human speech is beyond the scope of this book, a particularly simple and useful application of subtractive synthesis can be found in the creation of vowellike sounds. Vowels in human speech are characterized by certain resonant regions in the spectrum of a voiced sound. The frequencies of these resonant regions—or *formants*, as they are usually called—determine which vowel is heard. A list of the average frequencies for these formants in male speech is given in Table 3-10.

In the production of speech, the locations of the formant regions are determined by the detailed shape of the vocal tract. There is, of course, considerable variation among individual male, female, and juvenile speakers and even among groups of speakers from different geographic locations. Nevertheless, we can impart a vowellike

TABLE 3-10 Average formant frequencies for common vowels in American English (after Peterson and Barney, 1952). The vowels are shown in order of increasing formant frequency F_2.

Symbol	Typical Word	F_1	F_2	F_3
/ow/	bought	570	840	2410
/oo/	boot	300	870	2240
/u/	foot	440	1020	2240
/a/	hot	730	1090	2440
/uh/	but	520	1190	2390
/er/	bird	490	1350	1690
/ae/	bat	660	1720	2410
/e/	bet	530	1840	2480
/i/	bit	390	1990	2550
/iy/	beet	270	2290	3010

quality to virtually any harmonic-rich waveform simply by properly emphasizing the frequencies shown in Table 3-10.

For example, the following cmusic score produces a fairly realistic male voice singing /a/. The `sing` instrument has five basic parts:

- A pitch control section
- A simple vibrato section
- An amplitude envelope control section
- A source sound section
- A formant-filtering section

In this instrument, the main amplitude is given by p5, and p6 sets the number of components used in the band-limited pulse excitation waveform. p7 through p15 specify a three-part pitch inflection via the `trans` unit generator. Note that the vibrato depth and rate as well as the formant frequencies are fixed, though the instrument could easily be modified to allow these parameters to be controlled on a dynamic or note-by-note basis. A diagram of this instrument is shown in Figure 3-41.

```
#include <carl/cmusic.h>

ins 0 sing ;
{pitch inflection}
    trans b8 d d d 0,p7 p8 p9,p10 p11 p12,p13 p14 1,p15 ;
{vibrato}
    mult b10 b8 .015 ;              {+-1.5% depth}
    osc  b9 b10 5Hz f1 d ;          {5 Hz rate}
    adn  b7 b8 b9 ;
```

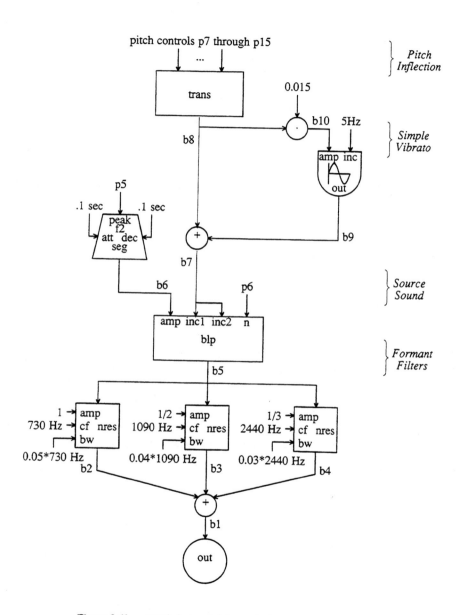

Figure 3-41   cmusic instrument for producing the sound of a male voice singing /a/.

```
{main envelope and source excitation}
    seg    b6 p5 f2 d .1sec 0 .1sec ; {p5-main amplitude}
    blp    b5 b6 b7 b7 p6 d d ;        {p6-n for blp}
{formants}
    NRES(b2,b5,1,730Hz,.05*730Hz) ;
    NRES(b3,b5,1/2,1090Hz,.04*1090Hz) ;
    NRES(b4,b5,1/3,2440Hz,.03*2440Hz) ;
{output}
    adn    b1 b2 b3 b4 ;
    out    b1 ;
end ;
SINE(f1) ;
GEN4(f2) 0,0 -1 1/3,1 0 2/3,1 -1 1,0 ; {3-segment envelope}

note 0 sing 2 1 40 C(-2) -2 .1,F(-2) 0 .9,F(-2) -1 D(-2) ;

ter ;
```

The relative amplitudes of the three formant regions are given in this example as 3, 2, and 1, and the bandwidths of the formant regions are specified as 5, 4, and 3 percent of their center frequencies, respectively. Note the use of a pitch inflection that starts and ends a bit lower than the main pitch. We could, of course, assign the formant frequencies, relative amplitudes, and bandwidths to note parameters as well, allowing the instrument to produce a wide variety of vowellike sounds.

None of the numeric values in the example are based in real speech or singing (except for the formant center frequencies); they are the result of experimentation with this instrument. Such experimentation has the advantage of not restricting the experimenter to "realistic" values for any of the parameters, thereby allowing the relative subjective "realism" of the singing sound to be adjusted as well as its other characteristics. To produce a truly realistic singing voice, however, it would be useful to have an objective method for measuring the formant characteristics of a real voice. We could use the short time spectrum analysis techniques already discussed to measure the formant characteristics of an arbitrary utterance or sung passage. However, there is a technique for designing IIR filters that is particularly well suited to this task.

3.4.7 Linear Prediction

One of the most powerful and general techniques for spectrum envelope estimation is *linear prediction*. The basic idea of linear prediction is that it is possible to design a filter whose frequency response closely matches the overall shape of the spectrum of an arbitrary sound. This filter may then be applied to an arbitrary excitation waveform in order to superimpose the same spectrum envelope on it that was present in the analyzed sound. By taking successive measurements at appropriate intervals, time-varying filtering may be achieved by applying the successive filters.

The major difference between linear prediction and the short time spectrum measurements is that linear prediction ideally measures only the overall shape, or envelope, of the spectrum of the input sound rather than the amounts of energy at a large number of equally spaced frequencies. The behavior of the spectrum between these frequencies is not represented directly in DFT-type measurements, though it is indirectly present in the form of the analysis artifacts that cause each measurement to record the presence of many frequencies lying "in between" those on the measurement grid. Linear prediction, by contrast, builds its estimation of the shape of the spectrum envelope on the actual underlying spectrum of the digital signal.

To understand linear prediction, we start by considering a new interpretation of the filter equation for an M-pole digital filter:

$$y(n) = a_0 x(n) + \sum_{i=1}^{M} b_i y(n - i) \qquad (3\text{-}109)$$

which has the z transform

$$H(z) = \frac{a_0}{1 + \sum_{i=1}^{M} b_i z^{-i}} \qquad (3\text{-}110)$$

According to our earlier interpretation of this equation, this specifies a digital filter in which input term $x(n)$ is combined with a weighted combination of the previous M filter output values. The spectrum of the filter can be found alternatively by taking the Fourier transform of its impulse response or by evaluating its z transform on the unit circle by setting z to $e^{j\omega}$. In particular, the amplitude response of this filter at various frequencies is given by the magnitude of its z transform $|H(e^{j\omega})|$.

However, we can reinterpret equation (3-110) as a formula for *predicting* the value of a signal at time n, $y(n)$, from the previous M samples of that signal, $y(n - 1)$, $y(n - 2)$, ..., $y(n - M)$, according to the coefficients b_1, b_2, ..., b_M. In this interpretation, the $x(n)$ term is interpreted as a *discrepancy* between the predicted value and the actual value of the signal at time n.

For example, suppose that we have a digital signal consisting of a pure, unwavering sinusoid at frequency $\omega_0 = 2\pi f_0 / R$, where R is the sampling rate. A conditionally stable digital filter with a complex pole pair at $e^{\pm j\omega_0}$ also has an impulse response consisting of a pure, unwavering sinusoid at frequency ω_0. The filter equation for such a filter is easily derived from its transfer function

$$H(z) = \frac{1}{1 - 2(\cos \omega_0) z^{-1} + z^{-2}} \qquad (3\text{-}111)$$

which is immediately translatable into the filter equation

$$y(n) = x(n) + 2(\cos \omega_0) y(n - 1) - y(n - 2) \qquad (3\text{-}112)$$

With these coefficients, then, our filter produces a pure, unwavering sinusoid at radian frequency ω_0. Therefore, the impulse response of this filter matches the characteristics of our digital signal rather well. In particular, the amplitude spectrum of the sinusoidal signal is virtually identical to the frequency response of the filter, because they both consist of infinitely thin lines at frequency ω_0. Furthermore, when equation (3-112) is interpreted as a filter equation, we see that except for a single nonzero input value needed to get the impulse response started, the values of input signal $x(n)$ are all zero. In fact, we can do away with the input term altogether if we simply initialize $y(n-1)$ and $y(n-2)$ to any two successive values of a sinusoidal signal with radian frequency ω_0. With these two initial values, the filter coefficients $b_1 = 2 \cos \omega_0$ and $b_2 = -1$ are seen to be *perfect predictors* of $y(n)$ in the sense that only two filter coefficients are needed to predict *all* future values of $y(n)$.

If the conjugate pair of poles lies *inside* the unit circle, the impulse response would still be a sinusoid, but one that *dies away* exponentially as time goes by, corresponding to a resonating filter with a center frequency of ω_0 and a nonzero bandwidth. Similarly, a conjugate-pole pair lying *outside* the unit circle describes a sinusoid with *exponentially increasing* amplitude. In principle, then, only two filter coefficients are needed to predict all future values of any steady or exponentially increasing or decreasing sinusoidal signal (see Figure 3-42).

We could therefore *replace* the waveform of a steady or exponentially increasing or decreasing sinusoid by only two filter coefficients that describe its frequency and rate of amplitude change, augmented possibly by two *initial values* for $y(n-1)$ and $y(n-2)$. Such replacement is one of the basic ideas behind so-called *linear predictive coding (LPC)*.

Of course, not all waveforms consist of sinusoids with exponentially increasing or decreasing amplitude. The foregoing discussing was intended only to show that for some waveforms, it is easy to see how in the equation

$$y(n) = x(n) + \sum_{i=1}^{M} b_i y(n - i) \qquad (3\text{-}113)$$

the $x(n)$ term—the discrepancy between the predicted and actual values for $y(n)$—can be made precisely zero, even for a waveform of long duration and for as few prediction coefficients as two. Imagine what this equation might be capable of doing in the case $M > 2$!

Linear prediction analysis boils down to the problem of finding prediction (that is, filter) coefficients that make discrepancy $x(n)$ as small as possible. In other words, we want to find a set of numbers, $b_1, b_2, \dots, b_M$ that makes the overall amplitude of the signal

$$x(n) = y(n) + \sum_{i=1}^{M} b_i y(n - i) \qquad (3\text{-}114)$$

as small as possible, where by "overall amplitude" we mean a quantity such as

$$E = \sum_{i=0}^{N-1} [x(n)]^2 \qquad (3\text{-}115)$$

where N is the number of samples in the signal being analyzed.

It turns out that there is a method for finding the set of b_i coefficients that minimizes the quantity E in equation (3-115). This method is based on the *Wiener-Khinchin theorem*, which says that the Fourier transform of the *autocorrelation* of a waveform is equal to its *power spectrum*.

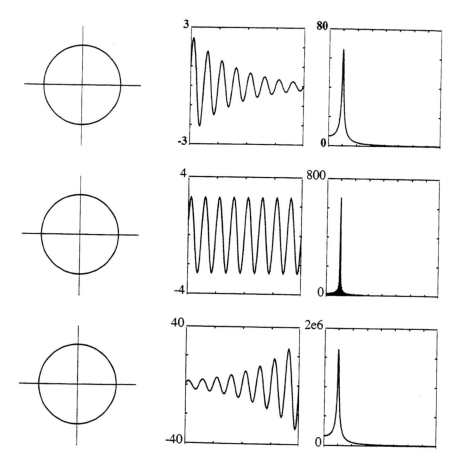

Figure 3-42   Two-pole filters with poles slightly inside, on, and slightly outside the
unit circle. In all cases, the pole angles are $\pm\pi/8$, corresponding to a frequency of 1/8 the
Nyquist rate. The top row shows a pole-zero diagram, impulse response, and amplitude
spectrum plot for a *stable* two-pole filter (pole radius = 0.98): the impulse response is a
sinusoid with exponentially decreasing amplitude, and the spectrum has a nonzero
bandwidth (the plotted pole radii are exaggerated slightly for clarity). The middle row
shows similar plots for a *conditionally stable* filter (pole radius = 1.0): the impulse
response and spectrum are those of a steady sinusoid. The bottom row shows similar
plots for an *unstable* filter (pole radius = 1.02): the impulse response is exponentially
increasing in amplitude, and the spectrum exhibits a nonzero bandwidth similar to the
first case.

We saw in Chapter 2 that the power spectrum is simply the square of the amplitude spectrum. We have been using the DFT as a means for estimating the power spectrum of a waveform, although we have seen in several instances that the finite length of
any practical digital waveform leads to various discrepancies between the DFT estimate
of the spectrum and the "true" underlying spectrum. Furthermore, we have seen that
the DFT is just a special case of the z transform of a waveform with z set to $e^{j2\pi k/N}$.

Linear prediction analysis works by exploiting the fact that the waveform, its spectrum, the Fourier and z transforms, and digital filter theory are all just different ways of viewing the same thing, which is the information present in any of these forms. The power spectrum of our filter is just the square of its magnitude, or

$$|H(e^{j\omega})|^2 = \frac{a_0}{\left|1 + \sum_{i=1}^{M} b_i z^{-i}\right|^2} \tag{3-116}$$

The autocorrelation of a waveform is *very* similar to the convolution of the waveform with itself. To compute the autocorrelation of an N-point waveform $y(n)$ at lag d, we simply slide a copy of the sampled waveform alongside itself offset by d samples, multiply the two waveforms together, add up the product terms, and divide by the number of product terms computed to get the average value. Stated mathematically, the autocorrelation at lag d of waveform $y(n)$ is

$$\phi(d) = \phi(-d) = \frac{1}{N-d} \sum_{k=0}^{N-1-d} y(k)y(k+d) \qquad d = 0, 1, ..., N-1 \tag{3-117}$$

Given N samples of $y(n)$, equation (3-117) tells us how to find its autocorrelation at N different lags d.

One way to take the Fourier transform of the autocorrelation of $y(n)$ is to take its z transform, as we have seen. We then can apply the Wiener-Khinchin theorem as follows:

$$\frac{a_0}{\left|1 + \sum_{i=1}^{M} b_i z^{-i}\right|^2} \approx \sum_{d=-M}^{M} \phi(d)z^d \tag{3-118}$$

The left-hand side of equation (3-118) is the power spectrum of the filter we are trying to design, and the right-hand side is the transform of the autocorrelation of the waveform we are trying to match.

Although the solution to equation (3-118) is not entirely obvious, it turns out that it can be solved as a set of simultaneous equations based on the series expansions of both sides. This can be expressed as a matrix equation to be solved for the filter coefficients as follows.

$$\begin{bmatrix} \phi(0) & \phi(1) & \phi(2) & \cdots & \phi(M) \\ \phi(1) & \phi(0) & \phi(1) & \cdots & \phi(M-1) \\ \phi(2) & \phi(1) & \phi(0) & \cdots & \phi(M-2) \\ \cdots & \cdots & \cdots & \cdots & \cdots \\ \phi(M) & \phi(M-1) & \phi(M-2) & \cdots & \phi(0) \end{bmatrix} \begin{bmatrix} 1 \\ b_1 \\ b_2 \\ \cdots \\ b_M \end{bmatrix} = \begin{bmatrix} a_0 \\ 0 \\ 0 \\ \cdots \\ 0 \end{bmatrix} \tag{3-119}$$

In case you've forgotten your matrix algebra somewhere, equation (3-119) stands for $M+1$ equations to be solved simultaneously. The first equation is

$$\phi(0) + \phi(1)b_1 + \phi(2)b_2 + \cdots + \phi(M)b_M = a_0 \tag{3-120}$$

the second is

$$\phi(1) + \phi(0)b_1 + \phi(1)b_2 + \cdots + \phi(M-1)b_M = 0 \qquad (3\text{-}121)$$

and so on. The big matrix in equation (3-119) has the property that it is symmetric and constant along its diagonals, making it a so-called *Toeplitz matrix*, which can be solved very efficiently on a computer in a number of ways.

We shall presently see how equation (3-119) can be solved on a computer. However, another matter must be taken into account before the solution is useful, namely, the *stability* of the resulting filter.

Even though we may obtain the filter coefficients by solving equation (3-119), we are by no means guaranteed that the resulting filter will be stable, because the N samples of the analyzed waveform may, for example, consist of a waveform in which one or more of the component amplitudes is increasing, or numeric inaccuracies in the autocorrelation matrix may cause it to be ill-conditioned. It is therefore necessary in many cases to check on the stability of the filter resulting from linear prediction analysis.

There are three basic ways to deal with unstable filters. The first is to ignore them on the grounds that we are going to use linear prediction analysis to compute new filters for each N-sample segment of the input signal. As long as we don't operate an unstable filter for a very long time, there is a chance that its output won't have time to grow large enough before the M filter coefficients are replaced with a new set derived from the next N samples. This becomes increasingly dangerous the larger N is compared with M. In general we want to choose N as large as we think the spectrum of the input signal remains relatively constant. Human speech, for example, has spectrum properties that vary relatively slowly in time, allowing us to choose N at typical values corresponding to 30 milliseconds or so. For a sampling rate of 10,000 Hz, 30 milliseconds is 300 samples, while for a sampling rate of 50,000 Hz, 30 milliseconds is 1500 samples. Values for M are typically chosen to be a few times the number of spectrum properties we wish to capture with the analysis (there is no reliable rule on how to set M). Because a single pole pair can represent a resonant region in the spectrum, M can be set to somewhere around 10 or 20 for typical speech analysis. For musical sounds, however, the number of spectrum features that we may wish to capture is typically much larger, leading us to prefer values of M nearer 50 or 100. The larger M is, the more likely that some of the poles will at time come to rest on spurious features of the spectrum of the analyzed sound, including ones that may result in unstable filters.

The second and third methods require that we check the filter coefficients for instabilities and decide what to do with poles that have wandered outside the unit circle. To do this, we must first *find* the poles that are implied by the filter coefficients computed by the autocorrelation method described. This is simply a matter of finding the roots of the polynomial associated with the denominator of the filter transfer function by any of a number of available root-finding methods. If we suspect that the input waveform contains a preponderance of steady sinusoids (as in the case of many sustained pitches), we can move the vagrant poles *onto* the unit circle, thereby causing them to represent steady sinusoids. Or if we suspect that the transient nature of the input signal is causing either spurious effects or anomalous analysis of decreasing components to result in vagrant poles, we can reflect these poles *inside* the unit circle, thereby maintaining the bandwidths and center frequencies of the poles while translating them from unstable to stable positions. There is no reliable way to determine which of these three methods will work better, so we should build a linear prediction analysis program in such a way that it is easy to switch strategies for handling instabilities.

The autocorrelation method of finding the linear prediction filter coefficients is also known as the *maximum-entropy*, *all-pole*, or *autoregressive* method. The reason for the first alternative name sheds some light on what the method is really doing. Given a digital signal $y(n)$, the extent to which the next sample may be predicted from the previous M samples is equivalent to the extent to which the successive samples of $y(n)$ are *redundant*, that is, the extent to which these samples provide little or no additional information compared with the ones already past. It is this redundancy that the method "captures" in the filter coefficients. For example, we saw earlier that a pure, unwavering sinusoid is so redundant that its entire future may be described precisely by only two filter coefficients. In an information-theoretic sense, such a signal contains very little *entropy* (randomness), also known as *information*. By capturing as much information as possible in the filter coefficients, the method ensures that the *discrepancy* between the predicted signal and the actual signal $x(n)$ contains as much information—or entropy—as possible (in the case of the sinusoidal signal, this discrepancy would always be zero because there is no information in a sinusoid that is not captured by a pair of poles). In terms of spectra, by capturing as much information as possible in the prediction coefficients, the spectrum of the discrepancy signal is *whitened*, that is, made as flat as possible.

Linear predict coding, (LPC) is based on the fact that most real acoustic signals such as speech and music contain a great deal of redundancy. By analyzing a signal in successive blocks of N samples, we may replace that block with M filter coefficients and the value of the *discrepancy signal $x(n)$*. To get the resynthesis of the first block started properly, we will also need the first M original samples to set the initial conditions of the predictor. We can then resynthesize the signal from the predictions of the filter together with the discrepancy signal. If we do this carefully, the output signal will be identical to the input signal.

The advantages of LPC lie in the fact that the values of the discrepancy signal tend to be very small most of the time, because $x(n)$ is merely the *difference* between the predicted value and the actual value of the input signal, and the predictor is pretty good! Therefore, it is usually possible to represent the samples of $x(n)$ with many fewer bits than are required for the original signal.

Even more extreme data compression may be obtained by capitalizing on the properties of $x(n)$. In the case of speech, for example, $x(n)$ tends to be a nearly pure string of pulses when the speech is voiced and random noise when the speech is unvoiced. In terms of our subtractive synthesis model, it is clear that $x(n)$ represents the source sound, while the filter coefficients control the variable filter through which they pass. However, the source sound itself may be encoded (albeit with various degrees of signal quality loss) in terms of its pitch, amplitude, and pulselike versus noiselike nature (in LPC literature, this is sometimes called the *buzz-hiss* ratio). We might encode a voiced excitation in terms of the duration between successive pulses (the *pitch period*) rather than retaining all the samples in between. Such information could be used to drive a pulse wave generator such as the `blp` unit generator found in cmusic, thereby replacing the discrepancy signal altogether. The more the excitation signal differs from the discrepancy signal, the more the resynthesized speech tends to sound like movie robots, which in this modern age is sometimes even desirable.

Another useful technique is to replace the discrepancy signal altogether with virtually any broadband excitation signal such as the sound of an orchestra playing. If the sound of an orchestra is passed through the time-varying filter driven by linear prediction coefficients derived from speech, a kind of *cross synthesis* occurs in which the orchestra seems to speak as well as play music.

Here is a complete C program for linear prediction analysis. It is based on an efficient method known as Robinson's recursion (Makhoul, 1975) for solving equation (3-119). The `lpa` subprogram accepts N sample values and computes an M-pole filter whose amplitude response approximates that of the input samples. Once the filter coefficients are computed, an argument to `lpa` determines which of the three methods discussed earlier will be used to handle filter instabilities. If the poles are to be examined, a root-finding program based on the very reliable Laguerre's method is used to find the pole locations.[29] Notice that the root-finding procedure requires complex arithmetic, implemented here in C using a rather complete set of routines for complex operations.

```
#include <stdio.h>
#include <math.h>

typedef struct { float re ; float im ; } complex ;
#define CABS(x) hypot( x.re, x.im )
complex cadd(), csub(), cmult(), scmult(), cdiv(), conjg(), csqrt() ;

complex zero = { 0., 0. } ;
complex one = { 1., 0. } ;
extern char *malloc(), *calloc() ;

extern float TWOPI ;
extern float PI ;
/*
 * given N samples of digital waveform x, lpa computes M+1
 * coefficients by autocorrelation method for spectral estimation--
 * these are returned in b[ ] (b[0] is always set to 1). lpa itself
 * returns the a0 (residual energy) coefficient.  If argument S is
 * nonzero, poles are checked for stability: S=1 specifies that
 * unstable poles are to be reflected inside the unit circle; S=2
 * specifies that unstable poles should be moved onto the unit circle.
 */
```

[29]The `findroots` and `laguerre` functions given here are adapted from FORTRAN programs given in Press et al. (1986).

```
float lpa( x, N, b, M, S ) float x[], b[] ; int N, M, S ; {
 int i, j ;
 float s, at, a0, *rx, *rc ;
/*
 * allocate temporary memory
 */
    rx = (float *) malloc( (M+2)*sizeof(float) ) ;
    rc = (float *) malloc( (M+2)*sizeof(float) ) ;
    for ( i = 0 ; i <= M + 1 ; i++ )
        for ( rx[i] = j = 0 ; j < N - i ; j++ )
            rx[i] += x[j]*x[i + j] ;
    b[0] = 1. ;
    b[1] = rc[0] = rx[0] != 0. ? -rx[1]/rx[0] : 0. ;
    for ( i = 2 ; i <= M ; i++ )
        b[i] = 0 ;
    a0 = rx[0] + rx[1]*rc[0] ;
/*
 * recursively solve autocorrelation matrix for coefficients
 */
    for ( i = 1 ; i < M ; i++ ) {
        for ( s = j = 0 ; j <= i ; j++ )
            s += rx[i - j + 1]*b[j] ;
        rc[i] = a0 != 0. ? -s/a0 : 0. ;
        for ( j = 1 ; j <= (i + 1)>>1 ; j++ ) {
            at = b[j] + rc[i]*b[i-j+1] ;
            b[i-j+1] += rc[i]*b[j] ;
            b[j] = at ;
        }
        b[i+1] = rc[i] ;
        a0 += rc[i]*s ;
        if ( a0 < 0. )
            fprintf( stderr, "lpa: singular matrix, a0 = %g\n", a0 ) ;
    }
/*
 * free working memory
 */
    free( rx ) ;
    free( rc ) ;
/*
 * if requested, check coefficients for stability
 */
    if ( S > 0 )
        checkroots( b, M, S ) ;
    return( a0 ) ;
}
/*
 * coef[] contains M+1 filter coefficients--find (complex) roots
 * in z plane and adjust as specified by argument S as needed to
```

```
 * maintain stability.
 */
checkroots( coef, M, S ) float coef[] ; int M, S ; {
 int i, j ;
 float x ;
 complex *a, *roots ;
/*
 * allocate working memory
 */
    a = (complex *) malloc( (M+1)*sizeof(complex) ) ;
    roots = (complex *) malloc( (M+1)*sizeof(complex) ) ;
/*
 * copy polynomial coefficients in working order
 */
    for ( i = 0 ; i <= M ; i++ ) {
        a[M-i].re = coef[i] ;
        a[i].im = 0. ;
    }
/*
 * find and adjust roots
 */
    findroots( a, roots, M ) ;
    for ( i = 0 ; i < M ; i++ ) {
        if ( ( x = CABS( roots[i] ) ) > 1.0 ) {
            if ( S == 1 )
/*
 * reflect unstable roots inside unit circle
 */
                roots[i] = cdiv( one, conjg( roots[i] ) ) ;
            else if ( S ==2 ) {
/*
 * move unstable roots onto unit circle
 */
                roots[i].re /= x ;
                roots[i].im /= x ;
            }
        }
    }
/*
 * reconstruct coefficients from (possibly revised) roots
 */
    a[0] = csub( zero, roots[0] ) ;
    a[1] = one ;
    for ( j = 1 ; j < M ; j++ ) {
        a[j+1] = one ;
        for ( i = j ; i > 0 ; i-- )
            a[i] = csub( a[i-1], cmult( roots[j], a[i] ) ) ;
        a[0] = csub( zero, cmult( roots[j], a[0] ) ) ;
```

```
    }
    for ( i = 0 ; i < M ; i++ ) {
        coef[M-i] = a[i].re ;
}

    free( a ) ;
    free( roots ) ;
}
/*
 * a[] contains M+1 complex polynomial coefficients in the order
 *          a[0] + a[1]*x + a[2]*x^2 + ... + a[M]*x^M
 * find and return its M roots in r[0] through r[M-1].
 * Based on program ZROOTS in Numerical Recipes: The Art of
 * Scientific Computing (Cambridge University Press, 1986),
 * copyright 1986 by Numerical Recipes Software.  Used by
 * permission.
 */
findroots( a, r, M ) complex a[], r[] ; int M ; {
 complex x, b, c, laguerre() ;
 float eps = 1.e-6 ;
 int i, j, jj ;
 static complex *ad ;
 static int LM ;
    if ( M != LM ) {
        if ( ad )
            free( ad ) ;
        ad = (complex *) malloc( (M+1)*sizeof(complex) ) ;
        LM = M ;
    }
/*
 * make temp copy of polynomial coefficients
 */
    for ( i = 0 ; i <= M ; i++ )
        ad[i] = a[i] ;
/*
 * use Laguerre's method to estimate each root
 */
    for ( j = M ; j > 0 ; j-- ) {
        x = zero ;
        x = laguerre( ad, j, x, eps, 0 ) ;
        if ( fabs( x.im ) <= pow( 2.*eps, 2.*fabs( x.re ) ) )
            x.im = 0. ;
        r[j-1] = x ;
/*
 * factor each root as it is found out of the polynomial
 * using synthetic division
 */
        b = ad[j] ;
        for ( jj = j - 1 ; jj >= 0 ; jj-- ) {
```

```
                    c = ad[jj] ;
                    ad[jj] = b ;
                    b = cadd( cmult( x, b ), c ) ;
            }
        }
/*
 * polish each root, (i.e., improve its accuracy)
 * also by using Laguerre's method
    for ( j = 0 ; j < M ; j++ )
        r[j] = laguerre( a, M, r[j], eps, 1 ) ;
 */
/*
 * sort roots by their real parts
 */
        for ( i = 0 ; i < M-1 ; i++ ) {
            for ( j = i + 1 ; j < M ; j++ ) {
                if ( r[j].re < r[i].re ) {
                    x = r[i] ;
                    r[i] = r[j] ;
                    r[j] = x ;
                }
            }
        }
}
/*
 * polynomial is in a[] in the form
 *          a[0] + a[1]*x + a[2]*x^2 + ... + a[M]*x^M
 * if P is 0, laguerre attempts to return a root to
 * within eps of its value, given an initial guess x;
 * if P is nonzero, eps is ignored and laguerre attempts
 * to improve the guess x to within the achievable
 * roundoff limit, specified as "tiny".  Based on program
 * LAGUER in Numerical Recipes: The Art of Scientific
 * Computing (Cambridge University Press, 1986), copyright
 * 1986 by Numerical Recipes Software.  Used by permission.
 */
complex laguerre( a, M, x, eps, P )
 complex a[], x ; float eps ; int M, P ;
{
 complex dx, x1, b, d, f, g, h, mh, sq, gp, gm, g2, q ;
 int i, j, npol ;
 float dxold, cdx, tiny = 1.e-15 ;
    if ( P ) {
        dxold = CABS( x ) ;
        npol = 0 ;
    }
/*
 * iterate up to 100 times
```

```
*/
   for ( i = 0 ; i < 100 ; i++ ) {
       b = a[M] ;
       d = zero ;
       f = zero ;
/*
 * compute polynomial and its first two derivatives
 */
       for ( j = M-1 ; j >= 0 ; j-- ) {
           f = cadd( cmult( x, f ), d ) ;
           d = cadd( cmult( x, d ), b ) ;
           b = cadd( cmult( x, b ), a[j] ) ;
       }
       if ( CABS( b ) <= tiny )        /* are we on the root? */
           dx = zero ;
       else if ( CABS( d ) <= tiny && CABS( f ) <= tiny ) {
           q = cdiv( b, a[M] ) ;   /* this is a special case */
           dx.re = pow( CABS( q ), 1./M ) ;
           dx.im = 0. ;
       } else {            /* general case: Laguerre's method */
           g = cdiv( d, b ) ;
           g2 = cmult( g, g ) ;
           h = csub( g2, scmult( 2., cdiv( f, b ) ) ) ;
           sq = csqrt(
               scmult( (float) M-1,
                   csub( scmult( (float) M, h ), g2 )
               )
           ) ;
           gp = cadd( g, sq ) ;
           gm = csub( g, sq ) ;
           if ( CABS( gp ) < CABS( gm ) )
               gp = gm ;
           q.re = M ; q.im = 0. ;
           dx = cdiv( q, gp ) ;
       }
       x1 = csub( x, dx ) ;
       if ( x1.re == x.re && x1.im == x.im )
           return( x ) ;                    /* converged */
       x = x1 ;
       if ( P ) {
           npol++ ;
           cdx = CABS( dx ) ;
           if ( npol > 9 && cdx >= dxold )
               return( x ) ; /* reached roundoff limit */
           dxold = cdx ;
       } else
           if ( CABS( dx ) <= eps*CABS( x ) )
               return( x ) ;                /* converged */
```

```
        }
        fprintf( stderr, "laguerre: root convergence failure\n" ) ;
        return( x ) ;
}
/*
 * complex arithmetic routines
 */
complex cadd( x, y ) complex x, y ; { /* return x + y */
 complex z ;
    z.re = x.re + y.re ;
    z.im = x.im + y.im ;
    return( z ) ;
}
complex csub( x, y ) complex x, y ; { /* return x - y */
 complex z ;
    z.re = x.re - y.re ;
    z.im = x.im - y.im ;
    return( z ) ;
}
complex cmult( x, y ) complex x, y ; { /* return x*y */
 complex z ;
    z.re = x.re*y.re - x.im*y.im ;
    z.im = x.re*y.im + x.im*y.re ;
    return( z ) ;
}
complex scmult( s, x ) float s ; complex x ; { /* return s*x */
 complex z ;
    z.re = s*x.re ;
    z.im = s*x.im ;
    return( z ) ;
}
complex cdiv( x, y ) complex x, y ; { /* return x/y */
 complex z ;
 float mag, ang ; /* polar arithmetic more robust here */
    mag = CABS( x )/CABS( y ) ;
    if ( x.re != 0. && y.re != 0. )
        ang = atan2( x.im, x.re) - atan2( y.im, y.re) ;
    else
        ang = 0. ;
    z.re = mag*cos( ang ) ;
    z.im = mag*sin( ang ) ;
    return( z ) ;
}
complex conjg( x ) complex x ; { /* return x* */
 complex y ;
    y.re = x.re ;
    y.im = -x.im ;
    return( y ) ;
```

```
}
complex csqrt( x ) complex x ; { /* return sqrt(x) */
 complex z ;
 float mag, ang ;
    mag = sqrt( CABS( x ) ) ;
    if ( x.re != 0. )
        ang = atan2( x.im, x.re)/2. ;
    else
        ang = 0. ;
    z.re = mag*cos( ang ) ;
    z.im = mag*sin( ang ) ;
    return( z ) ;
}
```

Here is a driver routine for `lpa` that calls it to analyze a block of N samples. The `lpa` routine given earlier computes and returns $M+1$ filter coefficients. The amplitude response of the resulting filter is printed out as a list of numbers that may be plotted.

```
#include <stdio.h>
#include <math.h>

extern char *malloc() ;

float TWOPI ;
float PI ;

/*
 * this program is invoked by "a.out bsize npoles scheck K";
 * it reads "bsize" (ASCII) samples from stdin and computes an
 * "npoles"-pole estimate of their spectrum; if scheck is 0,
 * the coefficients are not checked for stability; if scheck is
 * 1, prodigal poles are reflected inside the unit circle; if
 * scheck is 2, prodigal poles are moved onto the unit circle;
 * it then prints K equally spaced samples of the resulting spectrum
 * as ASCII data on stdout;
 */
main( argc, argv ) int argc ; char *argv[] ; {
 int i, bsize, npoles, scheck, K ;
 float *x, a0, *coef, lpa(), lpamp() ;

    TWOPI = 8.*atan(1.) ;
    PI = 4.*atan(1.) ;
    bsize = atof( argv[1] ) ;
    npoles = atof( argv[2] ) ;
    scheck = atoi( argv[3] ) ;
    K = atoi( argv[4] ) ;

    x = (float *) malloc( bsize*sizeof( float ) ) ;
    coef = (float *) malloc( (npoles+1)*sizeof( float ) ) ;
```

```
        readinput( x, bsize ) ;
        a0 = lpa( x, bsize, coef, npoles, scheck ) ;
        for ( i = 0 ; i < K ; i++ )
            printf( "%f\n", lpamp( i*PI/(K-1), a0, coef, npoles ) ) ;
}
/*
 * read up to size samples into array from stdin
 * zero-pad if EOF encountered while reading
 * return number of samples actually read
 */
readinput( array, size ) float array[] ; int size ; {
 float value ;
 int count ;
    for ( count = 0 ; count < size ; count++ ) {
        if ( scanf( "%f", &value ) == EOF )
            break ;
        array[count] = value ;
    }
    if ( count < size ) {
     int i = count ;
        while ( i < size )
            array[i++] = 0. ;
    }
    return( count ) ;
}
/*
 * coef[] contains M+1 filter coefficients (coef[0] = 1) obtained
 * via the lpa routine--lpamp evaluates magnitude of the
 * corresponding transfer function at frequency omega (lying between
 * plus and minus pi)
 */
float lpamp( omega, a0, coef, M ) float omega, a0, *coef ; int M ; {
 register float wpr, wpi, wr, wi, re, im, temp ;
 register int i ;
    if ( a0 == 0. )
        return( 0. ) ;
    wpr = cos( omega ) ;
    wpi = sin( omega ) ;
    re = wr = 1. ;
    im = wi = 0. ;
    for ( coef++, i = 1 ; i <= M ; i++, coef++ ) {
        wr = (temp = wr)*wpr - wi*wpi ;
        wi = wi*wpr + temp*wpi ;
        re += *coef*wr ;
        im += *coef*wi ;
    }
    if ( re == 0. && im == 0. )
        return( 0. ) ;
```

```
        else
            return( sqrt( a0/(re*re + im*im) ) ) ;
}
```

For comparison, this driver routine was used to analyze successive 512-sample blocks of the same speech utterance used to demonstrate phase vocoder analysis. The results are shown in Figure 3-43.

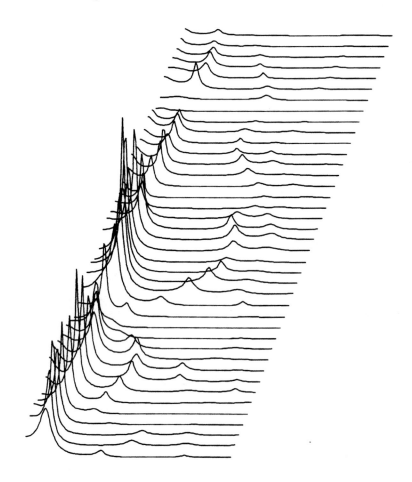

Figure 3-43   Graphical sound analysis using linear prediction. Measurements shown in this plot are based on successive 512-sample blocks of a sound sampled at 16,384 Hz. For comparison, the input signal is the same speech utterance used to demonstrate phase vocoder analysis. The measurements shown are the result of using the maximum-entropy method of linear prediction to model the spectrum of each sample block with a 20-pole filter. The plot shows the amplitude spectrum responses of the resulting filters up to 3/8 of the Nyquist rate (3072 Hz). In contrast to DFT-based analysis techniques such as the phase vocoder, linear prediction models the overall shape of the underlying, continuous spectrum envelope.

3.4.8 Combining Linear Prediction with Phase Vocoding

Linear prediction has many applications to speech and musical sounds. One of the most useful in our context is spectrum normalization for pitch shifts implemented with the phase vocoder. We have already seen that shifting the frequencies along with their associated amplitudes results in a movement of the entire spectrum up or down in frequency, resulting in a sometimes undesirable displacement of formant frequencies (resonant regions) as well as pitch. By combining linear prediction with phase vocoder analysis, we have a robust method for keeping the spectrum envelope in the same position while shifting the positions of the sinusoidal components under it during oscillator bank resynthesis.

By analyzing the input sound with both the phase vocoder and linear prediction, the frequency information may be altered as discussed earlier, and the `lpamp` routine may be used to assign new amplitude values to shifted pitches according to the spectrum envelope of the original sound. The reason this works is that the information gained through linear prediction represents the *continuous* spectrum envelope rather than the amplitudes associated with individual sinusoidal components. An arbitrary pitch shift is then possible using the smooth spectrum amplitude envelope represented by the response of the all-pole filter, which is designed during the linear prediction analysis process.

To implement this technique for a fixed pitch shift, we must modify the `oscbank` routine from the phase vocoder program given previously.[30] If the filter coefficients obtained through linear prediction analysis are known, the `lpamp` routine given in our last programming example can be used to replace the amplitude measurements of the phase vocoder with the amplitude measurements obtained by linear prediction analysis for an arbitrary pitch change P. P is used to scale both the frequency values obtained through phase vocoder analysis and the frequency of the associated amplitude, as shown in the following modified version of `oscbank`.

```
/*
 * oscillator bank resynthesizer for phase vocoder analyzer
 * uses sum of N+1 cosinusoidal table lookup oscillators to
 * compute I (interpolation factor) samples of output O
 * from N+1 amplitude and frequency value pairs in C;
 * frequencies are scaled by P
 */
oscbank( C, N, R, I, O, P, synt, Nw, coef, Np, a0 )
    float C[], O[], P, synt, coef[], a0 ;
    int N, R, I, Nw, Np ;
{
static int NP, L = 8192, first = 1 ;
static float Iinv, *lastamp, *lastfreq, *index, *table, Pinc ;
static float ffac, afac ;
int amp, freq, n, chan ;
```

---

[30]Time-varying pitch shifts are also possible; they are left as an exercise.

```
    float lpamp() ;
/*
 * FIRST TIME ONLY: allocate memory to hold previous values
 * of amplitude and frequency for each channel, the table
 * index for each oscillator, and the table itself (note
 * amplitude scaling); also compute constants
 */
    if ( first ) {
        first = 0 ;
        fvec( lastamp, N+1 ) ;
        fvec( lastfreq, N+1 ) ;
        fvec( index, N+1 ) ;
        fvec( table, L ) ;
        for ( n = 0 ; n < L ; n++ )
            table[n] = N*cos( TWOPI*n/L ) ;
        if ( P > 1. )
            NP = N/P ;
        else
            NP = N ;
        Iinv = 1./I ;
        Pinc = P*L/R ;
        ffac = P*PI/N ;
        if ( Np )
            afac = 20./(N*Nw*Np) ;
    }
/*
 * for each channel, compute I samples using linear
 * interpolation on the amplitude and frequency
 * control values
 */
    for ( chan = 0 ; chan < NP ; chan++ ) {
      register float a, ainc, f, finc, address ;
        freq = ( amp = chan<<1 ) + 1 ;
        C[freq] *= Pinc ;
        finc = ( C[freq] - ( f = lastfreq[chan] ) )*Iinv ;
/*
 * if channel amplitude under synthesis threshold, set it to 0
 */
        if ( C[amp] < synt )
            C[amp] = 0. ;
/*
 * if linear prediction specified and channel amplitude is nonzero,
 * normalize spectrum envelope using linear prediction coefficients
 */
        else if ( Np )
            C[amp] = lpamp( chan*ffac, a0, coef, Np )*afac ;
        ainc = ( C[amp] - ( a = lastamp[chan] ) )*Iinv ;
        address = index[chan] ;
```

```
/*
 * avoid extra computing
 */
        if ( ainc != 0. || a != 0. )
/*
 * accumulate the I samples from each oscillator into
 * output array O (initially assumed to be zero)
 */
            for ( n = 0 ; n < I ; n++ ) {
                O[n] += a*table[ (int) address ] ;
                address += f ;
                while ( address >= L )
                    address -= L ;
                while ( address < 0 )
                    address += L ;
                a += ainc ;
                f += finc ;
            }
/*
 * save current values for next iteration
 */
        lastamp[chan] = C[amp] ;
        lastfreq[chan] = C[freq] ;
        index[chan] = address ;
    }
}
```

The calling routine must be modified slightly as well. Here is a modified version of the main program given in the preceding phase vocoder example that allows specification of a pitch shift and the number of poles to be used for the linear prediction analysis (redundant comments are omitted). Assuming that it is compiled under the name pv, this program is invoked with the command

```
pv   R N Nw D I P T Np    < input > output
```

where, as before, R is the sampling rate, N is the FFT length, Nw is the window length, D is the decimation factor, I is the interpolation factor, P is the pitch scale factor, and T is the synthesis threshold. In addition, a new argument is specified: Np sets the number of poles to be used in the linear prediction analysis. As before, if P is set to zero, the more efficient overlap-add resynthesis procedure is used with no pitch change. If P is nonzero, oscillator bank resynthesis is used. In this case, if Np is zero, linear prediction analysis is not done, and the amplitudes of the pitch-shifted components "follow" their associated components to their new frequencies, resulting in a shift of the entire spectrum up or down by the factor P. This allows the enlargement or shrinking effect to be specified when it is desired. To compensate for the pitch shift, Np can be set to the number of poles desired in the linear prediction analysis, which will be used to maintain the overall shape of the original spectrum while the positions of the sinusoidal components are shifted beneath it by a factor P. Thus by combining additive synthesis with linear prediction analysis, we are able to shrink or expand the time scale of any musical sound while shifting its pitch up or down by an arbitrary factor, either normalizing the spectrum to its original amplitude envelope or not.

```
main( argc, argv )
    int argc ; char *argv[] ;
{
 int R, N, N2, Nw, Nw2, D, I, in, on, eof = 0, obank = 0, Np ;
 float P, synt, *Wanal, *Wsyn, *input, *buffer, *channel, *output ;
 float *coef, a0, lpa() ;

    R    = atoi( argv[1] ) ;    /* sampling rate */
    N    = atoi( argv[2] ) ;    /* FFT length */
    Nw   = atoi( argv[3] ) ;    /* window size */
    D    = atoi( argv[4] ) ;    /* decimation factor */
    I    = atoi( argv[5] ) ;    /* interpolation factor */
    P    = atof( argv[6] ) ;    /* oscillator bank pitch factor */
    synt = atof( argv[7] ) ;    /* synthesis threshold */
    Np   = atoi( argv[8] ) ;    /* linear prediction order */

    PI = 4.*atan( 1. ) ;
    TWOPI = 8.*atan( 1. ) ;
    obank = P != 0. ;
    N2 = N>>1 ;
    Nw2 = Nw>>1 ;

    fvec( Wanal, Nw ) ;         /* analysis window */
    fvec( Wsyn, Nw ) ;          /* synthesis window */
    fvec( input, Nw ) ;         /* input buffer */
    fvec( buffer, N ) ;         /* FFT buffer */
    fvec( channel, N+2 ) ;      /* analysis channels */
    fvec( output, Nw ) ;        /* output buffer */
    fvec( coef, Np+1 ) ;        /* filter coefficients */

    makewindows( Wanal, Wsyn, Nw, N, I ) ;

    in = -Nw ;
    on = (in*I)/D ;

    while ( !eof ) {

        in += D ;
        on += I ;

        eof = shiftin( input, Nw, D ) ;
        fold( input, Wanal, Nw, buffer, N, in ) ;
        rfft( buffer, N2, FORWARD ) ;
        convert( buffer, channel, N2, D, R ) ;
```

```
        if ( obank ) {
/*
 * oscillator bank resynthesis with optional linear prediction
 */
        if ( Np )
            a0 = lpa( input, Nw, coef, Np, 0 ) ;
        oscbank( channel, N2, R, I, output, P, synt,
            Nw, coef, Np, a0 ) ;
        shiftout( output, Nw, I, in+Nw2+D ) ;
    } else {

        unconvert( channel, buffer, N2, I, R ) ;
        rfft( buffer, N2, INVERSE ) ;
        overlapadd( buffer, N, Wsyn, output, Nw, on ) ;
        shiftout( output, Nw, I, on ) ;
    }
    }
}
```

3.5 NONLINEAR SYNTHESIS

The last major category of computer music sound synthesis techniques that we shall take up is called, for want of a better name, *nonlinear synthesis*. Of course, calling something nonlinear says nothing about what it is, only what it is not.[31] Because "nonlinear" does not describe any particular type of technique for making musical sounds, it acts as a catch-all repository for everything that fails to fit into other categories.

The term *nonlinear* is usually reserved for systems that do not obey the *principle of superposition*, which states essentially that the behavior of a system should be what one would expect from experience with it. In particular, if we put a signal x_1 into a system and observe signal y_1 coming out, and if we put another signal x_2 into a system and observe signal y_2 coming out, then we might expect that if we put $x_1 + x_2$ into the system, $y_1 + y_2$ will come out. If this behavior holds for *any* two input functions, the system is linear. A clear example of superposition can be seen when two stones are dropped simultaneously into a pool of water: the waves emanating from one stone seem to pass right through the waves coming from the other. This is not to say that the two sets of waves do not interact, only that they do not change each other as they interact.

Another requirement of the principle of superposition is that the noninterference be independent of amplitude. In mathematical terms, if input x_1 gives rise to output y_1 and x_2 gives rise to y_2, then input $ax_1 + bx_2$ will give rise to output $ay_1 + by_2$, where a and b are arbitrary constants. In other words, little waves pass through big waves (and vice versa) just as well as waves of like size pass through each other.

---

[31]Some mathematicians are fond of saying that talking about the class of nonlinear systems is like talking about the class of all animals that are not elephants.

All of the music synthesis techniques we have examined so far (except for band-limited pulse waveforms) have been linear. Additive synthesis is clearly linear because the addition operation itself is linear. All the filters we have examined—whether FIR or IIR—have been linear, so subtractive synthesis is in general linear. The major advantage of linear systems is that they are well behaved and well understood: if a process is linear, it is very likely to be mathematically tractable.

If a system is not linear, there is no guarantee that it can be handled with any known mathematics. There is also no guarantee that a nonlinear system cannot be solved, and some are quite well understood. In general, nonlinear systems are a bit more complicated than linear ones if only because there is no possible general theory of nonlinear systems.

If nonlinear systems are so unwieldy, why bother with them as means for synthesizing musical sounds? The answer is simple: they can be useful and very efficient. The discovery that *frequency modulation* can be used as an extremely efficient means of generating musically useful complex waveforms (Chowning, 1973; Chowning and Bristow, 1986) stands as one of the most important discoveries made to date in the field of computer music. It turns out that frequency modulation is a subclass of a more general type of a technique known as *nonlinear waveshaping*. We now consider these techniques in detail.

3.5.1 Frequency Modulation

One hallmark of a nonlinear system is that frequencies "come out" that do not "go in." A linear system can alter only the amplitude and phase of signal components, whereas a nonlinear system can generate components with entirely new frequencies. When an overdriven amplifier clips a waveform, for example, it tends to turn sine waves into waveforms that are closer to square in shape. The square waveform contains many frequencies that were not a part of the original sinusoid—the generation of new frequency components demonstrates the nonlinear nature of clipping.

We have already examined basic frequency modulation under the heading of vibrato. In its simplest form, frequency modulation involves arranging for the instantaneous frequency of a waveform to vary sinusoidally around a central value such as

$$f(n) = f_c + \Delta f \cos \frac{2\pi n f_m}{R} \qquad (3\text{-}122)$$

where

$f(n)$ is the *instantaneous frequency* of the desired waveform at sample n
f_c is the central or *carrier frequency*
f_m is the *modulating frequency*
Δf is the *peak frequency deviation* from the carrier frequency
R is the sampling rate (see Figure 3-44).

An instrument that implements such a frequency modulation process is shown in Figure 3-45. The defining equation for a frequency modulated waveform may then be stated as

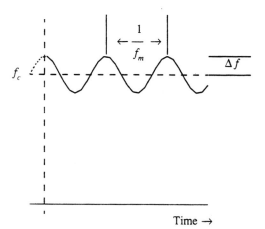

Figure 3-44   Representation of a time-varying instantaneous frequency $f_c + \Delta f \cos(2\pi n f_m/R)$.

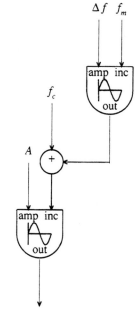

$$y(n) = A\sin(2\pi n f_c/R + I\sin 2\pi n f_m/R)$$

Figure 3-45   Definition of the basic frequency modulation process. Output signal $y(n)$ is determined by four parameters, any of which may be time-varying: A is the peak amplitude, f_c is the carrier frequency, f_m is the modulating frequency, and $I = \Delta f/f_m$ is the modulation index. Δf is the frequency deviation, R is the sampling rate, and n is the sample index. In this figure, the sampling rate and table length are assumed to be equal so that oscillator increments are numerically equal to frequencies in hertz.

$$y(n) = A\sin\left[\frac{2\pi n f_c}{R} + I\sin\frac{2\pi n f_m}{R}\right] \qquad (3\text{-}123)$$

where

A is the *peak amplitude* in arbitrary units

f_c is the *carrier frequency* in hertz

f_m is the *modulating frequency* in hertz

I is the *modulation index*, which is equal to $\Delta f / f_m$, where Δf is the frequency deviation in hertz.

Note that instead of having the value Δf as one might expect, the modulation index is equal to $\Delta f / f_m$. This is due to the way in which the instantaneous frequency values are summed (integrated) to obtain the instantaneous phase of the waveform (consider, for example, the calculation of the sum variable in the table lookup oscillator algorithm).[32]

Earlier in this chapter we saw how the instrument shown in Figure 3-45 can be used to produce a sound with a periodic vibrato, with f_c controlling the main *pitch*, f_m the *vibrato rate*, and Δf the *vibrato depth*. It is not obvious, however, what happens when the modulating frequency or frequency deviation parameters are given values that are large compared with the carrier frequency. While the general theory of frequency modulation has been known and applied for many decades in the field of radio enginee-ring,[33] no one understood the effect of listening directly to the frequency modulated waveform until John Chowning first became puzzled in the late 1960s by the unusual effects caused by extreme values of the vibrato rate and depth parameters. More impor-tant is the fact that Chowning persevered in understanding the theory of these remark-able sounds, eventually publishing a thorough account of the frequency modulation technique so that it could be used by other musicians. Today, a major portion of the commercial synthesizer industry is based on the patent that Chowning (and Stanford University) eventually received in return for making the process public. One such in-strument, the Yamaha DX-7, has sold many hundreds of thousands of units worldwide since its introduction in 1983, making it the most popular electronic musical

---

[32]We may recast equation (3-123) in terms of analog (continuous) time and radian frequencies as

$$y(t) = A \sin(\omega_c t + I \sin\omega_m t) = A \sin\theta$$

The instantaneous frequency is then defined as the time derivative of the phase according to

$$\frac{d\theta}{dt} = \frac{d}{dt}\omega_c t + \frac{d}{dt}(I \sin \omega_m t) = \omega_c + I \omega_m \cos \omega_m t$$

But because we also require that

$$\frac{d\theta}{dt} = \omega_c + \Delta\omega \cos \omega_m t$$

it is clear that $I \omega_m = \Delta\omega$. Therefore, in terms of equation (3-123),

$$I = \frac{\Delta\omega}{\omega_m} = \frac{\Delta f}{f_m}$$

In most practical implementations of frequency modulation, the modulating and carrier waveforms are both in sine phase rather than cosine phase. The instantaneous frequency is then given by

$$\frac{d\theta}{dt} = \omega_c + \Delta\omega \sin \omega_m t$$

and the resulting frequency modulated waveform is technically described by the equation

$$y(t) = A \sin (\omega_c t - I \cos\omega_m t)$$

Such fine mathematical distinctions have little practical effect on the perceptual characteristics of the resulting frequency modulated waveform.

[33]The terms *carrier frequency*, *modulating frequency*, *frequency deviation*, and *modulation index* are all borrowed from FM radio theory.

instrument—digital or otherwise—in history. Of considerably greater artistic significance is the fact that digital frequency modulation has been the basis for much wonderful music, such as Chowning's compositions *Turenas* and *Stria*.

To understand the frequency modulation process in a general way, we must examine it in terms of the spectrum that results for given combinations of carrier, modulating, and deviation frequencies. At least for simple cases, the spectrum of a frequency modulated waveform can be understood by considering the trigonometric identity

$$\sin(\theta + a\sin\beta) = J_0(a)\sin\theta$$

$$+ \sum_{k=1}^{\infty} J_k(a)[\sin(\theta + k\beta) + (-1)^k \sin(\theta - k\beta)]$$

$$\doteq J_0(a)\sin(\theta)$$

$$+ J_1(a)[\sin(\theta + \beta) - \sin(\theta - \beta)] \qquad (3\text{-}124)$$

$$+ J_2(a)[\sin(\theta + 2\beta) + \sin(\theta - 2\beta)]$$

$$+ J_3(a)[\sin(\theta + 3\beta) - \sin(\theta - 3\beta)]$$

$$+ \cdots$$

where $J_k(a)$ is a *Bessel function of the first kind of order k* evaluated at the point a. If we let θ equal $2\pi n f_c/R$, β equal $2\pi n f_m/R$, and a equal modulation index $I = \Delta f/f_m$, we can use equation (3-124) to compute the spectrum of the frequency modulated waveform directly, provided, of course, that we are able to evaluate the Bessel functions.

Equation (3-124) shows that the spectrum of a frequency modulated waveform consists of a component at carrier frequency f_c, whose amplitude is given by $J_0(I)$ (where I is the modulation index), and an infinite number of *sidebands*, which are sinusoidal frequency components spaced outward from the carrier frequency in both directions at intervals of the modulating frequency at frequencies $f_c \pm f_m$, $f_c \pm 2f_m$, $f_c \pm 3f_m$, and so on. The amplitude of the kth sideband pair is given by $J_k(I)$. The $(-1)^k$ term in front of the lower-frequency sideband term causes odd-numbered lower sidebands to have amplitudes that are negative with respect to the corresponding upper sideband.

Bessel functions of the first kind are solutions to *Bessel's differential equation*, which can be stated as

$$x^2 y'' + xy' + (x^2 - n^2)y = 0 \qquad n \geq 0 \qquad (3\text{-}125)$$

Solutions of this equation are called *Bessel functions of order n*, and there are two basic kinds, only the first of which is needed in our context.

Bessel functions of the first kind of order n are given by the equation

$$J_n(x) = \sum_{k=0}^{\infty} \frac{(-1)^k (x/2)^{n+2k}}{k!\Gamma(n+k+1)} \qquad n \geq 0 \qquad (3\text{-}126)$$

where $k!$ (k factorial) is equal to the product of all integers from 1 to k (that is, $k! = 1\times2\times \cdots \times k$) and $\Gamma(x)$ is known as the *gamma function*, whose value is given by

$$\Gamma(n) = \int_0^{\infty} t^{n-1}e^{-t}\,dt \qquad n > 0 \qquad (3\text{-}127)$$

For our purposes, we need only know that $\Gamma(n+1) = n!$ if n is an integer.

Bessel functions of the first kind can be computed from each other using the recurrence formula

$$J_{n+1}(x) = \frac{2n}{x}J_n(x) - J_{n-1}(x) \qquad (3\text{-}128)$$

If we can compute $J_0(x)$ and $J_1(x)$, equation (3-128) can be used to find the rest. These are given by the formulas

$$J_0(x) = 1 - \frac{x^2}{2^2} + \frac{x^4}{2^2\cdot4^2} - \frac{x^6}{2^2\cdot4^2\cdot6^2} + \cdots \qquad (3\text{-}129)$$

and

$$J_1(x) = \frac{x}{2} - \frac{x^3}{2^2\cdot4} + \frac{x^5}{2^2\cdot4^2\cdot6} - \frac{x^7}{2^2\cdot4^2\cdot6^2\cdot8} + \cdots \qquad (3\text{-}130)$$

Plots of the first 16 orders of Bessel functions of the first kind are shown in Figure 3-46. We can find the approximate amplitude of the carrier and any of the first 15 sidebands for modulation indices up to 25 by (1) selecting the plot from Figure 3-46 corresponding to the sideband of interest, (2) moving along the horizontal axis to the value of the modulation index, and (3) reading the value of the curve at that point, which is the sideband amplitude. We must also take into account the fact that odd numbered sidebands at frequencies less than the carrier are negative with respect to the value obtained from the Bessel function plots. For example, if $I = 1$, then

$$\sin(\theta + \sin\beta) \approx 0.77\sin\theta + 0.44[\sin(\theta+\beta) - \sin(\theta-\beta)] \qquad (3\text{-}131)$$

$$+ 0.11[\sin(\theta+2\beta) + \sin(\theta-2\beta)] + 0.02[\sin(\theta+3\beta) - \sin(\theta-3\beta)] + \cdots$$

For $I = 5$, we have

$$\sin(\theta + \sin\beta) \approx -0.18\sin\theta - 0.33[\sin(\theta+\beta) - \sin(\theta-\beta)] \qquad (3\text{-}132)$$

$$+ 0.05[\sin(\theta+2\beta) + \sin(\theta-2\beta)] + 0.36[\sin(\theta+3\beta) - \sin(\theta-3\beta)] + \cdots$$

and so on.

A great deal can be learned about the spectrum behavior of frequency modulated waveforms from observation of the plots in Figure 3-46. First, we see that Bessel functions of the first kind resemble "damped sinusoids" in that their peak amplitudes gradually decrease as the modulation index increases. Second, only $J_0(I)$, which determines

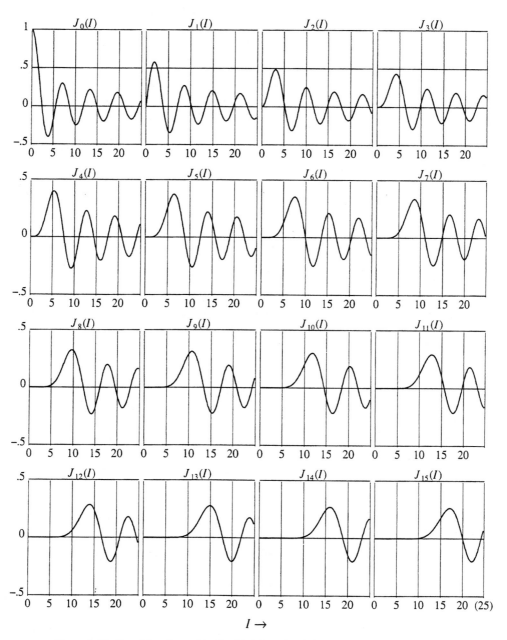

Figure 3-46 Bessel functions of the first kind for orders 0 through 15 and modulation indices 0 through 25.

the amplitude of the carrier frequency, is nonzero at $I = 0$; the rest all start out from 0. Therefore, as we might expect, a modulation index of zero results in a spectrum consisting of a pure sinusoid at the carrier frequency. Third, each order of Bessel function starts up more gradually than the one before, indicating that higher-order sidebands enter gradually as the modulation index is increased. Fourth, as the modulation index increases, amplitudes of all components oscillate between their extreme values, passing through zero in between. This indicates that it is possible for virtually any component of a frequency modulation waveform to have a small—even zero—amplitude while neighboring components have amplitudes that are quite significant. The overall envelope of the spectrum is therefore determined by the envelope of the Bessel functions, though individual components (including the carrier frequency) may be small or missing entirely for a given modulation index. Finally, a time-varying modulation index will cause individual sideband amplitudes to trace the Bessel function curves, indicating that the spectrum will change in complex ways even for simple, linear changes in the modulation index.

The spacing of the components in a frequency modulated waveform is determined by the value of the modulating frequency according to the series $f_c \pm f_m$, $f_c \pm 2f_m$, . . . If the modulating frequency is *equal* to the carrier frequency, for example, the upper sidebands will clearly fall at intervals that are *harmonics* of the carrier frequency. Because sidebands are generated on both sides of the carrier frequency, we must also take into account the effect of the lower sidebands on the overall spectrum.

In the case where the modulating and carrier frequencies are equal, the first lower sideband is at $f_c - f_m = f_c - f_c = 0$ Hz and thereby contributes a D.C. offset to the waveform according to its phase: if the net phase is 0 with respect to sine phase, this contribution will be zero because $\sin 0 = 0$; if the net phase is nonzero with respect to sine phase, this component will have a constant value. The second lower sideband will be at the frequency $f_c - 2f_m = f_c - 2f_c = -f_c$ Hz. Recalling that $\sin(-x) = -\sin x$ and $\cos(-x) = \cos x$, we deduce that this *negative-frequency component* will wrap around 0 Hz and interfere (either constructively or destructively) with the carrier frequency component, depending on its net phase and amplitude. All the remaining negative-frequency components due to lower sideband generation will similarly wrap around 0 Hz and interfere with components at the corresponding positive frequencies.[34]

The wraparound behavior of negative frequency components contributes an additional complication to the evolution of the spectrum of a frequency modulated waveform as the modulation index varies. The *overall* behavior is straightforward, however, which is what makes frequency modulation such a useful music synthesis technique: increasing the modulation index generally increases the *effective bandwidth* of the spectrum, and vice versa. Moreover, the spacing of the spectrum components is easily controlled by choosing modulating frequencies that have particular relationships to the carrier frequency.

---

[34]This wraparound effect distinguishes the behavior of frequency modulation in music synthesis applications from typical radio frequency applications, where the carrier frequency is so much greater than the (audio band) modulating frequencies that the wraparound effect is negligible.

To simplify the discussion of frequency modulation parameters, we may introduce the notion of a *harmonicity ratio* H, defined as the ratio of the modulating to carrier frequencies; that is, $H = f_m/f_c$. For $H = 1$, that is, when the carrier and modulating frequencies are equal, we have already seen that the resulting waveform is harmonic, with a fundamental frequency equal to the carrier frequency. If $H = 1/2$, that is, when the carrier frequency is twice the modulating frequency, the resulting waveform is still harmonic but now has the carrier frequency positioned at the second harmonic. In general, when $H = 1/N$, where N is any integer greater than or equal to 1, the resulting waveform is harmonic with the carrier frequency positioned at harmonic N. In all cases, any lower sidebands with negative frequencies simply wrap around to combine algebraically with the corresponding positive-frequency components.

Similarly, when $H = N$, where N is an integer greater than 1, the resulting waveform is still harmonic, but some harmonics will be missing. For example, when $H = 2$, the modulating frequency is twice the carrier frequency, causing the upper sidebands to be positioned at intervals corresponding to the odd harmonics of the fundamental frequency, which is equal to the carrier frequency. The lower sidebands occur at frequencies $f_c - f_m = f_c - 2f_c = -f_c$, $f_c - 2f_m = f_c - 4f_c = -3f_c$, and so on, which will wrap around to positive frequencies that also correspond to odd harmonics of the fundamental at f_c Hz. In general, when $H = N$, where N is a positive integer greater than 1, the fundamental frequency is equal to the carrier frequency, but only harmonics of the form $kN + 1$, $k = 0, 1, 2, \ldots$, will be present.

In general, if H has the form N_1/N_2, where N_1 and N_2 are any positive integers, the resulting waveform will be harmonic. If H is not of this form, the resulting spectrum is not harmonic. For example, if $H = 1/\sqrt{2}$, the spectrum consists of components at frequencies of the form $f_c \pm k\sqrt{2}f_c$, $k = 0, 1, 2, \ldots$ Because the relationship of the frequencies is irrational, there is no implied fundamental frequency. Such *inharmonic spectra* are useful for the synthesis of unpitched musical tones such as those of bells, gongs, and drums.

For a given carrier frequency and harmonicity ratio, the modulation index may be independently controlled via the frequency deviation. Because the peak amplitude of the frequency modulated waveform is independent of the other frequency modulation parameters, we are free to impose on the waveform any kind of amplitude envelope that we like. Figure 3-47 shows frequency modulated waveforms with unity peak amplitude and harmonicity ratios and integer modulation indices ranging from 0 to 24. Even though the peak amplitude always remains the same, the rms amplitude is not necessarily the same for each modulation index due to the 0 Hz wraparound effect.[35] Though it may not be entirely obvious from looking at Figure 3-47, the pitch of each of the waveforms is the same. However, the effective bandwidth, and hence the "brightness" of the corresponding sounds, distinguishes them from each other.

---

[35]An important feature of frequency modulation in radio applications is the fact that the rms amplitude of the transmitted waveform is constant, causing the power dissipated by the radio transmitter to be constant over time. Again, audio band frequency modulation is seen to differ from radio applications where the wraparound effect is practically negligible.

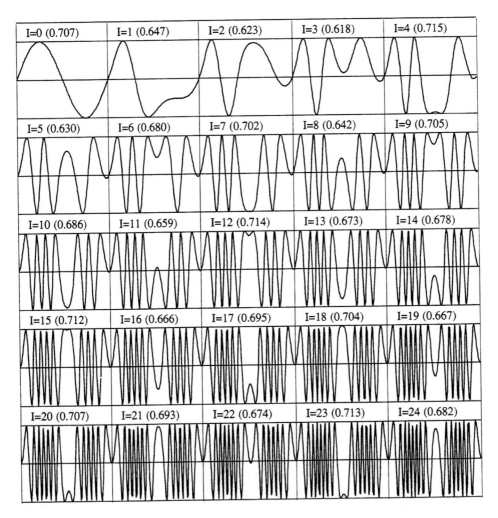

Figure 3-47 Frequency modulated waveforms for $A = 1$, $H = 1$ and $I = 0$ through 24 (see text). Each section of the plot shows one fundamental period (the numbers in parentheses indicate rms amplitude).

One feature of the Bessel functions that we can observe from Figure 3-46 is that as each order enters with increasing values of I, it momentarily attains the largest of all the orders when it reaches its first peak. Except for the first few orders, $J_k(I)$ reaches its greatest (first) local maximum at about $I + 2$. For example, $J_4(I)$ reaches its greatest value at about $I = 6$, $J_5(I)$ reaches its greatest value at about $I = 7$, and so on. Furthermore, when $J_k(I)$ reaches its first local maximum, its value is greater than that of any other order at the same value of I. This fact is helpful in approximating the effective bandwidth of a frequency modulated waveform. We can define this effective bandwidth to be some number of decibels below the strongest sideband. If we are concerned with audibility, sidebands with amplitudes about 20 or 40 dB below that of the strongest component are very likely to be masked into inaudibility. If we are concerned with foldover, we may wish to use a 40–dB or even a 60–dB criterion.

Figure 3-48 shows sideband numbers as a function of I, the modulation index. The curve marked 0 shows the number of the sideband that has the greatest amplitude as a function of modulation index I. The other curves show which sidebands have amplitudes 20, 40 and 60 dB below that of the one with the greatest amplitude. For example, for $I = 10$, the sideband with the greatest amplitude is number 8, and sidebands numbered 17 and above are all 60 dB below the amplitude of sideband 8. If we define S_0 as the number of the sideband with the greatest amplitude, we can see from Figure 3-48 that $S_0 \approx I - 2$, as we have already mentioned. If S_T is the number of the sideband with an amplitude T dB below the amplitude of sideband S_0, we can see that to within good approximations, $S_{20} \approx 1.3I$, $S_{40} \approx 1.5I$, and $S_{60} \approx 1.7I$. Using the 40–dB criterion, for example, we may conclude that components above about $f_c + 1.5If_m$ Hz will have "insignificant" amplitudes. As long as this frequency lies below the Nyquist rate, "significant" foldover is unlikely to occur, even though some measure of aliasing occurs with any frequency modulated waveform due to its theoretically infinite bandwidth.

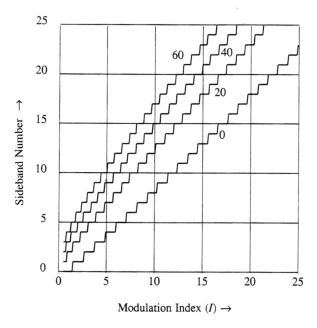

Figure 3-48   Curves for approximating the effective bandwidth of a frequency modulated waveform. The curve marked 0 shows the sideband with the greatest amplitude at a given modulation index. The other curves show the sidebands with amplitudes 20, 40 and 60 dB below the one marked 0.

3.5.2 Simple Applications of Frequency Modulation

Even in its simplest form, the frequency modulation technique can produce many attractive and useful musical sounds. To use frequency modulation effectively, we must decide how we wish to control its four basic parameters. We have seen earlier how a simple brasslike tone can be synthesized by causing the bandwidth of the spectrum to track the amplitude envelope of the waveform. It is a simple matter to obtain such behavior in a frequency modulated waveform.

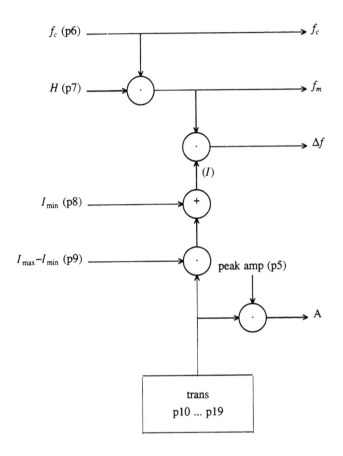

Figure 3-49 Control structure for making the modulation index track the amplitude envelope. p5 controls the peak amplitude; p6 controls the carrier frequency; p7 is the harmonicity ratio; p8 is the minimum modulation index value; p9 is the difference between the maximum modulation index value and p8; p10 through p19 control a four-segment envelope shape. The four control parameters generated by this structure may be fed directly into the basic frequency modulation instrument shown in Figure 3-45. Note parameters p6, p7, p8, and p9 could be replaced by time-varying controls.

Figure 3-45 defines the four basic parameters in need of control (A, f_c, f_m, and Δf). We can use a cmusic `trans` unit-generator to create a control function with an arbitrary shape and a unity peak value: this function can then be scaled as necessary for amplitude and modulation index control. By using the control structure shown in Figure 3-49, we can specify sound events directly in terms of peak amplitude (p5), carrier frequency (p6), harmonicity ratio (p7), minimum (p8) and maximum (p9) values for the modulation index, and envelope shape (p10 through p19). When the amplitude envelope is 0, the control structure shown in the figure will cause the modulation index to be I_{min} as specified by the value of p8. When the amplitude envelope reaches its peak, the modulation index will be I_{max} according to the value of p9. While the multiplier that computes the modulating frequency from the carrier frequency according to the value of the harmonicity ratio is not strictly necessary, it allows all three of these control values to be replaced by time-varying control signals. Therefore, the control structure shown in Figure 3-49 is quite general and flexible for situations where we wish the modulation index to track an arbitrary amplitude envelope.

The following cmusic instrument implements the control structure shown in Figure 3-49 along with the basic frequency modulation shown in Figure 3-45.

```
#include <carl/cmusic.h>

ins 0 fm ;                    {index tracks amplitude envelope}
                              {4-segment control function}
    trans b9 d d d 0,0 p10 p11,p12 p13 p14,p15 p16 p17,p18 p19 1,0 ;
    mult  b8 b9 p9 ;          {p9 = index range}
    adn   b7 b8 p8 ;          {p8 = minimum index}
    mult  b6 p6 p7 ;          {p7 = harmonicity}
    mult  b5 b7 b6 ;          {compute deviation from index}
    osc   b4 b5 b6 f1 d ;     {modulating oscillator}
    adn   b3 b4 p6 ;          {p6 = carrier frequency}
    mult  b2 b9 p5 ;          {p5 = peak amplitude}
    osc   b1 b2 b3 f1 d ;     {carrier oscillator}
    out   b1 ;
end ;


SINE(f1) ;
```

The `trans` unit generator is arranged to allow a four-segment control function to be generated with transition parameter control of each segment.

Rather than writing out 20 note parameters for each note we wish to play, we can specify macros that define various acoustic properties that the sound is to have. For example, the following macro definition defines minimum and maximum modulation indices as 0 and 5, respectively, along with a four-segment envelope that consists of an exponential rise over the first 20 percent of the note duration, an exponential fall by 3 dB over the next 10 percent of the note duration, a 1-dB sag in amplitude over the next 50 percent of the note duration, and an exponential decay to zero at the end of the note.

```
#define HORN( time,dur,amp,pitch )\
note time fm dur amp pitch 1 0 5 -1 .2,1 -1 .3,-3dB 0 .8,-4dB -1
```

With this definition in place, we can play brasslike tones using statements such as

```
HORN(0,.6,-10dB,C(0) ) ;
HORN(p2+p4,3,-10dB,G(0) ) ;
```

These two note statements specify a middle C for 0.6 second, followed by a G a fifth higher for 3 seconds. The peak amplitude is given as −10 dB. The modulation index "tracks" the amplitude envelope according to the shape of the control function given in the definition of the HORN macro. Because the modulation index controls the bandwidth and the bandwidth is therefore proportional to the amplitude, the resulting tones sound brasslike.

The same instrument can be used to produce a variety of other sounds as well. The following macro definition allows the production of double-reed-like sounds in the lower register (these examples are similar to those given in Chowning, 1973).

```
#define BASSOON(time,dur,amp,pitch )\
note time fm dur amp 5*pitch 1/5 0 1.5 -1 .1,1 0 .2,1 0 .9,1 -3
```

In this case, the carrier frequency is set to the fifth harmonic of the intended pitch and the harmonicity ratio is set so that the modulating frequency is one fifth the carrier frequency. This causes the attack of the note to have relatively greater energy at the fifth harmonic, with the remainder of the components entering as the amplitude builds up from zero. The envelope control function consists simply of an exponential rise over the first 10 percent of the note duration and a rapid release after 90 percent of the specified duration. Representative notes played on this instrument are as follows:

```
BASSOON(0,.6,-10dB,C(-1) ) ;
BASSOON(1,2,-10dB,G(-1) ) ;
```

To produce clarinetlike sounds we can choose the carrier frequency and harmonicity ratio so that only odd harmonics are generated. The carrier is placed at the third harmonic, and the modulation index in this case starts at a larger value (4) than it attains during the steady-state portion of the note.

```
#define CLARINET(time,dur,amp,pitch )\
note time fm dur amp 3*pitch 2/3 4 2 -1 .1,1 0 .2,1 0 .9,1 -3
```

The same instrument can also produce a variety of percussive sounds resembling bells, gongs and drums. In this case, the harmonicity is set so that the implied fundamental is very low, making the sound tend toward inharmonicity. A percussive envelope control function is specified consisting essentially of a very rapid attack followed by a gradual exponential decay. The modulation index falls from 10 to 0 as the amplitude falls from maximum to minimum.

```
#define BELL(time,dur,amp,pitch )\
note time fm dur amp pitch 1.4 0 10 -20 .01,1 -1 .9,-20dB -5 .99,0 0
```

A typical note played on this instrument, which sounds like a deep bell, may be produced with the following note statement:

```
BELL(p2+p4,3,-10dB,G(-1) ) ;
```

To achieve even more inharmonicity, the harmonicity ratio can be set to an irrational number (to within the finite precision of the computer, of course). The definition

```
#define GONG(time,dur,amp,pitch )\
 note time fm dur \
  amp pitch sqrt(2) 0 10 -20 .01,1 -1 .9,-20dB -5 .99,0 0
```

when played with a statement such as

```
GONG(p2+p4,8,0dB,G(-2) ) ;
```

produces a somewhat gonglike sound.

All of these examples are intended only to give some flavor of the remarkable flexibility of the frequency modulation technique for musical sound synthesis. The parameter settings given here are by no means definitive, and the resulting sounds do not match the sounds of traditional instruments in any precise way, yet they are evocative of the instruments after which their macro definitions have been named. One useful trick in improving the "realism" of sounds synthesized with frequency modulation is to set the harmonicity ratio slightly "off" from a ratio of integers so that the lower sidebands do not wrap around to precisely the same frequencies as the upper sidebands. This causes acoustic beats to occur that impart an undulation in the amplitude of the overall sound.

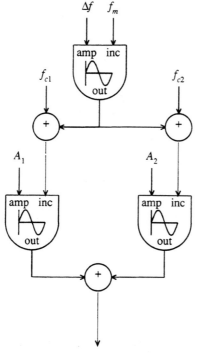

$$y(t) = A_1 \sin(\omega_{c1} t + I\sin\omega_m t) + A_2 \sin(\omega_{c2} t + I\sin\omega_m t)$$

Figure 3-50   Example of double carrier frequency modulation. Each of two independent carrier oscillators is modulated by the same sinusoidal signal. This technique may be extended to any number of carriers, each of which will have independently controllable amplitudes.

3.5.3 Extensions to Basic Frequency Modulation

The two extensions to basic frequency modulation that have been explored extensively consist of using multiple carriers or modulators to increase the complexity of the resulting sound in controllable ways. Adding a second carrier frequency oscillator (see Figure 3-50) effectively superimposes a second complete spectrum on the one generated by the first carrier. In this way, it is possible to impart emphasis to selected frequencies that can resemble the effect of adding a formant region to the spectrum. As many carriers as are desired can be added, each with independently controllable amplitudes.

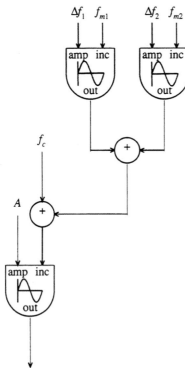

$$y(t) = A \sin[\omega_c t + I_1 \sin(\omega_{m1} t) + I_2 \sin(\omega_{m2} t)]$$

Figure 3-51 Example of double modulator frequency modulation. A single-carrier oscillator is modulated by the sum of two sinusoidal modulating oscillators, effectively causing the modulating signal to have a complex waveshape. This technique may be extended to any number of modulating oscillators, forming an output waveform in which all possible sum and difference frequencies exist.

Adding modulating oscillators has the effect of changing the modulating waveform from a sinusoid to a more complex shape (see Figure 3-58) Although the mathematical analysis of the resulting waveform can be quite complicated, it consists essentially of finding the effect generated by each component of the modulating waveform.

For example, when two sinusoidal modulators are used, it can be shown that all frequencies of the form

$$f_c \pm i f_{m1} \pm k f_{m2} \tag{3-133}$$

are generated, where i and k are integers and f_{m1} and f_{m2} are the two modulating frequencies. The resultant waveform (in analog form) is then described by the equation

$$y(t) = A \sin(\omega_c t + I_1 \sin\omega_{m1} t + I_2 \sin\omega_{m2} t) \qquad (3\text{-}134)$$

where I_1 and I_2 are the two relevant modulation indices. The amplitude of the component at $f_c \pm if_{m1} \pm kf_{m2}$ is then given by $J_i(I_1)J_k(I_2)$ according to (LeBrun, 1977)

$$y(t) = \sum_{i=-\infty}^{\infty} \sum_{k=-\infty}^{\infty} J_i(I_1)J_k(I_2) \sin(\omega_c t + i\omega_{m1} t + k\omega_{m1} t) \qquad (3\text{-}135)$$

The amplitude of carrier frequency f_c is then given by $J_0(I_1)J_0(I_2)$, for example. Such complex modulation waveforms have been explored as a means of simulating piano and string tones (Schottstaedt, 1977).

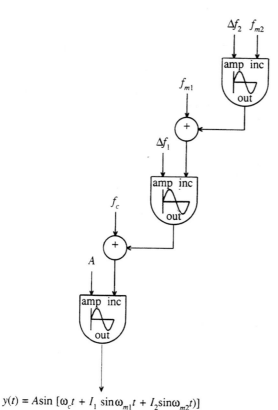

$$y(t) = A\sin[\omega_c t + I_1 \sin\omega_{m1} t + I_2\sin\omega_{m2} t)]$$

Figure 3-52   Example of cascade frequency modulation. A carrier oscillator is modulated by a frequency modulated waveform; the modulating signal therefore has an infinite number of components.

Of course, there are many other variations. Extremely dense spectra may be generated easily by modulating the frequency of a sinusoid with a frequency modulated waveform (see Figure 3-52). Unlike the last case, in which the modulating waveform had only two components, the modulating waveform now has an infinite number of components according to

$$y(t) = A \sin [\omega_c t + I_1 \sin(\omega_{m1} t + I_2 \sin \omega_{m2} t)] \qquad (3\text{-}136)$$

In this case, I_2 determines the effective bandwidth of the modulating waveform, and I_1 determines the effective bandwidth of the output waveform. Because the modulating waveform contains frequency components at $\omega_{m1} \pm k \omega_{m2}$, the output waveform will contain frequencies of the form $\omega_c \pm i (\omega_{m1} \pm k \omega_{m2})$, where both i and k are nonnegative integers. Even for small values of I_1 and I_2, the waveform described by equation (3-136) can be quite complex. Conversely, for moderate or large modulation indices, cascade frequency modulation can create spectra so complex that they sound like nonuniform noise. The following cmusic score, for example, uses cascade frequency modulation to produce a sound reminiscent of a note struck (forcefully) on a giant tam-tam. The envelopes for the modulation indices are chosen to simulate the buildup of the spectrum after the note is "struck" and the gradual decay of vibration modes during the long decay when several simultaneous pitches are audible. The irrational relationship of the carrier and modulating frequencies ($f_{m1}/f_c = \sqrt{2}$ and $f_{m2}/f_{m1} = \pi$) assures, however, that the spectrum is completely inharmonic.

```
#include <carl/cmusic.h>

ins 0 cascade ;
    trans b8 d d d 0,p20 p21 p22,p23 p24 1,p25 ;
    osc   b7 b8 p7 f1 d ;           {modulator 2}
    adn   b6 b7 p6 ;
    trans b5 d d d 0,p14 p15 p16,p17 p18 1,p19 ;
    osc   b4 b5 b6 f1 d ;           {modulator 1}
    adn   b3 b4 p5 ;
    trans b2 d d d 0,p8 p9 p10,p11 p12 1,p13 ;
    osc   b1 b2 b3 f1 d ;           {carrier}
    out   b1 ;
end ;

SINE(f1) ;

note 0 cascade 10
    60Hz                           {p5 - carrier frequency}
    p5*sqrt(2)                     {p6 - modulating frequency 1}
    p6*4*atan(1)                   {p7 - modulating frequency 2}
        0 -10       .01,1 -1      0   {amplitude envelope}
    1*p6   1 .045,12*p6 -2 .5*p6     {I1 envelope}
    1*p7   1 .03,8*p7 -1 1*p7 ;      {I2 envelope}

ter ;
```

3.5.4 Nonlinear Waveshaping

Despite the fact that frequency modulation is easily seen as a veritable cornucopia of musical sounds, it is nevertheless a small subset of a more general nonlinear synthesis technique. The more general technique of *nonlinear waveshaping* rests on a basic notion called *mathematical composition*.

In mathematics, a function is said to be *composable* with another function when one function may be used as the argument of the other. For example, if $y = f(x)$ is a function of independent variable x and $z = g(y)$ is a function of variable y, then $g(f(x))$ is said to be the *composition* of function g with function f (see, for example, Stone, 1973). For such composition to work, the *domain* of f (that is, the set of possible values of function f) must be a subset of the *range* of g (that is, the set of allowable arguments to function g). For example, suppose $y = f(x) = x + 1$ and $z = g(y) = y^2$. Then the composition of g with f is $z = g(f(x)) = g(x+1) = x^2 + 2x + 1$. Similarly, suppose $y = f(x) = cx + i\sin mx$, where c, i, and m are arbitrary constants, and $z = g(y) = a\sin y$ where a is an arbitrary constant. Then the composition of g with f is $z = g(f(x)) = a\sin(cx + i\sin mx)$, the frequency modulation formula.

In general, nonlinear waveshaping deals with the identification of useful composing functions g that can accept waveforms f as arguments. The particular class of composing functions that has received the most scrutiny in the computer music community is known as *Chebyshev polynomials*. Chebyshev polynomials are solutions to *Chebyshev's differential equation*, which may be stated as

$$(1 - x^2)y'' - xy' + n^2 y = 0 \qquad n = 0, 1, 2, \dots \qquad (3\text{-}137)$$

Solutions of this equation are *Chebyshev polynomials of the first kind*, given by

$$T_n(x) = \cos(n\cos^{-1}x) = x^n - \binom{n}{2}x^{n-2}(1-x^2) + \binom{n}{4}x^{n-4}(1-x^2)^2 - \dots \quad (3\text{-}138)$$

where the notation $\binom{n}{k}$ is called a *binomial coefficient*[36] and is defined as

$$\binom{n}{k} = \frac{n(n-1)(n-2)\cdots(n-k+1)}{k!} = \frac{n!}{k!(n-k)!} = \binom{n}{n-k} \quad (3\text{-}139)$$

Like Bessel functions, Chebyshev polynomials are related to each other so that we can calculate the "next" one from the "last two" according to

$$T_{n+1}(x) = 2xT_n(x) - T_{n-1}(x) \qquad (3\text{-}140)$$

Therefore, if we know the first two Chebyshev polynomials, equation (3-140) may be used to obtain the rest. The first few Chebyshev polynomials are

$$T_0(x) = 1$$

$$T_1(x) = x$$

$$T_2(x) = 2x^2 - 1$$

---

[36]The notation $\binom{n}{k}$ is often read "*n* choose *k*" because it refers to the number of possible ways to choose k objects from a set of n objects. For example, there are $\binom{52}{5} = 2{,}598{,}960$ distinct five-card poker hands and $\binom{52}{13}$ distinct bridge hands.

$$T_3(x) = 4x^3 - 3x$$

$$T_4(x) = 8x^4 - 8x^2 + 1$$

$$T_5(x) = 16x^5 - 20x^3 + 5x$$

$$T_6(x) = 32x^6 - 48x^4 + 18x^2 - 1$$

$$T_7(x) = 64x^7 - 112x^5 + 56x^3 - 7x$$

$$T_8(x) = 128x^8 - 256x^6 + 160x^4 - 32x^2 + 1$$

The reason that Chebyshev polynomials make useful composing functions for the synthesis of musical sound is that they have the cute mathematical property

$$T_k \cos\theta = \cos k\theta \qquad (3\text{-}141)$$

That is, if we feed a cosine waveform at frequency f into Chebyshev polynomial T_k, the kth harmonic of the input waveform "pops out." This is easily verified by comparing the composition of the Chebyshev polynomials and the cosine function with multiple-angle trigonometric identities, such as

$$T_0\cos x = 1 = \cos 0$$

$$T_1\cos x = \cos x$$

$$T_2\cos x = 2\cos^2 x - 1 = \cos 2x$$

$$T_3\cos x = 4\cos^3 x - 3\cos x = \cos 3x$$

We have already seen examples of nonlinear waveshaping in Chapter 2 when we considered nonlinear distortion in sound systems. Although such nonlinear distortion is usually considered undesirable in an audio amplifier, its controlled use allows us to turn one waveform into another in useful ways. For example, if we define a function that is a weighted sum of Chebyshev polynomials and use it as a composing function for a cosine wave, the result will be a waveform consisting of harmonics with the same weights as the Chebyshev polynomials. For example, if

$$f(x) = T_1(x) + \frac{1}{2}T_2(x) \qquad (3\text{-}142)$$

then

$$f\cos x = \cos x + \frac{1}{\cos}2x \qquad (3\text{-}143)$$

A plot of the input waveform, "mapping" function $f(x)$, and the composed (output) function are shown in Figure 3-53.

By a simple application of the `lookup` unit generator (discussed earlier), we are able to use this nonlinear waveshaping technique in cmusic. Figure 3-54 shows a simple cmusic instrument that consists of a cosinusoidal oscillator feeding a lookup unit generator—the result is scaled for amplitude and output. The frequency of the oscillator is arbitrary, and its amplitude is set to unity. If wave table f2 contains a weighted sum

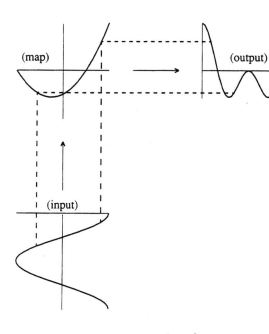

Figure 3-53   Example of nonlinear wave-shaping. The mapping function consists of the weighted sum of Chebyshev polynomials $T_1(x) + .5T_2(x)$, the input signal is a signal with a cosine waveform $\cos(2\pi ft)$, and the output signal is a signal $\cos 2\pi ft + .5\cos 2\pi 2ft$. Corresponding values of input and output waveforms are linked by dotted lines.

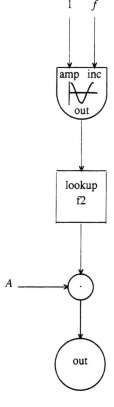

Figure 3-54   Nonlinear waveshaping in cmusic. An oscillator generating a cosine waveform is fed through the `lookup` unit generator, which refers to wave table f2 (this contains a weighted sum of Chebyshev polynomials). The amplitude is controlled by multiplying the output of the lookup process by an arbitrary (typically time-varying) value. The frequency of the oscillator is arbitrary. Amplitude values other than unity for the oscillator produce complex results.

of Chebyshev polynomials, the output waveform will contain harmonics in the same
proportions as the corresponding Chebyshev polynomials.

The cmusic function generator for computing weighted sums of Chebyshev polynomials is called `chubby`. Chubby has the following general statement:

```
gen 0 chubby fN DC A1 A2 A3... AN
```

The arguments to `chubby` specify the weights to be applied to an arbitrary number of
Chebyshev polynomials that are all summed to produce the resulting wave table. For
example, the cmusic statement

```
gen 0 chubby f2 0 .5 0 .5 ;
```

will define wave table f2 as

$$f(x) = \frac{1}{2}T_1(x) + \frac{1}{2}T_3(x) \qquad (3\text{-}144)$$

The sum of the coefficients should equal unity if the distorted waveform is to remain
within the range ±1. It is therefore often useful to normalize wave tables created by
`chubby` with `gen0`.

So far, we have used nonlinear waveshaping only to produce a waveform with an
arbitrary but fixed harmonic content, which is trivial to implement directly by defining
an appropriate wave table for the table lookup oscillator. In other words, if the input
waveform to the nonlinear lookup process always has a peak amplitude of 1 and the
nonlinear function is always the sum of Chebyshev polynomials, the resulting waveform
will always be one that could just as easily be placed into a wave table directly through
the use of, for example, `gen5`—this wave table could then be generated at any frequency or amplitude with a standard table lookup oscillator.

One interesting aspect of the waveshaping process is that the spectrum of the
output waveform changes in dramatic ways if the amplitude of the input cosinusoid
varies between 0 and 1. The details of this process are complicated and will not be
developed further here. Basically, if we replace $f \cos x$ with $f(a \cos x)$, where a is a
(possibly time-varying) quantity lying between 0 and 1, we find that the quantity a acts
similarly to the modulation index in the frequency modulation method. Generally
speaking, for sum-of-Chebyshev-polynomial-distorting functions, smaller values of a
yield more sinusoidal output, while values of a closer to 1 yield spectra close to the
target spectrum. A value of 0.5, however, does not yield a spectrum that can be derived
by linear interpolation of the spectra near 0 and 1. Of course, the amplitude of the
output waveform is usually affected by changes in a, making it sometimes difficult to
separate spectrum from amplitude effects using this technique.

Of course we need not restrict the contents of the distorting wave table to Chebyshev polynomials. Even though the input-output behavior of the waveshaping procedure can be complicated (or impossible!) to describe mathematically, computer
graphics and sound production allow it to be explored just like many other nonlinear
phenomenon. In fact, computer techniques are the basis for the investigation of many
nonlinear phenomena that could not be understood in any useful way before the
widespread accessibility of interactive computing. For example, we might draw an

arbitrary distorting waveform with a light pen or mouse, use it to distort an arbitrary waveform that could be displayed on a terminal screen along with its time-varying spectrum, and observe the effect of various scalings on the waveform and spectrum of the output waveform by either displaying them on the screen or to our ears through a digital-to-analog converter. Such computer-generated audiovisual displays of nonlinear phenomena are only beginning to be investigated and constitute an entirely new means for understanding these curious phenomena in the future.

3.6 INSTRUMENTS: SUMMARY

Computer synthesis of musical sound is based on the manipulation of digital signals, or lists of numbers describing the waveform of a desired sound. The essence of the sound synthesis problem is to understand the relationship between numbers, which directly represent the physical waveform of a sound, and the way the physical waveform is perceived by a listener.

Any process that can be defined in terms of signal and parameter inputs with a known relationship to an output signal can form the basis for digital sound synthesis. An "instrument" is then an abstraction consisting of all possible input-output relations for such a process.

Computer sound synthesis may be based on sounds that occur in nature or it may be based on arbitrary relationships among sound parameters. Analysis-based synthesis is usually the most useful method for capturing traditional qualities of musical sound, leading to "realistic" renditions of musical gestures. Synthesis that is not based on analysis of natural sounds often sounds "unnatural": however, useful results such as acoustical illusions can sometimes be obtained.

The basic methods of musical sound synthesis are separated from each other only conceptually and are often combined in practice. The basic methods are additive, subtractive, and nonlinear synthesis.

Additive synthesis rests on the basic idea of adding together multiple components, each of which is fairly simple to generate, in order to "build up" the desired sound. For the procedure to work, the connection between the desired sound and the basic components must be understood. If the components are restricted to harmonic sinusoids, for example, additive synthesis is well modeled by Fourier methods. The components need not be harmonically related, however, and need not even be sinusoids. In most cases, additive synthesis is carried out by a number—possibly a large number—of signal sources operating in parallel, each one of which is independently controlled and the sum of whose outputs is the desired signal. Typical examples of additive synthesis include the operation of the phase vocoder, in which the additive synthesis is based on the filter-bank analysis of an arbitrary sound, and the production of Shepard-Risset tones, which are not based on natural phenomena.

Subtractive synthesis rests on the basic notion of starting with a complex sound and removing unwanted components, leaving only the desired sound. For the procedure to work, the desired sound must be embedded in the original complex sound to begin with. Typical implementations of subtractive synthesis consist of a controllable noise or pulse source connected to a filter whose parameters are varied over time. Typical examples of subtractive synthesis include the creation of hornlike tones by sweeping the cutoff frequency of a lowpass filter according to the amplitude envelope of a harmonic-rich waveform, and linear prediction, which either analyzes or synthesizes a sound according to an all-pole filter model of its time-varying spectrum.

Nonlinear synthesis consists of the generation of complex waveforms from simple ones through controllable nonlinear operations such as modulation. Waveforms generated through nonlinear methods typically cannot match an arbitrary sound exactly; however, nonlinear methods often provide a convenient and highly efficient methods for the control of acoustically or psychoacoustically important parameters such as the overall bandwidth of a harmonic spectrum. Typical examples of nonlinear synthesis methods are frequency modulation and nonlinear distortion (waveshaping).

Sometimes regarded as a separate musical sound synthesis method, physical modeling consists of computing the waveform that is predicted from a mathematical model of the mechanical operation of a real or imaginary musical instrument. In most cases, tractable physical models reduce in practice to some combination of the three main techniques so they are not treated separately here. For example, a typical synthesis method that incorporates many aspects of a physical model is the Karplus-Strong string synthesis algorithm, which in turn is basically a subtractive synthesis technique.

The power of computer methods is not that they provide any particular method for producing musical sounds but that they provide a programmable means whereby the musician can design sounds according to the requirements of a particular musical idea. Programs for digital sound synthesis—"instruments," as they have been called in this chapter—allow musical sound to be analyzed, modified, and synthesized in ways that are limited only by the imagination of the creative musician.

REFERENCES

1. A. Benade, *Fundamentals of Musical Acoustics*, Oxford University Press, New York (1976).
2. J. Chowning, "The Synthesis of Complex Audio Spectra by Means of Frequency Modulation," *J. Aud. Eng. Soc., 21*, no. 7 (1973): 526–534.
3. ———— and D. Bristow, *FM Theory and Applications by Musicians for Musicians* (Yamaha Music Foundation, Tokyo, 1986).
4. M. Dolson, "The Phase Vocoder: A Tutorial," *Computer Music J. 10* (Winter 1986): 14–27.
5. H. Dudley, "The Vocoder," *Bell Labs Record 17* (1939): 122–126.
6. J. L. Flanagan and R. M. Golden, "Phase Vocoder," *Bell System Technical J. 45* (1966): pp. 1493–1509.
7. J. W. Gordon and J. Strawn "An Introduction to the Phase Vocoder," in *Digital Audio Signal Processing: An Anthology*, ed. J. Strawn (W. Kaufmann, Los Altos, Calif., 1985): 221–270.
8. J. M. Grey, *An Exploration of Musical Timbre*, Ph.D. dissertation, Department of Psychology, Stanford University (1975).

9. —— and J. A. Moorer, "Perceptual Evaluations of Synthesized Musical Instrument Tones," *J. Acoust. Soc. Amer. 63* (1977): 454–462.

10. W. M. Hartmann, "Digital Waveform Generation by Fractional Addressing," *J. Acoust. Soc. Amer. 82* (1987): 1883–1891.

11. D. Jaffe and J. Smith, "Extensions of the Karplus-Strong Plucked-String Algorithm," *Computer Music J., 7*, no. 2 (1983):56–)69.

12. L. B. W. Jolley, *Summation of Series* (Dover, New York, 1961).

13. R. Karplus and A. Strong, "Digital Synthesis of Plucked String and Drum Timbres," *Computer Music J., 7*, no. 2 (1983):43–55.

14. M. LeBrun, "A Derivation of the Spectrum of FM with a Complex Modulating Wave," *Computer Music J.* 1, no. 4 (1977): 51–52.

15. J. Makhoul, "Linear Prediction: A Tutorial Review," *Proc. IEEE, 63* (1975): 561–80.

16. M. V. Mathews, J. E. Miller, F. R. Moore, J. R. Pierce, and J.-C. Risset, *The Technology of Computer Music* (The MIT Press, Cambridge, Mass., 1969).

17. F. R. Moore, "Table Lookup Noise for Sinusoidal Digital Oscillators," *Computer Music J. 1* (September 1977): 26–29. Reprinted in *Fundamentals of Computer Music*, ed. C. Roads and J. Strawn MIT Press, Cambridge, Mass., 1985).

18. J. A. Moorer, "Signal Processing Aspects of Computer Music: A Survey," *Proc. IEEE 65* (1977): 1108–1137.

19. —— "The Use of the Phase Vocoder in Computer Music Applications," *J. Aud. Eng. Soc. 24* (1978): 717–727.

20. G. E. Peterson and H. L. Barney, "Control Methods Used in a Study of the Vowels," *J. Acoust. Soc. Amer. 24* (1952): 175–184.

21. M. R. Portnoff, "Short-Time Fourier Analysis of Sampled Speech," *IEEE Tran. on Acoustics, Speech and Signal Processing* 29(1981a) 364–373.

22. —— "Time-Frequency Representation of Digital Signals and Systems Based on Short-Time Fourier Transform," *IEEE Tran. on Acoustics, Speech and Signal Processing* 28(1980):8 55–69.

23. —— "Time-Scale Modification of Speech Based on Short-Time Fourier Analysis," *IEEE Tran. Acoustics, Speech and Signal Processing*, 29(1981b) 374–390.

24. W. H. Press, B. P. Flannery, S. A. Teukolsky, and W. T. Vetterling, *Numerical Recipes: The Art of Scientific Computing* (Cambridge University Press, Cambridge, 1986).

25. L. R. Rabiner and R. W. Schafer, *Digital Processing of Speech Signals* (Prentice-Hall, Englewood Cliffs, N.J., 1978).

26. J.-C. Risset and M. V. Mathews, "Analysis of Musical Instrument Tones," *Physics Today 22* (February 1969): 23–40.

27. J. G. Roederer, *Introduction to the Physics and Psychophysics of Music* (Springer-Verlag, New York, 1975).

28. B. Schottstaedt, "The Simulation of Natural Instrument Tones Using Frequency Modulation with a Complex Modulating Wave," *Computer Music J.1*, no. 4 (1977): 46–50.

29. J. O. Smith and J. B. Angell, "A Constant-Gain Digital Resonator Tuned by a Single Coefficient," *Computer Music J. 6*, no. 4 (1982): 36–40.

30. J. Stirling, *The Differential Method* (London, 1749).

31. H. S. Stone, *Discrete Mathematical Structures and Their Applications* (Science Research Associates, Chicago, 1973).

4

Rooms

Like "time," "energy," "force," or "particle," the concept of an element is the sort of textbook ingredient that is often not invented or discovered at all. Boyle's definition, in particular, can be traced back at least to Aristotle and forward through Lavoisier into modern texts. Yet that is not to say that science has possessed the modern concept of an element since antiquity. Verbal definitions like Boyle's have little scientific content when considered by themselves. They are not full logical specifications of meanings (if there are such), but more nearly pedagogical aids. The scientific concepts to which they point gain full significance only when related, within a text or other systematic presentation, to other scientific concepts, to manipulative procedures, and to paradigm applications. . . . What then was Boyle's historical function in that part of his work that includes the famous "definition"? He was a leader of a scientific revolution that, by changing the relation of "element" to chemical manipulation and chemical theory, transformed the notion into a tool quite different from what it had been before and transformed both chemistry and the chemist's world in the process.

—T. S. Kuhn, *The Structure of Scientific Revolutions*

We normally live at the bottom of an ocean of air. Even though the total mass of the atmosphere (some 5.1×10^{15} tons) represents only about a millionth of the mass of the earth, the weight of this great mass of air at the surface of the earth is about 2100 pounds per square foot, or about 14.69 pounds per square inch, or about 1.013250×10^6 dynes per square centimeter. The only reason we are not immediately crushed by this great weight is that the atmosphere exists inside us as well as outside—a "vacuum chamber" therefore needs to have extremely strong walls.

The atmosphere is the great canvas on which music is "painted." Whenever a mechanical disturbance destroys the repose of the atmosphere, "news" of the event propagates outward in all directions at the speed of sound, approximately 343.9 meters per second, or 1128.3 feet per second, at 20°C (68°F). If the mechanical disturbance is caused by oscillations in the approximate range from 20 to 20,000 per second, the resulting disturbance can potentially be detected through our sense of hearing, provided that the oscillations are strong enough to be heard and weak enough not to damage the hearing mechanism.

According to one of the most basic laws of physics (conservation of energy), the total energy of the oscillations in the "expanding bubble" of waves propagating from a sound source must remain the same. Therefore, the intensity of the sound, measured in terms of energy (or power) per unit area, is inversely proportional to the square of the distance from the sound source. That is, because the surface area of a sphere of radius r is just $4\pi r^2$ and because the total energy at the surface of the expanding sphere of radiating sound must remain constant, the amount of energy spread over each square unit of area falls off with the square of the sphere's radius. This is called the *inverse square law of sound intensity*.

As sound propagates outward from a source, it usually encounters obstacles. Depending on such factors as the wavelength of the sound (how far it travels during each oscillatory period) and the size, shape, and composition of the obstacle, a complex interaction takes place between the propagating sound and the obstacle. Some of the mechanical energy in the sound will be absorbed by the obstacle. Some of the energy will be reflected. If the obstacle is relatively small compared with the wavelength of the sound, the object will essentially "cast a shadow" in the direction of sound propagation, though this shadow will not be precisely "black" (silent) due to refraction and diffusion effects. Unlike light, which travels basically in straight lines, sound will pass around objects in its path just as the water in a river flows around a tree standing in its midst. Thus we are able to hear around corners, even though we cannot see around them.

The reason that we must consider the complex interaction between obstacles and propagating sound is that music is rarely played in places where sound encounters no obstacles. Even if there is no obstacle directly in the path between the sound source—such as a musical instrument—and a listener, what the listener hears is invariably affected by the nature of the sound that bounces off of nearby obstacles such as walls, ceilings, floors, furniture, and people. In fact, the realization that the acoustic context in which music is heard has a strong effect on our ability to perceive and enjoy it is the basis for *architectural acoustics*—the science of designing rooms so that they not only do not impede but actually enhance the experience of listening to music. If pieces of music were gems, concert halls would be their settings.

Consider, for example, the length of a staccato note. In musical terms, a note is designated staccato if it is to be detached acoustically from those that follow it. A composer specifies that a note should be performed staccato by placing a dot over or under its head. The performer then adjusts the manner in which the note is played so that the instrument stops vibrating momentarily before the following note is played. However, the duration of the note as executed by the performer depends on several things, including the rhythmic value of the note, the momentum of the instrument (physically small instruments are easier to silence than large instruments), and the amount of reverberation in the room where the music is being performed. For example, a sixteenth note at a slow tempo might have a nominal duration of 0.25 second. If such a note is to be played staccato in a small living room where the reverberant sound dies away rather quickly once the sound is stopped (a "dry" room), the performer may adjust the duration of the note to, say, 0.2 second to achieve the staccato effect. In a reverberant cathedral with stone walls that reflect a great deal of the sound, the performer may have to adjust the duration of the same note to 0.1 second or less to achieve the same "detached" effect.

Thus the ultimate instrument every performer plays, consciously or not, is the room in which the music is being heard. Fortunately, rooms may be characterized in many useful ways related to the changes they impress on a sound as it passes from source to listener. If we inject a known sound into a particular location in a room and record the resulting sound at another location in the room, the difference between the input and output sounds is the effect of the room. In particular, if the input sound is an impulse, the output sound is the impulse response of the room for given source and listener locations. In other words, we can model rooms as filters. By doing so, the enormous power of digital filtering theory can be brought to bear, not only on the problem of analyzing and synthesizing the source sound itself (as we did in Chapter 3) but also on the analysis and synthesis of the acoustic environment in which the sound is heard.

We start with a consideration of the characteristics of a room that make it a good concert hall.

4.1 CONCERT HALLS

The main source of information about which concert halls are good and which are poor is the subjective judgments of musically sophisticated listeners. After all, what ultimately matters in a concert hall is not physical measurements but the reactions of experienced listeners. Fortunately, and perhaps a bit surprisingly, what musically trained listeners report is usually borne out by physical measurements. For example, in one study of a famous acoustical disaster known originally as Philharmonic Hall in New York's Lincoln Center, Manfred Schroeder (1980) reports that ushers in the hall, many of whom were music students at the nearby Julliard School of Music, judged almost unanimously that a particular seat (A-15 on the Second Terrace) was the "best seat in the house." Schroeder and his colleagues eventually found that the *spectrum balance* at this seat was indeed superior to that of most other hall locations in ways that could be physically measured by observing the relative amounts of energy contained in various frequency bands that resulted from an impulsive sound generated on the stage. At a distance of about 30 meters from the stage (around the center of the main floor), the amount of energy centered around 125 Hz received by listeners was found to be much less than the amount of energy received in higher frequency bands. Somehow the hall was "soaking up" low frequencies much more rapidly than high frequencies at most locations, causing listeners difficulty in hearing basses and cellos playing on the stage. The problem was eventually traced to the poor low-frequency reflectivity of acoustic panels ("clouds") mounted in the ceiling—a defect that has since been corrected.

Another characteristic of concert halls that is strongly correlated in a negative way with listeners' reports of the quality of the sound is *interaural coherence*. In a major comparative study of 20 European concert halls, Schroeder and his colleagues found that even when halls had nearly identical reverberation and spectrum balance characteristics, listeners still had strong preferences for some halls over others. It was found that halls that tend to produce the same sound in each ear were generally judged to be inferior (all other factors being equal) to halls that present a different version of the sound to each ear. This finding correlated well with another one in which listeners generally seemed to prefer narrow halls to wider ones (again, all other factors being equal). Sound reflections from the ceiling and floor reach the listener sooner than those from the left and right walls in wide halls, tending to produce identical versions of the sound in both ears. Wider halls therefore tend to have a higher degree of interaural coherence and consequently are often judged to be inferior in sound quality by experienced listeners.

Along with spectrum balance and interaural coherence, a very important characteristic of a hall for musical purposes is its *reverberation time*. When one or more musical instruments produce a steady sound in a room, some of the acoustic energy generated by the sound sources is absorbed by the room and objects within it while the remaining sound energy is reflected back into the room. The overall sound level in the room gradually rises until the amount of sound energy produced by the instruments equals the sum of the reflected and absorbed energy. This process is called *sound buildup*, which generally explains why instruments sound louder in a reverberant room than they do when played outdoors.

When the instruments stop vibrating, a noticeable amount of time is needed for the reverberant sound energy to be absorbed. The amount of time needed for the acoustic energy to be absorbed by the room and the objects it contains is called the reverberation time of the room. Reverberation time is usually defined as the amount of time that it takes sound to die away by a factor of 60 dB—effectively "to silence"—from its initial intensity. This particular reverberation time is often denoted as T_{60} in the acoustics literature and is measured in seconds.

The most important factor determining reverberation time is the rate at which a room absorbs sound. The more rapidly sound is absorbed, the more rapidly it will die away once its source stops pumping acoustic energy into the room. Suppose that it takes 2 seconds for sound in a given room to die away by a factor of 60 dB. The reverberation time of the same room filled with 100 people would be less than 2 seconds, due to absorption of sound by the people. Suppose that the room when filled with 100 people has a reverberation time of 1.5 seconds. Returning the room to its empty state, we now begin to open windows around the room until the reverberation time is similarly reduced to 1.5 seconds. If we find that we need to open 50 windows, each having an opening of 1 square meter, to obtain the 1.5-second reverberation time, we may then reason that the sound absorbed by 100 people is equivalent to the sound absorbed by a 50-square-meter area of "perfect absorber"—an open window that does not reflect sound at all.

So reasoned Wallace C. Sabine in his pioneering investigations into reverberation time around the turn of the twentieth century. Sabine defined the *absorption coefficient* of a material as a dimensionless quantity representing the fraction of the sound absorbed by that material. Thus an absorption coefficient of 1 connotes complete absorption (an "open window"), while an absorption coefficient of 0 connotes perfect reflection. The *total absorption* of a material is then its absorption coefficient multiplied by its total area.

Of course, the absorption coefficient of a material, which may be thought of as the fraction of a square meter of open window equivalent to 1 square meter of the material, is frequency-dependent. Most materials absorb high frequencies better than low frequencies. For example, a heavy carpet over a concrete floor has an absorption coefficient of about .05 at 125 Hz and about .65 at 5000 Hz (see Table 4-1).

TABLE 4-1 Sound absorption coefficients for various materials. The numeric values represent the number of square meters of open window equivalent to 1 square meter of the material. Note how the absorption coefficient varies with frequency. To obtain total absorption in sabins, multiply the absorption coefficient by the area (in square meters) of the material.

Material	125 Hz	250 Hz	500 Hz	1000 Hz	2000 Hz	5000 Hz
Acoustic tile, ceiling	.80	.90	.90	.95	.90	.85
Brick, unglazed	.03	.03	.03	.04	.05	.07
Carpet, heavy, on felt over concrete	.08	.25	.60	.70	.72	.75
Carpet, heavy, on concrete	.05	.10	.30	.50	.60	.65
Concrete, smooth, unpainted	.01	.01	.01	.02	.02	.03
Concrete, painted	.10	.05	.10	.20	.40	.60
Curtains, heavy velour	.15	.35	.55	.75	.70	.60
Fiberglass, 3 cm thick	.20	.50	.90	.95	.90	.85
Glass, ordinary window	.35	.25	.20	.10	.07	.04
Linoleum or tile on concrete	.02	.03	.03	.03	.03	.02
Marble or glazed tile	.01	.01	.01	.01	.02	.02
Plaster on concrete or brick	.10	.10	.08	.05	.05	.05
Plywood paneling on studs	.30	.20	.15	.10	.09	.09
Wood floor	.15	.11	.10	.07	.06	.07
Wood floor over concrete	.04	.04	.07	.06	.06	.07

To calculate the total absorption of a room (in *sabins*, named in honor of the inventor of this technique), we have only to measure the surface area of each material in the room, multiply each area by the absorption coefficient associated with that material, and add the results together.

$$A = \sum_i a_i s_i \tag{4-1}$$

where A is the total absorption in sabins (in units of square meters of open window), a_i is the area (in square meters) of the ith material found in the room, and s_i is the absorption coefficient of the ith material found in the room.[1] Table 4-2 gives figures for the total absorption in sabins of people and seats in typical concert halls.

TABLE 4-2 Typical total absoption in sabins for audience and seats.

Absorber Type	125 Hz	250 Hz	500 Hz	1000 Hz	2000 Hz	5000 Hz
Audience, total absorption per person in sabins	.35	.43	.47	.50	.55	.60
Auditorium seat, solid, unupholstered, each	.02	.02	.03	.03	.04	.05
Auditorium seat, upholstered, each	.30	.30	.30	.30	.35	.35

As you might expect, Sabine found that the reverberation time of a room is inversely proportional to the total absorption in the room. He estimated that reverberation time is directly proportional to the volume of the room, the constant of proportionality being about 0.16 if the volume is measured in cubic meters. This yields the formula

$$T_{60} = \frac{0.16V}{\sum\limits_i a_i \, s_i} \tag{4-2}$$

At frequencies above about 1000 Hz, the effect of sound absorption by air becomes increasingly important: s_{air} (the absorption per cubic meter of air) is about .003 at 1000 Hz, .01 at 2000 Hz, and about .03 for frequencies above about 5000 Hz (it is negligible below 1000 Hz over distances in even very large rooms). Thus equation (4-2) may be improved slightly with the inclusion of this factor.

$$T_{60} = \frac{0.16V}{V \, s_{air} + \sum\limits_i a_i s_i} \tag{4-3}$$

Such formulas as equation (4-3), based on Sabine's original work, are commonly used today in architectural acoustics to solve such problems as finding the difference between the reverberation times of an empty auditorium and the same auditorium filled with people.

4.1.1 Ray Tracing

Unfortunately, even though equation (4-3) is simple to understand and simple to use (given a table of absorption coefficients), it is also highly inaccurate, tending to give

---

[1]Use caution to distinguish between absorption coefficients given in terms of square feet—which Sabine himself used—and square meters, which are more commonly used today.

reverberation time values that are too high, especially for large rooms. Schroeder points out, for example, that simple formulas such as equation (4-3) do not take into account the *geometry* of absorbing surfaces in a room.

An absorbing panel covering one wall of a rectangular room, for example, is much more effective at reducing reverberation time than the same area of absorbing surface configured in an L shape in one corner of the room (see Figure 4-1). The reason for this is that the absorber positioned entirely along one wall faces only highly reflective surfaces, while the absorber pressed into a corner—even though it has the same surface area—partly faces itself.

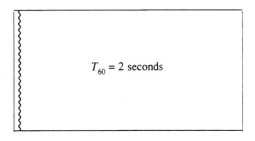

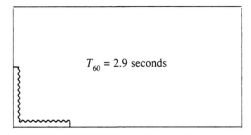

Figure 4-1   Effect of room and absorber geometry on reverberation time (after Schroeder, 1980). In the top figure, absorbing panels ($a = 1$) are aligned against the left wall of a rectangular room. In the bottom figure, absorbing panels with the same total area and absorption coefficient are arranged in the lower left-hand corner. Because the lower configuration partially faces some of the absorbing panels toward each other, they are much less effective at lowering the reverberation time in the room, resulting in a much larger T_{60} value. Such effects are well-predicted by ray-tracing techniques but are entirely ignored by simple formulas such as equation (4-3).

Such effects as room geometry and the spatial configuration of absorbing materials can be taken into account with a technique called acoustic ray-tracing. We can model the behavior of sound *waves* as sound *rays* under many useful circumstances. A "sound ray" is simply a line perpendicular to the wave front of a propagating sound giving the direction of propagation (see Figure 4-2).

Using ray-tracing techniques, a sound source may be modeled in terms of the intensity with which it radiates sound in all directions. This sound radiation pattern is modeled by mathematical vectors pointing outward from the source with an arbitrary shape—the length of each vector gives the strength (intensity or amplitude) of the sound radiating in the direction of the vector. Of course, it is possible to build such models in an arbitrary number of dimensions as well; two or three dimensions are commonly used (see Figure 4-3).

If the vectors pointing outward from the sound source in all directions are the same length, the sound source is said to be *omnidirectional*, whereas any other pattern

(Inside the top figure: $T_{60} = 2$ seconds. Inside the bottom figure: $T_{60} = 2.9$ seconds.)

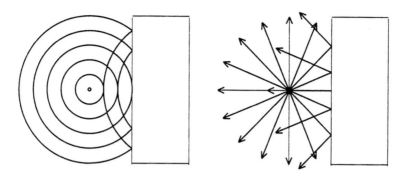

Figure 4-2   Sound waves versus sound rays. Under many circumstances, sound reflection may be modeled in two equivalent ways: in terms of waves (left) and in terms of rays (right). The wave model shows the relative positions of wave compressions or rarefactions at a given instant in time; the ray model shows directions of propagation of wavefronts.

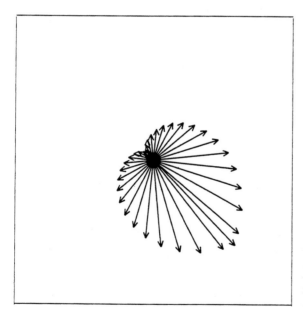

Figure 4-3   A sound source model for two-dimensional ray-tracing. The sound source in this example is modeled as a point in space with an arbitrary number of vectors radiating outward from it. The length of each vector radiating from the source represents the amplitude of sound radiation in the direction of that vector.

would indicate nonuniform directionality of the sound source to one extent or another. A trumpet, for example, radiates sound forward (out from the bell) much more strongly than in any other direction, whereas a violin tends to radiate strongly (though not equally) from both its top and bottom plates.

As the sound ray moves through space, it is generally attenuated according to the inverse square law for sound intensity. That is, if at a distance of 1 meter from the source the sound has an intensity of 80 dB, then at a distance of 2 meters from the source (assuming it encounters no obstacles) it has an intensity of about 74 dB, at a distance of 4 meters the intensity would be about 68 dB, and so on, a factor of 6 dB for each doubling of distance from the source.

4.1.2 Phantom Sound Sources

When any one of the rays emanating from the sound source strikes an object such as a wall, some of it is absorbed and some is reflected. The angle- and frequency-dependent reflectivity of a surface may be modeled in a variety of ways; a sound ray might simply bounce off a "perfect reflector" (absorption coefficient = 0) at an angle equal to the angle of incidence, but it would not bounce off a "perfect absorber" (absorption coefficient = 1) at all.

Assuming that reflection occurs, the ray leaves the wall at an angle of reflection that is the same as the angle of incidence. An observer (that is, a listener) in the path of this reflected ray would receive acoustic energy from a direction that is potentially indistinguishable from that emanating from a sound source behind the wall. This *phantom sound source* (see Figure 4-4) is equivalent to a secondary sound source from the standpoint of the direction of the ray. Of course, the sound emanating from a phantom source would have to be modified according to the interaction of the sound with the wall. Once the sound from an actual source bounces, the theory of phantom sources replaces it with a phantom source located behind the wall. Of course, the ray coming from the phantom source will bounce again, giving rise to second-order phantom sources, which in turn give rise to third-order phantom sources, and so on.

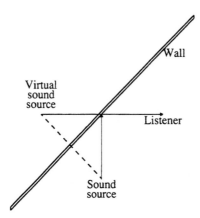

Figure 4-4   A phantom sound source. The distance from the listener to the phantom sound source is the same as the distance along the ray path from the actual source to the wall plus the distance from the reflection point on the wall to the listener.

The idea of phantom sound sources may be understood by considering what one would see inside a room completely covered with mirrors (some restaurants and barber shops give a good approximation of such a situation). One sees not only the objects in the room but also an infinitely receding pattern of reflections of each object within view. These "phantom" objects appear to be located at regular intervals, depending on the specific geometry of the room and location of objects within it, in an infinite "illusory space" that recedes in all directions from the observer.   .

Of course, such a model of sound reflection is too simple in and of itself to justify much confidence in the match between the model and what really happens when a sound bounces off a real, highly irregular surface. Ideally, a wall in a concert hall would not merely reflect sound but would do so in a manner that enhances the experience of listening to music in that hall. Schroeder and his colleagues found that there is a good correlation between audience acceptance of a concert hall and the extent to which the concert hall suppresses interaural coherence, which suggests that the "ideal" surface in a concert hall would reflect sound in a highly diffuse manner, spreading the sound energy as much as possible in many directions. Schroeder has even designed a specific type of sound reflector called a *reflection phase grating* whose detailed surface characteristics are based on the theory of quadratic residues, a branch of number theory. Such reflection phase gratings—widely known as "Schroeder boxes"— are available for use in concert halls and critical listening environments such as recording studios. According to the theory, quadratic-residue phase gratings are highly efficient at scattering sound—even more efficient than random surfaces!

To account for all the necessary ingredients, ray-tracing requires an approximation that can be built on an integral equation that describes the sound energy flux density along all inner surfaces of a room. This equation accounts for diffusion by integrating over all angles of incidence the incoming fluxes multiplied by the angle-dependent reflectivity of the surface. The resulting equation, strictly speaking, cannot be solved. However, E. N. Gilbert (1981) has developed a method to deal with the mathematical complexities of this equation using an approach based on splitting the equation into two complementary parts; solution of each part of the equation produces an increasingly good approximation of the solution of the other part. In this way, the "correct" ray-tracing solution has been obtained for several simple though useful room shapes. Such techniques promise to give future acoustical architects important new tools with which to design good-sounding concert halls that have to be built only once.

For most practical applications of computers to the simulation of the spatial characteristics of sounds, however, complete ray-tracing solutions involve prohibitive amounts of computation. Though in the creation of music it might be desirable to pose such questions as "How would a given synthetic sound sound in, say, Carnegie Hall as opposed to my living room?" the solution of the two corresponding ray-tracing problems currently exceeds the bounds of practical computability on standard computers.

There are three basic ways of dealing with this difficulty. First, supercomputer-class machines (such as Cray computers) might be applied to the problem. Even though the cost of such computation might be rather high, it could in many cases be much less than the cost of an architectural acoustical disaster such as the original Philharmonic Hall in New York s Lincoln Center. Second, nonstandard computers capable of a high degree of parallel computation (such as Connection Machines) might be used, also at a high cost. The cost of obtaining a computational solution with a computer having a nonstandard architecture often involves the additional component of specialized programming techniques. Finally, elements of ray tracing may be used with standard computers in ways that may be computationally expensive, but not prohibitively so. In a computer music context, this often provides enough precision to allow musically useful effects to be achieved, even though they may not be based on a very precise algorithmic model of a particular concert hall. In some cases, as we shall soon see, a precise simulation of physical reality can work less well in a musical context than some of the alternatives to it.

4.2 SPATIAL HEARING

In the production of computer music, the typical problem is not to simulate a particular concert hall or room with any degree of precision but to impart a spatial quality to sounds generated either by modification of digitally recorded sounds or by the methods of "pure" synthesis. To devise practical musical tools, it is necessary to consider the processing of signals both by computers and by our own hearing mechanism.

One may define the problem of sound spatialization in several useful ways. The simplest is to treat the *locations of the loudspeakers* as the set of possible locations from which sound can emanate (see Figure 4-5). Another is to create the impression of sound coming from *directions other than those of the loudspeakers*—these directions may be restricted to the *horizontal* plane or they may include the *vertical* dimension as well. Another possibility is to create impressions both of direction and of *distance*, allowing the "virtual" sound source to come from a location within a "virtual sound space" that generally lies beyond the perimeter formed by the loudspeakers. Finally, if a general control over sound position in either or both of the horizontal or vertical planes is in use, it is also possible to create the impression of *moving virtual sound sources*. For all but the first of these possibilities, it is necessary to have some means of giving the listener an impression that a sound is emanating from a direction different from those defined by the locations of multiple loudspeakers located in the listening space.

To make clear the distinction between locations from which sounds *seem* to be emanating and the locations of actual sources of acoustic energy, we will speak in terms of *virtual sound source* versus *actual sound sources*. The term *virtual sound source* refers to a listener's *subjective impression* of where a sound seems to come from, which may or may not coincide with the location of an *actual sound source*. For example, when we hear a jet plane passing rapidly overhead at fairly low altitude (a fairly common occurrence around airports), we often find that the airplane has already passed the place in the sky where we first search for it visually. This is due to the fact that the distance between our location and that of the airplane is fairly great, and the time it takes for the sound to reach our ears is significant. In effect, our aural impression of the location of the airplane differs considerably from our visual impression.

Similarly, when listening to a stereophonic recording of an orchestra played over a good stereo sound system, we are often able to discern the fact that the first violins are on the left, the basses are on the right, and the violas are in the middle. There are not actual sources of sound in all of these locations because the stereo system consists

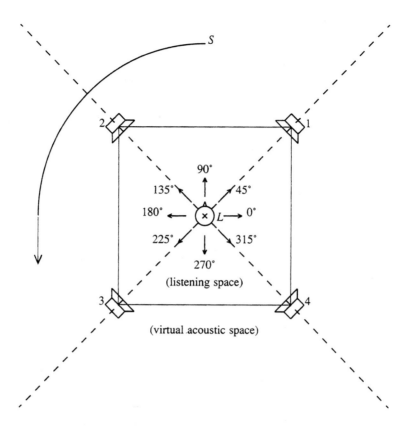

Figure 4-5 A basic playback configuration for sound spatialization. Four loudspeakers are positioned in a square in or near the corners of the listening space. To simplify mathematical calculations involved in spatialization, the loudspeaker positions are numbered according to the standard system of mathematical quadrants of a plane: 1 (right front), 2 (left front), 3 (left rear), and 4 (right rear). The listener (*L*) is located in the center of the square, facing forward. Again following the usual mathematical convention, angles are measured counterclockwise from 0, which points to the listener's right. A "virtual sound source" might be generated that starts at apparent position *S* and moves along the curved path shown.

of only two loudspeakers, that is, two actual sound sources. Nevertheless, we can often obtain a clear *impression* of the positions of instruments in a stereophonically recorded orchestra that differ considerably from the positions of the two loudspeakers. When we estimate the positions of the musical instruments while listening to recorded sound, we are clearly estimating something different from the locations of the actual sound sources (the loudspeakers).

The problem of sound spatialization in computer music is then the problem of gaining prescriptive control over the positions of virtual sound sources within an imaginary—or virtual, or illusory—space in which such events may occur. Generally speaking, it is quite difficult to create virtual sound sources that are localized at positions that are closer to us than the positions of the loudspeakers. The "illusory space" is therefore typically defined by the closed polygon that would result if we tied a piece of string around the outside of all of the loudspeakers. We will refer to the space on or outside the perimeter of this polygon as the *virtual acoustic space* and the space inside this perimeter as the *listening space*. Auditory event locations are then generally restricted to those within the virtual acoustic space.[2]

4.2.1 Localization Cues

To create virtual sound sources at arbitrary locations within the virtual acoustic space, it is necessary to use the loudspeakers in a special way that provides strong *localization cues* to a listener located inside the listening space. These cues may be divided into three basic categories:

- Perceptual and cognitive cues that help determine the direction of the virtual sound source on the horizontal plane (*azimuth angle cues*)
- Perceptual and cognitive cues that help determine the direction of the virtual sound source on the vertical plane (*elevation cues*)
- Perceptual and cognitive cues that help determine the *distance* of the virtual sound source

If we gain sufficient control of these cues to allow virtual sound sources to be "placed" anywhere within the virtual acoustic space, we also gain implicit control over successions of such locations. In other words, we may also create virtual sound sources that are not fixed in a single location but seem to move along continuous "paths" through the virtual acoustic space with varying degrees of speed. In this case, an additional cognitive cue, the Doppler shift (first explained by C. J. Doppler in 1842) becomes important in creating the subjective impression of velocity.

If an actual sound source (such as a train whistle) moves toward us at a velocity v and if the fundamental frequency of the whistle is f_w, then the apparent (Doppler-shifted) frequency f_a that we hear is given by the relation

$$f_a = f_w \frac{c}{c-v} \qquad (4\text{-}4)$$

where c is the speed of sound. The quantity $c/(c-v)$ is clearly unity if v is zero, but as v increases, it becomes larger than 1, gradually approaching infinity as v approaches c. If the train were traveling away from us instead of toward us, the Doppler shift is in the opposite direction, according to

$$f_b = f_w \frac{c}{c+v} \qquad (4\text{-}5)$$

[2]It is not strictly true that virtual sound sources may not be produced *inside* the perimeter defined by the string. However, due to severe constraints on how this may be done, it is not presently possible to create arbitrary virtual sound sources at arbitrary locations inside the listening space.

The apparent change in frequency as the train passes us is then easily seen to be

$$\Delta f = f_a - f_b = f_w \frac{2cv}{c^2 - v^2} \tag{4-6}$$

This characteristic shift in apparent frequency due to Doppler shift provides a strong *cognitive cue* to a listener who is familiar with sounds produced by rapidly moving sources.

4.2.2 Intensity Panning

One of the most important perceptual cues for both the direction and distance to a sound source is its intensity. Sounds in the real world coming from directly in front of or behind the listener reach both ears with equal intensity, for example, while those coming from the right or left reach one ear with slightly more intensity than the other.

A general impression of directional intensity may be simulated through the use of *intensity panning*. Using a multichannel loudspeaker system such as that depicted in Figure 4-5, we can provide ideal intensity cues only for the directions defined by the positions of the loudspeakers. At azimuth angles intermediate between any two of these directions, we can distribute the sound between adjacent pairs of loudspeakers. For example, to create the impression of a virtual sound source moving from left to right in front of the listener, we can simply crossfade the intensity of the sound in the two front loudspeaker channels.

Viewing the listening space from the top as shown in Figure 4-5 consider a sound coming from the direction of channel 2 (left front, or "northwest," or 135° as viewed from above). Assuming that the architectural acoustics within the listening space do not provide strong reflections from any particular direction (that is, the acoustics of the listening space are fairly "well behaved"), playing the sound through only the left-front loudspeaker will produce a clear impression that the virtual sound source is located in this direction. If the position of the virtual sound source now proceeds to move gradually to the right, the intensity-panning technique involves gradually decreasing the intensity of the sound coming from the left-front speaker while gradually increasing the intensity of the sound coming from the right-front loudspeaker. Because it is (in this case) the identical sound coming from both front loudspeakers during the transit from left to right and because we assume that the listener is positioned equally far from all loudspeakers, we may calculate the total intensity of the sound at the listener's position for intermediate azimuth angles simply by adding the intensities of the sound coming from the active loudspeakers. If this total intensity is constant, intensity panning can give a weak impression that the virtual sound source is moving along an arc that lies a constant distance from the listener.

We generally control the intensity of a sound in each playback channel with a gain factor that is multiplied directly by the waveform of the sound undergoing spatialization.[3] Because such a gain factor multiples the waveform directly, it represents a

---

[3]It is essential, of course, that identical waveforms in each playback channel produce identical intensities at the position of the listener, that is, that the playback system be carefully balanced.

direct control on the amplitude of the sound rather than its intensity. Combining the fact that the intensity of a sound is proportional to the square of its intensity with the inverse square law of sound intensity yields the following relation between sound amplitude and distance:

$$A^2 \propto I \propto \frac{1}{D^2} \tag{4-7}$$

where A is amplitude, I is intensity, and D is distance. Solving this relationship for linear amplitude yields

$$A \propto \sqrt{I} \propto \frac{1}{D} \tag{4-8}$$

For example, suppose that the gain factor for the left-front channel (2) is G_2 and the gain factor for the right-front channel (1) is G_1. To maintain a constant sound intensity at the listener's position for all intermediate positions of the virtual sound source as it pans from left to right, we require that the total intensity be constant, that is, that

$$G_2^2 + G_1^2 = \text{constant} \tag{4-9}$$

We may satisfy this requirement by employing the trigonometric identity

$$\sin^2 \theta + \cos^2 \theta = 1 \tag{4-10}$$

where θ represents the angle from the listener to the virtual sound source on the horizontal plane (the *azimuth* angle). If we make G_2 proportional to cos θ, where θ goes from 0 to 90° ($\pi/2$ radians), and G_1 proportional to sin θ for the same range of variation in θ, the intensity of a sound with constant source intensity will remain unchanged at the listener's position while the virtual sound source pans from left front to right front. This corresponds to the overall intensity behavior of a sound moving from left to right at a constant distance from the listener. The gain factors for the two front channels as a function of the direction (θ) from the listener to the virtual sound source are given by

$$G_2(\theta) = \cos (\theta - 135°) \tag{4-11}$$

and

$$G_1(\theta) = \sin (135°-\theta) \tag{4-12}$$

where θ goes from 135° to 45°. Making use of the trigonometric identity $\cos\theta = \sin (\theta + 90°)$, we may rewrite equation (4-12) as

$$G_1(\theta) = \cos (\theta - 45°) \tag{4-13}$$

For fixed distances, we may generalize this rule for intensity panning as follows:

$$G_n(\theta) = \begin{cases} \cos(\theta - \theta_n) & \text{if } |\theta - \theta_n| < 90° \\ \\ 0 & \text{otherwise} \end{cases} \tag{4-14}$$

where $G_n(\theta)$ is the gain factor for channel n for a virtual sound source located at an angle θ from the listener, θ_n is the angle between the loudspeaker for channel n and the listener, and $|x|$ denotes the absolute value of x. Equation (4-14) basically says that if the direction of a virtual sound source lies within 90° of the direction to one of the four loudspeakers configured as shown in Figure 4-5, the gain of the corresponding audio channel should be set to the value between 0 and 1 given by the cosine function of the difference in angles between the virtual sound source and the loudspeaker.

Equation (4-14) is incomplete, however, in that it does not explicitly show the relation between amplitude and distance. If we combine our earlier results with equation (4-14), a more general intensity-panning "law" based on both azimuth angle and distance may be stated as

$$G_n(\theta, D) = \begin{cases} \dfrac{D_n}{D} \cos(\theta - \theta_n) & \text{if } |\theta - \theta_n| < 90° \\ \\ 0 & \text{otherwise} \end{cases} \tag{4-15}$$

where $G_n(\theta, D)$ is the gain factor for channel n for a virtual sound source located at a distance D and an angle θ from the listener; θ_n and D_n are the angle and distance, respectively, between the loudspeaker for channel n and the listener; and $|x|$ denotes the absolute value of x. Figure 4-6 shows an application of equation (4-15) to achieve a constant-distance pan from left to right.

In addition to using equation (4-15) to determine gain factors for the loudspeaker channels, we may also use it to deduce the effects of various kinds of crossfades between adjacent channels. For example, if we use a simple crossfade in which the gain factor for the left-front channel decreases linearly from 1 to 0 while the gain factor for the right-front channel increases linearly from 0 to 1 during the transit of the virtual sound source from left to right, the sound intensity midway through the transit will be smaller than that required for an impression of constant distance. This effect, which has been called the "hole in the middle effect" (see Figure 4-7), is due to the fact that in the midway position both loudspeakers will produce the sound with one-half the amplitude associated with the endpoints of the path. Because sound intensity is proportional to the square of amplitude, the total intensity of the sound at the midway point will be proportional to

$$\left[\frac{1}{2}\right]^2 + \left[\frac{1}{2}\right]^2 = \frac{1}{2} \tag{4-16}$$

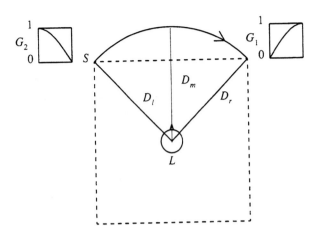

Figure 4-6   Intensity panning at a constant distance. The virtual sound source position (S) starts at the left-front loudspeaker and pans to the right-front loudspeaker. The distance from the listener (L) to the virtual sound source location at the beginning of the pan is shown as D_l, at the midpoint of the pan it is D_m, and at the end of the pan it is D_r. The figure shows how the gain factors in the two front loudspeakers (G_2 and G_1) must vary during the transit of the virtual sound source so that $D_l = D_m = D_r$. For convenience, we take all these distances to be 1.

That is, the sound will have half the intensity at the midpoint of its travel as it does at either endpoint. Because sound intensity obeys the inverse square law, the relative distance D_n/D between the listener and the sound would then be proportional to

$$\frac{1}{2} \propto \frac{1}{D^2} \Rightarrow D \propto \sqrt{2} \qquad (4\text{-}17)$$

In other words, the distance cue based on intensity would imply that the sound is $\sqrt{2} = 1.414 \ldots$ times farther from the listener at the midpoint of its travel than it is at either endpoint during such a linear crossfade.

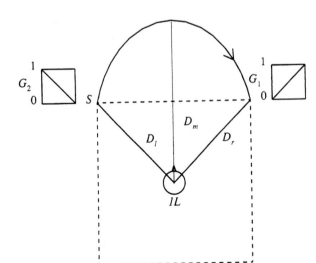

Figure 4-7   Intensity panning with a linear crossfade. If the gain factor in the left-front loudspeaker (G_2) *decreases* linearly from 1 to 0 while the gain factor in the right-front loudspeaker (G_1) linearly *increases* from 0 to 1, the total intensity at the position of the listener (L) would correspond to a sound traveling along the path shown, creating the "hole in the middle" effect. Here $D_l = D_r = 1$ and $D_m = \sqrt{2} = 1.414 \ldots$, according to the inverse square law of sound intensity.

We may also use equation (4-15) to deduce the gain factor changes needed to create the impression of a virtual sound source that travels in a *straight line* from the left-front loudspeaker to the right-front loudspeaker (see Figure 4-8). In this case, we note that the virtual sound source would be *closer* to the listener at the midpoint of its travel than it is at either endpoint. Using the Pythagorean theorem to analyze the triangle formed by the loudspeaker, the midpoint of linear travel, and the listener, we see that the relative distance between the listener and the midpoint is then $D_n / D = 1 / \sqrt{2} = 0.707 \ldots$. The inverse square law then requires that the total sound intensity at the midpoint be proportional to $1/D^2 = 2$ times the intensity at either endpoint. At the midpoint of travel, then, the intensity of sound coming from both of the active loudspeakers must be equal to 1.

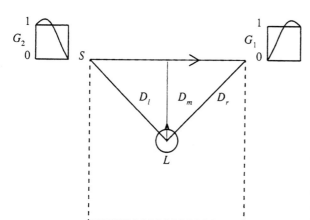

Figure 4-8   Intensity panning to achieve a straight-line path. For a straight-line path between the left-front and right-front loudspeakers, the midpoint distance (D_m) between the virtual sound source location and the listener is *smaller* than either D_l or D_r. If $D_l = D_r = 1$, then $D_m = 1 / \sqrt{2} = 0.707 \ldots$. According to the inverse square law for sound intensity, the necessary patterns of amplitude change during the crossfade are shown in the plots for G_2 and G_1.

To calculate the gain factors associated with intermediate positions, equation (4-15) requires that we compute the distance from the virtual sound source to the listener relative to the distance between the listener and the loudspeakers. For this purpose, we may use the general formula for distance between any two points on the horizontal plane, (x_1, y_1) and (x_2, y_2), which is

$$D = \sqrt{(x_2 - x_1)^2 + (y_2 - y_1)^2} \qquad (4\text{-}18)$$

If we assume that the listener is positioned at location $(0, 0)$, we may calculate the distance from the listener of any virtual sound source located at position (x, y) according to

$$D(x, y) = \sqrt{x^2 + y^2} \qquad (4\text{-}19)$$

Plots of the changing gain factors required for a straight-line transit from left-front to right-front loudspeaker positions are shown in Figure 4-8.

Let's examine a simple C function to compute gain factors according to equation (4-15). The main program requires the user to type four arguments giving the x and y position of the virtual sound source, the angle (this argument is typed in degrees and converted to radians for use by the program), and the distance to any of the loudspeakers (distances may be measured in arbitrary units, typically meters or feet).

```c
#include <stdio.h>
#include <math.h>

main( argc, argv ) int argc ; char *argv[] ; {
 float x, y, thetan, distn, gain() ;
 double TWOPI = 8.*atan( 1. ) ;
/*
 * pick up desired location of virtual sound source
 */
    x = atof( argv[1] ) ;
    y = atof( argv[2] ) ;
/*
 * pick up angle and distance to loudspeaker
 * (convert angle from degrees to radians)
 */
    thetan = TWOPI*atof( argv[3] )/360. ;
    distn = atof( argv[4] ) ;
/*
 * normalize angle within angle range of arc tangent function
 */
    thetan =
        atan2( sin( (double) thetan ), cos( (double) thetan ) ) ;
/*
 * print amplitude gain factor needed for specified loudspeaker
 */
    printf( "gain factor = %f\n", gain( x, y, thetan, distn ) ) ;
}
/*
 * compute intensity panning gain factor for channel n with
 * loudspeaker at distance distn and angle thetan (in radians)
 * from listener located at (0,0) for a virtual sound source
 * located at position (x,y)
 */
float gain( x, y, thetan, distn ) float x, y, thetan, distn ; {
 static double right_angle ;
 double diff ;
 static first = 1 ;
    if ( first ) {
        first = 0 ;
        right_angle = 2.*atan( 1. ) ;
    }
    diff = fabs( thetan - atan2( (double) y, (double) x ) ) ;
    if ( diff > right_angle )
        return( 0. ) ;
    return( cos( diff )*distn/sqrt( (double) x*x + y*y ) ) ;
}
```

The only step in this programming example that may not be immediately clear in the context of our discussion is the angle normalization step in the main program. Because inverse trigonometric functions (such as arc tangent) are inherently ambiguous (a given tangent value corresponds to infinitely many angles), a system of "principal values" is used (see Appendix A). By invoking the seemingly tautological relationship

$$\theta = \tan^{-1} \frac{\sin \theta}{\cos \theta} \tag{4-20}$$

we may ensure that θ lies within the principal value range for the inverse tangent function, thus allowing it to be compared easily with other angles similarly derived (for example, in the calculation of the angle difference variable `diff` in the programming example).

4.2.3 Direction Cues

Except for directions in which loudspeakers are situated, intensity panning provides the listener with only a rough cue for direction to the virtual sound source on the horizontal plane. Also, like all direction cues, intensity panning works best only for listeners situated at the center of the listening space, facing forward.

Other cues affecting the perceived direction of a virtual sound source include those based on *interaural timing differences* and spectrum cues based on the effects of the pinnae.

The interaural timing difference (ITD), is based on the fact that sound traveling from a source to a listener arrives at the two ears at slightly different times unless it is coming from a sound source located on the *median plane*, which is defined by all positions lying directly in front of, directly behind, directly above, and directly below the listener. The maximum ITD occurs when a sound source is located directly to the left or right of the listener, having then a value approximately equal to the time it takes sound to travel the distance between the two ears.

A classical experiment for determining the maximum useful value of ITD consists of inserting both ends of a rubber hose about 1 meter in length into the two ears. If the hose is tapped with a hard object at its midpoint, the sound is heard as if it were located in the center of the head. If we now tap at different points, we find that the sound seems to wander off center, toward the ear that is closer to the tapping point as measured along the hose. The lateral displacement continues to increase approximately linearly until the difference in hose lengths to the two ears reaches about 21 centimeters, corresponding to an ITD of about 630 microseconds. The lateral displacement then continues to increase more slowly until the ITD is about 1 millisecond, after which it stops increasing altogether (Blauert, 1983).

If steady tones are used instead of taps, however, the psychoacoustic situation becomes more complicated, because the hearing mechanism now has the more complex problem of comparing the arrival times at the two ears of a periodic waveform.

Apparently the hearing mechanism is capable of doing this, provided that the half-period of the waveform is greater than about 630 microseconds, which corresponds to a frequency of about 800 Hz. At frequencies above about 800 Hz, the maximum attainable ITD becomes smaller and smaller, causing ITD to become weaker and weaker as a directional cue at higher frequencies.

We can easily simulate the ITD cue by introducing small delays into the signals being presented in one loudspeaker channel versus another. We will consider this problem in two parts. The first part is to determine just how much ITD is desirable for all possible directions; the second part is to consider ways in which small amounts of delay may be introduced into the signals coming from the various loudspeakers. As we saw in the case of intensity panning, no amount of signal processing will produce a useful result if the playback system is not carefully calibrated. In this case, the calibration must assure that signals presented simultaneously to all channels reach the listener simultaneously as well.

Various loudspeaker designs have definite advantages and disadvantages for the simulation of ITD cues. For example, so-called time-aligned loudspeakers are designed so that the delay introduced by the crossover circuitry that distributes various frequencies to various driver elements is carefully compensated, often by positioning some of the drivers ahead of or behind the others so that all frequencies reach the listener aligned in time as they were aligned in the signal. Of course, such time alignment can only be approximate due to the nonlinear phase response of analog filters, which necessarily introduce a variable amount of delay at different frequencies. Also, a listener who is positioned as much as one-half of 21 centimeters off center would receive a completely distorted ITD, rendering reliance on this particular cue highly questionable for concert playback situations. Nevertheless, ITD can provide a useful cue to sound directionality under carefully controlled circumstances.

One way to determine the desirable amount of ITD is to solve triangles such as those shown in Figure 4-9. If we assume that sound coming directly from the left or right would cause an ITD of 630 microseconds, then sound coming from the direction of channel 1 would produce an ITD of less than 630 microseconds. To determine how much less, we can compute the different distances between a sound source located in this direction and the two ears, based on an interaural distance of 21 centimeters. The following C program does just that.

```
#include <stdio.h>
#include <math.h>

main( argc, argv ) int argc ; char *argv[] ; {
 int i, N ;
 double RA = 2.*atan(1.), a, dist, x, y, dx, dr, dl ;
    N = atoi( argv[1] ) ;          /* # of angles to compute */
    dist = atof( argv[2] ) ;       /* distance (cm) to source */
    for ( i = 0 ; i < N ; i++ ) {
        a = RA*i/(N-1) ;
        x = dist*cos( a ) ;        /* x-coordinate of source */
```

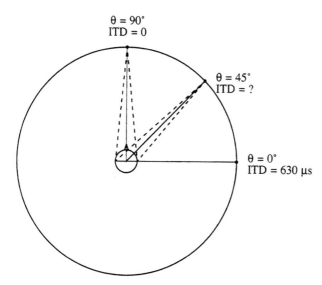

θ = 90°
ITD = 0

θ = 45°
ITD = ?

θ = 0°
ITD = 630 μs

Figure 4-9   Calculating interaural time differences (ITD). Assuming the maximum distance between the ears to be 21 centimeters, corresponding to a maximum ITD of 630 microseconds, we can compute the distances from any virtual source location to the two ears. The difference between these distances (marked with pairs of dotted lines in the figure) then determines the desired ITD value.

```
    y = dist*sin( a ) ;         /* y-coordinate of source */
    dx = x - 10.5 ;
    dr = hypot( dx, y ) ;       /* distance to right ear */
    dx = x + 10.5 ;
    dl = hypot( dx, y ) ;       /* distance to left ear */
    printf( "angle = %6.2f, diff = %9f, 21*cos(a) = %9f\n",
        90.*a/RA, dl-dr, 21.*cos(a) ) ;
    }
}
```

The arguments to this program are the number of angles to compute lying between 0° and 90° and the distance from the center of the head to the sound source, in centimeters. The program then lists the angles specified, together with the difference in distance from a source located at that angle to the two ears. It also lists the value for the cosine of the angle scaled by the maximum assumed interaural distance (21 centimeters).

The results of running this program with arguments $N = 11$ and $dist = 20$ (centimeters) are as follows:

```
angle =    0.00, diff = 21.000000, 21*cos(a) = 21.000000
angle =    9.00, diff = 20.646751, 21*cos(a) = 20.741455
angle =   18.00, diff = 19.634674, 21*cos(a) = 19.972187
angle =   27.00, diff = 18.077014, 21*cos(a) = 18.711137
angle =   36.00, diff = 16.099254, 21*cos(a) = 16.989357
angle =   45.00, diff = 13.808278, 21*cos(a) = 14.849242
angle =   54.00, diff = 11.286818, 21*cos(a) = 12.343490
angle =   63.00, diff =  8.598375, 21*cos(a) =  9.533800
angle =   72.00, diff =  5.793498, 21*cos(a) =  6.489357
```

```
angle =   81.00, diff =  2.914714, 21*cos(a) =   3.285124
angle =   90.00, diff =  0.000000, 21*cos(a) =   0.000000
```

We see that even at this small distance between the listener's position and that of the sound source, the difference in distances to the two ears is approximately equal to the cosine of the angle describing the direction to the source. This discrepancy becomes smaller very rapidly as the distance to the source becomes larger. For example, the following output results if we specify a source 100 centimeters away from the center of the head.

```
angle =    0.00, diff = 21.000000, 21*cos(a) =   21.000000
angle =    9.00, diff = 20.738627, 21*cos(a) =   20.741455
angle =   18.00, diff = 19.961576, 21*cos(a) =   19.972187
angle =   27.00, diff = 18.689728, 21*cos(a) =   18.711137
angle =   36.00, diff = 16.956859, 21*cos(a) =   16.989357
angle =   45.00, diff = 14.808259, 21*cos(a) =   14.849242
angle =   54.00, diff = 12.299028, 21*cos(a) =   12.343490
angle =   63.00, diff =  9.492256, 21*cos(a) =    9.533800
angle =   72.00, diff =  6.457207, 21*cos(a) =    6.489357
angle =   81.00, diff =  3.267594, 21*cos(a) =    3.285124
angle =   90.00, diff =  0.000000, 21*cos(a) =    0.000000
```

Even for sources as close as 1 meter, the cosine function approximates the differences in ear-source distances quite well. The desired ITD is then given by

$$\text{ITD} \approx 630 \cos \theta \quad \mu s \tag{4-21}$$

4.2.4 Delay Lines

Given a desired value for the ITD, we turn now to the problem of how it might be implemented. Once again, we have to restrict the implementation to the case where a listener is positioned exactly between the loudspeakers (or wears headphones). Furthermore, we now have the additional problem that some of the sound coming from a loudspeaker on the left will reach the right ear, and vice versa. While it is possible to compensate for the interaural crosstalk that invariably occurs when sounds are presented over loudspeakers (Schroeder, 1980), we will consider only the problem of implementing a desired delay in a given loudspeaker channel.

The simplest delay implementation consists of a "delay line" in which samples of the digital signal are passed at the sampling rate from one stage to the next (see Figure 4-10). Such a delay line allows straightforward implementation of delays of the form nT, where n is an integer and $T = 1/R$ is the sampling period (R is the sampling rate in hertz).

For example, a sound coming from the direction of channel 1 ($\theta = 45°$) would reach the listener's right ear about 445.5 microseconds sooner than the left ear, according to equation (4-21). The simplest approximation of this amount of ITD would in-

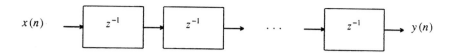

Figure 4-10   A simple delay line. The output $y(n)$ is the same as the input, delayed by an arbitrary number of samples.

volve delaying the signal coming from the channel 2 loudspeaker by this amount.[4] The delay of the signal in channel 2 in samples is given by

$$n = ITD \times R \qquad\qquad (4\text{-}22)$$

where n is the delay in samples, ITD is the desired interaural time delay in seconds, and R is the sampling rate. Most desired values of ITD will not result in an integral number of samples of delay. However, the human acuity of sound localization is coarse enough that small absolute errors in delay for sound sources with fixed locations may be ignored under most circumstances.

Let us now examine a simple C function that implements a fixed delay of n samples. It is called on a sample-by-sample basis. Each time it is called, it returns the value of the input argument that it was given n calls previously. The delay is implemented using the so-called *circular buffer* technique. Instead of actually copying all samples in the delay memory to successive locations as suggested by the delay line shown in Figure 4-10, indices are used that keep track of the current location in the delay buffer. The delay function advances the current index by one sample, resetting to the beginning of the delay buffer when necessary. The circular buffer technique allows the function to operate with an essentially constant amount of computation for each call, regardless of the length of the delay line in use. Note that zero delay is a special case.

```
/*
 * return input signal delayed by n samples
 * using circular buffer technique
 * buffer must be at least n samples long
 */
float delay( n, input, buffer, current )
 int n, *current ; float input, buffer[] ;
{
 float output ;
/*
 * recirculate samples among first n buffer locations
 * (zero delay is special case)
 */
    if ( n == 0 )
        return( input ) ;
```

---

[4]For simplicity, we ignore the small amount of crosstalk from the left speakers to the listener's right ear and vice versa.

```
    if ( ++(*current) >= n )
        *current = 0 ;
    output = buffer[*current] ;
    buffer[*current] = input ;
    return( output ) ;
}
```

4.2.5 Time-varying Delays

The circular buffer technique shown in the programming example is appropriate only for fixed delays of an integral number of samples. The technique may be useful for implementing a good approximation of an ITD for a virtual sound source at a fixed location, but it is inappropriate for virtual source locations that move. Time-varying delays require a different implementation to avoid discontinuities in the output signal that may result in audible clicks.

To avoid discontinuities, it is necessary to use some form of interpolation when dealing with nonintegral sample delays. Ideally, the interpolation method would give a good approximation of the value of the underlying analog signal at instants falling between the samples (we have already seen in Chapter 3 that such interpolation may be achieved with an appropriately defined filter). In many cases, however, delays of a nonintegral number of samples can be simulated using linear interpolation between two previous samples of a signal.

Although linear interpolation is simple to implement, it is important to recall how it differs from an ideal interpolator. An ideal interpolator constructs new sample values from those of a digital signal that correspond precisely to the underlying analog signal. As we saw in Chapter 2, the underlying analog signal typically does *not* move in a straight line from sample to sample of a digital signal, especially if the analog signal is sampled critically. The greater the extent to which the analog signal is oversampled (that is, sampled at a rate greater than the minimum required by the sampling theorem), the more nearly the underlying analog signal will follow close to a straight-line path between adjacent samples. Thus linear interpolation tends to distort high-frequency signals more than those containing only low-frequency (compared with the Nyquist rate) components.

An ideal interpolator corresponds in its frequency domain description to an ideal lowpass filter: it passes all frequencies up to the Nyquist rate without change and suppresses all higher frequencies perfectly. As we have already seen, the ideal lowpass filter is not implementable (realizable) in the usual sense because the instantaneous cutoff in the frequency domain corresponds to an impulse response with an infinite width in the time domain, extending into both the future and the past from the current input sample according to the shape of the function $\operatorname{sinc} x = \sin(x)/x$. In Chapter 3, we saw in the context of phase vocoder resynthesis how excellent approximations to the ideal interpolator can be implemented.

We can interpret a linear interpolator as a lowpass filter by considering its impulse response to be

$$h(m) = \begin{cases} 1 - \dfrac{|m|}{L} & \text{if } -L < m < L \\[2em] 0 & \text{otherwise} \end{cases} \qquad (4\text{-}23)$$

where L is called the *interpolation factor*. For example, if L has the value 2, equation (4-23) indicates that the linear interpolator will replace each input sample by two output samples, half of which are identical to the input samples and half of which lie halfway along straight lines drawn between the samples of the input signal. For $L = 3$, the output signal would have three times the sampling rate of the input signal, with pairs of intermediate samples filled in by linear interpolation, and so on.

It can be shown that the linear interpolator described by equation (4-23) has the frequency response

$$H(e^{j\omega}) = \frac{1}{L} \left[\frac{\sin(\omega L/2)}{\sin(\omega/2)} \right]^2 \qquad (4\text{-}24)$$

where L is the interpolation factor (Crochiere and Rabiner, 1983). In the case of linear interpolation between samples in a delay line, we may interpret the interpolation factor L as the reciprocal of the fractional part of the delay measured in samples. For example, if we require the value of a signal delayed by 4.2 samples, the equivalent interpolation factor would be $1/0.2 = 5$. Plots of the frequency response described by equation (4-24) for the cases $L = 5$ and $L = 10$ are shown in Figure 4-11. The linearly interpolated signal, in effect, contains "sharp corners" that are not present in the original (see Chapter 2). The weak side-lobe attenuation of the linear interpolator response shown in Figure 4-11 explains why it is more suitable for treating signals containing only low-frequency components than for broadband signals. Nevertheless, because it involves only two samples of the original signal, linear interpolation is widely used.

The following programming example implements nonintegral delays through linear interpolation. In this case, the buffer is assumed to be as long as the largest desired amount of delay. Furthermore, it is assumed that the samples are arranged according to a circular buffer technique in such a way that buffer[current] refers to the current input sample, buffer[current+1] refers to the previous input sample, and so on, with the proviso that the index to the delay buffer is taken modulo the buffer length (L).

```
/*
 * interp_delay looks up a sample delayed by n samples using linear
 * interpolation on a circular buffer of length L with current
 * input sample at buffer[current]
 */
float interp_delay( n, buffer, L, current )
 float n, buffer[] ; int L, current ;
{
 int t1, t2 ;
```

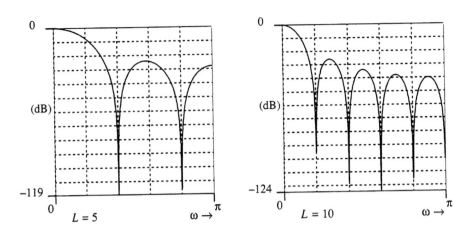

Figure 4-11 Frequency responses on a decibel scale for linear interpolators with interpolation factors (L) of 5 (left) and 10 (right). Note that the first side lobe of the response in both cases is just a little more the 20 dB below the main peak, indicating that unless the original signal (the one being interpolated) is band-limited to a band smaller than π/L, linear interpolation is only weakly capable of suppressing the periodic images of the signal spectrum.

```
/*
 * t1 is index in buffer of input signal delayed by n samples
 */
    t1 = current + n ;
/*
 * take t1 modulo the delay buffer length
 */
    while ( t1 >= L )
        t1 -= L ;
/*
 * t2 is index of input signal delayed by n+1 samples
 */
    t2 = t1 + 1 ;
    while ( t2 >= L )
        t2 -= L ;
/*
 * perform linear interpolation according
 * to possibly nonintegral value of n
 */
    return(
        buffer[t1] +
        (n - ( (int) n ) ) *
        ( buffer[t2] - buffer[t1] )
    ) ;
}
```

Using the `interp_delay` function, we can specify any amount of signal delay (up to `L-1` samples). As long as the amount of delay does not change too rapidly, the linear interpolation technique suppresses intersample discontinuities well enough to avoid audible clicks under most circumstances.

One of the more interesting characteristics of the interpolated delay technique is that it produces the equivalent of a Doppler shift as a side effect. To understand this usually delightful side effect, we have only to consider the basic mechanism through which the Doppler shift occurs.

Suppose that a stationary sound source emits a complete vibration pattern (that is, single periods of a periodic waveform) at a rate of 100 times a second. Because the sound energy propagates in all directions at the speed of sound, the wavelength of each vibration period is equal to the distance the wave front travels in 1/100 second. Anything traveling at a speed c meters per second will travel $c/100$ meters in 1/100 second. Therefore, the wavelength λ, frequency f, and speed of propagation c of any wave through any medium are related according to

$$\lambda = \frac{c}{f} \qquad\qquad (4\text{-}25)$$

Doppler shift occurs when the speed of wave propagation is essentially independent of the motion of the source relative to the medium of propagation. When a sound source moves toward a stationary listener, successive vibration periods are compressed in space due to the motion of the source (see Figure 4-12). Because the wavelength (that is, the spatial distance between successive peaks in the sound pressure wave) is shorter in the direction of travel, this causes peaks of the waveform to pass by the position of the listener at a greater rate than they would if the sound source were stationary. Conversely, when the sound source moves away from the listener, the wavelength is effectively lengthened due to the motion of the source.

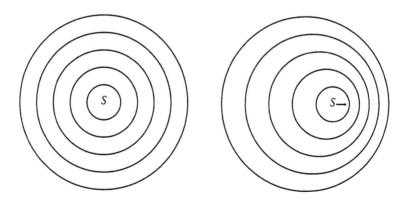

Figure 4-12   Doppler shift. The circles drawn around the sound sources represent an instantaneous picture of the peaks in the pressure wave propagating outward at the speed of sound. The source on the left is stationary, resulting in concentric circles with an equal distance between successive peaks (equal wavelengths) in all directions. The source on the right is moving toward the right, causing the center of each successive circle to move to the right also, effectively compressing the wavelength in the direction of travel and elongating it in the opposite direction.

If we recognize that the waveform in the delay buffer is a record of its recent history, it is evident that the delay value may be interpreted in terms of an equivalent distance P between a sound source and a listener. When this delay varies in time, the result is entirely equivalent to dynamically varying the distance between the sound source and the listener in terms of the time interval between successive peaks of the waveform. When the delay value decreases over time, the sound source and listener are effectively moving closer to each other; when the delay is increasing, the sound source and listener are effectively moving apart (see Figure 4-13.)

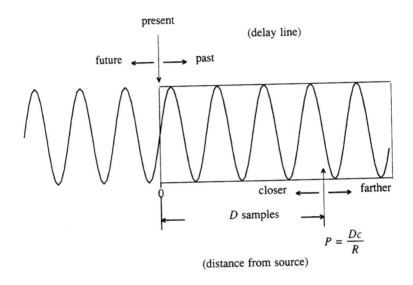

Figure 4-13 Equivalence between time and space in a delay line. D samples at a sampling rate R occur over a duration of D/R seconds, during which sound traveling at c will travel a distance $P = Dc/R$ (if c is given in meters per second, P will be in meters). If this distance is made smaller (or larger) by decreasing (or increasing) D while we listen to the sound entering the delay line, the resulting waveform will be compressed (or expanded) in time, resulting in a frequency shift that is equivalent to a Doppler shift. The size of this shift is the same as the one predicted by the Doppler shift equations for a velocity v given by the time rate of change of position P.

We may even use the basic mathematics of Doppler shift to calculate the amount of this frequency shift merely by considering the time rate of change of distance P (velocity). If sound travels at a rate of c meters per second, then for a digital waveform sampled at R samples per second, sound will travel a distance c/R meters during one sample period. A delay of D samples then represents D times this distance. The equivalent distance between the sound source and the listener is then given by

$$P = \frac{Dc}{R} \qquad (4\text{-}26)$$

where c is the speed of sound, R is the sampling rate, D is the delay in samples, and P will be in meters if c is expressed in meters per second. If P remains constant, the relative velocity between the sound source and the listener will be zero. If P changes over time, however, due to a variation in the value for D, the time rate of change of distance P signifies a nonzero relative velocity between the sound source and listener. For example, if P gradually gets smaller by 1 meter over a duration of 1 second, this represents motion of the sound source toward the listener (or the listener toward the source) at an average velocity v of 1 meter per second, with an attendant Doppler shift upward in frequency. If P gets larger (increasing delay), sound source and listener are moving away from each other, with a corresponding downward frequency shift.

Thus we see that just as the Doppler shift is a side effect of velocity, it is also a side effect of variation in time delay. Either way, the Doppler shift may be interpreted as the effect of a *changing distance* between a sound source and a listener. A Doppler shift is therefore not useful in conveying an impression of absolute distance. Even when the Doppler shift is fairly small, however, it provides a powerful perceptual cue regarding *motion* of a virtual sound source toward or away from the listener.

4.2.6 Distance Cues

To create the impression that a virtual sound source is coming from an arbitrary location in the virtual acoustic space outside the perimeter of the loudspeakers, it is necessary to have some control over the perceived distance between the listener and the virtual sound source. Interestingly, far less is known about the auditory perception of distance than is known about the auditory perception of direction.

It is known, however, that one of the most important factors used in the auditory determination of distance is the listener's *familiarity* with the sound source. We are able to judge distances rather well, for example, for familiar sounds such as human speech at normal loudnesses (Blauert, 1983). The sounds of traditional musical instruments seem to fall into this category of familiar sounds in the sense that we are generally able to discern the difference between a soft note played on a nearby trumpet and a loud note played far away, even though the two sounds might impinge on the ear with equal intensity. Our familiarity with the difference in tone quality (timbre) between a trumpet note played *pianissimo* and one played *fortissimo* is apparently correlated with the sound intensity in the formation of a distance judgment.

For unfamiliar sounds, however, the situation is more complicated. In this case, the primary distance cue is apparently just the *loudness* of the sound as perceived by the listener. Just as pitch and frequency are not the same (even though an increase in one generally corresponds to an increase in the other when all other characteristics of the sound remain the same), subjective loudness is not the same thing as sound intensity.

The classical method for defining a scale of subjective loudness rests on judgments of when one sound seems "twice as loud" or "half as loud" as another sound with identical spectrum characteristics. Somewhat surprisingly, when listeners are asked to make such judgments in the absence of other cues, the results are fairly consistent (this is the basis of the *sone scale* of subjective loudness). Even more surprisingly, the doubling or halving of subjective loudness does not correspond well with the relative changes in intensity associated with doubling or halving the distance to identical sound sources.

If we compare the intensity changes for the sone scale with the inverse square law of sound intensity associated with physical distances, we find that subjective loudness seems to follow a law that is much closer to the *inverse cube* of distance rather than the inverse square (Stevens, 1970). Expressed on a decibel scale, a halving or doubling of distance between a sound source and listener corresponds roughly to a relative change of ±6 dB in sound intensity, while a doubling or halving of subjective loudness corresponds much more closely to a relative change of ±9 dB in sound intensity.

There is at least some evidence that for spatialization of sounds by computer, the 6 dB (inverse square) law leads to more compelling results for familiar sounds while the 9 dB (inverse cube) law leads to more compelling results for unfamiliar sounds (Begault, 1987). In any case, it seems to be the case that a precise "simulation of reality" does not necessarily lead to the most compelling subjective impression of auditory distance, especially when the "reality" being simulated has unfamiliar aspects, such as the broad class of digitally synthesized sounds having no familiar counterparts.

Under different circumstances, therefore, we may choose to relate sound amplitude to distance according to the inverse square law, an inverse cube law, or an arbiarary law. By analogy with the inverse square law, for example, the inverse cube law would be based on the relationship

$$A^2 \propto I \propto \frac{1}{D^3} \qquad (4\text{-}27)$$

where A is amplitude, I is intensity, and D is distance. Solving this relationship for linear amplitude results in the corresponding inverse cube law of amplitude:

$$A \propto \sqrt{I} \propto \frac{1}{D^{1.5}} \qquad (4\text{-}28)$$

4.2.7 Reverberant Enclosures

When a sound source moves away into the distance, the sound that travels directly from the source to the listener becomes less intense according to the inverse square law. If both the sound source and the listener are in a reverberant enclosure, however, the listener also hears diffuse reverberation coming more or less uniformly from all directions. Assuming a source of continuous sound with constant intensity, a uniform enclosure with a simple shape, and the absence of significant obstructions of reflectors within the enclosure, the reverberant energy will be more or less uniformly intense at all locations within the enclosure. As mentioned earlier the intensity of the reverberant sound is determined by the source intensity and the total absorption of the room. Therefore, as a source of continuous sound with constant intensity moves away from a stationary listener *in a uniform reverberant environment*, the direct sound coming from the source to the listener drops off in intensity according to the inverse square law while the reverberant sound remains at a more or less constant intensity.

When sound source and listener are both inside the same auditory space defined by an enclosure (the typical case for music performance), we may divide the sound received by the listener into two distinct parts: the primary, or *direct*, sound that travels in a straight line from the source to the listener, and the diffuse, or *reverberant*, sound due to multiple reflections of the sound within the acoustic enclosure. The difference between the levels of the direct and reverberant sound supply information to the listener about the distance to the sound source. That the listener's auditory system actually takes this information into account in forming a subjective opinion regarding the distance to the sound source has been demonstrated many times (Hornbostel, 1926; Békésy, 1938; and Gardner, 1969). This led John Chowning (1971) to reason that a simplified cue to the distance of a sound source is "the ratio of the direct energy to the indirect or reverberant energy where the intensity of the direct sound reaching the listener falls off more sharply with distance than does the reverberant sound".

The actual situation is somewhat more complicated than this. First, the level of direct and reverberant sounds may be compared directly only in the case where the sound source radiates a signal into the room that is unchanging over time (stationary) and the listener is holding still. For impulsive sounds, the direct and reverberant sounds do not overlap in time at the position of the listener. For such sounds, the primary subjective impression regarding the position of the sound source is determined by the direct signal, which is the first to arrive at the listener's ears.[5] Furthermore, this direct signal elicits an inhibitory effect, suppressing additional information that follows it in time. After a certain length of time, called the *echo threshold*, strong reflections may lead to additional subjective impressions regarding the directionality of the echo itself, as opposed to additional information about the location of the sound source.[6] Therefore, the primary information regarding the location of the sound source is contained in the initial sound that arrives at the listener's position, and the ensuing reverberation provides diffuse information that tends to "fill" the listener's entire subjective auditory space. The higher the level of the direct sound in comparison to that of the reverberation, the more precisely located the sound source will be. If the reverberation is considerably louder than the direct sound, only a diffusely located sound source will be perceivable by the listener.

The basic approach to processing digital signals representing "pure" sound sources (that is, sounds in an anechoic environment) to create a strong impression regarding their locations within an illusory acoustic space therefore lies in the creation of a synthetic sound field that accompanies the direct sounds. The resulting (processed) signals may be designed for audition over loudspeakers in a listening space, over regular

---

[5]Cremer (1948), for example, describes a "law of the first wave front" thus: when the delay time between signals reaching the listener exceeds the maximum value for ITD that affects subjective directionality (about 630 microseconds), the subjective impression of the location of the source is determined primarily by the information arriving first at the position of the listener.

[6]The echo threshold—defined as the amount of time delay needed before a reflection is perceived as a separate echo—varies considerably, depending on such factors as the type of sound and the level of the direct sound. Blauert (1983) surveys a number of experiments leading to values for the echo threshold between 3 and 100 milliseconds. For our purposes, we consider the echo threshold to be the end of the "early echo response" of a room, which typically occurs at around 80 to 100 milliseconds.

headphones, or over special binaural headphones that inject the sound into the ear canal in such a way as to minimize the effects of the listener's pinnae. Whichever playback situation is chosen, the various temporal regimes of spatial hearing suggest that the processing needed to create the synthetic sound field that will result in effective spatialization of the source sound within a controllable "illusory acoustic space" includes the following steps:

- *Intensity:* control of intensity of the direct sound (a primary determinant of both direction and distance) in each playback channel
- *Early echo response:* control of the detailed pattern of reflections (a primary determinant of direction) that occur during the first 80 to 100 milliseconds after the direct sound in each playback channel
- *Reverberation:* reverberation control of the frequency-dependent decay time of the dense reverberation (a primary determinant of the impression of the size and acoustic characteristics of the enclosure surrounding the illusory acoustic space) that follows the early echo response
- *Interaural decorrelation:* control of the correlation of the signals (a primary determinant of the quality of the diffusion within the illusory acoustic space) reaching the two ears of the listener

We have already discussed most of the issues involving the control of intensity, including the fact that for unfamiliar sounds, the perception-based inverse cube law is sometime more effective than the physically based inverse square law in eliciting subjective impressions of sounds at various distances from the listener.

In addition, we have seen how simple digital delay lines may be used to simulate both stationary and nonstationary (using interpolation) time delays that may be combined to form any temporal pattern of echoes over the first 100 milliseconds or so after the arrival of the direct sound, which may itself be delayed due to its distance from the listener. The intensity of each of these echoes may be made nonuniform as well, corresponding to the lengths of the paths traversed by the sound rays that give rise to them according to either the inverse square law or some variation of it. You may have already noticed the similarity between the processing needed to generate the early echo response and that required for an FIR filter.

We have not yet considered the simulation of dense reverberation, but just as the control of the early echo pattern of the sound reaching the listener has turned out to be describable in terms of the specification of an FIR filter, the simulation of reverberation also turns out to be describable in terms of the specification of one or more IIR filters, as we shall soon see.

Finally, the decorrelation of signals reaching the listener can be accomplished through the application of allpass (IIR) filters that process the signals in each channel of the playback system.

In addition to these basic cues, we may also take into account the fact that the pinnae serve as direction-dependent filters, especially for the determination of the elevation of the sound source above the horizontal plane.

Thus by controlling the intensity, early echoes, reverberation, channel decorrelation, and pinnae cues that reach the listener, we can effectively place sounds at arbitrary (possibly time-varying) locations within an illusory acoustic space that itself has controllable acoustic characteristics. We now consider the simulation of each of these types of cues in terms of digital filtering.

4.3 EARLY ECHO RESPONSE

For the illusory acoustic space beyond the perimeter of the playback loudspeakers (or headphones) to be reverberant at all, it must contain reflective boundaries representing imaginary walls that enclose it. Thus our basic model for sound spatialization processing consists of a "room within a room," where the inner room consists of the listening space and the outer room consists of the enclosure surrounding the illusory acoustic space.

One of the fundamental problems encountered in practical sound spatialization for computer music involves the fact that for loudspeaker presentation, the position of the listener within the listening space is not a controllable factor. For a psychoacoustic experiment, it may be possible to position a single listener exactly in the center of the listening space and, through the use of various head-restraint devices such as bite-boards and head braces, to maintain the listener's head in a precisely located, fixed position. For the presentation of music over loudspeakers, we must take into practical consideration the fact the listeners will generally be located in many different positions within the listening space. This makes use of direction cues based on interaural time differences (ITDs) practically impossible, because even a listener sitting in a chair located at the center of the listening space may still engage in head movements that would distort this cue beyond all utility.

One way to unify the treatment of loudspeaker and headphone presentation is to consider the inner room to be either a listening space containing loudspeakers and one or more listeners located as near its center as possible or to consider the inner room to be the listener's head itself. In the latter case, the four loudspeakers in the corners of the listening space are effectively replaced by the two headphones located on either side of the listener's head (see Figure 4-14).

Given this basic model of the spatial relationships between the outer and inner rooms, we may signify a virtual sound source anywhere within the outer room simply by specifying its position, either in terms of rectangular $(x-y)$ or polar (distance and direction) coordinates. Taking the origin to be the center of the inner room, these position descriptions will be related by the formulas

$$x = r \cos \theta$$
$$y = r \sin \theta$$

$$(4\text{-}29)$$

and

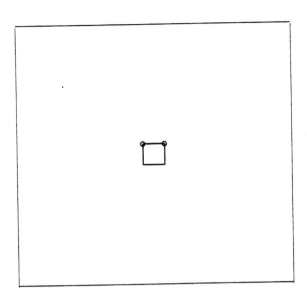

Figure 4-14 Computation model for sound spatialization. The outer rectangle represents the enclosure surrounding the illusory acoustic space. The inner rectangle represents alternatively the listening space with loudspeakers located at the positions marked with circles or the listener's head with headphone speakers located on either side. The relative sizes and geometries of the two "rooms" may be adjusted according to this interpretation and to achieve various types of spatialization effects.

$$r = \sqrt{x^2 + y^2}$$
$$\theta = \tan^{-1} \frac{y}{x}$$

(4-30)

where x and y are rectangular coordinates and r and θ are of a particular point in space (we arbitrarily take all distances to be measured in meters). For example, Figure 4-15 shows a single virtual sound source positioned at (15, 23), where 15 is the x-coordinate and 23 is the y-coordinate.

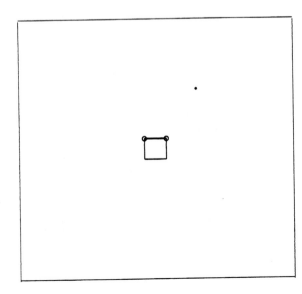

Figure 4-15 A single virtual sound source positioned within the illusory acoustic space ("outer room"). The outer room is specified to be 100 meters on a side, the inner room is 8 meters on a side, and the sound source is located alternatively at (15, 23) or at a distance 27.46 meters at an angle of 56.9° from the center of the inner room.

Once the dimensions of the inner and outer rooms are specified and the position of the virtual sound source is known, the distances between the virtual sound source and both of the loudspeakers are easily calculated according to the distance formula based on the Pythagorean theorem (see Figure 4-16). This distance determines both the amount of delay to be introduced in channels 1 and 2 for the direct sound and the amount of attenuation due to distance according to whatever intensity law is in effect (for example, inverse square or inverse cube).

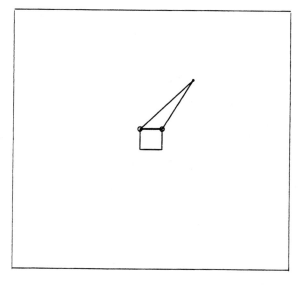

Figure 4-16   Calculating the distances between the virtual sound source position and the loudspeakers in the inner room. These distances may be used to determine delays and attenuations associated with the direct sound according to the speed of sound and the law relating distance and attenuation chosen (for example, inverse square or inverse cube).

In addition to the delays and attenuations associated with the direct sound, we can use our basic geometric model to calculate delays and distance attenuations associated with reflections of the sound from the walls of the outer room (see Figure 4-17). It is necessary to decide which reflective ray paths to choose for this step. The reflective ray paths shown in Figure 4-17 correspond to those that will arrive *first* at the positions of the loudspeakers from each of the four walls of the outer room. That is, these are the shortest reflective ray paths, which are the ones associated with reflection points at which the angles of incidence and reflection of the sound rays are equal. According to our earlier consideration of spatial hearing, it is these ray paths that result in the greatest information to the listener regarding the position of the virtual sound source.

There are several methods for finding the necessary reflection points along each wall. One of the simplest approaches to this problem involves finding the location of the "phantom" sound source behind each wall that is associated with the location of the virtual sound source. The phantom source is located in the symmetrical location behind each of the walls that we would find by rotating the outer room about the axis defined by the wall. For example, given the virtual sound source at (15, 23) as shown in Figure 4-18, we note that this position is 35 meters to the *left* of the right-hand wall located at $x = 50$. The phantom sound source would therefore be located 35 meters to the *right* of

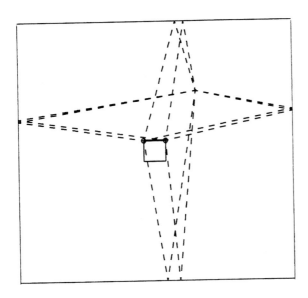

Figure 4-17   Calculating the distances along reflective ray paths between the virtual sound source position and the loudspeakers in the inner room. The reflection points chosen correspond to those associated with the shortest reflective ray paths from each wall of the outer room.

this wall at $(85, 23)$. If we draw a straight line from the phantom source location to either one of the loudspeakers in the inner room, the point where this line intersects the wall will be the reflection point associated with equal angles of incidence and reflection.

The analytic geometry behind this operation is quite straightforward. One general formula for a straight line is $y = mx + b$, where m is called the *slope* of the line and b is called the *y-axis intercept*. Any two points in space, (x_1, y_1) and (x_2, y_2), define a straight line with a slope $m = (y_2 - y_1)/(x_2 - x_1)$ and a y-axis intercept given either by $b = y_1 - mx_1$ or $b = y_2 - mx_2$ (special care must of course be taken when $x_1 = x_2$, indicating that the line is *vertical*, that is, that it has *infinite slope*). If (x_1, y_1) is the location of the loudspeaker and (x_2, y_2) is the phantom source location, the resulting line connecting these two points, $y = mx + b$, clearly crosses the vertical line at $x = 50$ at a point $(50, y_i)$, where y_i is found by solving $y_i = mx + b$ for $x = 50$.

The procedure described so far defines five values of delay and five values of attenuation (corresponding to the direct sound and one reflection from each wall) for each loudspeaker. Figure 4-19 shows the 20 ray paths that would result from using a four-channel playback configuration.

Figure 4-19 also shows how some of the direct and reflective ray paths cut through the listening space (inner room). We may choose to interpret such ray paths in two ways. If they are left in place, the resulting sound will be placed into the playback channels as if the inner room were "acoustically transparent," that is, as if the listening space had no effect on the acoustics of the illusory acoustic space. A practical alternative interpretation of the room-within-a-room model is to treat the outer walls of the inner room as absorbing surfaces, causing them to cast acoustic "shadows" by absorbing sound rays that strike them. This interpretation allows the inner room to affect the acoustics of the illusory acoustic space in a useful way by effectively modeling the loudspeakers as "holes" (apertures) in the walls of the inner room *through* which we

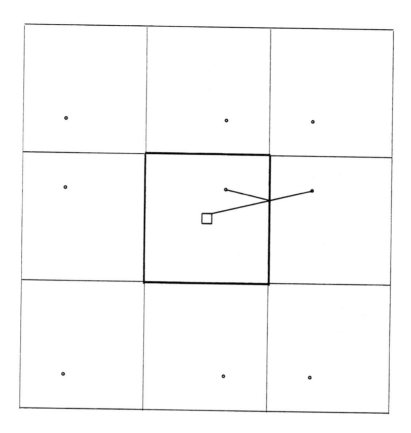

Figure 4-18. Finding reflection points using phantom sources. The phantom sources associated with the virtual source in the outer room (heavy rectangle) are located at positions found by reflecting the image of the outer room across each of its edges. The straight line between the phantom source and the loudspeaker shown defines the reflection point on the wall where angles of incidence and reflection will be equal.

hear the sounds in the outer "illusory" acoustic space. The advantage of this interpretation is that it creates an acoustical situation for listeners inside the listening space that differentiates among sounds coming from every possible position in the outer room, including, for example, weak front-back distinctions even when a stereophonic loudspeaker playback configuration is used.

The sound ray paths shown in Figure 4-19 include only *first-order* ("single bounce") reflections. By extending the phantom source grid, it is possible to extend this processing model to *n*th-order reflections as well. The utility of higher-order reflections is determined by two factors: their amplitude and their delays. Once these delays reach the echo threshold (beyond about 100 milliseconds), they no longer contribute information to the subjective localization of the virtual sound source itself. Instead, they begin to contribute information about the directionality of distinct echoes coming from various reflection points along the walls, with the possible effect of confounding the subjective

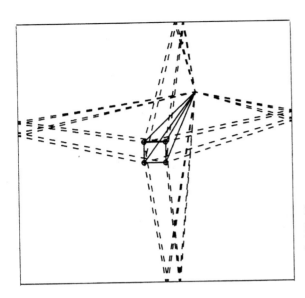

Figure 4-19   Direct and reflected ray
paths for a single virtual sound source and
four channels of loudspeaker playback.
There are one direct path and four reflected
ray paths for each of four loudspeakers, for
a total of 20 ray paths.

determination of the position of the virtual sound source. Second higher-order
reflections (resulting from more than one bounce) tend to be more greatly attenuated by
the distance law in effect, which also tends to reduce their perceptibility in any case.
Even though individual higher-order reflections may be quite small in amplitude,
however, their *density* grows exponentially over time, allowing their sum to add a perceptually significant component to the reverberant tail of a sound.

   The sound ray paths derived from this room-within-a-room model define an early
echo response that may be implemented in the form of a tapped delay line (FIR filter) in
which the delays and gains of the taps are determined by the lengths of associated direct
or reflective sound ray paths. Given a list of delays and gains derived from ray-tracing
considerations such as those shown in Figure 4-19, the FIR filter structure in Figure 4-
20 could easily be implemented by repeated calls to the `interp_delay` program
described in section 4.2.5 or its equivalent.

   If one were interested in determining the acoustic characteristics of a real room, it
would be important to take such factors as the reflections' dependency on frequency and
angle into account. This could be done by replacing the gain factor on each tap of the
FIR filter by a filter that accounts for frequency and angle-dependency on a reflection-
by-reflection basis. In the case of sound spatialization, however, it is unclear that the
inclusion of these factors would enhance the clarity of the localization information
presented to the listener.

   By contrast, the selection of dimensions for the inner and outer rooms, for example, can have a significant effect on the strength of the subjective cues presented to
the listener. If we wish to limit the overall duration of the early echo response to, say,
100 milliseconds in order to keep it within the limit of the echo threshold, then the
length of the longest possible reflected path may not exceed a delay value of $R/10$ samples, where R is the sampling rate. A convenient way to ensure this is to choose the

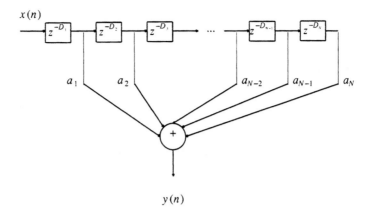

Figure 4-20 Tapped delay line (FIR filter) model of the early echo response. Direct and reflected sound ray paths (such as those shown in Figure 4-19) define the delays (D_i) and gains (a_i) associated with each tap according to the speed of sound and the law that associated intensity with distance.

dimensions of the outer room so that the longest first-order reflection ray path is no longer in time than the desired maximum value.

We may choose either the longest possible ray path for any virtual source location or the longest ray path that occurs for a given set of virtual source locations. The longest possible reflective ray path occurs when the virtual sound source is located maximally distant from any of the loudspeaker positions. Assuming that the outer and inner rooms are both squares measuring O and I meters on a side, respectively, then setting O so that the longest possible reflective ray path, as shown in Figure 4-21, is T seconds, we may solve the triangle involved to obtain the exact relation

$$T = \frac{\sqrt{2.5O^2 - IO + 0.5I^2}}{c} \tag{4-31}$$

which is approximately equal to

$$T \approx \frac{1.58O}{c} \tag{4-32}$$

if I is small compared with O. Solving Equation (4-32) for O yields

$$O \approx \frac{cT}{1.58} \tag{4-33}$$

Equation (4-33) suggests that if we wish to have a maximum reflective ray path delay of 100 milliseconds, we need an outer room approximately 22 meters on a side. An outer room dimension larger than this would create the possibility of reflections that fall outside of the subjectively early echo response range.

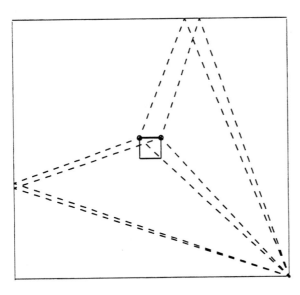

Figure 4-21   Finding the longest reflective ray path. For a given configuration of inner and outer room geometries, the longest possible reflective ray path generally occurs when the virtual sound source is maximally distant from any of the loudspeaker positions, such as in a corner of the outer room.

4.4 REVERBERATION

The output of the early echo response filter contains most of the directional information for a virtual sound source located at an arbitrary position in the illusory acoustic space in the outer room. In addition, it contains the intensity cue information related to the distances along the direct and reflected ray paths. The reverberant sound field in a real room consists of reflections that gradually increase in density over time according to the square of the time elapsed after a sound source begins to radiate sound into the room according to Cremer (1948):

$$\rho = \frac{4\pi c^3}{V} t^2 \tag{4-34}$$

where ρ is the number of reflections per second, c is the speed of sound, V is the volume of the room, and t is time in seconds. Once the density of the reflections becomes great enough, they begin to overlap in their time of arrival at all points in the room, indicating that the concept of an individual reflection has little meaning beyond the time when this overlap begins to occur. By considering a sound pulse of time width Δt, equation (4-34) suggests that this overlap begins to occur at a time

$$t_c = 5 \times 10^{-5}\sqrt{V/\Delta t} \tag{4-35}$$

where V is measured in cubic meters. Equation (4-35) indicates that even for pulses as short as 1 millisecond, this overlap begins to occur in a room with a volume of 10,000 cubic meters after about 150 milliseconds. For most sounds, the overlap begins even sooner, indicating that we may normally treat dense reverberation (reflections occurring at a rate high enough so that they may only be characterized statistically) as beginning by the end of the early echo response.

To simulate the dense reverberation that occurs in rooms, Schroeder (1961, 1962) and others (Schroeder and Logan, 1961) have suggested the use of both *comb filters* and *allpass reverberators*. We now consider the properties of these filters.

4.4.1 Comb Filters

The comb filter shown in Figure 4-22 has the difference equation

$$y(n) = x(n - D) + gy(n - D)$$ (4-36)

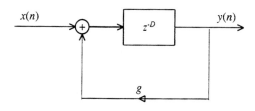

(comb filter)

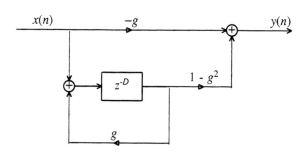

(allpass reverberation filter)

Figure 4-22   Comb and allpass filters for simulating dense reverberation. The comb filter (upper figure) consists of a simple feedback loop around a delay of D samples using a feedback loop gain of g (g must of course be less than 1 for the filter to be stable). The unity-gain allpass reverberator (after Schroeder; lower figure) consists of a comb filter embedded in a network that feeds forward a portion of the direct (input) signal (through a path with gain $-g$) combined with a portion of the comb-filtered signal (through a path with gain $1 - g^2$).

The impulse response of this filter clearly consists of an impulse delayed by D samples, followed by an impulse delayed by D samples and scaled by g, followed by another impulse D samples later scaled by g^2, and so on, according to

$$h(n) = u(n - D) + gu(n - 2D) + g^2 u(n - 3D) + \cdots$$ (4-37)

Thus we see the comb filter to be similar to a tape loop delay echo. As long as the feedback gain is less than 1, the impulse response consists of a series of repeating echoes that occur every D/R seconds, each of which is a factor of g weaker in amplitude than the previous one.

The z transform of the comb filter impulse response is easily written by inspection of the difference equation:

$$H(z) = \frac{z^{-D}}{1 - gz^{-D}}$$ (4-38)

The amplitude of the frequency response is then found by setting $z = e^{j\omega}$ and taking the magnitude of the result:

$$|H(e^{j\omega})| = \frac{1}{\sqrt{1 - 2g\cos\omega D + g^2}} \tag{4-39}$$

equation (4-39) shows how the frequency response of the comb filter varies with frequency. When the quantity $\cos\omega D$ is at its maximum (+1, which occurs whenever $\omega D = n\,2\pi$, where n is any integer), the denominator of equation (4-39) is clearly

$$\sqrt{1 - 2g + g^2} = 1 - g \tag{4-40}$$

When $\cos\omega D$ is at its minimum (−1, which occurs whenever $\omega D = (2n + 1)\pi$, where n is any integer), the same denominator is

$$\sqrt{1 + 2g + g^2} = 1 + g \tag{4-41}$$

The magnitude of the frequency response therefore swings periodically between

$$H_{max} = \frac{1}{1 - g} \tag{4-42}$$

and

$$H_{min} = \frac{1}{1 + g} \tag{4-43}$$

The ratio of the maxima to the minima is then given by

$$\frac{H_{max}}{H_{min}} = \frac{1 + g}{1 - g} \tag{4-44}$$

Equation (4-44) shows that for a loop gain of 0.7 (≈ -3 dB), the comb filter frequency response varies over a range of $1.7/0.3 = 5.666\ldots$, or about 15 dB (see Figure 4-23).

The loop gain of a comb filter determines not only the peak-to-valley ratio of the magnitude frequency response but the decay time of the impulse response (for a given loop delay) as well. Because the input signal is attenuated by a factor g each time it circulates once around the D-sample loop and because D samples represent a temporal extent of D/R seconds (where R is the sampling rate), we see that the time for the output of the comb filter to die away by a factor of 60 dB is given by

$$T_{60} = \frac{60}{-\gamma}\tau \quad \text{sec} \tag{4-45}$$

where $\gamma = 20\log g$ (the loop gain expressed in decibels), and $\tau = D/R$ (the loop delay expressed in seconds). For example, if $\gamma = -3$ dB (that is, $g \approx 0.7$), then $T_{60} = 20\tau$, indicating that the signal will decay by 60 dB after circulating through the loop 20 times. A reverberation time of 2 seconds would then require a loop delay τ of 0.1 second, corresponding to an echo rate ("echo density") of 10 per second.

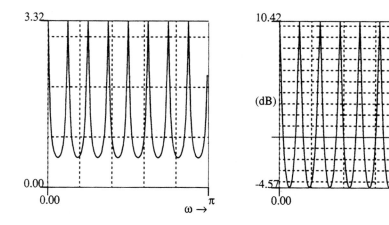

Figure 4-23 Frequency response for a comb filter with a delay D of 16 samples and a loop gain g of 0.7. The left figure shows the plot of the magnitude of the frequency response plotted on a linear scale; the right figure shows the same plot on a decibel scale. The shape of this response is the source of the name of the filter.

4.4.2 Allpass Reverberation Filters

The filter equation of the allpass reverberation filter is also easily written by inspection of its flow diagram:

$$y(n) = -gx(n) + (1 - g^2)[x(n - D) + gy(n - D)] \tag{4-46}$$

from which its impulse response is easily seen to be

$$h(n) = -gu(n) + (1 - g^2)[u(n - D) + gu(n - 2D) + \cdots] \tag{4-47}$$

In words, the impulse response of this filter consists of an impulse of height $-g$, followed D samples later by one of height $1 - g^2$, followed D samples later by one of height $g(1 - g^2)$, followed D samples later by one of height $g^2(1 - g^2)$, and so on.

The z transform of this impulse response is

$$H(z) = -g + (1 - g^2)\frac{z^{-D}}{1 - gz^{-D}}$$

$$= \frac{z^{-D} - g}{1 - gz^{-D}} \tag{4-48}$$

$$= z^{-D}\frac{1 - gz^{D}}{1 - gz^{-D}}$$

Setting $z = e^{j\omega}$ in the last form yields

$$H(e^{j\omega}) = e^{-j\omega D}\frac{1 - ge^{j\omega D}}{1 - ge^{-j\omega D}} \tag{4-49}$$

Because we can easily show that

$$| e^{-j\omega D} | = 1 \tag{4-50}$$

and

$$\left| \frac{1 - g e^{j\omega D}}{1 - g e^{-j\omega D}} \right| = 1 \tag{4-51}$$

this filter is seen to be allpass with unity gain at all frequencies, that is

$$| H(e^{j\omega}) | = 1 \tag{4-52}$$

Unlike the comb filter on which it is based, the allpass reverberation filter has a perfectly uniform frequency response. Of course, the phase response of any IIR filter is nonlinear, and this filter is no exception. We can easily show that

$$\phi = \text{pha}\,[H(e^{j\omega})] = \omega D + 2\tan^{-1}\frac{g \sin\omega D}{1 - g\cos\omega D} \tag{4-53}$$

By definition, the derivative with respect to frequency of the phase response is the group delay as a function of frequency, which we may think of as the time it takes for the filter to respond to inputs as a function of frequency:

$$\frac{d\phi}{d\omega} = D\frac{1 - g^2}{1 - 2g\cos\omega D + g^2} \tag{4-54}$$

The denominator of equation (4-54) indicates that the group delay of the allpass reverberation filter exhibits the same comblike behavior as a function of frequency as the magnitude-squared frequency response of the comb filter.

Thus we see that while the comb filter provides a frequency-specific magnitude response, the allpass reverberation filter provides a similarly frequency-specific group delay. As their impulse responses demonstrate, the echolike characteristics of the comb and allpass reverberation filters are essentially the same. To simulate dense reverberation using either type of filter, therefore, we need to combine several of them, either by feeding the output of one filter into the next (cascade connection), by summing the outputs of several filters operating simultaneously (parallel connection), or both. In either case, the delays of the combined filters should be incommensurate so that the echo distribution is as uncorrelated in time as possible. Schroeder and Logan (1961), for example, found after "considerable experimentation observing the response to a variety of sounds" that a cascade of five allpass reverberation filters with delays of 100, 68, 60, 19.7, and 5.85 milliseconds combined with loop gains of 0.7, −0.7, 0.7, 0.7, and 0.7, respectively, produced an echo response that was "quite random" and "not unlike that of real rooms," at least with respect to the distribution of echoes in time.

4.4.3 Frequency Dependence

Of course, the simulation of dense reverberation using allpass filters alone results in a sound that is quite *unlike* that of real rooms in the sense that the reverberation time is independent of frequency. Other difficulties with this type of reverberation, noticed by Moorer (1979) and others, include the fact that the decay may not be dense enough at first, it may not die away in an exponential manner, the response is critically dependent on the precise choices not only of the delay and gain parameters but also their order of occurrence in a cascade connection, and the fact that the reverberant sound may exhibit ringing at frequencies related to the loop delays and that such ringing also depends critically on the spectrum of the signal being reverberated. Although the theory of digital filtering usually allows us to find the source of such difficulties, it does not generally allow us to predict which configurations will sound good under all conditions. The design of good-sounding artificial reverberators therefore remains more an art than a science.

One approach to dealing with the unnaturally flat response of allpass reverberation filters is to use filters with frequency-dependent feedback loops, making the overall reverberation time depend on frequency. Because we are trying to create a filtering network with a nonuniform frequency response, the allpass reverberation filter has no particular advantage over the simpler comb filter as a basic element in a reverberator.

The simplest possible comb filter with the simplest possible IIR lowpass filter inserted in its feedback loop is shown in Figure 4-24. Of course, we would be remiss not to remark immediately on the similarity of the basic filter structure shown in Figure 4-24 to the one used as the basis for the plucked string synthesis algorithm discussed in Chapter 3.[7]

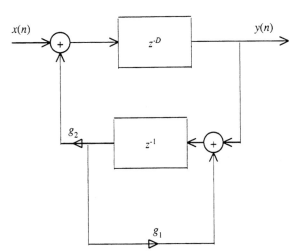

Figure 4-24   Comb filters with a lowpass feedback loop. Gain g_1 controls the lowpass filter; gain g_2 controls the overall loop gain of the comb filter. For stability, the magnitude of the quantity $g_2/(1 - g_1)$ must be less than 1.

As we saw in Chapter 2, the simple first-order filter in the feedback loop has the z transform

$$H(z) = \frac{1}{1 - g_1 z^{-1}} \qquad (4\text{-}55)$$

[7]The only difference between these filter structures is that the comb filter for reverberation uses an IIR lowpass filter in the feedback loop for the purpose of simulating the frequency dependence of reverberation time in rooms, whereas the plucked string synthesis algorithm uses an FIR lowpass filter in the feedback loop for the purpose of simulating the frequency dependence of decay time in string tones.

For this filter to be lowpass, g_1 must be positive; for it to be stable, g_1 must be less than 1. The maximum gain of this lowpass filter occurs, of course, at 0 Hz, where it is equal to

$$|H(e^{j0})| = \frac{1}{\sqrt{1 - 2g_1\cos 0 + g_1^2}} = \frac{1}{1 - g_1} \qquad (4\text{-}56)$$

If we call the overall loop gain g, we see that it is the product of the (frequency-dependent) loop filter gain and the factor g_2. By setting g_2 according to

$$g = \frac{g_2}{1 - g_1} \qquad (4\text{-}57)$$

(where g is less than 1), we are assured that the overall filter is stable at all frequencies. If g_1 is set to 0, the overall structure reduces to a simple comb filter. The nearer g_1 is set to 1, the more rapidly high frequencies are attenuated with respect to low frequencies. We may choose to set g_1 according to physical considerations (we may wish to model the absorption of high frequencies by air or the relatively greater absorption at higher frequencies of most building materials, for example), or we may simply set it according to some desired overall behavior of an "ideal" concert hall or to achieve relatively "bright" or "warm" reverberation. Whatever value is used for g_1, g_2 is then set, according to equation (4-57), at $g(1 - g_1)$ to assure overall filter stability.

4.4.4 Dense Reverberation

Extensive experimentation (Moorer, 1979) with lowpass comb filters indicates that they can provide a reasonable simulation of dense reverberation when several are operated in parallel, then summed into a single allpass output filter (see Figure 4-25). In this case, the parallel lowpass comb filters provide the basic dense echo pattern, while the allpass filter provides a frequency-dependent delay for the entire pattern, effectively "smearing" the pattern slightly in time. A feedforward path is also used to provide an adjustable measure of direct sound at the output (gains on this path and the output of the allpass stage may be used to control the relative proportions of direct and reverberated sound). Fewer than six lowpass comb filters operated in parallel seem to fail to provide the requisite echo density, but further improvement seems inaudible for more than about six. Representative values of lowpass comb filter delays and g_1 are shown in Table 4-3.

One of the advantages of using allpass reverberation filters to process the output of the bank of lowpass comb filters is that multiple allpass reverberation filters may be used to decorrelate the reverberation signal appearing in the playback channels. For example, by replacing the single output allpass reverberation filter in Figure 4-25 with several nearly identical such filters feeding each playback channel, the reverberant signal coming from the lowpass comb filter bank will be "smeared" in time in slightly different ways in each of the playback channels.

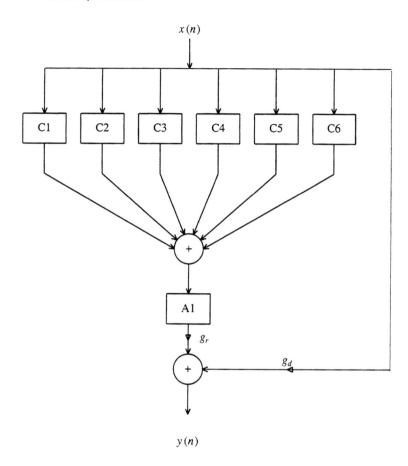

$x(n)$

$y(n)$

Figure 4-25 Combining lowpass comb and allpass filters to achieve reverberation. Six parallel lowpass comb filters (C1 through C6; see Figure 4-24) are operated in parallel with their summed outputs fed into a single allpass reverberation filter (A1). Gains g_d and g_r allow the relative proportions of direct and reverberated sound to be adjusted. Some appropriate filter parameter settings for this configuration are shown in Table 4-3.

4.5 SOUND SPATIALIZATION

Given the processing models and tools we have discussed so far, it is possible to build a practical multichannel sound spatializer that essentially allows us to place an arbitrary sound into an arbitrary (possibly time-varying) location within an illusory acoustic space that we hear but do not see.

Figure 4-26 shows the elements of a four-channel sound spatialization system (stereophonic playback would require only the processing for the first two channels). The input signal $x(n)$ is ideally anechoic, such as one that would result from a synthesis algorithm or a concrete sound that has been digitally recorded in an acoustic environment that is as "dry" as possible.

TABLE 4-3 Representative delay and g_1 gain values
for a six-lowpass comb filter reverberator operated at
25 kHz and 50 kHz sampling rates (after Moorer, 1979).
Six lowpass comb filters are operated in parallel with their
outputs summed into a single allpass filter stage with a
delay of about 6 milliseconds and a loop gain of about
0.7. The values of g_2 for the lowpass comb filters are
derived from those of g_1 according to $g_2 = g(1 - g_1)$,
where setting g to about 0.83 results in about a
2-second overall reverberation time for the delays and
gains shown here.

Filter	Delay	25 kHz	50 kHz
	(ms)	g_1	g_1
1	50	0.24	0.46
2	56	0.26	0.48
3	61	0.28	0.50
4	68	0.29	0.52
5	72	0.30	0.53
6	78	0.32	0.55

This signal is processed differently for each playback channel through an FIR filter that has tap delays and gains set according to the inner and outer room model. The delays and gains of each of the taps for these FIR filters represent propagation delays and distance attenuation factors derived from the relative positions of a specified virtual sound source location and the location of the loudspeaker for each playback channel. For example, the FIR filter for channel 1 has taps at delay values determined by the distances along direct and low-order reflective ray paths between the virtual source location and the location of the loudspeaker for channel 1 (by our convention, the right-front loudspeaker in the inner room). The attenuation for each tap is determined by applying whatever distance law is chosen, typically either an inverse square law or an inverse cube law.

Each FIR filter provides a portion of the early echo response of the outer room that is formed by summing the outputs of all FIR filter outputs. The dimensions of the outer room should be chosen so that the overall duration of this early echo response is approximately 80 to 100 milliseconds for most of the virtual source locations specified. If virtual source locations do not change over time, it is preferable to round the delays to the nearest integral sample value. For changing virtual source locations, some form of interpolation is generally needed in the FIR filters to avoid clicks. Linear interpolation is the most convenient and computationally efficient to apply and usually works well enough in practice.

Another option in the formation of the early echo response involves modeling the acoustic shadowing effect of the inner room. If a ray path cuts through the inner room, it may be either deleted for fixed virtual source locations or gradually attenuated for moving virtual source locations (once again, gradual attenuation is needed to avoid clicks). Such gradual attenuation may be implemented by associating a *cut factor* with

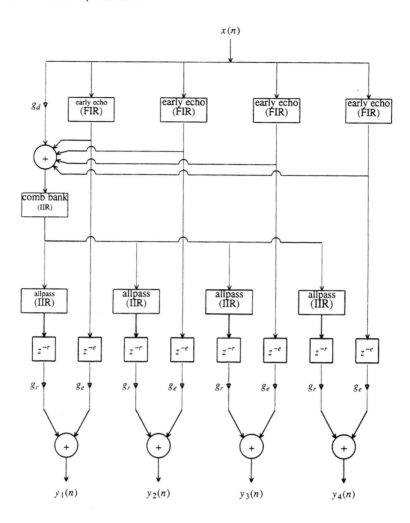

Figure 4-26 A four-channel sound spatialization system. A source sound $x(n)$ is fed to a separate FIR filter for each channel. These FIR filters provide early echo responses according to the relative positions of the virtual sound source and loudspeaker for each channel. The source sound and early echo responses are summed for processing by the bank of lowpass comb filters that produce dense reverberation. The dense reverberation signal is decorrelated by slightly different allpass reverberation filters for each channel. Delay and gain stages are used to time-align and balance the early echo responses with the dense reverberation signals, which are then summed for output to the four loudspeakers.

each ray path—when the ray path cuts through the inner room, the cut factor is set to 0 for the associated path. A separate *cut attenuation factor* may then be gradually decreased toward 0 if it is nonzero and the associated cut factor is zero or gradually increased toward 1 if the associated cut factor is 1 and the cut attenuation factor is less than 1.

The outputs of the FIR filters are added together to form the overall early echo response of the outer room. This overall response is also added to the direct sound (optionally scaled by a gain factor marked g_d in the figure) to form the input signal for the global reverberator, which consists of a bank of parallel lowpass comb filters as discussed earlier.

The output of the lowpass comb filter bank is distributed to a separate allpass reverberation filter for each channel. By configuring these allpass filters so that their responses are not quite identical, a slightly different version of the global reverberation signal is prepared for each output channel. The purpose of this slight difference is to ensure that the global reverberation signals in each channel are well decorrelated from each other.

The response of the comb-allpass global reverberator generally takes some time to build up to a significant amplitude. If this time is significantly longer than about 80 milliseconds, a constant delay can be inserted into the early echo signal path for each channel so that the end of the early echo response coincides properly in time with the beginning of the dense reverberation. If the dense reverberation takes significantly less than 80 milliseconds or so to build up, its output can be delayed so that the dense reverberation starts around the end of the early echo response signal coming from the FIR filters. Delays for these purposes are marked z^{-r} (reverberation delay) and z^{-e} (early echo delay) in Figure 4-26—usually only one of these delays is needed for a given global reverberator configuration. Similarly, the overall amplitude of the dense reverberation signal may be balanced with that of the early echo response signal by adjusting the (optional) fixed gains marked g_r and g_e.

Finally, let us consider the restrictions on the virtual source locations that may be specified. We must exercise caution in the precise formulation of the distance law to be used. Because we measure distances between virtual source locations and loudspeakers, we must decide how to handle virtual sources very near the loudspeaker positions. For example, if we use a simple $1/D$ formulation (where D is the distance between the virtual source and the loudspeaker) for the inverse square law pertaining to amplitude, virtual sources located precisely on top of loudspeakers would imply infinite FIR filter tap gains—clearly an undesirable situation! Probably the simplest solution to this problem is to approximate the inverse square law using the formula $1/(1 + D)$, which ensures that the maximum tap gain is unity rather than infinity. Similarly, the inverse cube law can be approximated with the amplitude relation $1/(1 + D^{3/2})$.

It is also desirable to have a way to deal with inadvertent or intentional specifications of virtual source locations located *inside* the inner room in order to avoid forbidden zones. A useful technique is to treat virtual sources located inside the inner room in exactly the same way as those outside it, except for global reverberation. When a virtual source is specified within the inner room, about the best that can be done seems to be to calculate the relevant distances to the loudspeakers as usual while shutting off the early echo and direct signal inputs (*gradually*, if the virtual source is moving) to the global reverberator. The output of the global reverberator will die away, as if the virtual sound source has left the illusory acoustic space (which it has!), as long as the virtual source location remains within the inner room. This processing trick is especially effective for virtual sound sources that move through the inner room at a fairly good clip, because the momentary disappearance of the global reverberation can sometimes provide the subjective impression that the sound source is closer to the listener than the nearest boundary of the illusory acoustic space.

4.5.1 The `space` Unit Generator

The cmusic program contains an experimental unit generator that implements most aspects of the processing model for sound spatialization described in this chapter. This is the general form of the `space` unit generator statement:

```
#include <carl/cmusic.h>

SPACE(input[b],1) RV* ;
```

where

```
RV = x[bvpn] y[bvpn] theta[bvpn] amp[bvpn] back[bvpn]
```

The `space` unit generator effectively replaces the `out` unit generator in an instrument definition. The `input` parameter is an input-output block representing a digital waveform to be spatialized—it is typically the output of a main oscillator or similar sound source (the 1 following the input specification is an experimental flag that has no function relevant to our discussion here). The `SPACE` macro definition includes a number of dynamic variables (d-type parameters) used to hold internal state information for the `space` unit generator.

The RV notation in the general statement stands for a *radiation vector* consisting of five pieces of information specifying the *x*- and *y*-coordinates in the outer room (in meters), a radiation direction called `theta` (given in radians), an amplitude scalar called `amp`, and a `back` radiation parameter specifying the relative strength of the radiation in the direction *opposite* to `theta`. For example, a radiation vector of

```
10 20 270Deg 1 1
```

specifies that the virtual sound source is to be located at position (10, 20), radiating in a direction pointing south (when viewed from above), with an amplitude scalar of unity, and a radiation in a northerly direction equal to that in a southerly direction (in effect, this specifies that the virtual sound source is *omnidirectional*). If the back radiation is less than 1, the `space` unit generator computes a "hypercardiod" amplitude radiation vector similar to the one shown in Figure 4-3 to find the relative amounts of radiation in all directions. More than one radiation vector may be given, indicating that the sound is to radiate from multiple positions in the illusory acoustic space simultaneously.

The remaining parameters, such as the sizes of the inner and outer rooms and the overall reverberation time, are specified with cmusic `set` commands (see Appendix D).

The `space` unit generator provides a simple user interface to the rather complicated spatialization processing model described in this chapter. Effectively, the cmusic user only has to specify a wish regarding the position of one or more virtual sound sources in an illusory acoustic space; the space unit generator then attempts to make the user's wish come true.

For example, the following cmusic score demonstrates how the `space` unit generator can be used to spatialize a note event lasting 4 seconds, during which the virtual sound source moves in a circular path centered about point (0, 20). The circle has a radius of 10 meters. The virtual sound source takes 2 seconds to complete one circular movement. Notice that some silence must be included at the end of the score to allow time for the global reverberation to die away.

```
#include <carl/cmusic.h>

set stereo ;            {set number of output channels}
set revscale = .1 ;     {relative strength of global reverb}
set t60 = 3 ;           {reverb time in seconds}
set cutoff = -60dB ;    {stop computation when amplitude of}
                        {reverb tail is very small}

ins 0 one;
    seg  b4 p5 f4 d .1sec 0 .1sec ; {amplitude envelope}
    osc  b5 b4 p10 f5 d ;           {amplitude modulator}
    osc  b2 p7 p8 f2 d ;            {time varying x-coordinate}
    osc  b3 p7 p9 f3 d ;            {time varying y-coordinate}
    adn  b3 b3 p11 ;                {offset to center of circle}
    osc  b1 b5 p6 f1 d ;            {main oscillator}
    SPACE(b1,1) b2 b3 0 1 0dB ;     {omni source-theta doesn't matter}
end;

SAWTOOTH(f1) ;
SINE(f2) ;
COS(f3) ;
GEN1(f4) 0,0 1/3,1 2/3,1 1,0 ;
PULSE(f5) ;
GEN3(f6) 3/4 -1/4 ;

note 0 one 4 0dB 440Hz 10 2sec 2sec 11Hz 20 ;

sec ;

ter 4 ; {allow 4 seconds for global reverb to die away}
```

Although the `space` unit generator does not provide a completely general spatialization facility, it has been found to be very useful in many of the compositions done to date with cmusic, such as *The Vanity of Words* by Roger Reynolds and *Study in White* by Joji Yuasa.

4.6 OTHER ISSUES

Two factors left out of our sound spatialization processor are the frequency and angle dependence of reflections and the frequency and angle dependence of the ear due to the shape of the outer ears, or *pinnae*. As previously mentioned, it would be possible to include filters to provide frequency- or angle-dependent tap gains for the early echo response. However, it is also clear that such filtering operations are computationally expensive, and it is questionable whether they actually improve the subjective impression of the location of the virtual sound source, especially when the result is heard over loudspeakers.

Pinna cues can be very useful, however, especially in cases where the result is heard over headphones and again especially if the headphones are of the binaural type that inject sound well into the listener's ear canals. Pinna cues also appear to be about the only ones available for suggesting virtual sound sources above or below the horizontal plane.

The pinnae operate by imposing a weak, direction-dependent filtering operation on sounds as they enter the ear canal. This filterlike response of the ear has been measured in a variety of ways by numerous investigators, many of whom are reviewed by Blauert (1983). Unfortunately, the details of this process are quite complicated and go well beyond the scope of this book. It does appear, however, that under some circumstances, simulated pinna cues may be used to impart a sense of direction, including elevation, to spatialized sounds.

Finally, we should not ignore the potential applicability of convolution to the spatialization of sound, especially for capturing particular qualities of reverberation that exist in the real world. If we find a hallway, a tunnel, a deep well, or any other acoustical enclosure with a reverberant quality of particular charm, a good digital recording of its impulse response can transform that charm into a potential setting for any sound. Of course, such an impulse response would contain a complete copy of the reverberant sound quality as produced by an impulsive sound source in a particular location and measured with a microphone in another particular location, including the early echo response and reverberant tail in one hermetic whole. Nevertheless, the FFT-based fast convolution program described in Chapter 2 could easily be applied to reverberation at a computational cost that is likely to be on the same order of magnitude as that required for the spatial processing model discussed in this chapter.

4.7 ROOMS: SUMMARY

We almost never hear sounds, especially musical sounds, in an anechoic acoustical environment. The typically reverberant environment in which most sound is heard affects not only the overall impression of music on a listener but the detailed manner in which performers execute musical directives and intentions as well.

The subject of rooms, then, is a metaphor for a consideration of the acoustical environment in which we are constantly immersed. We hear musical sounds not only in terms of their pitch, loudness, and timbre but also in terms of their direction and distance. In addition, we form an overall impression of the dimensions and physical nature of any enclosed space we may enter by listening to its characteristic sound.

Concert halls are rooms designed to enhance the sound of music. The main characteristics of rooms that have been identified as closely linked with their suitability for musical performance include such factors as overall reverberation time, "flutter echoes" that do not blend into the overall reverberant sound of the room, spectrum balance of the direct and reverberated sound that reaches the listener, and interaural coherence of the reverberant sound. Early studies of concert hall acoustics did not take the detailed geometry of rooms and their contents into account and consequently fail to provide accurate predictions regarding these subjectively important factors. Recent techniques based on computer ray tracing promise to provide valuable tools for the architectural acoustician.

In computer music applications, we are typically less interested in simulating a particular room than in imparting controllable spatial qualities to synthesized or digitally processed musical sounds. This spatialization of sound rests on understanding how our perceptual mechanism forms impressions about the direction and distance of a sound source and processing the digitized musical signal in such a way as to simulate perceptual cues. This allows specification of direction and distance to become a part of the musical aspect of sounds to the extent that we are able to succeed in making such wishes come true.

The principal perceptual cue for both direction and distance is sound intensity. A multichannel playback system consisting of several loudspeakers surrounding a listener can be manipulated by apportioning various intensities to the different loudspeakers in ways that can suggest virtual sound sources located in places where no loudspeaker is present. Properly done, intensity panning can provide a powerful cue suggesting changes in sound direction. The perceived distance to a sound source is also strongly affected by its intensity, combined with our familiarity with the sound source. By combining timbral and intensity information, for example, we are able to distinguish fairly well between a soft sound coming from a nearby location and a loud sound coming from far away, especially for familiar sources. For unfamiliar sources, however, the subjective loudness of the sound (rather than its physical intensity) seems to be a primary distance cue. Another example of a familiar cue is the Doppler shift associated with sources of sound that are in motion relative to the listener. Small differences in the time at which sound arrives at the two ears can also provide cues about the direction from which a sound emanates. However, it is nearly impossible to exploit this cue when sounds are presented to listeners over loudspeakers rather than headphones.

A useful and practical sound spatialization system can be devised by combining information from the realms of architectural and psychological acoustics with digital signal processing techniques. The main elements of the resulting processing model are an FIR filtering stage that simulates the early echo response of an imaginary acoustical enclosure inside which sound sources can be spatially manipulated, together with an IIR filtering stage that simulates dense reverberation. By manipulating the parameters of this processing model, it is possible to gain control over the spatial aspects of musical sound, thereby allowing musically expressive gestures to be composed out of space as well as time.

REFERENCES

1. D. R. Begault, *Control of Auditory Distance*, doctoral dissertation, Department of Music, University of California, San Diego (1987).

2. G. von Békésy, "Über die Entstehung der Entfernungsempfindung beim Hören" [On the origin of the sensation of distance in hearing], *Akustika Zeitung 3* (1938): 21–31.

3. J. Blauert, *Spatial Hearing*, (MIT Press, Cambridge, Mass., 1983).

4. J. Chowning, "The Simulation of Moving Sound Sources," *J. Aud. Eng. Soc. 199*, (1971):2–6.

5. L. Cremer, *Die wissenschaftlichen Grundlagen der Raumakustik* [The scientific foundations of architectural acoustics], vol. 1 (Hirzel Verlag, Stuttgart, 1948).

6. R. E. Crochiere and L. R. Rabiner, *Multirate Digital Signal Processing* (Prentice-Hall, Englewood Cliffs, N.J., 1983).

7. M. B. Gardner, "Distance Estimation of 0° or Apparent 0°-oriented Speech Signals in Anechoic Space," *J. Acoust. Soc. Amer. 45* (1969): 47–53.

8. E. N. Gilbert, "An Iterative Calculation of Reverberation," *J. Acoust. Soc. Amer. 69* (1981): 178–184.

9. E. M. von Hornbostol, "Das räumliche Hören" [Spatial hearing], in Bethe et al. (eds), *Handbuch der normalen und pathologischen Psychologie* [Handbook of normal and abnormal psychology], Vol. 2 (Springer-Verlag, Berlin, 1926), pp. 601–608.

10. V. O. Knudsen and C. M. Harris, *Acoustical Designing in Architecture*, (American Institute of Physics, 1978).

11. F. R. Moore, "A General Model for Spatial Processing of Sounds," *Computer Music J.* (Fall 1983): 6–15.

12. ——— *Spatialization of Sounds over Loudspeakers*, (System Development Foundation, 1988).

13. J. A. Moorer, "About This Reverberation Business," *Computer Music J. 3* (June 1979): 13–28.

14. J. R. Pierce, *The Science of Musical Sound* (Freeman, New York, 1983).

15. A. D. Pierce, *Acoustics: An Introduction to Its Physical Principles and Applications* (McGraw-Hill, New York, 1981).

16. M. R. Schroeder, "Improved Quasi-stereophony and Colorless Artificial Reverberation," *J. Aud. Eng. Soc. 33* (1961): 1061.

17. ——— "Natural-sounding Artificial Reverberation," *J. Aud. Eng. Soc. 10* (1962): 219–223.

18. ——— *Number Theory in Science and Communication* (Springer-Verlag, Berlin, 1986).

19. ——— "Toward Better Acoustics for Concert Halls," *Physics Today 33* (October 1980): 24–30.

20. —— and B. F. Logan, " 'Colorless' Artificial Reverberation," *J. Aud. Eng. Soc.* *9* (1961): 192–197.

21. S. S. Stevens, "Neural Events and Psychophysical Law," *Science*, *170* (1970): 1043.

5

Composing

Side by side with the evolution of sound-painting runs the development of "dramatic" music in a more subjective sense—music that is intended, and taken, to be a language of feeling. Not silverware, nor even parades and thunderstorms, are the objects of musical representation here, but love and longing, hope and fear, the essence of tragedy and comedy. This is not "self-expression"; it is exposition of feelings which may be attributed to persons on the stage or fictitious characters in a ballad. In pure instrumental music without dramatic action, there may be a high emotional import which is not referred to any subject, and the glib assurance of some program writers that this is the composer's protest against life, cry of despair, vision of his beloved, or what not, is a perfectly unjustified fancy; for if music is really a language of emotion, it expresses primarily the composer's knowledge of human feeling, not how or when that knowledge was acquired; as his conversation presumably expresses his knowledge of more tangible things, and usually not his first experience of them.

—S. K. Langer, *Philosophy in a New Key*

(Harvard University Press, reprinted by permission)

We have defined traditional musical composition as the task of generating symbolic representations. These symbolic representations may be based on the musical thoughts of the composer, together with the composer's knowledge and insight into the entire set of musical processes. To produce effective compositions, composers must therefore *anticipate* reactions of performers, instruments, rooms, and listeners to given representations of particular musical thoughts. If there is such a thing as an error in composition, it is probably related to an error in anticipation, which is a form of prediction. Like all predictions, musical predictions sometimes fail. Anticipation errors do not always lead to diminishment of the musical results, though they may arguably lead to a diminishment of the composer's connection with them. In other words, not all accidents are bad. In fact, some composers have relied on them.

5.1 COMPUTER-MEDIATED COMPOSITION

The fundamental differences between composing with computers and without them may be many or few. Certainly, computers do not make the composition of music any easier for the composer, although they may assist in carrying out some of the more tedious chores. As with the production of musical sound, the main reason to use computers to mediate in the act of composition is to augment the ways in which musical possibilities may be explored.

Some of the more interesting possibilities for computer-mediated music composition are depicted in Figure 5-1. The links in the figure represent information flow. All links are optional, though one or more paths must connect the composer to the musical sound.

For example, starting with the box labeled "composer" in Figure 5-1, we may follow down the left side of the diagram to obtain the path: composer → score → performer(s) → traditional instrument(s) → musical sound → acoustic environment → listener(s). Of course, we recognize along this path the stages of traditional composition and performance of music.

The computer assistance process may be usefully incorporated in this chain in two ways. First, the composer may employ the computer as an aid in creating the score by writing a program and editing or otherwise revising its output. Similarly, the composer may write a program that generates the entire score with no further compositional intervention. The first case might be called the computer-assisted composer. The second is the computer-composer, operating according to the rules of composition determined by the composer. A significant example of the latter possibility may be found in the pioneering work of Lejaren Hiller, who wrote programs that composed most if not all of such scores as the *Illiac Suite for String Quartet* and *Computer Cantata*.

Taking another route from composer to sound leads to the path-composer (with or without compositional assistance from the computer) → software sound specification → software instrument(s) → DAC (digital-to-analog conversion) → musical sound → acoustic environment → listener(s). We recognize along this path the stages of direct digital sound synthesis as one might implement with a program such as cmusic. A significant option along this path is to include the link to sounds that have been recorded through an analog-to-digital conversion system (ADC), as well as the same two options for computer assistance in creating the sound specification as the composer might use in creating a score for performers playing traditional instruments. Significant examples of this method of operation may be found in such works as *Turenas* by John Chowning, which employs only purely synthesized sounds, or *Sud* by Jean-Claude

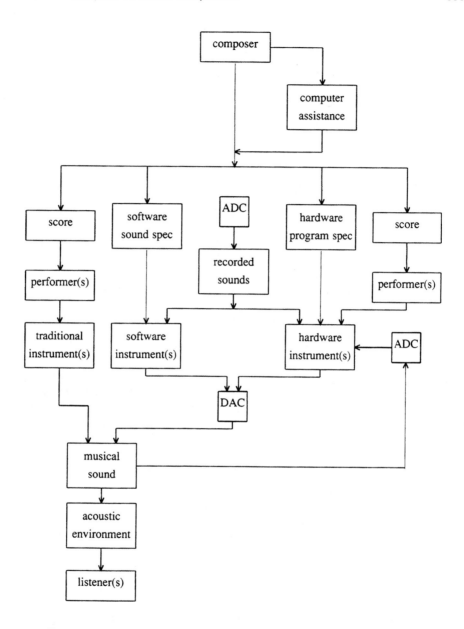

Figure 5-1   Computer-mediated music composition. The links in this diagram represent information flow. All links are optional, but one or more paths must connect the composer to the musical sound.

Risset and *The Vanity of Words* by Roger Reynolds, which are based on digitally processed sound materials obtained by recording natural sounds.

Other possibilities involve the use of specialized digital hardware that allows realtime sound synthesis. One route through the diagram essentially replaces the software specifications and instrument(s) with hardware, resulting in the path: composer (with or without compositional assistance from the computer) → hardware program specification → hardware instrument(s) → DAC (digital-to-analog conversion) → musical sound → acoustic environment → listener(s). One of the major advantages of this path is that the typical requirements of software synthesis for large amounts of sound data storage and nonrealtime operations can be avoided. The major disadvantages are due to the fact that the processing limitations and programming complexity imposed by particular realtime digital hardware can be severe. Once again, digitally recorded sound materials and computer assistance in the preparation of the hardware score may be used or not. Significant examples of works produced in this manner include those for the Systems Concepts realtime digital music synthesizer at the Center for Computer Research in Music and Acoustics (CCRMA) at Stanford University, such as *Silicon Valley Breakdown* by David Jaffe and *Nekyia* by Gareth Loy.

The final basic route once again involves human performers who "play" the digital synthesis or processing hardware in real time according to the path: composer (with or without compositional assistance from the computer) → score → live performer(s) → hardware instrument(s) → DAC (digital-to-analog conversion) → musical sound → acoustic environment → listener(s). In this case, the hardware instrument may require a special hardware program specification, or it may be possible to rely on built-in programs written outside the context of a particular work. One of the most significant options in the use of realtime hardware is that of processing live sounds that result either from digital synthesis or performance on one or more traditional instruments (this option is shown in Figure 5-1 as the optional link from the musical sound back to the hardware instrument(s) through an analog-to-digital conversion system). Some realtime digital synthesizers (the so-called sampling synthesizers) are specialized around the requirements of playing back digitally recorded sounds with variable pitch and loudness, while others are specialized around purely synthetic sound generation. Much popular commercial music is created in this general way, such as the *Security* album by Peter Gabriel.

These four basic methods are often combined in various ways. For example, *Reponse* by Pierre Boulez combines the programmable realtime processing capabilities of the so-called 4-X digital synthesizer built at the Institute for Research and Coordination of Acoustics and Music (IRCAM) in Paris with a sizable ensemble of traditional instruments. At various moments during the composition, the sound of the traditional instruments is picked up by the 4-X machine, which then proceeds to produce sonic cascades based on the sounds provided by the instrumentalists. The characteristics of the real time processing is itself modified in real time by "performers" who "play" the 4-X machine during the composition.

Another interesting possibility combines interactive realtime performance with composing software that also runs in real time (Moore, 1973; Fry, 1980; Chadabe, 1984), blurring the distinctions among composer, performer, and programmer.

Despite its complexity, Figure 5-1 is by no means a complete depiction of digitally mediated musicmaking. For example, many possible linkages are not shown, such as linking either the actions or sounds of live performers to the computer-assisted score specification or detecting characteristics of the acoustical environment as well as the direct sounds produced by the instrument(s). Traditional and nontraditional instruments may be linked directly to specialized hardware to detect a performer's actions, allowing synthesized sounds to follow a live performer in much the same way as a traditional accompanist or orchestra follows a soloist.

The number of ways that computers may be usefully employed in the creative act of music composition is limited only by the imagination, knowledge, and skill of the composer. Because of this, we can only hope to review some of the general techniques that have been found useful in the past rather than to develop a comprehensive view. The approach we shall take to computer-mediated composition, as elsewhere in this book, will be as general—and as hardware-independent—as possible.

5.2 MUSIC REPRESENTATIONS

One of the most fundamental problems of music composition is to determine appropriate representations for music. Along with common practice notation (CPN), many composers use a wide variety of invented notations, most of which are intended to convey musical thoughts as accurately as possible. The types of notation that a composer finds appropriate are usually associated with notions of how they will be interpreted by their intended recipients, which in the case of computer music may or may not include human performers. When human performers are included in the musicmaking chain, what determines the appropriateness of any particular form of notation is not changed materially by the fact that a computer has been used to mediate in its composition.

Insofar as human performers are not included in the chain, however, the problem of music composition is changed considerably from the traditional situation. In this case, the composer is specifying the musical sound itself, rather than recording instructions that describe how performers are to produce it. In directly specifying the musical sound, the composer becomes, in effect, the performer as well.

Two types of computer data structures that have been found useful in the representation of music are the *event* and the *gesture*. A musical event is typically represented as a time-tagged list of discrete parameters, such as one might find in a cmusic note statement. For example, a typical musical event might consist of a timbre or instrument specification, a starting time and duration (or ending time), and specifications for a musical pitch and dynamic (relative loudness) level.

A musical gesture, by contrast, is typically represented as a mathematical function in which the horizontal axis represents time and the vertical axis represents the time-varying change of an arbitrary parameter. In the context of acoustic compiler programs such as cmusic, gestures are typically represented as lookup tables or time-varying signals such as those produced by the `trans` unit generator. A typical musical gesture might represent time-varying pitch in such a way as to specify a musical phrase, complete with details regarding transitions between notes, inflections of the pitch that occur within single notes, and so on.

While the adoption of event-oriented or gesture-oriented strategies for the specification of musical sounds can have extensive practical implications regarding the implementation of musical ideas, the actual differences between these approaches is mostly conceptual. Having said this, however, it is often more convenient to think in terms of events or gestures, making it important to have both representations available. For example, with no convenient way to represent gestures, one is often forced to think exclusively in terms of "triggering" prefabricated events whose musical characteristics are entirely determined at the time of their onset. To prefabricate an operational "universe" of triggered-note possibilities is both time-consuming and difficult, especially when it is unlikely that all possible combinations of onset parameters will be used in any particular composition. The primary disadvantage of composing without recourse to eventlike specifications is that the notation is not likely to be nearly so compact for gestures as it can be for events.

In realtime synthesis, a pure event-oriented system can provide a reasonable basis for the production of musical sounds with which the performer typically has little interaction once they have begun, such as those of pianos or bells. A MIDI-based keyboard synthesizer, for example, models this type of performance control. For sustaining instruments such as bowed strings or wind instruments, however, pure event-based strategies are problematic because important factors that affect the sound directly (such as the length of the vibrating string or the bow or wind pressure and velocity) typically change continuously during the performance even of a single note. A gesture-based control system such as that of the GROOVE system Max Mathews and I developed (Mathews and Moore, 1970) models this type of performance control.

5.2.1 Direct Transcription

Let us begin our discussion of the details of music representation by developing an extremely simple, direct model for common practice notation. The purpose of this model, of course, is to be representative rather than definitive.

In most cases, it is convenient to choose a representation that is both compact (this eases the task of transcription) and readily interpretable by either a human reader or a computer. A useful convention for the notation of music based on equal temperament is the use of piano key numbers for pitches. This representation has the advantage that it is straightforward to translate the key numbers directly into corresponding fundamental frequencies. For example, the musical phrase

might be transcribed directly for computer entry in the following manner:

```
48,2 50,1 52,1  54,2                      (soprano notes)
43,2 43,1 41,.5 40,.5 47,2                (alto notes)
40,2 38,1 45,1  45,2                      (tenor notes)
36,2 35,1 37,1  39,2                      (bass notes)
```

In this case, the pitches are represented as piano key numbers (the keys are numbered from 0 to 87), and the note durations are transcribed as beats.

To ''play'' these notes, we have only to reformat the information in a way that is appropriate to drive either a software or hardware sound synthesis mechanism. For example, to ''play'' these notes with cmusic, we might use the following C program.

```c
#include <stdio.h>
#include <math.h>
/*
 * note definitions
 */
struct {
    int   pitch ;
    float dur ;
} chorale[4][6] = /* "Es ist genug"--J.S.Bach (first phrase) */
{
    48,2., 50,1., 52,1., 54,2., -1,0., -1,0.  , /* soprano notes */
    43,2., 43,1., 41,.5, 40,.5, 47,2., -1,0.  , /* alto notes */
    40,2., 38,1., 45,1., 45,2., -1,0., -1,0.  , /* tenor notes */
    36,2., 35,1., 37,1., 39,2., -1,0., -1,0.   /* bass notes */
} ;

main( argc, argv ) int argc ; char *argv[] ; {
 float t ;              /* note starting time variable */
 int
    i,                  /* general-purpose index */
    n,                  /* note index */
    v ;                 /* voice index */
```

```
/*
 * fetch cmusic score definitions from a file
 */
    printf( "\#include \"chorale.h\"\n" ) ;
/*
 * for each of the original four voices
 */
    for ( v = 0 ; v < 4 ; v++ )
/*
 * step through the original notes until the end of each
 * voice list is found
 */
        for ( t = n = 0 ; chorale[v][n].pitch >= 0 ; n++) {
/*
 * output a note-playing macro statement
 */
                printf( "NOTE(%.2f,%.2f,%.2fHz) ;\n",
                    t,
                    chorale[v][n].dur,
                    27.5*pow( 2., chorale[v][n].pitch/12. )
                ) ;

/*
 * update the starting time variable
 */
                t += chorale[v][n].dur ;
        }
/*
 * fetch post-notelist trailer information from a second file
 */
    printf( "\#include \"chorale.t\"\n" ) ;
}
```

In this programming example, we have used a two-dimensional struct array called chorale to hold the note specifications more or less verbatim, except that an additional entry is made for each voice with a pitch of –1, signifying that there are no more notes for a given voice. The first row of the chorale array is used to hold the soprano notes, the second row the alto notes, and so on.

It is a simple matter to produce a cmusic note list from such a representation. In this case, the notelist is sandwiched between two **#include** statements that access files containing instrument and waveform definitions, macro definitions, merge and termination statements, and so on.

The note-playing macro is given the simple name NOTE. It takes three arguments: one for the starting time of the note, another for the note duration, and a third for a fundamental frequency, which is derived from the piano key number according to the formula

$$f = 27.5(2^{k/12}) \qquad (5\text{-}1)$$

where k is the piano key number (numbered from 0) and f is frequency in hertz (27.5 is the frequency of the lowest note on the piano). Equation (5-1) makes clear another advantage of piano key number notation: while the whole numbered values of k from 0 to 87 represent the equal tempered pitches available on the piano, k may in general have any value, allowing specification of arbitrary pitches. For example, middle C in the notation corresponds to $k = 39$, while $k = 39.5$ corresponds to a pitch one-half tempered semitone (that is, a quarter tone) above middle C. k may of course be greater than 87 to specify pitches higher than those available on the piano. k may also be negative; for example, $k = -1$ specifies a pitch one tempered semitone lower than the A at 27.5 Hz.

Compiling and executing the example program yields the following output:

```
#include "chorale.h"
NOTE(0.00,2.00,440.00Hz) ;
NOTE(2.00,1.00,493.88Hz) ;
NOTE(3.00,1.00,554.37Hz) ;
NOTE(4.00,2.00,622.25Hz) ;
NOTE(0.00,2.00,329.63Hz) ;
NOTE(2.00,1.00,329.63Hz) ;
NOTE(3.00,0.50,293.66Hz) ;
NOTE(3.50,0.50,277.18Hz) ;
NOTE(4.00,2.00,415.30Hz) ;
NOTE(0.00,2.00,277.18Hz) ;
NOTE(2.00,1.00,246.94Hz) ;
NOTE(3.00,1.00,369.99Hz) ;
NOTE(4.00,2.00,369.99Hz) ;
NOTE(0.00,2.00,220.00Hz) ;
NOTE(2.00,1.00,207.65Hz) ;
NOTE(3.00,1.00,233.08Hz) ;
NOTE(4.00,2.00,261.63Hz) ;
#include "chorale.t"
```

The `chorale.h` file must contain instrument and wave table definitions, as well as an appropriate definition for the NOTE macro. The details of this definition will depend on, among other things, the note parameter requirements of the instruments. Provision may be made to play the notes at an arbitrary tempo simply by scaling the starting times and durations by an arbitrary factor. For example, the following definition for the NOTE macro scales the starting time and duration of each note by the manifest constant TEMPO, which is defined with a **#define** statement, as shown.

```
#define TEMPO (48MM)


#define NOTE(time,dur,freq) \
    note time*TEMPO ins1 dur*TEMPO p4sec -14dB freq
```

Notice that p5 has been set to `p4sec` and p6 to constant amplitude appropriate for a four-voice chorale. Other note parameters might also be defined as needed by `ins1`.

The `chorale.h` header file should end with a cmusic `merge` statement because the note statements as they appear in the note list are not in nondecreasing order of starting times. Similarly, the `chorale.t` file should contain `endsec` and `endmerge` statements as well as at least a `terminate` statement (a `section` statement might also be required, for example, if reverberation is being added to the synthesized sound).

5.2.2 Denominator Notation

While specifying event durations in beats is natural enough for many direct transcription applications, a useful alternative for duration notation is *denominator notation*. In denominator notation, the duration of a whole note is taken to be 1, a half note 2, a quarter note 4, and so on. In other words, the denominator notation N is interpreted to mean a duration of $1/N$ beats.

In denominator notation, N is usually specified either as LM or L/M, where L and M are integers. When multiplication is specified, we may think of LM as "L notes in the time of an Mth note"; when division is specified, we may think of L/M as a duration equal to M times L.

This scheme has the advantage of allowing easy, precise notation of duration values commonly encountered in CPN. For example, each note of an eighth note triplet (that is, three even notes in the time of one quarter note) has a denominator notation of $3{\cdot}4$ (read "three notes in the time of a quarter note"), specifying a duration equal to $1/(3{\cdot}4) = 1/12$ of a whole note. A quarter note triplet (three even notes in the time of a half note) would have denominator notation of $3{\cdot}2$, (read "three notes in the time of a half note"), specifying a duration specifying a duration of $1/(3{\cdot}2) = 1/6$ of a whole note, and so on.

Similarly, dotted note duration values from CPN may be specified with the division operator in denominator notation. For example, a dotted quarter note (that is, a note having the duration of three eighth notes) would have the denominator notation $8/3$, (read "three times the duration of an eighth note"), specifying a duration of $1/(8/3) = 3/8$ of a whole note.

Implementation of denominator notation is almost trivial. The note-playing macro defined previously might be modified to accept denominator notation simply by inverting the duration, as in

```
#define TEMPO (48MM)


#define NOTE(time,dur,freq) \
    note time*TEMPO ins1 (1/(dur))*TEMPO p4sec -14dB freq
```

which is, of course, equivalent to the definition

```
#define TEMPO (48MM)

#define NOTE(time,dur,freq) \
    note time*TEMPO ins1 TEMPO/(dur) p4sec -14dB freq
```

In cmusic, a useful trick is to specify the starting time of a note with the expression p2+p4, which causes the note to start immediately after the previous one is finished. Given the definitions

```
#include <cmusic.h>
#define TEMPO (60MM)

#define NOTE(freq,dur) \
    note p2+p4 ins1 TEMPO/(dur) p4sec -14dB freq
```

we may now easily transcribe a melody such as

with the note-playing statements

```
NOTE(C(0),20/5) ;
NOTE(D(0),5*4) ;
NOTE(C(0),5*4) ;
NOTE(B(-1),5*4) ;
NOTE(C(0),5*4) ;
NOTE(A(0),8/3) ;
NOTE(G(0),8) ;
NOTE(F(0),4) ;
NOTE(E(0),3*4) ;
NOTE(F(0),3*4) ;
NOTE(E(0),3*4) ;
NOTE(D(0),4) ;
NOTE(C(0),4) ;
```

The last example demonstrates a bare minimum of specification, of course. In most cases, the definition of a note-playing macro would be considerably more complex, perhaps allowing for the specification of musical dynamics, accents, duty factors (such as ''staccato,'' ''non-legato,'' ''legato''), and so on.

A variety of performance specifications (such as modulation indices, vibrato rates, and pitch inflection trajectories) could also be added, the values for some of which may be derived from the pitch, duration, and perhaps musical dynamic of the note. In addition, small random values may be added to parameters such as pitch and duration to emulate slight inaccuracies typical at the live performance of traditional music. For example, to cause the pitch of the notes in our example to lie anywhere within a quarter of a semitone of the specified pitch, we may define the note-playing macro as follows:

```
#define NOTE(freq,dur) \
    note p2+p4 ins1 TEMPO/(dur) \
        p4sec -14dB (freq)*2^((rand(2)-1)/(4*12))
```

Here the cmusic expression `rand(N)` indicates a random value between 0 and `N`.

5.3 RANDOM NUMBERS

Many useful techniques for computer-mediated music composition involve random numbers. In Lejaren Hiller's pioneering work on computer composition of music (Hiller and Isaacson, 1959), many note parameters were chosen by the *random sieve method*, which involves selecting candidate values at random and then discarding those that do not obey certain rules.

For example, we may choose representations for musical pitches and durations and then define an arbitrary set of rules that specify a type of melodic progression that we wish to obtain. We then proceed to generate random values and apply the rules, rejecting values that break one or more of the rules and accepting values that obey all of the rules.

To implement such a procedure, we need a source of random numbers. The problem of random number generation by computer has been studied extensively (see, for example, Knuth, 1971). For our purposes, however, we need only recognize a few of the basic properties of the process of random number generation.

First, it is important to recognize that in a sense there is no such thing as a truly random number. For example, is 4 a random number? Is 351 more random than 29? A *set* of numbers may be random—for our purposes—when there are *many* numbers in a *sequence* and their values are *independent* of each other in the sense that knowledge of the first N numbers in the sequence does not help to determine the value of the next number. Furthermore, a sequence of random numbers may be *uniformly distributed* between extreme values, or the numbers may be *nonuniformly distributed*, meaning that some values are more likely to occur in the sequence than others. In other words, a uniform distribution is one in which all possible numbers are equally probable, and a nonuniform distribution is one in which all possible numbers are *not* equally probable.

Second, we must recognize the fact that computers can only add, subtract, multiply, and divide, as well as make a few types of simple decisions, albeit very rapidly. Despite this fact, mathematicians have devised a number of effective ways of generating *pseudorandom numbers* with computers. The reason that these numbers are not truly random is that they must be generated according to a predetermined, well-defined, fixed algorithm.

One of the most popular of these techniques is known as the *linear congruential method*, introduced by D. H. Lehmer in 1948. The basic idea of this method is to generate the next number in a pseudorandom sequence from the last one according to a recurrence relation such as

$$X_{n+1} = (aX_n + c) \bmod m \qquad n \geq 0 \tag{5-2}$$

where $X_n \geq 0$ is the nth value in the sequence, $a \geq 0$ is the multiplier, $c \geq 0$ is the increment, and $m \geq X_0$ is the modulus (in general, m must also be larger than a and larger than c). For example, if we choose $X_0 = a = c = 7$ and $m = 10$, we obtain the *linear congruential sequence*

$$7, 6, 9, 0, 7, 6, 9, 0, 7, 6, 9, 0, \ \ldots$$

It is immediately clear that this sequence is not very random insofar as it repeats itself every four values! Furthermore, the philosophically inclined may object that once we have chosen values for X_0, a, c, and m, the entire sequence is forever predetermined, so in a sense it is not random at all!

To dispense with the first objection, we have only to note that there are many possible choices for X_0, a, c, and m, all of which affect the period and randomness of the resulting sequence. It has been shown, for example, that the period of a linear congruential sequence cannot exceed m, which is almost intuitively obvious if we consider that all the numbers in the sequence are taken modulo m, meaning that only m different values are possible. But, if m is very large (for example, on the order of 2^{31}), the period of the linear congruential sequence may be quite large as well. Also, judicious choices for a and c can cause each period of the sequence to appear quite random. Numerous tests for randomness can be applied to each period of the linear congruential sequence, many of them concerned with certain types of behavior, such as the average length of subsequences that contain exclusively increasing or decreasing values.

The second objection—that the sequence is completely predetermined once it has begun—is entirely valid. The numbers aren't really random at all—they simply appear to be in various mathematical senses. If one were really concerned about this point, it would be feasible to construct a nondeterministic random number generator by connecting the output of a source of "true" random noise (such as the noise encountered in electronic circuits or tape hiss) to an analog-to-digital converter and using the resulting samples as random values. Extreme care would be needed to ensure that the random noise source works properly before each use, and the random values obtained in this way would have many fewer "guaranteed" properties than the much more readily obtainable pseudorandom sequences. However, they would indeed be nondeterministic.

Because pseudorandom generators produce a periodic sequence of random values, we may think of their operation as one of reading from a circular list, starting from an arbitrary point determined by X_0 (see Figure 5-2). Because X_0 determines the starting point of the periodic sequence, it is called the *seed* of the pseudorandom generator. Having the ability to "seed" a pseudorandom generator allows us to generate the same pseudorandom sequence over and over again if we like (by specifying the same seed

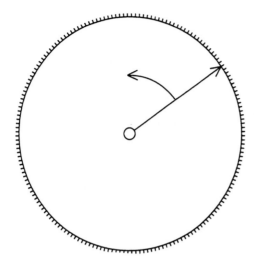

Figure 5-2 Pseudorandom numbers. We
may think of a pseudorandom sequence as a
(typically very long) circular list of random
values, represented here by tick marks
around the perimeter of a circle. Each time
we call a pseudorandom generator, the next
number on the list is returned, represented
here by the counterclockwise motion of the
pointer to the current random value. The arbitrary starting point in the sequence is
determined by the seed value X_0.

each time) or to generate different pseudorandom sequences simply by changing the
seed value.

The standard subprogram library in the UNIX operating system contains a linear
congruential pseudorandom number generator called rand.[1] It generates a pseudorandom sequence of integers with a period of $2^{32} \approx 4.29 \times 10^9$ (that is, over 4 billion
values), each lying in the range 0 through $2^{31} - 1$ (the largest positive integer representable in two's complement arithmetic on a 32-bit word-length computer). An associated
subprogram called srand(seed) may be used to seed the pseudorandom process: if
seed is set to 1, the default starting point is selected; if seed is set to any other
value, a different starting point is chosen. Note that it makes no difference what value
is used for seed except insofar as we may wish to generate the *same* pseudorandom
sequence more than once.

A useful programming trick for making the pseudorandom sequence "pseudonon-
deterministic" is to seed the rand generator with some fairly unpredictable value such
as the time of day when the program is run. On a UNIX system, for example, the
time(0) system library subprogram returns an integer specifying the time of day in
seconds since 00:00:00 GMT, January 1, 1970.

We can convert the pseudorandom value range from 0 to $2^{31} - 1$ to any other
range we like in several ways. One of the most useful transformations of the value returned by rand is simply to divide it by the double-precision floating-point value
$2^{31} - 1$, which may be easily specified with the C statement

```
double r, max ;
   max = 0x7fffffff ;
```

[1]Although these comments are specific to the UNIX operating system, most computer operating systems
provide a similar facility.

```
          .
          .
          .
    r = rand()/max ;
```

where the hexadecimal constant `0x7fffffff` is exactly equal to $2^{31} - 1$, and `r` will be a random value lying in the range 0 to 1. Given a random value between 0 and 1, we can easily generate a random value lying in the range a to b by simple scaling.

The following C program, for example, tests this strategy.

```
#include <stdio.h>
#include <math.h>

main( argc, argv ) int argc ; char *argv[] ; {
 double r, max, m, M ;
 int i, seed, N ;
    max = 0x7fffffff ;
    m = atof( argv[1] ) ;
    M = atof( argv[2] ) ;
    N = atoi( argv[3] ) ;
    seed = atoi( argv[4] ) ;
    srand( seed ) ;
    for ( i = 0 ; i < N ; i++ ) {
        r = rand()/max ;
        printf( "%f\n", r*(M - m) + m ) ;
    }
}
```

The four arguments to this program are the minimum and maximum random values to generate, the length of the desired sequence, and the seed value for the pseudorandom number generator. Invoking this program under the name `testran 1 10 10 1` results in the following output:

```
5.624831
2.581672
3.777864
5.810805
9.528651
2.545627
7.320081
3.037876
5.452961
2.122483
```

Invoking the program with the same arguments will always produce the same random sequence. Even extending the length of the sequence will leave the first 10 values unchanged. For example, the output produced by the program instantiation `testran 1 10 20 1` is as follows:

```
5.624831
2.581672
3.777864
5.810805
9.528651
2.545627
7.320081
3.037876
5.452961
2.122483
1.755089
4.506824
3.495032
4.312636
9.850935
5.818581
7.891137
6.818258
7.904249
8.022132
```

Changing the seed value, however, causes a different random sequence to be generated. For example, using the command `testran 1 10 10 2` produces

```
1.249610
7.266957
3.812398
4.546964
8.096386
8.442083
9.233164
8.653502
6.576329
9.934962
```

The sequence generated with a seed of 2 is entirely unrelated to the sequence resulting from a seed value of 1.

If we really want the random generator to give different results every time it is used (we usually don't want this effect), we can substitute the C statement

```
srand( time(0) ) ;
```

for the corresponding statement in the programming example.

Many procedures can test the randomness of the values generated by a random number generator. One of the more interesting and musically relevant tests of randomness is the *spectrum* of the pseudorandom sequence, which basically determines how "white" the "noise" produced by the random number generator is. That is, if we simply treat the pseudorandom sequence as a digital waveform by taking its Fourier transform, we can observe the flatness of the corresponding spectrum. If the numbers are truly decorrelated, we would expect the energy in this spectrum to be uniformly distributed over all available frequencies. Correlations in the pseudorandom sequence would show up as significant deviations from flatness in the overall spectrum.

Such a plot is shown in Figure 5-3. Although it shows that the power spectrum of the random values is quite lively, it contains significant energy at virtually all frequencies, indicating that the noise signal is fairly white. One of the reasons that the spectrum is not perfectly flat is that only 1024 random values were used.

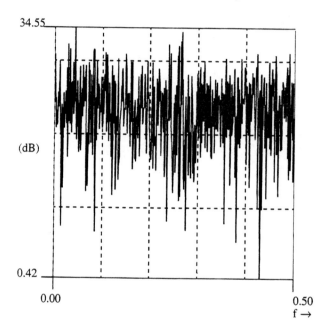

Figure 5-3   Spectrum of pseudorandom numbers produced by the `rand` program. This plot was obtained by taking the Fourier transform (using a rectangular window) of 1024 values all lying within the range −1 to +1 produced by the random number generator program given in the text. The resulting power spectrum is displayed on a decibel scale.

The concept of the power spectrum of a pseudorandom sequence allows us to see that it is possible to *introduce correlations* of various kinds into the sequence through the use of digital filtering, as we saw in Chapter 3 with regard to the synthesis of plucked string tones.

5.4 RANDOM SIEVES

Now that we have a practical method for generating random values, we can return to the specification of rules that bring order out of the chaos inherent in a random sequence. The basic idea of the random sieve (see Figure 5-4) is to generate candidate values for some musical parameter (such as pitch, duration, or timbre) at random, then to apply an arbitrary set of rules to each candidate. If a candidate breaks any one of the rules, it is rejected. If it does not break any rule, the candidate is accepted, the results are recorded

as necessary, and a new candidate is chosen for the next value. The rules essentially
filter out whichever random values do not obey the rules, thus acting like a sieve.
Somewhere in this procedure it is of course necessary to build in a criterion for when
the process is to stop.

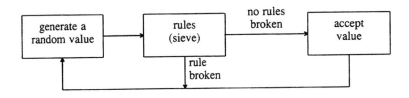

Figure 5-4   The random sieve procedure.

To demonstrate the random sieve procedure, let us develop a very simple program
that composes melodies.

What makes a sequence of pitches and durations melodic? Of course, this question has no simple answer. However, we may posit hypotheses about properties of
melodies by describing rules for choosing successive notes in a melody.

For example, let us suppose that we wish to examine melodies that obey the following rules.

1. The *ambitus* (pitch range) of the melody shall be evenly distributed between
   middle C and the G a tempered twelfth higher.
2. The duration of each note of the melody shall be the same for simplicity.
3. The melody shall be generated in 11 or 12 note groups. Each group shall be followed by a rest of three or four times the duration of each melody note.
4. The successive intervals of the melody shall be restricted to semitones, whole
   tones, and minor thirds except after rests, when a melodic skip upward as large as
   a perfect fifth shall be allowed, followed by a downward interval also as large as a
   perfect fifth.
5. After five groups of notes have been generated, the melody will repeat the first
   group in retrograde and terminate.

We can satisfy rule 1 simply by generating random integers corresponding to
piano key numbers in the range 39 to 58. Rule 2 merely specifies that we do not have
any decisions to make regarding durations for the individual notes of the melody. Rule
3 specifies that a random choice is to be made for each melodic group to determine its
length (11 or 12 notes). It also specifies that a choice is to be made regarding the
length of the rest after each group (3 or 4 note durations). Rule 4 sets limitations of the
successive notes of the melody that will require random values to be tested and possibly
rejected if they do not obey the stated restrictions. Rule 5 is most important: it specifies
how to determine when the melody is over. It will be necessary to "remember" the
first group so that it may be played backward (this ensures, for example, that the ending
note of the melody will be the same as the first note).

A C program that directly implements these rules for melody formation may be stated as follows:

```
#include <stdio.h>
#include <math.h>

double RMAX ;  /* set to 2^31 - 1 */

#define middleC 39  /* piano key number of middle C */
#define highG 58    /* piano key number of high G */

main( argc, argv ) int argc ; char *argv[] ; {
 int group,      /* group index */
     n,          /* note (within group) index */
     grplen,     /* group length */
     candidate,  /* candidate pitch */
     lastpitch,  /* last accepted pitch */
     interval,   /* interval between candidate & last pitch */
     restlen,    /* rest length */
     grp0len,    /* length of first group */
     grp0[12] ;  /* record of first group */
/*
 * set RMAX to 2^31 - 1 for random number generator
 */
    RMAX = 0x7fffffff ;
/*
 * for each of the first four groups
 */
    for ( group = 0 ; group < 4 ; group++ ) {
/*
 * choose a group length (11 or 12)
 */
        grplen = iran( 11, 12 ) ;
/*
 * for each note in the group
 */
        for ( n = 0 ; n < grplen ; n++ ) {
/*
 * first pitch is automatically accepted
 * first group (and its length) is memorized
 */
            if ( group == 0 && n == 0 ) {
                grp0[n] = candidate = iran( middleC, highG ) ;
                grp0len = grplen ;
/*
 * memorize first group pitches
 */
            } else if ( group == 0 ) {
                do {
                    grp0[n] = candidate = iran( middleC, highG ) ;
```

```
                        interval = candidate - lastpitch ;
/*
 * melodic notes must lie within minor third in first group
 */
                } while ( interval > 3 || interval < -3 ) ;
/*
 * first note of successive groups may skip upward by
 * as much as a tempered fifth
 */
            } else if ( n == 0 ) {
                do {
                    candidate = iran( middleC, highG ) ;
                    interval = candidate - lastpitch ;
                } while ( interval > 7 || interval < 0 ) ;
/*
 * second notes of successive groups may skip downward by
 * as much as a tempered fifth
 */
            } else if ( n == 1 ) {
                do {
                    candidate = iran( middleC, highG ) ;
                    interval = candidate - lastpitch ;
                } while ( interval > 0 || interval < -7 ) ;
/*
 * other intervals restricted to lie within minor third
 */
            } else {
                do {
                    candidate = iran( middleC, highG ) ;
                    interval = candidate - lastpitch ;
                } while ( interval > 3 || interval < -3 ) ;
            }
/*
 * accept candidate pitch and print note-playing macro statement
 */
            lastpitch = candidate ;
            printf( "NOTE(%d,1) ;\n", candidate ) ;
        }
/*
 * after each group, choose and print rest duration
 */
        restlen = iran( 3, 4 ) ;
        printf( "REST(%d) ;\n", restlen ) ;
    }
/*
 * after fourth group play first group in retrograde
 */
    for ( n = grp0len - 1 ; n >= 0 ; n-- )
        printf( "NOTE(%d,1) ;\n", grp0[n] ) ;
}
```

```
/*
 * return a random integer value between min and max
 */
iran( min, max ) int min, max ; {
 float fran() ;
    return( (int) fran( (float) min, max + 0.9999 ) ) ;
}
/*
 * return a random floating-point value between min and max
 */
float fran( min, max ) float min, max ; {
    return( ( max - min )*( rand()/RMAX ) + min ) ;
}
```

Here is a representative output of this program, compressed into multicolumn format (read *down* the columns for successive notes):

```
NOTE(42,1) ; NOTE(47,1) ; NOTE(48,1) ; NOTE(43,1) ; NOTE(47,1) ; NOTE(45,1) ;
NOTE(45,1) ; REST(3)    ; NOTE(47,1) ; NOTE(42,1) ; NOTE(46,1) ; NOTE(42,1) ;
NOTE(42,1) ; NOTE(53,1) ; NOTE(47,1) ; NOTE(44,1) ; NOTE(47,1) ; NOTE(40,1) ;
NOTE(43,1) ; NOTE(47,1) ; REST(3)    ; NOTE(41,1) ; NOTE(48,1) ; NOTE(41,1) ;
NOTE(41,1) ; NOTE(45,1) ; NOTE(49,1) ; REST(4)    ; NOTE(51,1) ; NOTE(43,1) ;
NOTE(40,1) ; NOTE(43,1) ; NOTE(47,1) ; NOTE(43,1) ; NOTE(48,1) ; NOTE(42,1) ;
NOTE(42,1) ; NOTE(45,1) ; NOTE(45,1) ; NOTE(41,1) ; REST(4)    ; NOTE(45,1) ;
NOTE(45,1) ; NOTE(47,1) ; NOTE(43,1) ; NOTE(44,1) ; NOTE(47,1) ; NOTE(42,1) ;
NOTE(45,1) ; NOTE(50,1) ; NOTE(44,1) ; NOTE(43,1) ; NOTE(50,1) ;
NOTE(47,1) ; NOTE(50,1) ; NOTE(45,1) ; NOTE(42,1) ; NOTE(47,1) ;
NOTE(50,1) ; NOTE(48,1) ; NOTE(46,1) ; NOTE(44,1) ; NOTE(45,1) ;
```

Transcribed into CPN, this output would read as follows:

A few comments are in order about the programming example. First, two subprograms are included for the generation of random numbers, `fran` and `iran`, which generate random floating-point and integer values, respectively, that lie in the range from `min` to `max` (note that the floating-point routine takes floating-point arguments, whereas the integer routine takes integer arguments). The integer routine simply calls the floating-point routine with the appropriate arguments and returns the truncated result. This truncation process necessitates increasing the range of choice so that the result is equally likely to lie anywhere within the desired integer range. For example, if we wish to generate a random integer that is equally likely to be 1, 2, or 3, we first generate a random floating-point value x that lies within the range $1 \le x < 4$. The truncation process reports all values of x in the range $1 \le x < 2$ as the integer 1, values in the range $2 \le x < 3$ as the integer 2, and values in the range $3 \le x < 4$ as the integer 3.

A general form for the rules in the sieve may be stated as follows:

```
(else) if ( <condition(s) under which to apply rule N> )
    do {
        <select new candidate and compute relevant parameters>
    } while ( <rule N is broken> ) ;
```

Because the conditions under which a given rule applies is only implicit in the statement of the rule itself (for example, we cannot apply to the first note a rule that deals with successive notes), we must be careful to make these conditions explicit in a computer program.

5.4.1 Biased Choices

The candidate selection process may be considerably more complex than just choosing a random number from a valid range within a uniform distribution. We may wish, for example, to specify that some choices are *more likely* than others within a range of possible values. In fact, biased choices are the defining characteristic of so-called *stochastic processes*, especially when the biases are chosen to model the statistical behavior of some observable phenomenon, such as the peak temperature of successive days or the succession of pitches in a melody.

One simple way to implement a biased choice with a uniform random number generator is to use what in probability theory is often called an *urn model*. Choices in the urn model are represented by a well-mixed collection of balls identical in all but color in an urn from which we draw at random. For example, imagine that an urn is filled with 50 red balls and 50 green balls. Because the number of balls of each color is the same, we would expect that a random selection from the urn is just as likely to be red or green. In fact, this corresponds closely to the usual *definition* of probability. If S is a set called the *sample space* (or *possible outcome space*) and A is a set denoting the ways in which a particular outcome can be achieved, then the probability of an event A is given by

$$Pr(A) = \frac{|A|}{|S|} \tag{5-3}$$

where $|A|$ denotes the number of distinct elements in set A and $|S|$ denotes the number of distinct elements in the sample space. For example, if there are 100 balls (total) in the urn, then $|S| = 100$. ways to achieve outcome A (a red ball is chosen) If 50 of the balls are red and 50 are green, then there are 50 and 50 ways to achieve outcome B (a green ball is chosen). The probability of drawing a red ball at random is therefore defined as $Pr(A = $ a red ball is chosen$) = 50/100 = .5$.

One way to implement a biased choice is therefore to "stuff the urn" with unequal numbers of balls of various colors, then to make simple random choices. If we put 50 red balls and 100 green balls in the urn, it stands to reason that the probability of drawing a green ball at random is twice that of drawing a red ball.

For example, if we wish to choose between a pitch C and a pitch C-sharp but we wish to make it three times as likely that C will be chosen, we have only to set up a sample space with four possible outcomes, three of which are C and one of which is C-sharp. If we then choose random integers lying in the range 1 to 4, we would expect that after a large number of choices have been made, C will have been chosen about three times as often as C-sharp. Such a biased choice might be implemented with the following C statement:

```
pitch = iran( 1, 4 ) <= 3 ? C : C_sharp ;
```

If the `iran` routine returns 1, 2, 3, or 4 with equal probability, it is clear that this statement will assign the value of the `pitch` variable about three times out of four.

A more general way to implement a biased choice is to associate a *relative weight factor* with each possible choice. If all the weight factors are equal, the resulting choice would be equally likely to be any of the possibilities. If the weight factor for choice A is twice as large as the weight factor for choice B, however, we can arrange for the probability of choosing A to be twice as large as the probability of choosing B.

If we restrict our attention to choices from among a relatively small number of values (say, up to a few thousand), we can use a *discrete probability distribution function* to specify the probabilities of the various possibilities. For example, suppose that the possible choices are all given by a set $C = \{x_1, x_2, x_3, \cdots\}$ (the x_i values are entirely arbitrary; that is, they may be integers, floating-point values, symbols, rules, or any other legitimate value). The only restriction on C is that it contain a finite number of elements. We then define a function

$$f(x) = Pr(X = x) \qquad\qquad (5\text{-}4)$$

where X is a *random variable* denoting some choice from set C, $Pr(X = x)$ means "the probability that X (the choice) is equal to x" (x is any element of set C; that is, $x \in C$), and $f(x)$ is called the *discrete distribution function*. One property of a probability distribution function is

$$0 \le f(x) \le 1 \qquad\qquad \text{for all}\quad x \in C \qquad\qquad (5\text{-}5)$$

That is, probability values always lie in the range 0 to 1, and

$$\sum_C f(x) = 1 \qquad\qquad (5\text{-}6)$$

—that is, the sum of all probability values in the distribution function must be equal to 1 (the notation $\sum_C f(x)$ denotes the sum of all numbers $f(x)$ for $x \in C$).

Suppose that C is the set of all piano key pitches from middle C up to G a tempered twelfth higher. Set C then contains 20 elements. We can think of the distribution function as an array containing 20 probability values, the first giving the probability that middle C will be chosen, the second giving the probability that C-sharp a semitone higher will be chosen, and so on. If all probability values are equal, all 20 choices are equally likely. If the sum of the probability values in the distribution array also add up to 1, an unbiased choice would be represented by setting each distribution function value to 1/20. The following table shows the contents of choice set C and distribution function f for this case.

C	f
39	1/20
40	1/20
41	1/20
42	1/20
43	1/20
44	1/20
45	1/20
46	1/20
47	1/20
48	1/20
49	1/20
50	1/20
51	1/20
52	1/20
53	1/20
54	1/20
55	1/20
56	1/20
57	1/20
58	1/20

In terms of programming, we can easily represent the choice set and distribution function with two arrays, say `C` and `f`, where `f[i]` gives the probability that choice `C[i]` will be made, for values of `i` in the range 0 through 19.

To represent a biased choice, we have only to change the values in the `f` array so that they are not all equal. A simple method for satisfying the requirement that the values in the distribution function add up to 1 is to fill out the `f` array with arbitrary values specifying *relative weights*, then to divide through by their sum (which must, of course, be greater than zero). For example, suppose that we wish to bias the pitch choice so that pitches in the lower half of the range are twice as likely to occur as those in the upper half. In other words, we wish to establish the relation

$$\sum_{i=0}^{i=9} f(x_i) = 2 \sum_{i=10}^{i=19} f(x_i)$$ (5-7)

Because all probability values in the distribution function must sum to 1, we also conclude that the left side of equation (5-7) must be equal to 2/3, while the right side must be equal to 1/3.

Therefore, we might set up the f array as follows:

```
for ( i = 0 ; i < 10 ; i++ )
    f[i] = 2.0 ;
for ( i = 10 ; i < 20 ; i++ )
    f[i] = 1.0 ;
```

This ensures that the sum of the values in the first half of the array will be twice as great as the sum of the values in the second half of the array. We then normalize the array so that the sum of all values is unity with the following programming steps:

```
for ( sum = i = 0 ; i < 20 ; i++ )
    sum += f[i] ;
for ( i = 0 ; i < 20 ; i++ )
    f[i] /= sum ;
```

The elements in the first half of the array are now set to 1/15 and those in the second half are set to 1/30, as required [10(1/15) + 10(1/30) = 2/3 + 1/3 = 1].

To make the biased choice, we first compute a corresponding *cumulative discrete probability distribution function F* from the discrete distribution function *f* (specified in array f). The cumulative distribution function has the property that each of its elements contains the *sum* of the probabilities up to the corresponding element in the distribution function.[2] In programming terms, we compute the values for an array F to hold the cumulative distribution function as follows:

```
for ( i = 0 ; i < 20 ; i++ )
    for ( F[i] = j = 0 ; j <= i ; j++ )
        F[i] += f[j] ;
```

The following table shows the contents of three arrays, the C array holding the possible pitch choices, the f array holding the probability distribution function (normalized weight factors), and the F array holding the cumulative distribution function.

---

[2] In terms of the mathematics of probability theory, what we here call a discrete probability distribution function is often called a probability mass function. When such a mass function is defined over a continuous interval (rather than discrete values), it is then often called a probability density function. The associated cumulative probability distribution function F is then defined as the *integral* of density function f, and we see that in general, $F(a) = Pr(X \le a)$. Because we deal here exclusively with discrete, finite sets of possible events, we can safely drop this distinction.

i	C[i]	f[i]	F[i]
0	39	1/15	1/15
1	40	1/15	2/15
2	41	1/15	3/15
3	42	1/15	4/15
4	43	1/15	5/15
5	44	1/15	6/15
6	45	1/15	7/15
7	46	1/15	8/15
8	47	1/15	9/15
9	48	1/15	10/15
10	49	1/30	21/30
11	50	1/30	22/30
12	51	1/30	23/30
13	52	1/30	24/30
14	53	1/30	25/30
15	54	1/30	26/30
16	55	1/30	27/30
17	56	1/30	28/30
18	57	1/30	29/30
19	58	1/30	30/30

We now make biased choices by computing uniformly distributed random values R lying in the range 0 to 1 (see Figure 5-5). Because of the summing procedure used to compute it, we may interpret the cumulative distribution function evaluated at point a, $F(a)$, as the probability that our biased random choice will be less than or equal to a. In mathematical terms,

$$F(a) = Pr(X \leq a) \qquad (5\text{-}8)$$

where X is a random variable. Therefore, the index of the *first element* in the F array that is greater than or equal to R is the index of our choice.

For example, if $R = 0.5$, we read down the list of values in the F array to find that the first element that exceeds R is F[7], indicating a choice of C[7] (piano key 46, or G above middle C).

This biased choice procedure might be implemented with the following C statements:

```
R = fran( 0., 1. ) ;
for ( i = 0 ; i < 20 ; i++ )
    if ( F[i] >= R )
        return( C[i] ) ;
```

The beauty of this procedure is that it may be used to implement any type of biased choice among a finite set of possibilities. We simply perform the following steps:

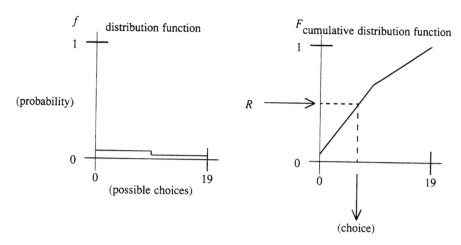

Figure 5-5 Biased choice procedure. *Discrete distribution function f* (on the left) specifies probability (vertical axis) as a function of possible choices (horizontal axis). The sum of all the probability values under the distribution function curve must be 1. The associated *cumulative distribution function F* (on the right) maps a uniform random value *R* in the range 0 onto 1 to a biased choice (in this figure, *R* has the value 0.5). In this case, the probability of choosing a value in the first half of the range of possible choices is twice as great as that of choosing a value in the second half of the range of possible choices. We see that the cumulative distribution function maps a uniform random choice into a biased random choice according to the associated distribution function weights.

1. List the possible choices in an array

2. Fill out a distribution function in an array describing the relative weights for each choice (normalizing the weights so that they add up to 1)

3. Compute the corresponding cumulative distribution function in an array from the distribution function

4. Choose a random value from the interval 0 to 1

5. Make the choice by finding the index of the first value in the cumulative distribution function array that is not less than the random value

To illustrate the use of biased random choices, the following program implements the same melody-composing method as the previous example, except that the choices for each of the first four groups of notes are biased toward higher and higher pitches (the fifth group is still the retrograde of the first). To produce this effect, the candidate notes are chosen by a new biased choice routine called `bchoice`, which computes a distribution function according to the group number. The distribution function in all cases has a triangular shape. For the first group, the peak of the triangle is centered in the first quarter of the range of possible choices; for the second group, it is centered in the second quarter of the range of possible choices; and so on. The `bchoice` routine executes all of the steps mentioned previously for obtaining biased choices each time it is called, including memory allocation of the arrays to hold the choice possibilities, distribution, and cumulative distribution functions (this allows the bias on the choice to change from call to call). Redundant comments are omitted.

```
#include <stdio.h>
#include <math.h>

double RMAX ;   /* set to 2^31 - 1 */

#define middleC 39
#define highG 58

main( argc, argv ) int argc ; char *argv[] ; {
 int group, n, grplen, candidate, lastpitch, interval, restlen,
    grp0len, grp0[12] ;
   RMAX = 0x7fffffff ;
   for ( group = 0 ; group < 4 ; group++ ) {
      grplen = iran( 11, 12 ) ;
      for ( n = 0 ; n < grplen ; n++ ) {
         if ( group == 0 && n == 0 ) {
            grp0[n] = candidate =
               bchoice( middleC, highG, group, 4 ) ;
            grp0len = grplen ;
         } else if ( group == 0 ) {
            do {
               grp0[n] = candidate =
                  bchoice( middleC, highG, group, 4 ) ;
               interval = candidate - lastpitch ;
            } while ( interval > 3 || interval < -3 ) ;
         } else if ( n == 0 ) {
            do {
               candidate =
                  bchoice( middleC, highG, group, 4 ) ;
               interval = candidate - lastpitch ;
            } while ( interval > 7 || interval < 0 ) ;
         } else if ( n == 1 ) {
            do {
               candidate =
                  bchoice( middleC, highG, group, 4 ) ;
               interval = candidate - lastpitch ;
            } while ( interval > 0 || interval < -7 ) ;
         } else {
            do {
               candidate =
                  bchoice( middleC, highG, group, 4 ) ;
               interval = candidate - lastpitch ;
            } while ( interval > 3 || interval < -3 ) ;
         }
```

```
            lastpitch = candidate ;
            printf( "NOTE(%d,1) ;\n", candidate ) ;
        }
        restlen = iran( 3, 4 ) ;
        printf( "REST(%d) ;\n", restlen ) ;
    }
    for ( n = grp0len - 1 ; n >= 0 ; n-- )
        printf( "NOTE(%d,1) ;\n", grp0[n] ) ;
}
/*
 * make a biased choice between min and max centered at
 * successively higher pitches for each group
 */
bchoice( min, max, grp, ngrp ) int min, max, grp, ngrp ; {
 int N, i, j, w, *C, choice ;
 float *f, center, *F, small, sum, R, fran() ;
 char * malloc() ;
/*
 * compute number of possible choices
 */
    N = max - min + 1 ;
/*
 * allocate choice, distribution, and
 * cumulative distribution arrays
 */
    C = (int *) malloc( N*sizeof(int) ) ;
    f = (float *) malloc( N*sizeof(float) ) ;
    F = (float *) malloc( N*sizeof(float) ) ;
/*
 * list possible choices
 */
    for ( i = 0 ; i < N ; i++ )
        C[i] = min + i ;
/*
 * compute center of bias
 */
    center = (float) (grp*N)/ngrp + N/(2.*ngrp) ;
/*
 * fill out distribution with triangular function with peak
 * located around center value
 */
    for ( w = 1, i = 0 ; i < N ; i++ ) {
        f[i] = w ;
        if ( i <= center )
            w++ ;
        else
            w-- ;
    }
```

```
/*
 * ensure that all distribution values are positive
 */
    for ( small = 1000., i = 0 ; i < N ; i++ )
        if ( f[i] < small )
            small = f[i] ;
    if ( small < 1. ) {
        small = 1 - small ;
        for ( i = 0 ; i < N ; i++ )
            f[i] += small ;
    }
/*
 * normalize distribution function to sum to 1
 */
    for ( sum = i = 0 ; i < N ; i++ )
        sum += f[i] ;
    for ( i = 0 ; i < N ; i++ )
        f[i] /= sum ;
/*
 * compute corresponding cumulative distribution function
 */
    for ( i = 0 ; i < N ; i++ )
        for ( F[i] = j = 0 ; j <= i ; j++ )
            F[i] += f[j] ;
/*
 * set R to random value between 0 and 1 (uniform distribution)
 */
    R = fran( 0., 1. ) ;
/*
 * find biased choice
 */
    for ( i = 0 ; i < N ; i++ )
        if ( F[i] >= R )
            break ;
    choice = C[i] ;
/*
 * free allocated memory and return chosen value
 */
    free( C ) ;
    free( f ) ;
    free( F ) ;
    return( choice ) ;
}
iran( min, max ) int min, max ; {
 float fran() ;
    return( (int) fran( (float) min, max + 0.999 ) ) ;
}
float fran( min, max ) float min, max ; {
```

```
    return( ( max - min )*( rand()/RMAX ) + min ) ;
}
```

The key to the bias in the `bchoice` routine is a variable named `center`, which takes on the values 2.5, 7.5, 12.5, and 17.5, respectively, as the `group` variable takes on the values 0, 1, 2, and 3. A triangular distribution function with a peak at the `center` value (rounded up to the next integer value) is constructed and normalized for each of the corresponding melody groups. Plots of the normalized forms of these distribution functions, together with their associated cumulative distribution functions, are shown in Figure 5-6.

Representative output of this biased choice melody-writing program—once again squeezed into multicolumn format—follows.

```
NOTE(41,1) ; NOTE(50,1) ; NOTE(48,1) ; NOTE(52,1) ; NOTE(54,1) ; NOTE(42,1) ;
NOTE(42,1) ; REST(4) ;    NOTE(46,1) ; NOTE(51,1) ; NOTE(51,1) ; NOTE(43,1) ;
NOTE(45,1) ; NOTE(54,1) ; REST(3) ;    NOTE(51,1) ; NOTE(48,1) ; NOTE(45,1) ;
NOTE(48,1) ; NOTE(47,1) ; NOTE(50,1) ; REST(3) ;    NOTE(51,1) ; NOTE(48,1) ;
NOTE(45,1) ; NOTE(46,1) ; NOTE(50,1) ; NOTE(51,1) ; NOTE(49,1) ; NOTE(45,1) ;
NOTE(43,1) ; NOTE(49,1) ; NOTE(50,1) ; NOTE(50,1) ; REST(3) ;    NOTE(42,1) ;
NOTE(42,1) ; NOTE(51,1) ; NOTE(48,1) ; NOTE(51,1) ; NOTE(50,1) ; NOTE(41,1) ;
NOTE(43,1) ; NOTE(53,1) ; NOTE(47,1) ; NOTE(53,1) ; NOTE(49,1) ;
NOTE(45,1) ; NOTE(53,1) ; NOTE(48,1) ; NOTE(55,1) ; NOTE(47,1) ;
NOTE(47,1) ; NOTE(50,1) ; NOTE(50,1) ; NOTE(56,1) ; NOTE(45,1) ;
NOTE(49,1) ; NOTE(51,1) ; NOTE(52,1) ; NOTE(57,1) ; NOTE(43,1) ;
```

Transcribed into CPN, this output would read as follows:

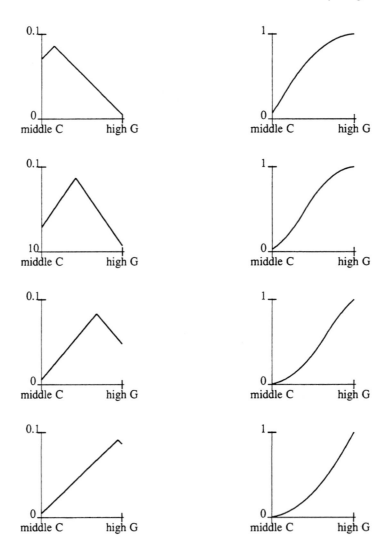

Figure 5-6   Distribution (left) and cumulative distribution (right) functions generated by the `bchoice` routine. The first four melody groups have probability peaks at choice 2.5, 7.5, 12.5, and 17.5, respectively (these are effectively rounded up to the nearest integer by the program). Note that the distribution and cumulative distribution plots do not have the same vertical scale.

The basic notion of the random sieve is both powerful and general. The programming composer is free to implement virtually any rules describing the characteristics of the desired music. These rules may describe methods for selecting the pitches and durations in melodies, rules of harmony, rules of counterpoint, rules of timbre or orchestration, rules of articulation, and so on.

Obviously, if the rules can become arbitrarily complex, so can the task of programming them. Some rules, for instance, may require keeping track of past choices. It is not uncommon for an elaborate random sieve procedure to keep track of all choices made in the past and, in some cases, all the rejected candidates as well. The reason for keeping such an elaborate history of program operation is that there is no simple way to guarantee the *consistency* in a given set of rules. For example, we might (arbitrarily) specify that if two melodic pitches in succession are the same, the next pitch must be lower than the previous two. If the program happens to generate two identical pitches that are also the lowest ones available in the pitch range, no next pitch choice will be possible under these conditions.

There are two basic approaches to handling difficulties that arise from the (probably accidental) inconsistency in a set of rules. One approach is to pore over the rules, trying to think of any inconsistencies that might be possible, and to amend the rules accordingly. For example, we might allow the previously stated rule specifying that a melodic progression must go down in pitch to have an exception when no lower pitch choices are possible (or we have only to think of such exceptions when we conceive the rules in the first place!). A variation of this approach is to have the computer program keep track of the reasons for rejecting candidate pitches in terms of the rule numbers; if we notice that the program seems to get stuck in a particular rule pattern (such as 2, 5, 2, 5, 2 . . .), we probably have cause to investigate the consistency of the rules in the repeating pattern.

Another useful approach is to employ the programming technique called *backtracking* whereby one or more earlier decisions is rescinded after the program fails to find an acceptable candidate after some number of tries. For example, the routine that supplies candidates could simply count how many candidates have been offered since the last one was accepted; if this number exceeds some threshold, the previous choice can be revoked, the conditions reset to those following the next previous choice, and a search made for a new previous choice. If this fails to solve the problem, two previous choices can be revoked, and so on.

Because of the general difficulty of anticipating rule inconsistencies, it is usually a good idea at least to keep track of how many times candidates have been rejected in the random sieve process in order to prevent the program from entering an endless loop. A sophisticated random sieve program might even enter an interactive mode when it deems itself to be stuck by displaying appropriate information to the user, who may then decide whether to keep trying, backtrack to a certain point, modify certain rules temporarily or permanently, or terminate.

5.5 MARKOV PROCESSES

Another basic approach to the automated composition of music employs *Markov processes*. A Markov process (or *Markov chain*) is an extension of the basic idea of the biased choice technique introduced in section 5.4.1. In fact, the biased choice procedure is entirely equivalent to what is known as a *zeroth-order Markov process* in which choices are made according to nonequal probabilities of occurrence of a set of possible events.

However, the idea of a Markov process also includes the element of *statistical analysis* of a set of data as well as the synthesis of a data set that has certain statistical properties. For example, we may choose to base the probabilities on one or more arbitrary pieces of music. If, for example, we find that of the 1000 notes in a given composition by Mozart, exactly 100 have the pitch A440, we may characterize that composition statistically by assigning a probability of 100/1000 = .1 to the pitch A440. In fact, we can derive a table that associates probabilities with all possible musical pitches (represented, for example, by piano key numbers). Each table entry would associate a piano key number with a probability computed by dividing the total number of occurrences of that pitch with the total number of notes in the piece (notes that do not occur in a given piece would be assigned a probability of 0).

We could then synthesize a set of pitches having the same statistical characteristics by using the probability table as a discrete distribution function, possibly eliminating zero-valued entries to save space. The resulting sequence of pitches—if it is long enough—will have the same statistical characteristics as the original composition, at least in the sense that if the original contains about 10 percent A440s, the synthesized composition would also contain about 10 percent A440s. It is a simple matter to extend this procedure to durations, timbres, dynamics, and other aspects.

Of course, the resulting composition is unlikely to sound very much like the model on which it is based. One reason for this is that the procedure just described completely ignores *transitions* from one note to another—each successive note is chosen *independently* of the ones before and after it.

A *first-order Markov process* represents the original composition in a different way in order to take note-to-note transitions into account. We start by making a list of all the notes that actually occur in a given composition (this eliminates consideration of pitches with zero probability). We then form an all-zero square matrix by assigning the names of the notes to both the rows and the columns of the matrix—that is, the rows and columns represent exactly the same set of possible notes. However, we shall arbitrarily designate the rows to refer to predecessor notes while the columns refer to successor notes.

We then proceed with the analysis by incrementing the entries that correspond to note-to-note transitions that actually occur in the composition. If the first note is, say, A440, we read down the rows until the position corresponding to A440 is found. If the following note is B (a whole tone higher), we increment the entry in the column that corresponds to B in the A440 row. Then we move to the row corresponding to B and increment the entry in the column that corresponds to its successor, and so on.

For example, the first half of the American folk tune "Yankee Doodle" is as follows:

The pitches of this tune are given by the list

CCDECEDCCDECBCCDEFEDCBGABCC

We note first that the only pitches that occur are given by the list (from lowest to highest)

GABCDEF

We form the initial transition matrix (with all-zero entries) as follows:

	G	A	B	C	D	E	F
G	0	0	0	0	0	0	0
A	0	0	0	0	0	0	0
B	0	0	0	0	0	0	0
C	0	0	0	0	0	0	0
D	0	0	0	0	0	0	0
E	0	0	0	0	0	0	0
F	0	0	0	0	0	0	0

We now proceed to analyze the notes in the melody. Treating the rows of the matrix as predecessors and the columns as successors, we observe that the first note, C, is followed by another C. We therefore increment the matrix entry at the C-C coordinates by 1, resulting in the following:

	G	A	B	C	D	E	F
G	0	0	0	0	0	0	0
A	0	0	0	0	0	0	0
B	0	0	0	0	0	0	0
C	0	0	0	1	0	0	0
D	0	0	0	0	0	0	0
E	0	0	0	0	0	0	0
F	0	0	0	0	0	0	0

The second note is a C followed by a D, yielding

	G	A	B	C	D	E	F
G	0	0	0	0	0	0	0
A	0	0	0	0	0	0	0
B	0	0	0	0	0	0	0
C	0	0	0	1	1	0	0
D	0	0	0	0	0	0	0
E	0	0	0	0	0	0	0
F	0	0	0	0	0	0	0

This D is followed by an E, yielding

	G	A	B	C	D	E	F
G	0	0	0	0	0	0	0
A	0	0	0	0	0	0	0
B	0	0	0	0	0	0	0
C	0	0	0	1	1	0	0
D	0	0	0	0	0	1	0
E	0	0	0	0	0	0	0
F	0	0	0	0	0	0	0

Continuing in this manner for all the notes in the melody results in the matrix

	G	A	B	C	D	E	F
G	0	1	0	0	0	0	0
A	0	0	1	0	0	0	0
B	1	0	0	2	0	0	0
C	0	0	2	4	3	1	0
D	0	0	0	2	0	3	0
E	0	0	0	2	2	0	1
F	0	0	0	0	0	1	0

The matrix entries sum to 26, as they should (because there are 27 notes in the melody, there are 26 note-to-note transitions). Furthermore, we see that because the note F appears only once in the melody, it has only a single successor listed in the matrix, E (A and G similarly have single successors). The sums of the rows of the matrix tell us how many times the corresponding note was a predecessor; the column sums tell us how many times it was a successor.

We now transform the matrix by dividing each entry by the sum of the entries in the corresponding row, yielding

	G	A	B	C	D	E	F
G	0	1/1	0	0	0	0	0
A	0	0	1/1	0	0	0	0
B	1/3	0	0	2/3	0	0	0
C	0	0	2/10	4/10	3/10	1/10	0
D	0	0	0	2/5	0	3/5	0
E	0	0	0	2/5	2/5	0	1/5
F	0	0	0	0	0	1/1	0

The rows of this matrix may now be interpreted as expressing the probabilities of transitions to any possible note, given the fact that the note at the beginning of the row has already occurred. For example, if the note F has occurred, the transition matrix states that it must (with probability 1) be followed by E. An E has a 40 percent chance of being followed by a C, a 40 percent chance of being followed by a D, and a 20 percent chance of being followed by an F.

Precisely the same information may be represented with a *state diagram* (see Figure 5-7). In this type of representation, circles are typically used to represent *states* of the Markov process, where in this case a state signifies that a particular pitch has occurred. The states are connected with *transition arcs*, showing possible transitions from

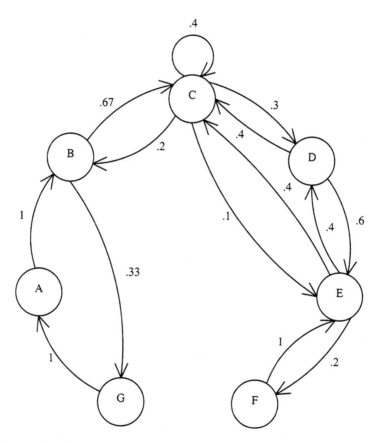

Figure 5-7   State diagram for the Markov representation of "Yankee Doodle." Each circle represents a state (the occurrence of a particular pitch). The arcs represent possible transitions to other states (occurrences of other pitches in succession). The numbers on the arcs represent the probability that a particular arc will be chosen. The sum of the probabilities of the arcs leaving any state must be 1.

a given state. With each arc is associated a *transition probability*, which gives the probability that that particular transition will be chosen. The sum of the probabilities on the arcs leaving any state must equal 1. However, as we can see in Figure 5-7, one of the possibilities may be that the next state is the same as the current state—this is indicated for the pitch C with a probability of .4.

The Markov representation may be extended to the *second order* by observing *all possible pairs* of successive pitches. A state in a second-order Markov process then has the meaning that a given *pair* of pitches has occurred in succession. As before, the transition arcs signify probabilities that a given pitch will follow a given pair of pitches that has already occurred.

For example, if we examine the pitches in the tune "Yankee Doodle" once more, we find that the following pairs of successive pitches occur one or more times (these are shown here sorted into alphabetical order).

> A-B
> B-C (twice)
> B-G
> C-B (twice)
> C-C (four times)
> C-D (three times)
> C-E
> D-C (twice)
> D-E (three times)
> E-C (twice)
> E-D (twice)
> E-D
> E-F
> F-E
> G-A

We can use this information to obtain second-order transition probabilities by forming the matrix

	G	A	B	C	D	E	F
A-B	0	0	0	0	0	0	0
B-C	0	0	0	0	0	0	0
B-G	0	0	0	0	0	0	0
C-B	0	0	0	0	0	0	0
C-C	0	0	0	0	0	0	0
C-D	0	0	0	0	0	0	0
C-E	0	0	0	0	0	0	0
D-C	0	0	0	0	0	0	0
D-E	0	0	0	0	0	0	0
E-C	0	0	0	0	0	0	0
E-D	0	0	0	0	0	0	0
E-F	0	0	0	0	0	0	0
F-E	0	0	0	0	0	0	0
G-A	0	0	0	0	0	0	0

As before, we now proceed to count the number of times each possible pair of successive pitches is followed by each of the other possible pitches in the melody, resulting in the following matrix:

	G	A	B	C	D	E	F
A-B	0	0	0	1	0	0	0
B-C	0	0	0	2	0	0	0
B-G	0	1	0	0	0	0	0
C-B	1	0	0	1	0	0	0
C-C	0	0	0	0	3	0	0
C-D	0	0	0	0	0	3	0
C-E	0	0	0	0	1	0	0
D-C	0	0	1	1	0	0	0
D-E	0	0	0	2	0	0	1
E-C	0	0	1	0	0	1	0
E-D	0	0	0	2	0	0	0
E-F	0	0	0	0	0	1	0
F-E	0	0	0	0	1	0	0
G-A	0	0	1	0	0	0	0

The entries in this matrix sum to 25 (the number of notes minus 2). We again "normalize" the rows so that they sum to 1—the results may be represented either in tabular (matrix) form or with a state diagram (in this case, the states represent the occurrence of pairs of notes). Note in this case that only four of the rows contain nonzero entries for more than one following state. The additional restrictions of the second order allow fewer alternatives for synthesis, and the synthesized melody would resemble the original more strongly than in the first-order case.

An alternative representation for a second-order Markov process would involve a three-dimensional matrix, in which each dimension is indexed by possible pitches. One dimension would represent the successor state, another dimension would represent the current state, and the third dimension would represent the previous state. Though this representation has a fine flexibility and elegance, it is considerably less compact. In this example, of the $7 \times 7 = 49$ possible pairs of 7 pitches, the 26 pairs of successive pitches in the 27-note melody fell into only 14 categories (the pairs that actually occurred), yielding a 14×7 matrix with 18 of the 98 entries having nonzero values (that is, the matrix is still only 18 percent "occupied"). A $7 \times 7 \times 7$ matrix would in this case still have only 18 out of 343 entries with nonzero values (5 percent "occupied").

The Markov process can be extended to whatever order we like. A third-order Markov process deals with the transitions between successive 3-tuples of pitches and the pitches in a given melody; a fourth-order Markov process statistically characterizes transitions between 4-tuples and their successors, and so on. Each time the order is increased, the transition matrix typically becomes sparser—there are fewer and fewer nonzero entries in it. This usually happens because the n-tuples tend to become more and more *unique* (for a given set of analysis data) as n increases. For example, if there are N notes in a given melody, then an $(N-1)th$-order Markov analysis is guaranteed to result in just one occurrence of the first $N - 1$ notes of the melody followed by a transition (with probability 1) to the final note—not very informative in any statistical sense!

Given a Markov analysis of any order in the form of a transition matrix, we can synthesize transitions by treating the rows of the matrix as discrete distribution functions such as those described in section 5.4.1. After each selected note, the Markov synthesizer is in the state that corresponds to that note. The row of the transition matrix that signifies the current state is then used to bias the choices of the following state.

One of the decisions a programming composer must make when doing Markov synthesis is how to terminate the process of selecting new notes. This may be done arbitrarily (say, after a suitable number of notes has been chosen), but one method has much to recommend it: we can treat the termination of the melody as a state in itself, which occurs just once after the last pitch in the melody. This might be represented in the transition matrix by adding a new "terminate" column, as in the following extended first-order matrix.

	G	A	B	C	D	E	F	Ω
G	0	1/1	0	0	0	0	0	0
A	0	0	1/1	0	0	0	0	0
B	1/3	0	0	2/3	0	0	0	0
C	0	0	2/11	4/11	3/11	1/11	0	1/11
D	0	0	0	2/5	0	3/5	0	0
E	0	0	0	2/5	2/5	0	1/5	0
F	0	0	0	0	0	1/1	0	0

There are many other ways to handle the termination condition. In the following programming example, the first-order transition matrix derived earlier is used to determine the probabilities of transitions between pitch states. The biased choice of next state is made for each current state by consulting a cumulative distribution matrix computed directly from the transition probability matrix. Because there are 11 Cs in the original tune and because the termination occurs after a C with a duration of 2 units, the program includes a statement that will terminate the process after any C with a duration of 2 units with a probability of 1/11. Unlike a rule for a random sieve, such a decision rule for a Markov process introduces no possible inconsistency—only uncertainty about when the synthetic melody will be over! Because it is impossible to know in advance how long the resulting melody will be, the program also contains an arbitrary length limitation of 100 notes.

To associate durations with pitches, we note that the pitches G, A, E, and F in the original melody always occur with a duration that we will call 1 unit. The remaining pitches (B, C, and D) may have a duration of either 1 or 2 units. B occurs in the melody once with a duration of 1 unit and once with a duration of 2 units; the program therefore includes a rule stating that if B is chosen, its associated duration should be equally likely to be either 1 or 2. C occurs 11 times in the original melody, 4 times with duration 2 and 7 times with duration 1. The program therefore includes another duration rule for C: when C occurs, it should be assigned duration 2 with probability 4/11 and duration 1 with probability 7/11. Similarly, D is given duration 1 with probability 4/5 and duration 2 with probability 1/5. The fran routine is slightly modified in this example to obviate the need for the calling program to set up its special RMAX constant.

```
#include <stdio.h>
/*
 * pitch-state associations
 */
#define G 0
#define A 1
#define B 2
#define C 3
#define D 4
#define E 5
#define F 6
/*
 * pitch-piano key associations for G, A, B, C, D, E, and F
 */
int key[7] = { 34, 36, 38, 39, 41, 43, 44 } ;
/*
 * first-order Markov transition matrix
 */
float trans[7][7] = {
        /*  G      A      B     C      D     E      F */
/* G */   0,     1.,    0,    0,     0,    0,     0,
/* A */   0,     0,     1.,   0,     0,    0,     0,
/* B */   .33,   0,     0,    .67,   0,    0,     0,
/* C */   0,     0,     .2,   .4,    .3,   .1,    0,
/* D */   0,     0,     0,    .4,    0,    .6,    0,
/* E */   0,     0,     0,    .4,    .4,   0,     .2,
/* F */   0,     0,     0,    0,     0,    1.,    0
} ;

main( argc, argv ) int argc ; char *argv[] ; {
 int i, j, k, n, state, dur ;
 float dist[7][7] ;
/*
 * optional seed for random generator
```

```
 */
    if ( argc > 1 )
        srand( atoi( argv[1] ) ) ;
/*
 * compute cumulative distribution matrix from transition matrix
 * (rows of the transition matrix must already sum to 1)
 */
    for ( i = 0 ; i < 7 ; i++ )
        for ( j = 0 ; j < 7 ; j++ )
            for ( dist[i][j] = k = 0 ; k <= j ; k++ )
                dist[i][j] += trans[i][k] ;
/*
 * pick an arbitrary state to start
 */
    state = C ;
    printf( "NOTE(%d,1) ;\n", key[state] ) ;
/*
 * limit length of output to 100 notes
 */
    for ( n = 0 ; n < 100 ; n++ ) {
/*
 * choose next state according to probability weights
 * associated with current state
 */
        state = wchoice( dist[state], 7 ) ;
/*
 * apply duration rules
 */
        if ( state == B )
            dur = iran( 1, 2 ) ;
        else if ( state == C )
            dur = iran( 1, 11 ) <= 7 ? 1 : 2 ;
        else if ( state == D )
            dur = iran( 1, 5 ) <= 4 ? 1 : 2 ;
        else
            dur = 1 ;
/*
 * print state and test for termination
 */
        printf( "NOTE(%d,%d) ;\n", key[state], dur ) ;
        if ( state == C && dur == 2 && iran( 1, 11 ) > 10 )
            break ;
    }
}
/*
 * return index of choice (new state) from cumulative distribution
 * in array dist[0] through dist[n-1]
 */
```

```
wchoice( dist, n ) float dist[] ; int n ; {
 float R, fran() ;
 int i ;
    R = fran( 0., 1. ) ;
    for ( i = 0 ; i < n ; i++ )
        if ( dist[i] >= R )
            return( i ) ;
}
iran( min, max ) int min, max ; {
 float fran() ;
    return( (int) fran( (float) min, max + 0.999 ) ) ;
}
float fran( min, max ) float min, max ; {
 static double RMAX = 0x7fffffff ;
    return( ( max - min )*( rand()/RMAX ) + min ) ;
}
```

Here is the representative output from this program, compressed into multicolumn format:

```
NOTE(39,1) ; NOTE(44,1) ; NOTE(39,1) ; NOTE(39,2) ; NOTE(39,2) ; NOTE(36,1) ;
NOTE(39,1) ; NOTE(43,1) ; NOTE(41,1) ; NOTE(39,2) ; NOTE(38,1) ; NOTE(38,1) ;
NOTE(39,2) ; NOTE(44,1) ; NOTE(43,1) ; NOTE(38,1) ; NOTE(39,1) ; NOTE(39,2) ;
NOTE(41,1) ; NOTE(43,1) ; NOTE(41,1) ; NOTE(39,1) ; NOTE(38,1) ;
NOTE(43,1) ; NOTE(41,1) ; NOTE(43,1) ; NOTE(38,2) ; NOTE(34,1) ;
```

Transcribed into CPN, this output reads as follows.

5.6 NOISE, FILTERS, RANDOM NUMBERS, AND PROBABILITY

Noise waveforms, digital filters, pseudorandom number sequences, and probability theory are intertwined in many ways, some of which have known musical relevance. Many of these connections can be found by observing correspondences between the statistical and signal processing interpretations of a sequence of numbers. In the statistical realm, we are usually interested in such things as the autocorrelation of a sequence or the cross-correlation between two sequences. In the signal processing realm, we are usually concerned with such things as the amplitude or phase spectrum of a waveform.

For example, suppose that we use a source of pseudorandom numbers that chooses integers from the range 1 to 6 (these integers may represent anything we like, such as pitches, or durations). Further, suppose that the likelihood of any of the six choices is equal, that is, that the choice is made according to the uniform discrete probability distribution function

Choice	1	2	3	4	5	6
Probability	1/6	1/6	1/6	1/6	1/6	1/6

Let X be a pseudorandom sequence of such choices, and let Y be an *independent* second sequence (of the same length) of such choices.

Now suppose that we add together the two sequences to form a new sequence, $X + Y = Z$. Because the minimum possible value in both the X and Y sequences is 1, the minimum possible value in the Z sequence is 2; similarly, the maximum possible value in the Z sequence is 12. We now ask the question, What probability distribution function describes the Z sequence? In particular, is Z described by a *uniform* distribution?

The answer is no. We might model the Z sequence by rolling a pair of dice, one of which we associate with the X sequence, the other with sequence Y. If the dice are fair, we would expect each one of them to come up with the value 1 about 1/6 of the time. For their sum to be 2, both dice must come up with 1. The probability that this happens will be equal to 1/6 (the probability of getting a 1 on the first die) times 1/6 (the probability of getting a 1 on the second die). Therefore, we would expect Z to be equal to 2 about 1/36 of the time.

However, the value 3 may occur in the Z sequence if the first die is equal to 1 with the second die equal to 2, or vice versa. Because there are two ways to get a sum of 3 under these circumstances, and each of these ways can occur with a probability of 1/36, we would expect Z to be equal to 3 about 2/36 of the time, or about twice as often as it is equal to 2. Continuing in this manner, we eventually can work the following discrete probability distribution for the Z sequence.

Z Value	2	3	4	5	6	7	8	9	10	11	12
Probability	1/36	2/36	3/36	4/36	5/36	6/36	5/36	4/36	3/36	2/36	1/36

(These are the probabilities of getting the various possible results from rolling two fair dice.)

Even though X and Y both have uniform densities, Z, their sum, does not. One of the fundamental results of probability theory states that if a random variable X has distribution $f(X)$ and random variable Y has distribution $f(Y)$, then the distribution of the sum of the two random variables, $f(X + Y)$, is equal to the *convolution* of $f(X)$ with $f(Y)$. We may verify this theorem in this case by observing the plots in

Figure 5-8. The probability of the occurrence of the possible outcomes of throwing a pair of dice is indeed given by the convolution of the probabilities of occurrence of the outcomes for the individual dice.

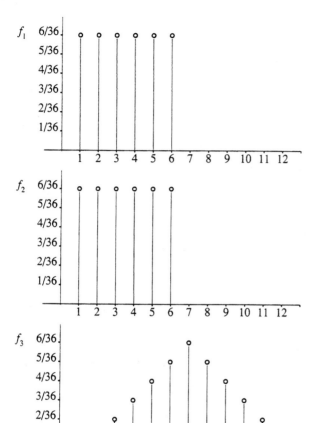

Figure 5-8   Convolution of probability distribution functions. f_1 and f_2 are uniform discrete probability distribution functions describing the probability of choosing integers from the range 1 through 6. f_3 is the convolution of f_1 and f_2, which gives the probabilities of occurrence of the numbers that result from adding together those chosen according to f_1 and f_2.

Where convolution lurks, can the Fourier transform be far away? We know from our consideration of digital signals that the Fourier transform of the convolved distribution function is equal to the product of the Fourier transforms of the individual distributions. However, we should not confuse the Fourier transform of a probability distribution function with the Fourier transform of a noise waveform, even if the numbers in the noise waveform were chosen according to that particular probability distribution function. The Fourier transform of a waveform relates a time domain view of a phenomenon to a frequency domain view; the Fourier transform of a probability distribution function is more abstract.

5.6.1 1/f Noise

One interpretation involving probability for the Fourier transform of a noise waveform, however, has surprising musical relevance. The long-term spectrum of musical signals tends to have a power spectrum that falls off with frequency as $1/f$, where f is frequency in hertz (Voss and Clarke, 1975). This spectrum behavior of musical sounds has been observed in music of many different kinds, including that of Bach, Beethoven, and the Beatles, and is related to a relatively recent mathematical concept known as a *fractal*.

A full explanation of fractals goes considerably beyond the scope of this book, but we can consider fractal behavior as typical of any structure that exhibits the characteristic of *self-similarity*. A self-similar structure is one in which the structure of the details resembles closely the overall structure, regardless of how closely we observe the structure. For example, if we take a picture of the desert from an airplane flying on a clear day at an altitude of 5000 meters, we get a picture that is very similar in its overall pattern to the one we would get if we took it from an altitude of 5 meters, or 0.5 meters. Benoit Mandelbrot (1983) suggests that the reason music exhibits fractal behavior is that musical compositions are typically composed hierarchically, with pieces broken down into movements, movements into sections, sections into phrases, and phrases into notes, thus imparting characteristics of the whole to each of the meaningful subdivisions.

Voss and Clarke investigated the use of random noise with a $1/f$ power spectrum characteristic as a source of melodic pitches, comparing it with other sources with a 1/1 (flat or white noise) spectrum and $1/f^2$ (Brownian noise) spectrum and concluded that the $1/f$ noise produced melodies that sounded "about right" in terms of the balance between redundancy and surprise as the melody progressed. Melodies based on white noise sounded too random to be musical, and melodies based on Brownian noise sounded too repetitive.

If the power spectrum of the random noise (the square of its amplitude spectrum) drops off as $1/f^\beta$, the larger the value of β, the more *constrained* the random numbers in the noise waveform will be. For example, if $\beta = 0$, implying that the spectrum does not drop off at all, the successive numbers in the noise waveform are truly independent. We may interpret the term *independent* to mean that the choice of the $(k + 1)th$ number in the sequence of numbers does not depend in any way on the first k numbers in the sequence. However, if β is greater than zero, the numbers in the pseudorandom sequence become more and more constrained by previous choices.

For example, if $\beta = 2$, implying that the noise power spectrum drops of as the square of frequency, the noise is constrained in exactly the same way as a *random walk*. The term *random walk* refers to the image of a drunk person who falls down, stands up, takes one step in a random direction, falls down again, stands up, takes another step in a random direction, and so on. In terms of a one-dimensional noise waveform, a random walk is represented by an arbitrary starting value to which a uniformly distributed number is added to get the next value. Noise of this type is also called Brownian noise because it typifies the Brownian motion of molecules being tossed about in random directions by heat: a molecule can move only so far (the length of the so-called mean free path) before it hits another molecule and bounces off in another random direction.

We can easily produce Brownian ($1/f^2$) noise with a program such as this one:

```
#include <stdio.h>

main( argc, argv ) int argc ; char *argv[] ; {
 int i, N ;
 float fran(), R, Rlast = 0 ;
    N = 10 ;
    if ( argc > 1 )
            N = atoi( argv[1] ) ;
    for ( i = 0 ; i < N ; i++ ) {
        do
            R = Rlast + fran( -.1, .1 ) ;
        while ( R > 1. || R < -1. ) ;
        printf( "%f\n", R ) ;
        Rlast = R ;
    }
}
```

The `fran` routine is the same as the one given before. This program simply adds a random value in the range –0.1 to +0.1 to the previous random value to get each output value. Boundaries are built in to make sure that the output signal stays within the range –1 to +1. A typical waveform produced by this program, along with its associated power spectrum, is shown in Figure 5-9.

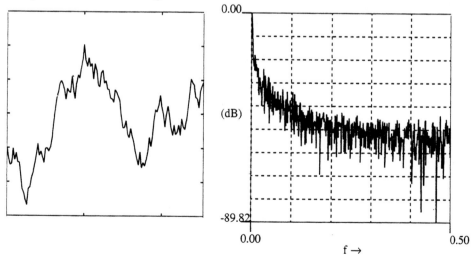

Figure 5-9 $1/f^2$ (Brownian) noise waveform and spectrum. The plot on the left shows 128 samples of a waveform generated according to the principle of a random walk. Each successive value of the waveform lies a small random distance away from its predecessor. The power spectrum of this waveform (right) drops off as $1/f^2$, which on a decibel scale corresponds to 6 dB per octave.

Whereas it is easy to produce white noise and Brownian noise, $1/f$ noise is somewhat more complicated. One method suggested by Gardner (1978) involves summing the output of N uniform random number generators in a particular way. We trigger new choices of each of the random generators by counting in binary using an N-bit number. Each bit in the number is associated with one of the random generators. Whenever one of the bits changes from 0 to 1 or 1 to 0, the associated generator chooses a new random number. The length of the sequence is equal to 2^N, where N is the number of generators used. The resulting sequence of random values interpreted as a noise waveform comes very close to having a $1/f$ characteristic.

Observation of a binary sequence reveals why this is so. In the following table, the ones and zeros represent the binary number and each X indicates random generator "triggering."

Bit				Generator			
3	2	1	0	1	2	3	4
(1	1	1	1)				
0	0	0	0	X	X	X	X
0	0	0	1				X
0	0	1	0			X	X
0	0	1	1				X
0	1	0	0		X	X	X
0	1	0	1				X
0	1	1	0			X	X
0	1	1	1				X
1	0	0	0	X	X	X	X
1	0	0	1				X
1	0	1	0			X	X
1	0	1	1				X
1	1	0	0		X	X	X
1	1	0	1				X
1	1	1	0			X	X
1	1	1	1				X

Generator 4, being associated with bit 0, triggers every time, so the sequence produced by the sum of the four generators is different at each step with high probability. However, generator 3 triggers only half as often as generator 4, so its contribution may be interpreted as having a lower rate of change (or a *lower frequency*) than that of generator 4. Similarly, generator 2 runs at half the frequency of generator 3, and generator 1 has the lowest frequency of all.

Conversely, once generator 1 has been triggered, the number it generates forms a part of the sum for the next eight numbers in the sequence, introducing considerable correlation between successive numbers. Only at the beginning and middle of the sequence are all generators changing, resulting in a value that is completely independent of the previous value. Each successive generator adds less correlation than the one before it.

This method has the advantage of being extremely simple to program. The following program provides a general method for obtaining $1/f$ noise waveforms of length 2^N, where N can be specified.

```c
#include <stdio.h>

main( argc, argv ) int argc ; char *argv[] ; {
 int i, n, lastn, N, length ;
 float fran(), halfrange, *r, R ;
 char *malloc() ;
/*
 * set default value for N
 */
    N = 4 ;
/*
 * use another value for N if specified
 */
    if ( argc > 1 )
                N = atoi( argv[1] ) ;
/*
 * allocate memory to hold results of individual random generators
 */
    r = (float *) malloc( N*sizeof(float) ) ;
/*
 * compute length of output sequence
 */
    for ( length = 1, i = 0 ; i < N ; i++ )
        length <<= 1 ;
/*
 * normalize halfrange so that sum of all generators
 * always lies in range from -1 to +1
 */
    halfrange = 1./N ;
/*
 * initialize previous index value
 */
    lastn = length - 1 ;
/*
 * generate the sequence
 */
    for ( n = 0 ; n < length ; n++ ) {
/*
 * at each step, check for changing bits and update corresponding
 * random numbers--their sum is the output
 */
        for ( R = i = 0 ; i < N ; i++ ) {
            if ( ( (1<<i) & n ) != ( (1<<i) & lastn ) )
                r[i] = fran( -halfrange, halfrange ) ;
```

```
        R += r[i] ;
    }
    printf( "%f\n", R ) ;
    lastn = n ;
    }
}
```

A typical output waveform generated by this program and its associated power spectrum are shown in Figure 5-10.

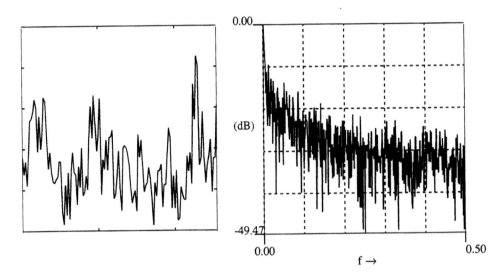

Figure 5-10   1/f noise waveform and spectrum. The plot on the left shows 128 samples of a waveform generated by summing together multiple uniform random generators triggered by changes in the bits of a binary sequence. Each successive value of the waveform is less constrained than in a Brownian waveform but more constrained than in a white noise (flat spectrum) waveform. The power spectrum of this waveform (right) drops off as 1/f, which on a decibel scale corresponds to 3 dB per octave.

Although the simplicity of this method has much to recommend it, another method can generate random sequences of arbitrary lengths that approximate a $1/f^\beta$ characteristic for an arbitrary value of $\beta \geq 0$. We can shape the spectrum of white noise by modifying its power spectrum obtained with a Fourier transform, retransform the result, and use the resulting modified sequence. The advantages of this approach are that we can give the power spectrum any shape we like, and the sequence can be of any length. For long sequences, however, the DFT can be quite slow. If long sequences are needed, the more efficient FFT algorithm can be substituted, which will constrain the length of the sequence to be a power of 2.

This method is demonstrated in the following example. This program uses the fran generator described earlier in this chapter and the dft and idft routines described in Chapter 2.

```
/*
 * this program accepts five arguments:
 * N - length of the desired noise-shaped sequence
 * min     - minimum sequence value
 * max     - maximum sequence value
 * beta    - noise spectrum parameter [spectrum is shaped
 *           according to 1/(f^beta) ]
 * seed    - seed value for random number generator
 */
#include <stdio.h>
#include <math.h>

main( argc, argv ) int argc ; char *argv[] ; {
 float min, max, beta, seed, *x ;
 int N, i ;
 char *malloc() ;
/*
 * collect arguments
 */
    N = atoi( argv[1] ) ;
    min = atof( argv[2] ) ;
    max = atof( argv[3] ) ;
    beta = atof( argv[4] ) ;
    seed = atoi( argv[5] ) ;
/*
 * seed random generator
 */
    srand( seed ) ;
/*
 * allocate space for result
 */
    x = (float *) malloc( N*sizeof(float) ) ;
/*
 * work is done by shapednoise routine
 */
    shapednoise( min, max, x, N, beta ) ;
    for ( i = 0 ; i < N ; i++ )
        printf( "%f\n", x[i] ) ;
    free( x ) ;
}
/*
 * typedef structure for dft and idft routines
 */
typedef struct {
    float re ;
    float im ;
} complex ;
/*
```

```
 * compute N values of random noise with values in range min to max
 * with power spectrum asymptotically bounded by 1/(f^beta)
 * return resulting values in x[0] through x[N-1]
 */
shapednoise( min, max, x, N, beta )
 float min, max, x[], beta ; int N ;
{
 float fran(), nmin, nmax ;
 double power, amplitude, phase ;
 complex *X ;
 char *malloc() ;
 int i ;
/*
 * allocate memory to hold noise spectrum
 */
    X = (complex *) malloc( N*sizeof(complex) ) ;
/*
 * start with flat random noise
 */
    for ( i = 0 ; i < N ; i++ )
        x[i] = fran( -1., 1. ) ;
/*
 * take its Fourier transform
 */
    dft( x, N, X ) ;
/*
 * scale noise power spectrum by 1/(f^beta)
 */
    for ( i = 1 ; i <= N/2 ; i++ ) {
        power = X[i].re*X[i].re + X[i].im*X[i].im ;
        phase = atan2( (double) X[i].im, (double) X[i].re ) ;
        power /= pow( (double) i, (double) beta ) ;
        amplitude = sqrt( power ) ;
        X[i].re = amplitude*cos( phase ) ;
        X[i].im = amplitude*sin( phase ) ;
    }
/*
 * force spectrum to be conjugate-symmetrical around 0 Hz
 */
    for ( i = 1 ; i <= N/2 ; i++ ) {
        X[N-i].re = X[i].re ;
        X[N-i].im = -X[i].im ;
    }
/*
 * take inverse Fourier transform
 */
    idft( x, N, X ) ;
/*
```

```
 * find minimum and maximum noise signal values
 */
    nmin = nmax = x[0] ;
    for ( i = 1 ; i < N ; i++ ) {
        if ( x[i] > nmax )
            nmax = x[i] ;
        if ( x[i] < nmin )
            nmin = x[i] ;
    }
/*
 * scale returned noise to lie between min and max
 */
    for ( i = 0 ; i < N ; i++ )
        x[i] = (max - min)*(x[i] - nmin)/(nmax - nmin) + min ;
/*
 * free temporarily allocated memory
 */
    free( X ) ;
}
```

Waveforms produced by this program, along with their associated spectra, are shown in Figures 5-11 and 5-12.

To test the "musicality" of these random sequences, we can display the data in yet another form. First, we choose a set of random integers in the range 0 to 19, corresponding to our "favorite" pitch range from middle C to G a tempered twelfth higher, with β set to 0. Then we vary β to 1, 1.5, and 2. As a final example, here are the four random melodies, broken up into 16-note phrases.

First, $\beta = 0$. The pitches are given by the list (reading down the columns)

```
18 13  7  7  7  4 15  3  3 13  1 19  4  6  7 19 14 19  9  0 10 17  4 11
11 19 11  8 11 12` 8 10  6 17  1 10  8  8 16  0  9  9 18 16 15 15 15 10
```

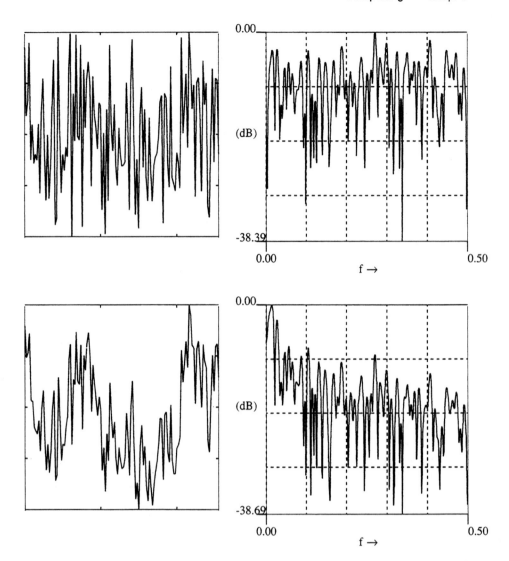

Figure 5-11 Noise waveforms and spectra obtained by direct spectrum shaping. Plots on the left show waveforms, plots on the right their associated spectra. β is 0 for the top pair and 1 for the bottom pair. As the β parameter increases, the waveforms become more and more constrained, and the associated spectrum drops off more rapidly with increasing frequency.

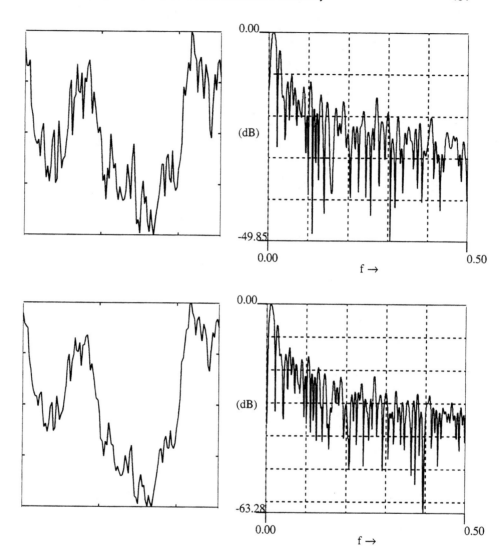

Figure 5-12   Noise waveforms and spectra obtained by direct spectrum shaping. β is 1.5 for the top pair of plots and 2 for the bottom pair.

Second, $\beta = 1$. The pitches for this melody are given by the list

```
19 16 10   6   5   3 11   1   0   8   0 12   2   4   8 17 12 18 12   7 14 19 10 15
15 18   9   6   7   8   5   4   3 11   0   7   4   6 15   4 12 12 17 16 18 17 17 14
```

Third, $\beta = 1.5$. The pitches are

```
19 16 10   6   5   3   7   0   0   5   0   8   2   3   7 14 12 17 13 10 16 19 13 16
16 16   9   5   5   6   3   2   1   7   0   5   3   6 13   7 13 13 16 16 18 18 17 16
```

Finally, $\beta = 2$. The pitches for this melody are given by the list

```
18 16 11   7   5   3   5   0   0   3   0   5   2   4   7  13  12  16  14  13  17  19  16  17
16 15   9   6   5   5   2   1   1   4   0   4   3   5  11   9  13  14  16  17  19  18  17  17
```

Are the pitches associated with the $\beta = 1$ list "about right"? Whether they are or not, this method of choosing random values provides a valuable tool for controlling the constraint of a random list.

5.7 COMPOSITIONAL ALGORITHMS

In addition to stochastic methods such as those described in this chapter, there exist a host of other approaches to composing music with the aid of a computer. Some of the methods that have been explored are based on formal grammars (Buxton et al., 1978; Roads, 1979) and their extensions, sometimes in the direction of stochastic methods (Jones, 1981). Other interesting approaches have been based on the techniques of artificial intelligence (Rodet and Cointe, 1984), while many concentrate on the direct manipulation of musical sound (Rodet et al., 1984). The field of compositional algorithms is so broad that this is necessarily the most incomplete section in this book.

The general area of compositional algorithms reflects the tremendous variation in approach to musicmaking that has been the hallmark of contemporary music for decades. Whatever else they may represent, computers are the most flexible and most powerful instruments of music yet devised. And as luck would have it, the rapidly decreasing cost of computing promises to make computer music the most widespread and accessible form of music in our world.

REFERENCES

1. W. Buxton, W. Reeves, R. Baeker, and L. Mezei, "The Use of Hierarchy and Instance in a Data Structure for Computer Music," *Computer Music J. 2*, no. 2 (1978): 10–20.

2. J. Chadabe, "Interactive Composing," *Computer Music J. 8*, no. 1 (1984): 22–27.

3. C. Fry, "Computer Improvisation," *Computer Music J. 4*, no. 3 (1980): 48–58.

4. M. Gardner, "White and Brown Music, Fractal Curves and 1/F Fluctuations," *Scientific American 238*, no. 4 (1978): 16–31.

5. L. A. Hiller and L. M. Isaacson, *Experimental Music: Composition with an Electronic Computer* (McGraw-Hill, New York, 1959).

6. K. Jones, "Compositional Applications of Stochastic Processes," *Computer Music J. 5* , no. 2, (1981): 45–61.

7. D. E. Knuth, "The Art of Computer Programming." Vol. 2 *Seminumerical Algorithms* Addison-Wesley, Reading, Mass., 1969.

8. B. B. Mandelbrot, *The Fractal Geometry of Nature* (Freeman, New York, 1983).

9. M. V. Mathews, and F. R. Moore, "GROOVE: A Program to Compose, Store, and Edit Functions of Time," *Comm. ACM 13* (1971): 715–721.

10. F. R. Moore, "Computer-controlled Analog Synthesizers," *Bell Laboratories Computing Science Report No. 10* (Murray Hill, N. J., May 1973)

11. C. Roads, "Grammars as Representations for Music," *Computer Music J. 3*, no. 1 (1979): 45–55.

12. X. Rodet and P. Cointe, "FORMES: Composition and Scheduling of Processes," *Computer Music J. 8*, no. 3 (1984): 32–50.

13. X. Rodet, Y. Potard, and J.-B. Barrière, "The CHANT Project: From Synthesis of the Singing Voice to Synthesis in General," *Computer Music J. 8*, no. 3 (1984): 15–31.

14. R. F. Voss and J. Clarke, "'1/f Noise' in Music: Music from 1/f Noise," *J. Acoust. Soc. of Amer. 63*, (January 1978): 258–263.

15. M. Woodroofe, *Probability with Applications* (McGraw-Hill Book Company, New York, 1975).

16. I. Xenakis, *Formalized Music* (Indiana University Press, Bloomington, 1971).

Appendix A

Mathematics

The following mathematical ideas are collected here for convenient reference.

A.1 SERIES NOTATION

The capital Greek letter sigma (Σ) is used to denote conveniently a number of quantities to be added together, as in

$$\sum_{k=1}^{n} k \tag{A-1}$$

which is read "the sum from $k = 1$ to n of k." k is called the index of summation and takes on integer values in the range specified below and above the capital sigma. To expand this notation, we write down the specified expression over and over, changing k each time as specified, adding as we go, as in

$$\sum_{k=1}^{n} k = 1 + 2 + 3 + \cdots + n \tag{A-2}$$

Many summation formulas have so-called closed forms, such as

$$\sum_{k=1}^{n} k = 1 + 2 + 3 + \cdots + n = \frac{n(n+1)}{2} \tag{A-3}$$

$$\sum_{k=0}^{\infty} ar^k = a + ar + ar^2 + \cdots = \frac{a}{1-r} \qquad (r < 1) \tag{A-4}$$

$$\sum_{k=0}^{n-1} ar^k = \frac{a(1 - r^n)}{1 - r} \qquad (r \neq 1) \tag{A-5}$$

Using these closed-form formulas allows us to compute directly the sum of the integers from 1 to 10 as $10(11/2) = 55$, the sum of the infinite series $1 + 1/2 + 1/4 + 1/8 + \ldots$ as $1/(1 - 1/2) = 2$, and the sum of the finite series $1 + 1/3 + 1/9 + 1/27$ as $1(1 - 1/81)/(1 - 1/3) = 240/162 = 1.481 \ldots$.

The capital Greek letter *pi* (Π) is used to denote conveniently a number of quantities to be multiplied together, as in

$$\prod_{k=1}^{n} k = k! \tag{A-6}$$

which is read "the product from $k = 1$ to n of k" (the notation $k!$ is read as "k factorial). Its properties are similar to those of the sum notation.

A.2 BASIC RULES OF ALGEBRA

Algebra deals with the solution of polynomial equations having the general form

$$f(x) = a_n x^n + a_{n-1}x^{n-1} + \cdots + a_2 x^2 + a_1 x + a_0 = 0 \tag{A-7}$$

All a values are constant coefficients, and the highest power of x that occurs is called the degree of the polynomial. The fundamental theorem of algebra states that any nth-degree polynomial always has exactly n roots, which may be complex and may not be distinct (different from each other).

A polynomial can always be rearranged so that the leading coefficient is unity by dividing through by a_n. The roots of the polynomial may then be obtained by factoring the polynomial, as in

$$f(x) = x^n + a_{n-1}x^{n-1} + \cdots + a_0 \tag{A-8}$$

$$= (x - r_1)(x - r_2) \cdots (x - r_n) = \prod_{k=1}^{n} (x - r_k) = 0$$

where r_k is the kth root of the polynomial.

A.2.1 Exponents

The basic rules of exponents are as follows. If p and q are any real numbers, a and b are positive real numbers, and m and n are positive integers, then

$$a^p a^q = a^{p+q} \tag{A-9}$$

$$\frac{a^p}{a^q} = a^{p-q} \tag{A-10}$$

$$(a^p)^q = a^{pq} \tag{A-11}$$

$$(a^m)^{1/n} = a^{m/n} \qquad (A\text{-}12)$$

$$a^{-p} = \frac{1}{a^p} \qquad (A\text{-}13)$$

$$a^0 = 1 \quad (\text{if } a \neq 0) \qquad (A\text{-}14)$$

$$(a/b)^{1/n} = \frac{a^{1/n}}{b^{1/n}} \qquad (A\text{-}15)$$

$$(ab)^p = a^p b^p \qquad (A\text{-}16)$$

A.2.2 Logarithms

If $a^p = x$, where a is not 0 or 1, then p is called the logarithm to the base a of x, written $\log_a x = p$. The following relationships follow from this definition and the rules of exponents given previously (x, y, and a are any real numbers).

$$\log_a xy = \log_a x + \log_a y \qquad (A\text{-}17)$$

$$\log_a \frac{x}{y} = \log_a x - \log_a y \qquad (A\text{-}18)$$

$$\log_a x^y = y \log_a x \qquad (A\text{-}19)$$

The irrational number $e = 2.7182818 \ldots$ is called the natural base of logarithms, and $\log_e x$ is often written as $\ln x$. The exact value of e is given by

$$e = 1 + \frac{1}{1!} + \frac{1}{2!} + \frac{1}{3!} + \frac{1}{4!} + \cdots \qquad (A\text{-}20)$$

where $n!$ means n factorial (the product of all integers from 1 to n).

The number e to any power is computable using the relation

$$e^x = \sum_{n=0}^{\infty} \frac{x^n}{n!} = 1 + \frac{x}{1!} + \frac{x^2}{2!} + \frac{x^3}{3!} + \frac{x^4}{4!} + \cdots \qquad (A\text{-}21)$$

where 0! is defined as 1.

To change the base of a logarithm, we may use the relation

$$\log_a x = \frac{\log_b x}{\log_b a} \qquad (A\text{-}22)$$

This may also be written as

$$\log_a x = K \log_b x \qquad (A\text{-}23)$$

where

$$K = \frac{1}{\log_b a} \qquad (A\text{-}24)$$

Values of K are given in the following table for base changes among 10, 2, and e (b is the base of the available logarithm of x, and a is the desired base).

	$b = 10$	$b = 2$	$b = e$
$a = 10$	1	0.30103...	0.43429...
$a = 2$	3.32193...	1	1.44270...
$a = e$	2.30259...	0.69315...	1

For example,

$$\log_2 x = 3.32193 \log_{10} x = 1.44270 \ln x \qquad \text{(A-25)}$$

A.3 BASIC PLANE TRIGONOMETRY

The following diagram shows a right triangle inscribed in a circle. The base of the triangle is marked A, the height O, and the hypotenuse H. θ refers to the angle between the base of the triangle and its hypotenuse.

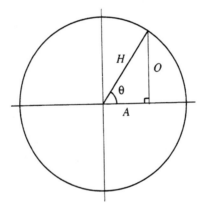

A.3.1 Angles

The ratio of the diameter to the circumference of a circle is an irrational number $\pi = 3.14159\ldots$. Because the circumference of a circle is π times its diameter and because the diameter is twice the radius of a circle, the circumference is 2π times the length of the radius of a circle.

Angles are commonly measured in degrees, radians, or grads. There are 360 degrees, 2π radians, and 400 grads in a circle (radians are preferred for most mathematical work). Positive angles are by convention measured counterclockwise from the positive horizontal axis. Thus in a typical diagram, a line inclined at an angle of 0° (0 radians) points to the right, 90° ($\pi/2$ radians) points straight up, 180° (π radians) points to the left, and so on. Negative angles denote measurement in the clockwise direction. Thus in a typical diagram, a line inclined at an angle of –90° ($-\pi/2$ radians) points straight down, and so on.

A.3.2 Trigonometric Functions

The sine of angle θ is defined as the ratio of the lengths of the side opposite the angle to the hypotenuse of a right triangle.

$$\sin \theta = \frac{O}{H} \tag{A-26}$$

The cosine of angle θ is defined as the ratio of the lengths of the side adjacent to the angle to the hypotenuse in a right triangle.

$$\cos \theta = \frac{A}{H} \tag{A-27}$$

The tangent of angle θ is defined as the ratio of the length of side opposite the angle to the length of the side adjacent to the angle.

$$\tan \theta = \frac{O}{A} \tag{A-28}$$

The cotangent of angle θ is defined as the reciprocal of the tangent of angle θ.

$$\cot \theta = \frac{1}{\tan \theta} = \frac{A}{O} \tag{A-29}$$

The secant of angle θ is defined as the reciprocal of the cosine of angle θ.

$$\sec \theta = \frac{1}{\cos \theta} = \frac{H}{A} \tag{A-30}$$

The cosecant of angle θ is defined as the reciprocal of the sine of angle θ.

$$\csc \theta = \frac{1}{\sin \theta} = \frac{H}{O} \tag{A-31}$$

A.3.3 Inverse Trigonometric Functions

If $\sin \theta = x$, then θ is the inverse sine of x, written as arcsin $x = \theta$, or $\sin^{-1} x = \theta$.[1] Because all trigonometric functions are periodic with periods of 2π, inverse trigonometric functions are many-valued, or inherently ambiguous. For example, if $\tan \theta = x$, then $\tan \theta + k 2\pi = x$ as well, where k is any integer.

To resolve this ambiguity, inverse trigonometric functions are considered to have values in a specified range of *principal values*. The following table compares the domains of the three basic trigonometric functions with the domains of the principal values of their inverses.

---

[1] The "inverse sine" is signified by either the notation $\sin^{-1} x$ or arcsin x. Similarly, the other inverse trigonometric functions may be signified by using the -1 superscript or by prefixing the name of the function with arc.

Function (domain)					Inverse Function (principal value range)			
-1	$\leq$	$x = \sin\theta$	$\leq$	1	$-\pi/2$	$\leq$	$\theta = \sin^{-1} x$	$\leq$	$\pi/2$
-1	$\leq$	$x = \cos\theta$	$\leq$	1	0	$\leq$	$\theta = \cos^{-1} x$	$\leq$	π
$-\infty$	$<$	$x = \tan\theta$	$<$	∞	$-\pi/2$	$<$	$\theta = \tan^{-1} x$	$<$	$\pi/2$

A.3.4 Trigonometric Identities

The following relationships derive from the basic definitions of the trigonometric functions, where A and B are any angles.

$$\tan A = \frac{\sin A}{\cos A} \tag{A-32}$$

$$\sin^2 A + \cos^2 A = 1 \tag{A-33}$$

$$\sin(-A) = -\sin A \tag{A-34}$$

$$\cos(-A) = \cos A \tag{A-35}$$

$$\tan(-A) = -\tan A \tag{A-36}$$

$$\sin 2A = 2\sin A \cos A \tag{A-37}$$

$$\cos 2A = \cos^2 A - \sin^2 A \tag{A-38}$$

$$\tan 2A = \frac{2\tan A}{1 - \tan^2 A} \tag{A-39}$$

$$\sin\frac{A}{2} = \left[\frac{1 - \cos A}{2}\right]^{1/2} \tag{A-40}$$

$$\cos\frac{A}{2} = \left[\frac{1 + \cos A}{2}\right]^{1/2} \tag{A-41}$$

$$\tan\frac{A}{2} = \left\{\frac{1 - \cos A}{1 + \cos A}\right\}^{1/2} = \frac{\sin A}{1 + \cos A} \tag{A-42}$$

$$= \frac{1 - \cos A}{\sin A} = \csc A - \cot A$$

$$\sin^2 A = \frac{1}{2} - \frac{1}{2}\cos 2A \tag{A-43}$$

$$\cos^2 A = \frac{1}{2} + \frac{1}{2}\cos 2A \tag{A-44}$$

$$\sin A + \sin B = 2\sin\left[\frac{1}{2}(A + B)\right]\cos\left[\frac{1}{2}(A - B)\right] \tag{A-45}$$

$$\sin A - \sin B = 2\cos\left[\frac{1}{2}(A + B)\right]\sin\left[\frac{1}{2}(A - B)\right] \tag{A-46}$$

$$\cos A + \cos B = 2 \cos \left[\frac{1}{2}(A + B)\right] \cos \left[\frac{1}{2}(A - B)\right] \qquad \text{(A-47)}$$

$$\cos A - \cos B = -2 \sin \left[\frac{1}{2}(A + B)\right] \sin \left(\frac{1}{2}(B - A)\right) \qquad \text{(A-48)}$$

$$\sin A \sin B = \frac{1}{2}[\cos (A - B) - \cos (A + B)] \qquad \text{(A-49)}$$

$$\cos A \cos B = \frac{1}{2}[\cos (A - B) + \cos (A + B)] \qquad \text{(A-50)}$$

$$\sin A \cos B = \frac{1}{2}[\sin (A - B) + \sin (A + B)] \qquad \text{(A-51)}$$

$$\sin (A \pm B) = \sin A \cos B \pm \cos A \sin B \qquad \text{(A-52)}$$

$$\cos (A \pm B) = \cos A \cos B \mp \sin A \sin B \qquad \text{(A-53)}$$

A.3.5 Trigonometric Series

The following relationships express the basic trigonometric functions in terms of an infinite series in angle θ, where θ is measured in radians.

$$\sin \theta = \theta - \frac{\theta^3}{3!} + \frac{\theta^5}{5!} - \frac{\theta^7}{7!} + \cdots \qquad \text{(A-54)}$$

$$\cos \theta = 1 - \frac{\theta^2}{2!} + \frac{\theta^4}{4!} - \frac{\theta^6}{6!} + \cdots \qquad \text{(A-55)}$$

A.4 COMPLEX NUMBERS

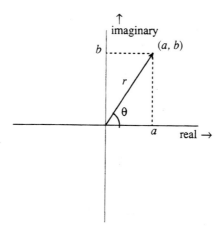

Just as a real number may be thought of as a point on an infinite line, a complex number may be thought of as a point on an infinite plane. The complex number plane is formed by adding an imaginary axis at a right angle to the real axis. The location of a point may be specified either in rectangular form by giving its coordinates along the real and imaginary axes or in polar form by giving its distance and direction (angle) from the origin of the plane.

In rectangular form, a complex number may be written as $a + ib$, where a and b are real numbers and i is the imaginary unit, defined to be equal to the square root of -1 (hence $i^2 = -1$). a and b are called the real and imaginary parts of the complex number $a + ib$.

In polar form, a complex number may be written as $r \angle \theta$ (read as "r at an angle θ"), where r is the distance of the point from the origin in the direction specified by angle θ. r is alternatively called the amplitude, modulus or magnitude of the complex number.

In rectangular form, the complex numbers $a + ib$ and $a - ib$ are called complex conjugates of each other.

In polar form, the complex numbers $r \angle \theta$ and $r \angle -\theta$ are called complex conjugates of each other. If z is a complex number, its complex conjugate is often written as z^*.

Two complex numbers are equal only if they refer to the same point on the complex plane. Therefore, $a + ib = c + id$ if and only if $a = c$ and $b = d$, and $r_1 \angle \theta_1 = r_2 \angle \theta_2$ if and only if $r_1 = r_2$ and $\theta_1 = \theta_2$.

A.4.1 Complex Arithmetic

Addition. The sum of two complex numbers is formed by adding the real and imaginary parts separately.

$$(a + ib) + (c + id) = (a + c) + i(b + d) \tag{A-56}$$

Subtraction. The difference of two complex numbers is formed by subtracting the real and imaginary parts separately.

$$(a + ib) - (c + id) = (a - c) + i(b - d) \tag{A-57}$$

Multiplication. The product of two complex numbers in rectangular form is computed by the ordinary rules of algebra (recalling that by definition, $i^2 = -1$).

$$(a + ib)(c + id) = ac + iad + ibc + i^2bd = (ac - bd) + i(ad + bc) \tag{A-58}$$

In polar form, the product of two complex numbers is computed by multiplying the magnitudes and adding the angles.

$$(r_1 \angle \theta_1)(r_2 \angle \theta_2) = (r_1 r_2) \angle (\theta_1 + \theta_2) \tag{A-59}$$

Division. The quotient of two complex numbers in rectangular form is also computed by the ordinary rules of algebra.

$$\frac{a + ib}{c + id} = \frac{(ac + bd) + i(bc - ad)}{c^2 + d^2} \tag{A-60}$$

This is obtained by multiplying by $(c - id)/(c - id)$, which is equivalent to 1.

In polar form, the quotient of two complex numbers is formed by dividing the magnitudes and subtracting the angles.

$$\frac{r_1 \angle \theta_1}{r_2 \angle \theta_2} = \frac{r_1}{r_2} \angle (\theta_1 - \theta_2) \tag{A-61}$$

A.4.2 Euler's Identities

The following identities relate trigonometric functions to the number e taken to an imaginary power:

$$e^{i\theta} = \cos \theta + i \sin \theta \tag{A-62}$$

and

$$e^{-i\theta} = \cos \theta - i \sin \theta \tag{A-63}$$

where $i^2 = -1$.

The following relationships follow directly from Euler's identities.

$$\sin \theta = \frac{e^{i\theta} - e^{-i\theta}}{2i} \tag{A-64}$$

$$\cos \theta = \frac{e^{i\theta} + e^{-i\theta}}{2} \tag{A-65}$$

$$\tan \theta = \frac{e^{i\theta} - e^{-i\theta}}{i(e^{i\theta} + e^{-i\theta})} = -i \left[\frac{e^{i\theta} - e^{-i\theta}}{e^{i\theta} + e^{-i\theta}} \right] \tag{A-66}$$

Using Euler's identities, we may write a complex number $a + ib$ in polar form as $re^{i\theta}$, where

$$a = r \cos \theta \tag{A-67}$$

and

$$b = r \sin \theta \tag{A-68}$$

Similarly,

$$r = \sqrt{a^2 + b^2} \tag{A-69}$$

and

$$\theta = \tan^{-1} \frac{b}{a} \tag{A-70}$$

Multiplication and division of complex numbers written in the form $re^{i\theta}$ follow directly from the basic laws of exponents.

The logarithm of a complex number may be defined as

$$\ln re^{i\theta} = \ln r + i\theta + k 2\pi i \tag{A-71}$$

where k is any integer.

A.4.3 De Moivre's Theorem

De Moivre's theorem states that if p is any real number,

$$(re^{i\theta})^p = r^p e^{ip\theta} \qquad (A\text{-}72)$$

Combining De Moivre's theorem with Euler's identity allows it to be stated as

$$[r(\cos\theta + i\sin\theta)]^p = r^p(\cos p\theta + i\sin p\theta) \qquad (A\text{-}73)$$

De Moivre's theorem provides a simple way to derive many new trigonometric expressions. For example, to derive an expression for $\cos 3\theta$, we can set r to 1 (for convenience) and p to 3, yielding

$$1^3(\cos 3\theta + i\sin 3\theta) = [1(\cos\theta + i\sin\theta)]^3 \qquad (A\text{-}74)$$

Evaluating the right-hand side of this equation yields expressions for both $\cos 3\theta$ and $\sin 3\theta$:

$$\cos 3\theta = \cos^3\theta - 3\sin^2\theta\cos\theta \qquad (A\text{-}75)$$

and

$$\sin 3\theta = 3\sin\theta\cos^2\theta - \sin^3\theta \qquad (A\text{-}76)$$

If p is set to $1/n$, De Moivre's theorem may be used to find roots of complex numbers according to

$$(re^{i\theta})^{1/n} = r^{1/n} e^{i(1/n)\theta} \qquad (A\text{-}77)$$

The n nth roots of a complex number may be found using

$$[r(\cos\theta + i\sin\theta)]^{1/n} = r^{1/n}\left[\cos\frac{\theta + k2\pi}{n} + i\sin\frac{\theta + k2\pi}{n}\right] \qquad (A\text{-}78)$$

and setting k to $0, 1, \ldots, n - 1$.

Appendix B

Units of Measure

Metric Prefixes

Multiplier		Prefix	Symbol
1,000,000,000,000.	$= 10^{12}$	tera-	T
1,000,000,000.	$= 10^{9}$	giga-	G
1,000,000.	$= 10^{6}$	mega-	M
1000.	$= 10^{3}$	kilo-	k
100.	$= 10^{2}$	hecto-	h
10.	$= 10^{1}$	deka-	da
0.1	$= 10^{-1}$	deci-	d
0.01	$= 10^{-2}$	centi-	c
0.001	$= 10^{-3}$	milli-	m
0.000 001	$= 10^{-6}$	micro-	μ
0.000 000 001	$= 10^{-9}$	nano-	n
0.000 000 000 001	$= 10^{-12}$	pico-	p
0.000 000 000 000 001	$= 10^{-15}$	femto-	f
0.000 000 000 000 000 001	$= 10^{-18}$	atto-	a

Système Internationale (SI) Unit Definitions

Unit	Symbol	Measure	Definition
Ampere	A	Electrical current	The constant current that, if maintained in two straight parallel conductors that are of infinite length and negligible cross section and are separated from each other by a distance of 1 meter in a vacuum, will produce between these conductors a force equal to 2×10^{-7} newton per meter of length.
Atmosphere	atm	Pressure	One standard atmosphere of pressure equals 101,325 newtons per square meter.
Bar	bar	Pressure	One bar equals 100,000 newtons per square meter.
Baud	Bd	Signaling speed	One baud equals one element per second.
Bel	B	Power ratio	The logarithm to the base 10 of the ratio of two values of power.
Bit	b	Information	A unit of information generally represented by a pulse; a binary digit (that is, a one or a zero in computer technology).
Dyne	dyn	Force	The amount of force necessary to impart an acceleration of 1 centimeter per second per second to 1 gram of mass. One dyne is equal to 10^{-5} newton.
Hertz	Hz	Frequency	The number of cycles per second.
Joule	J	Energy	The work done by 1 newton acting through a distance of 1 meter.
Kilogram	kg	Mass	A unit of mass based on a cylinder of platinum-iridium alloy located at the International Bureau of Weights and Measures in Paris.
Meter	m	Length	A unit of length defined as 1,650,763.73 wavelengths in vacuum of the orange-red line of the spectrum of ^{86}K (Krypton).
Neper	Np	Ratio	A dimensionless unit for expressing the ratio of two voltages, currents, or powers in a logarithmic manner. The number of nepers is the natural (Napierian) logarithm of the square root of the ratio of the two quantities being compared. One neper equals 8.686 decibels.
Newton	N	Force	One newton is the force that will impart an acceleration of 1 meter per second per second on a mass of 1 kilogram. One newton is equal to 10^5 dynes.
Pascal	Pa	Pressure	One pascal is equal to 1 newton per square meter.
Phon	phon	Loudness	One phon is the pressure level in decibels of a pure 1000 -Hz tone.
Volt	V	Voltage	One volt is the voltage between 2 points of a conducting wire carrying a constant current of 1 ampere and dissipating 1 watt of power.
Watt	W	Power	One watt equals 1 joule per second.

Appendix C

Tuning

> *Pythagoras found that the chords which sound pleasing to the ear—the
> western ear—correspond to exact divisions of the string by whole numbers.
> To the Pythagoreans that discovery had a mystic force. The agreement
> between nature and number was so cogent that it persuaded them that not
> only the sounds of nature, but all her characteristic dimensions, must be
> simple numbers that express harmonies. For example, Pythagoras or his fol-
> lowers believed that we should be able to calculate the orbits of the heavenly
> bodies (which the Greeks pictured as carried round the earth on crystal
> spheres) by relating them to the musical intervals. They felt that all the regu-
> larities in nature are musical; the movements of the heavens were, for them,
> the music of the spheres.*
>
> —J. Bronowski, *The Ascent of Man*
> *(Reproduced with the permission of BBC Enterprises Ltd.)*

One of the most fundamental problems in all music is the organization of pitch. A sequence of nonoverlapping pitches such as one might hear in speech is not constrained in
any particular way. As soon as sounds with differing pitches overlap in time, however,
as they might when a single voice is heard in a reverberant environment or when two or
more pitches are deliberately sounded together (as they are in most music), we are immediately struck by the many different qualities of the various pitch combinations.
Some pitch combinations sound simple, pleasant, relaxed, agreeable, euphonious, or
bland, while other combinations sound complex, unpleasant, tense, disagreeable, harsh,
or spicy. The musical adjectives *consonant* and *dissonant* are also used to describe

467

pitch combinations, as are the terms *harmonious* and *inharmonious*. The lore of musical aesthetics is rife with discussions of the relative merits and functions of musical consonance and dissonance as driving forces of music. There can be little doubt, however, about the origin of the notion of "harmonious" pitch combinations.

C.1 HARMONICS

All natural sounds are complex in the sense that they consist of several frequencies sounding simultaneously in time-varying proportions. Sounds that exhibit a strong musical pitch are precisely those whose component frequencies are related harmonically (or very nearly so). In other words, if a sound has the quality of musical pitch, it also has the the quality of being harmonic: its strongest vibrational components will exist at frequencies that tend to be integer multiples of some common frequency, called the *fundamental* frequency (see Figure C-1).

The existence of such harmonic components arises from physical properties of the vibrating object itself. Stretched strings, for example, can sustain vibrations in several modes simultaneously. Assuming that both ends are fixed (prevented from moving), a string, set in motion by plucking, striking, bowing, or the like, can sustain vibrations in modes such as these:

- The entire string moves back and forth (the fundamental mode).
- The two halves of the string exchange energy in seesaw fashion (the second harmonic).
- Three thirds of the string move symmetrically, typically with the center section moving in opposition to the outer two thirds (the third harmonic).

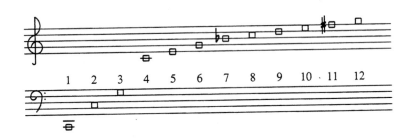

Figure C-1   Approximate pitches of harmonics. For a fundamental frequency of f Hz, harmonics occur at $1 f$ (the first harmonic, or fundamental), $2 f$ (the second harmonic), $3 f$ (the third harmonic), and so on. The approximate musical pitches of the harmonics are shown, relative to a fundamental frequency with a pitch of low C.

Though many other "inharmonic" vibration modes exist, they last only momentarily due to self-interference and cancellation. Thus a plucked or struck string tends to vibrate simultaneously in the easily self-sustaining modes while the others die out rapidly, with each sustained mode operating at one of the harmonic frequencies. Vibrating columns of air such as those in the human vocal tract, organ pipes, and woodwind and brass instruments also tend to vibrate in harmonic modes. Percussion instruments also vibrate in many modes simultaneously. However, due to their physical properties, many percussion instruments tend to vibrate in a variety of modes whose frequencies are not harmonically related. The instruments whose vibration modes are most inharmonically arranged are those that are most lacking in the property of musical pitch, such as cymbals and tam-tams, though musicians still speak of the "high" or "low" *indefinite pitch* of such instruments according to the relative strength of high- or low-frequency regions in the spectrum of the resulting sound.

Rather than hearing the collection of pitches associated with each harmonic frequency, we tend to *perceive* complex harmonic sounds as having a *single pitch*—associated with the fundamental frequency—and a tone color, or *timbre*—associated with the time-varying relative mixture of harmonic frequencies. Nevertheless, the consonance or dissonance of pitch combinations can be explained in terms of the interactions of individual frequency components, or sinusoids. For example, psychophysical studies have shown that if two sinusoidal frequency components match each other exactly, we simply hear a sinusoid, perhaps with a slightly different loudness than either component would produce alone.

As the frequencies of the two sinusoids gradually diverge, however, it is well known (and well documented) that at first we hear *beats*—or interference—between the two sinusoids, followed by a region of *roughness*—or acoustic dissonance—between the two sinusoids, followed by a region of *smoothness*—or acoustic independence—between the two sinusoids. The transition from roughness to smoothness defines the size of the *critical band*, or f_{cb}. The size of the critical band is usually described in terms of the ratio of the frequencies of the two nonidentical sinusoids, f_1 and f_2, with $f_1 > f_2$. If $f_1/f_2 < f_{cb}$, the two sinusoids will *interact*, producing a sensation of either beats or roughness, whereas if $f_1/f_2 > f_{cb}$, the two sinusoids will be *independent*, producing a smooth sensation. The size of the critical band is just under a tempered minor third at frequencies above about 500 Hz. The size of the critical band gradually grows larger at lower frequencies, becoming nearly an octave at 100 Hz, which explains why similar intervals can sound clear and harmonious at higher pitches but muddy or inharmonious at lower pitches.

When we hear a combination of two pitches, we judge the musical consonance or dissonance of the combination not solely by whether the two fundamental frequencies are within a critical band of each other but also by integrating the overall degree of interaction (or lack of interaction) among all possible pairs of harmonics from the individual tones. If a given pair of harmonics happens to match exactly in frequency, we hear no interaction at all, similar to hearing a single-frequency component. If the frequencies of another pair of harmonics do not match but lie within a critical band of each other, interaction in the form of beating or roughness is heard (the contribution of this interaction to the dissonance of the overall sound of the combination will depend on the strength of the interacting harmonics). If a pair of harmonics does not match and the component frequencies are separated by more than a critical band, we again hear no interaction. Because the relative strengths of the various components can vary greatly and in a time-varying manner, the overall degree of interaction between two complex tones can be difficult to predict. Nevertheless, it is precisely our overall impression of the degree of interaction that we call musical dissonance.

The history of musical tuning systems revolves principally around the search for ways of dealing with the fundamental insolubility of a problem that I call the fundamental problem of musical pitch. Simply stated, this problem is that there are no nonzero integer values of M and N that satisfy

$$\left[\frac{3}{2}\right]^M = \left[\frac{2}{1}\right]^N$$

The reason that this equation describes the fundamental problem of musical pitch is that the ratio 3/2 represents the musical interval of the perfect fifth (the interval between the second and third harmonics), and the ratio 2/1 (the interval between the first and second harmonics) represents the musical interval of the octave. If we are to devise a fixed tuning scheme for musical instruments, we must essentially find a reasonably small number of pitches that will allow a variety of harmonious combinations. To have even the possibility of harmonious combinations, the frequencies of the lowest (and therefore the strongest) harmonics must be taken into account, because every musical tone exhibiting the characteristic of definite pitch will contain such harmonics.

Suppose that we have two tones, one with a fundamental frequency of f_1 Hz and the other with a fundamental frequency of f_2 Hz. The harmonics of the first tone will fall at the frequencies $1f_1, 2f_1, 3f_1, \ldots$, while the harmonics of the second tone will fall at frequencies $1f_2, 2f_2, 3f_2, \ldots$ Obviously, two tones with exactly the same pitch $(f_1 = f_2)$ will sound harmonious, because the frequencies of all harmonics from the first tone will match the frequencies of all harmonics from the second tone precisely (the harmonics of the two tones need not have the same strengths, of course). Furthermore, it is obvious that if the fundamental frequencies of the two tones are related by an octave $(f_1 = 2f_2$ or $f_2 = 2f_1)$, all the harmonics of the upper pitch will be identical to the even-numbered harmonics of the lower tone. In fact, two tones separated by *any* number of octaves $(f_1 = 2^n f_2$, where n is an integer) will line up perfectly in this way, because all harmonics of the upper tone will invariably coincide precisely with harmonics of the lower tone. For this reason, different frequencies are considered to have the same pitch, or, more precisely, two pitches are said to belong to the same *pitch class* if they are separated only by an arbitrary number of octaves.

Finding harmonious combinations of octaves is therefore no problem, which is fortunate because the typically strong second harmonic of any complex tone falls one octave higher than the fundamental frequency. Furthermore, the second harmonic of most tones (when it is present) tends to be louder than all other harmonics except the fundamental; any disagreement with it would lead to audible beating or roughness in many cases.[1] The third harmonic, however, is also generally quite strong in amplitude and has a pitch that is *not* the same as that of the fundamental. The presence of frequency components near but not equal to this harmonic would be very likely to cause strong beating or roughness interaction and therefore a perceived sensation of dissonance. The frequency of the third harmonic is $3f$ Hz (where f Hz is the fundamental frequency). The frequency of the second harmonic—which has the same pitch as the fundamental—is $2f$ Hz. The ratio between the third and second harmonics is $3f/2f$, or simply $3/2$. The musical name for this interval (for reasons that will become evident later) is the *perfect fifth*.

What happens if we sound two complex tones together, one with a fundamental of f_1 Hz, the other with a fundamental frequency of $f_2 = 3f_1$ Hz? Clearly, all the harmonics of the second tone again fall precisely on top of harmonics of the first tone, just as in the case of the octave. This is easy to understand if we allow fundamental frequency f_1 to be 1 Hz to simplify the mathematics (even though this would be below our hearing range). The harmonics of 1 are 1, 2, 3, . . ., while the harmonics of 3 are 3, 6, 9, . . .—clearly the "harmonics of 3" are also "harmonics of 1." A moment's thought will generalize this principle even further: harmonics of harmonics are also harmonics. Thus if we choose two pitches so that the fundamental of one is a harmonic of the other, we are guaranteed perfect agreement, or musical consonance, always.

What if, however, the two fundamental frequencies are related as 3 is related to 2? 3 is clearly not a harmonic of 2. Every other harmonic of 3 is even, however, so every other harmonic of 3 is a harmonic of 2. How the two fundamentals interact will depend on their absolute frequencies: somewhere around 100 to 200 Hz and below the two fundamental frequencies will fall within the same critical band, causing interaction to occur. Higher-numbered harmonic pairs from the two tones will tend to be separated by more than a critical band, however, until fairly high numbered harmonics are reached. By the time this happens, the harmonics will have become fairly weak in amplitude.

Even more important is the fact that the combination of two tones a perfect fifth ($3/2$ frequency ratio) apart will result in a set of frequency components, all of which are harmonics of the frequency one octave below the lower tone. Once again, the harmonics of 2 are 2, 4, 6, 8, . . ., while the harmonics of 3 are 3, 6, 9, 12, ... The combination of both tones together (assuming that they are perfectly tuned) results in frequency components at 2, 3, 4, 6, 8, 9, 10, 12, . . ., all of which are harmonics of 1. Thus the combination sounds as harmonious as a single tone with a fundamental frequency of 1 that is missing a few of its harmonics—including the fundamental! Another psychophysical phenomenon—that of *residue pitch*—makes the combination tend to sound as if it has a single pitch associated with the "implied" fundamental, which lies one octave lower than the lower tone.[2]

---

[1]Remember that some musical tones are missing various harmonics altogether and that the tendency for harmonic components to become weaker in amplitude with increasing frequency is only an *overall* tendency that may not apply precisely to every harmonic of every tone.

[2]This effect, which works especially well at low frequencies, is sometimes used by pipe organ manufacturers to create sounds having the pitch of pipes twice the length of any in the organ.

C.2 PYTHAGOREAN TUNING

In general, the 3/2 ratio of fundamental frequencies results in the *best possible* harmonic agreement between tones with different pitches. Therefore, tone pairs separated by musical intervals of perfect fifths will sound as harmonious as different pitches ever can sound. We can therefore identify a set of pitches related to each other by 3/2 frequency ratios that provide many opportunities for harmonious tonal combinations.

So reasoned the ancient Greek mathematician and philosopher Pythagoras (580?–497 *B.C.*), whose method of tuning the notes of a musical "scale" is based solely on the perfect fifth. Pythagorean tuning works as follows. Starting with an arbitrary frequency, f, the frequencies of the notes in the Pythagorean tuning system are found by successive multiplication by 3/2:

$$N1: f$$

$$N2: \frac{3}{2} N1 = \frac{3}{2} f$$

$$N3: \frac{3}{2} N2 = \left(\frac{3}{2}\right)^2 f = \frac{9}{4} f$$

$$N4: \frac{3}{2} N3 = \left(\frac{3}{2}\right)^3 f = \frac{27}{8} f$$

$$N5: \frac{3}{2} N4 = \left(\frac{3}{2}\right)^4 f = \frac{81}{16} f$$

$$N6: \frac{3}{2} N5 = \left(\frac{3}{2}\right)^5 f = \frac{243}{32} f$$

$$N7: \frac{3}{2} N6 = \left(\frac{3}{2}\right)^6 f = \frac{729}{64} f$$

That is, if note N1 has a frequency of f Hz, then note N2 has a frequency of $(3/2)f$ Hz, note N3 has a frequency of $(9/4)f$ Hz, and so on. Each note in the sequence is a perfect fifth (3/2 frequency ratio) higher than the previous note, as depicted in Figure C-2.

The term *scale* comes from the Latin *scala*, meaning "ladder". Technically, we do not yet have a scale because the pitches obtained by taking successive perfect fifths will be spread out over quite a large pitch range. To obtain a proper scale, we must transform the pitches obtained by the sequence of fifths in two ways. First, we must transpose each pitch so that they all lie within the same octave. Second, we must rearrange the transposed pitches into ascending (or descending) order. Figure C-3 shows the results of applying these two operations to the sequence of seven pitches shown in Figure C-2.

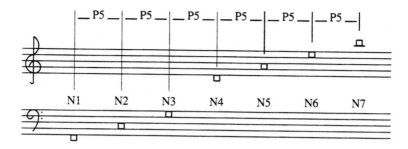

Figure C-2   Pythagorean tuning. Pitches are chosen at successive intervals of perfect fifths (P5) starting at an arbitrary pitch. The pitch interval between the second and third harmonics of any complex tone is a perfect fifth. The frequency of each tone in this sequence is therefore equal to 3/2 times the frequency of the previous pitch. If only the first five pitches of this sequence were used, a five-tone, or *pentatonic*, scale would result. Seven pitches are used to define the diatonic major scale, which has been used for centuries in Western music.

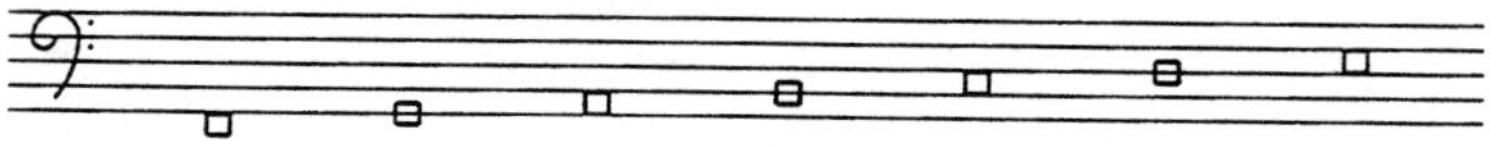

$$f \qquad \frac{9}{8}f \qquad \frac{81}{64}f \qquad \frac{729}{512}f \qquad \frac{3}{2}f \qquad \frac{27}{16}f \qquad \frac{243}{128}f$$

$$N1 \qquad \frac{N3}{2} \qquad \frac{N5}{4} \qquad \frac{N7}{8} \qquad \frac{N2}{1} \qquad \frac{N4}{2} \qquad \frac{N6}{4}$$

Figure C-3 Pythagorean tuning. The same seven pitches as in Figure C-2 are here shown transposed to lie within the same octave and rearranged into ascending (increasing frequency) order.

Finally, we have a choice about the starting note for the scale. It is of course possible to begin and end the scale on any of its pitches—in musical terms, the seven choices for starting notes are referred to as the *modes* of the scale. Only one choice, however, results in a scale that is divided into two "symmetric" halves. If we rearrange the pitches so that N2 is the beginning (and ending) note of the ascending scale and "normalize" the frequencies so that the frequency of N2 is 1, the so-called *Pythagorean diatonic major scale* results (see Figure C-4).

The Pythagorean diatonic major scale is symmetric in the sense that the intervals among the first four notes occur in the same order as the intervals among the last four notes. Each of these four-note groups is known as a *diatonic tetrachord* (four notes separated by a whole step, followed by a whole step, followed by a semitone). The two diatonic tetrachords are joined by a whole step (9/8 frequency ratio) between the fourth and fifth notes of the scale.

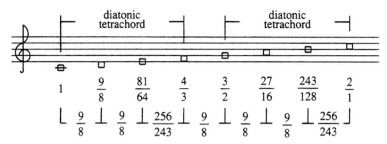

Figure C-4 Pythagorean tuning: the diatonic major scale. The frequency of each note is shown relative to the frequency of the beginning note, which is considered to be 1 (to obtain actual frequencies in hertz, simply multiply these rational values by f, the frequency of the first note of the scale). The intervals (frequency ratios between successive pitches) are also shown; note that there are only two interval types: the 9/8 *whole step* and the 256/243 *semitone*.

Observation of the diatonic major scale shown in Figure C-4 yields the reason that the 3/2 frequency ratio is called a *perfect fifth*. If we start at any note in the scale, call it number 1 (the ancient Greeks didn't know about 0), and count up five notes, the second note is said to be a "fifth" higher, in the sense that it lies five notes up the scale from the starting point. The fifth is a "perfect" interval when it has the "perfectly harmonious" 3/2 frequency ratio. All fifths in the Pythagorean diatonic major scale are perfect except for the one starting on the seventh note (B) and going up to the fourth note (F). The relative frequency of the seventh note is 243/128; the relative frequency of the fourth note (4/3) transposed up an octave so that it would lie higher than the seventh note is 8/3. Because the frequency ratio of this fifth

$$\frac{8/3}{243/128} = \frac{8}{3} \times \frac{128}{243} = \frac{1024}{729} \approx 1.40466\ldots$$

is less than the "perfect" ratio of 3/2 (= 1.5), this fifth is said to be *diminished*.

Similarly, the interval of the fourth is regarded as "perfect" because it is actually the same as a perfect fifth with the lower note transposed up an octave, resulting in a 4/3 frequency ratio. For example, the interval from the first to the fourth notes is clearly 4/3. Similarly, the interval from the second (9/8) to the fifth (3/2) notes in the scale is also a perfect fourth:

$$\frac{3/2}{9/8} = \frac{3}{2} \times \frac{8}{9} = \frac{24}{18} = \frac{4}{3} \approx 1.333333\ldots$$

All fourths in the Pythagorean diatonic major scale are perfect except for the one extending from the fourth note (F) up to the seventh note (B). Because the frequency ratio between these two notes

$$\frac{243/128}{4/3} = \frac{243}{128} \times \frac{3}{4} = \frac{729}{512} \approx 1.423828\ldots$$

is *greater* than the "perfect" ratio of 4/3 (= 1.333...), this fourth is said to be *augmented*.

Some historical tuning systems avoid the presence of augmented and diminished fifths and fourths by omitting the offending seventh note in the scale (which was obtained, after all, *last* in the sequence of seven perfect fifths used to obtain harmonious pitches). For example, a traditional Scottish tuning system that omits the seventh note in the Pythagorean scale is the basis for several old Scottish folktunes. Even more extreme in this regard is the *pentatonic scale*, which omits the *last two* notes in the sequence of perfect fifths. The pentatonic scale is still widely used in much Eastern music, especially the traditional music of the Orient.

Much harmonic music theory is based on the properties of the diatonic major scale, which finds its roots in the Pythagorean tuning system. All possible combinations of notes from this scale have been cataloged and analyzed thoroughly over the centuries. In addition to the 9/8 whole step and 256/243 semitone ratios necessary for the construction of the basic scale, one more interval plays an important role in Pythagorean tuning. If we wish to extend the scale to allow notes different from the first to play the "tonic" role, another interval accounts for some of the asymmetries between such intervals as the Pythagorean augmented fourth (729/512) and the Pythagorean diminished fifth (1024/729). By adding the next logical pitch to our sequence of perfect fifths, we gain the possibility of starting a new diatonic major scale on the fifth note of the original one (G). The pitch of this new note lies a perfect fifth higher than the last note of the sequence of fifths—in modern terminology, it would be called F# (F-sharp) because it lies a distance of five notes up the scale from B but has a pitch higher ("sharper") than the F already present in the scale. Its frequency is just $(243/128) \times (3/2) = 729/256$. The interval between F# and G is just the Pythagorean semitone

$$\frac{3/2}{729/512} = \frac{3}{2} \times \frac{512}{729} = \frac{1536}{1458} = \frac{256}{243} \approx 1.0534979\ldots$$

whereas the interval from F to F#

$$\frac{729/512}{4/3} = \frac{729}{512} \times \frac{3}{4} = \frac{2187}{2048} \approx 1.06787109\ldots$$

is somewhat larger and is called the Pythagorean *chromatic semitone*. We may think of the augmented fourth either as a perfect fifth minus a semitone or a perfect fourth plus a chromatic semitone, because 729/512 is equal either to (3/2)/(256/243) or (4/3) × (2187/2048). The Pythagorean scale is therefore made up of a whole tone (9/8) and two different semitone intervals, often called the diatonic semitone and the chromatic semitone (256/243 and 2187/2048, respectively).

The interval between the two types of Pythagorean semitones is known as the *Pythagorean comma*, which has the value

$$\frac{2187/2048}{256/243} = \frac{531,441}{524,288} \approx 1.013643265\ldots$$

The Pythagorean comma, to which we shall return later, is an extremely dissonant interval. Another small interval associated with Pythagorean tuning is the *syntonic comma*, equal to the ratio between the Pythagorean major third (81/64) and the harmonic (or "just") major third (5/4) or between the harmonic minor third (6/5) and the Pythagorean minor third (32/27). The syntonic comma has the value 81/80 = 1.0125.

Table C-1 lists the intervals in the Pythagorean scale in approximate order of increasing dissonance.

TABLE C-1   Intervals from the extended Pythagorean diatonic major scale.

Pythagorean Diatonic Major Scale	Examples in Scale Intervals	Ratios of Frequencies	Ratios as Decimal Numbers	Ratios in Terms of Perfect Fifths and Octaves
Octave	$\frac{C'}{C}$	$\frac{2}{1}$	2.0	$\frac{(3/2)^0}{(2/1)^{-1}}$
Perfect fifth	$\frac{G}{C}$	$\frac{3}{2}$	1.5	$\frac{(3/2)^2}{(2/1)^0}$
Perfect fourth	$\frac{F}{C}$	$\frac{4}{3}$	1.333333...	$\frac{(3/2)^{-1}}{(2/1)^{-1}}$
Pythagorean major sixth	$\frac{A}{C}$	$\frac{27}{16}$	1.6875	$\frac{(3/2)^3}{(2/1)^1}$
Pythagorean major third	$\frac{E}{C}$	$\frac{81}{64}$	1.265625	$\frac{(3/2)^4}{(2/1)^2}$
Pythagorean minor third	$\frac{F}{D}$	$\frac{32}{27}$	1.185185...	$\frac{(2/1)^2}{(3/2)^3}$
Pythagorean whole step	$\frac{D}{C}$	$\frac{9}{8}$	1.125	$\frac{(3/2)^2}{(2/1)^2}$
Pythagorean major seventh	$\frac{B}{C}$	$\frac{243}{128}$	1.8984375	$\frac{(3/2)^5}{(2/1)^2}$
Pythagorean diatonic semitone	$\frac{F}{E}$	$\frac{256}{243}$	1.053497942. ...	$\frac{(2/1)^3}{(3/2)^5}$
Pythagorean chromatic semitone	$\frac{F\#}{F}$	$\frac{2187}{2048}$	1.067871094. . .	$\frac{(3/2)^7}{(2/1)^4}$
Syntonic comma	$\frac{81/64}{5/4}$	$\frac{81}{80}$	1.0125	$\frac{(3/2)^2}{(2/1)^2}$
Pythagorean comma	$\frac{2187/2048}{256/243}$	$\frac{531,441}{524,288}$	1.013063585. . .	$\frac{(3/2)^{12}}{(2/1)^7}$

C.3 JUST TUNING

The Pythagorean system of tuning has many advantages, not the least of which is its simplicity. Tuning by fifths is easy to do in practice, and the resulting scale is therefore reasonably straightforward. All the fifths but one in the scale are perfect, allowing many harmonious combinations of two notes.

Not all these combinations are as harmonious as they could be, however. The Pythagorean method adjusts fifths to perfection, but not, for example, thirds. The third was for many centuries considered a dissonant interval, at least in the sense that it would have been unsatisfactory to resolve a piece of music by ending on a third.

The reason for this is simple: the Pythagorean major third (81/64) dissonates with the major third that naturally occurs between the fourth and fifth harmonics. Though the fourth and fifth harmonics are usually not as strong as the second and third, they nevertheless occur fairly early in the harmonic sequence, so disagreement with them is usually quite audible. A 5/4 frequency ratio would make a more harmonious major third than the one obtained through Pythagorean tuning.

So reasoned Zarlino, who lived in Italy about 2000 years after the time of Pythagoras. Zarlino adjusted the third note of the diatonic major scale to 5/4 times the frequency of the first, or tonic, note. This made the agreement between the harmonics of the tonic and the first, third, and fifth notes of the scale so good that this three-note triad soon replaced the two-note dyads of Pythagorean music as the basis for musical harmony.

The frequency ratios of the first, third, and fifth notes in Zarlino's system of *just* tuning (as it is called) are

$$1 : \frac{5}{4} : \frac{3}{2}$$

which are easily rearranged over a common denominator as

$$\frac{4}{4} : \frac{5}{4} : \frac{6}{4}$$

The three notes of this *just major triad* (in the key of C these notes would be, in ascending order, C-E-G) then have frequencies in the ratio 4:5:6. Zarlino left the pitches of the fourth and fifth notes of the scale unchanged, because these are obtained by tuning down and up a perfect fifth from the tonic. The rest of the notes of the scale are then derived by constructing pitches on the fourth (F-A-C) and fifth (G-B-D) notes of the scale in the 4:5:6 frequency proportion. Thus these triads, too, are just as harmonious as the tonic triad. The resulting just diatonic major scale is shown in Figure C-5.

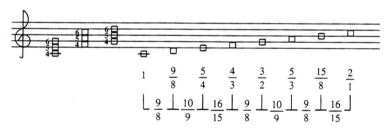

Figure C-5 The just major scale. This scale is constructed from the three triads shown on the left, each of which consists of tones with fundamental frequencies in the proportion 4:5:6. The frequency of each note in the resulting scale is shown relative to the frequency of the beginning note, which is considered to be 1. The intervals are also shown; note that there are now three basic interval types, compared with two for the corresponding Pythagorean scale.

Examination of Figure C-5 shows the essential differences between the Pythagorean and just systems of tuning. Four of the intervals (the octave, fifth, fourth, and one of the whole tones) are the same; the rest are different. The principal Pythagorean and just intervals are compared in Table C-2.

It is evident from Table C-2 that the numbers used in forming the interval ratios are generally smaller for the just system than for the Pythagorean, sometimes much smaller. Zarlino and others have argued that ratios of small numbers are generally more harmonious than ratios of larger numbers, much to the mystification of many readers over the centuries. The general tendency of lower-numbered harmonics to be stronger than higher-numbered ones in most musical sounds makes agreement with lower harmonics generally more important than agreement with higher harmonics. The fundamental of the upper tone in a just major third is in perfect agreement with the fifth harmonic of the lower tone, for example, whereas the fundamental of the upper tone in a Pythagorean major third is in perfect agreement with the (relatively weak) eighty-first harmonic of the lower tone. In the latter case, furthermore, the fundamental of the upper tone is in considerable disagreement with the much stronger fifth harmonic of the lower tone. If a major third were built on 200 Hz, for example, the frequency of the upper tone would be 250 Hz in the just system and 253.125 Hz in the Pythagorean system. The (relatively strong) fifth harmonic of the lower tone agrees exactly with the (relatively strong) fourth harmonic of the upper tone in the just system. The fourth harmonic of the upper tone in the Pythagorean system is 1012.5 Hz, which disagrees with the fifth harmonic of the lower tone by 12.5 Hz—enough to cause significant beating and plainly audible dissonance under most circumstances.

TABLE C-2 Comparison of Intervals from the Pythagorean and Just Tuning Systems.

Interval	Pythagorean Ratio	Just Ratio
Octave	$\frac{2}{1}$	$\frac{2}{1}$
Perfect fifth	$\frac{3}{2}$	$\frac{3}{2}$
Perfect fourth	$\frac{4}{3}$	$\frac{4}{3}$
Major sixth	$\frac{27}{16}$	$\frac{5}{3}$
Major third	$\frac{81}{64}$	$\frac{5}{4}$
Minor third	$\frac{32}{64}$	$\frac{6}{5}$
Whole tone	$\frac{9}{8}$	$\frac{9}{8}$ or $\frac{10}{9}$
Diatonic semitone	$\frac{256}{243}$	$\frac{16}{15}$

The just tuning system therefore tends to sound more harmonious when many thirds and sixths are used in music. The difficulty with the just system—at least in connection with the construction of musical instruments that must use a relatively small number of fixed pitch classes—is the additional complication that it introduces into the scale. The important intervals that occur in the just tuning system are shown in Table C-3. We see from this table that the just tuning system requires two types of whole steps (here denoted "major," and "minor") and three types of semitones ("diatonic," "chromatic major," and "chromatic minor").

Musical tones consisting of a single frequency component (sinusoids) are extremely rare (essentially nonexistent) in nature. Thus a single frequency might be readily interpreted as a fundamental or as a higher-numbered harmonic. If we consider the set of fundamentals of which a given frequency may be a harmonic, we immediately discover a second set of frequency relationships that are just as important as harmonics in music theory.

For example, if we consider frequency f to be the second harmonic of some other fundamental, it is clear that that fundamental must have a frequency of $f/2$ Hz. If f is a third harmonic, it is the third harmonic of $f/3$ Hz, and so on. This sequence of frequencies—f, $f/2$, $f/3$, $f/4$, and so on—defines the *subharmonic series* and gives rise to *minor scales* in music (see Figure C-6).

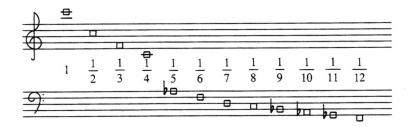

Figure C-6 Approximate pitches of subharmonics. For a fundamental frequency of f Hz, subharmonics occur at $f/1$ (the first subharmonic, or fundamental), $f/2$ (the second subharmonic), $f/3$ (the third subharmonic), and so on The approximate musical pitches of the subharmonics are shown, relative to a fundamental frequency with a pitch of high C. Note that the sequence of musical intervals between successive notes is the same as for the harmonic series, except that the intervals proceed in a downward direction.

Just as the fourth, fifth, and sixth harmonics define the basic triad for the just major scale, the fourth, fifth, and sixth subharmonics define the basic triad for the just minor scale. The sense of pitch is of course reversed for subharmonics, with the sixth subharmonic lower in pitch than the fifth and the fifth lower than the fourth. The frequency ratios of the just minor triad, from lowest to highest pitch, are therefore

$$\frac{1}{6} : \frac{1}{5} : \frac{1}{4}$$

TABLE C-3 Intervals from the extended just tuning system. The example in the second column is in the just diatonic major scale based on C. The *just chromatic major semitone* is given by the ratio of the *just minor whole step* to the *just diatonic semitone* [(10/9)/(16/15)]. Similarly, the *just chromatic minor semitone* is given by the ratio of the *just major whole step* to the *just diatonic semitone* [(9/8)/(16/15)]. The *syntonic comma* (repeated in this table along with the *Pythagorean comma* for convenience) is seen to be the discrepancy between the Pythagorean and just major thirds.

Interval	Example	Frequency Ratio (Fraction)	(Decimal)
Octave	$\frac{C'}{C}$	$\frac{2}{1}$	2.0
Perfect fifth	$\frac{G}{C}$	$\frac{3}{2}$	1.5
Perfect fourth	$\frac{F}{C}$	$\frac{4}{3}$	1.333333...
Just major sixth	$\frac{A}{C}$	$\frac{5}{3}$	1.6666...
Just major third	$\frac{E}{C}$	$\frac{5}{4}$	1.25
Just minor third	$\frac{G}{E}$	$\frac{6}{5}$	1.2
Just major whole step	$\frac{D}{C}$	$\frac{9}{8}$	1.125
Just minor whole step	$\frac{E}{D}$	$\frac{10}{9}$	1.1111...
Just major seventh	$\frac{B}{C}$	$\frac{15}{8}$	1.875
Just diatonic semitone	$\frac{F}{E}$	$\frac{16}{15}$	1.066666...
Just chromatic major semitone	$\frac{C\#}{C}$	$\frac{135}{128}$	1.0546875
Just chromatic minor semitone	$\frac{D\#}{D}$	$\frac{25}{24}$	1.0416666...
Syntonic comma	$\frac{81/64}{5/4}$	$\frac{81}{80}$	1.0125
Pythagorean comma	$\frac{2187/2048}{256/243}$	$\frac{531,441}{524,288}$	1.013063585...

which may be rearranged over a common denominator as

$$\frac{10}{60} : \frac{12}{60} : \frac{15}{60}$$

There are at least three alternative and entirely equivalent ways to interpret this result. First, we may regard the 10:12:15 proportion as resulting from the frequency ratios of the fourth, fifth, and sixth *subharmonics* of a given frequency, which will have the same pitch as the highest tone in the minor triad. Alternatively, we may note that the same relationship occurs among the tenth, twelfth, and fifteenth *harmonics* of any fundamental frequency. Finally, we may also note that the 4:5:6 just major triad consists of a 6:5 minor third stacked on top of a 5:4 major third, while the 10:12:15 just minor triad consists of a 5:4 (or 15:12) major third stacked on top of a 6:5 (or 12:10) minor third. The last interpretation emphasizes the fact that because both the major and minor triads consist of the same intervals (a minor third, a major third, and a perfect fifth), they may be regarded as equally consonant.

Using the 10:12:15 proportion, we can construct the just minor scale exactly the same way as the major scale was constructed:

1. From an arbitrary starting pitch we construct the first, third, and fifth degrees of the scale with the frequency ratios 10:12:15.

2. The bottom note of the first triad is then treated as the top note of another triad with the same frequency proportions, which yields the fourth and sixth degrees of the just minor scale.

3. The top note of the first triad is treated as the bottom note of a new triad, also constructed with the frequency ratios 10:12:15, yielding the second and seventh degrees of the just minor scale.

The resulting scale is shown in Figure C-7.

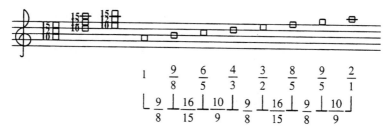

Figure C-7   The just minor scale. This scale is constructed from the three triads shown on the left, each of which consists of tones with fundamental frequencies in the proportions 10:12:15, which are the proportions among the sixth, fifth, and fourth subharmonics, respectively. The frequencies of the tones in the resulting scale are shown relative to the frequency of the beginning note, which is considered to be 1. The frequency ratios between successive pairs of adjacent tones in the scale are also shown.

C.4 MEAN TONE TEMPERAMENT

One approach to dealing with the difficulties introduced into the construction of instruments of fixed pitch by just tuning is to "temper" the frequencies of the notes of the scale. Developed in the nineteenth century, mean tone temperament is based on the idea of combining the sonorous major third of just tuning with the intervalic simplicity of Pythagorean tuning. To accomplish this, the frequency of the third tone in the scale is simply set at 5/4 times the frequency of the first tone. The interval between the first and second notes is chosen to be halfway to the third tone, yielding a whole step of $\sqrt{5/4}$:1. Similarly, just major thirds are maintained between the notes F and A, and between G and B, by using the $\sqrt{5/4}$ whole step. Because the major scale encompasses one octave and consists of five $\sqrt{5/4}$ whole tones plus two semitones, the size of the mean tone semitone s may be obtained directly using the mathematical relation

$$s^2(\sqrt{5/4})^5 = 2$$

$$s = \left[\frac{2}{(5/4)^{5/2}} \right]^{1/2} = 1.06998...$$

The resulting frequencies are shown in Table C-4, and the resulting scale is shown in Figure C-8.

TABLE C-4   Pitches of the diatonic major scale in mean tone temperament.

Pitch	Frequency Ratio To Starting Note of Scale(C)	Decimal	Decimal Ratio of Corresponding Pitch
C	1	1	(1)
D	$\sqrt{5/4}\,C$	1.11803...	(1.125)
E	$\sqrt{5/4}\,D = 5/4\,C$	1.2	(1.2)
D	$\sqrt{5/4}\,C$	1.11803...	(1.125)
F	$[2/(5/4)^{5/2}]^{1/2}E$	1.33748...	(1.333...)
G	$\sqrt{5/4}\,F$	1.49534...	(1.5)
A	$\sqrt{5/4}\,G = 5/4\,F$	1.67185...	(1.666...)
B	$\sqrt{5/4}\,A = 5/4\,G$	1.86919...	(1.875)
C	$[2/(5/4)^{5/2}]^{1/2}B$	2	(2)

Even though mean tone tuning simplifies somewhat the construction of fixed-pitch instruments while retaining several in-tune major third intervals, other intervals, fourths and fifths in particular, are no longer perfect. Mean tone temperament therefore has little advantage over equal temperament in practice.

C.5 EQUAL TEMPERAMENT

Another way to understand the Pythagorean comma is to consider what happens when the sequence of perfect fifths is extended until 13 different pitches are produced. Starting from 1, the second perfect fifth has the relative frequency 3/2, the third pitch has

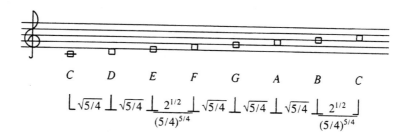

Figure C-8 Mean tone tuning: the diatonic major scale. Like Pythagorean tuning, mean tone temperament provides a scale built on only two types of intervals, the $\sqrt{5/4} = 1.11803\ldots$ *whole tone* and the $[2/(5/4)^{5/2}]^{1/2} = 1.06998\ldots$ *semitone*. Mean tone temperament provides just (5:4) major thirds C-E, F-A, and G-B, at the expense of introducing imperfection into fourth and fifth intervals such as C-F and C-G.

the relative frequency $(3/2)^2 = 9/8$, and so on. The thirteenth pitch obtained in this manner

$$\left[\frac{3}{2}\right]^{12} = \frac{531,441}{4,096} \approx 129.7463\ldots$$

is close to—but not quite equal to—the starting pitch raised by seven octaves, or $2^7 = 128$. The pitch discrepancy between the two (just a little over 1 percent) is the Pythagorean comma, which is therefore the amount by which the sequence of perfect fifths misses being "closed" after the sequence is carried out past 12 pitches. Thus, for example, a musical passage that constantly modulates (changes key, or changes the main tonic reference note) by perfect fifths never "returns" to the starting key. After 12 modulations, each up a perfect fifth, the resulting key would be slightly higher in pitch (by a Pythagorean comma) than the starting key. After 12 downward modulations by a perfect fifth, the resulting key would be a similar amount lower in pitch than the starting key.

One way to arrive at the basic idea of equal temperament is to consider the small size of the Pythagorean comma. If the perfect fifth were to be replaced by another slightly smaller interval, which we shall call $T5$ for "tempered fifth," the small discrepancy of the Pythagorean comma could be spread equally among twelve $T5$ intervals, each of which would be very close indeed to the perfect fifth.

In other words, we arrive at equal-tempered tuning by noting that the closest approximation of a solution to the previously mentioned fundamental problem of musical pitch

$$\left[\frac{3}{2}\right]^{M} = \left[\frac{2}{1}\right]^{N}$$

occurs when $M = 12$ and $N = 7$, the discrepancy being the Pythagorean comma. We then relax the constraints on the problem slightly by substituting $T5$ for 3/2 (the perfect fifth). Because the Pythagorean comma is small, we expect the discrepancy between $T5$ and the perfect fifth to be even smaller.

The size of $T5$ is found by solving the relationship

$$T5^{12} = 2^7$$

$$T5 = 2^{7/12} = 1.498307 \ldots$$

The discrepancy between $T5$ and the perfect fifth is indeed quite small, equal to the twelfth root of the Pythagorean comma:

$$\frac{P5}{T5} = \frac{3/2}{2^{7/12}} = \frac{1.5}{1.498307 \ldots} = 1.00113 \ldots$$

The ancient Greeks simply could not resolve such problems because they involve quantities that cannot be expressed as ratios of integers. More progress in mathematics was needed before musical equal temperament could be understood, progress that allowed "irrational" quantities such as the twelfth root of 2 to be calculated. It is interesting to note that tempered tuning was adopted in Western music soon after the invention of the logarithm by John Napier, a Scottish mathematician who lived from 1550 to 1617 (parts 1 and 2 of Johann Sebastian Bach's *Well-tempered Clavier*—a set of works commonly credited with the establishment of the system of equal temperament in Western music—appeared in 1722 and 1744).

If we construct a sequence of 12 such tempered fifths, the final note has exactly the same pitch as the starting note because

$$(2^{7/12})^{12} = 2^7$$

The resulting 12 pitches neatly divide the octave into 12 equally spaced pitches. Each interval between these pitches, when they are arranged within the same octave in an ascending sequence, is easily seen to be the *equal-tempered semitone*

$$2^{1/12} = 1.059463094 \ldots$$

The pitches that result from equal temperament are often described in music literature in terms of a "circle of fifths" (see Figure C-9). Pitches that are adjacent on the circle of fifths represent musical keys that are harmonically adjacent in the sense that their major or minor scales differ by the tuning of a single note. The notes in the C major scale are the same, for example, as the notes in the G major scale except that the sequence of scale intervals required by the two diatonic tetrachords in the latter requires an F-sharp where the former requires an F-natural. The D major scale is the same as G except for the introduction of a sharp on C, and so on. Moving in the other direction around the circle starting from C, the F major scale requires the pitch of B to be lowered to B-flat. If we then construct a major scale on B-flat, a new pitch, E-flat, is required. The order of appearance of the "sharpened" notes (which appear as we move clockwise around the circle of fifths) is F, C, G, D, A, E, B—exactly the order in which they are written in key signatures in music notation. The flats appear as we move counterclockwise starting from C in the order B, E, A, D, G, C, F.

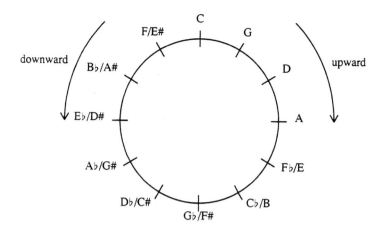

Figure C-9   The circle of fifths. Clockwise movement around the circle denotes an upward sequence of pitches separated by fifths; counterclockwise movement denotes a downward sequence of fifths. Pitches that are adjacent on this circle are harmonically adjacent in the sense that the major and minor scales based on those pitches differ only by a single note.

The frequencies of equal-tempered pitches are easily calculated from any reference frequency f_{ref} according to

$$f = 2^{\frac{n}{12}} f_{ref}$$

where n is the number of semitones between the reference frequency and the desired frequency, f. For example, the frequency of the equal-tempered pitch located a major third up (+4 semitones) from A440 is $440(2^{4/12}) = 554.365...$ Hz, while middle C, a major sixth down (–9 semitones), has a frequency of $440(2^{-9/12}) = 261.6255...$ Hz.

Unlike the other tuning systems, equal temperament does not yield several possible frequencies for each of the black keys on a piano keyboard. This allows a logically consistent and simple keyboard to be constructed on which music may modulate freely from any key to any other. Every key sounds exactly like every other key in equal temperament, at least as far as the scale intervals are concerned.

Unlike mean tone temperament, however, the thirds resulting from equal temperament do not agree with the harmonic frequencies given by just tuning. To compare equal-tempered intervals with those of other tuning systems, the logarithmic *cents* (¢) scale is often used. In the cents scale, the equal-tempered semitone is divided into 100 equal parts. There are therefore 1200 cents in an octave. One cent is therefore 1/1200 of an octave, or a frequency ratio of

$$2^{1/1200} = 1.00057779...$$

For example, a frequency one cent higher than 1000 Hz would have a frequency of 1000.57779 . . . Hz. If two such frequencies were sounded together, they would produce beats at a rate only slightly greater than 0.5 Hz. Alternatively, one cent is about five times smaller than the just noticeable difference in frequency for sequential tones.

A musical interval formed by the ratio of two frequencies f_1 and f_2 may be expressed in cents using the formula

$$\cent = 1200 \log_2 \frac{f_1}{f_2} = 3986.313713 \ldots \log_{10} \frac{f_1}{f_2} = 1731.234049 \ldots \ln \frac{f_1}{f_2}$$

(The constants in these formulas result from dividing 1200 by $\log_{10} 2$ and $\log_e 2$, respectively.)

The cents scale may be used to compare tuning systems such as those we have considered so far, as shown in Table C-5. Entries in this table are rounded to the nearest cent. From this table we can see, for example, that the size of the mean tone whole step is equal to 194 $\cent$—6 $\cent$ smaller than the whole step in equal-temperament. Similarly, the mean tone semitone interval is 17 $\cent$ larger than the equal-tempered semitone.

TABLE C-5 Pitches of diatonic major scale expressed in cents for four different tuning systems.

Note	Equal Temperament	Pythagorean	Just	Mean Tone
C	0	0	0	0
D	200	204	204	194
E	400	408	386	386
F	500	498	498	503
G	700	702	702	697
A	900	906	884	890
B	1100	1110	1088	1083
C	1200	1200	1200	1200

We can use the cents scale to compare various intervals, as shown in Table C-6. From this table we see, for example, that the equal tempered fifth is about 2 $\cent$ smaller than the perfect fifth of the Pythagorean and just systems. We also see that the just fifth between D and A (in a C major scale) is about 22 $\cent$ smaller than perfect.

C.6 TUNING BY COMPUTER

So far we have discussed musical tuning only in the traditional context, in which the fundamental problem is to find sets of pitches that are simultaneously rich enough to allow many useful musical combinations and small enough to allow practical instruments to be built. So far in the history of music, equal temperament has been declared the winner by acclaim among the competing systems, because it provides good

TABLE C-6 Intervals from the diatonic major scale based on C expressed in cents from four different tuning systems.

Interval	Name	Equal Temperament	Pythagorean	Just	Mean Tone
$\frac{E}{C}$	Major third	400	408	386	386
$\frac{G}{E}$	Minor third	300	294	316	311
$\frac{F}{D}$	Minor third	300	294	294	310
$\frac{F}{C}$	Fourth	500	498	498	503
$\frac{G}{C}$	Fifth	700	702	702	697
$\frac{A}{D}$	Fifth	700	702	680	697
$\frac{A}{C}$	Major sixth	900	906	884	890
$\frac{B}{C}$	Major seventh	1100	1110	1088	1083

approximations to just (harmonic) intervals while avoiding the complications associated with the just system.

Approximations are not the same as exact solutions, however. Many musicians have lamented the powerful grip that equal temperament has on Western music, in which all tonalities sound equally "in tune" and, at the same time, equally "out of tune." There is even some evidence that J. S. Bach himself—to whom the adoption of equal temperament is often attributed—did not champion equal temperament, as the title of his famous *Well-tempered Clavier* subtly indicates. Many musicians believe that the system of composition with 12 tones as postulated by the late Arnold Schönberg and his students arises naturally from the fact that equal-tempered tuning deals almost exclusively with pitch combinations that disagree harmonically. If true consonance is impossible in equal tempered tuning, according to this argument, pitch-organizing principles other than consonance are necessary without regard to harmonic agreement. The late composer Harry Partch spent much of his creative energy immersed in sawdust creating new instruments based on a system of tuning that owes much more to the system of just tuning than to any form of temperament.

One of the most interesting and as yet unexplored capacities of computer music lies in its absolute neutrality on questions of tuning. It is possible for a composer to specify virtually any frequency or combination of frequencies at every point in computer-synthesized music, though many practitioners accept equal temperament more or less habitually in their work. Most commercial music synthesizers completely ignore this potential of digital sound generation because they are intended primarily as cost-effective substitutes for other traditional instruments rather than augmentations of the musical palette.

One of the progenitors of computer music, John Pierce, has experimented with alternative tuning systems including such ideas as forming an equal tempered scale with eight equally spaced tones to the octave rather than 12. Dividing the octave into four equally spaced pitches results in a scale that is identical to the sound of the diminished seventh chord in 12-tone equal temperament. Eight equal divisions then result in scale steps that are separated by a musical interval exactly half the size of a minor third (there is no standard musical name for this interval, which consists of one and a half 12-tone equal-tempered semitones). Pierce's *Eight-Tone Canon* (which is included on a Decca record titled *The Voice of the Computer*) consists of four "voices" that play a canon in this scale. Pierce reasoned that because the size of the critical band is slightly smaller than a musical minor third (at least for frequencies above about 500 Hz), an eight-tone scale would make the rules of "consonant" and "dissonant" pitch combinations extremely simple: all the odd-numbered pitches in the scale would sound consonant together, as would all the even-numbered pitches. Combinations of even- and odd-numbered pitches would sound dissonant. Pierce and Mathews have experimented with sounds containing "stretched partials" in which each overtone of a fundamental frequency f in the inharmonic result is given by kSf, where $k = 0, 1, 2, \ldots$ and S is called the *stretch factor*. If S is set equal to 1, the usual harmonic frequencies result. If S is set to a value slightly greater than 1, say, 1.02, stretched partials result. In fact, S may be set to any value greater than zero, allowing partials to be stretched (or shrunk) from their harmonic positions. By applying the same stretch factor to the tuning of the pitches in the scale, it is possible to create new musical systems in which the overlap of stretched partials is identical to the overlap of harmonics that would occur if S were set equal to 1.

Pierce found that beyond a certain point, stretched music loses its ability to differentiate a cadence from an anticadence, and consonance and dissonance become intermixed in ways that defy normal musical description. His experiments were carried out on traditional music, however, rather than on music designed around the properties of his new sounds.

One exciting area for further study in computer music is so-called dynamic tuning. If a tonal composition begins in the key of C, for example, just tuning requires that the interval between C and D be a 9/8 major whole step while the interval between D and E is a 10/9 minor whole step. If the composition later modulates to the key of D, just tuning requires that the interval between D and E be based on the first and second notes of the major scale, or a 9/8 major whole step. Such adjustments are quite difficult to make when playing on a keyboard instrument because there must now be at least two keys within reach of the performer that sound the pitch E, depending on whether the composition has modulated to the key of C or the key of D. With a computer, such problems are trivial to solve, because tuning can easily be made context-dependent.

Music theory of the past has concentrated on the problems of finding practical ways to make fixed-pitch instruments. With computers, new music theory can be developed in which such constraints are removed. Instead of leaving the fundamental problem of musical pitch unresolved by adopting equal temperament, the problem can now be solved, even though the solution requires an infinite number of precisely controllable pitches.

REFERENCES

1. J. Askill, *Physics of Musical Sounds* (Van Nostrand, New York, 1979).
2. W. Carlos, "Tuning: At the Crossroads," *Computer Music J. 11*, no. 1 (1987): 29–43.
3. H. Partch, *Genesis of a Music* (Da Capo Press, New York, 1979).
4. J. R. Pierce, *The Science of Musical Sound* (Freeman, New York, 1983).

Appendix D

cmusic

D.1 GENERAL

cmusic is an acoustic compiler program I have written that translates a *score* into a *digital signal*. The digital signal is a sample stream suitable for digital-to-analog conversion. Properties of the digital signal are controlled by *instruments* that are defined in the score and by cmusic note events "played" on these instruments. The score is ASCII text that has been prepared directly by the cmusic user, or it may have resulted from a computer program. By convention, cmusic score files are named with a .sc extension (cmusic does not require this, however).

A cmusic score consists of *score statements*. Each score statement contains one or more *fields* that are separated by *white space* (blanks, tabs, or new lines) or commas. Each score statement is terminated with a semicolon (;). The first field of a cmusic score statement always specifies a *command*. The format of the remainder of the statement depends on the command given. Individual fields must not contain embedded white space. Statements are usually typed one per line, but several semicolon-delimited statements may be placed on one line, and one statement may continue over more than one line.

cmusic passes the score through the C language *preprocessor* before it interprets the score. The preprocessor allows specification of *include files* and *macros*, both with and without arguments. Macros allow user-defined shorthand notations for common or complex score statement idioms. A set of cmusic standard macro definitions is provided for commonly used idioms.

Comments may be inserted into the score between braces ({ }). Text between braces is ignored by cmusic. Comments may be nested to any depth (that is, comments within comments are allowed).

Table D-1 lists the basic cmusic commands.

TABLE D-1   Basic cmusic commands.

Command	Short Form	Meaning	Description
set	set	Set global parameter	Specifies global parameters for a cmusic run such as the sampling rate, default wave table length, or number of audio channels in the output signal.
instrument	ins	Begin instrument definition	Specifies that the following statements describe an interconnection of cmusic unit generators in a configuration designed to produce a particular type of sound.
end	end	End instrument definition	Terminates an instrument definition.
generate	gen	Generate wave table	Specifies that a wave table is to be filled with values computed by a specified program and passes any needed control information to that program.
note(play)	not(pla)	Play a note	Specifies that a note event is to be played on one of the defined instruments and passes any needed control information to that instrument.
section	sec	Terminate a score section	Specifies the end of a series of note events, resets the action time to zero, and continues score processing.
variable	var	Define global variable value(s)	Specifies the value(s) to which one or more global variables is (are) to be set (cmusic global variables may have either numeric or string values).
merge	merge	Begin a merge section	A merge section of note events is sorted into nondecreasing time order, merged with other (optional) sorted merge sections, and processed.
endsec	endsec	End merge section	Specifies the end of a merge section after a merge command has been used.
endmerge	endmerge	End of a group of merge sections	Specifies that the end of a group of merge sections has been reached.
terminate	ter	Terminate score	Specifies that the end of the score has been reached.

cmusic scores may be organized in a variety of ways. Table D-2 shows the general outline of an organization that may help a cmusic score to succeed.

TABLE D-2 General outline of a cmusic score.

Part	Operations	Commands
I.	Options	`set`

II.	Instrument definition(s)	`ins`
		unit generator statements
		`end`

III.	Wave table generation	`gen`

IV.	Note list	`note (play)`
		`sec`
		`var`
		`merge`
		`endsec`
		`endmerge`

V.	Termination	`ter`

D.2 EXPRESSIONS

Most fields in cmusic score statements contain numeric values (they need not be typed as numeric values if macro definitions are used). An *expression* may be typed in any field that requires a constant numeric value.

cmusic interprets the expression by executing the specified calculation—the resulting number becomes the value of the field containing the expression. For example, we may type either 4 or 2+2 to specify the same thing. Spaces are forbidden within expressions. Table D-3 summarizes the possibilities for cmusic expressions.

D.3 THE C PREPROCESSOR

In addition to expressions, cmusic provides macro and include-file capabilities by first feeding the score through the C language preprocessor.

Macros allow the user to define a private shorthand and often save a lot of typing. The simplest form of macros involves straight text substitution. If we include the statement

```
#define A 440Hz
```

in the score, any time we type A thereafter will cause cmusic to read 440Hz. Note that no semicolon is used—*the end of the line delimits the end of the definition.* Multiline definitions are possible by using backslash (\) characters, as in

```
#define A \
440Hz
```

TABLE D-3 cmusic expresssions.

	Parentheses	
	Parentheses must balance and may be used freely to establish operator precedence. Function arguments should be enclosed in parentheses.	
	Variables and Numbers	
	Variables may be either of type p *(note parameters) or* v *(global variables). Variables always contain their most recently assigned value.*	
Operands	**Description**	**Examples**
`pN or p[N]`	*Both refer to the current (that is, most recently assigned) value of note parameter* N. *If the brackets are used,* N *may be any valid cmusic expression.*	`p5,  p[6],` `p[p6+3]`
`vN or v[N]`	*Both refer to the current (that is, most recently assigned) value of global variable* N. *If the brackets are used,* N *may be any valid cmusic expression.*	`v1, v[v1],` `v[2*v[p8-1]-1]`
	Numbers may be written in any of three number bases (decimal is the default). All numeric values are of single-precision floating type whether they include a decimal point or not.	
`decimal`	*Any string of the digits* 0 *through* 9, *optionally including a decimal point.*	`3,` `3.1415926535`
`octal`	*Any string of the digits* 0 *through* 7 *that does not include a radix point and begins with the digit* 0.	`077, 03700`
`hexadecimal`	*Any string of the digits* 0 *through* 9 *plus the letters* a *through* f *that does not include a radix point and begins with the characters* 0x.	`0x3f, 0x10`
	Unary Operators	
	Unary operators are obeyed done before binary operators, which are normally obeyed before postoperators. The following unary operators are given in order of precedence; that is, functions are evaluated before the unary minus operator.	
Operators	**Description**	**Examples**
`sin, cos,` `atan, ln,` `exp, floor,` `abs, sqrt,` `rand`	*The standard sine, cosine, and arctangent functions from the UNIX math library, plus natural logarithm, exponential, floor, absolute value, and square root functions.* rand *returns a random value between 0 and its (positive) argument.*	`sin(45Deg),` `ln(p6)-ln(p5)` `3+rand(7-3)`
`-`	*Unary minus operator.*	`-3+p7`

Macros can also have *arguments*. If we write the definition

```
#define HORN( start, end ) note start horn end-start
```

TABLE D-3   (*cont.*) cmusic expresssions.

	Binary Operators	
	Binary operators are evaluated in the precedence order shown— any operator in the first brace-enclosed set is evaluated before any operator in the next brace-enclosed set, and so on, unless parentheses are used to specify otherwise.	
Operators	**Description**	**Examples**
{^, %}	a ^ b *means a to the b power;* a%b *means a modulo b.*	3^.5, 2^(1/12), p7%2
{*, /}	a*b *means a multiplied by b;* a/b *means a divided by b.*	p5*exp(1), ln(p6/v2)
{+, −}	a+b *means a plus b;* a−b *means a minus b.*	p5+exp(1), ln(p6−v2)

	Postoperators	
	Postoperators are normally evaluated last (after all other operators have been evaluated). They generally modify the value of the entire expression that precedes them. In the examples that follow, ξ stands for any valid cmusic expression.	
Operators	**Description**	**Examples**
ξdB	*The* dB *postoperator treats ξ as an amplitude value expressed in decibels with a reference value of 1.0 (= 0 dB) and converts this value to a linear amplitude; that is, ξdB means (ξ/20).*	0dB, p5/7dB
ξDeg	*The* Deg *postoperator treats ξ as a number of degrees and converts this value to the equivalent number of radians; that is, ξDeg means $\xi 2\pi/360$.*	sin(72Deg)
ξHz	*The* Hz *postoperator treats ξ as a frequency expressed in hertz and converts it to an oscillator increment; that is, ξHz means ξ * L / R, where* L *is the current default wave table length and* R *is the current default sampling rate.*	440Hz, 440*2^(1/12)Hz
ξIS	*The* IS *postoperator computes the sum of the first ξ inverse integers; that is,* 3IS *means* 1/1+1/2+1/3. 0IS = 0 *by definition.*	79IS
ξK	*The* K *postoperator multiplies the value of ξ by 1024.*	16K, 48/2K
ξMM	*The* 5M *postoperator treats ξ as a Maelzel metronome tempo indication and converts this value to the number of seconds per beat at the specified tempo; that is, ξMM means 60/ξ.*	72MM
ξms	*The* ms *postoperator treats ξ as a duration expressed in milliseconds and converts this value to a duration in samples; that is, ξms means $\xi * R /1000$.*	79ms
ξS	*The* S *postoperator treats ξ as a duration expressed as a number of samples at the current sampling rate and converts this value to a number of seconds; that is, ξS means ξ/R.*	16384S
ξsec	*The* sec *postoperator treats ξ as a duration expressed in seconds and converts this value to an oscillator increment; that is, ξsec means $\xi * R /L = 1/\xi Hz$.*	p4sec

then we can play notes on instrument "horn" with statements such as

```
HORN( 1, 2 ) -20dB 440Hz ;
```

which will be read by cmusic as

```
note 1 horn 2-1 -20dB 440Hz ;
```

In this example, the first argument has been given the value 1, and the second argument has been set to 2, causing the macro to expand in the manner shown. This definition changes the way in which timing is expressed from a starting time and a duration to a starting time and an ending time—the expression within the macro definition takes care of the minor computation needed to do this.

Care must be exercised to ensure that blanks do not creep into expression fields. For example, the definition

```
#define HORN( start, end ) note start horn end - start
```

wouldn't work because of the blanks surrounding the minus sign.

The preprocessor also processes statements of the form

```
#include "filename"
```

If this were typed in a cmusic score, the entire contents of the named file would be read in and substituted for the #include statement. It is generally necessary to give the full pathname of the file unless it is certain that the file will always be in the same directory as the one in which cmusic is run.

A file containing many standard cmusic definitions can be accessed with a special statement such as

```
#include <carl/cmusic.h>
```

The contents of this file can be examined directly to ascertain the nature of the definitions it contains. A portion of it is as follows.

```
/* cmusic.h - standard macro definitions for cmusic scores */
/*
 * unit generator statement abbreviations
 */
#define NRES(out,in,gain,cf,bw) nres out in gain cf bw d d d d d d d d d
/*
 * waveform components
 */
#define PLS(num) num,1,0
#define SAW(num) num,1/num,0
#define TRI(num) num,1/num^2,0
```

```
/*
 * useful signal waveforms
 */
#define SINE(func) gen p2 gen5 func 1 1 0
#define COS(func)  gen p2 gen5 func 1 1 90Deg
#define TRIANGLE(func) gen p2 gen5 func \
TRI(1) TRI(3) TRI(5) TRI(7); NORM(func)
#define SQUARE(func) gen p2 gen5 func \
SAW(1) SAW(3) SAW(5) SAW(7); NORM(func)
#define SAWTOOTH(func) gen p2 gen5 func \
SAW(1) SAW(2) SAW(3) SAW(4) SAW(5) \
SAW(6) SAW(7) SAW(8); NORM(func)
#define PULSE(func) gen p2 gen5 func \
PLS(1) PLS(2) PLS(3) PLS(4) PLS(5) \
PLS(6) PLS(7) PLS(8); NORM(func)
/*
 * use envelope waveforms
 */
#define ENV(func) gen p2 gen4 func 0,0 -1 .1,1 -1 .8,.5 -1 1,0
#define SLOWENV(func) gen p2 gen4 func 0,0 -1 1/3,1 -1 2/3,.5 -1 1,0
#define PLUCKENV(func) gen p2 gen4 func 0,0 -1 .005,1 -2 1,0
/*
 * gen statement abbreviations
 */
#define GEN0(func) gen p2 gen0 func
#define NORM(func) gen p2 gen0 func 1
#define GEN1(func) gen p2 gen1 func
#define GEN2(func) gen p2 gen2 func
#define GEN3(func) gen p2 gen3 func
#define GEN4(func) gen p2 gen4 func
#define GEN5(func) gen p2 gen5 func
#define GEN6(func) gen p2 gen6 func
#define CHUBBY(func) gen p2 chubby func
#define CSPLINE(func) gen p2 cspline func
#define GENRAW(func) gen p2 genraw func
#define QUADGEN(func) gen p2 quad func
#define SHEPENV(func) gen p2 shepenv func
/*
 * general period definition
 */
#define P (p4sec)
/*
 * pitch reference = middle C
 */
#define REF (220*2^(3/12))
/*
 * 12-tone temperament frequencies
 */
```

```
#define FR(pitch,oct) (REF*2^(oct)*2^(pitch/12))
/*
 * tempered scale pitch classes (0 octave = middle C up to B)
 */
#define C(oct) (FR(0,oct)Hz)
#define Cs(oct) (FR(1,oct)Hz)
#define Df(oct) (FR(1,oct)Hz)
#define D(oct) (FR(2,oct)Hz)
#define Ds(oct) (FR(3,oct)Hz)
#define Ef(oct) (FR(3,oct)Hz)
#define E(oct) (FR(4,oct)Hz)
#define F(oct) (FR(5,oct)Hz)
#define Fs(oct) (FR(6,oct)Hz)
#define Gf(oct) (FR(6,oct)Hz)
#define G(oct) (FR(7,oct)Hz)
#define Gs(oct) (FR(8,oct)Hz)
#define Af(oct) (FR(8,oct)Hz)
#define A(oct) (FR(9,oct)Hz)
#define As(oct) (FR(10,oct)Hz)
#define Bf(oct) (FR(10,oct)Hz)
#define B(oct) (FR(11,oct)Hz)

#define RAND(low,high) (rand(high-low)+low)
#define xy(distance, direction) distance*cos(direction) distance*sin(direction)
#define LOG10(x) (ln(x)/ln(10))
#define LOG2(x) (ln(x)/ln(2))
```

Among the useful definitions in the cmusic.h file are shorthands for wave table generation, certain unit generator definitions, mathematical operations, and pitch class names.

With these definitions in effect we may type, for example, SINE(f1) to fill wave table f1 with a sine waveform, RAND(9,13) to choose a random value between 9 and 13, LOG2(p7) to take the logarithm of p7 to the base 2, or C(0) to specify the frequency of middle C.

According to the definitions, Cs(1) expands into

```
(FR(1,1)Hz)
```

Because FR is also a defined macro, this expands further into

```
((REF*2^(1)*2^(1/12))Hz)
```

which again expands into

```
(((220*2^(3/12))*2^(1)*2^(1/12))Hz)
```

This expression calculates the cmusic oscillator increment associated with the precise frequency of C-sharp a minor ninth above middle C in equal-tempered tuning based on A440. The cmusic octave numbers change on octaves of the pitch class C; that is, `B(-1)` is a semitone lower than `C(0)`.

We could easily transpose an entire score that uses these macros simply by redefining the reference pitch. Other modifications to the standard definitions are easily implemented.

D.4 COMMAND DESCRIPTIONS

D.4.1 set

The cmusic `set` command has two basic forms:

```
set parameter = value ;
```

and

```
set option ;
```

Some of the options available through the `set` command are also available as command line flags. In case a score `set` statement and a command line flag conflict, the command line flag always takes precedence.

```
set barefile = filename ;
```

produces a "bare" score listing on the named file (a bare score has all macros and expressions replaced with their numeric values). By default, no bare file is produced.

```
set blocklength = N;
```

sets the input-output block length to `N`. By default, `N` is set to 256 (in command flag form, use `-BN`).

```
set channels = N; set nchannels = N; set stereo; set quad;
```

determines the number of output channels. By default, `N` is set to 1.0.

```
set cutoff = N;
```

sets the cutoff threshold for computing the tail of the global reverb to `N`. By default, N is set to 0.0001 (equivalent to –80 dB). This option affects the space unit generator only.

```
set floatoutput; set nofloatoutput;
```

specifies whether cmusic should produce 32-bit floating-point sample values (this is the default). If floating-point samples are not produced, 16-bit two's complement fixed-point fractions are produced.

```
set functionlength = N;
```

sets the default score function (wave table) length to N. By default, N is set to 1024 (in command flag form, use -LN).

```
set header; set noheader;
```

specifies whether a csound[1] header should be produced by cmusic (such headers are normally transparent to the user). By default, a header is produced.

```
set listingfile = filename;
```

produces a score listing on the named file. By default, no listing is produced. If this command is given with no listing filename specified, cmusic will create a file with the same first name as the score file and a .list extension.

```
set noclip;
```

turns off clipping of cmusic output (this allows floating-point sample output values to exceed the range ±1). By default, clipping is turned on.

```
set notify;
```

specifies that cmusic should produce its termination message on the terminal (in command flag form, use -n; the -q flag turns off any notify, timer, or verbose options in the score).

```
set outputfile = filename;
```

causes cmusic to place its sample output on the named file instead of stdout.

```
set rand = N; set seed = N;
```

[1]csound is the sound file system written at the Computer Audio Research Laboratory by Gareth Loy. It contains provisions for reading, writing, recording, and playing special files containing sample data.

These statements "seed" the random number generator with N. A particular seed value causes the random number generator to produce a particular pseudorandom output sequence.

```
set sfbuffersize = N;
```

sets the buffer size used by the `sndfile` unit generator to N. This option affects the `sndfile` unit generator only. By default, N is set to 4K (bytes).

```
set rate = N; set samplingrate = N; set srate = N;
```

sets the sampling rate to N. By default, N is set to 16K = 16384. (In command flag form, use -RN).

```
set revscale = N;
```

sets the relative amplitude of global reverb to N. By default, N is set to 0.25. This option affects the `space` unit generator only.

```
set room = Lx1,Ly1 Lx2,Ly2 Lx3,Ly3 Lx4,Ly4;
```

sets the quadrant 1, 2, 3, and 4 vertices of the inner room to the specified values, given in meters, with point (0, 0) being the center of all space. By default, the settings are (4, 4) (–4, 4) (–4, –4) (4, –4). This option affects the `space` unit generator only.

```
set space = Ax1,Ay1 Ax2,Ay2 Ax3,Ay3 Ax4,Ay4;
```

sets the quadrant 1, 2, 3, and 4 vertices of the outer room to the specified values, given in meters, with point (0, 0) being the center of all space. By default, the settings are (50, 50), (–50, 50), (–50, –50), (50, –50). This option affects the `space` unit generator only.

```
set speakers = Sx1,Sy1 Sx2,Sy2 ... Sxn,Syn;
```

sets the locations of n speakers (which must be on the perimeter of the inner room) to the specified values, given in meters, with point (0, 0) being the center of all space. By default, four speakers are defined at (4, 4), (–4, 4), (–4, –4), (4, –4). This option affects the `space` unit generator only.

```
set tempowith vN; set offsetwith vN;
```

causes cmusic to use the specified variable to set the tempo or time offset. If the tempo is specified with, say, v1, then the values of both p2 and p4 will be *replaced* with `p2*v1` and `p4*v1`, respectively. If the time offset is specified with, say, `v2`, then `v2` will be added to all `p2` values after they have been scaled by the tempo, if any. For example,

```
#define TEMPO set tempowith v10 ; var p2 v10
#define T (p2+p4)/(v10)
TEMPO 30MM;
note 0 one 1 440Hz 0dB ;
note T one 1 440Hz 0dB ;
note T one 1 440Hz 0dB ;
```

will use variable `v10` to set the tempo of the score. It is set up and defined with macro `TEMPO`. Note the use of `v10` in the `T` macro.

```
set t60 = N;
```

sets the global reverberation time to `N` seconds (approximately). This option affects the `space` unit generator only.

```
set timer;
```

causes cmusic to send computation timing numbers to the user's terminal. After each second of sound has been computed, a message of the form `:1(0.78563)` is printed, where `:1` indicates the time in seconds. The number in parentheses is the maximum amplitude generated during that second. A number in brackets following the timing value (such as `:5(1.284562)[127]`) indicates the number of out-of-range samples encountered during that second of output (in command flag form, use `-t`; the `-q` flag turns off any notify, timer, or verbose options in the score).

```
set verbose;
```

causes cmusic to send the interpreted input listing, timing, and termination notification messages to the user's terminal (in command flag form, use `-v`; the `-q` flag turns off any notify, timer, or verbose options in the score).

D.4.2 `ins`

The `ins` command specifies that unit generator statements defining a cmusic instrument are to follow. The command has the general form

```
ins time name ;
```

where `time` is the action time at which the instrument is to be defined (this is normally 0) and `name` is the name given to the instrument.

All instruments have definitions of the following general form

```
ins time name ;
  unit generator statements
end ;
```

Unit generator statements will be discussed in detail later on.

D.4.3 end

The `end` command is used to terminate an instrument definition.

D.4.4 gen

The `gen` command is used to invoke one of the available wave table generators. It has the general form

```
gen time name function parameters ;
```

where `time` is an action time (normally 0), `name` is the name of the wave table generating program to be invoked, `function` is the name of a cmusic wave table (`f1`, `f2`, and so on), and `parameters` are as required by the particular program invoked.

The standard cmusic generator programs will be discussed in detail later on.

D.4.5 note

The `note` command specifies that a note event is to be generated. It has the general form

```
note time instrument duration parameters ;
```

where `time` is the starting time of the note event, `instrument` is the name of the instrument to be played, `duration` is the duration of the note event in seconds, and `parameters` are as required by the particular instrument to be played.

All times and durations are specified in seconds. To be playable, the list of notes must be given in *nondecreasing order* of starting times (but see `merge`, Section D.4.8). If the action time of *any* command is less than one already encountered, cmusic will notify the user of a sequence error and stop.

An important concept in cmusic is that of note parameters, or *p fields*. Each *field* of a note statement is considered to be a *note parameter field*. Note parameters are numbered according to field positions, so the first field (the note command itself) is considered to be p1, the second field (the starting time) is p2, the instrument name is p3, and the duration is p4. The first four *p* fields of a note statement always have these fixed meanings. Subsequent *p* fields are given according to the needs of the instrument being played.

Because p2 and p4 are numeric values, they may be cmusic expressions. Further, cmusic expressions may refer directly to *p* field values simply by naming them as part of an expression (but beware of forward references, especially in instrument definitions!).

A common device is to specify either p2 or p2+p4 as an action time. If p2 is used, *the event will occur at whatever time was last specified as an action time of a previous cmusic statement*. If p2+p4 is used, the action will occur as soon as the previous note is finished, because p4 always refers to the most recent value to which p4 was set. For example, the following notes will be played in sequence, each with a duration of 1 second.

```
note      0 toot 1 ... ;
note p2+p4 toot 1 ... ;
note p2+p4 toot 1 ... ;
note p2+p4 toot 1 ... ;
note p2+p4 toot 1 ... ;
```

It would have been possible to use p2+p4 as the starting time of the first note in this example because all *p* fields initially have the value 0.0.

Here is a simple way to specify several two-note chords in sequence:

```
note      0 toot 1 ... ;
note p2    toot 1 ... ;

note p2+p4 toot 1 ... ;
note p2    toot 1 ... ;

note p2+p4 toot 1 ... ;
note p2    toot 1 ... ;
```

The first two notes have the same starting time (and duration), the next two notes will both start at time 1, the third pair of notes will start at time 2, and so on.

D.4.6 sec

The sec command has the general form

```
sec time ;
```

where time is the time at which the section is to be terminated. The time field may be omitted, in which case cmusic will automatically terminate the section after the last sounding note has ended. If time is later than the end of the last sounding note, cmusic will generate the requisite amount of silence (all-zero samples) needed to terminate the section at the specified moment.

Once the section is terminated, the action time of the score is reset to 0.0, and score processing continues. This allows major sections of a cmusic score to be rearranged easily, repeated, and so on. For example, we could repeat the two-note chords of the example in Section D.4.5 by interposing a `sec` statement after each repetition:

```
note      0 toot 1 ... ;
note p2    toot 1 ... ;

note p2+p4 toot 1 ... ;
note p2    toot 1 ... ;

note p2+p4 toot 1 ... ;
note p2    toot 1 ... ;

sec ;

note      0 toot 1 ... ;
note p2    toot 1 ... ;

note p2+p4 toot 1 ... ;
note p2    toot 1 ... ;

note p2+p4 toot 1 ... ;
note p2    toot 1 ... ;
```

D.4.7 `var`

The `var` command is used to set global variable values. Global values are maintained in static (that is, permanent) arrays. Global variable values may be used in cmusic expressions and in certain unit generator parameters. They have names like `v1`, `v2`, for numeric values and `s1`, `s2`, for string values.

The general form of the `var` command is

```
var time variable value(s) ;
```

where `time` is an action time, `variable` is the name of a global variable (either *v* type or *s* type), and `value(s)` stands for one or more values to be assigned to the named variable (and its successors).

For example, we may write

```
var 0 v1 440Hz ;
```

to assign the increment associated with the pitch A440 to global variable `v1` (at time 0). We could also write

```
var 0 v1 440Hz 880Hz ;
```

to set `v1` to the increment value associated with A440 and `v2` to the increment value associated with A880. (If more than one value is given, they are assigned to contiguously numbered variables starting with the one named.)

`var` statements act like assignment statements in programming. Macros may be used to christen variables with more imaginative and revealing names. For example, we might use global variables to obtain random selections from a particular pitch set.

```
#define PITCH(index) v[index]
#define PSET(position) var p2 PITCH[position]
#define S1 1
#define S2 (S1+5)

PSET(S1) A(0) Cs(1) E(1) F(1) Gs(1) ;  {pitch sets have}
PSET(S2) Af(0) C(1) Ef(1) E(1) G(1) ;  {5 elements today}

note p2+p4 honk 3 PITCH(S2+rand(5)) ... ;
```

`S1` and `S2` define the starting indices in the variable array for two pitch sets, each of which contains five arbitrary pitches. The pitch specified in `p5` of the note statement in the example would be selected randomly from the second set of pitches given.

String variables work in the same way, except that the values are strings instead of numbers. For example, the statement

```
var 0 s1 "file1" "file2" ;
```

would set the value of `s1` to the first string given and the value of `s2` to the second string given.

D.4.8 merge

Sometimes it is useful to write scores—especially note lists—out of time order. For example, the cmusic score writer may wish to write all of the notes for one musical voice, then all of the notes for a second voice, and so on. Or it may be desirable to give note statements not in time order for some reason. Perhaps the action times of notes are random (that is, computed with the `rand` function), and the proper order of notes literally cannot be determined in advance.

To accommodate such scores, the `merge` command may be used. The `merge` command reads in one or more merge sections, evaluating `p2` and `p4` fields as it goes. It then sorts each section into order and merges the sections together into a single, sorted score.

The `merge` command operates by reading all score statements until an `endsec` statement is encountered. An `endmerge` statement must follow the final `endsec` statement in each merged portion of the score. During this provisional reading of the score, all `var` statements are provisionally executed, because `p2` (starting time) and `p4` (duration) in note statements might depend on the values of some v-type variable.

The p2 and p4 fields of all note statements are evaluated (in case they are expressions—even random ones!) and replaced by numeric constants. The p2 fields on all gen and var statements are also evaluated.

All statements up to the endsec statement are placed into a special temporary file. More than one endsec-delimited section may be included before the endmerge statement. A new temporary file is created for each merge section given before the endmerge statement. ins, merge, sec, set, or ter statements are treated as *errors* within a merge.

After the temporary files have been created, they are individually sorted into non-decreasing time order, using the constant numbers in the p2 fields as keys for the sort. Then the files are merged together, so that cmusic plays the notes in the correct order.

The following note list shows two merge examples. In the first, notes with random starting times are placed into time order. In the second, two sections are merged together so that they will sound simultaneously. Note that it would be impossible to play either part of this score if the merge command did not exist, because the action times are unpredictable.

```
merge; {play random pitches at random times for 10 seconds}
    note 0+rand(10) toot rand(1) -23dB 220+rand(880)Hz;
    note 0+rand(10) toot rand(1) -23dB 220+rand(880)Hz;
    note 0+rand(10) toot rand(1) -23dB 220+rand(880)Hz;
    note 0+rand(10) toot rand(1) -23dB 220+rand(880)Hz;
    note 0+rand(10) toot rand(1) -23dB 220+rand(880)Hz;
    note 0+rand(10) toot rand(1) -23dB 220+rand(880)Hz;
    note 0+rand(10) toot rand(1) -23dB 220+rand(880)Hz;
    note 0+rand(10) toot rand(1) -23dB 220+rand(880)Hz;
endsec;
endmerge;

merge; {play the following two merge sections simultaneously}
    note 1 toot rand(1)+.2 -23dB A(rand(5)-3)+rand(12);
    note p2+p4 toot rand(1)+.2 -23dB A(1+rand(12));
    note p2+p4 toot rand(1)+.2 -23dB A(1+rand(12));
    note p2+p4 toot rand(1)+.2 -23dB A(1+rand(12));
    note p2+p4 toot rand(1)+.2 -23dB A(1+rand(12));
    note p2+p4 toot rand(1)+.2 -23dB A(1+rand(12));
    note p2+p4 toot rand(1)+.2 -23dB A(1+rand(12));
endsec;
    note 3 toot rand(1)+.2 -23dB C(rand(5)-3)+rand(12);
    note p2+p4 toot rand(1)+.2 -23dB C(1+rand(12));
    note p2+p4 toot rand(1)+.2 -23dB C(1+rand(12));
    note p2+p4 toot rand(1)+.2 -23dB C(1+rand(12));
    note p2+p4 toot rand(1)+.2 -23dB C(1+rand(12));
    note p2+p4 toot rand(1)+.2 -23dB C(1+rand(12));
    note p2+p4 toot rand(1)+.2 -23dB C(1+rand(12));
endsec;
endmerge;
```

D.4.9 `ter`

The `ter` command has the general form

```
ter time ;
```

where `time` is the time at which the score is to be terminated. The time field may be omitted, in which case cmusic will automatically terminate the score after the last sounding note has ended. If `time` is later than the end of the last sounding note, cmusic will generate the requisite amount of silence before terminating the score.

A combination of `sec` and `ter` statements can be used to supply a few seconds of silence at the end of a score:

```
note ...
note ...

sec ; {finish playing all notes and reset action time to 0}

ter 3 ; {pad with 3 seconds of silence for reverb to die away}
```

This is often necessary when the `space` unit generator is in use in order to allow reverberation to die away.

D.5 WAVE TABLE GENERATION

A growing library of free-standing programs exists for generating wave table values. cmusic users may write their own generating programs if they do not find suitable ones already available. These are shown in Table D-4.

cmusic invokes ones of these generating programs with the `gen` command. For example, the command

```
gen 0 gen3 f2 0 1 1 0 ;
```

instructs cmusic to execute the following UNIX-level command:

```
gen3 -L1024 0 1 1 0
```

The output of the command is a set of 1024 wave table values—cmusic places these into wave table `f2` (cmusic uses the `popen` facility of UNIX and C to do this). The `-L` flag informs the invoked program how many values it is to generate (this is usually the same as the current default wave table length).

Certain `gen` programs make a distinction between functions that are *open* and *closed* on the right. If so, they accept a `-o` flag to specify open and `-c` to specify closed. If no such flag is given, the program is free to use a default.

TABLE D-4   cmusic wave table-generating programs.

Name	Description
chubby	Chebyshev polynomial function generator
cspline	Smooth curve interpolator
gen0	Normalize a function to lie within the range +max to −max:
gen1	Straight line segment function generator
gen2	Fourier synthesis function generator
gen3	Simple line segment function generator
gen4	Exponential curve segment generator
gen5	Fourier synthesis generator
gen6	Random table generator
genraw	Read wave table values from a file
quad	Sound path interpreter
shepenv	Generator for Shepard tone spectrum envelopes

Open functions, such as waveforms, are typically used periodically, and closed functions, such as envelopes, are used once only over the course of single notes.

gen programs are written so that they may be invoked directly as UNIX commands. When they are invoked as commands by a user, they may print directly to the user's terminal screen. Such printout may be processed to produce graphs, for example, allowing the score writer to experiment with various parametric values while developing a cmusic score. When the output of a gen program is not connected to a terminal, it is usually a stream of binary single-precision floating-point values intended for storage in a cmusic wave table.

cmusic allows the score writer to type expressions and even string variables as parameters to be passed on to the gen program. cmusic always includes the −L flag with the number of function values to be generated, but further program flags may be specified in the score as in the following example:

```
var 0 s3 "-o -x" ;
GEN3(f2[256]) s3 0 -6dB -12dB 0 ;
```

cmusic translates the expressions into numeric values and includes the value of the string variable in the command as well. The command created by cmusic from the score statements would look approximately like this:

```
gen3 -L256 -o -x 0 .5 .25 0
```

This example illustrates that the cmusic gen statement will accept a *nonstandard function length* if it is enclosed in brackets after the function name. cmusic translates expressions into numerical values, and string values may be included anywhere in the parameter list. Of course, it is up to the invoked program to interpret the command.

D.5.1 chubby

The general form of the cmusic statement for this `gen` program is

```
gen time chubby function DC A1 A2 A3... AN
```

chubby is a `gen` program for waveshaping synthesis techniques.[2] Such functions are normally used in conjunction with the `lookup` unit generator.

The arguments specify the amplitude of each partial of a Chebyshev polynomial function according to the recursion relation

$$T_{n+1}(x) = 2xT_n(x) - T_{n-1}(x) \tag{D-1}$$

where $T_i(x)$ is a Chebyshev polynomial. $T_0(x)$ determines the relative amplitude of the 0-Hz component, $T_1(x)$ determines the fundamental energy, $T_2(x)$ determines the second harmonic, and so on. An example that produces 50 percent fundamental and 50 percent third harmonic is as follows (the resulting function is shown in Figure D-1).

```
CHUBBY(f2) 0 .5 0 .5 ;
```

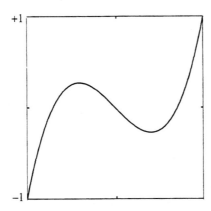

Figure D-1   Example of `chubby` output.

Whether the function returned by `chubby` is normalized to the range ±1 or not depends on the sum of its arguments being 1.0. It is customary to renormalize `chubby` functions with `gen0`.

D.5.2 `cspline`

The general form of the `cspline` statement is

```
gen time cspline function x0 y0 x1 y1 ... xN yN ;
```

---

[2]The `chubby`, `cspline`, `genraw`, and `quad` programs were added to cmusic by Gareth Loy.

cspline takes pairs of numbers as abscissas and ordinates of a function to be smoothed by a cubic spline function. It produces a smoothed function that includes the input values.

Here is a sample statement in a cmusic score (the resulting function is shown in Figure D-2):

```
CSPLINE(f1) 0 0 .1 .1 .2 1 .3 0 ;
```

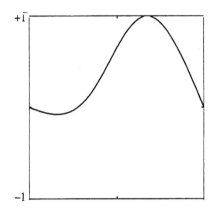

Figure D-2   Example of cspline output.

It is likely that cspline will produce function values that are not bounded by the supplied points; it is usually a good idea to normalize cspline functions with gen0.

D.5.3 gen0

Most cmusic gen programs produce functions with particular shapes, but the functions are often in need of *normalization*; that is, their extreme values are not necessarily guaranteed to lie in a particular range, such as ±1.   gen0 is provided to normalize functions generated by other gen programs.   gen0 is the only gen program that is built into cmusic itself, so it runs very efficiently.

The general form of the cmusic statement for this gen is as follows:

```
gen time gen0 function max ;
```

function is a *previously defined* wave table.   gen0 scales this wave table so that its maximum absolute value corresponds to max. If max is omitted, it is assumed to be 1.0. For example,

```
GEN0(f1) 1 ;    { may also be written as NORM(f1) ; }
GEN0(f2) 1000Hz ;
```

The first statement normalizes `f1` to 1.0, and the second normalizes `f2` so that its maximum value corresponds to 1000 Hz.

D.5.4 `gen1`

The general `gen1` statement is

```
gen time gen1 function    t1 v1    t2 v2    . . .    tN vN ;
```

`gen1` generates a (closed) function that starts with value `v1` at point `t1` (the beginning of the function), continues in a straight line to value `v2` at point `t2`, and so on, until the final value `vN` is reached.

As with all `gen` programs, the specification of *t* values goes from 0 to an arbitrary positive value—usually 1. The `gen` program maps these *t* values into the number of points required by the `-L` flag. For example, the statement

```
GEN1(f2)   0,0   1/3,1   2/3,1   1,0 ;
```

generates a trapezoidal function with a default length consisting of a straight line from 0 to 1 for the first third of the function, a steady value of 1 for the middle third, and a fall from 1 to 0 in the final third (see Figure D-3). Note the clarifying use of commas, which act as field separators in cmusic (equivalent to blank spaces).

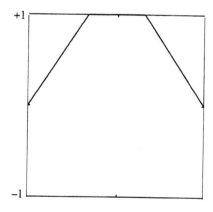

Figure D-3   Example of `gen1` output.

D.5.5 `gen2`

The general form of a `gen2` statement is

```
gen time gen2 function    a1 a2 ... aJ    b0 b1 ... bK    J ;
```

where `aM` is the amplitude of harmonic `M` in sine phase (the fundamental frequency, corresponding to the full length of the wave table, corresponds to M = 1), and bM is the amplitude of harmonic M in cosine phase. J is the number of aM terms given (gen2 uses this number to distinguish the a coefficients from the b coefficients). gen2 operates according to the relation

$$W(k) = \sum_{n=1}^{J} a_n \sin\frac{2\pi n k}{L} + \sum_{n=0}^{K} b_n \cos\frac{2\pi n k}{L} \qquad (D\text{-}2)$$

where k goes from 0 to $L-1$ (L is the wave table length).

Notice that the first cosine component is at 0 Hz. The shape of the final (open) function is determined by the sum of all the components specified. The peak amplitude of the final function depends on the coefficients chosen and in general is *not* equal to 1.0 (see Section D.5.3).

gen5 is generally easier to use and accomplishes the same thing as gen2. Examples of gen2 usage are as follows:

GEN2(f1) 1 1 ;	{f1 is a sine wave}
GEN2(f2) 0 1 0 ;	{f2 is a cosine wave}
GEN2(f3[4096]) 1 0	{f3 has length 4096 and the shape of the
1/3 0 1/5 5 ;	first five components of a square wave—
	note that this function will not be normal-
	ized (see Section D.5.3)}
GEN2(f4) 1 0 1/3 0	{f4 is the same as f3 with a 0.5 DC
1/5 .5 5 ;	offset—note that this function will not be
	normalized (see section D.5.3)}

Because the last two gen statements will result in functions that do not lie in the range ±1, normalization with gen0 will probably be necessary. The unnormalized result of the last statement (which defines f4) is shown in Figure D-4.

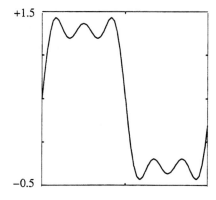

+1.5

−0.5

Figure D-4   Example of unnormalized gen2 output.

D.5.6 gen3

gen3 has the general statement

```
gen time gen3 function  v1 v2 ... vN ;
```

The arbitrarily long list of values, v1 through vN, specifies relative amplitude at *equally spaced points* along a (closed) function. Thus

```
GEN3(f2)    0 1 1 0 ;
```

specifies a trapezoidal function that has three parts: the first rises in a straight line from 0 to 1, the second is steady at 1, and the third falls from 1 to 0 (see Figure D-5).

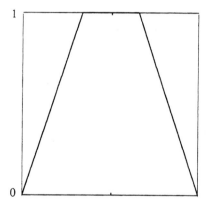

Figure D-5   Example of gen3 output.

If all gen3 parameters are positive, the function is scaled to be only positive. All-negative parameters result in an all-negative function. Values may be both positive and negative, resulting in a function that ranges above and below zero.

gen3 functions are easy to specify in ways that require no normalization, but the NORM macro defined in cmusic.h may be convenient for normalizing the resulting functions. In many cases, normalization is not only unnecessary, but also undesirable, as in the following example.

```
GEN3(f2) A(0) A(0) B(0) B(0) ;
```

f2 is defined here as a control function that is likely to be used to produce a portamento with an oscillator unit generator. Normalization would destroy the utility of f2 in such a case.

D.5.7 gen4

The general form of the gen4 statement is

```
gen time gen4 function    t1 v1 a1    t2 v2 a2    . . .    tM vM ;
```

gen4 operates analogously to gen1 except that transitions between points can be other than straight lines. The t values specify positions along the horizontal axis on an arbitrary scale (as with gen1), the v values specify values of the (closed) function at these points, and the x values specify *transitions* from one point to another. a = 0 will yield a straight line, a < 0 will yield an exponential transition, and a > 0 will yield an inverse exponential transition. If $S_{j,i}$ is the ith function value in the transition from v_j to v_{j+1}, its shape is determined by the relation

$$S_{j,i} = v_j + (v_{j+1} - v_j)\frac{1 - e^{i \cdot x_j/(N-1)}}{1 - e^{x_j}}$$
(D-3)

for $0 \le i < N$, where N is the number of function points between t_j and the following horizontal value. No a value is given after the final point. For example, the statement

```
GEN4(f2)    0,0   0   1/3,1   0   2/3,1   0   1,0 ;
```

fills wave table f2 with a function having straight-line transitions between the specified points, as shown in Figure D-6.

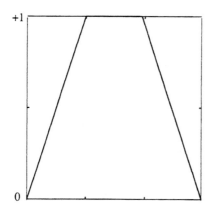

Figure D-6　gen4 Example with straight line transitions.

Using a negative transition parameter substitutes *exponential* transitions between the specified points. For example, the cmusic statement

```
GEN4(f2)    0,0   -1   1/3,1   0   2/3,1   -1   1,0 ;
```

would generate the shape shown in Figure D-7.

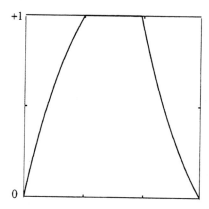

Figure D-7   gen4 example with exponential (−1) transitions.

Increasing the magnitude of the (negative) transition parameter increases the curvature of the exponential transitions. For example, the statement

```
GEN4(f2)   0,0  -5  1/3,1   0  2/3,1   -5  1,0 ;
```

generates the control function shown in Figure D-8.

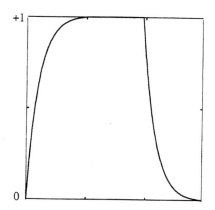

Figure D-8   gen4 example with exponential (−5) transitions.

Finally, a *positive* transition parameter specifies *inverse exponential* transitions. For example, the score statement

```
GEN4(f2)   0,0,10  1/3,1,0  2/3,1,10  1,0 ;
```

generates a function with the shape shown in Figure D-9.

Transition parameter values specify the number of *exponential time constants* between the endpoints of a transition. As shown in Figures D-7 and D-8, a small negative value specifies a curve that is not very different from a straight line but gets near the right hand value more quickly. A large negative value is more curved, and

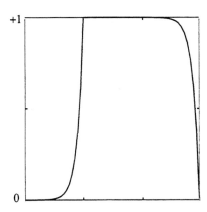

Figure D-9   gen4 example with inverse exponential (+10) transitions.

approaches the right hand value more quickly. The latter shape is useful for specifying very sharp attacks while avoiding clicks. Transition types may be mixed freely in a given function specification.

D.5.8 gen5

gen5 uses the general statement

```
gen time gen5 function    h1,a1,p1  h2,a2,p2  . . .  hM,aM,pM ;
```

Each Fourier component of the (open) function is described by a triplet specifying a harmonic number (h), an amplitude (a), and a phase offset (p) relative to sine phase according to the relation

$$W(k) = \sum_{n=1}^{M} a_n \sin\left[\frac{2\pi h_n k}{L} + p_n\right]$$ (D-4)

for $k = 0$ to $L-1$ (L is the specified wave table length). As many components may be supplied as desired, but all three values must be supplied for each component. Phase angles are in radians (recall the Deg postoperator in expressions). Harmonic numbers need not be integers, though noninteger harmonic numbers will generally result in wavetables that will produce clicks if they are used as acoustic waveforms.

Functions generated with gen5 are not normalized and will generally need to be treated with the NORM macro defined in cmusic.h. For example, the statement

```
GEN5(f1) 1,1,0 ;   { may also be written as SINE(f1) ; }
```

produces a sine waveform as shown in Figure D-10.
    The statement

```
GEN5(f2) 1,1,0 3,1/3,0 5,1/5,0;
```

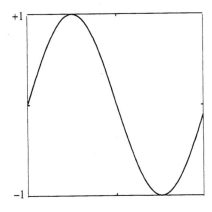

Figure D-10   Sine waveform produced with gen5.

creates a waveform consisting of the first three components of a square wave. Because more than one component is specified, normalization would usually be needed to bring the peaks within the range of ±1.0. This function is shown in Figure D-11.

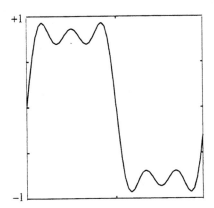

Figure D-11   First three components of a square waveform produced with gen5 (un-normalized).

The phase and amplitude parameters of gen5 may be used to create unusual waveforms as well. For example, the statement

```
GEN5(f3) 1,-.5,90Deg 0,.5,90Deg;    {f3 is a raised cosine wave}
```

generates the "raised," inverted cosinusoidal shape shown in Figure D-12.

D.5.9 gen6

gen6 fills the specified function with uniformly distributed random values in the range ±1. It has a general statement of the form

```
gen time gen6 function ;
```

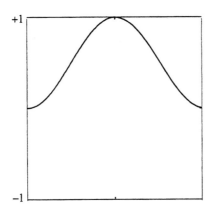

Figure D-12   Raised inverted cosinusoidal waveform produced with gen5.

D.5.10 genraw

genraw reads the named file, which must contain binary floating-point numbers. The values are then copied to its standard output. If called from inside cmusic, the contents of the file are copied into a wave table.

The genraw program is invoked in cmusic with statements such as

```
var p2 s1 "filename" ;
GENRAW(f1) s1 ;
```

genraw will force the number of values it outputs to equal the number specified by the -L flag by linearly interpolating the values in the input file as needed to stretch or shrink it.

D.5.11 quad

quad is a special gen program for use in conjunction with the CARL sndpath program. sndpath allows the user to design "sound paths" along which a sound seems to move. Paths designed with sndpath are read into cmusic with quad, and the generated wave tables are used to control the space unit generator.

D.5.12 shepenv

The general statement for this gen program is

```
gen time shepenv function cycles base ;
```

shepenv generates a function suitable for use with the illus unit generator in the production of Shepard-Risset tone illusions. Its output function has a raised inverted cosine shape that begins and ends with 0.0 and attains a single peak of 1.0 in between. shepenv scales this function along a logarithmic abscissa, so that equal pitch intervals occupy equal intervals along the horizontal axis. shepenv accepts two arguments: the number of logarithmic cycles and the logarithm base.

For example, if the spectrum envelope is to be scaled over six octaves, then cycles would be 6 and base would be 2 (see Figure D-13).

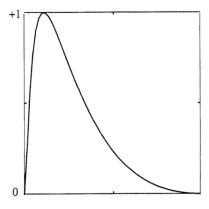

Figure D-13   shepenv output for cycles = 6 and base = 2.

If the envelope is to span seven perfect fifths, set cycles to 7 and base to 3/2, as shown in Figure D-14).

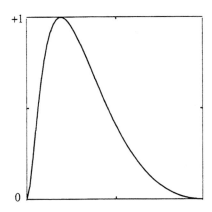

Figure D-14   shepenv output for cycles = 7 and base = 1.5.

D.6 UNIT GENERATORS

Unit generators are subprograms that perform signal generation or processing tasks. The heart of cmusic operation lies in the operation of the unit generators. Table D-4 lists many of the unit generators currently implemented.

Some of the unit generators are extremely simple (adn), while others are quite complex (space). Most have been highly optimized for speed. They are written in the

TABLE D-4 cmusic unit generators.

Name	Description
abs	Absolute value of a signal
adn	Sums arbitrary number of signals and constants
airabsorb	A filter that simulates air absorption
blp	Band limited pulse generator
delay	Fixed signal delay
diff	Calculates difference between successive samples
div	Divides one signal by another signal or a number
flt	General second-order digital filter
fltdelay	Recirculating delay line with filtered feedback
freq	Truncating oscillator with unity amplitude
illus	Control signal generator for pitch illusions
integer	Integer part of a signal
inv	1 minus input signal
iosc	Interpolating oscillator
lookup	Nonlinear transfer function
mult	Multiplies arbitrary number of signals and constants
neg	Negative of input signal
nres	Second-order filter with normalized, constant resonance gain
osc	Truncating oscillator
out	Multichannel signal output
rah	Random noise signal generator with hold feature
ran	Random noise signal generator with controlled bandwidth
sah	Sample and hold unit
seg	Envelope generator with arbitrary number of segments
shape	Waveshape generator
signum	Signum unit generator
smooth	One-pole smoothing filter
sndfile	Oscillator for sound files (digital recordings)
space	Spatial processor
sqroot	Square root of a signal
square	Square of a signal
trans	Transition generator
white	White noise generator
zdelay	Interpolating dynamic signal delay

C programming language, so it is possible to understand the operation of a unit generator by examining its source code, and it is relatively straightforward to add new unit generators to private copies of cmusic (guidelines about how to do this are included in the cmusic source code).

Unit generators are described in terms of their inputs, output(s), and state variable(s). For example, the `osc` unit generator is tersely described with the line

```
osc output[b] amplitude[bvpn] increment[bvpn] table[fvpn] sum[dpv] ;
```

This description tells us how the `osc` unit generator may be used in a cmusic instrument definition. The name of the unit generator appears first, followed by its parameters. Each parameter is given a more or less descriptive name, which is followed by a bracketed list of the types of data sources or sinks to which it may be connected. The abbreviations indicate possible connections for each parameter, as follows:

    b   Signal outputs of other unit generators
    p   Note statement parameters
    v   Global numeric variables
    s   Global string variables
    d   Dynamically allocated state variables
    f   Wave table functions
    n   Numbers (constant values, which may be expressions).

As a general rule, any unit generator parameter that *may* be a dynamic (that is, d-type) variable *should* be a dynamic variable. This allows cmusic instruments to be reentrant, allowing multiple notes to be played "simultaneously." Exceptions to this rule occur when there is reason to save the value of state variables between note events.

Certain unit generators have a variable number of parameter fields. For example, the `adn` unit generator is described as follows:

```
adn out[b] in[bnpv]* ;
```

The asterisk (*) indicates that the parameter that precedes it may be repeated (it must appear at least once, however). Thus `adn` may be used to add together as many inputs as desired, any of which may be of type `b`, `n`, `p`, or `d`.

Table D-5 shows terse parameter descriptions—including possible connection types—for several cmusic unit generators.

Descriptions of the operation of these unit generators follow.

D.6.1 abs

```
abs out[b] in[bnpv] ;
```

The output of `abs` is the absolute value of its input.

TABLE D-5   cmusic unit generator parameter descriptions.

Unit Generator	Parameter Description
abs	out[b] in[bnpv] ;
adn	out[b] in[bnpv]* ;
airabsorb	out[b] in[b] x[bnpv] y[bnpv] t[d] t[d] t[d] t[d] t[d] t[d] t[d] t[d] t[d] t[d] ;
blp	out[b] amp[bnpv] inc1[bnpv] inc2[bnpv] n[bnpv] t[dpv] t[dpv] ;
delay	out[b] in[bnpv] gain[bnpv] table[fnpv] len[npv] pos[npv] ;
diff	out[b] in[bnpv] t[dpv] ;
div	out[b] num[bnpv] denom[bnpv] t[dpv] ;
flt	out[b] in[bnpv] gain[bnpv] a0[bnpv] a1[bnpv] a2[bnpv] b1[bnpv] b2[bnpv] t[dpv] t[dpv] t[dpv] t[dpv] ;
fltdelay	out[b] t[dpnv] t[dpnv] t[dpnv] t[dpnv] t[dpnv] t[dpnv] t[dpnv] t[dpnv] t[dpnv] t[dpnv] t[dpnv] t[dpnv] t[dpnv] t[dpnv] t[dpnv] in[bnpv] pitch[bnpv] decay[bnpv] table[fnpv] level[npv] final[npv] onset[npv] place[npv] filtr[npv] noise[npv] stiff[npv] ;
freq	out[b] incr[bnpv] table[fnpv] sum[bdnpv] ;
illus	ampout[b] incrout[b] ampin[bnpv] incrin[bnpv] which[bnpv] ratio[bnpv] table[fnpv] incrmin[bnpv] incrmax[bnpv] ;
integer	out[b] in[bnpv] ;
inv	out[b] in[bnpv] ;
iosc	out[b] amp[bnpv] incr[bnpv] table[fnpv] sum[bdnpv] ;
lookup	out[b] table[fnpv] in[bnpv] min[npv] max[npv] ;
mult	out[b] in[bnpv]* ;
neg	out[b] in[bnpv] ;
nres	out[b] in[bnpv] gain[bnpv] cf[bnpv] bw[bnpv] t[dpv] t[dpv] t[dpv] t[dpv] t[dpv] t[dpv] t[dpv] t[dpv] t[dpv] t[dpv] ;
osc	out[b] amp[bnpv] incr[bnpv] table[fnpv] sum[bdnpv] ;
out	in[bdnpv]* ;
rah	out[b] amp[bnpv] incr[bnpv] t[dpv] t[dpv] t[dpv] ;
ran	out[b] amp[bnpv] incr[bnpv] t[dpv] t[dpv] t[dpv] ;
sah	out[b] in[b] period[bnpv] t[dnpv] t[dnpv] ;
seg	out[b] amp[bnpv] table[fnpv] sum[dpv] incr[npv]* ;
shape	out[b] table[fnpv] sum[bdnpv] ;
signum	out[b] in[bnpv] ;
smooth	out[b] in[bnpv] coef[bnpv] t[bdnpv] ;
sndfile	out[b] amp[bnpv] incr[bnpv] filename[s] channel[npv] startframe[bnpv] endframe[bnpv] t[bdnpv] t[d] ;
space	in[bnpv] dummy[npdv] t[d] t[d] t[d] t[d] t[d] t[d] t[d] t[d] t[d] t[d] t[d] t[d] x[bnpv] y[bnpv] theta[bnpv] len[bnpv]* ;
sqroot	out[b] in[bnpv] ;
square	out[b] in[bnpv] ;
trans	out[b] t[dpv] t[dpv] t[dpv] t[npv] v[npv] a[npv] *t[npv] v[npv] ;
white	out[b] amp[bnpv] ;
zdelay	out[b] in[bnpv] maxtime[npv] table[dnpv] tlen[dnpv] pos[dnpv] gain[bnpv] delay[bnpv]* ;

D.6.2 `adn`

```
adn out[b] in[bnpv]* ;
```

The output of `adn` is the (algebraic) sum of all its inputs. Any number of inputs may be given.

D.6.3 `airabsorb`

```
airabsorb out[b] in[b] x[bnpv] y[bnpv]
   lx[d] ly[d] r[d] scale[d] c1[d] c2[d]
      xm1[d] xm2[d] ym1[d] ym2[d] ;
```

`cmusic.h` macro definition:

```
#define AIRABSORB(OUT,IN,X,Y) airabsorb OUT IN X Y\
   d d d d d d d d d
```

`airabsorb` is a useful filter that simulates the sound absorption characteristics of air. The filter is essentially lowpass, with parameters adjusted to simulate the nitrogen and oxygen absorption characteristics of air according to the approximation

$$\text{Absorption(freq) (in dB/m)} \approx \text{freq}/100000$$

Thus a 1–kHz signal at a distance of 100 meters suffers a 1–dB attenuation, while a 10–kHz signal at the same distance suffers a 10–dB attenuation. Such absorptions are very small for sounds closer than about 50 meters, but they become significant for larger distances. It calculates the distance from coordinate $(0, 0)$ to (x, y) and calculates a lowpass filter that it applies to the input signal (all coordinate values are in meters).

D.6.4 `blp`

```
blp out[b] amp[bnpv] inc1[bnpv] inc2[bnpv]
     n[bnpv] sum1[dpv] sum1[dpv] ;
```

`blp` generates a band-limited pulse wave that contains n equal-amplitude sinusoidal components starting at frequency f_1 (specified by `inc1`) and spaced upward by frequency f_2 (specified by `inc2`) according to the closed-form summation formula:

$$y(n) = \sum_{k=0}^{N-1} \sin(\alpha + k\beta) = \sin\left[\alpha + \frac{(N-1)\beta}{2}\right]\sin\frac{N\beta}{2}\csc\frac{\beta}{2} \qquad \text{(D-5)}$$

where $y(n)$ is the output, $\alpha = 2\pi n f_1/R$, and $\beta = 2\pi n f_2/R$.

If f_2 is equal to f_1, a harmonic spectrum will result; that is, the first n harmonics of f_1 will be present, all at equal amplitude. `blp` is useful to generate efficiently harmonic-rich waveforms that do not produce foldover as long as the value of n is less than $1 + (R/2 - f_1)/f_2$ (where R is the sampling rate).

D.6.5 `delay`

```
delay out[b] in[bnpv] gain[bnpv] table[fnpv] len[npv] pos[npv] ;
```

    `delay` output is equal to its input delayed by `len` samples and scaled by `gain`. `table` should be a wave table (or a wave table index) whose length is at least equal to `len`.

    An all-zero function of length 39 milliseconds could be created with the command

```
GEN3(f2[39ms]) 0 0 ;
```

    Care should be exercised with this unit generator because the wave table may not contain two things at the same time. Instruments containing delays are not reentrant (they can play just one note at a time). Also, it will usually be necessary to clear `table` before each note begins. A macro to do this might read

```
#define Dnote(Time,Func)GEN3(func) 0 0 ; note Time
```

D.6.6 `diff`

```
    diff out[b] in[bnpv] temp[dpv] ;
```

    The `diff` unit generator outputs the differences between successive samples of its input. `temp` is normally a d-type variable. If the input signal is `x(0)`, `x(1)`, `x(2)`, . . ., then output is `x(0)-0`, `x(1)-x(0)`, `x(2)-x(1)`, . . .

D.6.7 `div`

```
div out[b] num[bnpv] denom[bnpv] temp[dpv] ;
```

    The output of the `div` unit generator is equal to `num` divided by `denom`. Each value of `denom` is checked to see of it is equal to 0.0, and if so, a huge value is output.

D.6.8 `flt`

```
flt out[b] in[bnpv] gain[bnpv]
    a0[bnpv] a1[bnpv] a2[bnpv] b1[bnpv] b2[bnpv]
      t1[dpv] t2[dpv] t3[dpv] t4[dpv] ;
```

    `flt` is a general second-order digital filter that operates according to the input-output relation

```
out[n] = gain *
 ( a0*in[n] + a1*in[n-1] + a2*in[n-2]
  + b1*out[n-1] + b2*out[n-2] )
```

where out[n] is the current output, out[n-1] is the previous output, in[n-1] is the previous input, and so on. The filter requires five coefficients, as shown, and four temporary locations (t1 through t4), which are normally of type d.

D.6.9 fltdelay

```
fltdelay out[b]
        dbuf[dpnv] dlen[dpnv] now[dpnv] del[dpnv] coef[dpnv]
        durcnt[dpnv] noicnt[dpnv] begcnt[dpnv] shrink[dpnv]
      strtch[dpnv] sdelay[dpnv] oldpit[dpnv] oldval[dpnv]
        oldin[dpnv] oldout[dpnv] in[bnpv] pitch[bnpv]
        decay[bnpv] table[fnpv] level[npv] final[npv]
          onset[npv] place[npv] filtr[npv] noise[npv]
            stiff[npv] ;
```

cmusic.h macro definition:

#define FLTDELAY(b) fltdelay b d d d d d d d d d d d d d

where

input[bvpn]	Optional input block (for use as resonator)
pitch[bvpn]	Desired fundamental freq (use Hz postop)
decay[bvpn]	Duration factor (0 to 1: 1 = full duration)
table[fvpn]	Function to initialize table (for example, from gen6)
level[vpn]	Amplitude of pluck (0 to 1: 1 = loudest)
final[vpn]	Number of dB down at p4 (0 to 100: 40 = norm)
onset[vpn]	Attack time for pluck (0 to 0.1 sec: 0 = fast)
place[vpn]	Pluck point on string (0 to 0.5: 0 = normal)
filtr[vpn]	Lowpass prefilter cutoﬀ. freq (0 to 0.5 S rate)
noise[vpn]	Time of initial noise burst (−1 to +0.1 sec)
stiff[vpn]	Stiffness (0 to 10: 10 = stiffest/sharpest)

fltdelay implements the Karplus-Strong plucked-string algorithm.[3] In its simplest form, operation is as follows: gen6 is used to fill a table with random numbers. The first N random numbers (where N is approximately R/pitch) are fed into a delay line of length N. The output of the delay line is the output of the unit generator; but the output is also sent to a filter that computes a weighted average of the current output sample and the previous output sample. The output of this averaging filter is placed back into the delay line. The result is that in every N samples, a given sample in the loop will be replaced by an average of that sample and the adjacent sample. The delay line therefore begins with white noise in it and ends with all zeros (or some small D.C. value) in it. The resulting sound can be very similar to that of a plucked string (see Chapter 3).

---

[3] fltdelay was added to cmusic by Mark Dolson.

Many options can be explored. An `input` can be connected so that the recirculating delay line acts as a resonator (but beware of overflow—either `input` should have small amplitude, or the value of `final` should be very large to produce rapid decay). `pitch` can be allowed to vary down to about R/L Hz, where R is the sampling rate and L is the wave table length. `decay` can vary (but note that the effect of the `decay` parameter depends on `pitch`—higher pitches are attenuated more rapidly for the same value of `decay`). `final` provides control of the decay independently of pitch (the decay is always exponential, and the duration is always `p4`; `final` specifies whether the note is to be 40 dB down by `p4` or perhaps 80 dB down—in which case it will sound shorter). `onset` applies a linear ramp of duration `onset` seconds to the output, which can be used to soften the characteristic pluck attack. It is also possible to output a noise burst of duration `noise` seconds prior to starting up the recirculating delay line. Conversely, a negative value for `noise` causes the recirculating delay line to run for `-noise` seconds prior to the start of the note. Finally, string stiffness can be simulated by specifying sharpened partials (but values of `stiff` less than 4 will probably be inaudible).

The other options apply only to the numbers in the delay line immediately prior to the start of the note. A function other than `gen6` can be used to fill `table`. The initial amplitude can be set with `level`. A comb prefilter can be applied to the numbers in `table` to simulate plucking at a different `place` along the string (for example, setting `place` to 0.5 is like plucking the string in the middle, in that even harmonics are eliminated). A lowpass prefilter can be applied to the numbers in the `table` to decrease the brightness of the plucked sound (for example, setting `filtr` to 0.1 applies a lowpass prefilter with a cutoff frequency of $0.1R$). When prefiltering is *not* desired, the value of `filtr` should be 0.5.

`fltdelay` can also be used to implement drumlike sounds by setting `decay` to −1 or letting it switch randomly between +1 and −1.

D.6.10 `freq`

```
freq out[b] incr[bnpv] table[fnpv] sum[bdnpv] ;
```

`freq` is a a truncating table lookup oscillator. Dynamic variables are recommended for `sum` locations. `table` may be explicit, or a number may be given. If the number is N, the integer part of N is used as a wave table index. This unit generator is equivalent to (but faster than) an `osc` with its amplitude set to 1.0.

D.6.11 `illus`

```
illus ampout[b] incrout[b] ampin[bnpv] incrin[bnpv] which[bnpv]
    ratio[bnpv] table[fnpv] incrmin[bnpv] incrmax[bnpv] ;
```

`illus` is a special Shepard-Risset tone illusion control function generator. It generates amplitude (`ampout`) and frequency (`incrout`) control signals from an input frequency (`incrin`) and a spectrum-shaping function (`table`) that determines which of *M* ratio-related components in the frequency range incrmin to incrmax is to be output.

ampout and incrout are fed (presumably) to an oscillator that generates a single component of the illusion. Each component has a frequency equal to ratio times the last one (unless it exceeds incrmax, in which case it wraps around to a frequency between incrmin and incrmax). The amplitude of each component is obtained from table by mapping the table abscissa onto the frequency range [incrmin, incrmax]. All output amplitudes are also scaled by the constant factor ampin.

The following cmusic score generates a full ascending chromatic scale of Shepard tones, using the special gen function for the spectrum envelope (shepenv) that produces a raised inverted cosine envelope on a logarithmic frequency abscissa.

```
#include <carl/cmusic.h>

ins 0 shep ;
    seg    b3 p5 f2 d 0 ;                    {note envelope}
    illus b1 b2 b3 p10 p6 p7 f3 p8 p9 ; {spectrum envelope}
    osc    b1 b1 b2 f1 d ;                   {carrier}
    out    b1 ;
end ;


{ reserve spectrum space for 6 components }
#define NCOMP 6
{ each component separated by an octave }
#define BASE 2
{ spectrum enveloped based at 50 Hz }
#define FMIN 50Hz
{ max frequency NCOMP octaves higher }
#define FMAX FMIN*(BASE^NCOMP)
{ amplitude scaler for each component }
#define AMP 1/NCOMP

SINE(f1) ;                 {component waveshape}
GEN4(f2) 0,0 -3 .1,1 0 .9,1 -1 1,0 ;      {overall note envelope}
SHEPENV(f3) NCOMP BASE ;           {special spectrum envelope}

{macro for tone complex}
{NOTE : NCOMP-1 components fit under spectrum envelope}

#define SHEP(time,pitch,dur)\
note time shep dur AMP 1 BASE FMIN FMAX pitch ;\
note p2 shep dur AMP 2 BASE FMIN FMAX pitch ;\
note p2 shep dur AMP 3 BASE FMIN FMAX pitch ;\
note p2 shep dur AMP 4 BASE FMIN FMAX pitch ;\
note p2 shep dur AMP 5 BASE FMIN FMAX pitch ;\
note p2 shep dur AMP 6 BASE FMIN FMAX pitch
```

```
SHEP(0,A(-3),.5) ;
SHEP(p2+1,As(-3),.5) ;
SHEP(p2+1,B(-3),.5) ;
SHEP(p2+1,C(-2),.5) ;
SHEP(p2+1,Cs(-2),.5) ;
SHEP(p2+1,D(-2),.5) ;
SHEP(p2+1,Ds(-2),.5) ;
SHEP(p2+1,E(-2),.5) ;
SHEP(p2+1,F(-2),.5) ;
SHEP(p2+1,Fs(-2),.5) ;
SHEP(p2+1,G(-2),.5) ;
SHEP(p2+1,Gs(-2),.5) ;
SHEP(p2+1,A(-2),.5) ; {last note sounds same as first}

ter ;
```

D.6.12 `integer`

```
integer out[b] in[bnpv] ;
```

The output of this unit generator is equal to the integer part of its input.

D.6.13 `inv`

```
inv out[b] in[bnpv] ;
```

The output of this unit generator is equal to 1 minus its input.

D.6.14 `iosc`

```
iosc out[b] amp[bnpv] incr[bnpv] table[fnpv] sum[bdnpv] ;
```

An interpolating, table lookup oscillator. Dynamic variables are recommended for sum locations. `table` may be explicit, or a number may be given. If the number is N, the integer part of N is used as a wave table index.

`iosc` requires a much shorter table than `osc` for equivalent distortion but runs more slowly.

D.6.15 `lookup`

```
lookup out[b] table[fnpv] in[bnpv] min[npv] max[npv] ;
```

`lookup` is a table lookup generator that uses its input to address the table to find the output. The input is clipped to `min` and `max`.

Conceptually, `table` is a function of x, with x in the domain `min` to `max`. The input to `lookup` is then x, and the output is $f(x)$. Because `table` is used to provide the mapping from input to output, quite arbitrary correspondences—in particular nonlinear ones—may be specified.

If $f(x)$ is a sum of Chebyshev polynomials (see Chapter 3), an arbitrary spectrum may be generated by making use of the relation

$$T_n(\cos \theta) = \cos n\theta \qquad \text{(D-6)}$$

where $T_n(x)$ is the nth-order Chebyshev polynomial (which may be generated with the gen program `chubby`). For example, if $f(x)$ is set equal to $a_0 T_0(x) + a_1 T_1(x) + \cdots + a_k T_k(x)$, then $f(\cos \theta)$ will have the spectrum components $a_0 \cos 0 + a_1 \cos \theta + \cdots + a_k \cos k\theta$.

D.6.16 mult

```
mult out[b] in[bnpv]* ;
```

The output of this unit generator is the product of its the inputs. Any number of inputs may be given.

D.6.17 neg

```
neg out[b] in[bnpv] ;
```

The output of this unit generator is equal to the negative of its input.

D.6.18 nres

```
nres out[b] in[bnpv] gain[bnpv] cf[bnpv] bw[bnpv]
    t1[dpv] t2[dpv] t3[dpv] t4[dpv] t5[dpv] t6[dpv]
    t7[dpv] t8[dpv] t9[dpv] t10[dpv] ;
```

`cmusic.h` macro definition:

```
#define NRES(out,in,gain,cf,bw) nres out in gain cf bw
                                d d d d d d d d d
```

`nres` (see Chapter 3). is a resonator that automatically adjusts its gain while bandwidth and center frequency change according to

```
y[n] = gain*scale*(x[n] - r*x[n-2]) + c1*y[n-1] + c2*y[n-2]
```

where

gain	is an arbitrary gain factor
cf	(center frequency) is specified in hertz
bw	(bandwidth) is specified in hertz
r	$= e^{-\pi bw / R}$, where R is the sampling rate in hertz

$$\text{scale} = 1 - r$$
$$\text{c1} \quad = 2r \cos(2\pi \cdot cf / R)$$
$$\text{c2} \quad = -(r^2)$$

The gain at the peak of the resonance region will always be gain, so other frequencies may be severely attenuated if the bandwidth is small.

D.6.19 osc

```
osc out[b] amp[bnpv] incr[bnpv] table[fnpv] sum[bdnpv] ;
```

osc is a truncating table lookup oscillator. Dynamic variables are recommended for sum locations. table may be explicit, or a number may be given.

D.6.20 out

```
out in[bdnpv]* ;
```

The number of inputs to the out unit generator *must* be equal to the number of sound channels. The first input is summed into output channel 1, the second input is summed into output channel 2, and so on. The set command may be used to specify the number of channels.

When necessary, cmusic assumes the following correspondence between sound channels and loudspeaker placement:

(front)

Channel 2   Channel 1

(left)   *Listener*   *(right)*

Channel 3   Channel 4

(back)

D.6.21 rah

```
rah out[b] amp[bnpv] incr[bnpv] pos[dpv] from[dpv] to[dpv] ;
```

rah chooses new random values at a rate of f Hz, where f is determined by incr. rah is the same as ran except that instead of moving in straight lines between random values, the random values are held steady until a new one is chosen.

D.6.22 `ran`

```
ran out[b] amp[bnpv] incr[bnpv] pos[dpv] from[dpv] to[dpv] ;
```

The output signal of `ran` consists of straight line segments that travel from one random value to another. The frequency with which new random values are chosen is determined by `incr`. A new random value is chosen every $L/incr$ samples, or at a rate of $R*incr/L$ Hz, where L is the prevailing wave table length and R is the sampling rate. Setting `incr` to 100 Hz, for example, would cause a new random value to be chosen every 10 milliseconds. The random values lie in the range ±1, and the output signal is scaled by `amp`. The last three arguments are typically dynamic (d-type) variables, used for temporary storage by `ran`. The spectrum of the output signal is sinc-squared, symmetrically centered around 0 Hz with a bandwidth given by `incr`. It may by centered around an arbitrary center frequency by convolution with a sinusoid at that frequency.

The following score fragment produces bandpass noise centered around 1000 Hz with an approximate bandwidth from 900 to 1100 Hz.

```
ins 0 noise ;
    ran b1 p5 p7 d d d ;
    osc b1 b1 p6 f1 d ;
    out b1 ;
end ;
GEN2(f1) 1 1 ;
note 0 noise 4 0dB 1000Hz 200Hz ;
```

D.6.23 `sah`

```
sah out[b] in[b] period[bnpv] temp1[dnpv] temp2[dnpv] ;
```

The `sah` unit generator looks at its input and holds it for `period` samples. For instance, for an input sequence `x0, x1, x2, x3, . . .` , setting `period` to 1.0 will cause it to output `x0, x0, x2, x2, x4, x4, . . .` `period` is the length of time to hold, in samples, and may be set to zero. A negative `period` is treated like a zero `period`. The `ms` postoperator may be used, for example, to specify the `period` in milliseconds.

Care must be exercised in the use of this sample and hold unit generator to avoid clicks due to discontinuities in the output sample stream. It may be desirable to smooth `sah` output with a lowpass filter (see `flt`, section D.6.8).

D.6.24 `seg`

```
seg out[b] amp[bnpv] table[fnpv] sum[dpv] incr[npv]* ;
```

seg is a special version of the oscillator specialized around the tasks of amplitude envelope generation. A wave table is defined for use with seg so that it contains *N* *equal-length* segments. seg then scans these segments at variable rates over the duration of a note event, allowing one segment to control the shape of the attack, another to control the shape of the pseudosteady state, another the initial decay, and so on. table may be either a wave table function (for example, f3), or a wave table function index (for example, 3).

The wave table function is divided into *N* equal-length segments. *N* is then the number of incr fields given in the seg statement (typically 3, corresponding to attack, steady-state, and decay times). incr fields with zero values may be used to signify that the corresponding segment duration is to be computed automatically from the duration that remains after all nonzero increments have been subtracted from the total note duration. For example, the following instrument plays with 100-millisecond attack and decay times, with the steady-state adjusted to fill up the note duration.

```
ins 0 env ;
    seg b1 p5 f2 d .1sec 0 .1sec ;
    osc b1 b1 p6 f1 d ;
    out b1 ;
end ;
GEN3(f2) 0 1 1 0 ; {a 3-segment trapezoidal envelope}
```

The following instrument allows attack and decay to be set directly, with steady-state duration computed automatically.

```
ins 0 env ;
    seg b1 p5 f2 d p7 0 p8 ;
    osc b1 b1 p6 f1 d ;
    out b1 ;
end ;
GEN3(f2) 0 1 1 0 ;
```

More than one envelope segment may be computed automatically. In the next example, a four-segment envelope would be adjusted over a 1-second note duration thus:

segment 1 = 0.1 sec
segment 2 = 0.4 sec
segment 3 = 0.4 sec
segment 4 = 0.1 sec

```
ins 0 env ;
    seg b1 p5 f2 d p7 0 0 p8 ; {p7 & p8 control att & dec times}
    osc b1 b1 p6 f1 d ;
    out b1 ;
end ;
GEN3(f2) 0 1 1 .5 0 ; {4 segment envelope}
```

```
SINE(f1) ;
note 0 env 1 0dB 440Hz .1sec .1sec ;
```

seg assumes that the sum of all nonzero `incr` fields will be strictly greater than the total duration `p4`. If this condition is not satisfied, the results may or may not be acceptable. In particular, if the sum of all nonzero increments is exactly equal to the total duration `p4`, a division by zero may result.

D.6.25 shape

```
shape out[b] table[fnpv] sum[bdnpv] ;
```

shape is a truncating table lookup oscillator with amplitude automatically set to 1 and frequency automatically set to `p4sec`. In other words, this unit generator simply scales the function given in `table` to the note duration. Dynamic variables are recommended for `sum` locations. `table` may be explicit, or a number may be given. shape is equivalent to (but faster than) `osc` with its amplitude set to 1.0. It is not significantly faster than the `freq` unit generator, but it obviates the need for a `p` field set to p4sec.

D.6.26 signum

```
signum out[b] in[bnpv] ;
```

If the input is greater than or equal to zero, the output is set to 1.0; otherwise, the output is set to −1.0.

D.6.27 smooth

```
smooth  output[b] in[bvpn] tau[bvpn] temp[d] ;
```

The output is a smoothed version of the input according to the lowpass filter relation

```
y(n) = x(n) + tau*y(n-1) ;
output = y(n)*(1 - tau) ;
```

`tau` should normally be less than 1. `temp` is used to hold the previous output.

D.6.28 sndfile

```
sndfile out[b] amp[bnpv] incr[bnpv] filename[s] channel[npv]
        startframe[bnpv] endframe[bnpv] pos[bdnpv] ptr[d] ;
```

sndfile reads the specified `channel` of the file named by the `filename` string variable, starting at sample `startframe`, and ending at sample `endframe` (if endframe = −1, the end of the file is used). The specified increment (incr) is applied to the file (this is normally 1.0); if the end of the specified segment is reached, sndfile starts reading again from startframe.

The buffer size used by sndfile can be controlled with the set sfbufsize = N ; score statement (the default value for *N* is 4 kb, and may cause swapping if many simultaneous read operations are used).

D.6.29 space

```
space in[bnpv] nskip[npdv]
    t[d] t[d] t[d] t[d] t[d] t[d] t[d] t[d] t[d] t[d] t[d] t[d]
    [ x[bnpv] y[bnpv] theta[bnpv] len[bnpv] ]* ;
```

cmusic.h macro definitions:

```
#define SPACE(b,n) space b n d d d d d d d d d d d

#define QUAD(In,Out)\
set quad ;\
set space = Out/2,Out/2 -Out/2,Out/2 -Out/2,-Out/2 Out/2,-Out/2 ;\
set room = In/2,In/2 -In/2,In/2 -In/2,-In/2 In/2,-In/2 ;\
set speakers = In/2,In/2 -In/2,In/2 -In/2,-In/2 In/2,-In/2 ;\
set revscale = .1 ;\
set t60 = (Out/10)^.5

#define STEREO(In,Out)\
set stereo ;\
set space = Out/2,Out/2 -Out/2,Out/2 -Out/2,-Out/2 Out/2,-Out/2 ;\
set room = In/2,In/2 -In/2,In/2 -In/2,-In/2 In/2,-In/2 ;\
set speakers = In/2,In/2 -In/2,In/2 ;\
set revscale = .1 ;\
set t60 = (Out/10)^.5
```

space is the cmusic spatialization unit generator (see Chapter 4) The SPACE macro takes two arguments. The first argument is an I/O block (b) that contains a source sound to be located in space at the coordinates x, y. The second argument is an obsolete parameter which should be set to 1. The set of parameters x, y, theta, amp, and back is called a *radiation vector*. Any number of radiation vectors may be given to cause the sound to seem to radiate from several locations at once, with each source having its own directional characteristics.

x and y are specified directly in meters; coordinates may lie in the range ± Out (see the STEREO and QUAD macro definitions). theta is a direction for a radiation vector (in radians, with 0 pointing to the right). amp is the length of the radiation vector (it simply scales the amplitude). back is the relative radiation amplitude in the direction opposite to theta (0 gives a very directional source, 1 gives an omnidirectional source, values in between give cardoid shapes in between; omnidirectional sources generally give better results). The relative amount of global reverb is specified with a `set` statement. The following example gives some good settings for everything.

```
#include <carl/cmusic.h>

STEREO(3,12) ;

ins 0 one ;
    seg  b4 p5 f4 d .1sec 0 .1sec ;
    osc  b5 b4 p10 f5 d ;
    osc  b2 p7 p8 f2 d ;
    osc  b3 p7 p9 f3 d ;
    adn  b3 b3 p11 ;
    osc  b1 b5 p6 f1 d ;
    SPACE(b1,1) b2 b3 0 1 0dB ;
end ;

SAWTOOTH(f1) ;
SINE(f2) ;
COS(f3) ;
GEN1(f4) 0,0 1/3,1 2/3,1 1,0 ;
PULSE(f5) ;
GEN3(f6) 3/4 -1/4 ;

{play 4 second note that moves in circular path centered
about point (0,20). Circle has radius of 10 meters. Sound
takes 2 seconds to complete one circular movement}

note 0 one 4 0dB 440Hz 10 2sec 2sec 11Hz 20 ;

sec ;

ter 4 ; {allow 4 seconds at end for global reverb to die}
```

D.6.30 sqroot

```
sqroot out[b] in[bnpv] ;
```

The output of `sqroot` is equal to the square root of its input. Naturally, the input had better be greater than zero.

D.6.31 square

```
square out[b] in[bnpv] ;
```

The output of `square` is equal to the square of its input.

D.6.32 trans

```
trans out[b] no[dpv] len[dpv] i[dpv]
     [ t[npv] v[npv] a[npv] ]* t[npv] v[npv] ;
```

trans is the unit generator equivalent of gen4, which is a general exponential transition generator. The parameters give a description of a transition path exactly like a gen4 definition, except that the transition path occurs over the duration of a note event. Any number of time-value (t-v) pairs may be given, and the transition parameters (a) work as they do in gen4: 0 yields a straight-line transition, negative numbers yield exponential transitions, and positive numbers yield inverse exponential transitions.

The power of this generator lies in the fact that the transition points and parameters may be connected to p fields, allowing such things as easy glissando specification and loudness contouring. For example, the following score plays a 1-second glissando from 440 Hz to 880 Hz, followed by a 2-second gliss to 100 Hz.

```
ins 0 gliss ;
    trans b1 d d d 0,p6 0 1/3,p7 0 1,p8 ;
    osc   b1 p5 b1 f1 d ;
    out   b1 ;
end ;
SINE(f1) ;
note 0 gliss 3 -6dB 440Hz 880Hz 100Hz ;
ter ;
```

trans runs considerably slower for nonzero transition parameter values than it does for straight-line transitions.

D.6.33 white

```
white output[b] amplitude[bvpn] ;
```

white outputs random numbers in the range ±amplitude.

D.6.34 zdelay

```
zdelay out[b] in[bnpv] maxtime[npv] table[dnpv] tlen[dnpv]
pos[dnpv] gain[bnpv] delay[bnpv]* ;
```

zdelay output is equal to its input delayed by delay seconds and scaled by gain. An arbitrary number of gain/delay taps may be given—the output is the sum of all tap outputs. zdelay is therefore an arbitrary FIR (that is, a tapped delay-line) filter with continuously adjustable taps.

Because the amount of delay is continuously and dynamically variable, zdelay is useful for effects such as pitch shifting and flanging. The maximum allowable delay is set by the user in `maxtime` (also given in seconds). It is an error for any delay time to exceed the value given in `maxtime` for any given note (negative delays are also illegal). Note that whereas `gain` and `delay` values may be dynamic signals or constants (`b`, `v`, `p`, or `n`), `maxtime` *must* be a constant (`v`, `p`, or `n`).

D.7 ADVANCED TOPICS

D.7.1 Global Control

cmusic operates by observing the action time of the command at hand in the score, starting from the beginning, of course. Once an action time is encountered that is greater than the current action time (the greatest time to which sound has been synthesized), cmusic starts generating samples. Sample generation continues until either a command is to be executed or a note terminates, in which case resources for that note must be deallocated.

cmusic does not produce one sample at a time but runs in *blocks* of samples. The length of a sample synthesis block is equal to the length of the I/O blocks.

For example, if it is time to start synthesizing a note, cmusic looks up the definition for the relevant instrument and calls the unit generator programs one at a time in the order in which they are stated in the instrument definition. Information is passed to the individual unit generators about where to find information about parameter information—a `b` will be a pointer to an array (I/O block), a `p` will point to a single value within the list of note parameters for the current note, and so on. Each unit generator is instructed to generate either B samples (where B is the number of samples in an I/O block) or fewer, if the note is to terminate before B samples have gone by from the current synthesis time.

This manner of operation allows the cmusic score writer to use an interesting form of global control. A "dummy" instrument may be defined that outputs into an I/O block. Let's say a `shape` unit generator outputs into `b10`, as in the following example:

```
ins 0 cresc ;
    shape b10 f2 d ;
end ;
GEN4(f2) 0,-30dB -2 1,-20dB ;
```

Notice that there is no `out` unit generator included in the definition of instrument `cresc`. The values in `b10` seem to be going nowhere!

Other instruments, however, may refer to `b10` as part of their definitions. In this case, because the `b10` values will gradually change from −30 to −20 dB over the course of any note played on instrument `cresc`, we may deduce that it is designed for long-term amplitude control. In fact, `cresc` will produce a crescendo when used in conjunction with other instruments in the following manner:

```
ins 0 cresc ;
    shape b10 f2 d ;
end ;
GEN4(f2) 0,-30dB -2 1,-20dB ;
ins 0 toot ;
    seg b1 b10 f3 d p6 0 p7 ;
    osc b1 b1 p5 f1 d ;
    out b1 ;
end ;
GEN4(f3) 0,0 -3 1/3,1 0 2/3,.1 -2 1,0 ;
SAWTOOTH(f1) ;

note 0 cresc 5 ; {crescendo over 5 seconds}

note 0 toot 1 A(0) .1sec .1sec ;
note 0 toot 1 Cs(1) .1sec .1sec ;

note 2 toot 1.5 B(0) .05sec .1sec ;
note 2.3 toot 2 Ds(1) .05sec .1sec ;

note 3.6 toot 1.4 E(1) .01sec .1sec ;

sec ;
```

Several advanced techniques are demonstrated in this example.

First, b10 is used to control the amplitude of another instrument, which plays chords with various pitches and attack times. b10 is simply fed into the Camp input of the seg unit generator controlling the peak note amplitude—the amplitude envelopes are continuously being fed a greater and greater peak value as the first 5 seconds of the score go by.

Second, b1 is used both as an input and an output of the osc unit generator. This is perfectly legal because the information in b1 is examined before the output is produced—we only have to be careful not to use the same I/O block to hold more than one thing at one time! No unit generator may use b10 while the cresc unit generator is operating, for example.

This demonstrates that even though I/O blocks are dynamic, they are allocated at the beginning of any note that uses them and remain usable as long as that note event is active. Their contents will always be whatever was last put there from any source.

Such global control techniques may be used for more than the production of crescendi, of course. Any and all instrument parameters may be modulated in this way, yielding an entire layer of control possibilities independent of the note event level.

D.7.2 Advanced Uses of sndfile

The sndfile unit generator allows cmusic to be used as a general mixing program for digital recordings and sound files that result from other synthesis runs. Global control functions may be used to specify long-term mixing levels, filtering (equalization) parameters, panning, spatialization, and so on.

In addition, the `sndfile` unit generator can be used to read in the results of sound analysis programs such as the *phase vocoder*, which may be viewed as the output of a large number of special bandpass filters, where each filter describes the time-varying amplitude and frequency of an individual sinusoidal component that lies within its bandpass region.

D.8 THE CMUSIC COMMAND[4]

cmusic [–o] [[–v] [–n] [–t] [–q] [–Rx] [–Lx] [–Bx] [score_file] > output
   cmusic flags given on the command line override options in the `score_file`.

   –o tells cmusic to produce no sample output (debug mode)

   –v sets the verbose option; –v– turns it off (default = off)

   –n sets the notify option; –n– turns it off (default = off)

   –t sets the timer option; –t– turns it off (default = off)

   –q turns off any verbose, timer, or notify options set elsewhere

 –Rx sets the sampling rate to x (default = 16K)

 –Lx sets the default function length to x (default default = 1K)

 –Bx sets the IO block length to x (default = 256)

   Flag symbols must not be combined, that is, –tn will not work, but –t –n will.
   If no `score_file` is given, cmusic reads its standard input.
   If its standard output is connected to a terminal, cmusic generates ASCII sample values on the screen; if the standard output is not a terminal, binary values (floats by default) are produced.
   Detected score errors generally cause sample synthesis to stop; the remainder of the score is scanned for further errors, if possible.

D.9 SCORE FILE EXAMPLES

A few briefly annotated score examples are included here for reference. These scores are intended only to give a flavor of the idiomatic use of the cmusic score language and are not compositional models.
   The following score synthesizes several notes with just pitch and just and tempered timbres.

```
#include <carl/cmusic.h>
set list ;
```

---

[4]Details of this command (such as default values) are likely to be installation-dependent.

```
set funclength = 8K ;
set srate = 48K ;
ins 0 comp ;
{envelope}        osc  b1 p5 p7 f2 d ;
{carrier}         osc  b1 b1 p6 f1 d ;
{output}          out  b1 ;
end ;

GEN2(f1) 1 1 ;
GEN4(f2) 0,0 -2 .2,1 -1 .5,.5 -2 1,0 ;

#define AMP (-18dB)

#define TEMP(time, dur, amp, pitch)\
note time comp dur amp pitch P ;\
note time comp dur amp/2 pitch*2 P ;\
note time comp dur amp/3 pitch*2*2^(7/12) P ;\
note time comp dur amp/4 pitch*4 P ;\
note time comp dur amp/5 pitch*4*2^(4/12) P

#define JUST(time, dur, amp, pitch)\
note time comp dur amp pitch P ;\
note time comp dur amp/2 pitch*2 P ;\
note time comp dur amp/3 pitch*3 P ;\
note time comp dur amp/4 pitch*4 P ;\
note time comp dur amp/5 pitch*5 P

{
JUST(0,2,(-30dB),(C(0))) ;
sec ;
sec .5 ;
TEMP(0,2,(-30dB),(C(0))) ;
sec ;
sec .5 ;
}

JUST(0,1.5,(-30dB),(P1(-2)*C(0))) ;       {(C(-2))) ;}
JUST(0,1.5,(-30dB),(P1(-1)*C(0))) ;       {(C(-1))) ;}
JUST(0,1.5,(-30dB),(P5(-1)*C(0))) ;       {(G(-1))) ;}
JUST(0,1.5,(-30dB),(P1(0)*C(0))) ;        {(C(0))) ;}
JUST(0,1.5,(-30dB),(M3(0)*C(0))) ;        {(E(0))) ;}
JUST(0,1.5,(-30dB),(P5(0)*C(0))) ;        {(G(0))) ;}

JUST(2,8,(-24dB),(P1(-2)*P4(0)*C(0))) ;   {(F(-2))) ;}
JUST(2,8,(-24dB),(P5(-2)*P4(0)*C(0))) ;   {(C(-1))) ;}
JUST(2,8,(-24dB),(M3(-1)*P4(0)*C(0))) ;   {(A(-1))) ;}
JUST(2,8,(-24dB),(P5(-1)*P4(0)*C(0))) ;   {(C(0))) ;}
JUST(2,8,(-24dB),(M7(-1)*P4(0)*C(0))) ;   {(E(0))) ;}
```

```
JUST(2,8,(-24dB),(M2(0)*P4(0)*C(0)))  ;    {(G(0))) ;}

JUST(10,1.5,(-24dB),(P1(-3)*P4(0)*C(0)))  ; {(F(-3))) ;}
JUST(10,1.5,(-24dB),(P1(-2)*P4(0)*C(0)))  ; {(F(-2))) ;}
JUST(10,1.5,(-24dB),(M3(-1)*P4(0)*C(0)))  ; {(A(-1))) ;}
JUST(10,1.5,(-24dB),(P5(-1)*P4(0)*C(0)))  ; {(C(0))) ;}
JUST(10,1.5,(-24dB),(m7(-1)*P4(0)*C(0)))  ; {(Ef(0))) ;}
JUST(10,1.5,(-24dB),(M2(0)*P4(0)*C(0)))  ;  {(G(0))) ;}

JUST(12,8,(-24dB),(P1(-3)*C(0)))  ;          {(C(-3))) ;}
JUST(12,8,(-24dB),(P5(-2)*C(0)))  ;          {(G(-2))) ;}
JUST(12,8,(-24dB),(P1(0)*C(0)))  ;           {(C(0))) ;}
JUST(12,8,(-24dB),(M3(0)*C(0)))  ;           {(E(0))) ;}
JUST(12,8,(-24dB),(P5(0)*C(0)))  ;           {(G(0))) ;}
JUST(12,8,(-24dB),(M7(0)*C(0)))  ;           {(B(0))) ;}


sec ;
sec 2 ;

TEMP(0,1.5,(-30dB),(P1(-2)*C(0)))  ;          {(C(-2))) ;}
TEMP(0,1.5,(-30dB),(P1(-1)*C(0)))  ;          {(C(-1))) ;}
TEMP(0,1.5,(-30dB),(P5(-1)*C(0)))  ;          {(G(-1))) ;}
TEMP(0,1.5,(-30dB),(P1(0)*C(0)))  ;           {(C(0))) ;}
TEMP(0,1.5,(-30dB),(M3(0)*C(0)))  ;           {(E(0))) ;}
TEMP(0,1.5,(-30dB),(P5(0)*C(0)))  ;           {(G(0))) ;}

TEMP(2,8,(-24dB),(P1(-2)*P4(0)*C(0)))  ;      {(F(-2))) ;}
TEMP(2,8,(-24dB),(P5(-2)*P4(0)*C(0)))  ;      {(C(-1))) ;}
TEMP(2,8,(-24dB),(M3(-1)*P4(0)*C(0)))  ;      {(A(-1))) ;}
TEMP(2,8,(-24dB),(P5(-1)*P4(0)*C(0)))  ;      {(C(0))) ;}
TEMP(2,8,(-24dB),(M7(-1)*P4(0)*C(0)))  ;      {(E(0))) ;}
TEMP(2,8,(-24dB),(M2(0)*P4(0)*C(0)))  ;       {(G(0))) ;}

TEMP(10,1.5,(-24dB),(P1(-3)*P4(0)*C(0)))  ; {(F(-3))) ;}
TEMP(10,1.5,(-24dB),(P1(-2)*P4(0)*C(0)))  ; {(F(-2))) ;}
TEMP(10,1.5,(-24dB),(M3(-1)*P4(0)*C(0)))  ; {(A(-1))) ;}
TEMP(10,1.5,(-24dB),(P5(-1)*P4(0)*C(0)))  ; {(C(0))) ;}
TEMP(10,1.5,(-24dB),(m7(-1)*P4(0)*C(0)))  ; {(Ef(0))) ;}
TEMP(10,1.5,(-24dB),(M2(0)*P4(0)*C(0)))  ;  {(G(0))) ;}

TEMP(12,8,(-24dB),(P1(-3)*C(0)))  ;          {(C(-3))) ;}
TEMP(12,8,(-24dB),(P5(-2)*C(0)))  ;          {(G(-2))) ;}
TEMP(12,8,(-24dB),(P1(0)*C(0)))  ;           {(C(0))) ;}
TEMP(12,8,(-24dB),(M3(0)*C(0)))  ;           {(E(0))) ;}
TEMP(12,8,(-24dB),(P5(0)*C(0)))  ;           {(G(0))) ;}
TEMP(12,8,(-24dB),(M7(0)*C(0)))  ;           {(B(0))) ;}


ter ;
```

     The following score defines a frequency modulated instrument and plays a note on it.

```
#include <carl/cmusic.h>
set funclength = 8K ;
set list ;

ins 0 fm ; {p5:p4sec, p6:peak amp, p7:fc}
    {amp env}    osc b1 p6 p5 f2 d ;
    {df env}     osc b2 1 p5 f3 d ;
    {fm env}     osc b3 1 p5 f4 d ;
    {mod osc}    osc b5 b2 b3 f1 d ;
    {sum}        adn b6 b5 p7 ;
    {carrier}    osc b7 b1 b6 f1 d ;
    {output}     out b7 ;
end ;
{f1 - sine}
SINE(f1) ;
{f2 - amp env}
GEN4(f2) 0,0 -1 .05,1 0 .95,1 -2 1,0 ;
{f3 - df env}
GEN4(f3) 0,0 0 1/8,6Hz 0 2/8,12Hz 0 3/8,300Hz 0 4/8,900Hz 0
            7/8,900Hz 0 8/8,0 ;
{f4 - fm env}
GEN4(f4) 0,1.5Hz (ln(2)) 4/8,3Hz (ln(100)) 7/8,300Hz 0 1,300Hz ;

note 0 fm 32 p4sec -12dB 300Hz ;

ter ;
```

     The following score exploits cmusic macros to create a score shorthand similar to music notation.

```
#include <carl/cmusic.h>

set notify ;
set func = 4K ;

ins 0 t ;
    seg b2 1 f2 d 0 ;
    mult b5 b2 p5 ;
    mult b3 b2 p8 ;
    osc b4 b3 p7 f1 d ;
    adn b4 b4 p6 ;
    osc b1 b5 b4 f1 d ;
    out b1 ;
end ;
{p5-amp ; p6-Fc ; p7-Fm ; p8-dF ;}
```

```
ins 0 o ;
    seg b2 1 f4 d 0 ;
    mult b5 b2 p5 ;
    mult b3 b2 p8 ;
    osc b4 b3 p7 f1 d ;
    adn b4 b4 p6 ;
    osc b1 b5 b4 f1 d ;
    out b1 ;
end ;
ins 0 b ;
    seg b2 1 f4 d 0 ;
    mult b5 b2 p5 ;
    mult b3 b2 p8 ;
    osc b4 b3 p7 f1 d ;
    adn b4 b4 p6 ;
    osc b1 b5 b4 f1 d ;
    out b1 ;
end ;
SINE(f1) ;
GEN4(f2) 0,0 -2 .1,1 0 .8,.5 -2 1,0 ;
GEN5(f3) 1,1,0 2,1,0 3,1/2,0 4,1,0 5,1/3,0 6,1/4,0 7,1/5,0 ;
NORM(f3) ;
GEN4(f4) 0,0 -3 .1,1 0 .9,1 0 1,0 ;


#define amp (1/10)
#define T (4*(180MM))
#define STAC .6
#define NON .9
#define LEG 1.1
#define INDEX 7
#define HARM 1
{Macro to play a note AFTER the last one in the score}
#define NEXT(ins,pitch,dur,duty)\
note p2+p4 ins T*duty/(dur) amp   pitch HARM*p6  INDEX*p7 ;\
note p2 ins T*duty/(dur) amp   pitch/2 HARM*p6  INDEX*p7 ;\
var  p2  p4  T/(dur)


{Macro to play a note WITH the last one in the score}
#define SAME(ins,pitch,dur,duty)\
var  p2    v1 p4 ;\
note p2    ins T*duty/(dur) amp   pitch HARM*p6  INDEX*p7 ;\
note p2    ins T*duty/(dur) amp   pitch/2 HARM*p6  INDEX*p7 ;\
var  p2    p4 v1


{Chord Macros}
#define CH2(p1,p2,ins,dur,duty)\
 NEXT(ins,p1,dur,duty) ; SAME(ins,p2-.5,dur,duty)
```

```
#define CHS2(p1,p2,ins,dur,duty)\
 SAME(ins,p1,dur,duty) ; SAME(ins,p2-.5,dur,duty)

#define CH3(p1,p2,p3,ins,dur,duty)\
 NEXT(ins,p1,dur,duty) ; SAME(ins,p2-.5,dur,duty) ; \
  SAME(ins,p3-.7,dur,duty)

#define CHS3(p1,p2,p3,ins,dur,duty)\
 SAME(ins,p1,dur,duty) ; SAME(ins,p2-.5,dur,duty) ; \
  SAME(ins,p3-.7,dur,duty)

#define CH4(p1,p2,p3,p4,ins,dur,duty)\
 NEXT(ins,p1,dur,duty) ;SAME(ins,p2,dur,duty) ;\
  SAME(ins,p3,dur,duty) ;SAME(ins,p4,dur,duty)

#define CHS4(p1,p2,p3,p4,ins,dur,duty)\
 SAME(ins,p1,dur,duty) ;SAME(ins,p2,dur,duty) ;\
  SAME(ins,p3,dur,duty) ;SAME(ins,p4,dur,duty)

{Notelist begins here - tune is by Mendelssohn}

    CH3(C(0),C(0),C(0),t,4*3,STAC) ;
     CH3(C(0),C(0),C(0),t,4*3,STAC) ;
      CH3(C(0),C(0),C(0),t,4*3,STAC) ;
CH3(C(0),C(0),C(0),t,4/3,NON) ;

 CH3(C(0),C(0),C(0),t,4*3,STAC) ;
  CH3(C(0),C(0),C(0),t,4*3,STAC) ;
   CH3(C(0),C(0),C(0),t,4*3,STAC) ;
CH3(C(0),C(0),C(0),t,4/3,NON) ;

 CH3(C(0),C(0),C(0),t,4*3,STAC) ;
  CH3(C(0),C(0),C(0),t,4*3,STAC) ;
   CH3(C(0),C(0),C(0),t,4*3,STAC) ;
CH3(C(0),E(0),E(0),t,4,STAC) ;

 CH3(C(0),E(0),E(0),t,4*3,STAC) ;
  CH3(C(0),E(0),E(0),t,4*3,STAC) ;
   CH3(C(0),E(0),E(0),t,4*3,STAC) ;
    CH3(C(0),E(0),E(0),t,4,STAC) ;

     CH3(C(0),E(0),E(0),t,4*3,STAC) ;
      CH3(C(0),E(0),E(0),t,4*3,STAC) ;
       CH3(C(0),E(0),E(0),t,4*3,STAC) ;
CH3(C(0),E(0),G(0),t,4,STAC) ;

 CH3(C(0),E(0),G(0),t,4*3,STAC) ;
  CH3(C(0),E(0),G(0),t,4*3,STAC) ;
```

```
     CH3(C(0),E(0),G(0),t,4*3,STAC) ;
      CH3(C(0),E(0),G(0),t,4,STAC) ;


        CH3(C(0),E(0),G(0),t,4*3,STAC) ;
         CH3(C(0),E(0),G(0),t,4*3,STAC) ;
          CH3(C(0),E(0),G(0),t,4*3,STAC) ;
CH4(C(1),E(1),Fs(1),C(2),o,2,LEG) ;
CHS3(E(0),Fs(0),C(1),t,2,STAC) ;
CHS2(A(-3),A(-2),b,2,LEG) ;
 CH4(B(0),Ds(1),Fs(1),B(1),o,16/7,LEG) ;
 CHS2(B(-3),B(-2),b,2,LEG) ;
  CH4(B(0),Ds(1),Fs(1),Fs(1),o,16,NON) ;
CH4(B(0),Ds(1),Fs(1),A(1),o,4,LEG) ;
CHS2(E(-3),E(-2),b,2,LEG) ;
 CH4(B(0),E(1),G(1),G(1),o,4,LEG) ;
  CH4(A(0),D(1),F(1),F(1),o,4,NON) ;
  CHS2(F(-3),F(-2),b,2,LEG) ;
   CH4(F(0),A(0),D(1),D(1),o,4,NON) ;
 CH4(E(0),G(0),C(1),C(1),o,2*9,LEG) ;
 CHS2(G(-3),G(-2),b,2,LEG) ;
  CH4(F(0),F(0),D(1),D(1),o,2*9,NON) ;
   CH4(E(0),E(0),C(1),C(1),o,2*9,NON) ;
    CH4(F(0),F(0),D(1),D(1),o,2*9,NON) ;
     CH4(E(0),E(0),C(1),C(1),o,2*9,NON) ;
      CH4(F(0),F(0),D(1),D(1),o,2*9,NON) ;
       CH4(E(0),E(0),C(1),C(1),o,2*9,NON) ;
        CH4(D(0),D(0),B(0),B(0),o,2*9,NON) ;
         CH4(E(0),E(0),C(1),C(1),o,2*9,NON) ;
 CH4(F(0),G(0),B(0),D(1),o,4,STAC) ;
 CHS2(G(-3),G(-2),b,2,LEG) ;
  CH4(F(0),G(0),G(0),G(0),o,16/3,STAC) ;
   CH4(F(0),G(0),B(0),D(1),o,16,NON) ;
 CH4(E(0),G(0),C(1),E(1),o,4,LEG) ;
 CHS2(C(-3),C(-2),b,2,LEG) ;
  CH3(C(0),C(0),C(0),t,8,NON) ;
   CH3(E(0),E(0),E(0),t,8,NON) ;
    CH3(G(0),G(0),G(0),t,8,NON) ;
     CH3(C(1),C(1),C(1),t,8,NON) ;
      CH3(C(1),E(1),E(1),t,8,NON) ;
       CH3(C(1),E(1),G(1),t,8,NON) ;
CH2(A(-3),A(-2),b,4,LEG) ;
CHS4(C(1),E(1),Fs(1),C(2),o,2,LEG) ;
CHS3(E(1),Fs(1),C(2),t,2,STAC) ;
 CH2(Fs(-3),Fs(-2),b,4,LEG) ;
  CH2(B(-3),B(-2),b,4,LEG) ;
  CHS4(B(0),Ds(1),Fs(1),B(1),o,2,LEG) ;
   CH2(Ds(-3),Ds(-2),b,16/3,LEG) ;
    CH4(B(0),Ds(1),Fs(1),Fs(1),o,16,NON) ;
```

```
CH4(B(0),Ds(1),Fs(1),A(1),o,4,LEG) ;
CHS2(E(-3),E(-2),b,4,LEG) ;
 CH4(B(0),E(1),G(1),G(1),o,4,LEG) ;
 CHS2(G(-3),G(-2),b,4,LEG) ;
  CH4(A(0),D(1),F(1),F(1),o,4,NON) ;
  CHS2(F(-3),F(-2),b,4,LEG) ;
   CH4(F(0),A(0),D(1),D(1),o,4,NON) ;
   CHS2(A(-3),A(-2),b,4,LEG) ;
 CH4(E(0),G(0),C(1),C(1),o,2*9,LEG) ;
 CHS2(G(-3),G(-2),b,2,LEG) ;
  CH4(F(0),F(0),D(1),D(1),o,2*9,NON) ;
   CH4(E(0),E(0),C(1),C(1),o,2*9,NON) ;
    CH4(F(0),F(0),D(1),D(1),o,2*9,NON) ;
     CH4(E(0),E(0),C(1),C(1),o,2*9,NON) ;
      CH4(F(0),F(0),D(1),D(1),o,2*9,NON) ;
       CH4(E(0),E(0),C(1),C(1),o,2*9,NON) ;
        CH4(D(0),D(0),B(0),B(0),o,2*9,NON) ;
         CH4(E(0),E(0),C(1),C(1),o,2*9,NON) ;
 CH4(E(0),G(0),C(1),E(1),o,4,NON) ;
 CHS2(G(-3),G(-2),b,4,LEG) ;
  CH4(F(0),G(0),B(0),D(1),o,16/3,NON) ;
  CHS2(G(-3),G(-2),b,4,LEG) ;
   CH4(G(0),G(0),C(0),E(1),o,16,STAC) ;
    CH2(G(-2),G(-1),b,4,STAC) ;
    CHS4(F(0),G(0),B(0),D(1),o,2,LEG) ;
     CH2(G(-3),G(-2),b,4,NON) ;
CH4(E(0),G(0),C(1),C(1),o,4,NON) ;
CHS2(C(-3),C(-2),b,4,NON) ;
CH4(C(1),E(1),G(1),C(2),o,4,STAC) ;
CHS2(C(-2),G(-2),b,4,STAC) ;
CHS3(C(1),E(0),G(0),t,3,STAC) ;
ter ;
```

Index

547